A Concise Introduction to
World Religions

Fourth Edition

Edited by

Amir Hussain *Loyola Marymount University*
Roy C. Amore *University of Windsor*
Willard G. Oxtoby *University of Toronto*

Oxford   New York
OXFORD UNIVERSITY PRESS

Oxford University Press is a department of the University of Oxford.
It furthers the University's objective of excellence in research, scholarship,
and education by publishing worldwide. Oxford is a registered trade mark of
Oxford University Press in the UK and certain other countries.

Published in the United States of America by Oxford University Press
198 Madison Avenue, New York, NY 10016, United States of America.

Library of Congress Cataloging-in-Publication Data
CIP data is on file at the Library of Congress
ISBN 9780190919023 (pbk.) | ISBN 9780190919054 (eBook)

Printing number: 9 8 7 6 5 4
Printed by LSC Communications Inc., United States of America

Brief Contents

Contents

3. Religions of Antiquity   76

4. Jewish Traditions   126

5. Christian Traditions   182

6. Muslim Traditions   244

7. Hindu Traditions   302

8. Sikh Traditions 364

9. Jaina Traditions   400

10. Buddhist Traditions   434

11. Chinese and Korean Traditions   496

12. Japanese Traditions   560

13. New Religions and Movements   592

Contributors

Roy C. Amore is a professor of political science at the University of Windsor in Ontario, where he teaches religion and politics. His extensive research in the areas of comparative religion and Asia has enabled him to author *Religion and Politics in the World's Hot Spots* (2016) and *Two Masters, One Message* (1985), a book comparing the lives and teachings of Christ and Buddha, in addition to other works.

Ken Derry received his Ph.D. from the University of Toronto's Centre for the Study of Religion with a thesis on religion, violence, and First Nations literature. He is an associate professor of religion in the teaching stream of the Department of Historical Studies at the University of Toronto Mississauga.

Michael Desrochers is an adjunct professor of history at California State University, Dominguez Hills, and received his Ph.D. from UCLA in the history of Mesopotamia. He is currently at work on two book-length projects: an overview of the religions of antiquity and an examination of historical irony.

Wendy L. Fletcher is a professor of the history of Christianity as well as the principal and vice-chancellor of Renison University College, University of Waterloo. She has published extensively in the areas of women and Christianity, spirituality, and religion and ethnicity.

Amir Hussain is a professor in the Department of Theological Studies at Loyola Marymount University in Los Angeles, where he teaches courses on Islam and world religions. A dual citizen of Canada and the United States, he is the author of *Muslims and the Making of America* and *Oil and Water: Two Faiths, One God*. He is on the board of directors of the American Academy of Religion and was twice selected by LMU students as professor of the year.

Michele Murray is the dean of arts and science at Bishop's University, where she is also a professor in the Department of Religion and holds the William and Nancy Turner Chair in Christianity. Her research areas include Jewish–Christian relations in the ancient world and interaction among Eastern and Mediterranean religions in late antiquity.

Vasudha Narayanan is a distinguished professor in the Department of Religion and director of the Center for the Study of Hindu Traditions at the University of Florida. A past president of the American Academy of Religion, she is the author or editor of seven books, a coeditor of the six-volume *Brill's Encyclopedia of Hinduism*, and the author of more than 100 articles and chapters in books.

John K. Nelson is a professor in the Department of Theology and Religious Studies at the University of San Francisco. Trained as a cultural anthropologist, he is the author of two books on Shinto and a documentary film on the Yasukuni Shrine. He is also the author of *Experimental Buddhism: Innovation and Activism in Contemporary Japan* (2013), which was co-winner of the 2014 Toshihide Numata Book Prize in Buddhism.

The late **Willard G. Oxtoby,** the original editor of the works on which this book is based, was a professor emeritus at the University of Toronto, where he launched the graduate program in the study of religion. His books include *Experiencing India: European Descriptions and Impressions, 1498—1898* and *The Meaning of Other Faiths*.

The late **Alan F. Segal** was a professor of religion and the Ingeborg Rennert Professor of Jewish Studies at Barnard College, Columbia University. He wrote extensively in the fields of comparative religion, Judaism, and early Christianity. His books include *Rebecca's Children: Judaism and Christianity in the Roman World*; *Paul the Convert*; and *Life after Death: A History of the Afterlife in Western Religion*.

Pashaura Singh is a professor and the Dr. Jasbir Singh Saini Endowed Chair in Sikh and Punjabi Studies at the University of California, Riverside. He has authored three Oxford monographs, coedited five conference volumes, and contributed articles to academic journals, books, and encyclopedias. His book *Life and Work of Guru Arjan: History, Memory, and Biography in the Sikh Tradition* (2006) was a bestseller in India.

Anne Vallely is an associate professor in the Department of Classics and Religious Studies at the University of Ottawa, where she teaches courses on South Asian traditions (especially Jainism and Hinduism), as well as nature and religion and death and dying. Her book *Guardians of the Transcendent: An Ethnography of a Jain Ascetic Community* (2002) is an anthropological study of Jain female ascetics. Her coedited volume *Animals and the Human Imagination* was published in 2012.

Terry Tak-ling Woo teaches in the Humanities Department at York University. Her research interests include women in Chinese religions and Chinese religions in diaspora. Recent publications include a coedited volume, *Canadian Women Shaping Diasporic Religious Identities* (2016), and articles in *Chinese Philosophy and Gender* and the *Journal of Chinese Overseas*.

Preface

It has been an honor for us to edit this fourth edition of *A Concise Introduction to World Religions*. The late Will Oxtoby was an outstanding researcher, but his true excellence was as a teacher. It is no coincidence that the publications for which he will be remembered best are the textbooks *World Religions: Eastern Traditions* and *World Religions: Western Traditions*. It was also as a teacher that Will first met Alan Segal, who became a colleague, a close friend, and eventually a collaborator on those books. After Will's death early in the planning of the first edition of *A Concise Introduction to World Religions* (2006), it was Alan who took over as general editor and saw the work through to completion. He also oversaw the development of the second edition of the present work, but just before it went to press, in 2011, he died—barely three months into his retirement from Barnard College.

With Alan's death, new authors were required for the chapters on Judaism and Christianity. In choosing his original contributors, Will Oxtoby looked for people who combined scholarship with sympathetic appreciation of the traditions in question. We have tried to be true to that vision in choosing our own contributors. This is the first *Concise* edition to include Michael Desrochers's excellent work on the religions of antiquity.

In his original foreword, Will wrote that people often used to ask him why he would waste his life on something as unimportant as religion, but that no one ever asked that question after the Islamic revolution in Iran. We have had the same experience: since the terrorist attacks of 9/11, not a single student has raised the issue of relevance. On the contrary, the study of world religions is now seen as more important today than ever before.

Important Features of This Edition

This fourth edition of *A Concise Introduction to World Religions* builds on and further refines the significant changes made to the third edition. The introductory chapter has been enhanced in several ways. Now titled "Studying Religion," it has been newly written to give more attention to theories about religion and methods for the study of religion. In addition, at the suggestion of reviewers, we've added a new chapter on the religions of antiquity.

We have also added three new features: Interview boxes, Practice boxes, and Women in the Traditions boxes. The Interview boxes offer a short interview with an important or influential member of one of the traditions discussed in each chapter. The Practice boxes invite students to glimpse facets of religion as observed in daily life. The Women in the Traditions boxes expand the coverage found in the chapters by examining an issue related to women's practice or lives within a tradition.

Dynamic Pedagogical Program

- **Traditions at a Glance boxes** provide thumbnail summaries of numbers and distribution of participants, founders and leaders, deities, important texts, and noteworthy doctrines.
- **Timelines** help to place religious developments in historical context.
- **Informative maps** provide useful reference points.
- **A vibrant art program** highlights practitioners' lived experiences.
- **Sacred Texts tables** give students a convenient summary of the most important texts in each tradition, how and when they were composed, and how they have been used.
- **End-of-chapter discussion questions** enhance students' critical understanding of key concepts, **glossaries** explain key terms, and lists of **further readings and recommended websites** provide excellent starting points for further research.

Compelling Boxed Features

- **Document boxes** provide generous excerpts from scripture and other important writings.
- **Sites boxes** draw attention to locations of special significance to each tradition.
- **Focus boxes** give students greater understanding of certain aspects of each tradition.

Extensive Ancillary Package

Online resources provide an outstanding array of teaching and learning tools for both instructors and students.

Instructors can benefit from a suite of ancillaries designed to support their teaching goals. An **instructor's manual** contains chapter summaries, learning objectives, student activities, class discussion topics, essay topics, and lists of multimedia resources for each chapter. **PowerPoint slides** cover all key concepts and are easily adapted to suit a particular course.

Students have access to a wealth of additional information in the **student study guide**, which offers chapter summaries, learning objectives, short-answer questions (with answers), reflection questions, research paper topics, and multimedia resources.
www.oup.com/he/Amoree

Acknowledgments

First, our thanks to the contributors without whom this book would not exist: Ken Derry, Michael Desrochers, Wendy Fletcher, Michele Murray, Vasudha Narayanan, John Nelson, Pashaura Singh, Anne Vallely, and Terry Tak-ling Woo. At Oxford University Press we would like to thank Katherine Skene and Stephen Kotowych for their encouragement, Leah-Ann Lymer and Meg Patterson for their developmental guidance, and Sally Livingston for her editorial work on earlier editions of this text, including abridgement of the two-volume material. For their work on this new edition, we would like to thank Robert Miller, Lisa Ball, Anna Deen, Meg Botteon, Sydney Keen, Alyssa Palazzo, and Sarah Vogelsong. Finally, we are grateful to all the reviewers whose comments helped to shape this volume, both those whose names are listed here and those who wished to remain anonymous:

Tara Baldrick-Morrone, Florida State University

Clayton Crockett, University of Central Arkansas

Philip Drey, Mount Mercy University

Grant Hardy, University of North Carolina at Asheville

Joshua Heter, Iowa Western Community College

Ernest P. Janzen, University of Winnipeg

Stephen Joseph, Butler County Community College

Samantha Langsdale, University of North Texas

Rev. Dr. Ryan M. Lozano, Alamo Colleges Central Texas Technology Center

Judson B. Murray, Wright State University

David Perley, University of Toronto, Scarborough

Michelle Rebidoux, Memorial University of Newfoundland

Isabelle Rucks, University of Phoenix

L. D. Russell, Elon University

Jeffrey Scholes, University of Colorado, Colorado Springs

Laura Stevens, Northwest Florida State College

Theresa A. Vaughan, University of Central Oklahoma

Mathias Warnes, California State University, Sacramento

Mike Williams, Lipscomb University

We dedicate this volume to Will Oxtoby and Alan Segal. May their memories be a blessing.

Roy C. Amore, University of Windsor
Amir Hussain, Loyola Marymount University, Los Angeles

A Concise Introduction to
World Religions

1 Studying Religions

Roy C. Amore and Amir Hussain

In this chapter you will learn about:

- Some basic characteristics of human religion from ancient times
- Some reasons for studying religion
- Some methods used for studying religion
- A number of patterns that can be observed in more than one religious tradition
- Various theories of why humans are religious

⊕ What Is Religion?

Many scholars trace the derivation of the word "religion" to the Latin verb *religare*, "to bind." Others argue that the root is *relegere*, "to go over again." From the beginning, then, there has been no universal definition of religion. We can describe religion as being concerned with the divine, but even that raises questions. Is there one god that is worshiped or many gods—or is there just a set of deep spiritual or moral practices? Most of us would probably not think of atheism as a religion, but what about Theravada Buddhism or Jainism, which are considered to be religions but do not promote belief in an Abrahamic-style god? The same problem arises with religious texts. Is there one text or a set of texts that is particularly authoritative for a particular tradition? Is that set a closed "canon," or can

new materials be added to it? What are the distinctions between established religions and newer ones (sometimes referred to pejoratively as "cults")? We may accept, for example, the validity of a man (Moses) receiving revelations from God on Mount Sinai 3,200 years ago or another man (Muhammad) receiving similar revelations in Mecca 1,400 years ago but reject the idea of a third man (Joseph Smith) receiving revelations in upstate New York 200 years ago. There is some truth in the saying "Today's cult, tomorrow's religion." Although this work focuses mainly on established traditions, some new religions will be introduced in the final chapter, along with a discussion of the terms "cult," "sect," and "new religious movement."

Another way of looking at religion is in terms of its functions. For example, a simple functional definition might be that religion is one way of creating community. For some people, belonging to a religion has less to do with piety or worship than with a community that offers a sense of belonging and social activities. Many other understandings of religion have been put forward. Karl Marx defined religion in terms of economics; Sigmund Freud, in terms of interior psychological states. Other scholars have approached the question from the perspective of sociology or anthropology, looking at religion as a social phenomenon or a cultural product.

The academic study of religion is usually a secular, nonconfessional enterprise, one undertaken without a

Jonathan Z. Smith. (Chris Salata / The Chicago Maroon)

 Ethiopian Orthodox pilgrims at the Church of the Holy Sepulchre in Jerusalem. (Yaacov Dagan / Alamy Stock Photo)

particular faith commitment. One of the key scholars in this area was Jonathan Z. Smith of the University of Chicago. His work on the history of religions has had a profound impact on scholarly understanding of key terms such as "myth" and "ritual," as well as the way comparisons are made both within a single religious tradition and across different traditions.

⊕ Why Study Religion?

The first and most obvious reason to study religion is that it exists. Not all humans might lay claim to religious beliefs, but humans in general have been religious from time immemorial.

A closely related reason is that religion has played a crucially important role in human affairs. People organize their communities around religious identities, go to war over religious beliefs or identities, make great art in the service of religion, and seek to change social norms or prevent or encourage change out of religious conviction. In short, religion so pervades the human world that it demands our attention regardless of whether it plays a direct role in our own lives.

It is also common to study religion for more personal reasons. You may want to know more about the tradition you or someone close to you grew up in. You may want to study other religions in order to understand other people's beliefs or to look at your own beliefs from a different perspective. You may also want to arm yourself with knowledge in order to bring others around to your way of thinking or to defend your beliefs against the arguments of those who might try to convert you to theirs.

Insider Versus Outsider

Most people learn about their own religion from their parents, their teachers at religious schools, or other members of the same religious community. Naturally, we tend to accept the teachings of our own religion as true and assume that the teachings of other religions are false, or at least less true. As "insiders," we may find it disturbing when "outsiders" challenge our beliefs or suggest that the history of "our religion" may not have been exactly as we were taught. Most people raised in a religious context tend to idealize their own tradition. In his 1962 book *The Meaning and End of Religion*, the late Canadian scholar of religion Wilfred Cantwell Smith famously wrote: "Normally persons talk about other people's religions as they are, and about their own as it ought to be" (Smith 1962: 49).

One of the advantages of a work such as this is that it helps us appreciate our own traditions from both insider and outsider points of view. When approaching an unfamiliar religious tradition, outsiders need to be sensitive to the ways in which it serves the needs of its followers. For their part, insiders need to understand how their own tradition looks from the outside.

Insiders also need to develop an understanding of the various traditions within their own religion. The insider–outsider matter is more complex than we might imagine, for there are many kinds of insiders. Is your Muslim friend a Sunni or a Shi'i? If a Shi'i, does she belong to the Twelver branch or one of the Sevener branches? Which variety of Buddhism does your classmate practice— Theravada, Mahayana, or Vajrayana? If Mahayana, which school? Is your Christian neighbor Protestant, Catholic, or Orthodox? A Protestant may well be an outsider to other Protestant groups, let alone to Catholics. A Zen Buddhist could have trouble seeing any connection between his or her practice and an elaborate Vajrayana ritual. Because each religion has many subdivisions, we will speak of traditions in the plural. We hope our readers will keep in mind the diversity behind the monolithic labels.

Methods for the Study of Religion

There are many different ways in which religion is studied in higher education. The American Academy of Religion (AAR) is the largest scholarly organization in the world devoted to the study of religion. It recommends the **religious studies** or **study of religion** approach, which it defines as follows:

> A religious studies approach provides students with tools to analyze religion from an academic perspective. There are many different methods that can fall under the category of the academic study of religion (e.g., anthropological, sociological, textual, historical, etc.), but religious studies scholars share the following five overarching assertions about religion:
>
> 1. There is distinction between the devotional expression of a religious belief and the study of diverse devotional expressions.
> 2. Religions are internally diverse.
> 3. Religions are always evolving and changing.
> 4. Religions are enmeshed in virtually all dimensions of human agency and expression.
> 5. Religions are historically embedded. (American Academy of Religion n.d.)

A religious studies approach gives students the ability to discern and analyze the intersections of religion with personal, social, political, and cultural life. Other methods for the study of religion are **faith-based**, **interfaith**, and **experiential**. Faith-based teaching promotes an explicit belief in and/or practice of religion. Faith-based approaches can often be found on college campuses in either chaplaincy or campus ministry programs, or in some classes offered in religiously affiliated schools. The faith-based approach advances understanding of particular interpretations of faith and tradition. It also responds to the religious and spiritual needs of students. The faith-based approach differs from the academic study of religion described earlier by promoting a specific religious perspective.

The central assumption of an interfaith approach is that people of differing religious traditions (within and among traditions) can communicate important elements of their faith experience to others through story and other forms of mutual exploration and sharing. This approach can include a decision to embrace a religious studies content focus, but the framework of exploration always emerges from one's own experience and understanding of faith and conversations with others about their faith.

The experiential approach focuses on introducing students to religious traditions and expressions through encounters with religious leaders, practitioners, and/or significant physical sites such as places of worship or other locations designated as holy. The educational purpose of this approach is to provide students with experiential learning encounters that can ground their studies in the lives of real people and places. This approach can be compatible with a religious studies approach when these encounters are framed within the context of ethnographic research. Without this framework, however, this approach can be problematic, since individual practitioners and specific religious settings always represent particular interpretations of a tradition, and highlighting them through an experiential encounter privileges them in unintentional but nevertheless concrete ways.

There are other issues in the academic study of religion, of course. One of the important scholars in this area is Russell T. McCutcheon of the University of Alabama. He makes an important distinction between the study of religion and theology:

The academic study of religion is fundamentally an *anthropological enterprise*. That is, it is primarily concerned with studying people (*anthropos* is an ancient Greek term meaning "human being"; *logos* means "word" or a "rational, systematic discourse"), their beliefs, behaviors, and institutions, rather than assessing "the truth" or "truths" of their various beliefs or behaviors. An anthropological approach to the study of religion (which is not to say that the study of religion is simply a sub-field of anthropology) is distinguished from a confessional, religious, or theological approach (*theos* is an ancient Greek term for "deity" or "god") which is generally concerned with determining the nature, will, or wishes of a god or the gods. Traditionally, the term "theology" refers to specifically Christian discourses on God, though the term now generally applies either to any religion's own articulate self-study or to its study of another religion (e.g., evangelism or religious pluralism are equally theological pursuits). (McCutcheon n.d.)

⊕ Basic Human Religion: Origins of Faith

There are a few concepts, shared by virtually all human cultures, that seem fundamental to what we call religion: powerful gods, sacred places, a life of some kind after death, and the presence in the physical world of spirits and deities that interact with humans in various ways. These concepts are so old and so widespread that no one can say where or when they first emerged.

Three Worlds

Historically, it seems that humans around the globe have imagined the world to consist of three levels—sky, earth, and underworld. The uppermost level, the sky, has typically been considered the home of the greatest deities. Exactly how this concept developed is impossible to know, but we can guess that the awesome power of storms was one contributing factor. The apparent movement of the sun, the stars, and the planets across the sky was very likely another. Observing the varying patterns could well have led early humans to believe that the heavenly bodies were living entities animated by their own individual spirits—in effect, gods and goddesses.

The very highest level, located in the heavens above the clouds and stars, was generally thought to be the home of the highest deity, typically referred to by a name such as Sky Father, Creator, or King of Heaven. This deity—invariably male—was the forerunner of the god of the monotheistic religions. Under the earth the spirits of serpents (surviving as the cobras, or **nagas**, in the religions of India) or reptilian monsters (surviving in dragon lore) were thought to dwell; perhaps because they were associated with dark and hidden places, they were usually imagined as evil. Finally, between the sky and the underworld lay the earth: the intermediate level where humans lived.

Sacred Places

Around the world, there are certain types of places where humans tend to feel they are in the presence of some unusual energy or power. Such places are regarded as set apart from the everyday world and are treated with special respect. One famous example is **Stonehenge**, a structure erected for ceremonial and burial purposes on the plains of England beginning about 3000 to 2500 BCE. Its circle of massive standing stones is oriented toward the point where the sun rises at the summer solstice, leading many to think it might have been designed as a kind of astronomical observatory. Another recent theory, based on the discovery of the remains of as many as 240 people buried at the site, suggests that Stonehenge served as the dwelling place of the ancestors.

Birds over Stonehenge. (Tore Johannesen/Getty Images)

Other places often considered sacred (meaning "set aside") are mountains and hilltops—the places closest to the sky-dwelling deities. In the ancient Middle East, for instance, worship was often conducted at ritual centers known simply as **high places**. People gathered at these sites to win the favor of the deities by offering them food, drink, praise, and prayer. One widely known example is the altar area on the cliff above the ancient city of Petra in Jordan.

Great rivers and waterfalls are also often regarded as sacred. And in Japan virtually every feature of the natural landscape—from great mountains and waterfalls to trees and stones—was traditionally believed to be animated by its own god or spirit (*kami*).

Animal Spirits

Another common and long-standing human tendency has been to attribute spirits to animals, either individually or as members of a family, with a kind of collective guardian spirit. For this reason, traditional hunting societies have typically sought to ensure that the animals they kill for food are treated with the proper respect, lest other members of those species be frightened away or refuse to let themselves be caught.

In addition, body parts from the most impressive animals—such as bulls, bears, lions, and eagles—have often been used as "power objects" to help humans make contact with the spirits of these animals. People in many cultures have attributed magical properties to objects such as bear claws or eagle feathers, wearing them as amulets or using them as protection against evil spirits.

Death and Burial

From ancient times, humans have taken great care with the burial of their dead. Excavations have revealed bodies positioned with the head facing east, the "first direction," where the sun rises, or

A seal from the Harappan culture depicting a ritual killing of a bull in the presence of the tree god. (John Marshall/Harappa.com)

placed in the fetal position, suggesting a hope for rebirth into a different realm. These burial positions in themselves would not be enough to prove a belief in an afterlife; however, many graves have also contained, along with the remains of the dead, "grave goods" of various kinds for use by the deceased. Some of these provisions for the afterlife likely belonged to the person in life, while others appear to be specially made replicas. Grave goods sometimes include sacrificed animals or costly items such as precious stones. Apparently the living were willing to sacrifice important resources to help the dead in the afterlife.

The belief that deceased ancestors can play a role in guiding living family members appears to be especially widespread. Traditions such as the Japanese **Obon**, the Mexican **Day of the Dead**, and the Christian **All Saints' Day** and **Halloween** all reflect the belief that the souls of the dead return to earth once a year to share a ritual meal with the living. Humans have traditionally felt the need to perform rituals to appease these spirits while they are back among the living.

Focus

A Modern Reflection on Ancient Burials and Religion

Wilfred Cantwell Smith wrote about prehistoric burials:

> Some years ago I had the privilege of standing in the Rockefeller Museum in Jerusalem before a case in which the plaster was still wet, setting the skeleton of *Palaeoanthropos palestiniensis* or "Mount Carmel man," dating somewhere from a hundred to two hundred thousand years BCE. It had been found under a floor in a distinct excavated cyst, quite clearly buried. This is the earliest instance we have of human activity of a kind that today we call religious. While there is no way of knowing what went on in the minds or hearts of this man's community who took the trouble to bury him

> carefully, this much we can say: that present religious practices of humankind can be traced back for at least a thousand centuries in a continuous tradition.
>
> . . . [P]rehistoric burial shows that men and women from the very earliest traces of their beginnings have recognized that there is more to human life than meets the eye, that our total significance is not exhausted within the six feet of space or sixty years of time whereby we each play our part on the stage of earth. The sober observation of the historian now agrees with the insight of the philosopher, and the faith of the saint, that human beings are not human until they have recognized that the proper response to death is poetry, not prose. (Smith 1998: 33–34)

Why Are Humans Religious?

The reasons behind human religiosity are complex and varied. All we can say with any certainty is that religion seems to grow out of human experiences: out of the fear of death, which religion transforms into the hope for a good afterlife, and out of the uncertainty surrounding natural events, over which religion offers a sense of control through the intervention of a priest capable of predicting the change of seasons and the movement of the planets. Religion emerges from the experience of good or bad powers that are sensed in dreams, in sacred spaces, and in certain humans and animals.

Religion has many emotional dimensions, including fear, awe, love, and hate. But it also has intellectual dimensions, including curiosity about what causes things to happen, the recognition of a sense of order in the universe that suggests the presence of a creator, and the drive to make sense out of human experience.

The nature of religious belief and practice has changed through the centuries, so we must be careful not to take the religion of any particular time and place as the norm. What we can safely say is that religion is such an ancient aspect of human experience that it has become part of human nature. For this reason some scholars have given our species, *Homo sapiens*, a second name: *Homo religiosus*.

⊕ Basic Human Religion: Patterns of Faith

Looking forward from the ancient origins of religion, we can see a number of patterns that have emerged in different parts of the world, some of them almost simultaneously.

Since most of the chapters in this work focus on individual religious traditions, it may be useful to begin with a broader perspective. What follows is a brief overview of some of the major developments in the history of what Wilfred Cantwell Smith called "religion in the singular," meaning the history of human religiosity in the most general sense.

Shamanism

One very early pattern of human religiosity involves a ritual specialist—in essence, a kind of priest—that we know today as a **shaman**. The word "shaman" comes from a specific Central Asian culture, but it has become the generic term for a person who acts as an intermediary between humans and the spirit world. Other terms include "medicine man," "soul doctor," and "witch doctor."

Shamans are still active in a number of cultures today. The way they operate varies, but certain patterns seem to be almost universal, which in itself suggests that the way of the shaman is very ancient. Sometimes the child of a shaman will follow in the parent's footsteps, but more often a shaman will be "called" to the role by his or her psychic abilities, as manifested in some extraordinary vision or revelation, or perhaps a near-death experience.

Candidates for the role of shaman face a long and rigorous apprenticeship that often includes a vision quest, in the course of which they are likely to confront terrifying apparitions. Typically the quester will acquire a guiding spirit, sometimes the spirit of a particular animal (perhaps a bear or an eagle, whose claws or feathers the shaman may wear to draw strength from its special powers) and sometimes a more humanlike spirit (a god or goddess). That spirit will then often continue to serve as a guide and protector throughout the shaman's life.

To communicate with the spirit world, the shaman usually enters a trance state (often induced with the help of rhythmic chanting, drumming, or hallucinogenic drugs). According to Mircea Eliade's classic book *Shamanism: Archaic Techniques of Ecstasy*, contact is then made in one of two ways. In the first, described as "ecstatic" (from a Greek root meaning "to stand outside"), the shaman's soul leaves his or her body (which may appear lifeless) and travels to the realm where the spirits live. In

This picture, taken on August 13, 2016, shows professional shaman La Thi Tam performing a "Len Dong" dance at a temple in Hanoi. The Len Dong dance is said to cure prolonged illness, spiritual possession, and stress over family troubles. The ancient practice—previously restricted by colonial French and Vietnamese authorities—is enjoying a renaissance in the communist nation as officials ease constraints against it. (NHAC NGUYEN/AFP/Getty Images)

the second, the shaman calls the spirit into his or her own body and is possessed by it; in such cases the shaman may take on the voice and personality of the spirit or mimic its way of moving.

In either case, after regaining normal consciousness, the shaman announces what he or she has learned about the problem at hand and what should be done about it. Typically, the problem is traced to the anger of a particular spirit, and the shaman then explains the reason for that anger and what must be done to appease the spirit. In most cases the appropriate response is to perform a ritual sacrifice of some kind.

Hunting Rituals

Many ancient cave drawings depict hunting scenes in which a human figure seems to be performing a dance of some kind. Based on what we know of later hunting societies, we can guess that the figure is a shaman performing a ritual either to ensure a successful hunt or to appease the spirits of the animals killed.

It is not hard to imagine why such societies would have sought ways to influence the outcome of a hunt. Indeed, it seems that the more dangerous the endeavor, the more likely humans were to surround it with rituals. As the anthropologist Bronislaw Malinowski pointed out in his classic book *Magic, Science and Religion*, the Trobriand Islanders he studied did not perform any special ceremonies before fishing in the lagoon, but they never failed to perform rituals before setting out to fish in the open ocean. This suggested to Malinowski that religious behavior is, at least in part, a way of coping with dangerous situations.

In addition, though, as we have seen, many early humans believed that the spirits of the animals they hunted had to be appeased. Thus a special ritual might be performed to mark the first goose kill of the season in the hope that other geese would not be frightened away from the hunting grounds.

Such rituals not only reflect humans' concern over the future food supply, but also reveal something about the nature of human belief in spirits. From very ancient times, it seems, humans have believed that the spirit—whether of an animal killed for food or of a human being—survives death and can communicate with others of its kind.

Coping with Unfriendly Spirits

The spirits associated with natural phenomena—whether animals or storms, mountains or rivers—have typically been thought to behave toward humans in the same ways that humans behave toward one another. Strategies for dealing with unfriendly spirits have therefore usually been based on what works with humans, such as threats or offerings of food, dance, music, or other pleasing things.

Many cultures have believed wild, uninhabited areas to be guarded by resident spirits. In some cases, these spirits have taken the form of monsters or mythical beasts; in others, such as the folklore of Scandinavia, they have assumed the guise of "little people" such as trolls.

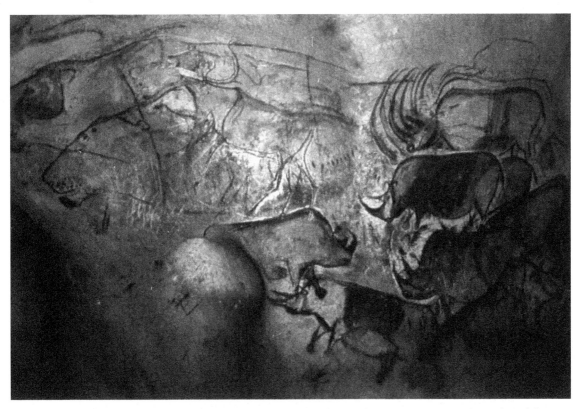

Animal images from the Chauvet cave in southern France, dated to c. 30,000 BCE. (Arterra Picture Library/Alamy Stock Photo)

In ancient times, unfriendly spirits were of particular concern to those who ventured into the forest as hunters or gatherers, but they were not understood to be confined to the wilderness. Pain and disease of all kinds—from toothache to appendicitis to mental illness—were also attributed to possession by malevolent spirits or demons. In Sri Lanka, those suffering from certain illnesses were advised to have a shaman sacrifice a chicken as an offering to the "graveyard demon," effectively bribing him to go away. In such cases a second chicken, still alive, would be given to the shaman who performed the ritual. Another approach was to frighten the demon away, either by threatening to invoke another, stronger spiritual power, such as the spirit guide of the shaman, to drive him off or by making threatening gestures or loud noises. The firecrackers still used in some East Asian rituals are examples of the latter approach.

Connecting to the Cosmos

A second pattern that emerged as religion developed across the globe is the one that inspired the building of structures like Stonehenge. People of the Neolithic era went to extraordinary lengths to create sacred areas by assembling huge stones in complex patterns. In some cases the motivation may have been political: perhaps a leader wanted to demonstrate his power over the people under his command. In others, however, the main reason undoubtedly had something to do with religion, such as the need for a public space where the rituals essential to the society—weddings, puberty rites, funerals—could be performed.

Discerning the Cosmic Cycles

Ritual centers such as Stonehenge may also have served purposes that we might today think of as scientific or technical, but that their builders would have associated with religion. One very important function of priests was to track the seasons and determine the best time for seasonal activities such as planting. In addition to tracking the north–south movements of the sun, the people of the Neolithic era paid careful attention to the phases of the moon and the positions of certain constellations at their rising. The horizon was divided into segments named after various planets or constellations associated with that segment. What we now call astrology developed as a way of understanding the cycle of the seasons and how humans fit into it, collectively and individually. In ancient times no important decision would have been made without consulting an expert in the movements of the sun, moon, planets, and constellations. Even in modern times, many people, including political leaders, will consult an astrologer before making a major decision.

Hilltop Tombs

We suggested earlier that two powerful motivators of human religion are the fear of death and the idea of an afterlife. Ancient cultures around the world appear to have favored high places as burial sites. Where there were no hills, artificial ones were sometimes built, at least for the most important members of the society. The pyramids of Egypt and the stupas of Asia are both examples of this practice. In the pyramids, shafts extending from the burial chambers toward important stars connected the deceased with the cosmos. Similarly, in Buddhist stupas, a wooden pole—later replaced by a vertical stone structure—extended above the burial mound to connect the earth with the heavens. Scholars refer to this kind of symbolic link between earth and sky as an *axis mundi* ("world axis").

Animals and Gods

Another common feature of Neolithic religion was a tendency to associate certain animals with specific deities. One very early example comes from the ancient (c. 7000–5000 BCE) city of Catalhoyuk ("forked mound"), near Konya in modern Turkey, where a small sculpture of a woman flanked by two large felines was found. James Mellaart, the archaeologist who first excavated the site in the 1960s, believed she represented a mother goddess seated on a throne. Although this interpretation has been disputed, we know that the ancient Egyptians had a cat goddess named Bast who was revered as a symbol of both motherliness and hunting prowess. And the fierce Hindu goddess Durga is usually depicted riding either a lion or a tiger. (One Christmas card from modern India shows the Virgin Mary riding a tiger in the same fashion.)

A similar pattern of association linked the most powerful male deities of Neolithic societies with the strength and virility of the bull. In Greek mythology, the great god Zeus took the form of a white bull when he abducted the Phoenician princess Europa. A creature known as the minotaur—half man, half bull—was said to have been kept in a labyrinth beneath the ancient palace of Knossos, on the island of Crete, where frescos show people leaping over the horns of a bull. Greek temples often displayed bull horns near their altars. And in India a bull named Nandi is the sacred mount of the great god Shiva.

The association of the bull with the creator god can be seen even in Judaism, which strictly forbids the use of any image to represent its invisible deity. In the Bible, when Moses returns from the mountain where he encounters God and finds that his brother Aaron, the first high priest, has allowed the people to worship an image of a golden calf or bullock, he denounces this practice as

Hindus venerate the bull Nandi as a manifestation in animal form of the divine power of the god Shiva. (Jeremy Horner/Corbis/VCG)

idolatry. Centuries later, one of Solomon's sons is severely chastised for installing bull images in the temples he has built.

Temple Religion

A third pattern that emerged as religions spread was the emergence of the temple cult, featuring the construction of larger temples, the creation of more elaborate sacrificial rituals, and the development of a priestly class endowed with unusual power, prestige, and wealth. This pattern, beginning at least 3,000 years ago, played an enormous role in shaping many traditions, including Judaism, Chinese religion, and Hinduism.

Indo-European Priests

"Indo-European" (IE) is a modern term referring to a language family and cultural system that eventually stretched from India all the way through Europe. The Indo-European cultural system has been one of the most important in human history. It most likely originated in the region of the steppes of modern Russia and Ukraine, but other theories about the IE homeland have been proposed. Based on the vocabulary of "proto-IE," as reconstructed by linguists, it is clear that IE people hunted, herded, practiced metallurgy, rode horses, drove chariots, and waged war, among other activities. Farming, however, appears not to have been part of their culture: the fact that the IE vocabulary related to agriculture differs from one place to another suggests that when it came to farming, the Indo-Europeans simply adopted existing local practices.

In at least some of the places where the IE culture came to dominate, its members set up a social system with four basic divisions, the top three of which consisted of priests, warriors, and middle-class commoners. In India these groups are known respectively as the *brahmins*, *kshatriyas*, and *vaishyas*. In ancient times each of these groups had a special clothing color; thus, today in India *varna* ("color") is still the standard term for "class." The priests performed rituals, kept the calendar, taught the young, and advised the kings. Within the warrior class, the top clans were the rulers. The middle-class "commoners" earned their living as merchants or farmers. Finally, all people of local origin, no matter how wealthy or accomplished, were relegated to the servant (*shudra*) class.

The four-level social system was given mythic status in the *Rig Veda*, according to which the world came into being through the sacrifice of a "cosmic person" (Purusha). Out of his mouth came the brahmin priests, whose job was to chant the sacred hymns and syllables. The warriors came from his arms, the middle class from his thighs, and the servants from his feet. Even today, this ancient hymn continues to be invoked to buttress the social structure of India.

Over a period of about 1,000 years, beginning around 2500 BCE, the Indo-Europeans took control of the territories that are now Afghanistan, northwest India, Pakistan, Turkey, Greece, Rome, central Europe, and, for a while, even Egypt. Their religious culture was similar to those embraced by most of their contemporaries 4,000 to 5,000 years ago, with many deities, including a "sky father" (a name that survives in the Greek Zeus Pater, the Latin Jupiter, and the Sanskrit Dyaus Pitar) and a storm god (Indra in India, Thor in Scandinavia). They also sang hymns to female deities, such as the goddess of dawn, and had a hereditary priesthood that offered sacrifices to the gods.

Although the IE people did not necessarily invent the system of hereditary priesthood, they certainly contributed to its spread. Priests such as Hindu brahmins, ancient Roman priests,

Document

The Social Role of Sacrifice

These selections show how ritual sacrifice helps define social roles. In the first selection, from the Hindu Vedas, the sacrifice of a primal Person defines the norms for the social roles of the four social classes. In the second selection, from the Hebrew Bible, Moses's instructions to the Israelites make it normative for them to bring a sacrificial offering to the temple three times each year.

When they divided the Man [Purusha, the primal Person sacrificed by the gods to create the world], into how many parts did they disperse him? What became of his mouth, what of his arms, what were his two thighs and his two feet called? His mouth was the brahmin, his arms were made into the nobles, his two thighs were the populace, and from his feet the servants were born. (Doniger O'Flaherty 1975: 26)

Three times a year all your males shall appear before the Lord your God at the place which he will choose: at the feast of unleavened bread, at the feast of weeks, and at the feast of booths. They shall not appear before the Lord empty-handed: All shall give as they are able, according to the blessing of the Lord your God that he has given you. (Deuteronomy 16:16–17) and Celtic Druids inherited their priestly status. These individuals enjoyed great power and prestige, and sometimes were resented by the other classes. (One ancient Indian text includes a parody in which dogs, acting like priests, dance around a fire chanting, "*Om* let us eat, *om* let us drink.")

Priests and Temples Elsewhere

We actually know when the first Jewish temple was built. After David was chosen as king of both the northern kingdom of Israel and the southern kingdom of Judah, he captured the Jebusite city now known as Jerusalem. He transformed the city into a proper capital, complete with a grand palace for himself and an organized priesthood. His son Solomon took the next step, building the first temple in the mid-tenth century BCE. The priests attached to the temple soon made it the only site where sacrificial rituals could be performed.

The Jewish priesthood was hereditary. All those who served in the temple as assistants to the priests were required to be Levites (members of the tribe of Levi), and priests themselves had to be not only Levites but direct descendants of Aaron, the brother of Moses, who had been the original high priest.

Priests became a powerful social class in many other parts of the world as well, including Africa, Asia, and the Americas. In some cultures they inherited their role, and in others they were recruited into it. Typically, the role of priest was reserved for males, with females considered impure because of the menstrual cycle; the Vestal Virgins of ancient Rome, who tended the sacred fires and performed rituals, were among the very few exceptions to the general rule. There is evidence that in India and elsewhere, women sometimes served as temple prostitutes, embodying the goddess in sexual union with males who represented the god.

Middle Eastern Prophets and Asian Sages

By 700 BCE or even earlier, several new religious traditions had begun to form under the leadership of great prophets or sages—a fourth pattern in the development of religiosity. The word "prophet" derives from Greek and has two related meanings, one referring to a person who speaks on behalf of a deity and one referring to a person who foresees or predicts the future. The terms are often conflated because prophets delivering messages from the deity often warned of disasters to come if God's will was not obeyed. The site of the temple at Delphi, Greece, where a virgin priestess said to be under the inspiration of Apollo delivered prophecies, must have seemed a natural spot for making contact with the divine and receiving sacred knowledge: high up a mountainside, close to the gods, with a natural cave that resembled the entrance to a womb (*delphys* in Greek) representing the mysterious female energy and a standing stone or *omphalos* (navel of the earth) representing the male energy and the connection between heaven and earth.

This sacred site dates back at least 3,000 years, to a time before the rise of classical Greece when the oracle was believed to be inspired not by Apollo but by the earth goddess Gaia. Eventually males took control of the sacred site, but even in classical times the virgin priestesses would prepare themselves to receive Apollo's message by bathing in an artesian spring and breathing intoxicating fumes emitted from a fissure in the earth—with both the water and the fumes believed to issue from Gaia, the earth.

Those wishing to consult the oracle had to climb the mountain, make known their request, pay a fee, and sacrifice a black goat before their question could be put to the oracle.

Document

Ritual Sacrifice in the Hebrew Bible

Long before the establishment of the temple in Jerusalem, where priests would perform ritual sacrifices, God commanded the Hebrew patriarch Abram (later renamed Abraham) to sacrifice several animals to mark the covenant that was about to be made between them.

> Then [God] said to [Abram], "I am the Lord who brought you from Ur of the Chaldeans, to give you this land to possess." But he said, "O Lord God, how am I to know that I shall possess it?" He said to him, "Bring me a heifer three years old, a female goat three years old, a ram three years old, a turtledove, and a young pigeon." He brought him all these and cut them in two, laying each half over against the other; but he did not cut the birds in two. And when birds of prey came down on the carcasses, Abram drove them away.
>
> As the sun was going down, a deep sleep fell upon Abram, and a deep and terrifying darkness descended upon him. Then the Lord said to Abram, "Know this for certain, that your offspring shall be aliens in a land that is not theirs, and shall be slaves there, and they shall be oppressed for four hundred years; but I will bring judgment on the nation that they serve, and afterward they shall come out with great possessions. As for yourself, you shall go to your ancestors in peace; you shall be buried in a good old age. . . ."
>
> When the sun had gone down and it was dark, a smoking fire pot and a flaming torch passed between these pieces [the halved carcasses]. On that day the Lord made a covenant with Abram, saying, "To your descendants I give this land, from the river of Egypt to the great river, the river Euphrates, the land of the Kenites, the Kenizzites, the Kadmonites, the Hittites, the Perizzites, the Rephaim, the Amorites, the Canaanites, the Girgashites, and the Jebusites." (Genesis 15:7–21)

The priestess would take her place over the fissure and, in an ecstatic trance, deliver Apollo's message, which was typically unintelligible and had to be translated into ordinary language by a male priest. Interpreting the real-world significance of a prophecy was not so simple, however. In one famous case, a Greek leader who asked what would happen if he went to war with another state was told that a great country would fall; accordingly, he went to war—but the country that fell was his own. Similarly, in the Oedipus myth, the oracle's prophecy that the infant will grow up to kill his father and marry his mother is fulfilled in spite of the measures taken to avoid that fate.

Abrahamic Prophetic Traditions

In 586 BCE the people of Israel were forcibly removed from their homeland and exiled to Babylon. The centuries that followed the "Babylonian captivity" were the defining period for the concept of prophecy as it developed in the three monotheistic traditions that trace their origins to the prophet Abraham. Often, the Jewish prophets' messages were directed toward the people of Israel as a whole, warning of the disasters that loomed if they did not meet God's demands. Christianity saw

Jesus and certain events surrounding his life as the fulfillment of Hebrew prophecies. And Islam in turn recognized the Hebrew prophets, beginning with Abraham and including Jesus, as the forerunners of the Prophet Muhammad, the last and greatest of all prophets, the messenger (*rasul*) who received God's final revelations. Muslims understand Muhammad to have been the "seal of the prophets": no other prophet will follow him, since he has delivered the message of God in its entirety. As in earlier prophetic traditions, the Day of Judgment (or Day of Doom) and the concepts of heaven and hell are central to Islam.

Zarathustra, Prophet of the Wise Lord

Zarathustra (or Zoroaster) was a prophet figure who lived more than 2,500 years ago, probably in the region of eastern Iran or Afghanistan. Although we know little about his life, he left behind a collection of poems devoted to a "wise lord" called Ahura Mazda. The religion that developed around his teachings, which came to be known as Zoroastrianism, played an important part in the development of monotheism. The concepts of heaven and hell also owe a lot to the Zoroastrians, who believed that evildoers would be condemned to hell at their death, but that eventually a great day of judgment would come when the souls of all the dead would be made to pass through

The remains of Har Megiddo, the site known to Christians as Armageddon. The circular rock structure is thought to have been an altar. (Judith Reishtein)

a fiery wall. Those who had been virtuous in life would pass through the fire without pain, while the rest would be cleansed of their remaining sin and permitted to enter paradise (a term believed to derive from a Persian word meaning "garden"). The threat of hell and the promise of heaven were powerful tools for any prophet seeking to persuade people to behave as he or she believed the deity demanded.

Among Asian religions the great moral leaders are typically referred to as sages rather than prophets. Whereas a prophet brings a message from a god, a sage is a wise person who speaks the wisdom of the ages. The ethical content of both figures' messages may concern how humans should live together harmoniously, but for the sage the authority of the message resides in its inherent wisdom rather than in it being the word of a god. While Western (Middle Eastern) religions have typically been founded by prophets, Asian religions are generally traced back to sages such as Buddha (Buddhism), Mahavira (Jainism), Confucius (Confucianism), or Laozi (Daoism).

The First Principle: Greek Philosophy and Daoist Thought

Yet another important pattern emerged around 2,500 years ago. In it the divine is understood not as a humanlike entity but as the energy or first principle of the cosmos. This energy is not a god who issues commandments, answers prayers, or in any way interacts with humans as a human. It does not create in the usual fashion of gods; it does not direct the course of history or dictate the fate of individuals. In fact, some have suggested that this divine force may have more in common with the principles of modern physics than it does with the traditional gods of most religions. This divinity simply exists—or rather "underlies" everything that exists. Among the traditions that developed around the energy concept were Chinese Daoism, the Upanishadic wisdom of Hinduism, and the pre-Socratic philosophy of the early Greek world.

Around 2,500 years ago the Greek-speaking philosophers of Ionia (now southwestern Turkey) began to ask the following question: What is the first principle, the first cause, the source from which all else comes? Starting from the science of the day, they tried to determine which of the four primal elements—earth, air, fire, and water—came first. Although their methods were those of philosophy rather than scientific experimentation, their attempt to understand the causal principle underlying all things—without bringing in a god as the final cause—marked a major advance toward the development of the scientific worldview.

Mystery Religion

"Mystery religion," a sixth pattern that emerges in the history of religiosity, refers to a type of Greek and Roman tradition in which the core teachings and rituals were kept secret from outsiders and were revealed only to those who were prepared to undergo initiation in the hope of securing blessings during this life and a heavenly paradise in the afterlife. Such religions became so popular during the Roman period that they presented a threat to the power and influence of the official Roman priesthood (not to be confused with the Roman Catholic priesthood).

The Eleusinian mystery tradition may be the oldest of these religions. Named for an ancient Greek town called Eleusis, it grew out of the myth of the young Persephone, or Kore ("girl"), who is abducted by the god of the dead, Hades, and taken down into the underworld. With the disappearance of this young girl—a potent symbol of growth and fertility—everything on earth begins to die. This imperils not only humans but also the gods themselves, who depend on humans to feed them through sacrifices. The girl's mother, Demeter, is therefore allowed to descend into the underworld and bring her back. Scholars understand the Persephone myth to be based on the seasonal cycles of stagnation during the winter and renewal in the spring. Members of her cult believed that by identifying themselves with the dying and rising goddess through the celebration of seasonal rituals, they too would triumph over death.

Initiates into the mysteries associated with the god Dionysus also followed a very ancient tradition. Through rituals that included the drinking of wine, ecstatic dancing, and perhaps the eating of mind-altering plants, participants were able to enter into ecstatic states of consciousness that they believed would lead their god to ensure them a pleasant afterlife. Another popular mystery cult, dedicated to the goddess Isis, had Egyptian origins.

Many scholars have suggested that mystery cults such as these may have influenced the development of Christianity. The early Christians were initiated into the new cult by undergoing baptism. They then joined an inner circle of people whose faith centered on the death and resurrection of Jesus and who hoped that by following Christ they would secure blessings during this life and a place in heaven after death. Although Christianity developed out of Judaism, its theological structure does seem to have been influenced, however indirectly, by mystery religion.

Avatar: God on Earth

Long before anyone thought of an "avatar" as either a blue-skinned movie humanoid or an on-screen image representing a player in a computer game, *avatar(a)* was a Sanskrit theological term for the "coming down" to earth of a god. By the first century of the Common Era, the idea of a god born in human form had taken root in many parts of the world. In the earlier stages of the development of religion, there were many stories of gods and goddesses who came down to earth, but there are two major differences between these accounts and the avatar stories.

First, whereas the ancient gods came down to earth as gods, the avatar is a god in a truly human form—as a later Christian creed put it, "fully God and fully man." For example, in the ancient Indian

Document

Avatar Gods

These two selections, one Hindu and one Christian, reflect the idea that the divine can come down (avatar) to earth in human form in order to help the world.

For the protection of the good,
For the destruction of evildoers,
For the setting up of righteousness,
I come into being, age after age.
   (Krishna to Arjuna in the Bhagavad Gita;
     Zaehner 1966: 267)

Have this mind among yourselves, which you have in Christ Jesus, who, though he was in the form of God, did not count equality with God a thing to be grasped, but emptied himself, taking the form of a servant, being born in the likeness of men. And being found in human form he humbled himself. (St. Paul to the Christians of Philippi; Philippians 2:6–7)

story of Princess Dhamayanti, her father holds a party to which he invites all the marriageable princes from various kingdoms. Four gods also attend the party, however, all disguised as the handsome Prince Nala, whom the princess already plans to choose. At first she is disturbed to see five look-alikes, but finally she finds that she can distinguish the four divine imposters because they do not sweat and float slightly above the ground. She marries the human prince, and they live happily ever after.

Unlike the gods at Dhamayanti's party, the avatar gods walk on the ground, sweat, get hungry, sleep, and are in every way human. They are incarnated in a human womb, are born, grow up, teach, save the world from evil, and eventually die. As a Christian layman once explained, "You have to understand that we Christians worship a god in diapers." His choice of words was unusual, but his theology was solid, and it leads us to the second major innovation that came with the development of the concept of the avatar god.

This second innovation is the idea that the avatar god is a savior figure in at least two ways. Not only does he save the world from some evil power, such as Satan or a demonic king, but he also saves from hell those who put their faith in him and secures them a place in heaven. In avatar religions, the ritual of sacrifice is replaced by the ritual of placing faith in the savior god.

The biography of the savior god follows a well-known pattern. Typically, the avatar god has a special, nonsexual conception. His mother is chosen to bear him because she is exceptionally pure, and an angel or prophet announces to her that the child she is carrying has a special destiny. The savior's birth, usually in a rustic setting, is surrounded by miracles, which often include the appearance of a fortuitous star or constellation pattern in the night sky. Wise persons foresee the child's greatness. An evil king tries to kill the baby but kills another baby, or other babies, instead. The child has special powers and as an adult is able to work miracles. He typically marries and has a child before embarking on his religious mission. His death represents a triumph over evil, and the cosmos responds with earthquakes and other natural signs. Upon dying, he returns to the heavens to preside over a paradise in which his followers hope to join him after they die.

The avatar concept took root in Asia and the Middle East at least 2,000 years ago. Among some Hindus its impact was reflected in the worship of Krishna; among some Buddhists, in the veneration of Amitabha Buddha (the figure who would become Amida in Japan); and among some Jews, in the rise of Christianity.

Jesus the Christ: God Come Down

The Christian doctrine of the trinity affirms that the one God exists in three persons: the father, the son, and the holy spirit. In formulating this doctrine, the Christians departed radically from the theology proclaimed by Abraham and Moses. There is no room in Jewish thought for an avatar god, but that was the direction in which Christian thought developed. The prologue to the Gospel of John identifies Jesus with the divine Logos—the Word of God that was present before creation. The New Testament says that Jesus "emptied himself of divinity" and came down for the salvation of the world after being conceived in the womb of a virgin by the spirit of God. An angel announces the pregnancy and its significance to his mother. The birth is associated with the appearance of a special star. According to the Gospel of Luke, shepherds overhear the angels rejoicing and come to revere the infant. In Matthew's Gospel, magi (wise men) from the East follow a special star and bring gifts to the child.

For Christians, Jesus became the ultimate god, one who died on the cross on behalf of his followers and rose on the third day after his death. By participating in the sacred rituals—the sacraments of baptism and the Eucharist (in which consecrated bread and wine are consumed in commemoration of the Last Supper)—and placing their trust in Jesus as Lord, Christians hope to secure a place in heaven after their death.

In this way Christianity started with the Hebrew scriptures and the monotheism of Moses and incorporated into them the avatar pattern, along with elements of the mystery traditions, to form a new religion. Many Jews resisted these changes, but some accepted them in the belief that God had in fact offered the world a new dispensation.

Scriptural Religion

Traditionally, religious wisdom was communicated from generation to generation orally. Many ancient cultures did not have writing. Others preferred to keep their stories about the gods, goddesses, and spirits and their morality tales in oral form while using writing for more mundane matters such as tax records or treaties. The beginning of scriptural religion is hard to date. Some of the earliest scriptures include the Zoroastrian Avesta of Persia and the Torah of Judaism, which took shape approximately 3,000 years ago. The Hindu Vedas are at least that old as well, but because of their sacredness, they were passed along orally and were not written down until centuries after their composition.

Religions based primarily on scripture were relative latecomers, arising after a fixed set of writings was adopted. A phenomenon we might term scripturalism began when some religious traditions began to insist that their particular scriptures were the literal words of God, and to make adherence to those scriptures the focus of their religious life.

Scripturalism manifested itself in rabbinic Judaism in the centuries that followed the destruction of the Second Jerusalem Temple in 70 CE. It emerged in full force with the rise of Islam, destined to become one of the two most influential religions of all time, in the seventh century. It also played a large role in Protestant Christianity, starting in the sixteenth century, in which the authority of scripture replaced that of tradition and the papacy.

Living by Torah

During the Jews' exile in Babylon, the priests were not able to perform the traditional temple rituals, and so the Jews turned to the rabbis—scholars of the Torah with special expertise in Jewish law and ritual. In this way scripture began to play a more important role in Jewish life, a role that became even more important after the destruction of the Second Temple in 70 CE. Since that time, Jewish religious life has centered on the interpretation of scripture.

Document

The Word of God

We have sent it down as an Arabic Qur'an, in order that you may learn wisdom. (Qur'an 12:2)

In the beginning was the Word, and the Word was with God, and the Word was God. The same was in the beginning with God. All things were made by him, and without him was not any thing made that was made. (John 1:1–3, King James Version [KJV])

And the Word was made flesh and dwelt among us. (John 1:14, KJV)

The Word of God

The Gospels were not written until two or three generations after the death of Jesus, and the Christian canon did not take final shape until well into the third century CE. But once the books of the canon were fixed, the church came to emphasize scripture as a divinely inspired source of faith and practice. The Bible became as central to Christianity as the Torah was to Judaism. Christians commonly refer to their scriptures as the word of God, and some believe that the Bible was literally dictated by God to its human authors.

God's Final Prophet

The scriptural approach to religion is a very important aspect of Islam. The *surahs* that make up the Qur'an are believed to be the sacred words of God as revealed to the Prophet Muhammad by an angel, recorded by scribes, and compiled as a collection after his death. In its essence, then, the Qur'an is considered to be an oral text, meant to be recited—always in the original Arabic—rather than read silently. Nevertheless, the written Qur'an is treated with great respect. No other book is to be placed on top of the Qur'an, and before opening the book, the reader is expected to be in the same state of ritual purity required to perform the daily prayers.

Schoolchildren in Dhaka, Bangladesh, learn to read the Arabic of the Qur'an. (Majority World/UIG via Getty Images)

Creation Through the Word of God

A number of scriptural traditions have maintained that their scriptures were in existence before the world was created. The medieval book of Jewish mysticism known as the *Zohar*, for example, teaches that the Torah played a role in the creation. The prologue to the Gospel of John in the New Testament talks about creation through the Word (*Logos* in Greek). And Islam understands the Qur'an to have existed in the mind of God before the world itself was brought into existence.

How could the scriptures—the actual words of the Torah, Bible, or Qur'an—be present in the mind of God at the time of creation, thousands of years before the historical events they describe? The answer for believers is that God knows the future. Outsiders might argue that this calls into question the concept of free will: If the deity knows everything in advance, how can humans be free to choose? What use is it to try to persuade people to do the right thing if the deity has already determined what each of them will do? Such questions have led to lively theological debates in many religious traditions.

This idea has very old roots. In ancient Israel, Egypt, India, and elsewhere, it was assumed that the deities would not have performed the physical work of creation themselves, as ordinary humans would have done; rather, like kings, they would have commanded that the work be done: "Let there be light." Thus the divine word took on a special role in later theologies. In traditional Hindu thought, the goddess of speech, Vac, played this role.

Some branches of scriptural religions place such total authority in their scriptures that outsiders have branded their followers **fundamentalists**. The term "fundamentalism" was first used in the early twentieth century to refer to a variety of American Protestantism characterized by a fervent belief in the absolute, literal truth of the Bible. Similar movements exist within most religious traditions.

Some Practical Matters

We choose to avoid using the conventional distinction between Eastern and Western religions in this work for several reasons. One is that most religions may now be found anywhere in the world. Another is that the so-called Western religions arose in what we now term the Middle East: they are Western only in the sense that they have been widely adopted in the West. A related problem is that there is no clear dividing line between East and West. As the late Will Oxtoby pointed out in an earlier edition of this text,

> Well into the twentieth century, the East was everything to the east of Europe. The Orient began where the Orient Express ran: Istanbul. For some purposes, it even included North Africa and began at Morocco. A century ago, Islam was thought to be an Eastern religion, and Westerners who studied it were called orientalists.

For dates we use BCE ("before the Common Era") rather than BC ("before Christ") and CE ("Common Era") rather than AD ("Anno Domini," Latin for "in the year of our Lord"). For dates that are obviously in the Common Era, the "CE" will be implied.

Finally, it is difficult to decide whether a book like this should use diacritical marks in rendering foreign words. Scholars of religion writing for other scholars typically use diacritics for precision in transliterating foreign terms into English. Since this is an introductory text, we have chosen

Sites

Petra, Jordan

One of the best preserved of the high places (sacrificial altars) of the ancient Near East is found on the cliff above the ancient city of Petra in modern Jordan. Many tourists are content to walk along the valley road to view the many cave dwellings cut out of the cliffs, but some choose to make the rigorous climb to the top for the panoramic views and to see this ancient altar complex.

Tell Megiddo, Israel

Tell Megiddo is an archaeological mound in Israel, southeast of the modern city of Haifa. The ancient city of Megiddo was strategically located near a pass used by the trade route connecting Egypt and Assyria. The site of a battle with Egypt in the sixteenth century BCE, Har ("Mount") Megiddo is mentioned numerous times in the Hebrew Bible and is referred to by the Greek version of its name, Armageddon, in Revelation 16:16—a passage that some Christians interpret to mean that a final battle will be fought there at the end of time.

not to use diacritics because students often find them more confusing than helpful. Anyone who wishes to do more research on a religious tradition will soon encounter them, however.

Whether or not you are religious yourself, we invite you to delve into the study of several religious traditions that have played central roles both in the lives of individual humans and in the civilizations they have built around the world.

Discussion Questions

1. What are some concepts that are fundamental to what we call religion?

2. What are some of the major developments or patterns in the history of human religiosity?

3. What is an avatar? Give an example from both an Asian and a Western tradition to illustrate your answer.

4. What are some of the ways to study or approach religions?

Glossary

All Saints' Day A Christian festival honoring all the departed saints, held in the West on November 1.

Day of the Dead A Mexican festival honoring the dead.

experiential An approach to understanding religions through the experience of various devotional services, often at that religion's place of worship, prayer, or meditation.

faith-based A way of studying religion from the perspective of a particular faith.

fundamentalists Persons who ascribe total authority to their scriptures or doctrines, rejecting any conflicting secular or religious alternatives.

Halloween A holiday originally celebrated as the "Eve" of All Saints' Day and now a popular secular celebration held on October 31.

high places Sacred areas located on hill- or mountaintops; such places existed throughout the ancient Near East.

interfaith An approach in which, typically, persons of one faith share their experiences and worldview with persons of other faiths.

naga A mythical cobra living in the underworld, often associated with water and fertility in Indian religions.

Obon A Japanese festival honoring ancestors.

religious studies, or study of religion An academic, rather than confessional or doctrinal, approach to describing religions and their personal, social, political, and cultural roles.

shaman A type of priest, widespread among hunter-gatherer societies, who communicates with the spirit world on behalf of his or her people.

Stonehenge One of several ancient rock structures thought to have been constructed for ritual purposes.

Further Reading

Braun, Willi, and Russell T. McCutcheon, eds. 2000. *Guide to the Study of Religion.* New York: Cassell. An excellent introduction to terms that occur in the study of religion.

Juschka, Darlene M., ed. 2001. *Feminism in the Study of Religion: A Reader.* New York: Continuum. A collection of essays about feminism and the study of religion.

Miles, Jack, gen. ed. 2014. *The Norton Anthology of World Religions.* New York: W. W. Norton. An anthology of primary texts from the world's religions.

Orsi, Robert A. 2005. *Between Heaven and Earth.* Princeton, NJ: Princeton University Press. A study of Catholic devotion to various figures, as well as an examination of how scholars straddle the line between faith and scholarship.

Smith, Jonathan Z. 1978. *Map Is Not Territory: Studies in the History of Religions.* Leiden: E. J. Brill. A key volume by one of the most important theorists of the study of religion.

Smith, Jonathan Z. 1987. *To Take Place: Toward Theory in Ritual.* Chicago: University of Chicago Press. A key text for the study of ritual in the study of religion.

Stone, Jon R., ed. 2000. *The Craft of Religious Studies.* New York: Palgrave. A collection of essays from noted scholars on the study of religion.

Tweed, Thomas A. 2006. *Crossing and Dwelling: A Theory of Religion.* Cambridge, MA: Harvard University Press. A transnational model of religion from another key theorist of the study of religion.

Recommended Websites

https://www.aarweb.org/
The website of the largest professional organization for the study of religion.

https://religiousstudiesproject.com/
A podcast on the study of religion.

http://pluralism.org/
The website of the Pluralism Project at Harvard University, which looks at religious diversity in the United States and around the world.

References

American Academy of Religion. n.d. "Religious Literacy Guidelines for College Students". https://www.aarweb.org/about/religious-literacy-guidelines-for-college-students.

Doniger O'Flaherty, Wendy. 1975. *Hindu Myths: A Source Book, Translated from the Sanskrit.* Harmondsworth, UK: Penguin Classics.

Eliade, Mircea. 1964 [1951]. *Shamanism: Archaic Techniques of Ecstasy.* Translated by Willard R. Trask. Princeton, NJ: Princeton University Press.

Malinowski, Bronislaw. 1948. *Magic, Science and Religion.* Boston: Beacon Press.

McCutcheon, Russell. n.d. "What Is the Academic Study of Religion?" University of Alabama Department of Religious Studies. https://religion.ua.edu/links/the-students-desk/what-is-the-academic-study-of-religion/.

Smith, Wilfred Cantwell. 1962. *The Meaning and End of Religion.* New York: MacMillan.

Smith, Wilfred Cantwell. 1998. *Patterns of Faith Around the World.* Oxford: Oneworld.

Zaehner, R.C., ed. 1966. *Hindu Scriptures.* London: Everyman's Library.

2 Indigenous Traditions

Ken Derry

Traditions at a Glance

Numbers

Reliable statistical information is virtually nonexistent, but the United Nations estimates that there are approximately 370 million Indigenous people in the world. On average, perhaps 15 to 20 percent practice their ancestral traditions, but the figures are much higher in some communities and much lower in others.

Distribution

There are more than 5,000 distinct Indigenous cultures in some 90 countries around the world. By far the largest populations are in Asia and Africa; fewer than 10 percent are in Central and South America, while approximately 2 percent are found in North America and Oceania, and just a small fraction are located in Europe.

Recent Historical Periods

Written records of most Indigenous traditions do not begin until after first contact with non-Indigenous people, so the only developments we can trace with any certainty are relatively recent. However, Indigenous religions had been evolving for millennia before that time. First contact between Muslims and Indigenous Africans occurred around 600–700 CE. First contact between Europeans and Indigenous people of Africa, North America, and Oceania occurred between 1450 and 1850; this period saw the development of Atlantic slave trade and other colonial practices that devastated Indigenous populations. Between 1930 and 1960, several governments begin to reduce restrictions on Indigenous people and religions. Finally, starting around 1960, there was a revival of many Indigenous traditions around the world and the development of global pan-Indigenous movements.

Founders and Leaders

Few pre-contact traditions identify a human founder, although most attribute key elements of their religious life to superhuman ancestors. Virtually all of them recognize religious authority figures such as Elders and rely on ritual specialists such as diviners and healers who invoke spiritual powers to aid their communities. In response to colonialism, several new movements were founded by specific people, such as Wovoka (Paiute) or Nongqawuse (Xhosa).

Deities

Indigenous conceptions of gods vary widely. Some traditions recognize a single supreme deity as the source of all life and power. Others attribute creation to a series of gods, spirits, or ancestors. Almost all believe that personal deities (or spirits or ancestors) have ongoing influence in the world.

Authoritative Texts

Most pre-contact Indigenous religions passed along their sacred stories orally. These stories often include accounts of the creation of the world and/or the origins of the community. Many also recount the ongoing activity of personal spiritual forces in the world. New tales continue to be told (and written), particularly about trickster figures, and some post-contact movements (such as the Handsome Lake religion of the Iroquois) have their own sacred texts.

Noteworthy Teachings

Indigenous traditions are typically bound to specific places where important spiritual forces have manifested themselves (e.g., where acts of creation occurred). They also tend to be more concerned with

 A ceremony involving tobacco and **smudging** conducted in September 2014 beside the Red River in Winnipeg, Canada, for missing and murdered Indigenous women. The ceremony was conducted close to where the body of 15-year-old Tina Fontaine, from Sagkeeng First Nation, had been found in the river a few weeks earlier. (Mike Deal/Winnipeg Free Press)

what happens during life than after death; therefore, they place greater emphasis on behavior than on belief and assess actions in terms of their impact on the community. Many Indigenous traditions understand time as rhythmic rather than linear; in this conception, the sacred interacts with the world on an ongoing basis, responding to changing circumstances.

In this chapter you will learn about:

- The difficulties involved in defining the term "Indigenous"
- Some of the false assumptions that non-Indigenous people have held (and continue to hold) about Indigenous cultures
- The necessity of considering the specific historic and cultural context of any aspect of an Indigenous tradition
- The importance of relationships in Indigenous communities, stories, rituals, and art
- Why religious location and practice are much more important than belief for many Indigenous people
- The impact of colonialism on Indigenous religions
- How contemporary Indigenous people around the world are reclaiming, rebuilding, and revising many of their traditions

Indigenous traditions, which constitute the majority of the world's religions, are interwoven with the entire history of humanity and are almost unimaginably diverse. Some cultures recognize a single supreme being, some recognize a variety of deities, and some do not bother at all with such things. Among the peoples who do believe in one or more gods, there are some who pray to those higher powers and some who do not. How reasonable is it to group such diverse traditions together? The task of generalizing about Indigenous traditions must be approached with both caution and humility, recognizing that there are exceptions to every rule. Many past interpretations have been deeply mistaken. Looking through the lenses of their own assumptions and cultural biases, scholars can easily see things that aren't there or miss what is right in front of them.

⊕ "Indigenous" Religion

There is no definitive understanding of the term "Indigenous." Often, the term is understood to mean "original to the land." Yet places such as India and Africa have very ancient histories of migration and interaction between various groups. How could anyone possibly determine the "original" inhabitants of such lands? The question of who is and who is not Indigenous has both legal and political implications, and so how it is answered has a direct and lasting impact on the lives of people around the world. If we cannot identify a particular group as Indigenous, for example, how can its members assert their treaty rights or see their land claims settled fairly? Unfortunately, it is usually non-Indigenous governments that impose definitions of "Indigenous," and those definitions tend to change over time and do further harm to the people who are most impacted by such decisions.

That stated, there are two elements of central importance to cultures that have typically been considered Indigenous: kinship and location. Thus, we might say that an "Indigenous" (or "Aboriginal") community is one that is defined both by its members' *genealogical* relations to one another and by its connection to a particular *place*. The people who make up this community may or may not be the first or "original" inhabitants of this place. They may not even inhabit it now. Yet they see themselves as belonging to it, and they distinguish themselves from people who do not share this connection.

Timeline

The events listed here relate only to the cultures discussed in this chapter—a tiny fraction of the thousands that have existed. Although most of the dates relate to events since contact with non-Indigenous people, the histories in question began many millennia earlier.

c. 190,000 BCE	Earliest evidence of Indigenous people in Africa
c. 70,000 BCE	Earliest evidence of Indigenous people in Australia, Europe, and Asia
c. 12,500 BCE	Earliest evidence of Indigenous people in the Americas
616 CE	First Muslims arrive in Africa (Ethiopia)
c. 1250	First contact between the Ainu and the Japanese
c. 1300	First Indigenous settlers arrive in New Zealand (from Polynesia)
1444	Portuguese exploration of sub-Saharan Africa begins
c. 1480	Atlantic slave trade begins
1492	Christopher Columbus (Italian) arrives in the Caribbean, initiating Spanish colonization of the Americas
1642	Dutch explorer Abel Janszoon Tasman arrives in New Zealand
1788	British First Fleet arrives in Sydney, Australia
1799	Handsome Lake experiences his first vision
1819	British and Xhosa (led by Nxele) fight Battle of Grahamstown
1856–1857	Nongqawuse's vision leads to Xhosa cattle massacre
1869	Australia begins taking Aboriginal children from their families, producing the first of many "Stolen Generations"
1883	Pauline Johnson (Mohawk) publishes first poems; United States bans Sun Dance
1884	Canada bans potlatch
1885	European powers partition Africa at Congress of Berlin; intensive Christian missionary efforts begin in non-Muslim areas of Africa; earliest recorded "cargo cult" begins in Fiji
1889	Wovoka revives the Ghost Dance
1890	US cavalry massacre more than 300 Lakota Sioux at Wounded Knee, North Dakota
1899	Japan appropriates Ainu lands, denies Ainu status as Indigenous people
1934	United States lifts ban on Sun Dance and potlatch
1951	Canada lifts ban on potlatch
1956–1965	Beginning of African postindependence era
1958	Chinua Achebe (Igbo) publishes *Things Fall Apart*
1969	Kiowa novelist N. Scott Momaday's *House Made of Dawn* wins Pulitzer Prize for Fiction
1970	United States returns 75 mi² of land to Taos Pueblo
1985	Maori novelist Keri Hulme's *The Bone People* wins the Booker Prize for Fiction
1992	Australian High Court overturns *terra nullius* ruling

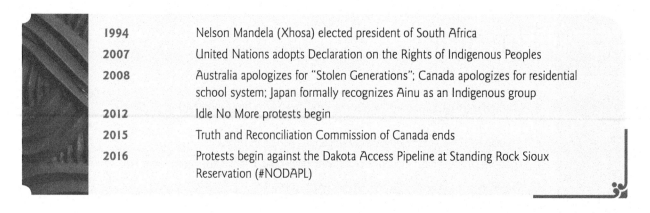

1994	Nelson Mandela (Xhosa) elected president of South Africa
2007	United Nations adopts Declaration on the Rights of Indigenous Peoples
2008	Australia apologizes for "Stolen Generations"; Canada apologizes for residential school system; Japan formally recognizes Ainu as an Indigenous group
2012	Idle No More protests begin
2015	Truth and Reconciliation Commission of Canada ends
2016	Protests begin against the Dakota Access Pipeline at Standing Rock Sioux Reservation (#NODAPL)

For the purposes of this chapter, then, "Indigenous" refers to peoples who (1) identify themselves as Indigenous and (2) rely (at least in part) on kinship and location to define their place in the world. Despite the immense diversity of the cultures involved, it may still be possible to suggest some commonalities that characterize many Indigenous traditions. As Wiradjuri author Anita Heiss has stated, "There is a shared sense of Aboriginality nationally (and internationally with other Indigenous peoples), regardless of the geographical location or socio-economic experience of the individual" (2001: 207).

Change and Syncretism

It is important to keep in mind that Indigenous religions no longer exist as they did before contact with the "outside" world. This situation is partly the result of **syncretism**: the merging of elements from different cultures. Many Native North American religions have been deeply affected by Christianity; some African rituals have incorporated elements of Islam; the sacred oral stories of Japanese Shinto became written texts under the influence of Chinese Buddhism. However, this does not mean that "real" Indigenous religions have disappeared.

It is true that Indigenous religions today are not the same as they were in the past. But the traditions as they exist now are no less authentic than they were. Change and syncretism have affected *all* religions throughout history.

Before we can say much more about what Indigenous religions are, however, we first need to consider what they are not. That means breaking down some common non-Indigenous misconceptions.

"Us" and "Them"

Recent decades have seen some opposition to the efforts of non-Indigenous scholars to "explain" Indigenous people. The main concern is that even unfounded theories can have significant social and political influence. In this regard, Chippewa author Lenore Keeshig-Tobias points out: "The people who have control of your stories, control of your voice, also have control of your destiny, your culture" (Lutz 1991: 81).

An example of the kind of harm that academic theories can do was outlined by the Oglala Sioux lawyer, historian, and activist Vine Deloria, Jr. (see Document box). Anthropologists seeking to explain the social ills plaguing the Oglala community ignored what Deloria called the "real issue, white control of the reservation," and theorized that the people were simply "warriors without weapons" (Deloria 1988 [1969]: 90). In this view, the Oglala were incapable of adapting to a market-economy lifestyle because, deep in their souls, they remained violently primitive. Accordingly, attention was diverted away from the pressing needs of the people—credit, employment, housing, medical services—and focused instead on figuring out how to make "modern Indians" out of them (Deloria 1988 [1969]: 92).

Map 2.1 Distribution of North American Language Families at European Contact

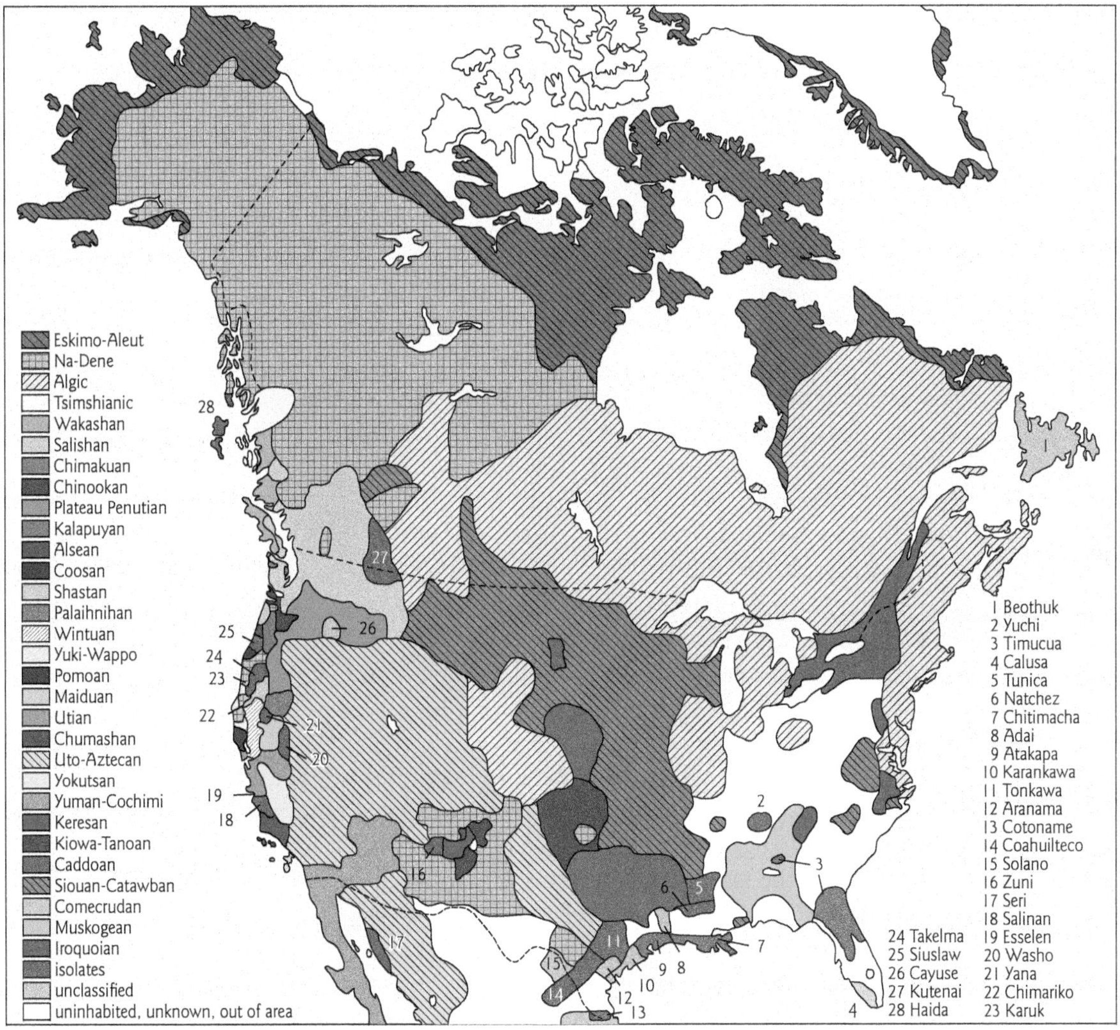

Language borders were in reality much fuzzier than this image suggests. The map points to the tremendous diversity of Native North American cultures, since each language family may contain dozens of distinct languages.

Today concern is often expressed when non-Indigenous scholars speak about Indigenous people. The main objection might seem to be that "outsiders" lack the necessary "insider" knowledge and insight. As Deloria suggests, however, the real problem is one of power and control. The fact is that, historically, such scholars have had the authority to define Indigenous people not only to non-Natives, but even to Native people themselves.

Another important problem with academic work about Indigenous people is that it tends to reinforce the idea that "they" are different from "us." Thus the study of Indigenous religions has produced many terms and concepts that typically are applied only to those traditions, and not to "world" religions more broadly—"animism," "fetish," "mana," "myth," "shaman," "taboo," and "totem," among others. This chapter will rarely use any of those terms, in part because they are

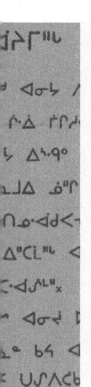

Document

From *Custer Died for Your Sins*, by Vine Deloria, Jr.

(Oglala Sioux)

Published in the early days of the American Indian Movement, Custer Died for Your Sins *(1969) remains one of the most influential works of Indigenous nonfiction ever written.*

From lack of roads to unshined shoes, Sioux problems were generated, so the anthros discovered, by the refusal of the white man to recognize the great desire of the Oglala to go to war. Why expect an Oglala to become a small businessman, when he was only waiting for that wagon train to come around the bend?

The very real and human problems of the reservation were considered to be merely by-products of the failure of a warrior people to become domesticated. . . .

What use would roads, houses, schools, businesses, and income be to a people who, everyone expected, would soon depart on the hunt or warpath? . . .

The question of the Oglala Sioux is one that plagues every Indian tribe in the nation, if it will closely examine itself. Tribes have been defined as one thing, the definition has been completely explored, test scores have been advanced promoting and deriding the thesis, and finally the conclusion has been reached—Indians must be redefined in terms that white men will accept, even if that means re-Indianizing them according to the white man's idea of what they were like in the past and should logically become in the future. (Deloria 1988 [1969]: 92)

not necessary for an introductory understanding of Indigenous religions, but also because they are not used in reference to the other religions discussed in this work, even when they might be relevant. For example, Indigenous origin stories are usually labeled "myths," while similar stories in the Hebrew Bible or the *Mahabharata* are considered "sacred literature." Similarly, the rule that prohibits an African mask carver from having contact with a woman during his work is often called a "taboo," yet that term is not applied to the rule that forbids a Catholic priest from pouring unused Communion wine down the drain. In short, it's important not to perpetuate the notion that Indigenous religions are of a different order than non-Indigenous religions.

"Primitives" and the Problem of History

For many years non-Indigenous people assumed that Indigenous people and cultures had changed very little over the centuries before colonization began. In fact, until quite recently anthropologists were the only ones who studied Aboriginal people: historians did not think there was any Aboriginal history to look at.

Assuming that such cultures had remained essentially unchanged from their beginnings, the Europeans called them "primitive" (from Latin *primus*, "first") and supposed that for them history had begun only when they encountered "modern" or "civilized" cultures. This notion was supported by the fact that the majority of Europeans at the time were Christians who believed both in the superiority of their own culture and in the divine imperative to spread their religion to those who had not yet heard the gospel. Indigenous cultures were seen as blank slates and as lacking any real religion of their own. This missionary worldview often went hand in hand with academic inquiry and tended to color the scholars' interpretation (and sometimes fabrication) of the details of Indigenous lives.

We know now that those assumptions that Indigenous cultures were static and ahistorical were completely untrue. All the available evidence shows that Indigenous peoples had dynamic, eventful histories full of change long before they were "discovered." Over the millennia they have used stories, songs, and physical markings to record past events, changes in the culture or the land, family genealogies, and so on.

One example of the persistent notion that Indigenous cultures are "primitive" is the tendency to think of them as nonliterate. This belief is deeply problematic in three key ways. First, writing is not inherently more "advanced" than orality. Second, many Indigenous cultures did use a form of writing before contact with non-Indigenous people. Finally, the vast majority of contemporary Indigenous cultures are fully literate.

Another example of the tendency to regard Indigenous people as "primitive" is the belief that they do not distinguish between the "religious" and "nonreligious" aspects of their lives—that they consider everything to be sacred. Thus some commentators have claimed that the Navajo "Blessing-way" ceremony, which is performed before a new dwelling is occupied, transforms the home into a sacred site in which every activity is equally sacred. This notion is both inaccurate and patronizing.

The fact is that Indigenous cultures are no less able than non-Indigenous ones to draw distinctions in relation to the category of religion. Observant Muslims may take their prayer mats wherever they go, but they use the mats only at specified times. Similarly, an Australian **Aborigine** knows that certain acts are performed only in particular ritual contexts.

Many non-Indigenous scholars now realize that Indigenous cultures were (and are) just as complex and innovative as their own, and that the idea of the "primitive" typically suggests a belief in one's own superiority that can be used to justify the need for "improvement" of Indigenous cultures. In a similar fashion, those who romanticize "primitive" cultures often do so in the belief that their own "civilized" culture has alienated people from themselves or from the natural world. The concept of the "primitive" tells us more about the people who hold it than it does about the people they apply it to.

The rest of this chapter will try to identify some elements common to many (if not necessarily all) Indigenous religions. Among them are the following:

- Orality
- Connection to specific places

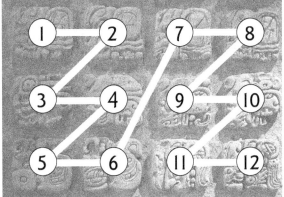

Mayan writing consisted of elaborate images, or glyphs, which were "logosyllabic" (each image represents either a word or a syllable). These images were painted on ceramics, carved in wood, or—as here—molded in stucco. Most often they were arranged in blocks of two columns, each one to be read from left to right, top to bottom (© Ariadne Van Zandbergen/Alamy).

- Emphasis on community and relationship
- A sense of time as rhythmic
- Greater emphasis on what happens in life than after death
- Greater emphasis on behavior than belief
- Authority of **Elders**
- Complementary dualism
- A view of the sacred as an ongoing process rather than static revelation
- Gendered roles

⊕ Transmission

Orality may not be a defining characteristic of Indigenous religions, but it remains a vital one for the vast majority of them. Even cultures that have long had writing have usually passed on critical values and beliefs orally, through stories.

Stories

In many cultures, stories serve as vehicles for the transmission of beliefs and values. Yet it is not always easy to determine what is being passed along. There are many factors that may undermine our ability to interpret a particular story from an Indigenous community.

First, we should not assume that the literal meaning of a story is its most important aspect. Some stories may well be understood to be fiction or to be true only in a figurative or symbolic sense. The Kewa, for example, clearly distinguish between true stories, called *ramani* (oral history), and fictional tales, called *lidi* (oral literature). Similarly, the Nyanga of Zaire contrast *nganuriro* (true stories) with *karisi* (epic poems).

We must also be careful not to assume that a given story is a reflection of a culture. It may be only a single storyteller's version, and the narrative details may reflect the teller's own preferences as much as they do the values or worldview of his or her culture. In other words, the story may be "true" only to the person who is telling it.

Finally, the most important point is that we almost never encounter Indigenous stories in their natural form: spoken to a group in their original language. Instead, most of us encounter them in a time and a place far removed from the circumstances in which they would normally have been performed. The act of storytelling is itself a ritual: many stories are told only in a particular place and time, and only by certain people. Similarly, not all stories are for everyone: some may be just for women, some for men, and some for children.

Every Indigenous culture has thousands of stories, and each of those stories may have many variations. It is impossible to do justice to such variety here. We will simply consider a few examples of two types of stories: those that in some way explain origins and those that feature "trickster" figures.

Origin Stories

North America

Among the best-known origin stories in North America are "Earth Diver" tales. Several of their key elements are common to cultures across the eastern woodlands. Typically, the story begins with the world destroyed by flooding; then an animal or deity brings some earth up from beneath the waters to begin rebuilding the land.

In one version, Sky Woman, a spirit being, descends to earth during the flood. Seeing that she is pregnant, a giant turtle offers to let her rest on his back. She then asks the other animals to dive for some soil. Many try but fail, and they drown. In the end, it is the lowly muskrat—who has been ridiculed by the others—that succeeds. Sky Woman breathes into the soil, which spreads across the turtle's back to become what is now called North America. Her breath infuses the earth with life. She gives birth to twins (the ancestors of the people who tell this story) and awards joint stewardship of the land to all the beings who live there—human, animal, and spirit.

Africa

The African Dogon people also refer to a form of pregnancy in their origin stories, which tell how the supreme being, Amma, created the world and humanity. Out of loneliness, Amma transformed himself into a womb holding four new beings called Nummo; two of these were mostly male but partly female, and the other two were mostly female but partly male. Before their 60-year gestation period was complete, one of the males became so impatient to be with his sister that he tore away part of the womb searching for her. This torn part of the womb became the earth.

Life began when Amma sacrificed this sister and scattered the pieces of her body on the ground to purify the earth. The two remaining Nummo clothed the earth with vegetation and infused it with a creative, universal life force. Amma and the Nummo also created eight beings who were placed in separate celestial chambers and prohibited from eating a certain type of grain. They became lonely, however, and when their food ran out, they gathered together and cooked the forbidden grain. When they were expelled from the heavens and crashed to earth, the world as we know it was created.

Australia

The origin stories of the Australian Aborigines center on events that occurred in a time that nineteenth-century anthropologists famously mistranslated as "**The Dreaming**"; a more accurate translation might be "The Uncreated." Although anthropologists understand The Dreaming as

Document

"Love Magic" (Australian Aborigine)

"Ngarlu" has three meanings in this story from central Australia. It is the flower of the ngarlkirdi (witchetty grub tree) as well as the name of a sacred site and of the ceremonies performed there. A "subsection" is a kinship group, while "hairstring" is string made from human hair.

There was a Dreaming man named Linjiplinjipi of the Jungari subsection at this site. He had adorned his body with *Ngarlu* and was spinning hairstring. The whirling sound of his spinning tool [made of crossed sticks] attracted a woman of the Ngapangardi subsection [and therefore his mother-in-law]. He climbed the hill and as he was watching her she stopped to urinate. Sexually aroused, he continued to attract her with the noise. Finally, he caught her, forced her legs apart and raped her. Upon ejaculation, however, she closed her legs and her tight vagina dismembered his penis.

Today, at Ngarlu her vagina remains transformed into rock and the severed stone-penis is still embedded in it. Linjiplinjipi himself, in agony, went to the other side of the hill where he turned into a large boulder that has paintings upon it depicting his hairstring cross and his erect penis. *Yilpinji* ["love magic"] is performed modelled on Linjiplinjipi's methods of attracting his mother-in-law, using sticks from *Ngarlu* and adorning the torso with the flowers of the witchetty grub tree. (Swain and Trompf 1995: 22–23) archaic time, Aborigines have usually referred to the events of The Dreaming as if they occurred not long before their own time. In other words, those events are out of reach of living memory but recent enough to remain vital and meaningful to the communities that speak of them.

Unlike most Africans and Native North Americans, Australian Aborigines generally do not recognize a single divine authority from whom all life, values, rules, and so on derive. Instead, stories of origin usually concern the first ancestors, whose actions shaped both the physical world and the cultural practices of their descendants. There are countless stories of The Dreaming, but many tales reflect some basic patterns. For example, "Love Magic" (see Document box) explains how the love magic ritual and a specific sacred site originated in the actions of two ancestors while reinforcing the community's prohibitions on incest and rape. The metamorphosis of the ancestors into physical formations on the land is typical of Dreaming tales.

Meanings

What do origin stories mean? While it's certainly possible that they were understood to be straightforward historical accounts, we should also consider what other aspects of these stories might be important.

First, relationships are central to all of these stories. In each case, creation results from a desire for community or companionship, and the central beings are the ancestors of the people who tell the story. Second, the stories typically underline the relatedness of all aspects of existence. Just as the Aborigines are related to ancestors from The Dreaming who remain connected to the landscape, all of existence is connected. The world in its entirety is infused with the spirit of the ancestors. Third, origin stories typically do not imagine the beginning of time: they presuppose the existence of the universe and focus on the origin of certain elements—language, culture, landscape—that still exist, connecting us to the actions of our ancestors. Past and present are forever linked.

Finally, it's worth noting that these stories rarely present a simple, idealized picture of the world. They tell us that it is (at least in part) the product of violence: a torn womb, a rape, a devastating flood. The Dogon tradition associates the creation of humans with loneliness and disobedience, while in North America many animals sacrifice themselves to help Sky Woman and her baby. Order, creation, and life are almost always connected to chaos, destruction, and death.

Contemporary Yolngu artist David Malangi paints the Milmildjark Dreaming on bark in 1997. When the Australian government eventually compensated Malangi for using his work "Gurrmirringu's Mortuary Feast" on the $1 note, the payment marked the first recognition of Aboriginal copyright (© Penny Tweedie/Alamy).

Tricksters

The concept of the **trickster** was developed by scholars to categorize a certain type of character that appears in the stories of many cultures, including the Norse (Loki) and the ancient Greeks (Hermes). Tricksters are sometimes referred to as "culture heroes," typically because they are the central figures in many of the community's stories, and also because they often teach important lessons.

Many tricksters are capable of shape-shifting and often take the form of animals. In North America, for example, the raven and the coyote are often tricksters. In addition, many tricksters are able to change their gender (always from male to female).

Tricksters are typically more powerful than humans but not quite gods. They can be selfless or greedy, kind or cruel, funny or deadly serious. And while their behavior often violates the social order, this is not always a bad thing. Sometimes the social order *needs* to be violated, and sometimes the most effective way to do that is through laughter. For example, a common scenario

Document

"Red Willows" (Anishinaubae)

Nanabush was wandering in the far north. He was hungry. Nanabush was always hungry.

He was with his mother at the time. That old lady is known by many names. Some call her "Dodomum" or "Dodum"; others call her "Gushiwun" or "Gushih."

They wandered until Nanabush chanced to meet a bear. "Ha!" he announced. "I'm going to eat you!" "Oh no you don't," replied the bear. "I will fight back if you try to kill me. Get out of here, Nanabush."

Nanabush would not leave. "Listen," he pleaded, "I'm hungry. Can't you see that? I'm hungry. I've eaten next to nothing for about three days. Maybe four days! I'm going to kill you."

They started fighting somewhere over there, somewhere near Kenora. They battled tooth and nail. They fought in a number of different places along the way, even where Sault Ste Marie now stands. At the rapids. That really happened. That was all land then. At that time there was no channel of water flowing there.

First, Nanabush would hit the bear; then the bear would hit Nanabush. One time, Nanabush threw the bear so hard against the ground he broke the earth, and water began to flow through. That in fact is the reason the water now flows past Sault Ste Marie.

Finally, Nanabush said to his mother, "You go on ahead and stay there. When I get there too, I will kill this bear." As soon as the word was given, she was gone.

She could hear them battling in the distance. At one point, the bear sent Nanabush flying with such force that he landed on his mother, causing her to fall backwards onto her rump. That is why the lake there is called "The Old Lady Sat Down."

They fought all along the way. The evidence of it is still there. At the place that is now called Sudbury they hurled rocks at one another.

Where they pulled boulders up from the earth, ore was later found. Where they dragged each other along the ground, depressions were made in the land.

Eventually, Nanabush killed the bear, in the general vicinity of Parry Sound.

Meanwhile, his mother came along behind, carrying supplies. She made a fire and put a pot of water over it. Nanabush butchered the bear. When it was cooked, he ate and ate. But he ate too much and very soon suffered the runs.

"Oh!" He ran over there. "Ah!" Such discomfort. He could not stop going to the toilet. When he sat down to defecate, blood also flowed. He couldn't find anything to use to wipe himself, so he grabbed a sapling and used that. Then he stuck the sapling— with the blood and feces on it—into the earth, somewhere near Parry Sound.

A red willow grew at that spot. Its colour came from the blood of Nanabush.

That is how the red willows came to be. (Johnston 1995: 33–37)

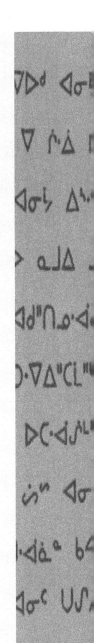

Red Willows, by contemporary Anishinaubae artist David Johnson (with permission of the Royal Ontario Museum).

centers on the disastrous results of the male trickster's efforts to satisfy his enormous sexual appetite. Such stories testify to the understanding that unrestrained (male) sexuality poses a serious threat to society.

By contrast, in the Anishinaubae story "Red Willows," Nanabush displays consideration for his mother. However, he is also extremely self-indulgent and shows no restraint when eating the bear—a transgression for which he pays a painful price.

Like many trickster stories, "Red Willows" explains the origins of certain elements of the community's physical world, from the river at Sault Ste. Marie to the rugged terrain around Sudbury. And since those (colonial) towns are named, we know that this is either a modern retelling of an old tale or one of the new stories of Nanabush that continue to appear. Finally, we learn that the red willows got their color from Nanabush's bloody feces. This is an example of a view of nature that recognizes connections between the beautiful and the ugly or painful.

Chaos and Order

Like origin stories, trickster tales often attribute aspects of our world to destructive activity. And so the trickster invents the bow and arrow, breaks the teeth in women's vaginas to make intercourse possible, and introduces death. Despite his association with chaos, then, the trickster also brings a kind of order to the world.

The Yoruba trickster Eshu, for example, is constantly playing pranks in the hope that disorder will result. But his tricks work only when the people forget the importance of community stability and become greedy or lazy or behave stupidly. In one story Eshu wears a special hat, black on one side and red on the other, while walking between two friends who, each seeing only one side of the hat, fight over what color it is and wind up bitter enemies for no good reason.

Thus trickster stories can play many roles: they can show us how we *should* or *should not* behave, they can help explain the origins of the world and connect a community more deeply to its place, and they are almost always entertaining and provocative. They embody the contradictions of humanity: our weaknesses and strengths, selfishness and compassion, humiliations and triumphs.

It's also worth noting again that almost all the traditional trickster figures we know of are male. One reason could be the fact that until recently the academics who recorded the stories were invariably male: perhaps they had no interest in female trickster stories, or perhaps such stories were the preserve of women and the male scholars never inquired about them. On the other hand, it may be that in some communities the trickster's typical activities—hunting, traveling, unrestrained sex—were in fact associated only with men.

⊕ Practice

Ritual

Rituals perform the same functions in every culture. To an extent, they identify and remind us of what is important to the community we live in. In religious terms, their purpose is often to communicate in some way with gods, ancestors, or spirits. At the same time, rituals remain rooted in *human* needs and relationships.

Varieties

Indigenous rituals can mark critical moments in the lives of individuals (birth, marriage, death), the community (departure of a powerful leader, liberation from slavery, completion of a great project), or the natural world (annual cycles, great disasters, rich harvests). Sometimes these rituals reflect transformations, and sometimes they help to bring transformation about. It is this less frequent, more dramatic type of ritual that will be discussed here. First, though, let us briefly turn our attention to gender in Indigenous communities in order to understand the different ways in which rituals are performed by and for people at various stages of their lives.

Gendered Roles

Traditionally, all members of an Indigenous community had clearly defined roles that were often gendered. In general, hunting and warfare were male occupations, while food preparation and healing were the responsibility of women. Maori carvers were men, and Maori weavers were women. Among the Bunu Yoruba, men were responsible for growing cotton and women for turning it into cloth. Men and women depended on one another and yet were also independent in important ways.

A similar balancing act can often be seen in regard to political and social power. The heads of most Indigenous societies have typically been male. Yet in many instances women have been inherently involved with any decision-making affecting the entire community. And in some cases such decisions have normally been made by women and then carried out by men.

It is also important to note that gender classification could be somewhat fluid within Indigenous communities. Sometimes women might participate in men's work, and vice versa. Sexual roles and orientations could also be fluid. Accounts of men identifying as women, wearing female clothes, and taking on women's roles are not unusual. There are also accounts of Indigenous women identifying as men and becoming hunters or warriors.

Among Indigenous communities, there is no definitive gender pattern with respect to kinship. Some Indigenous societies are matrilineal, tracing ancestry primarily through the mother, while others are patrilineal, focusing on the father. Similarly, important spirits and gods—including the supreme being—may be either male or female.

Traditionally, it was also not uncommon for Indigenous societies to separate the religious activities of women and men. Yet most studies have looked only at male practices—whether because male scholars were unaware that women had their own practices, because they were not permitted to study the women, or because they assumed that the men were the most important members of their communities and hence that their practices were the only ones worth investigating. It is only relatively recently that scholars have begun to examine what Indigenous women think and do in the context of religion.

Meaning and Structure

The rituals of Indigenous cultures reveal a system of formal activities through which community members relate to the world and to one another. Such activities tap into their deepest beliefs about the origins of the world, the existence of order, and the beginnings of life. Repeating them therefore serves in some way to re-create key aspects of the world, of order, and of life. In this sense, ritual can be understood as an indicator both of the human need for meaning and structure in a world that is often random and frightening and of the human capacity to create such meaning and structure.

Rites of Passage

The Journey

Many cultures regard life as a journey or quest. Rituals highlight points along the way, but they also constitute journeys of their own. This understanding is most evident in rites of passage, which explicitly mark a change of state and often involve *literal* journeys.

Typically, such rituals take participants away from their community to a new place with unfamiliar rules, where some sort of transformation occurs. For males this place is often outside, in the forest or the bush or the desert, whereas for females it is often a domestic space of some sort. Once the ritual is complete the participants return home, often with a physical change, such as a tattoo or scar, that symbolizes their new mode of being. While away, they exist in a kind of in-between or "liminal" state, after the death of the old self but before the birth of the new.

In South Africa, young Pondos preparing to become sacred healers are moved into a special hut. If they go into town before the ritual is complete, their faces and bodies must be covered in

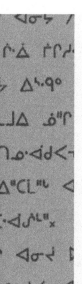

Document

Yoruba Verse

This verse from the sacred literature of the Yoruba (known as the Odu Ifa) describes life as a quest.

A small child works his way off the edge of his sleeping mat.
A bird soars high above it all.
They divined for our elderly people,
When they were preparing to leave heaven to go to the world. They said, what are we going to do?
They asked themselves, where are we going?

We are going in search of knowledge, truth, and justice.
In accordance with our destiny,
At the peak of the hill
We were delayed.
We are going to meet success.
We will arrive on earth knowledgeable.
We will arrive on earth in beauty.
We are searching for knowledge continuously.
Knowledge has no end. (Drewal 2002: 129)

white pigment—the color of transformation in many parts of Africa—to indicate that they are in the midst of a journey between the realms of the living and the ancestors. This initiation is most often undertaken by women and is considered complete only when the initiates receive a dream of a particular animal, understood as the incarnation of the ancestor who will authorize them to become healers.

Many Anishinaubae undertake a similar initiation, known as a **vision quest**. In this ritual, after years of preparation, a boy on the verge of adulthood travels far from home to a designated site in the wilderness where the spirits dwell. Typically, this will be the first time he has ever been completely alone. He is given no food, only water. He endures cold, hunger, and fear. With luck, the spirits will give him dreams or visions that will reveal his true self and the role he is to play in his community. After several days, an adult male will arrive and take the initiate home. If the religious leader determines that the boy experienced true spirit visions during the quest, the ritual is complete and the boy is recognized as an adult man.

The rite of passage for Wiradjuri males in eastern Australia also involves a journey, punctuated by fear and pain. At the appointed time, the women and children of the village are covered with branches and blankets. They hear a roaring sound, identified as the voice of the spirit being Daramulun; he takes the boys away to the bush, where they are told that

Young Pondo women from Transkei in South Africa during their initiation to become sacred healers (Daniel Lainé).

he will devour them and regurgitate them back as men. The boys are led away, and each one has an incisor tooth knocked out. Then fires appear and the boys are told that Daramulun is coming to burn them. At the height of their terror, however, the boys receive a shock. Their blankets are removed, and the men of the village reveal that they have been acting as Daramulun all along. It was the men who took the boys' teeth, set the fires, and made the voice of the spirit being.

When the boys return to the village, they do so as men, are given new adult names, and take up residence outside their parents' homes. They are transformed: they have been initiated into a secret (male) knowledge about the spirit world and have formed bonds with one another through their shared experience. The ritual may also demonstrate that what is genuinely meaningful lies beneath the surface of reality. By exposing their own trickery, the men produce "a disenchantment with a naive view of reality, that is, with the view that things are what they appear to be" (Gill 1982: 81). In this way, the boys experience a true death of their youthful selves.

Sacrifice

Sacrificial rituals are extremely common among Indigenous communities. At one time the central religious ceremony of the Ainu of northern Japan, for example, was bear sacrifice. They would capture a cub, raise it for two or three years, shoot it with ceremonial arrows, and finally kill it. The carcass would then be specially prepared—often the head would be emptied out and filled with flowers—and cooked and eaten by the entire village.

Among the Aboriginal peoples of the North American plains, the **Sun Dance** is an annual ritual lasting several days. Inside a specially created lodge, participants dance to the point of exhaustion while the community provides support. The Sioux Sun Dance includes a kind of self-sacrifice: male dancers fast, pierce their chests and backs, and attach themselves to a central pole with ropes tied to sticks that are inserted through the piercings. They may be partially or entirely suspended above the ground, and they dance until they pass out or their fastenings tear loose.

In Africa, the Nuer regularly sacrifice an ox to celebrate, to heal, and to atone for moral transgressions. The Xhosa perform a similar but more complex ritual when a young woman falls ill and a **diviner** determines that she is being punished by an ancestor spirit. To restore good relations between the woman's home and the ancestor, a cow is consecrated and then speared. The animal's cry opens up the path of communication with the spirit world. Inside the woman's home, a special part of the animal is cooked. One piece of the meat is given to the woman, who sucks it and throws it to the back of the house as a sign that she is throwing away her illness. She is then given a second piece, which she holds while being chastised for behaving in a manner displeasing to the ancestor(s). She consumes the meat and is congratulated for having "eaten the ancestor." Then the rest of the cow is cooked and eaten by the entire community in celebration.

Community and Ritual Action

As we have seen, communal participation is crucial for the Ainu, the Sioux, and the Xhosa. Everyone becomes involved in a ritual in some way, whether by providing support or simply by sharing in the group meal. The ritual ultimately brings people together. In addition, the object of sacrifice itself is clearly not of central importance. When necessary, the Nuer can replace the ox with a cucumber, and if the Xhosa have no suitable cow, they can use beer instead.

The fact that such substitutions are possible suggests that, in some cases at least, the materials involved in a ritual are far less meaningful than the ritual actions themselves. When the Xhosa sacrifice a cow, they don't simply kill and eat it. What appears to be primarily at stake is the woman's behavior in relation to notions of social order set down by the ancestors and reinforced by (male) ritual Elders. The community thus shares both in naming the transgression that led to her illness and in the meal generated by the ritual that heals her.

For the Sioux, the building of a special lodge for the Sun Dance replicates the creation of the world and is accompanied by songs that tell of this creation. The pole used in the dance is a newly cut tree; in its state between life and death and its physical positioning at the center of the lodge, it links the material world to the world of the spirits. Physically attached to this tree, the dancers are thus also tied to the spirits and to the earliest times.

In their traditional ritual of sacrifice, the Ainu filled the chosen bear's head with flowers because the animal was understood as the mountain god in disguise, and the ritual killing of his bear form was necessary to release the god's spirit back to his own realm. The Ainu were not offering a bear to the god; rather, from primordial times onward the god became a bear, over and over again, as a gift to the Ainu. The flowers were an expression of the community's gratitude.

In each case, the ritual actions relate to the spiritual and sometimes physical establishment of the community, or of the world itself. Sacrificial practices thus play a key role in re-creating order and meaning. In reenacting ancient events, these rituals join people to the past, and yet they also respond to current situations and needs. Thus they reflect the common Indigenous sense of time as rhythmic, neither purely linear nor entirely cyclical. Individuals and communities are always changing; through ritual, they return to a source that sustains them.

⊕ Cultural Expressions

Among the art forms traditionally produced by Indigenous cultures are architecture, songs, baskets, clothing, statues, paintings, drums, pipes, mats, headdresses, amulets, masks, and tapestries. In each community, some art forms exist almost entirely for religious purposes, some are entwined with religion only at specific times, and others may have very little to do with religion.

Indigenous cultural expressions are fundamentally about relationships. There is a network that connects an object to the person(s) who created it, the ritual in which it is used, the people it is made to serve, and the stories that underlie their worldview. These relationships are vital to the culture in question, and some or all aspects of the network—object, creation, ritual, stories—may be considered religious. To illustrate the complex ways in which Indigenous art forms are related to Indigenous religion, we will consider three examples: weaving, carving, and building.

Weaving

To weave is to intertwine, to connect. Even in modern English, we speak of the "social fabric," the "warp and weft" of history, friendships, or community life. In most cultures, weaving is a social activity; weavers work together, helping (and watching) one another, sharing stories, and passing on their skills to younger generations, and the products of their work often have both a religious meaning and a practical purpose. These functions reflect and reinforce the bonds among community members, as well as the bonds between them and their environment, ancestors, and gods.

Sacred Thread

In Maori tradition, all weavers are female. A prospective weaver is selected as a baby, and a special prayer is spoken over her. As she grows up, she learns the art from her mother, aunts, and grandmothers until it becomes a natural part of her. But her destiny is not fixed. The more she learns, the more the women *discourage* her from weaving. This is a test. The girl must demonstrate her commitment. When the older women are satisfied, she is at last initiated into the collective of weavers. Only then does she come to understand why the weft used to create the pattern and design in Maori weaving is called "sacred thread."

Maori weaving traditions include not only physical techniques but rituals. The materials used must be specially prepared, sex is prohibited the night before dyeing fibers, no food may be consumed while weaving, and no strangers can view any work until it is completed.

Maori weaving patterns and techniques are said to have been given to humanity by Niwareka, daughter of the lightning god Uetonga. The goddess of weaving is Hine-te-iwaiwa, who also presides over healing and childbirth and is often associated with the moon and menstruation. The colors used in traditional weaving—black, red, and white—symbolize the forces of creation. Black represents the realm of potential being, the darkness from which the earth emerged; white represents the process of coming into being, the energies that make life possible; and red represents the realm of being and light, the physical world itself. The sacred thread thus runs not only through the people's garments but also through time and the various realms of existence, entwining the Maori in the cosmos itself.

Undying Cloth

In many Indigenous cultures, the final product of weaving also has religious significance. Around the world, a key function of clothing is to declare who we are—Muslim or Hindu, artist or lawyer, man or woman—and how we fit into the "social fabric." Yet clothing can hide as much as it can reveal, helping us to construct a public face while obscuring certain aspects of ourselves.

Many non-African people think of African textiles as colorful, but the most common traditional cloth among peoples on this continent is actually white. Among the Bunu Yoruba, for example, white may represent anything from human secretions (milk, semen) to aspects of nature (air, water) and religious phenomena (spirits, heaven). White cloth—traditionally woven by Bunu women only—is thus often used to bridge the gap between the physical and spirit worlds, between living people and their ancestors. It is worn to remedy disorders caused by destructive spirits (miscarriage, anger, illness), wrapped around the trunks of sacred trees to appease the spirits living inside them, wound around a pot of objects to help bring rain, and used for burial shrouds to facilitate the deceased's rebirth as an ancestor. In short, white cloth helps members of the Bunu community cope with pain, disruption, and loss.

Spirit Baskets

Baskets figure in the sacred stories of many cultures. Tane, the Maori god of light and wisdom, brought three baskets of knowledge from heaven to earth (knowledge of ritual matters, of acts of harm and aggression among people, and of peace and well-being). In a Navajo story about the origin of small birds, a woman plucks the feathers of several winged monsters and puts them in her basket, but when she passes through a forbidden territory filled with sunflowers, the feathers are transformed into tiny birds and fly out of the basket.

Mabel McKay (1907–1991) was a traditional Pomo healer whose practice was interwoven with basket making: she gave each of her patients a miniature basket (sometimes the size of a pea) or instruction on how to make one. In Pomo communities, men traditionally wove the heavy baskets used for purposes such as fishing; baskets that had explicitly religious purposes were woven by women. As in most Indigenous communities, rituals were prescribed for obtaining and preparing the materials, and the weaving process was surrounded by restrictions. Weavers were forbidden to make baskets at all when menstruating or consuming alcohol. They were also forbidden to include representations of humans in their designs or to reproduce the designs of medicine weavers such as McKay.

This last rule reflected the fact that those designs were the product of personal spiritual visions. Such visions were for the weaver alone and were relevant to particular situations. Although McKay followed the traditions of her culture, everything she produced was unique. Even more than usual, then, her baskets were living things that both reflected and communicated her sacred visions. When asked if she had been taught to weave by her grandmother or mother, she replied: "No, spirit teach me, since I was small child" (Sarris 1992: 25).

Carvings

Masks

The difference that context makes in understanding the meaning of cultural objects is well illustrated by African masks. In the museums where non-Africans usually see these objects, they are mere shadows of themselves, but they come alive when used as intended, in ritual activities. While aspects of a mask's meaning may be apparent even to outsiders, we must be cautious in our inter-pretations of them. Although masks are typically meant to bring a spirit into the community, in African traditions the supreme being is never represented by any physical object; therefore, masks can relate only to lesser deities. Also, the fact that certain masks clearly represent certain animals does not mean (as was once assumed) that the people who use them worship those animals. In Mali, both the Dogon and Bamana cultures use antelope masks in agricultural ceremonies that have little to do with actual antelopes, but the symbolic meanings of this animal are not identical: for the Dogon the antelope represents hard work, whereas for the Bamana its horns symbolize tall sprouts of grain.

When we focus only on the form of a mask, without reference to its use, we can easily miss the meaning of certain critical elements. For example, the fact that the intricately carved Epa masks of the Yoruba are extremely heavy reflects their function in rituals celebrating the male passage into adulthood. The strength required to dance with such a mask is a literal representation of the wearer's ability to take on his responsibilities as an adult member of the community.

Another unseen but equally important aspect of the mask is the process of its creation. Carvers have traditionally been male, trained as apprentices to master carvers. Ritual is no less central in the creation of a mask than it is in the ceremony for which it is made. Typically, carvers must work in isolation while fasting, abstaining from any sexual activity, and avoiding contact both with women and with anything connected to death.

Totem Poles

The **totem poles** produced by the Aboriginal peoples of the Pacific Northwest Coast pose similar challenges of context and symbolism. The various markings and carving styles used in this art form are specific to particular communities and locations; those familiar with these traditions would immediately know, on encountering a totem pole, whose territory they had entered. As carver Norman Tait explains, "Every time I carve a totem pole, there's always a kind of signature to identify my family or my nation, the Nisga'a" (1993: 11).

Yet for many years now, totem poles have been removed from their homes. Poles from different cultures, and with different functions, are often displayed together in places such as Stanley Park in Vancouver. Some groups have fought this trend—in 2006 the Haisla of northern British Columbia successfully retrieved from Sweden's Museum of Ethnography a sacred totem pole that had been stolen from them almost 80 years earlier.

Ironically, the word "totem" is derived from the Anishinaubae word *dodaem*, which has been variously translated as "heart," "nourishment," and "kinship group." But the Anishinaubae (who live thousands of miles to the east) never made totem poles, and the cultures of the Pacific North-west themselves never used the word "totem." The Tsimshian people—to pick just one example—call such a pole a *ptsan*.

Normally carved from a single cedar tree, a pole can survive for a century or so. It is tradi-tionally regarded as a living thing and is allowed to rot naturally; some believe that to physically preserve a totem pole is to interfere with the natural order of the world. Certain communities even forbid the "preservation" of poles in drawings or photographs.

The meaning of a particular pole depends on its intended use. Some are designed primarily to serve as supporting structures or grave markers; others, as symbols of status or power. Most, how-ever, tell stories. Some stories are mainly historical, recounting achievements, murders, arguments, victories, defeats, marriages, ancestral lineages, and so on. But other stories are explicitly religious,

Totem poles in Vancouver's Stanley Park reflect different creative ends: to support a roof (a) and to tell the story of the Tait family crest (b) (© imagebroker/Alamy; © Douglas Lander/Alamy).

relating to particular beliefs or to the tales of supernatural figures such as Raven or Thunderbird (who is responsible for great storms).

The photos here show two totem poles. The pole marked (a) may appear more ornate than the other but is actually much simpler, depicting only two main figures. Grizzly Bear is at the base, holding a human, which usually represents self-preservation or survival. Thunderbird, a symbol of strength, is at the top. The pole's relative simplicity reflects the fact that it was one of a pair created primarily to support the roof beam of a house.

The pole marked (b), carved by Norman Tait (with Robert and Isaac Tait), tells a more complicated story. The family is represented by the man at the top, who is holding Eagle to signify their clan. Five disembodied faces represent five ancestral brothers who once saw two beavers emerge from their home, remove their skin, and become men. The figures told the five brothers that they were being slaughtered by the humans, so the brothers sang a sad song that froze the river, protecting the beavers (who can be seen climbing the pole). This is how the Tait ancestors came to adopt the beaver for their crest.

Moko

Maori carvings are rarely displayed outside their original physical context. This is because many of them are an integral part of the ancestral meeting house, or *whare whakairo* ("carved house"),

Tame Iti, an outspoken and sometimes controversial Maori activist who is well known for his full facial *moko* (Phil Walter/Getty Images).

for which they were created. The figures that decorate these houses are depictions of ancestors such as Tihori, of the Ngati Awa in Bay of Plenty, New Zealand. The carving of Tihori in the Bay of Plenty meeting house holds a weapon used in hand-to-hand combat, which symbolizes his role as a warrior. Tihori is also covered with traditional Maori tattoos, or **moko** (literally, "to strike" or "to tap"). The same markings can be seen on some contemporary Maori men and women, including the famous Tuhoe activist Tame Iti.

Originally chiseled (not just inked) into the skin, these markings identify both the individual and his or her relationship to the community. Some *moko* elements may signify education level, personal and family rank, tribal history, or ancestral connections; others may simply be marks of beauty or ferocity in battle. Traditionally, women were allowed tattoos only on or around their lips and chin, while men could receive markings on their entire face.

A key design that is repeated on Iti's face is the *koru*, or frond/spiral, the most common (and important) of all *moko* elements. A Maori proverb—"As one fern frond dies, another is born to take its place"—suggests that the *koru*'s primary meaning has to do with birth, regeneration, and sustainability, but that it can also represent the ancestors who gave birth to the Maori and continue to sustain them.

Beyond this symbolism, the art of *moko* itself is directly linked to the Maori ancestors. Uetonga, the god of lightning, developed *moko* in imitation of the marks that his grandfather Ru, the god of earthquakes, had left on the face of the primal parent, the earth. One day Uetonga's daughter

Niwareka (who brought weaving to humanity) fell in love with the Maori ancestral chief Mataora. The two married and lived together until Mataora, in a jealous rage, hit Niwareka and she fled home to the underworld. In sorrow, Mataora followed her and came upon Uetonga tattooing a man by cutting deep patterns into his flesh. When Mataora asked to have his own story marked on his face in the same way, Uetonga agreed.

To ease the pain of the carving, Mataora sang of his loss and regret, and the sound reached Niwareka, who forgave him. The couple reunited and received permission to return to the surface world. But Mataora neglected to leave an appropriate offering for the guardian of the portal between the two realms, and so from then on living humans were forbidden to enter the underworld. *Moko*—in fact, all traditional carvings—thus remind Maori people of their ancestors, the importance of meeting one's obligations, the need to treat one another with respect, the power of the natural world, and the boundaries between life and death.

Buildings

The significance of religious buildings to Indigenous peoples can be difficult to apprehend. The majority of Indigenous people throughout history have performed all or most of their rituals outdoors, in the natural world. Specific locations can be crucial; when the purpose of a ritual is to make contact with particular entities, for example, the ritual must generally be performed where they dwell or intersect with our world. Although some communities may erect complex structures to mark such sites, others will put up something extremely unassuming; to do anything more elaborate would in many instances not be in keeping with their religious worldview.

Such structures can be deceptively simple to an outsider's eye. For example, an African shrine may contain nothing more than a couple of small, plain, human-shaped carvings, but if the community understands that from time to time these figures will be inhabited by particular ancestors or spirits, then at those times it will see them as visible manifestations of the gods.

Other shrine statues may have quite a different meaning, however. Consider the **mbari** shrine in the photo here. How would you interpret these figures? Are they gods? Which one is the most important? Who is the man sitting in front of the statues, and why is he there?

The figure in the lower middle represents the founder of the community, with his wife above and servants on either side. He was renowned as a great healer some two centuries ago but was attacked by another community and forced to flee across the marshes, carrying his wife on his shoulders. Relics of the healer, kept with the statues, protect the community from disease. Because most of the *mbari* shrines in this region have been destroyed, an Elder stands guard over them at all times. But this is a modern development. Traditionally, *mbari*—like totem poles—were never repaired; after several rains, they would simply dissolve back into the earth.

Ancestral Houses

The *whare whakairo* is part of a larger complex called a **marae**, a cleared area containing structures such as a dining room, shelters, and a site where the recently deceased are placed to lie in state. The *marae* is the religious and social home of a Maori person, the site of ritual ceremonies such as weddings, funerals, family celebrations, and formal welcomes for visitors. Authority over the *marae* is held by the community's Elders, who use the space to pass on traditions, stories, and arts such as weaving and carving.

As in the case of African masks, the builders and carvers of the *whare whakairo* were traditionally male; the rest of the community was banned from the site until the work was officially declared complete. The workers operated under ritual restrictions and obligations from the moment the first trees for the building were cut down. Traditionally, *marae* artists could be put to death if the community did not judge their work to be acceptable.

The location of the *marae* is critical: it must be located in a place where previous generations carried out the religious and social activities that continue to define and restore the world itself. This connection to the land is not merely metaphorical: it is Maori custom to bury the placenta in the ground at birth, as well as the bones after death. The *marae* is also identified with a single common ancestor to whom all members of the community are ostensibly connected.

This identification is given physical form in the *whare whakairo*, which represents the body of the ancestor. On the front of the house, where the roof slopes meet, is the mask-head of the ancestor; the boards along the front of each side of the roof are his arms; the central ridge of the roof is his spine, with ribs/rafters spreading out from it; the front door is his mouth; and the window is his eye.

A *mbari* shrine in southeastern Nigeria (Daniel Lainé).

Hogans

The Navajo **hogan** is not "explicitly" religious: although many ceremonies are performed there, a hogan is also simply a traditional dwelling in which any Navajo family might live. As such it is the site of all the daily activities that go on in a home, some of which are religious and some of which are not.

Before a newly constructed hogan is occupied, the community will perform the Blessingway ritual, which includes a song that refers to "a holy home" (Gill 1982: 10), although this term merely hints at what the hogan represents. The point becomes clearer when we learn that the Blessingway is in many ways the foundation of Navajo religious thought and practice. Before any other ritual can be conducted, some version of the Blessingway must be performed.

The Blessingway song names four divine beings: Earth, Mountain Woman, Water Woman, and Corn Woman. But it also speaks of everyday things: vegetation, fabrics, long life, happiness. In this way it represents a joining of perspectives, the cosmic with the mundane.

The cosmic–mundane connection is furthered by the song's identification of the four deities with the four supporting poles of the hogan; in Navajo cosmology, the same deities provide support for the world itself. In fact, the Navajo understand the creation of the world to have begun with the building of a structure, which is to say that the world *is* a structure—a hogan. It should come

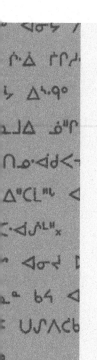

Document

From the Nightway Prayer (Navajo)

Like the Blessingway song performed as part of the creation of a new hogan, the first part of this prayer connects the ordinary with the extraordinary through the central symbol of the home. And, like the Yoruba verse in a prior Document box, its concluding section envisions life as a journey.

In Tse 'gíhi
In the house made of the dawn
In the house made of the evening twilight
In the house made of the dark cloud
In the house made of the he-rain
In the house made of the dark mist
In the house made of the she-rain
In the house made of pollen

In the house made of grasshoppers
Where the dark mist curtains the doorway
The path to which is on the rainbow . . .
In beauty (happily) I walk
With beauty before me, I walk
With beauty behind me, I walk
With beauty below me, I walk
With beauty above me, I walk
With beauty all around me, I walk
It is finished (again) in beauty
It is finished in beauty
It is finished in beauty
It is finished in beauty. (Matthews 1995 [1902]: 143–145)

as no surprise that creation was accompanied by the first performance of the Blessingway ritual. Thus to build a hogan is to reproduce the origin of all things and to fulfill one's ongoing (sacred) responsibility to continually make and remake the world.

Despite its apparent simplicity, then, the Navajo hogan—like Pomo baskets and Nisga'a totem poles, like Yoruba white cloth and Dogon shrines, like Maori tattoos and *whare whakairo*—is a vital link between present and past, between community and place, between our world and the world of the spirits.

⊕ Colonialism

"**Colonialism**" refers both to the process by which people from one place establish and maintain a settlement in another and to the effects of this process on any people already living there. Typically, those effects include their subjugation, if not removal, and the imposition of new laws, economies, and social practices that are often modeled on those of the colonists' home territory.

Between the fifteenth and twentieth centuries, western Europeans established colonies in Africa, North and South America, Australia, and the islands of the Pacific Ocean. Until this activity began, western Europe was a relatively insignificant region in terms of global influence; afterward, it was the center of the world.

Quests for power and profit have often been the key factors driving colonialism. Religion has also played a critical role, however, both as a motivating factor and as a justification. The consequences of this activity for the religious traditions of the conquered peoples have been profound. It is not possible to understand Indigenous traditions today, therefore, without understanding colonialism.

Invasion

Columbus

The journals of Christopher Columbus record the start of the most devastating colonial project in history. His first contact with the Arawaks after his arrival in the Caribbean foretells much of what happened later: "On the first Island which I found, I took some of the natives by force in order that they might . . . give me information of whatever there is in these parts" (Zinn 1995: 1).

What Columbus most wanted to know was where the gold was. Unfortunately for the Arawaks, there was very little gold to find, but Columbus was not deterred. Those who managed to bring him a specified amount of gold were given a copper token to hang around their necks; those who were then found without a token had their hands cut off and were left to bleed to death.

Eventually Columbus came to see that the islands' most valuable "resources" were the people themselves, and he shipped them back to Europe by the boatload. Thus he exclaimed: "Let us in the name of the Holy Trinity go on sending all the slaves that can be sold" (Zinn 1995: 4). Within two years of his arrival, roughly half of the estimated original population of 250,000 had been either exported or killed. A century later, all of the Arawaks on the islands were gone.

Genocides

Colonial efforts elsewhere—in Africa, Australia, New Zealand, and the Americas—were similarly catastrophic. Millions of people, representing thousands of distinct cultures, were wiped out.

In Africa, as in the Caribbean, the chief source of wealth for the Europeans was the population itself. By the late nineteenth century, upward of 20 million Africans had been taken from their homes and sent to the Americas as slaves, though only about 11 million made it there alive. Scholars estimate that by the time the trans-Atlantic slave trade ended, the population of Africa had been reduced by half.

In Australia, less than half of the original population of about 500,000 remained after just a few years of contact with Europeans. The southeast—where the First Fleet arrived in 1788—was hit the hardest. During the first year of colonization, approximately two-thirds of the estimated 250,000 Aboriginals in the region were killed by a smallpox epidemic. By 1850, 96 percent were dead.

In the Americas, records suggest that by 1600 as many as 90 million Indigenous people—more than 90 percent of the original population—had died as a direct result of the Europeans' presence. More people had been killed than existed in all of Europe at the time (approximately 60 to 80 million). The destruction of the original inhabitants of the Americas was genocide on a scale that has not been seen before or since. The biggest single cause of the depopulation of both Australia and the Americas was disease, but other factors included military action, slavery, mistreatment, starvation or malnutrition, and loss of will to live. And the destruction has not ended yet. Indigenous citizens are still seen as expendable, such as when governments want more land.

"Masters of the Continent"

In many parts of North America, European occupation was initially accomplished through relatively peaceful negotiations with the original inhabitants. After all, the first settlers were greatly outnumbered, and the Indigenous people possessed valuable knowledge and skills. As the settler population grew, however, and the Indigenous population declined, negotiation became less important; eventually it ceased entirely in most instances, and Native people living on land that Europeans wanted were either forcibly removed or simply killed.

Colonists justified this behavior in many ways, some of which explicitly invoked religion. Many equated their situation with that of the Jews who were ordered by God to destroy the native inhabitants of Canaan. Only then could they inherit the Promised Land.

The notion of **terra nullius** ("no one's land") was also invoked by European settlers. Colonists argued variously that Indigenous people were not "really" using the land; that they could not own the land because they did not have any concept of ownership; or that because of their "primitive" nature, they did not count as people and therefore the land on which they lived was technically unoccupied. All these arguments were, of course, specious, self-serving, and inherently racist, with devastating consequences.

In 1890, US calvary moved to relocate an encampment of Lakota Sioux near Wounded Knee Creek, South Dakota, in order to free up the land for colonial settlers. The result was a massacre. More than 300 Sioux were killed, among them unarmed women and children; some were shot as they tried to run away.

Not far from the site of the massacre, at the Standing Rock Sioux Reservation in North and South Dakota, another colonial confrontation played out more recently. Since April 2016, members of Indigenous communities across North America have been at Standing Rock protesting the construction of the Dakota Access Pipeline (DAPL). An earlier proposal involved routing the pipeline near the city of Bismarck, but when the non-Indigenous residents of the city complained that the project risked jeopardizing water supplies, the pipeline was rerouted. Indigenous people have maintained that the pipeline's revised path would similarly harm water sources used by local communities, as well as desecrating sacred Sioux territories. After several confrontations with government authorities, the pipeline was completed in April 2017.

Around the world, Wounded Knee and Standing Rock remain powerful symbols of colonialism and its consequences for Indigenous people. Similar conjunctions of land acquisition and violence can be found at some point in the history of virtually every colonial encounter.

Conversion

As a result of colonialism, the majority of the world's Indigenous peoples were converted to the religion of one colonial power or another. That religion was usually some form of Christianity, but other missionary religions took hold in some areas of the world, notably Islam in parts of Africa and Buddhism throughout Asia.

Accurate information on adherence to Indigenous religions is virtually nonexistent. Such data are normally obtained from national censuses. On the topic of religion, however, many countries have had trouble either with their census questions or with the answer choices they offer. In Indonesia, for example, Indigenous religions are not recognized by law; thus, Indigenous people are counted as members of the dominant tradition (Islam) by default. As well, Indigenous people in many parts of the world may give the answers they think are desired to avoid possible reprisals or repercussions.

That said, approximately 70 percent of Indigenous people in the world today identify with a colonial religion; only 15 to 20 percent report that they practice an Indigenous religion. The rest declare adherence either to an alternative tradition or to none at all.

Loss of Religion

Some early European missionaries tried to persuade Indigenous communities that Christianity made more sense than their own traditions, but that approach was rarely successful. A more effective strategy was to demonstrate the "superiority" of Christian beliefs in practical terms. In many cases, that task was accomplished through the association of military strength with religious authority. The message was simple: our people are stronger than your people because our god is stronger than yours.

Another major factor in the decline of Indigenous religions was the people's belief that they needed the education available only through missionaries. Then, as colonial abuses accumulated, many oppressed Native people looked to the missionaries for *protection* from the new system. In both situations, Christianity flourished at the expense of traditional beliefs and practices.

Document

From *Things Fall Apart*, by Chinua Achebe (Igbo)

Achebe's 1958 novel—which focuses on an Igbo man named Okonkwo from a fictional village in Nigeria in the late 1800s—is the most influential work of African literature ever written. In this passage Okonkwo has just returned home after a seven-year exile, and his best friend Obierika is explaining the dramatic changes that colonialism has brought during his absence.

"Perhaps I have been away too long," Okonkwo said, almost to himself. "But I cannot understand these things you tell me. What is it that has happened to our people? Why have they lost the power to fight?"

"Have you not heard how the white man wiped out Abame?" asked Obierika.

"I have heard," said Okonkwo. "But I have also heard that Abame people were weak and foolish. Why did they not fight back? Had they no guns and machetes? We would be cowards to compare ourselves with the men of Abame. Their fathers had never dared to stand before our ancestors. We must fight these men and drive them from the land."

"It is already too late," said Obierika sadly. "Our own men and our sons have joined the ranks of the stranger. They have joined his religion and they help to uphold his government. If we should try to drive out the white men in Umuofia we should find it easy. There are only two of them. But what of our own people who are following their way and have been given power? They would go to Umuru and bring the soldiers, and we would be like Abame." He paused for a long time and then said: "I told you on my last visit to Mbanta how they hanged Aneto."

"What has happened to that piece of land in dispute?" asked Okonkwo.

"The white man's court has decided that it should belong to Nnama's family, who had given much money to the white man's messengers and interpreter."

"Does the white man understand our custom about land?"

"How can he when he does not even speak our tongue? But he says that our customs are bad, and our own brothers who have taken up his religion also say that our customs are bad. How do you think we can fight when our own brothers have turned against us? The white man is very clever. He came quietly and peaceably with his religion. We were amused at his foolishness and allowed him to stay. Now he has won our brothers, and our clan can no longer act like one. He has put a knife on the things that held us together and we have fallen apart." (Achebe 1996 [1958]: 12, 124–125)

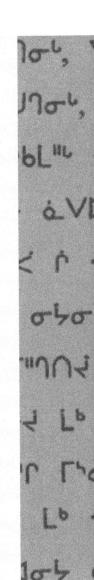

Some colonial governments outlawed the practice of Indigenous religions. This was invariably the case whenever such religions were suspected of involvement with anticolonial resistance. And sometimes such laws were put into effect in a more preemptive manner. In 1883, for example, the United States banned many Native ceremonies, including the Sun Dance. The next year, Canada amended its **Indian Act** to criminalize the **potlatch**. In both cases the declared motive was not to regulate religion but to protect Aboriginal citizens—from physical harm in the case of the Sun Dance, and from economic hardship in the case of the potlatch, which the government depicted as driving people into poverty.

Finally, the conversion of Indigenous people had an enormous impact on gender relations, which in turn has had repercussions in all areas of life. Most colonial powers brought a form of patriarchy with them that resulted in the gendered stratification of local societies and the devaluation of women and their roles. As the Métis author Maria Campbell has pointed out, this devaluation was often supported by colonial religious teachings: "The missionaries had impressed upon us the feeling that women were a source of evil. This belief, combined with the ancient Indian recognition of the power of women, is still holding back the progress of our people today" (1973: 168).

Loss of Language

As a result of colonialism, an untold number of Indigenous languages have disappeared forever. It has been estimated that Australia had almost 300 distinct Aboriginal languages at first contact; today all but 20 are either extinct or endangered. According to the United Nations, as many as 90 percent of all existing languages are in danger of dying out within 100 years; the vast majority of these languages are Indigenous.

For cultures that rely heavily on oral traditions to transmit their beliefs and values, the loss of language constitutes a devastating blow to their religion. In his memoir *Our Land Was a Forest*,

Practice

The Potlatch

The potlatch is practiced by many peoples of the Pacific Northwest, including the Haida, Kwakwaka'wakw, Salish, Tlingit, and Tsimshian. A way of demonstrating hospitality and redistributing wealth, it takes the form of a feast at which the hosting family presents the guests with gifts.

A potlatch is typically held to mark important moments, such as marriage, childbirth, or death, and may include music, theater, and ceremonial dancing. It may also serve to indicate social status: families demonstrate their wealth and importance by giving away (or even destroying) more resources than other families.

Recognizing the potlatch as a central element of many Native cultures, Christian missionaries thought that banning it would facilitate assimilation. Their governments agreed: the potlatch was made illegal in Canada in 1884, and in the United States a few years later. But the law was hard to enforce (Indigenous communities were large enough that they could often hold potlatches in secret), and many non-Natives—including the government agents tasked with enforcing the ban—considered it harsh and unnecessary. The ban was finally lifted in the United States in 1934 and in Canada in 1951.

Kayano Shigeru tells a story about the last three fluent Ainu speakers in his town, one of whom was his father. The three agreed that the first among them to die would be the luckiest, because the other two would be able to perform the death ritual for him in the Ainu language and thereby ensure that he would "return to the realm of the gods" (Shigeru 1994: 107).

What has caused this situation? In many cases, as communities died, their languages died with them. In others, the process of language loss was accelerated by government programs designed specifically to promote assimilation. Thus in Canada, Indigenous children were taken from their families against their will and placed in church-run **residential schools** where they were forbidden to speak their own languages. The United States began a similar program in the 1880s, a few decades later than Canada, forcibly sending Indigenous children away to schools operated by churches or government officials. In Australia, beginning in 1869, children were permanently removed from their homes and placed in foster care or (more often) in government- or church-run institutions, where they remained as wards of the state until they reached the age of 18. Record-keeping was often either inadequate or nonexistent, with the result that some children were never able to return to their families.

In all three countries, many agents of the institutions involved inflicted physical, psychological, and/or sexual abuse on the children in their care. Separated from their families, these children grew up with no knowledge of their language and traditions; at the same time they were deprived of the social knowledge required to establish healthy relationships and raise their own families. Lyn Austin, one of the children taken from her family by the Australian government, summarized the impact of these practices as follows: "Everything's gone, the loss of your culture, the loss of your family, all these things have a big impact" (Cooke 2008). It is no wonder that in Australia the children who were abducted by the government have been termed the "**Stolen Generations**."

Loss of Land

We have already noted how closely Indigenous religions are tied to specific locations: the sacred places where gods, spirits, and ancestors become present in the lives of each community. Limiting or preventing access to such locations therefore undermines the very foundations of Indigenous religion.

Thousands of Indigenous religious sites have been taken over or destroyed as a result of colonialism; no doubt there are many more such sites that we know nothing of, because the people who held them sacred have been destroyed. Yet even where both the people and the land survive, gaining recognition of land rights is an ongoing problem.

In the United States, more than 90 percent of the land inhabited by Indigenous peoples had been taken from them by 1890. A key (negative) moment in the Native Americans' struggle to reclaim some of this territory came almost a century later, when the US Forest Service proposed putting a paved road through the Six Rivers National Forest in Northern California to open the space for commercial logging. The project would effectively destroy the center of religious existence for two Native communities, the Yurok and the Karuk.

The case was eventually brought to the Supreme Court. The Native people were not asking that the land be returned to them—only that they retain access to it. Yet the Court found that their attachment to the territory was no different from the attachment that any individual might feel for any space. Thus, to agree to their request would set a precedent allowing anyone to request protection of any site on religious grounds. The petition was denied.

This case highlights two central problems in the understanding that many non-Indigenous people have of Indigenous religions. The first is that religion in general is often seen primarily as an individual commitment to a set of beliefs. Indigenous religions, by contrast, are communal and are as much about practice as belief.

The second problem is the difficulty that non-Indigenous people have in understanding why Indigenous practices often depend on access to particular sites. There is an important difference between religions that see the world as a unity—for example, all people are loved equally by Allah, or the Four Noble Truths apply to everyone—and religions that see the world in more particular, or locative, terms. For most Indigenous people, specific places are sacred to specific people, not to everyone in the world. For such people, one might say that the place itself is the religion; without it, the religion is fundamentally different.

Appropriation

Identity

For some people, a match between the Cleveland Indians and the Atlanta Braves is not just a baseball game: it's a stark reminder of the ongoing legacy of colonialism, of all that has been and that continues to be taken from them. Adding insult to injury, Braves' fans are known for doing the "tomahawk chop," while until 2018 the Indians' mascot was a caricature named "Chief Wahoo." And so Chippewa author Philip Bellfy remarks: "We lost most of our land, most of our 'Aboriginal' rights, many of our languages, most of our traditional cultural ways, our religion, our relationship to the land and the spirits of the land, and, it seems, that we've even lost control of much of our identity through the process of "trade-marking" images of us, and elements of our culture" (2005: 30).

This phenomenon is of course not limited to baseball. Many North American sports teams—including the Chicago Blackhawks and Washington Redskins—have taken Indigenous-oriented names. Many other businesses have used "Indigenous" names or logos to market their products, from Eskimo Pie ice cream to the Ford Thunderbird. In effect, the dominant colonial culture has appropriated Indigenous identities and reconstructed them to evoke whatever "primitive" stereotype is best suited to the product in question: the primal "warrior" for a sports team, the noble "chief" for tobacco, or the pure, natural "Indian maiden" for a line of dairy products or even beer.

Such appropriation is thus not simply arrogant, impolite, or politically incorrect. It perpetuates an image of Indigenous people that is far removed from current reality and thus helps to blind non-Indigenous people to ongoing injustices. People who see Indigenous cultures as primitive and uncivilized, as vanished or vanishing, will have difficulty recognizing the reality of modern communities and their concerns.

Around the world, sacred Indigenous items are often turned into souvenirs for cultural tourists. There is a lot of money to be made by selling cheap versions of African masks to non-Africans. Imitation Maori *moko* are popular among non-Indigenous tattoo enthusiasts and were even used on fashion models for a 2007 Jean-Paul Gaultier collection. Even more striking is the proliferation of dream catchers. Originally used in Anishinaubae culture to help protect children from nightmares, they are now sold by the thousands for use as decorative knickknacks. Often they can be seen hanging from a rearview mirror like a pair of fuzzy dice.

Indigenous opinion concerning the commercial use of religious objects and symbols is divided. Some people see it as disrespectful and damaging; others argue that it has some value, not only in economic terms but in educating the public about Indigenous culture. Still, there are forms of appropriation that almost all agree are inappropriate. Some of these are part of what is often called the **New Age** movement (see Chapter 13).

The Washington Redskins are the only major professional sports team named after a racial slur. The name, logo, and mascot "Chief Zee" have been the subject of ongoing legal action. Some Native Americans have proposed that if the team will not change its name, it could at least change its mascot—to a red-skinned potato (© Chris Szagola/NewSport/Corbis).

Many New Age teachings that seem to reflect Indigenous religions in fact turn them upside down, coopting elements of a locative and communal tradition to promote notions of universal truth and individual fulfillment. Non-Indigenous people are often willing to pay New Age "shamans" lots of money for the opportunity to get in touch with a "primal" part of themselves and overcome their own psychological and emotional problems. To this end they practice all manner of pseudo-Indigenous rituals: telling stories, chanting, passing around a talking stick, banging drums, dancing, and yelling in a forest.

These imitative practices can actually be quite dangerous. In October 2009, 3 people died and 18 more were hospitalized when self-help guru James Arthur Ray conducted a New Age **sweat lodge** ceremony in Arizona. In the traditional practice, participants sit in an enclosed space and water is poured over rocks heated in a fire to create steam. The ritual is used for various medicinal and religious purposes, including purification and reconnection to the spirits. Many Native communities, including the Anishinaubae, Lakota, Crow, and Chumash, conduct sweat lodge ceremonies safely in enclosures covered with hides, dirt, or blankets, but it seems that Ray's lodge was covered with plastic sheeting. In 2010, Ray was charged with manslaughter for the three deaths.

The largest Indigenous-themed New Age event is the annual Burning Man festival in northern Nevada. Taking its name from its central ceremony, during which a large wooden effigy is set aflame, since 2007 the event has attracted well over 40,000 people each year. Some have complained about the festival's appropriation of Indigenous cultures. In April 2009 organizers of an offshoot party in Oakland, California, circulated an online flyer encouraging participants to "GO NATIVE" and offering a discount to those "in Native costume." Given the immense popularity of Burning Man, it is impossible to overestimate the degree to which such appropriation influences the views of non-Natives about Native people—and thereby affects the lives of the latter.

⊕ Recent Developments

Given that Indigenous traditions are the world's oldest religions, the changes that have taken place within them since the 1500s certainly qualify as "recent developments." Also, as a result of colonialism, the religious traditions of Indigenous people have arguably changed more dramatically over the last centuries than the traditions of any other cultures in the world. That said, it's important to bear two points in mind.

First, there is a critical difference between recognizing that awful things have been done to Indigenous people and defining them as "victims"—a label that robs them of full humanity. A second, and related, point is that Indigenous people were never simply the passive objects of colonialism: they engaged with it at every step, and they have remained active agents in the developments that have shaped their histories, including recent developments in their religions.

Interaction and Adaptation

Dualisms

Soon after contact with Europeans, many Indigenous people began to incorporate elements of the colonial religion into their own traditions. An important example was the shift that sometimes took place from the more typically Indigenous worldview of **complementary dualism** (seeing the universe as necessarily including both creative and destructive forces that can work together) to the "Western" worldview of **conflict dualism** (seeing the universe as divided between good and evil forces that are in constant battle with one another).

Such a shift occurred around 1600 among many of the Indigenous people of Peru, who previously had had no real concept of "evil." In certain regions, local populations were demonized as enemies of Christ, giving the Spanish invaders license to use extreme violence to subjugate and convert them. The plan worked: many Indigenous Peruvians did adopt Christian beliefs, including good–evil dualism. While they came to regard Jesus as a positive and humane figure, however, they saw the Spanish as the true embodiments of evil.

A similar change took place among the Iroquois in the late 1700s. A man named Ganioda'yo, or Handsome Lake, experienced a series of visions in which he met Jesus as well as four angels sent by the creator, Tarachiawagon. As a result of these visions, he taught the Iroquois to publicly confess their sins, avoid evil (including witchcraft and alcohol), and worship only Tarachiawagon, not his malevolent brother, Tawiskaron. This division of the world between the good and evil brothers represented a potent fusion of Indigenous religion with Christian conflict dualism. Today approximately a third of all Iroquois practice what came to be called the Handsome Lake or Longhouse religion.

The Atlantic slave trade carried African traditions to the Americas, where they mixed with elements of both Christianity and Native American religions. Many relocated Africans continued to worship Yoruba gods under the guise of Christian saints, but in time elements of the two traditions often merged in fact, giving rise to new religions such as Macumba (in Brazil), Voudou (in Haiti), and Santeria (in Cuba).

Many Africans also moved toward conflict dualism. In the early 1800s, in the region that became South Africa, a Xhosa diviner named Nxele experienced what he understood to be an intervention by Christ. Although he continued to practice divination, he also began preaching a message that echoed the teachings of the nearby Christian missionaries.

Like the Indigenous Peruvians, however, Nxele came to see the Europeans as Christ's betrayers. Preaching that the god Mdalidiphu was on the Xhosa's side, Nxele led 10,000 warriors against the British at Grahamstown. The attack failed, and Nxele was imprisoned. He later drowned off the Cape coast while attempting to escape.

Cargo Cults

A famous recent example of an Indigenous religion changing in response to contact with outsiders is the **cargo cult**. Most cargo cults developed in the southwest Pacific region, although a few similar groups have also appeared in Africa and the Americas. The cargos in question were the supplies and manufactured goods that regularly arrived for various foreigners.

Colonists and missionaries first appeared on many Pacific islands in the late nineteenth and early twentieth centuries, but their activity intensified during the Second World War when military forces established bases on the islands. The local people believed that the goods arriving for the forces were provided by deities or ancestors, and that in order to receive similar shipments they should imitate the newcomers. Thus they painted military insignia on their bodies, marched like soldiers, and made guns from wood and radios from coconuts. Some even built replicas of airplanes, control towers, and headphones, waved landing signals, and lit torches along runways at night.

Their hopes were fueled by the belief that acquiring the desired goods would allow for reciprocal exchanges with the Europeans—a practice that for many Indigenous cultures was central to establishing relationships—and help bring about a new age of social harmony, healing the wounds caused by the arrival of the colonists.

Unfortunately, the focus on obtaining cargo eclipsed other elements of the local religions. Even though the cults reflected the content of their tradition (which explained the cargo as originating with gods or ancestors), they radically changed its form (their ritual behavior). In the end, many of the local traditions completely disappeared.

Paths of Resistance

Not all Indigenous religions changed so dramatically or quickly. Several Australian communities neither merged their tradition with the colonial one nor rejected one or the other. Instead, they declared the contradictory truth of both. Some have suggested that the Aborigines were better able than most to entertain two radically different cosmologies because their cultural heritage had accustomed them to paradoxes and nonlinear thinking.

In a number of instances Christianity was subsumed by the Indigenous tradition. The Warlpiri of Central Australia, for example, used ritual song and dance to tell Bible stories, just as they did with Dreaming tales. They also tended to conflate events, as if Adam, Abraham, and Jesus had

A young man worships at Saut d'Eau, Haiti, in July 2008 as part of the annual Voudou pilgrimage to the site (© Aurora Photos/Alamy).

lived at the same time as the Warlpiri's own ancestors. In effect, by telling the biblical stories in their own way, they reconfigured them to focus on place rather than the sequence of events.

This emphasis on place is a clear indication that the Aboriginal worldview took precedence over the Christian. To most Christians, it is theologically critical to understand the sequence in which the stories of Adam, Abraham, and Jesus occur. For the Aborigines, however, this sequence was irrelevant; the biblical figures were thus easily incorporated into their universe. In other words, unlike the cargo cult practitioners, they kept the form of their traditional religion (how stories were told), even as they altered its content to include biblical references. It's possible that this approach allowed them to resist conversion longer than many other communities.

"The End Is Near"

In the wake of the destruction wrought by Europeans, many Indigenous cultures experienced a religious crisis. One response was to understand colonialism as punishment for inadequate observance of Native traditions. Among the people who took this view were some who reasoned that repentance might help to usher in a new golden age. In some cases this view may have reflected the influence of Christian eschatology—the idea that the end of the world is near and the Kingdom of God will soon arrive. Of course, it may also have reflected the fact that the world as Indigenous people had known it really was coming to an end.

The Cattle Massacre

In the mid-1800s—a time when the Xhosa were suffering greatly under the British—a young woman named Nongqawuse had a vision in which her ancestors told her that because some of her people had practiced witchcraft, the British had been sent to punish them all. If the Xhosa renounced witchcraft and destroyed their food supplies, then the Europeans would be destroyed, the ancestors would return, their food would be replaced, and their land would be restored to them.

Many Xhosa responded by burning their granaries and slaughtering their cows—ultimately killing almost half a million. The result was starvation. The Xhosa population fell from 105,000 to 27,000 in a year. Many blamed the tragedy on those who had failed to heed Nongqawuse's prophecy, although there was a later backlash against Nongqawuse herself. In the end, most of the survivors turned to Christianity.

The Ghost Dance

Nongqawuse's vision shares some basic similarities with a vision promoted in 1889 by a Paiute religious leader named Wovoka in the region that is now Nevada. Reviving a movement from two decades earlier, he prophesied that in a few years the ancestors would return, the buffalo herds would be restored, and the settlers would disappear. To hasten this renewal, Wovoka urged his people to live peacefully and perform a ritual focused on the spirits of their ancestors. The Lakota Sioux termed this ritual the "spirit dance," which the Euro-Americans translated as "**Ghost Dance.**"

Delegates from various Native communities were sent to hear Wovoka. The Navajo, who were enjoying a period of relative stability, were not convinced. But the Lakota were on the verge of starvation after the US government had broken a treaty and given away their fertile reservation lands to white settlers. With the bison gone, crops scarce, and government supplies running low, the Lakota were strongly attracted to Wovoka's message, particularly the idea that the whites could be made to disappear. They danced with greater urgency as their situation deteriorated, and many took to wearing "Ghost Shirts," which they believed would repel bullets. Alarmed, the Bureau of Indian Affairs dispatched thousands of US Army troops to the Lakota territory. Among the consequences of this deployment were the death of Sitting Bull and the massacre at Wounded Knee.

From Earth to Sky

The British arrived in Australia in 1788 at the site that would become Sydney. They then appropriated the original inhabitants' territories so efficiently that within a decade the people were practicing special rituals to drive them out, appealing to the serpent Mindi to destroy them with (fittingly) smallpox.

But these efforts failed, and a religious crisis developed. Some Aborigines came to believe not only that the world would soon end, but also that the source of sacred power and authority had moved from the earth to a heavenly utopia in the sky. Evidence suggests that these beliefs were a direct result of exposure to Christianity.

Traditionally, the Aborigines had understood that after death their spirits would return to their homelands. Now, in a sad irony, they found comfort in the colonizers' promise that their spirits would journey to a paradise in the sky. The only difference was that, for the Aborigines, that paradise would be free of Europeans.

Autonomy and Equality

Unable to prevent colonialism, many Indigenous people eventually found other ways of pursuing autonomy, equality, and fair treatment. In many cases, religion has been at the heart of these efforts.

Non-Indigenous Religions

Often the religion involved in the quest for equity has been Indigenous, but not always. In his resistance to the racist apartheid system of South Africa, for example, Anglican Archbishop Desmond Tutu (Xhosa) quoted Romans 8:31 when he declared, "If God be for us, who can be against us?" (Allen 2008: 334). Many Indigenous Christians have similarly fought passionately against colonial (and Christian) abuses using ideas from the imported religion itself. Like Archbishop Tutu, they have drawn on biblical notions of justice, sympathy for the oppressed, and deliverance from evil to support their campaigns for equality and redress.

By the same token, some Indigenous Christians have incorporated Indigenous views into their critiques of colonial attitudes and practices. To this end, Desmond Tutu has frequently cited the African concept of **Ubuntu**, according to which all human beings are interconnected and therefore to harm others is to harm oneself. Anna Lee Rain Yellowhammer, a member of the Standing Rock Sioux tribe, voiced a critical Indigenous value (and rallying cry) for the protests against the Dakota Access Pipeline in 2016 when, at only age 13, she declared: "*Mni wiconi*" ("water is life"). Stan McKay (Cree), an ordained minister and former moderator of the United Church—the first Native person in Canada to head up a mainline denomination—similarly draws on Aboriginal notions of the interrelatedness of all life in his censure of Christianity's contributions to current environmental problems through its denial of "the integrity of creation" (McKay 1996: 55).

Land Claims

Many Indigenous activists combine a general concern for the environment with more specific concerns related to sacred Indigenous lands. Some efforts to reclaim such lands have failed completely, some have done well, and others have had more complex results. One early success came in 1970, when 48,000 acres of land in New Mexico were returned to the Taos Pueblo by President Richard Nixon. Originally confiscated by President Theodore Roosevelt and designated the Carson National Forest, the region includes Blue Lake, which Taos tradition holds to be the site of creation.

In Canada, a major land dispute erupted in 1990 between the Mohawk community of Kanesatake and the town of Oka, Quebec. At issue was Oka's plan to expand a golf course onto land sacred to the Mohawk. After a court ruling allowed construction to proceed, some Kanesatake people erected a barricade denying access to the disputed territory. The 78-day standoff eventually pitted Native people from across North America against the Canadian army. Ultimately, the federal government purchased the land and stopped the golf course development. But the victory was only partial for the Mohawk, since the land still did not return to them.

Australian Aborigines have perhaps had more success at reclaiming land than any other Indigenous group. Since a High Court case in 1992 overturned the idea of Australia as *terra nullius*,

Aborigines have successfully negotiated approximately 3,000 land claims. In the Northern Territory, most of the coastline and more than 40 percent of the land area is now (once again) owned by Indigenous people.

Other Victories

Most countries have also repealed their laws inhibiting the practice of Indigenous religions. The ban on the Sun Dance was lifted in Canada in 1951, and the ban on the potlatch was lifted in the United States in 1934. Much more recently, in 1993, when a local government in Florida outlawed animal sacrifice in an effort to stop the practice of Santeria and Voudou, the US Supreme Court ruled the legislation unconstitutional.

On a much larger scale, South Africa's apartheid laws were eliminated and its colonial regime overturned in 1994, and in 2008 Australia's prime minister, Kevin Rudd, officially apologized to the Aboriginal people for the policies that had led to the Stolen Generations. Later the same year, Canada's prime minister, Stephen Harper, issued an official apology for the residential school system, acknowledging that "it was wrong . . . to separate children from rich and vibrant traditions." Harper's apology led to the creation of the Truth and Reconciliation Commission (TRC), which operated from 2008 to 2015. The TRC met with thousands of residential school survivors and in the end issued 94 calls to action designed to acknowledge and to some extent redress the vast, traumatizing, and ongoing harm of residential schools.

Such victories are reflected in changes in attitude. School teams around the world have replaced their Indigenous-themed names or mascots. An especially imaginative solution was devised in 2006 for the Syracuse Chiefs baseball team in New York State, which kept its name but changed its logo from an "Indian chief" to a silver locomotive (with a "chief engineer"). The change actually made the team's name more relevant to the town's history as a railway hub.

In April 2009, when several Native people got wind of the "GO NATIVE" party promoting the Burning Man festival, they decided to attend and explain why they believed the event was harmful. After they had lectured the participants about colonialism and the history of invasion, genocide, and appropriation associated with it, most of those present apologized, and several broke down sobbing.

Contemporary Indigenous Traditions

Resurgence

With increasing legal and social recognition has come a rise in the actual practice of Indigenous traditions. Most of the religious traditions discussed in this chapter have recently experienced revivals, from carving masks in Africa to telling Dreamtime stories in Australia to the performance of the Sun Dance in North America.

The revival of Indigenous religions is understood, at least in part, as a way of coping with the cultural damage done by colonialism. At the same time some people—both Indigenous and non-Indigenous—have pointed out that the more material consequences of colonialism must be addressed as well. For many Indigenous people, these consequences include extreme poverty and deprivation; therefore, it is important to channel the positive effects of religious revitalization in ways that will also contribute to the improvement of Indigenous living conditions.

It's important to recognize that Indigenous people themselves are not of one mind on the revival of traditional religions. Many want no part of them, either because they do not find value in them or because they now practice another religion. Nevertheless, growing numbers of Indigenous people do seem eager to incorporate traditional beliefs and practices into their lives.

The ways in which Indigenous traditions are practiced today are rarely identical to the ways in which they were practiced in the past, for several reasons. First, all religions change over time. Second, colonial disruptions have been so severe that in many instances it is not possible to recover precolonial traditions. Third, Indigenous traditions are typically interested in the manifestation of the sacred in the here and now; the intersection of spirits and ancestors with the world is an ongoing reality that necessitates adaptation.

Among the Yoruba, for example, the god of iron and war, Ogun, has come to be associated with the protection of welders, mechanics, and chauffeurs. Also, as a result of lifestyle upheavals, very little cloth is now woven by hand, and younger people in particular often wear American clothing even to ceremonial events. Yet the Bunu still ascribe great value to handwoven cloth and so continue to produce it for the most important religious occasions.

New trickster stories frequently embody the ways in which Indigenous religions have responded to historical developments. When colonization began, some stories began to be told of tricksters using their powers to get the better of the newcomers; in others, these figures imitated colonizing practices—for example, negotiating worthless agreements—to fool the Indigenous people into giving them things they wanted. Tricksters in modern stories appear in many nontraditional guises, as politicians, bartenders, or university teachers. In addition, there are now many female tricksters.

Gender shifts are evident in other areas of Indigenous life as well. In the past, men and women often had quite different, though interdependent, functions, but because of disruptions to traditional lifestyles, the same role differentiation is often no longer possible. For example, if at one time in a community women were responsible for preparing the food that the men killed or grew, that arrangement fell apart once their land was taken. This dissolution combined with the advent of colonial patriarchies to put severe stress on Indigenous gender relations.

Some communities are now moving toward more balanced gender representation, much of it related to religious practices. Thus increasing numbers of Native American men are weaving ritual baskets. Similarly, there are now several female *moko* artists, and it is no longer uncommon for women to receive full *moko* themselves. Such changes are among the ways in which Indigenous people are working to overcome the gender hierarchies that developed under colonialism.

Cultural Expressions

One especially notable recent development is the presence of Indigenous religions in art forms that originated in non-Indigenous cultures, including film, written literature, oil painting, and electronic music. Works *by* Indigenous people *about* Indigenous people are receiving much attention and acclaim. Religion has been employed in some of these works both to engage issues arising from colonialism (past or present) and to explore aspects of Indigenous life on their own terms.

An example of the latter approach is the painting *Red Willows* by David Johnson. The work is clearly modern, produced in the mid-1990s to accompany Basil Johnston's retelling of the traditional story. The pairing of art and text adds meaning to both, often in a way that highlights the religious aspects of the tale. Thus the significance of the color red in the painting is revealed only by the text, while the branch that appears both inside and outside the man suggests the interrelatedness of all things, a theme that readers of the story—distracted by its vivid, humorous physicality—could easily miss.

Interview

Cat Criger, Traditional Elder for the University of Toronto Mississauga

Mark "Cat" Criger was born in 1956 in St. Catharines, Ontario, and for many years has worked as an Elder with various government and Indigenous agencies in Ontario and Canada, including the 2015 Pan American Games in Toronto. He served as an executive member of the board of directors for Anishnaawbe Health Toronto and received the Queen's Diamond Jubilee Medal for his work in the community on diversity, equity, respect for women, antiracism, and anti-oppression. Since 2008 Cat has worked with the University of Toronto Mississauga (UTM) and in 2013 became UTM's official Traditional Elder. In this role, among many other activities, he advises students, conducts ceremonies, and works with staff and faculty to help Indigenize spaces, courses, and curricula. In his spare time Cat is an archer, astronomer, artist, hiker, and kayaker. He participates in extreme sports when possible, is pursing a degree in photography, and loves spending time with his family and kittens.

For our interview, I asked Cat one question: "How did you become an Elder?" Here is a very abbreviated and slightly edited version of his response. The original interview was much longer and was painstakingly transcribed by Kelly Jay.

My spirit name is Mukwa Giizhigad, or Daytime Bear or Sun Bear. I am Cayugan on my dad's side, from the Haudenosaunee people, the People of the Longhouse. My dad's mom moved off reserve soon after he was born, and he grew up in St. Catharines. So part of that means the tradition was not part of his generation, it was not part of his growing up. My dad married a German English woman, my mother, and then not too long after that, joined the Canadian army, which meant that he was enfranchised and lost his Indian status.

We immediately start bouncing around the world. So we lived in Kingston, we lived in Trenton, we went to Winnipeg, and then to Germany. It was a fair amount of moving around. I turned five on the boat to Germany. And then back to Canada by about 1964/1965. So we went from continental European culture to the middle of backwoods Manitoba. Quite a cultural change.

When we moved there, to an army base west of Brandon, Manitoba, the opportunity to hunt was great. There's tons of deer, what we call prairie chicken. My dad taught me the values of hunting, he taught me respect for animals, respect for everything. The idea is that everything takes work, everything comes from the land, everything has value, and should be treated as if it's alive. I can remember being about nine, and I damaged a garbage can, and I got in trouble for not respecting that object. I was told that everything deserves respect. I remember that distinctly. I ruined an object that took a lot of design, technology, materials, fabrication, somebody had to pay for it, we had to bring it home. It was serving a purpose, it was doing something in the house, even though it was just holding garbage. I always, always remember that moment.

By the 1980s I started thinking more about my own culture. And then one day in Toronto in the early '90s I was given a pamphlet about Indigenous events put on at First Canadian Place. One of these events was a display of hoop dancing by Quentin Pipestem, who is a champion hoop dancer. So I had this pamphlet in my hand, and this woman comes up and asks me if I'm Native, if I'm Indian. I say, "Yeah." And she says: "There's a place just downtown near Queen and Sherbourne called Anishnawbe Health Toronto [AHT]. We have teaching circles there with Elders. Why don't you drop in?" And I did.

At that point I lived in the Beaches in Toronto, which is purely non-Native. I knew of no other

Continued

Native people in the Beaches at all, and all of a sudden I find myself in a setting where everybody's Native. I thought, "Ah, this is kind of neat. There are other people like me in the world."

One day an Elder at AHT asked if I would help him do work up north. I said yes. You know, at the time I'm racing motorcycles and doing extreme whitewater kayaking, and that world still exists for me, but now there was this other door opening. So it's a joke in Native culture, if I tell somebody this story: "Oh, this Elder said, 'Come and help me,' and I said yes," they'll laugh, because right away they know I've made a life commitment. But at the time I didn't really understand this, I didn't realize it would be so intense. It was a huge change in my life.

Also: I'm Cayugan, as I said. But this Elder, Roger Jones, was Ojibwe. Originally our peoples would

have been in conflict with each other. So him and I working together was this kind of funny combination. It was intercultural in a sense. Indigenous intercultural. And some people in our community had trouble with that. Traditionally, if you were of a particular tribe, you would learn those tribal teachings, or ways. You wouldn't be learning a completely different one.

In any case, I learned a lot of traditional teachings from this man, and from other tribal Elders. One of the other people I did some work with was an Elder from Mille Lacs, Minnesota, named Adam Lydia. He was an incredible medicine/plant person. It was quite astounding to work with him. It was a privilege. A lot of teachings about the pipe came from that gentleman. He is the one who found a spirit name for me in ceremony, Mukwa Giizhigad.

Cat Criger. (Courtesy of Cat Criger)

I didn't receive a spirit name when I was young. There was no access to that. Originally we would be given our spirit name before or during birth, but that practice was broken up by colonialism.

The whole idea of this apprenticeship with Roger Jones was so powerful—the exposure to experiencing life, taking a life direction, making changes within my mind. Old-style apprentice, old-style helper, old-style way of learning. People would work with the hunters to learn hunting, with the fishers to learn fishing, with the canoe builders to learn canoe building. I worked with an Elder to learn "eldering." And that included plant medicine, ceremonies, working with people on assorted concepts and styles of healing—physically, emotionally, spiritually. We met in the early 1990s and worked together for about 15 years, before he passed away.

When Roger died, some of his responsibilities and sacred items were passed on to me. The concept of carrying a pipe came from that. And so there were years of training, working towards carrying traditional pipe, which is a big honor and responsibility. Then waiting longer after that, a number of years after Roger passed away, and finally getting to a spiritual point where through dream, through ceremony, it came time to pick up this next responsibility of the pipe.

Meanwhile, working within the community, people get to know you. People start to ask you to do things that an Elder would do. And as you do more and more of those things, people recognize that you can do those things that this person once did; you did pick up the training, you are walking in a good way. And then the term "Elder" starts to be used to refer to you. It's one of those slow morphings, it's like a doctorate. It's also a big responsibility, because you're helping people. So to be an Elder is to accept that responsibility by saying, "Okay, I guess I'll do this for the rest of my life."

Prominent recent films that focus primarily on Indigenous religion include *Atanarjuat: The Fast Runner* (Canada, 2001), *Whale Rider* (New Zealand, 2002), and *Ten Canoes* (Australia, 2006). Two notable documentaries that consider the appropriation of Indigenous religion are *White Shamans and Plastic Medicine Men* (United States, 1996), on the theft and commercialization of Native American traditions by non-Natives; and *Reel Injun* (Canada, 2009), on the depictions of Native people in movies.

Several other films refer to Indigenous religion while focusing primarily on the consequences of colonialism, among them *Dance Me Outside* (Canada, 1994), *Rabbit-Proof Fence* (Australia, 2002), *Moolaadé* (Senegal/France/Burkina Faso/Cameroon/Morocco/Tunisia, 2004), and, perhaps most famously, *Once Were Warriors* (New Zealand, 1994). Directed by Lee Tamahori (Maori) and starring mostly Maori actors, *Once Were Warriors* presents a complex picture of the return to Indigenous traditions. For some key female characters, this return is beneficial, helping them to regain a sense of community and self-worth in the wake of the havoc wreaked by colonialism. For a number of male characters, however, the return is clouded by anger and misunderstanding, and sadly perpetuates the violence resulting from colonialism.

Literary works by Indigenous writers are also receiving wide acclaim. One of the first Indigenous writers to be recognized internationally was the poet Pauline Johnson (Mohawk), who began publishing in 1883 and was described by critics of her time as "perhaps the most unique figure in the literary world on this continent" and even as "the greatest living poetess" (Francis 1992: 113). Her poetry very often returned to the sacred theme of place, as in her most famous work, "The Song My Paddle Sings."

The modern era of Indigenous literature began in earnest in 1958 with the appearance of Chinua Achebe's *Things Fall Apart* (see Document box), which depicts the effects of British colonialism,

Women in the Traditions

Missing and Murdered Indigenous Women and Girls

One of the most insidious and harmful effects of colonialism on Indigenous communities has been patriarchy. Aside from the ways in which patriarchy has created division and suffering within the communities themselves, it has combined with the pervasive, ongoing colonial view of Indigenous people as less than fully human to make the lives of Indigenous women particularly difficult and precarious.

This precariousness is acutely apparent in the disproportionately high rates of violence suffered by Indigenous women. In Canada, according to the Royal Canadian Mounted Police (RCMP), Indigenous women represent 16 percent of all female homicide victims despite comprising only 4.3 percent of the total female population. In the province of Manitoba alone, Indigenous women make up 16.7 percent of the population but 49 percent of all female homicide victims. In its review of cases across Canada from 1980 to 2013, the RCMP concluded that 164 Indigenous women had gone missing, and 1,017 had been murdered. This situation has been called a "national crisis" and in September 2016 resulted in the federal government initiating an independent investigation, the National Inquiry into Missing and Murdered Indigenous Women and Girls.

Indigenous women in Canada have worked in various ways to bring attention to this situation, to humanize Indigenous women, and to resist colonial/patriarchal violence. In October 2015, Oji–Cree activist Kristen Villebrun and 10 other Indigenous women began constructing *inuksuit* (human-shaped stone forms) on the Chedoke Radial Trail in Hamilton, Ontario. As of December 2017, they had made and placed 1,181 *inuksuit*. In February 2016, Lucy Annanack worked with another team of women to build and place 1,200 *inuksuit* in Montreal.

A few years earlier, in March 2012, the Native Women's Association of Canada (NWAC) launched the collaborative traveling Faceless Dolls Project. With creative contributions from Cree artist Gloria Laroque, the project involves the making of faceless paper dolls by people across Canada. These dolls, the NWAC website explains, are a "visual representation of strong and beautiful Aboriginal women who have become 'faceless' victims of crime."

The REDress Project at the University of Toronto in March 2017 is one installment of Métis artist Jaime Black's ongoing attempt to bring attention to the issue of missing and murdered Indigenous women and girls. (Courtesy of Stephen Hong)

One of the oldest responses to the high number of missing and murdered Indigenous women in Canada is the REDress Project, started in 2000 by Métis artist Jaime Black. The project is an ongoing installation of red dresses in public spaces. Like the *inuksuit* and the faceless dolls, these dresses visually memorialize the women who have gone missing or been murdered. The title of the project also acts as a play on words, serving as a call to redress the violence committed against Indigenous women. Red was chosen for the project because an Indigenous friend of Black explained that red was the only color that spirits could see. Thus, said the artist, using red "is really a calling back of the spirits of these women and allowing them a chance to be among us and have their voices heard through their family members and community."

Document

From *The Bone People*, by Keri Hulme (Maori)

Published in 1983, this Booker Prize–winning novel follows three interconnected characters—Simon, Joe, and Kerewin—whose experiences are symbolically linked to Maori religious beliefs and practices. These characters are briefly introduced in the book's prologue.

He walks down the street. The asphalt reels by him.
  It is all silence.
  The silence is music.
  He is the singer.
  The people passing smile and shake their heads.
  He holds a hand out to them.
  They open their hands like flowers, shyly.
  He smiles with them.
  The light is blinding: he loves the light.
  They are the light.
  . . .
  He walks down the street. The asphalt is hot and soft with sun.
  The people passing smile, and call out greetings.
  He smiles and calls back.
  His mind is full of change and curve and hope, and he knows it is being lightly tapped. He laughs. Maybe there is the dance, as she says. Creation and change, destruction and change.
  New marae from the old marae, a beginning from the end.
  His mind weaves it into a spiral fretted with stars.

He holds out his hand, and it is gently taken.
  . . .
  She walks down the street. The asphalt sinks beneath her muscled feet.
  She whistles softly as she walks. Sometimes she smiles.
  The people passing smile too, but duck their heads in a deferential way as though her smile is too sharp.
  She grins more at the lowered heads. She can dig out each thought, each reaction, out from the grey brains, out through the bones. She knows a lot.
  She is eager to know more.
  But for now there is the sun at her back, and home here, and free wind all round.
  And them, shuffling ahead in the strange-paced dance. She quickens her steps until she has reached them.
  And she sings as she takes their hands.
  . . .
  They were nothing more than people, by themselves. Even paired, any pairing, they would have been nothing more than people by themselves. But all together, they have become the heart and muscles and mind of something perilous and new, something strange and growing and great. Together, all together, they are the instruments of change. (Hulme 1983: 2–4)

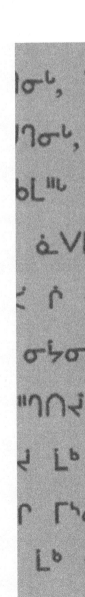

and particularly Christian missionaries, on the life and religion of the Indigenous people of Africa. *Things Fall Apart* was a landmark and regularly appears high on lists of the top 100 books of all time.

Religion is a central issue in the works of most Indigenous authors. The very title of N. Scott Momaday's breakthrough novel *House Made of Dawn*—winner of the 1969 Pulitzer Prize for Fiction—is taken from the Navajo Nightway Prayer.

Keri Hulme's novel *The Bone People* similarly displays elements characteristic of the resurgence of Indigenous traditions in general and Maori traditions in particular. Many of these elements are evident even in the book's brief prologue (see Document box):

- a rhythmic sense of time, in which the past is connected to the present;
- complementary dualism (the "dance" of "creation and change, destruction and change");
- an allusion to the central *koru* (frond/spiral) element of Maori *moko*; and
- the importance of community and rebuilding the *marae*.

Like other works of contemporary Indigenous art, *The Bone People* applies traditional religious views and practices to current situations. With both pathos and humor, it shows us characters struggling with their place in the world as individuals and as members of a community. Some of them manage better than others; some make terrible mistakes. But nothing is forever, and (as in many Indigenous stories, past and present) when we get to the end, we are also at a beginning. For there are always new stories to tell.

⊕ Summary

A key challenge in understanding Indigenous people and their religions is that they have long been defined, regulated, altered, and in many instances destroyed by non-Indigenous people. In the process, many incorrect and damaging views of Indigenous people and their traditions have been passed along, among them the belief that, before colonialism, Indigenous cultures were unchanging and illiterate—which is to say, "primitive."

There is enormous diversity among Indigenous cultures, but many of them share certain broad beliefs and social structures. In addition, although some of these cultures were literate long before colonialism, orality remains important to virtually all of them. Stories continue to transmit these communities' beliefs and values, although interpretation remains tricky. As with all religious texts, it is difficult to know which stories people understand to be objectively true and which ones they think about in a more figurative way. Different communities may perform similar rituals but attribute entirely different meanings to them. There is also, as we have noted, great diversity among Indigenous religions. Despite the harmful changes that have taken place in Indigenous communities over the past several hundred years, many of these communities are reviving and re-creating their religious traditions in various ways. Not only are elements of religious traditions being presented in new forms or contexts—novels, paintings, films—but, perhaps most important, religious activity is increasingly linked with political activism. Indigenous people are working passionately to reclaim the lands and rights taken from them, and religion continues to be a critical component of those efforts.

Sites

Bandiagara Escarpment, Western Africa

In the Dogon creation story, the supreme being Amma sacrificed one of his four children and scattered the remains on the earth. The Bandiagara escarpment in Mali is one of the sites where the Dogon people erected shrines to house the pieces.

Uluru, Central Australia

Uluru is an enormous sandstone formation that is sacred to the local Pitjantjatjara and Yankunytjatjara people. In 1985 the Australian government finally agreed to transfer the title to the site to them in exchange for a 99-year lease arrangement and tourist access, but the latter continues to be a point of contention.

Bighorn Medicine Wheel, Wyoming, United States

The Bighorn Medicine Wheel is a circular arrangement of stones with radial lines from the center to the rim found in Wyoming, designed to facilitate communication with spirits. It is still used by Blackfoot, Crow, Cheyenne, Sioux, and Arapahoe communities for vision quests, healing rituals, and prayer.

Ife, Nigeria

Ife is the ancient site where the Yoruba deities Oduduwa and Obatala began the creation of the world—an event that is celebrated at the annual Itapa festival in Ife.

Nibutani, Japan

Nibutani is the site on the northern island of Hokkaido where the Ainu god Okikurmikamuy arrived on earth. Today it is home to the Nibutani Museum of Ainu Cultural Resources, established by the Ainu author Kayano Shigeru.

Tiwanaku, Bolivia

Tiwanaku is the most sacred place for the Aymara people. Located roughly 70 km (45 miles) west of La Paz, it is seen as the center of the world, the site of humanity's creation, and the place where the Aymara go to communicate with their ancestors.

Kanesatake, Quebec, Canada

Kanesatake is the home of a Mohawk community that objected when the neighboring town of Oka planned to expand a golf course onto land containing a Mohawk cemetery. After a 78-day standoff, the government of Canada bought the site and stopped the development.

Saut d'Eau, Haiti

Saut d'Eau is the site of a group of waterfalls where Yoruba spirits are understood to dwell along with several Catholic saints. Voudou adherents make an annual pilgrimage to Saut d'Eau in June.

Tanna, Vanuatu

Tanna is an island in the South Pacific that is home to one of the last cargo cults. The Jon Frum movement began in the 1930s by urging a return to traditional practices and became a cargo cult during the Second World War, when approximately 300,000 American troops were stationed in Vanuatu. Its followers still hold a military-style parade every year.

Blue Lake, New Mexico, United States

Blue Lake is the site of the most sacred rituals and stories of the Taos Pueblo, confiscated in 1906. After more than 60 years of campaigning, they regained their title to it in 1970. Juan de Jésus Romero, the Pueblo's religious leader in the late 1960s and 1970s, once said: "The story of my people and the story of this place are one single story. No man can think of us without also thinking of this place. We are always joined together."

Discussion Questions

1. Are all Indigenous religions essentially the same? Why or why not?

2. Why was the colonial appropriation of land so harmful to Indigenous religions?

3. What are some elements of contemporary non-Indigenous culture that Indigenous people have used for their own purposes?

4. How do some trickster tales use chaos to promote social order in a community?

5. What is the literal and symbolic significance of a "journey" in Indigenous rites of passage?

6. What meaning is lost when Indigenous art is placed in a museum?

7. With reference to religious beliefs and practices, how did Indigenous gender relations become more unequal because of colonialism? What are some instances in which gender relations have recently become more equitable in Indigenous communities?

Glossary

Aborigine An Indigenous person; often specifies an Indigenous person of Australia.

cargo cults Religious movements, mainly in Melanesia, inspired by the shipments of goods arriving for foreigners and founded on the belief that one day the spirits would send similar shipments to the Indigenous people, initiating a new age of peace and social harmony.

colonialism The process by which people from one place establish and maintain a settlement in another, and its consequences for Indigenous people.

complementary dualism A worldview in which the universe necessarily comprises both creative and destructive forces, which can work together; a feature of many Indigenous religions.

conflict dualism A worldview in which the universe is divided between good and evil forces that are in constant battle with one another; a feature of many Western religions.

diviner A religious specialist who uses various ritual tools and practices to gain insight into the hidden or spiritual

aspects of particular circumstances, events, problems, etc.

Dreaming, The The term that anthropologists gave to the time and place of Australian Aboriginal origin stories. Although often assumed to represent the archaic past, The Dreaming is understood by many traditional Aborigines to lie just out of reach of living memory.

Elders Men or women whose wisdom and authority in cultural matters are recognized by their community. Elders are not necessarily old but are understood to possess greater knowledge of tradition than others and often to be more closely in touch with spiritual forces.

Ghost Dance A religious movement that emerged in the western United States in response to colonialism. Launched in 1869 and revived in 1889, the Ghost Dance was performed in an effort to hasten the removal of the settlers and the restoration of what Native people had lost. Smaller revivals occurred periodically throughout the twentieth century.

hogan A traditional Navajo home. The first hogan was the earth itself, and so building a new home reproduces the creation. This structure is at the center

of the community's domestic, social, and religious life.

Indian Act Canadian federal legislation created in 1876 that defines and regulates Native people and their lands and outlines the federal government's responsibilities toward them. The act is administered by the Department of Indian and Northern Affairs and has undergone several amendments and revisions.

marae The religious and social home of a Maori community consisting of a cleared area bordered with stones or wooden posts and containing several structures, including the *whare whakairo* ("carved house").

mbari A mode or style of cultural practice, especially architecture; principally identified with the Owerri Igbo of Nigeria.

moko Traditional Maori tattoos, originally chiseled into the skin, that identify the individual and his or her relationship to the community. Said to have been brought to earth from the underworld by the ancestors, *moko* were prohibited by colonial rulers but have resurfaced with the revival of other Maori practices.

New Age A common term for Western spiritual movements concerned with universal truths and individual potential that draw from a wide range of religions and philosophies, including astrology, Buddhism, metaphysics, environmentalism, and Indigenous traditions.

potlatch A ritual practiced by many Indigenous groups of the Pacific Northwest (e.g., Haida, Salish, Tlingit, Tsimshian) in which a family hosts a feast and offers guests gifts. The ritual typically marks important moments such as marriage, childbirth, or death and may include music, theater, and ceremonial dancing.

residential schools Schools funded by the American and Canadian federal governments, often run by churches, designed to facilitate assimilation to colonial, Christian societies. Indigenous families were forced to send their children to the schools, where they were forbidden to speak their own languages and often subjected to neglect and abuse. These schools operated from the 1840s (Canada) and 1880s (United States) until the late twentieth century.

smudging Indigenous North American purification and/or healing ceremony that involves burning a small amount of a particular plant, such as sage, cedar, or sweetgrass, in a small bowl.

Stolen Generations The generations of Australian Aborigines who as children were taken from their families and sent either to foster homes or to government- or church-run institutions. Because records were frequently lost (or not kept), many children were never able to reconnect with their families. The practice continued from approximately 1869 to the early 1970s.

Sun Dance Annual summer ritual practiced by peoples of the North American plains (e.g., Blackfoot, Cheyenne, Crow, Kiowa, Sioux). The details of the ritual vary from one community to the next, as does the meaning of the solar symbolism. In the late nineteenth century the Sun Dance was severely discouraged by the Canadian government and outlawed in the United States; it has experienced a revival since the 1960s.

sweat lodge A structure traditionally covered with skins, blankets, or dirt, used to induce sweating by pouring water over heated stones to create steam. Sweat lodge ceremonies are performed by several Native North American communities for medicinal and religious purposes, including purification and reconnection to the spirits.

syncretism The combination of elements from two or more religious traditions. Too often the term is used negatively to suggest that the "purity" of a particular religion has been compromised or contaminated.

terra nullius Latin for "no one's land," referring to territory over which no person or state has ownership or sovereignty; a concept invoked in several instances by European colonists to claim land occupied by Indigenous people. In Australia, the High Court invalidated this justification in a 1992 ruling.

totem pole A tall pole traditionally carved from a single cedar tree by an Indigenous community of the Pacific Northwest Coast (e.g., Haisla, Nisga'a, Tsimshian) to record historical events, indicate social status, represent ancestral lineage, support a physical structure, etc. Markings are often highly symbolic and specific to particular communities and locations.

trickster Term coined by scholars to classify a variety of usually superhuman figures who appear in the stories of cultures around the world; tricksters disrupt the norms of society and/or nature and often serve to teach important lessons about what is and is not acceptable in a particular community.

Ubuntu The African concept that all human beings are interconnected, employed most famously by Nelson Mandela and Archbishop Desmond Tutu as one of the founding principles of the new South Africa. *Ubuntu* has since gained prominence in the United States as well.

vision quest Fasting ritual undertaken to induce visions through contact with spirits; typically involving a solitary journey into the wilderness, it may be undertaken as a rite of passage to adulthood or during other key life events, such as preparation for war.

Further Reading

Ballinger, Franchot. 2004. *Living Sideways: Tricksters in American Indian Oral Traditions*. Norman: University of Oklahoma Press. An excellent, engaging introduction to Native American trickster figures; focuses on traditional (oral) stories but also includes references to contemporary literature.

Baum, Robert M. 1999. *Shrines of the Slave Trade: Diola Religion and Society in Precolonial Senegambia*. New York: Oxford University Press. This detailed study is one of the few to examine the pre-contact history of any African Indigenous religion.

Bell, Diane. 1983. *Daughters of the Dreaming*. Melbourne: McPhee-Gribble. An accessible (and bestselling) work of groundbreaking scholarship on the religious lives of Aboriginal women in central Australia.

Bockle, Simon. 1993. *Death and the Invisible Powers: The World of Kongo Belief*. Bloomington: Indiana University Press. An insider's introduction to the religious life of the Kongo people of Lower Zaire and to African religions generally, focusing on views and behaviors concerning death.

Deloria, Vine, Jr. 1994 [1972]. *God Is Red: A Native View of Religion*. 2nd ed. Golden, CO: Fulcrum. Indispensable overview of Native American religious perspectives, particularly regarding the importance of sacred places and the effects of colonialism.

Fiola, Chantal. 2015. *Rekindling the Sacred Fire: Métis Ancestry and Anishinaabe Spirituality*. Winnipeg: University of Manitoba Press. Currently the only text on Métis traditions, offering historical and contemporary overviews, discussions of colonialism and efforts at recovery, and interviews with Métis people about their religious lives.

Francis, Daniel. 1992. *The Imaginary Indian: The Image of the Indian in Canadian Culture*. Vancouver: Arsenal Pulp. A detailed, accessible discussion of the ways in which non-Natives in Canada have appropriated Native identity.

Gill, Sam D. 1982. *Beyond the "Primitive": The Religions of Nonliterate Peoples*. Englewood Cliffs, NJ: Prentice-Hall. Still one of the best general introductions to Indigenous traditions; especially useful on what religious practices mean to their communities.

Jacobs, Sue-Ellen, Wesley Thomas, and Sabine Lang, eds. 1997. *Two-Spirit People: Native American Gender Identity, Sexuality, and Spirituality*. Urbana and Chicago: University of Illinois Press. A vital collection of essays examining the connections between Native North American religions and constructions of gender and sexuality, from the traditional acceptance of diversity in many communities to current efforts to reclaim that acceptance.

King, Thomas. 2012. *The Inconvenient Indian: A Curious Account of Native People in North America*. Toronto: Doubleday. A simultaneously moving, horrifying, insightful, and funny overview, from an Indigenous perspective, of the history of Indigenous people in North America since first contact with Europeans, by one of the continent's most respected and prominent writers of fiction and nonfiction.

LeRoy, John, ed. 1985. *Kewa Tales*. Vancouver: University of British Columbia Press. A valuable collection of traditional oral narratives from Papua New Guinea, catalogued to highlight various story patterns.

Mead, Hirini Moko. 2003. *Tikanga Maori: Living by Maori Values*. Wellington, New Zealand: Huia. A useful overview of Maori *tikanga* ("way of doing things"), especially the connections between religion and the creative arts; promotes *tikanga* as a guide for non-Maori people.

Olajubu, Oyeronke. 2003. *Women in the Yoruba Religious Sphere*. New York: State University of New York Press. Examines women's roles—along with issues of gender and power relations—in both traditional and contemporary Yoruba thought and practice.

Olupona, Jacob K., ed. 2004. *Beyond Primitivism: Indigenous Religious Traditions and Modernity*. New York: Routledge. One of the very few works to look at the contemporary situation of Indigenous religions, with contributors from a broad range of backgrounds considering traditions from across America, Africa, Asia, and the Pacific.

Renne, Elisha P. 1995. *Cloth That Does Not Die: The Meaning of Cloth in Bùnú Social Life*. Seattle: University of Washington Press. A clear, insightful look at the role of a key material object in the culture (and especially religion) of the Bunu Yoruba people.

Rosaldo, Renato. 1980. *Ilongot Headhunting 1883–1974: A Study in Society and History*. Stanford, CA: Stanford University Press. An influential analysis of the meaning and function of headhunting for the Ilongot people in the Philippines; discredits the notion that Indigenous societies were/are static, as opposed to European societies that have changed over time.

Ryan, Allan. 1999. *The Trickster Shift: Humour and Irony in Contemporary Native Art*. Vancouver: University of British Columbia Press. The first book-length study of the influence of trickster conceptions in modern Native art, with photos of recent work alongside commentaries from the artists.

Shigeru, Kayano. 1994. *Our Land Was a Forest: An Ainu Memoir*. Translated by Kyoko Selden and Lili Selden. Boulder, CO: Westview. A moving personal account by an Ainu man who has spent much of his life documenting his people's culture and history, as well as creating a school to ensure the continuation of the Ainu language.

Smith, Jonathan Z., William Scott Green, and Jorunn Jacobsen Buckley, eds. 1995. *The HarperCollins Dictionary of Religion*. San Francisco: Harper-Collins. The following entries provide excellent brief introductions to topics relevant to Indigenous religions: "Africa, traditional religions in"; "Australian and Pacific traditional religions"; "circumpolar religions"; "Mesoamerican religion"; "Native Americans (Central and South America), new religions among"; "Native Americans (North America), new religions among"; "non-literacy"; "North America, traditional religions in"; "Religions of Traditional Peoples"; "South American religions, traditional"; and "traditional religions, Western influence on."

Swain, Tony, and Garry Trompf. 1995. *The Religions of Oceania*. London: Routledge. The first (and possibly best) book in English on the religions of the southwest Pacific as a whole; provides clear interpretive tools and general information on the history and content of these traditions, from before colonialism through modernity.

Wright, Ronald. 1992. *Stolen Continents: The "New World" Through Indian Eyes*. Boston: Houghton Mifflin. A powerful, accessible account of the colonization and survival of the Aztec, Maya, Inca, Cherokee, and Iroquois civilizations; includes much Indigenous testimony.

Recommended Websites

http://cwis.org

The Center for World Indigenous Studies Virtual Library, offering a list of websites with further information on Indigenous cultures and current issues, organized by region.

http://www.everyculture.com

A site offering brief but substantive information on most Indigenous cultures, including an overview of religious beliefs and practices, and a bibliography for each group.

http://indigenouspeoplesissues.com

Articles, updates, and information on current issues affecting Indigenous communities around the world, provided by a global network of scholars, activists, and organizations.

http://www.hanksville.org/sand/index.html

Information and resources about (and critiques of) the appropriation of Indigenous cultural property, particularly religious images and practices.

http://www.nativeweb.org

News and information from and about Indigenous people and organizations around the world. This effort initiated the NativeWiki project, a library of Indigenous data to which users can also contribute.

http://www.peoplesoftheworld.org

A site providing education for and about Indigenous people, including lists of resources such as documentaries and volunteer programs, as well as detailed information about Indigenous people organized by language, country, and name.

References

Achebe, Chinua. 1996 [1958]. *Things Fall Apart*. Oxford: Heinemann.

Allen, John. 2008. *Desmond Tutu: Rabble-Rouser for Peace: The Authorized Biography*. Chicago: Lawrence Hill.

Bellfy, Philip. 2005. "Permission and Possession: The Identity Tightrope." In *Walking a Tightrope: Aboriginal People and Their Representations*, ed. Ute Lischke and David T. McNab. Waterloo, Ontario: Wilfrid Laurier University Press.

Campbell, Maria. 1973. *Halfbreed*. Halifax, Nova Scotia: Goodread.

Cooke, Dewi. 2008. "'Sorry' Statement Should Acknowledge Cultural Loss, Says State Leader." *Age*, February1. http://www.theage.com.au/articles/2008/01/31/1201714153311.html (accessed October 11, 2009).

Deloria, Vine, Jr. 1988 [1969]. *Custer Died for Your Sins: An Indian Manifesto*. Norman and Lincoln: University of Oklahoma Press. Originally published in 1969, pp. 89–93.

Drewal, Margaret Thompson. 2002. "The Ontological Journey." In *Readings in Indigenous Religions*, ed. Graham Harvey. London: Continuum.

Francis, Daniel. 1992. *The Imaginary Indian: The Image of the Indian in Canadian Culture*. Vancouver: Arsenal Pulp.

Gill, Sam D. 1982. *Beyond the "Primitive": The Religions of Nonliterate Peoples*. Englewood Cliffs, NJ: Prentice-Hall.

Heiss, Anita. 2001. "Aboriginal Identity and Its Effects on Writing." In *(Ad)dressing Our Words: Aboriginal Perspectives on Aboriginal Literatures*, ed. Armand Garnet Ruffo. Penticton, British Columbia: Theytus.

Hulme, Keri. 1983. *The Bone People*. Wellington: Spiral.

Johnston, Basil. 1995. *The Bear-Walker and Other Stories*. Illustrated by David Johnson. Toronto: Royal Ontario Museum.

Lutz, Hartmut. 1991. *Contemporary Challenges: Conversations with Canadian Native Authors*. Saskatoon, Saskatchewan: Fifth House.

Matthews, Washington. 1995 [1902]. *The Night Chant: A Navaho Ceremony*. Salt Lake City: University of Utah Press.

McKay, Stan. 1996. "An Aboriginal Christian Perspective on the Integrity of Creation." In *Native and Christian: Indigenous Voices on Religious Identity in the United States and Canada*, ed. James Treat. New York: Routledge.

Sarris, Greg. 1992. "'What I'm Talking about When I'm Talking about My Baskets': Conversations with Mabel McKay." In *De/Colonizing the Subject: The Politics of Gender in Women's Autobiography*, ed. Sidonie Smith and Julia Watson. Minneapolis: University of Minnesota Press.

Shigeru, Kayano. 1994. *Our Land Was a Forest: An Ainu Memoir*. Translated by Kyoko Selden and Lili Selden. Boulder, CO: Westview.

Swain, Tony, and Garry Trompf. 1995. *The Religions of Oceania*. London: Routledge.

Tait, Norman. 1993. Foreword to Hilary Stewart, *Looking at Totem Poles*. Vancouver: Douglas & McIntyre.

Zinn, Howard. 1995. *A People's History of the United States: 1492–Present*. New York: HarperPerennial.

Note

I would like to express my very great thanks to all those who read, commented upon, or inspired any part of this chapter: Lisa Ball, Meg Botteon, Meagan Carlsson, Ted Chamberlin, Michel Desjardins, Graham Harvey, Amir Hussain, Agnes Jay, Kelly Jay, Daniel Heath Justice, Sarah King, Sally Livingston, Jennifer Mueller, Michael Ostling, Keren Rice, Mark Ruml, and Sarah Vogelsong. I also wish to dedicate this chapter to Willard Oxtoby, who shaped much of my time as a graduate student at the University of Toronto, and who was always generous with both his scholarship and his terrible, terrible puns.

3 Religions of Antiquity

Michael Desrochers

Traditions at a Glance

"Antiquity" refers to the general region of the Near East (Iran, Mesopotamia, and Egypt) and the Mediterranean (Greece and Rome) as it existed from the late fourth millennium BCE to the mid-first millennium CE. In that time many religious traditions emerged and evolved, sometimes independently and sometimes intersecting with one another.

Founders and Principal Leaders

Zoroastrianism attributed its founding to Zarathustra/Zoroaster, while Manichaeism was founded by Mani.

Names of the Deity

Most traditions recognized hundreds of deities, many of which also had multiple aspects, expressed using various epithets. Zoroastrianism and Manichaeism acknowledged several divinities, but Zoroastrianism focused on Ahura Mazda and Manichaeism on the Father of Greatness.

Authoritative Texts

Certain texts were essential components of these cultures' canonic traditions: the *Epic of Gilgamesh* for Mesopotamia, Homer's *Iliad* for Greece, and Vergil's *Aeneid* for Rome. Zoroastrianism had several important scriptures: *Yasna*, *Yashts*, *Vendidad*, *Denkard*, and *Bundahishn*. Mani composed several works, which survive only in fragmentary later translations.

Noteworthy Doctrines

All ancient traditions were originally polytheistic, worshiping multiple gods, and they all promoted moral/ethical behavior. In practice, they placed equal or greater emphasis on ritual of various types. Manichaeism and Zoroastrianism stressed dualism, a philosophy based on the conflict between good and evil.

In this chapter you will learn about:

- The commonalities and special emphases of six religious traditions
- The nature and purposes of myth and ritual
- Shared and conflicting interpretations of the divine
- Various ways ancient peoples expressed their religiosity
- Reasons for the longevity and ultimate collapse of the ancient traditions

⊕ Introduction

As we learned in Chapter 1, while there has been no universal definition of "religion," the term is generally understood to imply a sense of obligation within a relationship, whether a communal bond among humans or one between humans and divinities. The bond's proof is demonstrated in performance. Religious performance entails a ritual act. In practicing religious traditions, cultures and societies express the idea that every ritual performance of the obligation preserves the practices undertaken, and bonds secured, by previous generations.

Two of the religious traditions examined in this chapter—Zoroastrianism and Manichaeism—fit the designation of "world" religions, with their influence stretching at some point from the western Mediterranean to China. Such a broad diffusion, which could later be seen in Judaism,

Al-Dayr ("the monastery") is a first-century BCE building by the Nabataeans in Petra, Jordan (Richard Vinson/iStockphoto).

Christianity, and Islam, only occurred with the appearance of empires. Before that development, though, certain traditions (e.g., Mesopotamian) and behaviors (e.g., sacrifices and offerings) were distinctly widespread. The adjective "world" can also connote that such religions have survived to the present. Manichaeism did not; Zoroastrianism has.

When we consider religions of "antiquity," however, we are not referring to the entire globe but rather to a specific geographical area. Two terms identify this broad region: "Fertile Crescent" for pre-history and "ancient Near East" for the historical era. Agriculture first developed in the highlands of the Fertile Crescent and then spread both eastward and westward. Religions similarly spread outward from the ancient Near East. Judaism arose in a region first dominated by ancient Near Eastern powers and later by the Greek and Roman empires. Just as Jews were first dispersed during the Assyrian and Babylonian empires and Christianity spread under the rule of the Roman Empire, so Islam appeared on the borders of two rival empires, the Byzantine to the northwest and Sasanian to the northeast, and quickly conquered large portions of them. Manichaeism emerged in southern Mesopotamia in the third century CE, long after the advance of Zoroastrianism in the Persian Empire. Mesopotamia was for a millennium a borderland between Western (Greek and Roman) and Eastern (Iranian) empires. The ancient Near East, including both Mesopotamia and Iran, was neither West nor East, but rather the center from which religions radiated to both the West and the East via imperial routes.

"Antiquity" can be perceived not only as a time period but also as a tradition, the Greco-Roman pre-Christian tradition, for it was fourth-century CE Christian authors who used the term *antiquitas* to disparage that tradition, which they condemned as "the mother of all evils." Those same Christian authors labeled that tradition's participants "pagans," a term that suggested unsophisticated ignorance. "Pagans" had been blithely ignorant that they were pagans or could be identified by any particular designation. They were simply following their respective traditions.

A principal characteristic of the three religions of the Abrahamic tradition is that they are "religions of the book." Both Zoroastrianism and Manichaeism were also based on sacred books, but the other religions of antiquity were not scripture-directed. They were, however, text-based, drawing from a host of different types of texts that offer insights into both the continuities and alterations of their religious sensibilities, behaviors, and understandings over time. These texts served as the carriers of traditions, several of which lasted for well over 2,000 years. Those "living texts" were passed down in copies that oftentimes challenged or revised earlier traditions.

⊕ Prehistory

The religious roots of antiquity reach deep into prehistory. In the absence of documentary evidence we must rely on material remains; thus, interpretations of prehistory will always be conjectural. Anatomically modern humans first appeared around 200,000 years ago. Some scholars contend that human symbolic behavior, such as the association of red ocher with burials—the very origins of religion—can be traced to an equally distant time, making religion inherent to our species. In a cave in South Africa, archaeologists discovered an infant burial dated to 100,000 years ago; the child's bones were stained with ocher, and a pierced shell, a pendant, had been placed atop him. Awe-inspired, and awe-inspiring, cave paintings created over a span of 25 millennia—from roughly 35,000 to 10,000 BCE—also include many symbolic elements associated with religion, even if there is no consensus on how they should be interpreted.

If the cave paintings that stretched from the Iberian Peninsula and southern France as far as the Ural Mountains of Russia can be taken as indications of the very first religious tradition, we

Timeline

	Mesopotamia	Egypt	Greece	Rome	Iran
3000 BCE	**Sumerian Era**				
2700		**Old Kingdom** Pyramid Age			
2300	Sargon	Pyramid Texts			
2000		**Middle Kingdom** Coffin Texts *Merikare*			
1800	Hammurabi *Gilgamesh*				
1300		**New Kingdom** Akhenaten *Book of the Dead*			
	Enuma Elish				
1000	Omen collections **Assyrian Empire**				
700 BCE			Homer Hesiod		Zoroaster? *Avesta?*
	Nabonidus				
500 BCE			Xenophanes Heraclitus	**Roman Republic**	Darius
400 BCE			Plato		
		Late Period			
300 BCE			Alexander		
100 BCE		Roman conquest			
BC/CE					
				Cicero	
				Roman Empire Augustus Ovid Vergil	
100 CE					
200 CE					
	Mani				**Sasanian Dynasty**
300 CE					
				Diocletian	
400 CE					
500 CE					

Map 3.1 Classical World of Greece and Rome

can pinpoint a second identifiable tradition that appeared in the northwestern section of the Fertile Crescent, an area roughly covering southeastern Turkey and northern Israel, from 13,000 to 5000 BCE, a period of transition from hunting and gathering to agriculture. There are four significant components to this tradition: shrines, symbolism, female figurines, and burials.

Gobekli Tepe

The most famous early shrine is Gobekli Tepe in southeastern Turkey. Dating from 9500 to 8000 BCE, Gobekli Tepe consisted of a series of rings or circles, edged by benches that connected massive *T*-shaped pillars, the sides of which resembled human arms. It is the oldest known example of monumental architecture, and if its excavator is correct in claiming that Gobekli was a temple complex, it is also the oldest known religious structure. Corresponding features have been found at several nearby sites.

The builders of these sites were pre-agricultural foragers. Given the limited evidence that anyone lived there, the complexes must have served as a central meeting place for social functions, including feasts and ceremonies. One interesting hypothesis suggests that the necessity of feeding large numbers of workers and pilgrims served as the catalyst for the development of agriculture; the earliest evidence for the domestication of wheat, dated to 9000 BCE, has been found at a site

Map 3.2 Ancient Near East

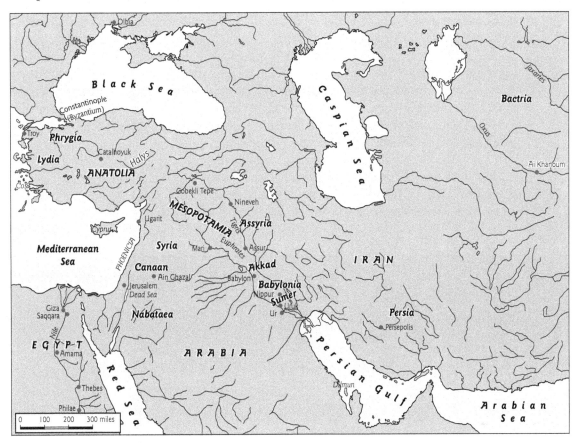

barely 20 miles from Gobekli. If this hypothesis is valid, it reverses the long-held position that organized religion began in response to the needs of settled agricultural life. Religion, in this new view, may have been the inspiration for agriculture and, ultimately, the beginnings of "civilization."

Catalhoyuk

Located slightly outside the Fertile Crescent, 300 miles west of Gobekli, Catalhoyuk was an early agricultural town, inhabited from 7400 to 6000 BCE. Its growth seems to have coincided with the desertion of other nearby settlements, and its unusual layout may reflect a new approach to social integration, prompted by the need to absorb disparate groups of people. Catalhoyuk's structures are clearly residential, divided into two distinct zones: a drab domestic space and a "sacred" area with platforms superimposed over burial sites and walls painted with scenes of humans baiting wild animals and adorned with bulls' heads. Burial sites, platforms, thresholds, and plaster-covered bulls' skulls were all painted with red ocher, presumably a symbol of vitality.

Catalhoyuk seems to have been as much a ritual center as a place of production, and as much a cemetery as a settlement. Many of the homes contain evidence of both numerous burials and frequent rebuilding. To date, 350 burials have been uncovered at Catalhoyuk. Eighteen had their heads removed, typically one year after the original burial. In one such burial, a woman's skull, which was plastered and painted red on at least four occasions, was nestled in the arms of a newly interred woman. These "history houses," so named by the excavators, were effectively virtual archives, with their symbolic texts taking the form of bones and such material objects as obsidian and crystals, thereby preserving transgenerational memory and bringing ancestors temporarily back to life with each rebuilding.

The signature item found at Catalhoyuk was the seated figure of a large-breasted female about to give birth, flanked by two leopards. Several similar figurines have been found at sites throughout the region, with one such find dating from the early tenth millennium BCE. Even more important than this symbolic figure of fertility is the more common and more prominent representation of the bull, which later became the paradigmatic sacrificial animal of the Mediterranean region. The majority of the 450 individuals buried at the nearby site of Çayonu were deposited along with dozens of bulls' skulls in a complex named the "Skull Building."

Catalhoyuk exemplifies many features of religious significance: religion's role as an integrator of both families and communities, boundaries between the mundane and the sacred, rituals and memorialization, and a repertoire of symbols and figurines used in the region for several millennia.

A reconstructed room at Catalhoyuk, with numerous skulls of aurochs or bulls (© Photo by DEA/G. DAGLI ORTI/De Agostini/Getty Images).

Nabta Playa

Nabta Playa, in the western desert of southern Egypt, was a meeting place for Saharan cattle herders, who erected there a series of significant monuments between the late seventh and mid-fourth millennia BCE. One part of the complex, labeled the Valley of Sacrifices, held several burials, including the remains of entire cows; one even contained a life-sized sculpture of a cow. Next to the Valley of Sacrifices were several megalithic complexes, including standing stones with **anthropomorphic** (human-shaped) shoulders (similar to those seen at Gobekli) oriented to the brightest stars of the northern sky. There was also a "calendar circle" used to predict the summer solstice, when life-giving rains arrived. Abandoned around 3400 BCE, Nabta was foundational for much of what would become central to Egyptian civilization, including its religion, for the next several millennia. Egypt's most widely adored deity would become the goddess **Hathor**: depicted as a cow, she was considered the patron of rulers. Later, the royal pyramids, the best-known Egyptian burial sites, were designed with a series of internal passageways that opened to the outside and were oriented to the very same stars as the stones at Nabta, stars that were understood to be the homes of the gods and the ultimate destination of deceased pharaohs.

⊕ Common Features of the Religions of Antiquity

The people of antiquity accepted as fact that there was another world besides their own. That supernatural realm both existed on its own level and interacted with the natural world, of which human society was the principal part. The human quest to explain the supernatural world and supernatural creatures started with humans themselves and was then extended to supernatural entities, the gods, by means of analogy. Gods were personified, made to look and act like humans. Besides resembling humans physically (anthropomorphism), they received human form as statues; lived in their own houses, temples; and had the same bodily needs as humans, especially the need for nourishment. Gods were members of families, some quite normal, others (especially in Greece) highly dysfunctional. Whatever humans did, gods did. At other times, gods were identified with nature: some personified force had to be responsible for the regular path of the sun, the cycle of the seasons, life and death, violent floods and storms, and famine-inducing droughts.

Particular gods could perform numerous functions; certain functions, such as creation, were the responsibility of several different gods. Myths offered multiple, competing explanations of natural phenomena. What a leading scholar wrote of Greek religion—"The attempt to confer logical coherence on polytheism is a hopeless enterprise. But the incoherence made it all the more flexible a tool for coping with the diversity of experience" (Parker 2011: 98)—applies to all the religions of antiquity.

Deities

Nothing so characterized antiquity as divine omnipresence. Antiquity was, in the words of the sixth-century BCE Greek philosopher Thales, a "world full of gods," a polytheistic world. The best known of these gods are the major Greek deities and their Roman counterparts: **Zeus**–Jupiter, **Hera**–Juno, Aphrodite–Venus, Ares–Mars, Athena–Minerva, Poseidon–Neptune, Artemis–Diana, Hermes–Mercury, Hephaestus–Vulcan, **Demeter**–Ceres, Apollo, and Dionysus. These were the 12 great gods who inhabited Mount Olympus. Still, 12 hardly compares to the hundreds and even thousands of gods invoked by other ancient civilizations. The Babylonian creation epic *Enuma Elish* describes the city of Babylon as the meeting place of 300 gods from "on high" and 300 more from "below," Egyptian texts and monuments name at least 1,500 deities, one early **Sumerian** text refers to 3,600 gods (a symbolic number signifying totality), and in Rome there was a specific "little god" for almost every aspect of life.

Not all deities were equally godlike. Divinity was a continuum along which great gods, secondary gods, minor gods, demigods such as heroes, personified abstractions, and special groups such as nymphs, the dead, and divinized emperors all occupied different locations. Even among the great gods—the 12 Olympians, for instance, or the "seven great gods" of Mesopotamia—one was always supreme: Olympian Zeus, Mesopotamian Enlil (later supplanted by **Marduk**), Egyptian **Amun-Ra**, or Roman Jupiter.

Early Gods

The earliest gods corresponded to natural phenomena: sun, moon, planets, sky, grain, fresh water, storms. Mesopotamia's Enlil was "Lord Wind." The Sumerian goddess Inanna, depicted in the fourth millennium BCE as a reed gatepost, guarded the storehouses on which a community's survival depended. The oldest Sumerian sign for "god" was an eight-sided star. As the Tigris–Euphrates floodplain became urbanized in the late fourth millennium BCE, the deified elements of nature acquired social and political functions. Each city had its own patron deity, typically accompanied by a spouse and counselors. Over time the gods of several cities or districts were connected to one another through complex family relationships, leading to the development of a pantheon ("totality of gods").

The early patron gods were the equivalent of petty rulers, but as the more successful cities came to dominate entire regions, their gods were elevated accordingly. For instance, the status of

A cylinder seal depicting Inanna/Ishtar's prowess as she tames a lion (© The Trustees of the British Museum).

Marduk, the previously unimportant patron god of Babylon, received an important boost under Hammurabi (r. 1792–1750 BCE) and thereafter continued to rise in significance until, in the Babylonian creation epic (composed toward the end of the second millennium BCE), he became the supreme ruler of the Mesopotamian pantheon. Egypt's New Kingdom rulers similarly elevated Amun, the patron of their home city of Thebes, linking him with the sun deity Ra, the dominant god of the Old Kingdom, in the new form of Amun-Ra.

Power

The defining characteristic of gods in antiquity was their power; the more important the god, the greater the power. The greatest power was associated with the fiercest forces of nature—in particular, storms. Enlil and Zeus were storm gods. Since the most powerful humans were rulers, the supreme gods also ruled. The status of Zeus, ruler of the Olympian gods, depended on his preeminent command of violence and force, manifested in his thunderbolt. Secondary gods played supporting roles, acting as judges dispensing justice to humans or as advisors to the sovereign god seeking to contain his "stormy" power. Like subordinate administrators serving the ruler, numerous deities—each with a different local base and area of responsibility, directed by the one supreme leader and assisted by numerous divine servants—collectively ensured societal order.

Divine Light

Intrinsic to Mesopotamian deities was a second characteristic of gods, "divine splendor" (*melammu*; literally, "luminous power"), an awesome and fearsome supernatural brilliance emanating from the gods, often portrayed as a halo surrounding their heads. At Marduk's birth, the "auras of the gods" were said to have clothed his body and encircled his head. The narrator of the Roman poet **Ovid**'s *Fasti*, while praying to the goddess **Vesta**, "felt the influence of celestial divinity, and the glad earth gleamed with a purple light" (Feeney 1998: 99). A comparable Egyptian term was *akhu*, "radiant power." "How great is your [Amun's] power! . . . You have surrounded me with your radiance," declared one prayer (Assmann 2001: 117). The Greek word for god, *theos*, likely originally meant "bright"; thus, Greek gods were "the shining ones."

Omniscience

A third major characteristic of gods was their superior knowledge. According to a second-millennium BCE Mesopotamian work known as the *Babylonian Theodicy*, "The divine mind, like the center of heaven, is remote. Knowledge of it is difficult; humans do not know it" (Lambert 1960: 87). A character in the *Symposium* of the Greek historian Xenophon (430–354 BCE) notes that "the gods, whose knowledge and power are absolute, are such friends to me that, because they care for me, they notice all my doings both day and night" (Parker 2011: 6). In his ninth Pythian ode the Greek poet Pindar (518–438 BCE) praises Apollo:

> You know the appointed end
> of each thing and the ways they are brought to pass;
> . . . ; and things to be
> and whence they shall come to pass. All this you know. (Lattimore 1947: 82–83)

Focus

The *Epic of Gilgamesh*

There was an actual third-millennium BCE Sumerian king named Gilgamesh. Proclaimed a god shortly after his reign, he became the subject of several separate tales. Unfortunately, no complete version of the *Epic of Gilgamesh* has survived, but the two main versions that are extant are sufficiently complete to permit reconstruction of the plot. The story opens with Uruk's citizens appealing to the gods for relief from their king's oppression. The gods then create Enkidu to counteract Gilgamesh's misuse of power. Quick to become friends, Gilgamesh and Enkidu decide to gain lasting fame by killing the Guardian of the Cedar Forest. Fame comes in an act of murder, for they slay the creature as it begs for its life. Their actions capture the attention of Ishtar, goddess of love. When Gilgamesh rejects her amorous advances, she threatens to open the gates to the underworld and unleash the restive spirits there on the world unless her father sends the Bull of Heaven to punish Gilgamesh and his city. Her father does so, and Gilgamesh and Enkidu slay the bull, but rather than piously offer its thighbone to the gods as a sacrifice, Enkidu hurls it at them. For such sacrilege, Enkidu has to die. Enkidu's death transforms Gilgamesh, as it forces him to confront his own mortality. He sets off on a journey to discover the secret of immortality. Along the way several characters advise him that his quest is hopeless. Undaunted, he reaches the island of Dilmun, home of Utnapishtim and his wife, the survivors of an annihilating flood sent by the god Enlil in his rage against humans. The basic message that Gilgamesh learns from them is that immortality only came to Utnapishtim as a gift of the gods. It is unavailable to Gilgamesh. In parting, Gilgamesh receives from Utnapishtim the gift of a plant named "Old Man Grown Young," an early version of the fountain of youth, but Gilgamesh loses even that consolation prize when a snake steals it from him as he rests near a pool. In the end Gilgamesh returns home, chastened, wiser, and resigned to being the best possible ruler, husband, and father for the rest of his life.

Immortality

A final major divine trait—some would argue the defining trait—distinguishing gods from humans was their immortality. Some immortals, however, could die. **Gilgamesh**, offspring of a human father and a divine mother, was destined to die, like the Greek hero Heracles. Succession myths recount the death of gods; however, death did not constitute complete annihilation. Such deaths simply relegated those gods to an inferior position or transformed their flesh and blood into human flesh and blood.

Appropriation of Gods

Third-millennium BCE Sumerians organized their thousands of gods in lists, typically with two columns: names in the left column and descriptions in the right. Later, bilingual lists correlated Sumerian gods with their Semitic counterparts in the same way that the Romans would link their gods with those of the Greeks: the Sumerian goddess Inanna, for instance, was identified with the Semitic **Ishtar**, the Sumerian sun god Utu with the Semitic Shamash, and the Sumerian Enki with the Semitic Ea.

Eventually, the Mesopotamians produced multilingual lists, recording multiple names for the same god. As political boundaries expanded and contact among different peoples increased, correlations among the gods of different cultures became increasingly frequent. Some scholars see this trend as marking a fusion of religious traditions termed "syncretism"; others interpret it simply as a reflection of the need for different cultural traditions to communicate with one another.

Gods and Goddesses

In antiquity, there were household gods, such as the Roman Penates and Lares; there were gods of the countryside, such as Pan in Greece; there were patron gods assigned to the cities, such as Apollo in Miletus or Marduk in Babylon; and there were state gods advanced by different political regimes, such as Amun-Ra, promoted by Egypt's New Kingdom rulers. All these were male deities, but there were as many goddesses as gods. The two most important female deities in Egypt were **Isis** and Hathor.

First worshiped in Egypt during the Old Kingdom, Isis became so popular that in time her worship spread throughout the Greek and Roman worlds. One reason for her popularity was her role as a nurturing mother, a role that led to her assimilation into Hathor, who represented beauty, love, and motherhood. In her guise as the lion-headed goddess Sekhmet, Hathor also represented violent destruction, although she was normally depicted as either a cow or a woman wearing a crown with a sun disk between cow horns. One scholar has suggested that the most significant feature of Mesopotamian religion was its many powerful goddesses. Some were nurturers, such as Ninsun, the mother of Gilgamesh; Ninhursaga, described as the wet-nurse of kings; and the more prominent Inanna–Ishtar, who like Hathor was simultaneously a goddess of love and war and like Isis and Hathor sustained kingship. The most popular Greek goddesses were "child-nourishing" deities. To the common people, Hera (also symbolized by a cow) was not the nagging scold depicted in epic poetry but, like Demeter and Artemis, a solicitous guardian of women. The male deity most favored by Greek women was Asclepius, because of his assistance in the most critical issues in a woman's life—fertility, pregnancy, and childbirth. An Egyptian "child-nourishing" goddess named Taweret, especially popular among commoners, was depicted as a hippopotamus, a species whose females were known for their ferocity in protecting their young. The Greek geographer Strabo (64 BCE–21 CE) aptly remarked: "All agree that women are the chief founders of religion; it is women who encourage men to more attentive worship of the gods" (Connelly 2007: 166–167).

Myth

The people most interested in understanding the cosmos were antiquity's intellectuals. The earliest of them were tellers of oral tales; a literate elite, typically anonymous in Mesopotamia and Egypt but including many Greeks and Romans whose names are familiar today, produced the later works. The mode of explanation of both was myth. Myth touched on the everyday even as it addressed the ultimate human questions: how the world originated (cosmogony), how it was structured (cosmology), how the gods came into being (theogony), the nature of the gods (theology), how humans came into existence (anthropogony), the conditions of human life (anthropology), the relationship between fate and free will, how the gods could be viewed as just when they allowed evil to exist (theodicy), and the end of life and what came next (eschatology). Myth offered no single explanation for any of these concerns. Eventually, however, the poets' mythic accounts of the world were challenged by rational accounts proposed by a rival set of intellectuals—philosophers.

Cosmogony: How the World Originated

Antiquity's mythmakers addressed questions concerning origins and identity. They had no conception of creation *ex nihilo* (out of nothing). Instead, creation represented the transformation of shapeless preexistence into substantial existence. Creation gave shape to the amorphous, which Egyptians and Mesopotamians alike envisioned as primeval waters. To explain how that transformation came about, both civilizations used two analogical models.

The first analogical model for creation was nature, as seen in the daily circuit of the sun or the annual changes of the seasons. Since life in Egypt depended on the annual flooding of the Nile to irrigate the land, one Egyptian creation story envisioned an earthen mound with a lotus plant emerging from the receding primeval waters. The sanctuary of every Egyptian temple replicated that primeval mound, while tomb chambers, shrines, and even mummy wrappings were decorated with scenes of the sun god's journey across the heavens. The dung beetle, or scarab, which lays its eggs in a ball of dung from which new beetles hatch, became Egypt's principal symbol of rebirth.

The second analogical model for creation was human behavior. One Egyptian creation myth personified the undifferentiated waters as the androgynous primeval god Atum, whose name meant both "nonexistent" and "completed." Yet he was far from complete: aware of his loneliness, he impregnated himself and gave birth to twin gods, a male named Ankh ("life") and a female named Ma'at ("order"). Atum passed on to his offspring his "life force" (*ka*), which they in turn implanted in their children Geb ("earth") and Nut ("sky"). The rivalry among the fourth-generation children of Geb and Nut—**Osiris** and Seth, with their sister-consorts Isis and Nephthys—formed the basis of Egypt's most pervasive myth, in which Osiris, murdered by Seth, was temporarily resurrected by Isis, who conceived their son Horus before Osiris returned forever to the underworld; when Horus was grown, he assumed responsibility for the struggle with Seth. Eventually Atum was further differentiated into Ra, the sun god whose daily passage represented eternal recurrence; Heka, the embodiment of transformational power; Sia, representing the imagination; and Hu, the word that turned image into creature.

Ptah, the patron god of Memphis, was another Egyptian creator deity who brought everything into existence through thought and speech. According to this myth, in the beginning was the thought; then came the word. Creation stories themselves eventually multiplied to the point that every late Egyptian temple had a different story in which its own god played the role of creator. Isis was "mistress of the word in the beginning." Another goddess created the entire world by proclaiming just seven magic words. Words—the union of name and object—were the basis of identity.

Cosmology: How the World Is Structured

In Greek accounts such as **Hesiod**'s *Theogony*, as in Mesopotamian and Egyptian counterparts, the first order of creation was the divine. Cosmogony started with theogony. Next came cosmology, the organization of the universe. Egyptians, Greeks, and Mesopotamians all envisioned a tripartite cosmos: heaven, earth, and some kind of **netherworld**. According to a Mesopotamian text known as *Atrahasis*, the process of organization began with a lottery in which Anu won heaven, Enlil the earth, and Ea the underground waters.

Cosmic order was the goal, but conflict was the norm. So threatening was **Tiamat** (a goddess who gave birth to a brood of sea monsters) that Marduk killed her and fashioned the universe out of her carcass. In Greece, Zeus led his generation of gods in overthrowing the older Titans, headed by his father Cronus, who in his time had unseated his own progenitor, Uranus. In Egypt, Ma'at ("order") waged an unending struggle against Isfet ("chaos"). Ra, the sun god whose light represented life, descended into the netherworld every night to do battle with the evil serpent monster Apophis, who threatened the source of life itself.

In a world where order was so tenuous, it was essential to establish institutions, protocols, and responsibilities for the gods. One Sumerian myth listed 94 components of the cosmic state, including kingship, power, knowledge, triumph, rebellion, godhood, priesthood, sanctuary, truth, slander, righteousness, dishonesty, and justice (i.e., political and religious institutions and ethical standards). Within this cosmic state, every god was assigned a specific responsibility. Such appointments were made permanent when they were inscribed on the Tablet of Destinies, which played a role in several myths. In one, the cosmic state ceased operating when the tablet was hidden. According to *Enuma Elish*, once Marduk had defeated the forces of chaos, he secured the tablet, thereby legitimizing both his claim to kingship over the gods and his decrees for reorganizing the cosmos.

In Egypt, the most visible manifestation of order was the sun's daily course across the sky. As Ra's earthly representative, the king was responsible for ensuring order. Thus, each day his regimen reenacted the sun's routine. Egypt's temples were not only the homes of particular gods but models of the cosmos itself. Their walls separated order from chaos; processional passageways replicated the course of the sun; dim inner sanctums corresponded to the primeval darkness from which life and order emerged. In maintaining their kingdom's temples, Egyptian rulers secured *ma'at*, the continuing order of the cosmos.

Anthropogony: How Humans Came to Exist

In Mesopotamia, the important gods might have enjoyed their existence, but the lesser gods endured unrelieved drudgery on their behalf. Eventually the latter rebelled, forcing the major gods to find substitutes. Thus humans were created, formed of clay lubricated with the blood of a rebel leader. Humans were partly divine, but they were flawed from the start because their progenitor had challenged the cosmic order. Just as their life source was put to death for his "original sin," humans would one day die and become spirits. At the same time, because humans had inherited the mind of their dead ancestor, they knew that they had been created to serve the gods, to toil daily on their behalf. Name and ancestry defined human nature; divine will determined human function.

The creation of humans was not a major theme in the mythology of ancient Egypt. Among the few references to the subject that have been found are two **Coffin Texts** (spells inscribed on Middle Kingdom coffins to assist the deceased in the afterlife). Coffin Text 1130, a speech by the sun god Ra, includes a play on words: "I created gods from my sweat while humans [*rmt*] are the tears [*rmwt*] of my eye" (Assmann 2001: 177). Coffin Text 714 explains that the creator wept because the other gods were angry at him. Tears streaming, he became temporarily blind, unable to see what his tears had produced. Humans were thus the imperfect products of blind anger and self-pity—quintessential "human" qualities.

Classical myth also regarded humanity as flawed from the beginning. One tradition, recounted in Ovid's *Metamorphoses*, traced human ancestry to the Titans, representatives of brute force, barbarism, and chaos who were defeated by the Olympians, proponents of law, order, and civilization. Thus humans were variously described as sprouting from soil irrigated by the Titans' blood, materializing out of their incinerated remains, or being formed from their flesh and blood and brought to life by the lightning bolt of Zeus. Ovid reproved humans for being—like the Titans—"contemptuous of the gods."

Another set of traditions associated human beginnings with an "original offense" of some kind. When Prometheus stole fire for humans, he gave them the ability to offer sacrifices to the gods, but that ability was tainted because it was the result of a transgression. Similarly, Pandora was entrusted with a "box" (actually a jar) by Hermes, who instructed her never to open it, but she disobeyed, opened the jar, and let loose all the evils that would forever afflict humans. So dismal was Hesiod's view of humanity that in his *Works and Days* he laments the contrast between the humans of his time, the "Iron Race," who were condemned to toil and misery, and those of the first "Golden Race," who neither toiled nor aged but feasted and lived like gods. Decline was thus envisioned as inherent to the human condition.

Anthropology: The Conditions of Human Life

Greek authors confronted the fundamental flaws that humans could not overcome. In myth, epic, tragedy, and history, Greeks examined the truth of Zeus's remark to Athena, near the beginning of **Homer**'s *Odyssey*, that greed and folly doubled the suffering that was the lot of humans. Humans always wanted more than they had and consistently overrated their own intelligence. Their arrogant pride ("hubris") led them to ignore divine warnings, assume they could deceive the gods, and refuse to accept the limits imposed on them. Greek authors delineated those limits and demonstrated the tragic consequences of ignoring them. An example of this theme appears in the tale of Daedalus and Icarus, made famous by Ovid in his *Metamorphoses*. To escape from Crete, Daedalus constructed feather-and-wax wings for himself and his son. As they departed, he warned Icarus to "fly a middle course. If you're too low, sea spray may damp your wings; and if you fly too high, the heat is scorching" (Mandelbaum 1993: 255). Disobeying his father, the hubristic Icarus soared higher and higher until the sun's fiery rays melted the wax and he plunged to his death in the sea.

Mesopotamian myths reflected a similar view of human nature. According to *Atrahasis*, for instance, the first humans did not recognize any limits on procreation, and their numbers multiplied so rapidly that they disturbed the divine rest of Enlil. He then sent a great flood to drown them all but relented—allowing the hero Atrahasis and his family to survive—when Ea offered two solutions to the population problem: miscarriage and death. (This story is echoed in the *Epic of Gilgamesh*, which describes the hero encountering Utnapishtim, another flood survivor who owed his life to the intercession of Ea.) The same pattern can be seen in Greece, where the Olympian gods were said to have sent a "liquidating" flood in retaliation for a deceitful sacrifice. The survivors, Deucalion and Pyrrha, revived humanity by tossing stones over their shoulders.

According to Egyptian myth, humans and gods originally lived together until some humans rebelled against their subservient status. Angered, Ra decided to wipe out the entire species but was advised by other gods to target only the rebels. Accordingly, Ra dispatched the goddess Hathor to punish the offenders, but she became uncontrollably furious and began killing humans indiscriminately. To prevent the complete annihilation of humans, Ra tricked Hathor by mixing ocher into beer until it resembled blood. Bloodthirsty Hathor consumed the beer and became inebriated, losing her focus and ferocity. The surviving humans were thus spared, but before long they again exasperated Ra. This time, instead of punishing them, Ra decided that she would separate them from the divine, abandoning earth and moving all the gods to heaven.

Like the biblical story of Adam and Eve's expulsion from the Garden of Eden, this myth explained humanity's separation from the divine as the consequence of the deity's displeasure with human behavior, although in this case, instead of expelling the humans, the gods removed themselves. At the same time, the myth confronted the conflict between justice and power. Similarly, the *Epic of Gilgamesh* reports that Enlil thundered when he learned that humans had survived his flood. But the other gods, upset because human offerings had ceased during the flood, chastised him: "How could you so lack judgment as to inundate [all humans]? Punish [only] transgressors; punish [only] wrongdoers." Cosmic justice was necessary to limit otherwise unlimited cosmic power. But the criticism directed at Enlil also applied to Gilgamesh, who had abused his powers as the earthly ruler of Uruk. Divine justice and human justice were equally essential to prevent abuses of human power.

Legitimation

If the *Gilgamesh* myth sought, on one level, to temper power, power also used myth for its own purposes. Nothing so effectively legitimized rulers as association with the gods. Royally sponsored mythmakers asserted that kingship "came down from heaven" and that rulers consequently functioned either as divine agents or as gods themselves. Egyptian rulers had claimed a direct relationship with the gods since the inception of historical kingship; according to Egyptian myth, Atum, depicted wearing the double crown of kingship, created the ordered political system as well as the ordered cosmos. As early as the fifth dynasty (c. 2400 BCE), pharaohs were referring to themselves as "sons of Ra," and even before that time one king's self-description was "the perfect god." A later royal myth attributed the conception of Amenhotep III directly to the god Amun. According to this account, the god, attracted to the queen, entered her bedchamber. She awakened and exclaimed, "Your sweet fragrance stiffens all my limbs." After impregnating her, Amun announced: "Amenhotep-ruler-of-Thebes is the name of the child I have placed in your womb. . . . He shall exercise potent kingship in this entire land. . . . He shall rule the Two Lands [Egypt] like Ra forever" (Wilkinson 2010: 250). The boy was then fashioned in Amun's image by the potter god Khnum, and after his birth he was raised among the gods until he was ready to be presented to the Egyptians as their new king. Centuries later, Alexander the Great—who was identified as the son of Zeus–Amun when he entered Egypt—circulated a similar story, claiming that a god had visited his mother at his conception. The Alexandrian model made its way to Rome under Augustus Caesar.

Households

In antiquity, the common people did not generate myth, but they were familiar with it, typically learning the stories through reenactments at public festivals or the theater. Myth also served to teach children proper conduct.

Myth entered daily life in tangible form. A common Egyptian item was a carved hand, a representation of the hand of god—more specifically, the hand into which the primeval god Atum "spat" (a euphemism for "masturbated") to conceive Shu and Tefnut. The hand symbolized the feminine role in creation. By the New Kingdom period, influential women bore the title "hand of god," and ivory hands depicting Hathor were used in dances honoring her: a dancer would hold the ivory hand above her head so that it was reflected in a mirror (another symbol associated with Hathor) held in her other hand. Numerous Hathor-handled mirrors have been uncovered in Egyptian homes.

Since mothers and children were envisioned as reflections of Isis and Horus, numerous spells sought Isis's protection for human children. Some spells were recited over an amulet worn by the child. Figurines depicting Isis cradling the infant Horus in one arm spread from her Egyptian homeland throughout the ancient world, where she epitomized motherhood. One memorable scene in Egyptian myth had Isis, upon finding the child Horus dying, accuse Ra of imperious disregard of suffering and death. Stung by her attack, Ra restored Horus to health. Isis's life-saving intercession figured prominently on a type of small **stela** called a *cippus*. Found in homes and tombs, *cippi* were typically engraved with images of the child Horus combating dangerous animals that threatened both cosmic order and family tranquility. Mothers who gave their children water poured over a *cippus* could safeguard them just as Isis had preserved Horus. Finally, Egyptian homes were filled with the scent of incense—an aromatic substance that was burned both to please the senses and (as the Egyptian term for "incense" indicated) "to make divine."

Services to the Gods

In a world full of gods, humans could encounter the divine anywhere; some places, however, were more likely venues for contact, such as caves, springs, groves, mountaintops, and crossroads. Such places were considered sacred, or set apart. While the gods could similarly be worshiped anywhere, the preferred place of homage was a sanctuary, where, according to the Greek philosopher Theophrastus, humans worshiped the gods "to give them honor, or to render thanks, or to ask for something that we need." Sanctuaries were powerful places demarcated by boundaries. Everything within sanctuaries—altars, temples, offerings, divine images—was also seen as sacred. By extension, so too were participants in any cult that transpired there, whether priests, sacrifices, or ritual assistants.

Temples

A god-filled world was a sanctuary-filled world. Mesopotamian and Egyptian temples appeared as early as the fifth and fourth millennia BCE, respectively. Greek temples, based on Egyptian models, materialized in the eighth century BCE. Rome's would follow two centuries later. There were home sanctuaries, countryside sanctuaries, neighborhood sanctuaries, and city sanctuaries, with major temples concentrated in city centers. Some cities, such as Babylon, Rome, and Akhetaten, were themselves considered sanctuaries. Others, such as Olympia and Delphi, were regional shrines. By late antiquity, the number of functioning temples was staggering. A catalogue of buildings in fourth-century CE Alexandria listed 2,500 temples, or one shrine for every 20 houses, while a small Egyptian village typically had more than a dozen temples. Taken together, all the temples across the Roman Empire surely held several million statues, images, and votive offerings.

Ritual

The ancients knew that safe navigation of their dangerous world required divine assistance. Pious humans therefore fed, clothed, and sheltered their deities; bestowed gifts on them; and glorified and obeyed them in exchange for crops, progeny, economic security, health, and safety. The means through which humans performed their part in this exchange, which was understood as a contract with the gods, was ritual. Temples provided places for gods to spend their time on earth. In Mesopotamia and Egypt, gods dwelt in their temples as living statues, which became divine through

The Temple of Hephaestus is the best-preserved ancient temple in Greece. It was later converted into a Christian church (© Andriy Kravchenko/Alamy Stock Photo).

"Opening of the Mouth" rituals. One word for "god" in Egyptian derived from a term for "image." Priests began each day by greeting and worshiping the divine statue in its inner sanctum and then anointing and dressing it; in Egypt the clothing rite alone required 45 separate steps.

In the most important of all the daily rituals, the statue was offered food, which mysteriously nourished the gods even though it was not consumed. So close was the association between ritual and mystery that the Egyptians referred to ritual itself as "mystery." Most rituals were performed in secret, away from public scrutiny, and required the meticulous performance of a sequence of steps that simultaneously imitated the cosmic order and helped to secure it by pleasing the gods.

Sacrifice

The foremost ritual act was sacrifice, which transformed profane objects into holy ones. Sacrificial offerings ranged from simple foods (fruits, vegetables, honeyed barley cakes) and libations (wine, milk, or oil) to animals, which were ritually slaughtered by priests and then cooked and eaten by priests or devotees. Animal sacrifice was also the central ritual and the highlight of public festivals in Greece and Rome. The altars on which sacrifices were performed were as important as temples to Greeks and Romans. Since the sacrificial smoke had to rise to heaven to reach the gods, altars were left open to the elements. Offerings destined for the gods of the underworld were poured on the ground. Greek and Roman temples also served as treasuries housing the gifts offered to the gods by their devotees, either in thanks for favors granted or in fulfillment of vows ("votive" gifts).

Festivals

Festivals typically began with a procession in which the god's statue was displayed to the public, followed by hymns to the deity, a sacrificial ritual, games or competitions carried out while the sacrificial animals cooked, and a communal banquet. The first three stages were solemn, while the last two were celebratory. During these events, humans reveled in one another's company, confirmed communal bonds, reestablished connections with the gods, and acknowledged the preeminence of the divine. Athens' religious calendar set aside 170 festival days every year. The Roman calendar distinguished between Fasti, days of the month for conducting public business, and Nefasti, "sacred" days set aside for religious festivals. A Roman calendar for the year 354 CE listed 177 festival days, during which there were public celebrations honoring 33 gods and goddesses. Attendance lists noted that workmen in Egyptian royal necropolises took time off to attend family festivals in addition to celebrating two major public festivals and at least 65 lesser ones.

Priests

Except during public festivals, ritual was the exclusive prerogative of priests. In Mesopotamia and Egypt, priests were originally private citizens appointed for limited periods of service, but eventually priesthood became a full-time profession. Priests were scrupulous in the performance of their duties, which included ensuring the absolute integrity of sanctuaries. Egyptian priests, known as "pure ones," were circumcised, dressed in white, and observed food taboos; to remove physical pollution and restore spiritual purity, they washed themselves several times daily, often in basins located at temple entrances. Mesopotamians, too, ritually removed surface and internal impurities in "bathing houses" before entering temple grounds. Such ritual cleansing was referred to as "making holy" and was reinforced with the burning of pleasant-smelling incense.

Anyone entering sacred ground had to be morally and physically pure. The Greek physician Hippocrates wrote, "We ourselves mark out the precincts of the temples so that no one should enter without purifying himself; as we go in, we sprinkle ourselves with holy water" (Chadwick and Mann 1950: 240). A North African benefactor who dedicated a local shrine during the early Roman Empire set the following conditions: "Whoever wishes to ascend into the shrine, let him abstain from women, pork, bean, barber, and public bath for three days; do not enter the enclosure wearing shoes" (Rives 2007: 102). A first-century BCE inscription posted outside a temple in Ephesus prohibited entry to anyone who had murdered, robbed, withheld knowledge of a crime, committed adultery, or used a contraceptive or abortion-inducing drug or charm. An inscription at an Egyptian temple at Edfu warned: "Whoever enters by this door must beware of entering impurely, for god loves purity more than millions of rituals." Inside the temple were further injunctions: "Do not utter falsehood in his house, do not covet things, do not slander, do not accept bribes, do not be partial between a poor man and a great, . . . do not reveal what you have seen in the mysteries of the temple" (H. te Velde, in Sasson 1995: 1733).

Attached to late Egyptian temples were two "Houses": a House of Life and a House of Books, in which priests transmitted their knowledge to neophytes and preserved the sacred writings, inscribed in hieroglyphs (Greek for "holy writing," from the Egyptian "words of god"). Each temple library contained 42 indispensable books—42 being the number of Egyptian provinces and hence symbolic of perfection or totality. Among them were books explaining how to inscribe texts on temple walls. The priests engaged in codifying their cultic tradition were transforming the "words of god" into holy scripture.

Female Priests

Since there were as many goddesses in the ancient world as there were gods, it is unsurprising that women had significant roles and responsibilities in cultic life. Women were particularly devoted to goddesses associated with marriage, pregnancy, and birth. Greek and Roman women served female deities, and they celebrated their own festivals. Sumerian women held high priestly office, and the highest-ranking priestess was described as the "lady goddess." Sargon, a third-millennium BCE ruler, installed his daughter as high priestess of the moon god of Ur. So integral were women to their religion that Mesopotamians dismissed as uncivilized any people whose god knew no priestess.

The best-known Roman priestesses were the six Vestals, who were chosen as young girls to serve for 30 years. They performed three functions considered essential to the city's survival: preparing the objects used in public sacrifices, guarding Rome's symbolic storehouse, and, above all, preserving the sacred fire. Greek priestesses kept the keys to temples, groomed cult statues, led prayers, and even took part in sacrifices.

Afterlife

The religions of antiquity sought to transcend the material world by overcoming death and matter itself. Some traditions, especially that of the Mesopotamians, viewed death as an ending, while others, particularly that of the Egyptians, saw death as a transition, a passage into another world. Overcoming the fear of death was important to certain groups in the Greco-Roman world. Inspired by Plato's dualism of material body and immaterial spirit, Stoics and Neoplatonists attempted to liberate pure spirit from its imprisonment in matter.

Death as an Ending

One of the main topics in the *Epic of Gilgamesh* is death. The story's central event occurs after Gilgamesh and Enkidu rescue Uruk from the threat of the Bull of Heaven. Upon killing the beast, they cut off its thighbone; instead of offering it to the gods, however, Enkidu tosses it heavenward in an act of defiance (hubris) against the gods. For such impiety, the gods determine that Enkidu has to die. Enkidu's death throws Gilgamesh into emotional turmoil: he experiences the full range of disbelief, rage, and grief before he can accept it. He orders craftsmen to fashion a statue of Enkidu, has valuable items from his own treasury interred with his friend so Enkidu can impress the netherworld gods, and holds a funeral that includes a sacrifice of animals for a banquet at which Gilgamesh orders further offerings to the gods.

Ancient funeral rites institutionalized the sequence of emotional responses to death illustrated in the *Epic of Gilgamesh*. Greek rites, for instance, included several phases. In the "laying out" phase, women washed, anointed, and dressed the body; wrapped it in cloth; and placed in its mouth or hand a coin to pay Charon for ferrying it across the river Styx to the land of the dead; then they positioned the body on a bier over which family members paid their final respects. The following night, accompanied by mourners, a family procession transported the deceased to the

Document

A Tavern-keeper's Advice to Gilgamesh

In this Old Babylonian version of the tale, Siduri advises Gilgamesh to "seize the day" ("carpe diem" in Latin).

You'll never find the life you seek.
When the gods created humankind,
they assigned them death,
retaining immortality for themselves.

Gilgamesh, fill your belly,
enjoy yourself day and night!
Savor every day,
dance merrily day and night!
Wear clean clothes, anoint your head, bathe in water!
Dote on the child who holds your hand;
tender your wife loving embraces.

burial site, where the body was cremated and then interred with offerings of food, wine, and other items deemed useful in the afterlife. The family then returned home for a funeral banquet that typically included animal sacrifices. Families further showed their respect for the dead by maintaining their gravesites and making offerings on the anniversaries of their deaths.

Mesopotamians believed that the spirits of the dead lived on, but their depictions of the afterlife were so consistently gloomy that no one looked forward to it. Most Greeks and Romans shared that view. In Book 11 of the *Odyssey*, the spirit of the dead Achilles tells Odysseus that he would rather toil as a hired worker on someone else's land than rule the underworld. Surviving funerary inscriptions suggest that most Greeks did not envision any meaningful existence after death.

Death as a Passage

In Mesopotamian thinking, this world mattered more than the next, so life should be lived to its fullest. The Egyptians also enjoyed this world, so much so that they never wanted it to end. During the Old Kingdom period the possibility of never-ending life extended only to the rulers and their immediate court circles. Tomb scenes emphasized the presentation of offerings, both of life's necessities (bread and beer) and of elite status symbols (furniture and jewelry). If the actual grave offerings ever ran out, it was thought that the offerings painted on the tomb walls would come to life. The Old Kingdom's **Pyramid Texts**, Egypt's oldest religious works of literature, include prayers, spells, and hymns to assist the deceased ruler on his afterlife journey to the cosmic realm of the gods.

The Middle Kingdom saw major changes to this system. No longer was afterlife divinity restricted to rulers: any member of the elite could achieve that status. With this democratization of the afterlife, the main focus of mortuary religion shifted from Ra to Osiris, ruler of the underworld. To facilitate the treacherous journey from the Land of Life to the Field of Offering, the deceased had two aids: 1,200 spells known as the Coffin Texts and maps of the underworld sketched on their coffins. Finally, the deceased had to prove his or her worthiness to enter the realm of Osiris by vindicating him or herself before a divine tribunal. These beliefs continued to be held for the remainder of ancient Egyptian history.

The New Kingdom version of the judgment of the dead, in which the heart is weighed on the scales of truth before Osiris (© Public domain via Wikimedia Commons).

Mastering Death

Not everyone feared death. The Greek philosopher Epicurus wrote, "The most terrifying of evils, death, is nothing to us, since when we exist, death does not. But when death is present, then we do not exist." A favorite epitaph in Roman times consisted of a simple sequence of verbs: "I was not; I am not; I care not." The Stoic philosopher Seneca left this epigram: "Death is either an end or a transition"—and hence is not to be feared (Segal 2004: 222–223). Seneca was known as a moralist, someone who sought to transform inner life through moral endeavor. For such an individual, "salvation" entailed the triumph of the human spirit over ignorance and moral malaise.

Plato's *Phaedrus* describes souls after they have separated themselves from their bodies:

> They could see beauty shining, when with the divine chorus they beheld the blessed sight and vision—we following after Zeus and others after other gods—and we went through the initiations which it is right to call the most blessed, which we celebrated in complete wholeness . . . seeing, as initiates (*mystai*), entire and whole and calm and happy visions of pure light. (Bowden 2010: 205)

Plato's words capture the experience of participants in the "mystery religions" associated with deities such as Demeter, Dionysus, and Isis. Unlike most Greek ritual traditions, these cults were nonexclusive, equally accepting of males and females, slaves and free citizens.

Three notable features of mystery cults were secrecy, specialized knowledge, and direct experience of the divine. Initiates were required to swear oaths of secrecy (as were priests in Egypt and Mesopotamia). At some point in both traditions, the initiates would be given directions on gold-leaf tablets for navigating the "Sacred Way" of the underworld. The tablets told them that they would encounter the divine twice: immediately in the brilliant light described by Plato and ultimately at the end of their underworld journey.

⊕ Mesopotamian Tradition

Among the oldest Mesopotamian documents are records of food offerings to gods, the human side of an ongoing reciprocal relationship between gods and humans. While that relationship was expected to benefit humans, suffering was also recognizably part of the human condition. The Sumerians attempted to explain that inconsistency. One answer lay in the nature of gods. A Sumerian myth suggested that Enki, the god of wisdom, had assigned to Inanna, goddess of love and war, ambivalence as her universal role, in contrast to the singular functions of most other gods. Another god who disconcerted humans was Enlil, who assuaged his divine anger by inflicting various disasters, including demons such as Namtar ("Fate"), on humankind. A second response lay in the Mesopotamian understanding of fate, which held that an individual's destiny was determined at birth, when it was inscribed on the Tablets of Existence. Thus life's pleasures and pains were preordained—to an extent. Gods granted humans occasional glimpses of their destiny and even permitted the use of that knowledge to anticipate and change a negative outcome. These beliefs formed the basis of the Mesopotamian practice of divination.

Third-millennium BCE documents mention diviners, whose actual practices remained within the bounds of an oral rather than written tradition. Mesopotamian diviners traced their genealogy back to a mythical sage-king named Enmeduranki, "Lord of the Powers of the Bond of Heaven and Earth." Cities and temples were places where cosmic bonds, analogically identified as mooring ropes, connected heaven and earth. An early Mesopotamian center of the world was Nippur, later replaced by Babylon, literally "the gate(way) of/to the gods." It was in Babylon that later Neo-Babylonian rulers built a ziggurat (the inspiration for the biblical Tower of Babel) named Etemenanki, "temple of the foundation of heaven and earth."

Since, according to an early text known as the *Sumerian King List*, kingship descended from heaven, the person analogically holding the mooring rope was the ruler, a responsibility that lasted to the final days of Mesopotamia's independent history. The god most closely associated with kingship was Inanna–Ishtar. Rulers depended on their female relatives in various ways: royal wives led processions to cities throughout the realm or commissioned new temples, while daughters served as priestesses. Sargon's appointment of his daughter as high priestess of Ur was emulated for the next 500 years, since that position symbolized dynastic hegemony in Babylonia.

Sargon's grandson Naram-Sin became the first Mesopotamian ruler to claim actual divine status. His famous Victory Stele depicted him wearing the horned crown of divinity, and he erected a statue of himself inscribed with the claim that his subjects requested heaven's permission to worship Naram-Sin as a god to honor his valor. Self-deification by kings continued during the Ur III Dynasty (twenty-second to twenty-first centuries BCE), when rulers, seeking legitimation, circulated movable shrines containing their divine images throughout the land.

The Old Babylonian period (approximately 1900–1600 BCE), an era of rampant warfare, saw a shift in the seat of political power from southern to central Mesopotamia and a reformulation of earlier traditions. Divination became textual, based on reading signs. Mesopotamians recorded two types of omen: diagnostic and predictive. Diagnostic omens were based on physical or behavioral characteristics: a mole on the right thigh, for instance, might indicate prosperity, while a generous person could expect to be treated generously. Predictive omens, by contrast, hinted at one's fate.

Sometimes such omens were unprovoked, discovered through observation of natural phenomena. Predictive omens could also be solicited by various means. Divination was highly formal. After a preparatory ritual, the diviner would request the god Shamash to establish the "truth" of the reading, which would then take place. Pouring oil on water was one such method of divining, but the most influential and enduring was astrology, the practice of translating the "heavenly writing" of the gods.

Rulers availed themselves of celestial signs to "prove" their legitimacy. One such ruler was Hammurabi (r. 1792–1750 BCE), who initiated a reformulation of tradition. His "Code of Laws" paralleled contemporaneous omen compendiums. Both laws and omens had the same goal and assumed the same format. Hammurabi's 282 "laws" comprised the central section of an inscribed stela, framed by an extensive prologue and an equally lengthy epilogue. In this text Hammurabi portrayed himself as an exemplary and just king. As in Egypt, Mesopotamian rulers received the tools of justice from the gods. Hammurabi's stela showed the king, in the traditional pose of a worshiper, receiving those instruments from Shamash, the god of justice, wearing the horned crown of divinity.

Toward the end of the second millennium BCE the Old Babylonian version of *Gilgamesh* was modified into a standard version, the opening line of which, "He who saw the Deep," places this work within the wisdom genre. Most relevant is Tablet XI, in which, still pursuing his mission of becoming an immortal god, Gilgamesh encounters Utnapishtim, the survivor of the global flood.

Top of stela containing Code of Hammurabi (© RMN-Grand Palais/Art Resource, NY).

As the scene opens, Utnapishtim advises his wife that, human nature being inherently deceitful, Gilgamesh will attempt to deceive them. Gilgamesh lies to them, but they turn the lie against him. Utnapishtim then counsels Gilgamesh. First, he contrasts kings with their diametrical opposites, fools. Gilgamesh, a king, is foolish for wandering the wilderness in the skin of a lion and eating raw meat. Next, in relating the story of the flood, Utnapishtim offers further knowledge: a king's most important duty is to help those least able to help themselves. When Enlil, furious at the din caused by humans, decided to annihilate humankind, Ea, god of wisdom, secretly warned Utnapishtim about the forthcoming flood and told him how to survive it. When the waters subsided, Utnapishtim's first act was to offer a sacrifice of thanksgiving to the gods, who, having gone without food offerings for 40 days, turned their frustration toward Enlil for attempting to destroy their sustainers. The criticism directed at Enlil, Utnapishtim says, also applies to Gilgamesh, who earlier in the story had abused his powers as the earthly ruler of Uruk. Finally, Utnapishtim reiterates the impossibility of immortality. Tablet XII identifies Gilgamesh as the deified ruler and judge of the underworld shades. Ironically, the hero who failed to become a god during his lifetime becomes one in death.

Another important late-second-millennium BCE work ponders the ambivalence of the human–divine relationship. *Enuma Elish*, also called the *Epic of Creation*, was likely composed to celebrate the return of Marduk's statue from lengthy captivity in enemy territory. The piece is a paean to Marduk, who defeated the monsters Tiamat and Kingu in an epic battle, was acclaimed ruler of the gods by his peers, and then used the carcass of Tiamat to organize the cosmos and a mixture of Kingu's blood and soil to create humans. Humanity was thus born from a violent rebel.

The *Epic of Erra* explores the consequences of a god's abandonment. According to this account, Marduk, appalled at human society's abandonment of self-restraint and its tendency to engage in uncontrolled violence toward one another and impiety toward the gods, departs for the netherworld. Atrocities continue unabated and are further instigated by Erra, the god of violence; eventually Babylon itself is plundered. The text of *Erra*'s final tablet, which tells how Marduk's return curtailed the mayhem and rescued Babylon, was inscribed on stones shaped into amulets to be hung on house walls. The conclusion of the composition pledges: "To the house in which this tablet is placed . . . the sword of destruction shall not come near; salvation shall alight on it" (Cagni 1977: 14).

The third composition, *Ludlul Bel Nemeqi* ("I Will Praise the Lord of Wisdom"), also called the *Poem of the Righteous Sufferer*, portrays Marduk as simultaneously wrathful and merciful. Marduk directs his wrath at the narrator, a Babylonian version of Job who is afflicted by social alienation and physical ailments. When his own lament fails to move Marduk, the righteous sufferer consults various specialists: an exorcist, a diviner, a dream interpreter, and a personal deity. None of their efforts sway Marduk. At issue is theodicy: how humans are expected to react when gods cause human suffering for no obvious reason. The answer, according to *Ludlul*, lies in the sufferer's behavior. No matter the tribulation and no matter the failed rituals, he never repudiates Marduk. His salvation inheres in his patience, a faith that Marduk will ultimately be merciful.

When the writers of *Enuma Elish* and *Ludlul* extolled Marduk as superior to all other gods, they were reinforcing a shift in Mesopotamia's polytheistic theology in the direction of a single universal god:

> Sin is your divinity, Anu your sovereignty,
> Dagan is your lordship, Enlil your kingship,
> Adad is your might, wise Ea your perception,
> Nabu, holder of the tablet stylus, is your skill.
> Your leadership in battle is Ninurta, your might Nergal,
> Your counsel is Nusku . . .
> Your judgeship is radiant Shamash . . .
> Your eminent name is Marduk, sage of the gods. (Foster 2005: 692)

All other gods had become mere aspects of Marduk.

Soon, however, all of these gods became aspects of the Assyrian national god Assur, as Assyrian emperors coopted *Enuma Elish* to suit their imperial ambitions, supplanting Marduk as hero of the story and king of the gods. When Babylonia rebelled against Assyrian dominance, Sennacherib (r. 705–681 BCE) destroyed Babylon, including the temple of Marduk. Sennacherib's assassination by two of his sons convinced his heir, Esarhaddon (r. 681–669 BCE), that the murder was divine retribution for Sennacherib's sacrilegious treatment of Babylon, for which Esarhaddon atoned by rebuilding Babylon and the temple of Marduk and privileging the priesthood of Marduk.

Assurbanipal (r. 668–639 BCE), the last major ruler of the Assyrian Empire, in an act of cultural imperialism, sought to collect in one place the entirety of available knowledge. He stripped the major Babylonian temples of their archives, which were henceforth stored in his library in Nineveh. He further assigned teams of scholars to prepare a canon of essential texts. A substantial number of the 30,000 tablets in Assurbanipal's library were omen collections. Like other Assyrian rulers, Assurbanipal included diviners in his inner circle of advisors on state policies. In addition, he depended on reports from astrologers and astronomers dispersed throughout his entire realm.

The *Enuma Elish* played a key role in the 10-day Akitu, or New Year Festival, the most significant celebration of Babylon's culture. The first days of the festival were preparatory, with rites conducted in secrecy by the priests of Marduk. Day four was devoted to a reading of *Enuma Elish*. The highlight came toward the festival's end. At that time the ruler laid down his scepter before Marduk's statue, after which a priest slapped the king, who then prostrated himself before Marduk. The priest slapped the king a second time; if tears came to the king's eyes, the ensuing year would be favorable. Marduk's statue was then paraded through richly decorated streets en route to his festival house outside the

Nabonidus worshiping Sin (moon), Shamash (sun), and Ishtar (Venus-star) (© Trustees of the British Museum).

city's walls. The festival concluded with the return of Marduk to his temple, entering the city via the Ishtar Gate and then following the Processional Way, which was faced with glazed bricks decorated with 120 roaring lions.

A decade-long refusal by Nabonidus, the last Babylonian king (r. 556–539 BCE), to participate in the festival cost him the throne and Babylon its empire. Influenced by his mother, a native of Harran, Nabonidus sought to replace Marduk with the moon god Sin. He restored temples to Sin in Harran and Ur, revived the practice of appointing a daughter as high priestess of the moon god, and appropriated several Marduk temples for his favorite deity. Nabonidus's reforms aroused such deep hostility that when the Persian ruler Cyrus arrived at the gates of Babylon, the priests of Marduk welcomed him into their city as their liberator.

⊕ Egyptian Tradition

An ancient Egyptian's greatest wish was to be remembered. The surest way to be remembered was by preserving one's name and one's body through a physical memorial: a tomb. One's name depended upon adhering to the Egyptian ethos, expressed by the word *ma'at*. *Ma'at* had several overlapping meanings—order, truth, justice—and in essence meant an omnipresent goodness or rightness. Introduced into the world by Atum, *ma'at* was maintained by the gods, but humans were expected to implement it daily. Egyptians perceived the ethical treatment of others, as required by *ma'at*, as their profoundest offering to the gods. The rationale for that outlook is expounded in Coffin Text 1130, wherein the sun god proclaims that he has created every human like every other human, an early intimation of the "golden rule."

Unas, the last major ruler of the Old Kingdom (twenty-fourth century BCE), initiated the practice of transforming formerly unadorned tomb chambers into symbolic microcosms of the universe. Unas's black coffin represented Egypt's rich alluvial soil, sustainer of life; his tomb's ceiling portrayed the night sky's stars, to which the dead ruler would ascend. Especially noteworthy were the walls, covered with texts painted blue to evoke the waters of creation. Ancient Egyptians believed that those Pyramid Texts, which offered spells against earthly threats and guides to the afterlife, would assist Unas to become one with Ra in the heavens even as he identified himself with Osiris. Feared and venerated as the god of the underworld, Osiris's ability to overcome death inspired a belief in a comparable resurrection for rulers.

The Old Kingdom set the foundation for Egypt's enduring association of tomb and virtue. That relationship continued into the Middle Kingdom, when emphasis shifted from tomb to coffin, which

Document

The *Instructions for Merikare*

The Middle Kingdom Instructions for Merikare, *a guide on how to be a good ruler, emphasizes justice.*

May you be justified before the god
That a man may say in your absence
That you punish in accordance with the crime.

. . .

Justice comes to the wise man distilled,
Shaped in the sayings of ancestors.
See, their words endure in books;
Open, read them, copy their knowledge,
He who is taught becomes skilled.
Don't be evil, kindness is good,
Make your memorial last through love of you.

. . .

Make people come to you through your good nature.
A wretch . . . desires the land of his neighbor,
A fool . . . covets what others possess.

. . .

Do justice, then you endure on earth.
Calm the weeper, don't oppress the widow,
Don't expel a man from his father's property.

. . .

When a man remains over after death,
His deeds are set beside him as treasure,
And being yonder lasts forever.

. . .

He who reaches them without having done wrong
Will exist there like a god.

. . .

Make your monuments worthy of the god,
This keeps alive their maker's name.

. . .

Visit the temple, observe the mysteries,
Enter the shrine, eat bread in the god's house;
Proffer libations, multiply the loaves,
Make ample the daily offerings,
It profits him who does it.

. . .

Make worthy your house of the west (tomb),
Make firm your station in the graveyard,
By being upright, by doing justice,
Upon which men's hearts rely.
The loaf [of bread] of the upright is preferred
To the ox of the evildoer. (Lichtheim 1973: 99–104)

became the principal focus of decoration. The magical spells that covered these coffins, collectively known as the Coffin Texts, were believed to assist the deceased to reach the afterlife. Also, the physical tomb had by this time come to matter less than a person's character. Only the virtuous could attain the afterlife, if they proved their worthiness. The judgment of the dead before a divine tribunal, headed by Osiris, became a central component of funerary religion. After death, Egyptians of this period believed that a person's heart would be placed on a scale, to be weighed against the feather of truth (ma'at). Whereas the only body capable of becoming "the Osiris" during the Old Kingdom had been the king's, the Middle Kingdom extended such a possibility of afterlife to Egypt's social elite.

New Kingdom texts continued to emphasize ethics. A forceful articulation of justice appears in chapter 125 of the **Book of the Dead**, wherein the deceased appears before a tribunal consisting of Osiris and 42 divine judges. Facing the court, the deceased makes a public confession, during which he avows innocence with respect to 82 commandments prohibiting criminal acts, taboos, or professional improprieties. Then the divine council either purifies the deceased, enabling him to enjoy the afterlife, or condemns him to oblivion.

The bond between piety and intimacy with the divine helps us understand the most controversial of Egyptian rulers. At the beginning of his reign, Amenhotep IV (r. 1353–1336 BCE) constructed in Thebes a monumental complex at the center of which was a temple named Gempaaten ("The Aten is found"), its courtyard lined with towering statues of the king and his wife, Nefertiti, wearing distinctive crowns that identified them as Shu ("light"), the eldest son of Atum, and Tefnut, the sister of Shu. The building program anticipated later name changes: Amenhotep ("Amun is content") became **Akhenaten** ("Effective for Aten" or "Illuminated Manifestation of Aten"), and Nefertiti assumed the epithet Neferneferuaten ("Beautiful are the beauties of Aten"). More building ensued, and a new capital named Akhetaten (modern Amarna) transformed virgin desert into an open-air temple to Aten. Represented as the sun's disk with rays ending in human hands holding signs of life and bounty, Aten—light itself—was henceforth to be worshiped in the open rather than in some dark inner sanctuary.

Akhenaten's religious reform has been the subject of multiple modern interpretations. The standard view treats Akhenaten as a "heretic" who overturned Egypt's religious traditions (closing temples, ending festivals, forbidding worship of deities other than Aten) and even threatened the security of Egypt itself by alienating the traditional gods. After his death he was charged with having the names of other gods expunged from monuments (the earliest attested act of iconoclasm), forbidding personal names that included elements of other divine names, and ordering the eradication of any plural form of "god." The reaction against Akhenaten was dramatic, beginning with a name change for his son (from Tutankhaten to Tutankhamun), which signaled a return to Egypt's traditional religion, and concluding with a campaign to obliterate any vestige or memory of the former ruler.

While Akhenaten did make a determined effort to get rid of two gods, ordering the removal of the names of Amun and Mut (Amun's consort) from temple inscriptions and the renaming of individuals whose names included "Amun" and "Mut," this component of his reforms was limited to the gods most closely associated with kingship and Thebes. Moreover, Akhenaten's own inscriptions use the plural "gods," and almost all the houses excavated in Amarna have shrines dedicated to gods other than Aten. If there was a component of monotheism to Akhenaten's reforms, it was restricted to the official state religion.

At first Akhenaten identified Aten with Atum, the primeval god who initiated the creation of the world. Later, Akhenaten switched Aten's identification from Atum to Ra, another creator god. Moreover, the way Akhenaten had himself portrayed by court artists, with a body that blended male and female features, symbolized his role as sustainer of Egypt's fertility. The motive behind

An intimate portrayal of Akhenaten's royal family enjoying the beneficence of the sun disk, Aten (© Photo by Universal History Archive/Getty Images).

his elevation of Aten, however, remains uncertain. One possibility is that he disdained the anthropomorphic representation of Amun-Ra and, by focusing attention on the source of light (and renewal) itself, sought to purify the representation of the supreme deity.

A fourth-century BCE Greek visitor to Egypt noted the care Egyptians gave to the tombs of the dead, which they saw as "everlasting homes," in contrast to the actual homes of the living, which were seen as temporary "inns." Even as Egypt fell to foreign powers, the Ptolemies and the Romans, its people retained their heritage. Passages from the *Book of the Dead* were reproduced in Ptolemaic-era tombs, and funerary texts of the Roman era, modeled on the *Book of the Dead*, had such titles as the *Book of Passing Through Eternity*.

The upheavals of the late first millennium BCE led to an intensification of piety. Egyptians flocked to their temples, where, in acts of adoration, they left their names along with short prayers or simply touched the temple wall. They also participated in an increasing number of festivals, many lasting several days.

The most important celebration was the pan-Egyptian festival of Khoiak, in which 42 separate limbs of Osiris were embalmed, taken on a procession accompanied by statues of the patron deities of Egypt's 42 districts, and then buried as the onlookers beat themselves in a display of grief. Mourning gave way to hope inasmuch as the people believed that Osiris would be resurrected whole. This festival, both a memorial to the past and a lament on present mistreatment by Roman authorities, who considered Egyptians so many "sheep for shearing," symbolized Egypt's longing for a restoration of *ma'at*.

⊕ Greek Tradition

The Greek historian Herodotus asserted that Hesiod and Homer were the first authors to describe the birth, physical appearance, individual epithets, specific powers, and typical behaviors of the Greek gods—the Olympian gods. He could have added to this list the foundation of their shrines as well as such practices as sacrifice, votive gifts, and divination. Hesiod's *Theogony*, Homer's *Iliad*, and the several Homeric Hymns attributed to the latter author were written in the late eighth or early seventh centuries BCE, chronologically proximate to the traditional date (776 BCE) of the first Olympic Games.

An ancient Greek traveling from Mount Olympus to Olympia would have passed by dozens of Greece's cities, each intensely protective of its independence. The route would also have taken him or her past the international sanctuaries where the four Panhellenic Games were staged: Delphi, where the Pythian Games were held in honor of Apollo; Corinth, which hosted the Isthmian Games

Focus

The *Iliad*

The *Iliad*, Homer's eighth-century BCE composition, describes the events of several days toward the end of the 10-year war between the Greeks and the Trojans, which has pitted not only humans but also gods against one another. Hera, Poseidon, and Athena, for instance, favor the Greeks, while Apollo, Ares, and Aphrodite side with the Trojans. The gods—who do not have to face death—are depicted as considerably less noble than the human characters. Lying, browbeating, carping, threatening, and engaging in promiscuous and generally petty behavior, the gods are hardly suitable models for humans to emulate. Their dominant characteristic is their vastly superior power, most evident in Zeus, who shows no concern for human death or anguish.

The human who most resembles the gods is Achilles, the mighty Greek warrior whose father was human but whose mother was a minor goddess. The *Iliad* is manifestly his story, its first line announcing the theme of "Achilles's wrath." When aroused, Achilles projects the power of a god, and in the concluding chapters he is truly uncontrollable, willing to meet his own prophesied death once he unleashes his deadly fury on as many Trojans and gods as possible. Even after he kills Hector, the greatest and noblest Trojan hero and the specific target of his "mankillings," Achilles, his wrath still undiminished, straddles Hector's corpse, refusing to release it for burial. But when Priam, Hector's aging father, crawls in terror toward him to plead for the release of his son's body, Achilles is reminded of his own father, and so he sets aside his wrath and grants Priam's petition. This act of compassion tames Achilles's "godlike" anger and restores his humanity.

in honor of Poseidon; Argos, where the Nemean Games honored Zeus and Heracles; and, finally, Olympia, where the games were held in honor of both Zeus and Hera (with the women-only Heraean Games staged prior to the men's events). These fiercely independent Greek cities were constantly at war, which would be temporarily suspended for extended sacred truces during every Panhellenic celebration.

The principal Olympian gods bore the same names across the Greek world, but their functions differed from place to place. Function and location were typically denoted by epithets: Phoebus ("Bright") Apollo, god of light; Apollo Smintheus ("Mouse"), god of plagues; Apollo Apotropaios, the god who averted plague; Apollo Iatros ("Healer"), the god of physicians. Apollo was also associated with major oracular sites, known as Apollo Pythios or Delphinios through his association with Delphi and as Apollo Delios through his link to Delos. A god with several sanctuaries in the same city, such as Athens, was known by different epithets depending on where he or she was invoked: Athena Polias ("of the city") on the Acropolis, Athena Ergane ("Crafts") in the agora (marketplace), and Athena Soteira ("Savior") in Piraeus (Athens' port). Oracles frequently enjoined cities to add a particular god's cult under a new epithet. Cult was invariably local. One worshiped Athena and Apollo in their local rather than their generic guise.

Greeks patronized various divinatory practitioners, relying on figures ranging from individual seers, favored by such important leaders as Pericles and Alexander the Great, to the ubiquitous oracles. One could visit the sanctuary of Zeus at Dodona in northern Greece, where priests first gave ear and then voice to windblown leaves, or a southern Greek shrine, where a priestess of Apollo conducted nocturnal sacrifices during which she drank the blood of the victims.

The most famous oracle was located at Delphi and operated from the seventh century BCE to the late fourth century CE. On "oracle days," petitioners paid a substantial fee to queue up with a sacrificial goat, on which a priest sprinkled water; if the animal shook off the water, Apollo would hear the inquiry. On entering the temple, the supplicant presented a question to a priest, who passed it on to the Pythia, who, in turn, took her seat in the *adyton* (the term meant "inaccessible"), where Apollo Loxias ("Ambiguous") communicated to her. As expressed by the Delphian priest **Plutarch** (45–120 CE), Apollo's communication was intended neither to conceal nor to reveal, but to intimate. One of the three maxims placed above the entrance to Apollo's temple—"Know thyself"—suggested that the final interpretation of the oracle rested with the petitioner.

Communal piety, involving both men and women, was at the center of Greek life. Priestesses were as numerous as priests. Women prayed, performed at festivals, paid for and participated in sacrifices, and made dedications (especially for their children). The ritual actions of women were most closely linked to their domestic roles: carrying water, preparing food, and weaving. Yet women were excluded from political participation. Athenian citizenship, for instance, was exclusive to males.

The most important female-centered festival in cities throughout Greece was the Thesmophoria, honoring Demeter and her daughter Persephone/Kore. Demeter represented both fertility (of women and the land) and political solidarity secured though the law. Every year on this occasion women briefly controlled the cities. In Athens, for example, emulating the exact practice whereby male representatives were chosen for public responsibilities, each of the 140 *demes* (communities) selected two of its women to preside over the Athenian assembly to do whatever was "consecrated by tradition." Day one began with a procession from Athens to Eleusis, with the women bearing the tablets of sacred laws on their heads. That night they participated in the mysteries. Back in Athens for day two, the women fasted and sat on cushions made from the branches of weeping willows as they reenacted Demeter's mourning for Persephone's abduction to the underworld; toward day's end they carried sacred barley seeds in sacrificial baskets to Demeter's altar. Day three revolved around a blood sacrifice consecrated to Demeter as Kalligeneia ("She who gives birth to beautiful children"), symbolic of the goddess's return from the underworld and the promise of fertility.

The Greeks had competing interpretations of fate. One view held that the Fates spun, assigned, and then cut the thread of life, while another, influenced by Egyptian tradition, held that Zeus or Hermes weighed the souls of the dead. At death the soul departed the body for the land of the dead, where it led a dismal existence among the netherworld shades ruled by Hades and Persephone. The desire for a less dreary afterlife drew many Greeks to mystery cults, which promised brighter prospects. So strong was that longing that mystery cults abounded throughout the Greek world. Arcadia, a sparsely inhabited rural region, accommodated 13 such cults. The most famous site where such rites were held was **Eleusis**, a day's walking distance from Athens. This rite, known as the Eleusinian Mysteries, began with a procession from Eleusis to Athens, during which priestesses carried objects sacred to Demeter in containers secured with red ribbons. Five days

A red-figure amphora depicting women preparing oxen for sacrifice (© Science History Images/Alamy Stock Photo).

later, initiates paraded to Eleusis, where they fasted in anticipation of the secret rites held that night. Eventually, initiates could advance to gain knowledge of the "unrepeatable secrets" of the cult, which could never be divulged on pain of death. The ritual ended with dancing, a sacrifice of bulls, and libations to the dead. Mystery cults became even more important during the Hellenistic and Roman eras. The Eleusinian Mysteries, introduced in the eighth century BCE, finally ceased in 396 CE, when Christian Goths sacked Eleusis.

Certain intellectuals, especially Greek philosophers, questioned and challenged the Olympian religion presented in the mythical epics of Homer and Hesiod. The author of the Homeric "Hymn to Dionysus" contrasted his "true" account of the god's birth with five "lying" renditions, but the major shift in thinking about the gods did not occur until the late sixth century BCE, when critics Heraclitus and **Xenophanes** rejected the anthropomorphic view of the divine, according to which "mortals suppose that gods are born, wear their own clothes, and have voice and body." Xenophanes and Heraclitus particularly censured those who "attributed to the gods all sorts of things which are matters of reproach and censure among men: theft, adultery, and mutual deceit." In place of those all-too-human gods, Xenophanes proposed a supreme universal god:

> One god is greatest among gods and men, not at all like mortals in body or thought.
> Whole he sees, whole he thinks, and whole he hears.
> Always he abides in the same place, not moving at all. . . .
> Completely without effort he shakes all things [keeps everything moving] by the thought of his mind. (Lesher 1992: 23, 25, 31, 33)

Document

"Hymn to Zeus"

In the "Hymn to Zeus," the Stoic philosopher Cleanthes (331–230 BCE) lauds the universal dominion of a single omniscient god (Zeus) and his role in dispensing universal justice.

Noblest of immortals, many-named, always all-powerful
Zeus, first cause and ruler of nature, governing everything with your law,
greetings! For it is right for all mortals to address you:
for we have our origin in you, bearing a likeness to god,
we, alone of all that live and move as mortal creatures on earth.
Therefore I shall praise you constantly; indeed I will always sing of your rule.
This whole universe, spinning around the earth, truly
obeys you wherever you lead, and is readily ruled by you;
such a servant do you have between your unconquerable hands,
the two-edged, fiery, ever-living thunderbolt.
For by its stroke all works of nature are guided.
With it you direct the universal reason, which permeates
everything, mingling with the great and the small lights.
Because of this you are so great, the highest king forever.
Not a single thing takes place on earth without you, god,
nor in the divine celestial sphere nor in the sea,
except what bad people do in their folly.
But you know how to make the uneven even
and to put into order the disorderly; even the unloved is dear to you.
For you have thus joined everything into one, the good with the bad,
that there comes to be one ever-existing rational order for everything.
This all mortals that are bad flee and avoid,
the wretched, who though always desiring to acquire good things,
neither see nor hear god's universal law,
obeying which they could have a good life with understanding.
But they on the contrary rush without regard to the good, each after different things,
some with a belligerent eagerness for glory,
others without discipline intent on profits,
others yet on indulgence and the pleasurable actions of the body.
They desire the good, but they are born now to this, then to that,
while striving eagerly that the complete opposite of these things happen.
But all-bountiful Zeus, cloud-wrapped ruler of the thunderbolt,
deliver human beings from their destructive ignorance;
disperse it from their souls; grant that they obtain
the insight on which you rely when governing everything with justice;
so that we, having been honored, may honor you in return,
constantly praising your works, as befits
one who is mortal. For there is no greater privilege for mortals
or for gods than always to praise the universal law of justice. (Thom 2005: 40–41)

The most influential Greek philosopher to reflect on the nature of the divine was **Plato** (425–347 BCE). Plato's earliest writings defended his mentor Socrates against charges of atheism and impiety. In later works, such as the *Republic* and *Phaedo*, Plato developed a theory of abstract, otherworldly forms that exist in a loftier realm than that of this world. He further proposed a comparable theory of an immortal soul superior to physical flesh. He elaborated on his dualism in *Timaeus*, in which he attributed to a demiurge (creator god) the fashioning of a perfect, orderly universe. In such an interconnected cosmos, every soul would be paired with a star. Upon death the souls of the virtuous would be released from the body and ascend to the soul's linked star. Unrighteous men would be reincarnated as women, while immoral women would be reborn as animals.

Plato also offered cosmological proof of God's existence based on the regular motions of heavenly bodies. Expanding upon ideas suggested by Xenophanes and Heraclitus, he posited the existence of a prime mover, arguing that all that moves has to be animated. In this view God animates the heavens just as the soul animates living creatures. In his final work, *Laws*, Plato shifted from cosmology to morality, declaring that if humans do not accept their share in the divine, in the form of souls, then they cannot strive for moral perfection. Plato assailed Greece's Olympian religion but accepted the necessity of its *polis*, or state-sponsored, religion with its traditional rituals, so long as they were publicly, rather than privately, staged. Those who challenged or ignored these positions were deemed impious atheists, subject to a sentence of death. Thus Plato ironically endorsed the very legislation that had been used to punish Socrates.

Plato could not envision divinity as evil, nor could he accept that God would introduce evil into the world. Later Stoics embraced this sanguine appreciation of God, whom they termed the Divine Mind; they originally considered Zeus the embodiment of the divine and later used his name as a synonym for God.

In the ensuing cosmopolitan era initiated by Alexander, the once-independent *polis* (city-state) succumbed to powerful Hellenistic monarchs who were acclaimed as gods and honored with ruler cults. A hymn to one such king captured this attitude, contending that the other gods were so distant that they no longer heeded humans (and even when they did, their contact came through fabricated statues), but the king was real and present, and hence far more likely to respond to a person's pleas. Nevertheless, cult practice continued much as it had for hundreds of years, centered on traditional festivals and rituals, and the major oracles thrived. As rulers became more godlike, though, they too came to be seen as distant; thus, the emotional immediacy of mystery cults became especially attractive to common citizens. Everyone wanted divine favor, including rulers, who sponsored cults and perpetuated propaganda claiming that the imperial world they ruled was, as Stoic philosophers also claimed, the result of divine will and favor.

⊕ Roman Tradition

Rome's defining characteristic was power. An ever-expanding empire, Rome was characterized by a personality split between ruthless force and generosity. Rome expected unquestioned loyalty from allies and subjects. Any disobedience or threat faced swift and brutal reprisal. At the same time Rome also displayed forbearance by absorbing rather than destroying conquered foes. A key component of Rome's absorptive state was its continuous embrace of foreign influences, including non-Roman gods and philosophies.

The heyday of Roman acceptance of foreign gods came during the Second Carthaginian War (218–202 BCE). The Sibylline oracle predicted that Rome would defeat Carthage if it imported

Focus

The Magna Mater (Cybele)

Worship of the Magna Mater ("Great Mother") had a long, distinguished history. Her cult's origins are commonly traced to seventh-century BCE Phrygia (a land in western Turkey), but its roots were much older. From Phrygia the cult spread to Greece in the sixth century BCE and from there to Rome. By the second century CE her sanctuaries covered the breadth of the Roman Empire and beyond, from the Vatican Hill to Lugdunum in Gaul (present-day Lyons, France) to Ai Khanoum in northern Afghanistan.

In Phrygia she was known simply as Matar, "Mother," but one of her epithets, *kubileya*, a term associated with mountains, was rendered by the Greeks as Kybele/Cybele. The only Phrygian deity to be depicted iconographically, in many images she is accompanied by a lion—a symbol of her power.

Cybele, undoubtedly due to her association with Troy, the home of Aeneas, whom Roman myth identified as the ancestor of Rome's founder, Romulus, and the pacifier of Carthage (a role in which he would appear in Vergil's *Aeneid*). In 204 BCE, Cybele, in the form of a black meteorite from Asia Minor, arrived in Rome, where she was named Magna Mater. There she joined other foreign gods, including Apollo, for whom special games were instituted in 212 BCE; Demeter, whose Thesmophoria was introduced in 205 BCE; and Dionysus/Bacchus, whose rites reached Rome in 200 BCE. In 186 BCE the Roman Senate charged the followers of Bacchus with conspiring against the Roman state, arrested 7,000 Bacchantes, executed unknown numbers of them, and placed stringent limitations on future practice of the god's rites. The first Roman devotees of Bacchus had been women and slaves, who had sought release from their debased status in the cult's emotional ritual, the Bacchanalia, which was typically conducted in secret (like a mystery rite). As long as its numbers had remained low, the **cult** had been tolerated. When its soaring popularity coincided with yet another Roman crisis, however, its secret and nocturnal rites were denounced as anti-Roman.

Rome's tendency to lash out in times of upheaval affected several of its Vestal Virgins, the state's only major female priesthood. The six Vestals were viewed as indispensable pillars of the *pax deorum*, Rome's singular relationship with its gods. They were responsible for ensuring that Rome's sacred fire never died out; preparing the special flour that was sprinkled on animals offered to the gods during state sacrifices; participating in such public festivals as the Parentalia, which honored dead ancestors; and safeguarding private wills and important state documents. Each year their own Vestalia festival was held for eight days in June. On day one the temple of Vesta's inner sanctum was opened to ordinary women, who assisted the Vestals in preparing the hallowed flour. Vestals themselves had to be pure—hence the requirement of strictest chastity that was placed on them. Breaches of Vestal duties merited merciless discipline. The *pontifex maximus* ("high priest") publicly whipped any Vestal whose neglect caused the sacred flame to die out. Violating the vow of chastity was a capital crime, punished by being thrown into the Tiber River or by live entombment in an underground cell, where the accused died of starvation or suffocation. At least 19 Vestals are recorded to have been executed. While some may have willfully ignored their vows, others were likely scapegoats during precarious moments in Rome's history.

The first century BCE was a particularly perilous era, marked by decades of upheavals that ended when Octavian defeated Marc Antony and Cleopatra. No ruler was more astute in the use of myth to justify his political regime than Octavian, better known as Augustus Caesar. Augustus transformed foundation myths into legitimation myths. Rome's principal foundation myth centered on the legend of Romulus, whose choice of the Palatine Hill as the site of the future city had been validated by the appearance of 12 vultures. Accordingly, Octavian made it known that 12 vultures had also appeared to him, implying that he would reestablish Rome—although now as the Roman Empire, as opposed to the Roman Republic.

Augustus used religious props throughout his reign, including a second foundation myth that was the subject of the greatest literary work of the Augustan Age. Vergil's *Aeneid* traced Rome's origins to Aeneas, a refugee from Troy who was the son of a human father and a divine mother identified as Aphrodite/Venus. Augustus's clan, the Julians, had long claimed Aeneas and Venus as ancestors. Furthermore, as *pontifex maximus*, Augustus was required to live next to the house of the Vestal Virgins, but, unwilling to vacate his own home, he rededicated his house as public property and turned part of it into a shrine to Vesta. In this way he not only brought Rome's hearth, the symbol of the empire's divine favor, into his own home but also reinforced his connection with the foundation myth in which the fire of Vesta was first transferred from Troy to Italy by Aeneas and then brought into Rome by Romulus.

Finally, the very name "Augustus" was part of the new ruler's legitimation scheme. Until he took the name for himself, "august" had been an epithet attached to places touched by a god and subsequently consecrated by priests known as augurs. By renaming himself Augustus, Octavian emphasized his heaven-sent good fortune. Sacrifices were offered to both his *genius* (the personification of his innate qualities) and his *numen* (divine power). He was elevated to divine status upon his death in 14 CE, when a senator—his vision sharpened by an extremely large bribe from Augustus's widow—declared under oath that he had witnessed Augustus physically ascending to heaven.

Augustus's rise to power terminated a century of civil war, in the course of which he obtained a near monopoly on the instruments of power. He also looked to poets to justify his new position. Some obliged, but others censured him. Ovid's *Metamorphoses* directly challenged Augustus's legitimation myth and Rome's developing imperial cult. Ovid's gods, far from concerning themselves with justice, used their power to prey on the weak. Male gods, particularly Jupiter, regularly resorted to sexual violence. The only truly compassionate deity was Isis, a female goddess who comforted the distressed—and she was a non-Roman goddess, imported from Egypt, Rome's most recent imperial conquest (under Augustus). Augustus exiled Ovid for his pointed criticism of power's darker side.

Three times reprieved from execution, Marcus Terentius Varro (116–27 BCE) was eventually celebrated by Augustus for his *Human and Divine Antiquities*, a 41-book compilation of Roman religious practices that effectively made "Roman religion" a subject of study. Borrowing from Greek thought, Varro specified three ways of thinking about the gods: mythical, philosophical, and civic/practical (referring to popular understanding and practices). Even though they were mutually incompatible, Varro argued, each of these approaches served a purpose that rendered it valid in its own sphere.

Not so lucky was another admirer of Varro, Cicero, who was murdered for his political role in the civil wars, but not before he wrote several works on religion. As a philosopher, Cicero held skeptical views on much religious lore and behavior, but he saw the value of traditional civic religion, which he encouraged in *The Laws*, echoing Plato's sentiments in his work of the same name:

Let men approach the gods in chastity, let them bring a spirit of loyalty, let them do without riches. If a man does otherwise, a god will punish him.

No one should have gods of his own, not new ones, not imported ones, unless they have been publicly invited in and accepted. Private worship should only be for those approved by the fathers.

. . .

Observe the rites of family and fathers.

The gods who are regarded as heavenly—worship those, and those who have earned heaven by their deeds . . . and worship those virtues by which men achieve ascent to heaven: Intelligence, Courage, Piety, Faithfulness.

. . .

Let there be no quarrels on festal days, and let servants observe them when their work is done, for so they were placed on the annual calendar.

Let there be priests for the gods, pontiffs for all, and a priest for each.

Let the vestal virgins in the city look after the fire on the public hearth forever.

Let there be no nighttime sacrifices by women except those done properly on behalf of the people.

Let there be no initiations except for the customary one for Ceres in the Greek [Eleusis] way.

At the public games . . . keep the popular celebration under control and connected to the honor shown the gods. (O'Donnell 2015: 48–49)

Cicero, the self-designated upholder of the Republic, in these assertions focused on Rome the city rather than Rome the empire, but the city could not be separated from the empire of which it was the center.

The Roman Empire, with a population of about 50 million in the time of Augustus, was a vast network of roads that all led to Rome, a multicultural metropolis of approximately 750,000 residents. Rome the city was the emporium of the world, the place where everything, including religions, was marketed. Besides the cults already mentioned, Greece's Asclepius, Iran's Mithra(s), and Egypt's Serapis were represented in the capital and throughout the empire. Shrines to Isis and Mithras were erected in Britain, and Mithras was also particularly popular in military camps and settlements along the Rhine and Danube frontiers. Greek philosophical schools, such as Stoicism, Epicureanism, and Platonism, with their varying perspectives on religion, were also present. Cults and philosophies were significantly modified, however. For example, the cult of Mithras in Rome bore no resemblance to Mithraic worship in the god's Iranian homeland, and Plato's "rational" philosophy turned mystical in its **Neoplatonist** guise.

Many such cults, including those of Mithras, Cybele, and Isis, can be classed as mystery religions, offering a promise of "salvation" and a release from the restrictions placed on, and the insignificance felt by, individuals under the domain of an all-powerful imperial state and an equally imperious Fate. Countless people also still placed their trust in the stars and divination. And traditional festivals continued according to long-established calendars. In choosing a tradition to adhere to, a resident of Rome or other major city of the empire had a wealth of options. By the fourth century CE, however, most of those religions were becoming stale. Some, like Mithraism, disappeared, while components of others, such as Neoplatonism, became accessories to the fashion that caught the eye of emperors and then the empire: Christianity.

Women in the Traditions

Women in the Traditions of Antiquity

According to the principal character of a play by Euripides of which only fragments have been preserved, women had the greatest involvement in matters concerning the gods, a position that reinforced a much earlier Sumerian proverb: "My wife is at the outdoor shrine . . . And here am I starving of hunger" (Kramer 1963: 255). The perspective of these lines is male. Our knowledge of the role of women in ancient religion derives from texts written by males, a few of which are supportive, many of which are neutral, and a significant number of which are hostile toward their female contemporaries.

The Sumerian proverb, whether serious or humorous, captures typical gender relations of the ancient world, where women were expected to subordinate their interests to those of males, who expressed frustration when women looked to their own interests, especially religious devotion. Such devotion could be formal, in that some women had the opportunity to become practitioners, such as priestesses, or informal, as when women acted as worshipers.

In both the ancient Near East and the later Greco-Roman era, women's formal participation in religion declined over time. For most of the third and second millennia BCE, Mesopotamian priestesses, like their counterparts in Egypt, made offerings, prayed to the gods, led rituals, and even supervised the construction and operation of temples. Some women prophesied. Those responsibilities faded with the centralization of state power during the Old Babylonian period and Egypt's New Kingdom. With rare exceptions (royal women), even as goddesses continued to be worshiped, women in later centuries tended to be depicted negatively, commonly as witches intent on doing evil. The one important role left to women in religious services

was as musicians, either singers or instrumentalists, such as the 200 female percussionists who served one Babylonian temple.

Men controlled both civic and family religion in Greece and Rome; consequently, classical culture, both written and visual, served to inform women of their proper gender roles, especially as mothers and wives, and further identified boundaries between men and women, such as the rule that only men could participate in animal sacrifice. Certain females who transgressed boundaries—the ecstatic devotees of Dionysus (*maenads*), the jealous shrew Hera, or the child-murdering Medea—served as warnings of how women should not behave.

For all that, women were not passive but actively partook in religious matters in a number of ways: as attendees of specifically female festivals, which were often age-related; as priestesses; or as dedicators. Dedications, in fact, present a different picture of female religious participation than that put forward by the male-generated cultural constructs. Between the eighth and fifth centuries BCE, the greater Greek world produced some 800 inscribed dedications, of which roughly 10 percent named women. The tens of thousands of dedications made at sanctuaries to Hera to honor this patron of marriage included spindle whorls, bobbins, loom weights, and fibulae (dress fasteners), all of which point to the significance of women's domestic economy in the areas of weaving and spinning. Devotees also offered her cakes associated with fertility. One particular Heraion held close to 3,000 terracotta figurines of seated or standing female worshipers of Hera.

Such dedications permit women who would have remained forever anonymous to emerge for brief moments: Demetria, who offered three obols (coins) to Asclepius; the women who made their

Continued

personal marks on spindle whorls; Menekrateia, identified as a priestess, who paid for a small shrine in honor of Aphrodite in that goddess's sanctuary on the Athenian acropolis. Dedications also offer insight into contemporary gender relations. Menekrateia is identified as the daughter of Dexicrates. Prior to 500 BCE, women's dedications did not note parentage. As Greek states centralized during the fifth century BCE, women's independent identity was subordinated to that of male authority figures (father or husband).

The Greek author Dionysius of Halicarnassus, writing during the reign of Augustus Caesar, contrasted conservative Rome with the much looser Greece:

> And no festival is observed among the Romans by the wearing of black garments or as a day of mourning and with beating of breasts and lamentations of women because of the disappearance of deities, in the way that the Greeks commemorate the rape of Persephone and the experiences of Dionysus. . . . And one will see among the Romans no ecstatic possession, no Corybantic frenzies, no begging rituals, no bacchanals or secret mysteries, no all-night vigils of men and women in the temples, nor any other trickery of this kind. (Dillon 2002: 3–4)

Not much later, all such practices, or "trickery," would be subjected once again to the scathing criticism of male upholders of cultural tradition, as in Juvenal's *Satires*, which ridiculed women for their worship of Isis and Bona Dea (the "Good Goddess"). Neither hungry husbands nor ridicule, however, were grounds for stopping women from displaying their religiosity as they saw fit.

It was Constantine (r. 306–337) who eventually used the power of his imperial office to favor Christianity. From then on the imperial mantle was Christian, except for a brief, failed effort by Julian (r. 360–363) to reverse the trend.

⊕ Iranian Tradition (Zoroastrianism)

Iran was home to many religious traditions, but this section emphasizes Zoroastrianism, which influenced Judaism, Christianity, and Islam. The major source of our knowledge of Zoroastrianism is the **Avesta**, a compilation of several sources composed over at least 10 centuries that received canonic form in the seventh century CE and was further revised over the next two centuries as Zoroastrianism continued to define itself in the face of attacks from Islam. The oldest surviving copy of this *Great Avesta*, three-quarters of which has been lost, dates to 1323 CE. Determining how much revision each component of the *Avesta* underwent is a particularly thorny problem.

The major text of the *Avesta* is the **Yasna** ("worship"), 72 chapters split between the languages of Old Avestan and Younger Avestan. Seventeen hymns comprising the **Gathas**, plus nine other chapters, form the *Avesta*'s Old Avestan substratum. The Younger Avestan sections include all remaining chapters of the *Yasna* plus the *Yashts*, 21 hymns to several deities, and the *Vendidad*, a collection of purity taboos. These are the fundamental sources for any interpretation of ancient Zoroastrianism.

The *Gathas* introduce Zarathustra as the recipient of revelatory visions from **Ahura Mazda**. Zarathustra (hereafter called Zoroaster, as the Greeks rendered his name) can be understood as a prophet in the same vein as Muhammad or as an inspired poet comparable to Homer. Much of what is "known" of Zoroaster comes from much later **hagiographies** (idealized biographies of spiritual figures). Zoroaster's life is shrouded in the mists of time. No one can determine when (or indeed even if) he lived, with suggestions ranging from the seventeenth to the sixth centuries BCE. The date of the composition of the *Gathas* is also problematic. Since they are written in the language of Old Avestan, which is closely related to Vedic Sanskrit, scholars assume that they were composed quite early, no later than 1000 BCE, and preserved in an unchanging oral tradition until put into writing at an undetermined date centuries later.

The similarities between the *Gathas* and the *Rig Veda* place the former in an Indo-Iranian rather than an ancient Near Eastern context, so the original homeland of Zoroastrianism was likely much closer to the Indus River Valley than to the Tigris–Euphrates region. A key term common to both sources is *asura/ahura*. In the *Rig Veda*, *asura* is an epithet used for several important gods, while *ahura* (the Sanskrit *s-* became *h-* in Avestan) refers to one god elevated above all others, who are reduced to six aspects ("Beneficent Immortals") of the principal god, Ahura Mazda. *Mazda* marks someone who is wise, while *ahura* implies creative power. The most common translation of Ahura Mazda is "Wise Lord."

The central tenet of Zoroastrianism was cosmic dualism, a near-eternal tension or conflict between good and evil, *asha* ("Truth") and *druj* ("Lie"), light (sun and fire) and darkness. *Asha* was beneficent (*spenta*) and life affirming; *druj* was maleficent (*angra*) and life denying. Ahura Mazda was said to have created twin offspring: Spenta Mainyu ("Good Spirit") and **Angra Mainyu** ("Evil Spirit"). Their constant battle was also believed to engage humans, who received free will to choose between them. Righteous humans, known as *ashavans* ("possessors of the truth"), had a moral duty to follow the principal ethos set forth by Ahura Mazda: good thoughts, good words, and good deeds. If they adhered to that ethos and participated in sacrifices, then, in the same way that Ahura Mazda and his six emanations ("Good Thinking," "Highest Truth," "Dominion," "Prosperity," "Humility," and "Immortality") fostered life, humans would produce blessings for themselves, their communities, and the world. Dishonesty was ruinous; so too was debt, since it made a person susceptible to deceit, violence, and loss of free will.

This brief overview of Zoroastrian ideas is based on the later, Younger Avestan, portions of the *Avesta* as well as the *Gathas*. Also composed in Younger Avestan were the *Yashts* (hymns of "veneration"), which praise an assortment of gods, identified as *yazatas* ("beings worthy of worship"), including Mithra, Anahita, and other gods of non-Zoroastrian Iran. Younger Avestan was linguistically related to Old Persian, the home of which was southwestern Iran and which was the official language of the first Achaemenid Persian Empire (550–330 BCE).

Although Achaemenids never mentioned Zoroaster, their inscriptions, in wording identical to that found in Younger Avestan examples, underscore the relationship between the ruler and Ahura Mazda. The inscriptions of Darius (r. 522–486 BCE) praise Ahura Mazda as the god who assured his victory in combat and as the "all-great god who established the cosmos." To obey Darius was to obey Ahura Mazda. Darius and his successors governed earth as agents of Ahura Mazda, fought against the Lie, and spurned evil gods, thereby maintaining order, securing prosperity, and promoting happiness. Their construction of palaces recapitulated Ahura Mazda's creation of the cosmos, and Greek authors described their royal gardens as *paradeisos* ("paradise"). The most important element of the official state religion was sacrifice—of grain, beer, wine, or fruit, but never animals. Although other gods received offerings, the major dedication was the *lan* sacrifice, performed by the king in honor of Ahura Mazda. Zoroastrianism may not have been the official religion of the first Persian Empire, but it was markedly associated with the ruling dynasty.

Alexander's termination of the Achaemenid Empire inaugurated the Hellenistic Age, an era that saw the diffusion of Greek influence far to the east and of some eastern ideas, including Zoroastrianism, to the west. Eventually a new Persian Empire emerged, alternately named the Parthian (for its Central Asian homeland) or the Arsacid (for its founder). Like the Achaemenids, the Arsacids (247 BCE–224 CE) did not force their private devotion to Ahura Mazda on their subjects. Religion throughout the Parthian Empire remained heterogeneous. Excavations at Nisa, the empire's first capital, located in today's Turkmenistan, show that the Arsacid royal family sponsored priests bearing the titles *magus* and "master of fire," supported several temples, and participated in Zoroastrian rituals, including worshiping ancestors and maintaining dynastic fires, but also revered such Greek and Mesopotamian deities as Artemis, Aphrodite, Dionysus, Anahita, and Nanaya.

A similar admixture was evident in the northern Anatolian kingdom of Pontus, particularly during the reign of Mithradates VI (120–63 BCE), who claimed descent from the Achaemenids. Mithradates ("Gift of Mithra") worshiped Greek gods, local Anatolian gods, and Iranian deities. On special occasions he joined Zoroastrian priests named "Fire-keepers" at a mountaintop fire altar dedicated to Zeus, who was equated with Ahura Mazda. Wearing the pure white cape of a magus, Mithradates poured libations onto the altar, over which he tossed incense, and recited prayers to Mithra and Ahura Mazda.

Some scholars contend, based on diverse sources, that Parthian Zoroastrianism influenced Jewish, Gnostic, and early Christian apocalyptic literature. It is equally possible that Zoroastrianism was influenced by earlier Mesopotamian traditions. The transmission of ideas was complex and undoubtedly moved in several directions.

The term "apocalypse" normally refers to a cataclysmic end of the world; it is thus related to eschatology, which is concerned with an individual's lot upon death. A Parthian-era work called the *Vendidad* ("Against the Demons") expands upon such a fate, which was first portrayed in the

Practice

Coming of Age in Zoroastrianism

Among Zoroastrians, ethics was not the only determiner of one's fate; piety was seen as equally important in strengthening both individual and cosmos. Days customarily began with prayers to Ahura Mazda, voiced while facing either the sun or fire, in a symbolic re-creation of the world of light after a period of darkness. The *Yasna* was recited at set hours of the day, while the *Yashts* were important components of seasonal festivals. The coming-of-age ritual, normally conducted when a youth attained the age of 15, was especially significant. Until then, children's good and bad deeds accrued to their parents' accounts. After this ceremony the young person's thoughts, words, and deeds went into his or her own account. The youth, whose body was perceived as a microcosm of the universe, would ceremoniously don a white shirt that symbolized the sunlit sky, the visible representation of good thought. The central moment of the ritual was the placement of the *kushti*, the sacred waistband, on the initiate. The *kushti's* 72 threads of white lamb's wool represented the 72 chapters of the *Yasna*, while its six tassels referred to the six life-affirming seasonal festivals. The initiated young person could now enter the temple, although only consecrated priests could access the holy of holies for recitation of the *Yasna* hymns.

Gathas. This work describes how at death the *urvan* ("breath-soul") of an individual hovers around the corpse for three days, after which it proceeds to the Account-Keeper's Bridge. A beautiful, sweet-smelling maiden guides righteous souls across the bridge to the House of Good Thought, while a malodorous hag leads evil souls to the House of Lies. As expressed in a later work named the **Denkard**, every individual's thoughts, words, and actions have consequences in the larger world, especially in the struggle between good and evil. Honesty, truthfulness, generosity, and charity all help good attain a final victory over evil.

According to Zoroastrian teaching, the world has passed through several phases: the age of creation, when all was perfect; the age of debasement, when evil and corruption entered the world; and the age of conflict, when good and evil competed with one another. In the coming age of separation, good thought will defeat evil thought, the world will return to its primordial state of

Ardashir faces Ohrmazd (the Middle Persian rendering of Ahura Mazda), who invests Ardashir (on the left) with the ring of sovereignty. Ardashir's horse tramples the defeated Parthian ruler, while Ohrmazd's horse crushes the snake-headed Ahriman (the Middle Persian form of Angra Mainyu). That the horses are mirror images of each other implies that Ardashir was the earthly counterpart of Ohrmazd, a piece of propaganda highlighted in the inscription: "This is the figure of the Mazda-worshiper, divine Ardashir, King of Kings of the Iranians, whose lineage issues from the gods." That same formula appeared on the front of Ardashir's coins, while the reverse featured a fire altar, which became the symbol of the Sasanian dynasty. Ardashir subsequently destroyed all the fire altars in his empire except those of his own founding; in this way, he used religion to centralize his realm (© Richard Slater/Alamy Stock Photo).

perfection, and evil will be cast into permanent oblivion. At such time, there will be a general bodily resurrection. The good will spend eternity in a brilliant heavenly abode, while the evil will drown in the darkness of extinction.

Priests, titled "those who offer libations" and "those who tend the sacred fire," became a privileged caste and highly influential political force during the Sasanian era (224–651 CE). The ancestors of Ardashir I (r. 224–242 CE), founder of the Sasanian dynasty, had been such priests, supervisors of a local fire temple they maintained as Parthian vassals. They had also identified much more closely with the Achaemenid than the Arsacid dynasty. The rock relief of Ardashir at Naqsh-e-Rustam set the tone for his reign.

Since church and state were one under the Sasanians, the church could make use of the state just as the state made use of the church. This unification became the goal of Kartir, a Zoroastrian high priest who used his position in the administrations of four successive kings to establish a single paramount state religion. Such centralization entailed both exclusivity and expansion. Kartir launched persecutions of non-Zoroastrians, beginning with Manichaeans and then expanding to Jews, Christians, and Buddhists. He also pursued "heretical" Zoroastrians, countenancing only a single form of state-approved fire temples, magi-priesthood, and rituals. Under this system uniform devotion to an exclusive god depended on performance, especially the proper maintenance of the fire temples, rather than belief.

The Sasanian Empire and its state-backed Zoroastrianism suffered a major blow when the last Sasanian ruler surrendered to Arab Muslims in 651. Zoroastrianism was not entirely suppressed, however. Zoroastrian priests continued to hold administrative positions, and Zoroastrian intellectuals continued to offer thoughtful assessments of their religion. Theology, especially the issue of theodicy, gained urgency. A ninth-century work argued that dualism was better suited than monotheism to dealing with the problem of evil, since God, the ultimate good, could never authorize evil. Zoroastrianism's cosmogonic subordinate creator god (comparable to Plato's demiurge), who engendered the twins Good and Evil, made more sense.

Zoroastrian thought influenced other religious traditions, but it also appropriated external ideas, including the figure of a savior who effectuates the final resurrection of the bodies of the righteous at the end of time. However, no such savior protected Zoroastrians from actual attacks, which were launched by Muslims and especially by Mongols in the thirteenth and fourteenth centuries. Many Zoroastrians found safety in flight, leaving Iran for western India (where they became known as Parsis) as the beginning of a diaspora that currently finds the surviving 150,000 or so modern adherents, including 16,000 in North America, struggling to keep their tradition alive.

⊕ Manichaean Tradition

Mani was born in 216 in southern Mesopotamia, an interaction zone of religious cultures—Judaism, Christianity, Zoroastrianism, and the vestigial Babylonian star-worship tradition. Raised in a branch of Jewish Christianity, Mani experienced two epiphanies, the first at age 12 and the second at 24, during which the "Living God" made manifest to him the true origins and future of the universe, "the mystery of Light and Darkness." Inspired to undertake a public career, Mani first journeyed to the Indus River Valley (present-day southern Pakistan), where he acquainted himself with Buddhism. He then returned home to Ctesiphon, capital of the newly installed Sasanian dynasty. Even though the ruling house adopted Zoroastrianism as the official state religion, several early rulers sanctioned the teachings of Mani, who took advantage of such protection to fulfill God's command to found a universal religion.

Among the secrets God revealed to Mani was the "mystery of the apostles"—Buddha, Zoroaster, and Jesus. According to Mani, these figures were authoritative for their time but insufficiently valid for the present, and hence had to be supplanted. One way to supersede them was to craft a canon of written texts, a failure for which Mani criticized his predecessors. He thus produced a corpus of several texts, supplemented with picture books for the unlettered. None of his works has survived intact, but excerpts from several offer a glimpse of his vision.

Mani obsessed over the origin of evil. Like Neoplatonism, Zoroastrianism, and Gnosticism, his worldview proposed a thoroughgoing dualism, on which he elaborated via cosmological myth. In his account, creation had produced two coeternal principles that existed separately from one another. The good (peace, justice, wisdom), which Mani called God or "Father of Goodness," resided in the realm of light. Evil, labeled Satan or "matter," inhabited darkness but later invaded the realm of light and imprisoned light within matter, thereby initiating the present age of human existence. God then tasked special individuals, culminating in Mani and his "Elect" followers, to liberate light. Ultimately, a great conflagration would consume the universe, and the end would replicate the beginning, with light and darkness again coexisting separately.

The Manichaean Elect, comprising both male and female monks, had to live a stringently ascetic life according to five commandments—no lying, killing, eating meat, sexual intercourse, or personal possessions—and three seals. The "seal of the mouth" demanded vigilance over thoughts and expression (e.g., no blasphemy), plus avoidance of prohibited foods (those lacking light, including wine and meat). The "seal of hands" required vigilance over actions, prohibiting the killing of any living thing. The "seal of thought" sought constant harmony with the realm of light. The Elect were further required to pray seven times daily and to fast at least 100 days yearly, including the entire month preceding the principal Manichaean feast day, known as the Bema, named for the throne on which Mani's portrait was placed on the anniversary of his death. Laypersons known as "Hearers" supported the Elect. They too were forbidden to lie, murder, rob, or commit adultery, but they could perform manual labor, own property, and "kill," since they prepared food (those grains, vegetables, and fruits with the most light) for the Elect. The other expectations for this group were also milder: they were required to pray only four times each day and to fast only 50 days per year.

While Mani preached in Iran and Mesopotamia, his disciples sought converts throughout the Sasanian Empire and then ventured farther afield, east to India and west to Egypt. Mani's success threatened the Zoroastrian state religion; prodded by Kartir, the leading Zoroastrian at his court, Bahram I (r. 274–277) ordered Mani's arrest and subsequent execution in 276.

Shortly afterward, Manichaeism earned the displeasure of the Roman emperor Diocletian, who saw it as a contagion from Persia, Rome's long-standing enemy. Prior to his persecution of Christians, Diocletian ordered Manichaean leaders to be burned alive along with their scriptures. The tradition fared no better under Constantine and later Christian emperors, who came to regard it as a heresy. Nevertheless, Manichaeism spread from Egypt to Italy, Gaul, Spain, and North Africa. So influential did it become in North Africa that five of the region's Christian bishops were former Manichaeans. The most famous ex-Manichaean was Augustine, whose 10 years as an adherent left a deep imprint on his understanding of good and evil. Continuing attacks, however, led to the disappearance of Manichaeism from the West by the end of the sixth century.

A Sasanian state offensive encouraged by the Zoroastrian leadership convinced Manichaeans to head east, from Iran to Central Asia along the Silk Road. When the Umayyad caliphate overthrew the Sasanian dynasty, Manichaeans returned to Iran, but their stay ended a century later when attacks resumed under the Abbasid caliphate. The Silk Road again beckoned. Manichaeism became the official religion of an Uighur state from 763 to 840 and even reached China, where it was called the "Religion of Light." Several sporadic persecutions in the latter state forced it underground, where it survived by adapting to local conditions. Just as Mani had borrowed freely from Zoroastrianism, Christianity, and Buddhism, his heirs in China claimed to be Daoists. Thus, Manichaeism persisted in China until the seventeenth century.

⊕ The End of Paganism

By the time of Constantine, religious disciplines that sought self-transformation by releasing the divinity within humans, such as Mithraism, had become far less fashionable. Constantine himself, acting on contrary personal and imperial positions, publicized his personal distaste for paganism's "injurious errors" even as he permitted public performance of traditional practices such as sacrifice and divination. Later laws were often contradictory. One, passed in 341, outlawed animal sacrifice in Italy, although the prohibition was rarely enforced. Another, enacted the following year, protected rural temples even as urban temples were transformed into Christian churches. Such ambivalence ended with Theodosius, who ordered the suppression of paganism. The first assault on these traditions was physical, with bands of monks destroying temples throughout the empire, starting in cities along the Euphrates frontier. The second assault came in the form of a series of laws passed in 391 and 392 that forbade sacrifices, worship of idols, visits to temples, and other traditional practices such as burning incense.

Simultaneously, a polytheistic correspondent of Augustine made an appeal for Christians and pagans to coexist in paradoxical "harmonious discord," since their common Father could be worshiped in 1,000 ways. Discord, however, trumped harmony. Augustine's monolithic religion—characterized by one exclusive path, one exclusive truth, and one exclusive God—won out. Laws proscribing traditional practices helped in this battle, as did denunciatory sermons. Perhaps the most effective tactic in the campaign against the traditions of antiquity was the withholding of imperial monies from pagan temples and shrines. By 400, anyone seeking to commune with the divine in the presence of others had nowhere to go but a Christian church. Finally, the Theodosian Code of 438 outlawed all traditional modes of piety as superstitions and legally defined religion from the single perspective of the Christian church.

The power of the state determined the final outcome of the rivalry between Christianity and paganism. Constantine and his Christian successors used their position to elevate their preferred, and omnipotent, God over the myriad petty gods of old, now rendered powerless.

Power may claim to be absolute, but its reach is never total. Paganism persisted—in the secrecy of private homes, in the countryside, and in a few long-established public festivals. During the fifth century, Christians persistently disparaged traditionalists as "incense offerers." Citizens in Rome continued to build private shrines to Isis and Osiris into the fifth century. The traditional festival of Lupercalia was finally outlawed in Rome in 496 but persisted in Constantinople until the tenth century. During that century, the Muslim geographer al-Mas'udi also marveled at the number of pilgrims, primarily star-worshipers, who were still visiting active pagan temples in Harran, a mere 20 miles from Gobekli. Thus, this story of the religions of antiquity ends where it began.

⊕ Recent Developments

The current study of ancient religion(s) reflects the influence of several recent developments. Archaeological evidence has simultaneously complemented textual evidence and challenged interpretations derived exclusively from texts (produced by the literary elite). Such evidence also affords a more detailed picture of everyday religious life. Greater attention has been paid to the official and unofficial roles of women. More emphasis has been placed on the features that the religions of antiquity shared with Judaism and Christianity (fewer commonalities can be found with Islam). This emphasis has resulted in efforts to contextualize practices and concepts and an appreciation that differences among religious traditions are more often differences of degree than of kind. Finally, there is intense debate about the extent to which the religions of antiquity were monotheistic.

⊕ Summary

This chapter has demonstrated that the religious traditions of antiquity sought to address every aspect of what most laypeople today consider "religion": a "belief" in the supernatural, an effort to understand the interaction between divine and human planes of existence, consideration of what

Sites

Harran, Mesopotamia

An important trade center in northern Mesopotamia for four millennia, Harran was a major site for the worship of the moon god Sin, which linked the city to Sin's southern Mesopotamian home in Ur, an association mirrored in the biblical story of Abraham. A later goddess named Allat (Arabic for "goddess") was also worshiped there. Harran's "pagan" worship continued for several centuries after the city came under Islamic dominion.

Akhetaten (Modern Amarna), Egypt

Literally "the horizon of Aten," Akhetaten was the short-lived city created by Akhenaten as his capital in the fourteenth century BCE. The "Amarna Letters"—some 400 cuneiform tablets discovered at the site—shed light on Egypt's relations with its neighbors during this period.

Dodona, Greece

Dodona was the site of the oldest Greek oracle, originally associated with a mother goddess but later dedicated to Zeus. Though located in an isolated region of northwestern Greece, Dodona is mentioned in both the *Iliad* and the *Odyssey*, and it became second in importance only to Delphi. The earliest oracles were obtained by interpreting the rustling of the leaves of a sacred oak tree or the cooing of doves.

Rome, Italy

The religious as well as the political capital of the Roman world, ancient Rome contained hundreds of temples. Among them was the magnificent Pantheon, commissioned by the Emperor Hadrian in the second century CE to replace a temple built under the Augustan-era consul Marcus Agrippa. Although the earlier temple had burned down, its façade survived and was incorporated into the new building, which was eventually converted into a Christian church.

Sacred Texts of Antiquity

Religious Tradition	Text	Composition/Compilation	Compilation/ Revision	Use
Egypt	Pyramid Texts	24th century BCE		mortuary myth
Egypt	Coffin Texts	22nd–17th centuries BCE		mortuary myth
Egypt	*Book of the Dead*	16th century BCE		mortuary myth
Mesopotamia	*Epic of Gilgamesh*	18th century BCE (Old Babylonian version)	13th–10th centuries BCE (Standard Version)	myth
Mesopotamia	*Enuma Elish*	13th century BCE (Babylonian version)	7th century BCE (Assyrian version)	myth ritual
Mesopotamia	*Epic of Erra* (also known as *Erra and Ishum*)	8th century BCE		myth magic
Greece	Homer's *Iliad* and *Odyssey*	8th–7th centuries BCE		myth
Greece	Hesiod's *Theogony*	8th–7th centuries BCE		myth
Rome	Ovid's *Metamorphoses*	1st century CE		myth
Rome	Ovid's *Fasti*	1st century CE		ritual
Zoroastrianism	*Yasna*	Uncertain BCE	7th century CE	ritual
Zoroastrianism	*Yashts*	Uncertain BCE	7th century CE	ritual
Zoroastrianism	*Denkard*	9th–10th centuries CE		compendium
Zoroastrianism	*Bundahishn*	8th–9th centuries CE		myth
Manichaeism	*The Fundamental Epistle*	3rd century CE		doctrine

makes people worthy of divine support, the idea of conflict between good and evil, and contemplation of the ultimate end of material existence. The six traditions examined in this chapter all reached comparable conclusions. The questioning of those conclusions that began around 600 BCE, however, set the stage for a challenge to the most fundamental components of the religions of antiquity: the number of gods and the most proper form of worship. Eventually, a different set of answers, which would form the basis of the three monotheistic Western traditions, would supplant the ancients' answers.

Discussion Questions

1. What radically new understanding of the divine did Greek philosophers introduce?

2. Which aspect of ancient religion would prove most offensive to Jews, Christians, and Muslims: (a) the worship of statues as if they were actual gods themselves (idolatry), (b) the practice of offering sacrifices to the gods, (c) the recognition of numerous gods (polytheism), or (d) the ancients' openness to diverse explanations of how the universe operated?

3. Many late antique defenders of "pagan" religion argued that since God was ultimately unknowable to humans, all reasonable ways to reach some understanding of the divine were legitimate. "The paths to God are many," according to that view. Is such a position defendable?

4. Which are more important: the differences or similarities between the religions of antiquity and the three major monotheisms?

5. How similar to ancient Near Eastern and Greco-Roman religions were Zoroastrianism and Manichaeism?

Glossary

Ahura Mazda (Ohrmazd) Principal Zoroastrian god.

Akhenaten Controversial fourteenth-century BCE Egyptian ruler whose devotion to Aten convinces some scholars that he was the world's first monotheist.

Amun/Amun-Ra Principal Egyptian state god during the Middle and New Kingdoms.

Angra Mainyu (Ahriman) Evil god of Zoroastrianism.

anthropomorphism Attribution of a human form or character to nonhuman phenomena.

Avesta Most important collection of Zoroastrian scripture.

Book of the Dead A modern designation of *The Book of Going Forth by Day*, a New Kingdom collection of spells designed to ensure the resurrection of the dead and their security in the afterworld.

Coffin Texts Spells inscribed on the coffins of nonroyal elite Egyptians during the Middle Kingdom, intended to protect the dead traversing the netherworld and to secure them an afterlife comparable to that of the (divinized) dead rulers.

cult Synonym for "ritual worship."

Demeter Greek "mother goddess" associated with the harvest whose principal center of worship was Eleusis.

Denkard Zoroastrian *Acts of Religion*, often called the "Encyclopedia of Zoroastrianism."

Eleusis Site of the Eleusinian Mysteries, centered on the myth of Persephone's abduction to the underworld by Hades and her rescue by her mother, Demeter. Initiates participated in rituals designed to ensure a favorable stay in the netherworld.

Enuma Elish Mesopotamia's creation epic, named for its first two words (translated "When on high"), in which the Babylonian god Marduk triumphs over the forces of chaos, "creates" and orders the universe, and becomes ruler of the pantheon.

Gathas Oldest portion of the *Avesta*, containing Ahura Mazda's revelation to Zoroaster.

Gilgamesh Subject of several Sumerian stories reformulated during the Old Babylonian period into a unified narrative commonly known as the *Epic of Gilgamesh* and later revised into the "Standard Version."

hagiography An idealized biography of a spiritual figure. Often used to describe the devotional biography of a saint.

Hathor Egyptian cow goddess associated with both creation (love, sex, and fertility) and violent destructive power.

Hesiod Eighth-century BCE author of *Works and Days* and *Theogony*; one of the two primary sources for the "standard" portraits of the Greek gods.

Homer Eighth-century BCE author of the *Iliad* and the *Odyssey*; the other primary source for the "standard" portraits of the Greek gods.

Ishtar Mesopotamian goddess of both love and war, early identified with her Sumerian counterpart Inanna.

Isis The best-known Egyptian goddess, first associated with living and dead rulers. In myth she was the devoted sister and wife of Osiris and the loving mother of Horus. During the Ptolemaic and Roman eras, Isis assumed the functions of numerous other deities and became a universal goddess.

magus Originally a term for Median priests that became the major designation of Zoroastrian priests.

Marduk Patron god of Babylon, later elevated to the supreme position in the Mesopotamian pantheon.

Neoplatonism Philosophical school most influential between the third and sixth centuries CE. Many of its concepts regarding divinity and cosmology intersected with Jewish, Christian, and Islamic thought.

netherworld Region where spirits of the dead were believed to enter, also known as the afterworld or afterlife. While "netherworld" suggests it lay beneath the earth, the land of the dead could also be located in the heavens.

Osiris Egyptian god who was the preeminent judge of the dead and who ruled the realm of the dead.

Ovid (43 BCE–17 CE) Roman author of *Metamorphoses* and *Fasti*.

Plato (c. 425–347 BCE) Greek philosopher whose most important contribution to religious thought was his separation of the world into conflicting material and spiritual realms.

Plutarch (46–120 CE) Senior priest of Apollo at Delphi and a prolific author of works including the *Moralia*, which featured "On the Worship of Isis and Osiris"—the most complete version of the principal Egyptian myth.

Pyramid Texts Spells or incantations (literally, "utterances") carved on the walls of the royal burial suites of Old Kingdom rulers and recited by priests to guarantee the resurrection and well-being of dead rulers.

stela Inscribed stone sculpture; plural "stelas" or "stelae."

Sumer Urban civilization of southern-most Mesopotamia in the fourth and third millennia BCE; Sumerian religion was a substratum of Mesopotamian religion.

Tiamat Female monster who represented primeval chaos/disorder and was subdued by Marduk in *Enuma Elish*. ("Tiamat" is related to *tehom*, the Hebrew word usually translated as "the void" or "nothing" in the first verses of *Genesis*.)

Vesta Roman goddess of household and hearth, served by priestesses known as the Vestal Virgins, who maintained the sacred fire that secured the safety of Rome itself. Vesta's Greek equivalent was Hestia ("hearth").

Xenophanes (c. 570–c. 475 BCE) Early Greek philosopher who challenged the anthropomorphic depictions of the gods in Greek myth.

Yasna Principal Zoroastrian ceremony accompanied by recitation of the *Yasna* section of the *Avesta*.

Zeus Most powerful Greek god, who ruled from Mount Olympus. His principal shrine was at Olympia, the site of the ancient Olympic Games.

Further Reading

Beard, Mary, John North, and Simon Price. 1998. *Religions of Rome.* 2 vols. Cambridge: Cambridge University Press. Volume 1 offers a thoughtful assessment of classical Roman religion; Volume 2 provides hundreds of texts.

Dalley, Stephanie. 2000. *Myths from Mesopotamia: Creation, the Flood, Gilgamesh, and Others.* Rev. ed. New York: Oxford University Press. Translations of Mesopotamian texts.

Foltz, Richard. 2010. *Religions of the Silk Road: Premodern Patterns of Globalization.* 2nd ed. New York: Palgrave Macmillan. A work detailing the eastward spread of religions and dealing with Manichaeism.

Hinnels, John R., ed. 2007. *A Handbook of Ancient Religions.* Cambridge: Cambridge University Press. Includes several chapters devoted to the ancient Near East and classical worlds.

Johnston, Sarah Iles, ed. 2004. *Religions of the Ancient World: A Guide.* Cambridge, MA: Harvard University Press. A single-volume compendium that includes sections on 11 major aspects of religion, the histories of 11 religious traditions, and comparative examinations of 20 important topics.

Kraemer, Ross Shepard, ed. 2004. *Women's Religions in the Greco-Roman World: A Sourcebook.* Oxford: Oxford University Press. A wide-ranging collection of documents from the classical world.

Mikalson, Jon D. 2005. *Ancient Greek Religion.* Oxford: Blackwell. A basic, topical introduction.

Ogden, Daniel, ed. 2009. *Magic, Witchcraft, and Ghosts in the Greek and Roman Worlds: A Sourcebook.* 2nd ed. Oxford: Oxford University Press. A fascinating collection on the classical world.

Rose, Jenny. 2010. *Zoroastrianism: An Introduction.* London: I. B. Tauris. The most accessible presentation of the religion available.

Salzmann, Michele Renee, ed. 2013. *The Cambridge History of Religions in the Ancient World.* 2 vols. Cambridge: Cambridge University Press. Includes several chapters, some challenging, on ancient Near Eastern and Greco-Roman religious traditions.

Simpson, William Kelley, ed. 2003. *The Literature of Ancient Egypt.* 3rd ed. New Haven, CT: Yale University Press. A fine anthology of ancient Egyptian texts.

Snell, Daniel C. 2011. *Religions of the Ancient Near East.* Cambridge: Cambridge University Press. An excellent work for beginners.

Recommended Websites

http://www.etana.org
The site of the Electronic Tools and Ancient Near Eastern Archives, offering a range of materials, including texts in translation.

http://www.uee.ucla.edu
The UCLA Encyclopedia of Egyptology, offering brief topical articles.

http://www.perseus.tufts.edu
A Tufts University site providing texts in Greek, Latin, and English.

http://www.iranicaonline.org
An online encyclopedia containing numerous articles pertaining to Zoroastrianism and Manichaeism.

References

Assmann, Jan. 2001. *The Search for God in Ancient Egypt*. Ithaca, NY: Cornell University Press.

Bowden, Hugh. 2010. *Mystery Cults of the Ancient World*. Princeton, NJ: Princeton University Press.

Cagni, Luigi. 1977. *The Poem of Erra*. Malibu, CA: Undena Publications.

Chadwick, J., and W. N. Mann. 1950. *Hippocratic Writings*. London: Penguin.

Connelly, Joan Breton. 2007. *Portrait of a Priestess: Women and Ritual in Ancient Greece*. Princeton, NJ: Princeton University Press.

Dillon, Matthew. 2002. *Girls and Women in Classical Greek Religion*. London: Routledge.

Feeney, Denis. 1998. *Literature and Religion at Rome: Cultures, Contexts, and Beliefs*. Cambridge: Cambridge University Press.

Foster, Benjamin. 2005. *Before the Muses*. 3rd ed. Bethesda, MD: CDL Press.

Kramer, Samuel Noah. 1963. *The Sumerians*. Chicago: University of Chicago Press.

Lambert, W. G. 1960. *Babylonian Wisdom Literature*. Oxford: Oxford University Press.

Lattimore, Richard. 1947. *Pindar's Odes*. Chicago: University of Chicago Press.

Lesher, J. H. 1992. *Xenophanes of Colophon*. Toronto: University of Toronto Press.

Lichtheim, Miriam. 1973–1980. *Ancient Egyptian Literature*. 3 vols. Berkeley: University of California Press.

Mandelbaum, Allen. 1993. *The Metamorphoses of Ovid*. San Diego: Harcourt.

O'Donnell, James. 2015. *Pagans: The End of Traditional Religion and the Rise of Christianity*. New York: HarperCollins.

Parker, Robert. 2011. *On Greek Religion*. Ithaca, NY: Cornell University Press.

Rives, James B. 2007. *Religion in the Roman Empire*. Oxford: Blackwell.

Sasson, Jack M., ed. 1995. *Civilizations of the Ancient Near East*. Vol. 3. New York: Charles Scribner's Sons.

Segal, Alan F. 2004. *Life after Death: A History of the Afterlife in Western Religions*. New York: Doubleday.

Thom, Johan. 2005. *Cleanthes' Hymn to Zeus*. Tubingen, Germany: Mohr Siebeck.

Wilkinson, Toby. 2010. *The Rise and Fall of Ancient Egypt*. New York: Random House.

4 Jewish Traditions

Michele Murray

Traditions at a Glance

Numbers

There are approximately 14 million Jews worldwide.

Distribution

The majority of Jews live in either the United States (5–6 million) or Israel (6 million). There are about 1.5 million Jews in Europe, 400,000 in Latin America, and 375,000 in Canada.

Founders and Leaders

Abraham, his son Isaac, and Isaac's son Jacob are considered the patriarchs of the Jews; the prophet Moses, who is said to have received the Torah from God and revealed it to the Israelites, is known as the Lawgiver.

Deity

Judaism's sole deity is Yahweh.

Authoritative Texts

Judaism takes as its central texts the Hebrew Bible (Tanakh), the Mishnah, and the Talmud.

Noteworthy Teachings

Two passages from the Hebrew Bible are central to the Jewish tradition. The first is Deuteronomy 6: 4–9: "Hear O Israel, the LORD our God, the LORD is One. You shall love the LORD your God with all your heart and with all your soul and with all your strength. These words which I command you this day are to be kept in your heart. You shall repeat them to your children, speaking of them indoors and outdoors, morning and night. You shall bind them as a sign upon your hand and wear them as signs upon your forehead; you shall write them on the doorposts of your houses and on your gates." The second is Leviticus 19:18: "You shall not take vengeance or bear a grudge against any of your people, but you shall love your neighbor as yourself: I am the LORD."

In this chapter you will learn about:

- Jewish history from biblical times to the present day
- The diverse expressions of Jewish identity throughout that history
- How Jews responded to struggle and adversity in their past, how their responses shaped Judaism, and how Judaism affected their responses
- Jewish rituals and practices, and their connections to events in Jewish history
- How it is possible to identify oneself as a Jew and even take part in religious services and observances without necessarily believing in God
- How Jewish women are now challenging some ancient traditions within Judaism

⊕ Jewish Identity as Ethnicity and Religion

Jewishness can be grounded in religious, ethnic, or cultural elements, or any combination of these three. Some Jews feel their Jewishness to be inseparable from Jewish religious practices and customs. Others—in fact, the majority of Jews in North America and Israel—rarely if ever attend **synagogue** (the place of congregational worship) and make no attempt to follow the rules set down by

Jerusalem: view from the Mount of Olives (Fred Froese/Getty Images).

Alina Treiger—the first female rabbi to be installed in Germany since the Holocaust—introduces herself to her congregation at the synagogue in Oldenburg on November 4, 2010 (AP Photo/Marcel Mettelsiefen, pool).

Timeline

c. 1850 BCE	Abraham (Abram) arrives in Canaan
c. 1260	Moses leads the Exodus from Egypt and Yahweh reveals the Torah to the Israelites
c. 1000	David takes Jerusalem and makes it his capital
921	Northern kingdom separates following Solomon's death
722	Assyrians conquer northern kingdom and disperse its people
586	Babylonians conquer Jerusalem and deport its leaders
539	Persians conquer Babylonia, permitting exiles to return in 538 BCE
c. 515	Rededication of the Second Temple
c. 333	Alexander the Great's conquests in the eastern Mediterranean begin the process of Hellenization
c. 200	Torah translated from Hebrew into Greek (the Septuagint)
167–164	Maccabean Revolt

70 CE	Romans lay siege to Jerusalem and destroy the Second Temple
132–135	Bar Kochba Revolt
c. 220	Mishnah of Rabbi Judah ha-Nasi compiled
c. 400	The Palestinian (or Jerusalem) Talmud compiled
c. 500	The Babylonian Talmud compiled
1135	Birth of Moses Maimonides, author of *The Guide of the Perplexed* (d. 1204)
1492	Jews expelled from Spain
1569	Kabbalah scholar Isaac Luria establishes a center of Jewish mysticism in the northern Palestinian city of Safed
1666	Sabbatai Zvi is promoted as the messiah
1698	Birth of Israel ben Eliezer, the Baal Shem Tov, in Poland (d. 1760)
1729	Birth of Moses Mendelssohn, pioneer of Reform Judaism in Germany (d. 1786)
1881	Severe pogroms in Russia spur Jewish emigration
1889	Conservative Judaism separates from Reform Judaism in the United States
1897	Theodor Herzl organizes the first Zionist Congress
1935	Nuremberg Laws revoke many rights of Jews in Germany
1938	November 9–10: *Kristallnacht*, the "Night of Broken Glass," when Jewish businesses and synagogues are attacked across Germany as a prelude to the Holocaust
1939–1945	Second World War and Holocaust
1947	Discovery of the Dead Sea Scrolls
1948	Establishment of the state of Israel
2016	Shimon Peres, former president and prime minister of Israel and key negotiator of the Oslo Accords, dies at age 93
2017	Unprecedented interfaith dialogue and cooperation among Jews and Muslims in United States

Halakhah (Jewish Law). They consider themselves to be ethnically Jewish because they were born to Jewish parents, and they may or may not identify with aspects of secular Jewish culture (music, literature, food, and so on), but the religious dimension is not important to them.

The spectrum of Jewish identity is broad, and what one Jew may consider an essential part of that identity may not hold any significance for another. Who ought to be called Jewish and what constitutes acceptable Jewish behavior are subjects of ongoing debate among Jews themselves.

⊕ Earliest Jewish History: The Biblical Story

Any discussion of Jewish history must begin with the **Hebrew Bible**, also known to Jews as the **Tanakh** and to Christians as the Old Testament (Jews do not use the latter term, which reflects the Christian idea that the Hebrew Bible was superseded by the New Testament). Although often referred to as a book, the Hebrew Bible is in fact an anthology of 24 books, many of which were initially separate. They represent an assortment of literary forms, including poems, songs, legal prose, and vivid narratives full of drama and supernatural events. Most scholars believe they were composed by a variety of authors from different segments of society from approximately the tenth to the second century BCE. Eventually the separate books were assembled into a single canonical collection. There were many additional writings that could have been selected for inclusion in this canon, but the Jewish community by this time had come to recognize only a certain set of documents as theologically meaningful and authoritative.

The Hebrew Bible is divided into three sections: Torah, Nevi'im, and Ketuvim. ("TaNaKh" is an acronym based on the first letters of the three section names.) "Torah" is a Hebrew word that has two meanings. In its broad sense it designates the law or instruction of God and as such is another way of referring to the Hebrew Bible as a whole. In its narrow sense it refers specifically to the first five books of the Hebrew Bible (Genesis, Exodus, Leviticus, Numbers, and Deuteronomy), which recount the history of the **Israelites** from the creation of the world until the entry into the Promised Land and tell them how to live moral and ritually acceptable lives. Also known collectively as the **Pentateuch** (Greek for "five books"), they are considered the most sacred part of the entire Hebrew Bible. "Nevi'im" is the Hebrew word for "prophets": men such as Moses, who were believed to speak for God to the Israelites. The third section, "Ketuvim" ("writings"), includes songs, prayers, and wisdom literature (i.e., the books of Job, Proverbs, and Ecclesiastes, which offer practical advice for dealing with common human concerns) as well as historical texts.

The Biblical Narrative as Sacred History

The biblical people of Israel, the Israelites, were the precursors of modern Jews, and the majority of Jewish festivals, rituals, and customs are derived from biblical stories. Although in most cases there is no evidence that the events they describe ever occurred, or even that the people involved in them actually existed, it was not the goal of the stories' human authors to record an objective account of historical events. Rather, they sought to convey a theological message and teach the Israelites how to live a devout life. Although some of the Tanakh stories do contain accurate historical information, we should not assume any of them to be entirely factual.

The biblical narrative is more properly understood as "sacred" history—it provides insight into the characters and events that came to be considered theologically meaningful for the Jewish community. Among the figures whose existence cannot be confirmed are Abraham, his son Isaac, Isaac's son Jacob, and Moses. The earliest biblical figure for whom we may have archaeological evidence is David, the king of Israel. Yet even this evidence—an inscription on a monumental stela—is disputed by a few scholars.

The Origins of "Israel," "Hebrew," "Jew," and "Semitic"

The earliest reference to the people of Israel outside the Bible is found on an Egyptian stela from approximately 1208 BCE, which is inscribed with a hymn recording the pharaoh's triumphs. In a verse that reads "Israel is wasted, its seed is not . . ." (Hallo 2003: 41), "Israel" almost certainly refers to an ethnic group or people. By the end of the thirteenth century BCE, then, it seems that a people calling themselves "Israel" existed in Canaan (roughly the region comprising modern Israel, the Palestinian territories, Lebanon, and part of Syria).

The origins of the term "Israel" are not certain, although one interpretation ("the one who struggled with God") links the name with a story in which Abraham's grandson Jacob wrestles with a divine being and is then renamed "Israel." Two other terms used on occasion in the Tanakh are "Hebrew(s)" and "Jew(s)." Abraham, for example, is called a Hebrew, and the prophet Jonah identifies himself as a Hebrew. In modern usage, "Hebrew" is reserved for languages: the ancient Hebrew of the Bible and the modern Hebrew that is one of the two official languages of the modern state of Israel (the other is Arabic). The word "Jew" is derived from "Judah," the name of the territory that in ancient times was considered the Jewish homeland. "Semitic" is derived from "Shem," the name of the man from whom both Jews and Arabs are said to have descended. (According to the biblical story, Shem was one of three sons of the legendary Noah, builder of the ark that survived the great flood sent by God to destroy creation.)

When Was the Torah Written Down?

Traditional Jews (for example, those belonging to the Orthodox branch of Judaism) hold that the Torah was divinely revealed to the prophet Moses at Mount Sinai and written down by him as a single document. However, most contemporary biblical scholars believe the Torah to be a composite of texts composed at different times by different human beings. Although the basic assumption that the Bible is a human rather than a divine creation has drawn vigorous criticism from traditional Jews, Christians, and Muslims alike, it is now widely accepted that the Torah texts represent multiple voices. The second book of the Torah, Exodus, tells how Moses, with divine help, led the Israelites out of slavery in Egypt and eventually, after 40 years of wandering in the desert, to the Promised Land of Canaan. Some scholars suggest that part of Exodus may have been written as early as the thirteenth century BCE.

Other scholars suggest that the writing process may have begun during a time of crisis when it was feared that the oral traditions might be lost if they were not recorded. Two such periods were the eighth century BCE, after the northern kingdom of Israel fell to the Assyrians, and the sixth century BCE, after Jerusalem fell to the Babylonians and the leaders of the Israelites were sent into exile in Babylonia.

It is probably safe to assume that the earliest material to have been written down was the Torah. The first five books likely took their final form in the post-exilic period, sometime between the sixth and fourth centuries BCE. The Nevi'im were probably finalized around 200 BCE, and the Ketuvim by the second century CE. The most recent book in the Hebrew Bible is that of Daniel, the final chapters of which (7–12) were composed after 167 BCE (even though the narrative is written as if the events it describes took place during the time of the Exile).

Passover is the first of three major festivals known collectively as the *Shalosh Regalim* ("Three Pilgrimages"), for which the Torah commanded the ancient Israelites to make a pilgrimage to Jerusalem; the other two are Shavuot and Sukkot.

Relationship as Covenant: The Israelites and Their God

The Bible identifies the Israelites as God's chosen people. On the one hand, they have been chosen by Yahweh: "For you are a people holy to the LORD your God; the LORD your God has chosen you out of all the peoples on earth to be his people, his treasured possession" (Deuteronomy 7:6). On the other hand, the Israelites have themselves chosen Yahweh: "Then Joshua said to the people, 'You are witnesses against yourselves that you have chosen the LORD, to serve him.' And they

Practice

Passover

Passover (*Pesach* in Hebrew) commemorates the liberation of the Israelites from slavery in Egypt. It falls in the spring, and its focal point is the ritual meal called the **Seder** ("order"), during which a text called the **Haggadah** is read aloud. Relating the story of the **Exodus** from Egypt, it celebrates the fact that death passed over the Israelites when God sent a plague to destroy all of the firstborn children of Egypt. During Passover Jews eat only unleavened bread (bread without yeast) to remind them that the Israelites had to flee Egypt so quickly that they could not wait for their bread to rise. In fact, all cereal products are forbidden over the holiday, because they could ferment: only the unleavened bread called matzo is allowed.

The Seder is a joyous occasion, a gathering of family and friends that should include a spirited discussion of the holiday's meaning. The centerpiece of the Seder table is a plate of five or six symbolic foods. A vegetable, typically a piece of parsley or celery, represents spring or hope, and before it is eaten it is dipped in saltwater, which symbolizes the tears

of the Israelites. Horseradish recalls the bitterness of slavery, while *kharoset*—a mixture of fruit, nuts, wine, and spices—recalls the mortar from which the Israelite slaves made bricks for the pharaoh. A shankbone from a lamb echoes the lamb's blood with which Israelites marked their doorways, signaling their presence to God so that he would "pass over" their houses without taking their firstborn. A hard-boiled egg symbolizes either fertility or mourning for the loss of the two historic Temples in Jerusalem. Finally, a bitter vegetable, often a piece of romaine lettuce, is an optional second symbol of the harsh life of a slave. Jews retell the story of the Exodus as if all those present had been liberated from slavery in Egypt themselves.

It is the custom to reserve some wine in a special cup for the prophet Elijah, whose return to earth will herald the coming of the Messianic Age, a time of peace and prosperity for all. At one point in the evening the door to the house is even held open for him to come in and partake of the Passover meal.

said, 'We are witnesses'" (Joshua 24:22). It is unlikely that the Israelites understood their selection by Yahweh to mark them out as superior to other peoples; rather, it obliged them to assume the responsibilities of serving God. Nor was the notion of being a "chosen people" unique to the Israelites; other peoples in the ancient world also understood themselves to have been chosen by their deities.

One of the central themes in the Bible's account of the relationship between the Israelites and their God is the **covenant**. The first biblical covenant, described in Genesis 9:8–17, is made when God promises Noah that he will never again send a flood to destroy the world.

Covenants played an important part in the governance of ancient Near Eastern societies. Typically they were made between two parties of unequal power; thus, a powerful ruler would promise protection to a less powerful one on condition that the latter fulfilled certain obligations. What was unique about the Israelites' covenants was that, in exchange for the deity's protection and presence in their lives, they were required to live in accordance with a moral code. Other Near Eastern peoples offered sacrifices to their national or tribal deities in hopes of receiving rainfall, fertility, and prosperity, as well as protection, but they did not promise to behave in an ethical manner as part of the pact.

The Book of Genesis traces Israelite ancestry back to a single patriarch, a descendant of Noah named Abraham. According to this account, Abraham left his birthplace in Mesopotamia (present-day Iraq and Syria) and traveled with his extended family toward the land of Canaan. Although much of the family decided to stay at a midway point, God told Abraham to continue on to Canaan, where they made a covenant that shared many of the elements outlined earlier. God, who was obviously the more powerful of the two parties, promised that he would give the land of Canaan to Abraham's still-unborn offspring on condition that Abraham show perfect obedience to him. Many years later, Abraham agreed to God's request that he undergo circumcision as a sign of their covenant (Genesis 17). Then, in fulfillment of another promise that God made to Abraham, his wife Sarah miraculously produced a son, Isaac, even though she was now well past childbearing age. Later still, God asked Abraham to sacrifice the young Isaac as a burnt offering, and Abraham prepared to fulfill his part of the bargain (Genesis 22). But just as he was about to plunge the knife into his son's body, an angel intervened, instructing him to free Isaac and sacrifice a ram instead. Abraham, who had shown that he was willing to obey God even if it meant sacrificing his beloved son, became the ultimate model of obedience for the Israelite people.

A seder plate makes a colorful centerpiece for the Passover table. The six symbolic foods can be seen clockwise from the top: a hard-boiled egg; a shankbone; a "mortar" of apples, nuts, wine, and spices; a piece of lettuce; parsley, and horseradish (© ZUMA Press, Inc./Alamy).

Abraham's son Isaac and Isaac's son Jacob in turn made further covenants with God, but it was only centuries later that Moses made a covenant with God on behalf of the Israelites. The Decalogue—Latin for "ten words," also known as the Ten Commandments—which Moses transmitted to the Israelites at Mount Sinai, stipulated the people's duties both to God and to one another. This aspect of the Torah confirms that ethical behavior was an obligatory component of the Israelites' covenant with God.

The second book of the Torah, Exodus, describes how God, through Moses, led the Israelites out of Egypt to Mount Sinai, where he revealed his commandments, beginning with the Decalogue. Then Moses went up the mountain and stayed there for 40 days and 40 nights.

Lost without Moses, the Israelites persuaded his brother Aaron to make a god to lead them. Aaron collected the people's gold earrings, melted them down, and used the gold to create an idol in the form of a golden calf. They were worshiping the calf when Moses descended from the mountain with the stone tablets on which God had engraved his commandments—the second of which forbade the making of idols. Enraged, Moses hurled the tablets to the ground, shattering them; he then destroyed the golden idol and, with the help of those who had not taken part in the idol worship, put to death 3,000 who had. The Israelites subsequently spent the next 40 years wandering in the desert; then, within sight of the Promised Land of Canaan, Moses died. Leadership of the people of Israel was transferred to Joshua, who guided them across the Jordan River to take possession of Canaan.

According to the book of Joshua, the Israelites annihilated the people of Canaan. But there is no archaeological evidence to support this account, and many biblical scholars argue that it was constructed to convey the theologically important idea of the Israelites' taking full possession of

Practice

Circumcision

Judaism, like other religious traditions, uses rituals to commemorate important transitional moments in a person's life. Circumcision is one of the best known of these rituals, and the first one performed on a Jewish male, usually eight days after birth. Just as Abraham underwent circumcision as a sign of the covenant between him and God, so too does every male born into a Jewish family. Known as a *Brit milah* ("covenant of circumcision") in Hebrew, the ritual is called a "**bris**" in **Yiddish**, the vernacular language of central and eastern European Jews. It involves the removal of the foreskin from the penis by a ritual circumciser called a **mohel**. Usually the ceremony is conducted at home in the presence of family members and friends, although it can also take place in a synagogue. The only people who are required to be present are the father, the mohel, and the *sandek*, the person who holds the baby while the circumcision is performed. Traditionally, the baby is then named and a celebratory meal is served that connects the presence of a new life with the joy of sharing food with family and friends. Blessings for the child and his parents are also recited as part of the ritual.

Today, many Jewish families are finding formal ways of expressing their joy at the birth of daughters as well. The more liberal branches of Judaism hold a naming ceremony called a **Simchat Bat** ("joy of a daughter") that celebrates the bringing of a daughter both into the family and into the covenant with God. Since there is no explicit ritual formula to follow, families tend to create their own traditions: some invite relatives and friends to share a meal, while others make the event more of a traditional ceremony, including various prayers and blessings.

the land that had been promised to their ancestor Abraham. Archaeological findings reveal that the earliest Israelite communities were built not on the ruins of Canaanite settlements, but on formerly uninhabited land in the central highlands. As a result, most scholars now understand the acquisition of Canaan to have been accomplished through settlement rather than military conquest.

The Personal Name of God

The God with whom all these biblical figures made their covenants has a personal name, which is represented in Hebrew by four consonants: YHWH. Although this **Tetragrammaton** ("four-letter word") is conventionally written as "Yahweh," no one knows how it ought to be pronounced, since there are no vowels between the consonants. In any case, many Jews consider the Tetragrammaton too sacred to ever be pronounced. Indeed, the Decalogue commands that God's name not be taken in vain. Modern Jews reading the Tanakh aloud substitute "Adonai" ("Lord") or "haShem" ("the Name") for "YHWH." English translations normally use capital letters ("the LORD" or "GOD").

In the sixteenth century, a mistaken belief that the vowels of "Adonai" were those belonging to the Tetragrammaton produced the name "Jehovah." At that time Protestants were in a power struggle against the Church of Rome, and to buttress their arguments they turned to the original Hebrew and Aramaic texts. But they were not well versed in these languages and did not realize that the vowels they were combining with the Tetragrammaton were in fact those of another word

Document

The Decalogue (Ten Commandments)

The terms of the covenant into which Yahweh and the Israelites enter are presented in the Decalogue, also called the Ten Commandments. The Decalogue appears twice in the Torah: in the second book, Exodus (20:2–17) and in the fifth, Deuteronomy (5:6–21). The first five commandments concern responsibilities to God; the second, to fellow human beings.

I am the LORD your God who brought you out of Egypt, out of the land of slavery.

You shall have no other god to set against me.

You shall not make a carved image for yourself nor the likeness of anything in the heavens above, or on the earth below, or in the waters under the earth. You shall not bow down to them or worship them; for I, the LORD your God, am a jealous god. I punish the children for the sins of the fathers to the third and fourth generations of those who hate me. But I keep faith with thousands, with those who love me and keep my commandments.

You shall not make wrong use of the name of the LORD your God: The LORD will not leave unpunished the man who misuses his name.

Remember to keep the sabbath day holy. You have six days to labor and do all your work. But the seventh day is a sabbath of the LORD your God; that day you shall not do any work, you, your son or your daughter, your slave or your slave-girl, your cattle or the alien within your gates; for in six days the LORD made heaven and earth, the sea, and all that is in them, and on the seventh day he rested. Therefore the LORD blessed the sabbath day and declared it holy.

Honor your father and mother, that you may live long in the land which the LORD your God is giving you.

You shall not commit murder.

You shall not commit adultery.

You shall not steal.

You shall not give false evidence against your neighbor.

You shall not covet your neighbor's house; you shall not covet your neighbor's wife, his slave, his slave-girl, his ox, his ass, or anything that belongs to him. (Exodus 20:2–17)

altogether. To this day, certain Christians (in particular, Jehovah's Witnesses) continue to use the name "Jehovah," but it has never been used by Jews.

Of Kings and Messiahs

It is possible that the biblical David—an obscure shepherd who, according to one tradition, killed the giant Goliath with his slingshot and became king—is based on a historical figure. David, whose reign is said to have begun around 1000 BCE, is identified as the Israelites' greatest king, the ruler against whom every future leader of Judah is compared. As part of the inauguration ritual, the new king was anointed with oil. The Hebrew term *mashiach*, from which the English "**messiah**" is derived—as is the Greek form, "Christos," hence "Christ"—is directly related to this ritual, as it means "anointed

Practice

Shavuot

Shavuot celebrates God's revelation of the Torah to Moses, although its origins can be traced to the barley harvest held in the ancient land of Israel. Also known as the Festival of Weeks, it is the second of the *Shalosh Regalim*.

By the mid-second century CE, Shavuot was being marked by readings of the Decalogue and the Book of Ruth (set during the barley harvest). Another tradition, still observed today by religious Jews, is to stay up the entire night of Shavuot reading from a special volume that contains passages from every book of the Bible and every section of the rabbinic commentary on it (the Mishnah); this ritual, introduced by sixteenth-century mystics, represents devotion to the Torah. A third tradition is to eat sweet dairy foods such as cheesecake and cheese blintzes, possibly because they recall the description of the Torah as "honey and milk . . . under your tongue" (Song of Songs 4:11). Usually falling in late May or early June, Shavuot is celebrated for just one day in Israel, but for two days by most Jews living elsewhere.

[one]." Thus David was a messiah. He was also a warrior king credited with conquering an impressive number of neighboring peoples and establishing a kingdom that his son Solomon inherited.

Solomon built the First Temple in Jerusalem as a focal point for national identity and worship, the latter primarily being carried out in the form of sacrifices. After his death in the second half of the tenth century BCE, the kingdom split in two: Israel in the north and Judah in the south. From this point on, the historicity of events described in the Hebrew Bible is on firmer ground.

The Exile in Babylonia

Some two centuries later (c. 722 BCE), the northern kingdom fell to the superpower of the region, the Assyrians. The victors deported some of the Israelites to other parts of their empire and imported people from elsewhere into Israel, destroying its national cohesion. The Israelites remaining

Practice

Sukkot

Sukkot commemorates the Israelites' wanderings in the wilderness. It is an eight-day holiday during which—weather permitting—Jews eat and sleep in the open air in a temporary structure called a *sukkah* ("booth" or "tabernacle"; *sukkot* is the plural form). The *sukkah* should have a roof made of organic material such as leaves and branches, and the sky must be visible through gaps in it. This symbolizes the Israelites' willingness to put themselves directly under divine protection. Usually falling in September or October, Sukkot is said to have taken its name from the temporary shelters that farmers used in autumn to guard their ripening crops. It is the third and last of the *Shalosh Regalim*.

in the south fell to a later superpower, the Babylonians, in 586 BCE, at which time the Temple in Jerusalem was destroyed and the Israelites' political and religious leaders were deported to Babylonia (modern-day Iraq) to prevent them from stirring up trouble in their homeland. Thus began the Babylonian captivity, or "**Exile**."

Focus

Samaritans

The Samaritans are an ancient people who still inhabit the region of Samaria, in the center of modern Israel. Although they identify themselves as Jews, some believe that they were the product of intermarriage between the people who were not deported by the Assyrians and those brought to the region from elsewhere. In any event, the Samaritans broke away from mainstream Jewish beliefs and practices in about the fifth century BCE. The Jerusalem Temple was never their holy place—they had their own temple on Mount Gerizim in Samaria, although it was destroyed in the second century BCE and never rebuilt—and their Bible consists of the Torah or Pentateuch alone. Although they number only about 600 today, during Passover they still offer sacrifices at the foot of Mount Gerizim.

Samaritan priests prepare a firepit for their Passover sacrifices, held at the foot of Mount Gerizim in Samaria (© www.BibleLandPictures.com/Alamy).

Document

From Psalm 137:1–4

Although tradition attributes the poetic prayers called the Psalms to King David, modern scholars believe they were composed by a multitude of post-exilic authors. Indeed, the Exile is a frequent theme of these works. Psalm 137, for example, expresses an exile's longing for his home, Jerusalem.

By the rivers of Babylon,
   there we sat,
      sat and wept,
      as we thought of Zion.
There on the poplars
   we hung up our lyres,
      for our captors asked us there for songs,
      our tormentors, for amusement,
      "Sing us one of the songs of Zion."
How can we sing a song of the Lord on alien soil? . . .

The Exile is of paramount importance in Israelite–Jewish history. Marking the beginning of the **Diaspora**—the dispersion of Jews outside Israel—it reverberates throughout the Hebrew Bible in passages evoking the trauma of alienation from the homeland, which Jews have dealt with throughout their history (see Document box containing Psalm 137:1–4). One important theological development associated with the Exile was the first unambiguous statement of monotheism: the belief in a single god, creator of the universe. Scholars theorize that, far from their homeland, the exiles recast their national deity as universal. The earliest writer to describe Yahweh as the only god was the unnamed prophet who is believed to have composed chapters 40 to 55 of the Book of Isaiah: in Isaiah 45:21, for example, he has Yahweh declare that "there is no other god besides me, a righteous God and a Savior; there is no one besides me."

The Exile came to an end in 539 BCE, when Cyrus of Persia (modern-day Iran) conquered the Babylonians and freed their captives. Many Judeans then returned to their homeland, but after nearly five decades in Babylonia, a sizable number had put down roots there, and they decided to stay. In time, Babylonia would become one of Judaism's most vibrant intellectual centers. It was the Babylonian Jewish community that produced one of the central texts in the history of Judaism: the Babylonian Talmud, completed in the sixth century CE.

⊕ The Second Temple Period (515 BCE–70 CE)

Those who did return to Israel found that their ancestral homeland had been reduced to the area immediately around Jerusalem. Nevertheless, they rebuilt the Temple and (with the help of the Persians) furnished it with many of the gold and silver items that the Babylonians had taken. Rededicated in 515 BCE, the "Second Temple" would endure until 70 CE.

The Impact of Alexander the Great

Alexander the Great (356–323 BCE) brought major cultural shifts to the ancient Near East. The son of the king of Macedon, as a youth Alexander had been tutored by the Greek philosopher Aristotle, and he had no doubt that Greek culture surpassed all others. When his father died, the 20-year-old Alexander set out to become the master of the then known world.

Across Asia Minor (modern-day Turkey) and down into the eastern Mediterranean basin, Alexander established more than 30 cities (20 named after himself), in each of which he established institutions central to Greek civilization, such as theaters and gymnasia. Before long, Greek became the new lingua franca of the region. In this way Alexander laid the foundations for the *cosmopolis* ("world city") and made possible a new sense of interconnectedness among formerly disparate peoples.

Jewish responses to the introduction of Greek culture ("Hellenization") varied widely. While some Jews greatly admired Greek culture and sought to assimilate, many other Jews, particularly in non-urban areas, staunchly rejected all Greek ideas and customs.

The Maccabean Revolt

For over a century, Judea was controlled by the Ptolemies, the Greek dynasty that had ruled Egypt since 305 BCE. In 198 BCE, however, a rival Greek dynasty named the Seleucids, who already ruled Syria, took control of Judea. The territory around Jerusalem became known in Greek as *Ioudaia*, and a person from there was an *Ioudaios*.

Antiochus IV Epiphanes (r. 175–163 BCE) was a Seleucid who strongly advocated assimilation to Greek culture in the territories he ruled. He prohibited the reading and teaching of the Mosaic Law, commanded that Torah scrolls be burned, and made observation of the **Sabbath** (the seventh day) a crime punishable by death.

The most egregious actions of all were directed against the Temple, where Antiochus erected altars to other gods, placed a statue of Zeus in the sanctuary courtyard, and even sacrificed pigs—animals that Israelites were forbidden to eat, let alone offer to their deity—on Yahweh's altar. Antiochus also intervened in the selection of the Temple's high priest and, when Jews objected, imposed further restrictions on them. His ultimate goal might well have been to promote political unity, but since religion was intertwined with all aspects of life in that era, the Judeans interpreted his actions as a comprehensive attack on their way of life.

Jews who refused to transgress the laws of their faith were often tortured and put to death, and some Jews interpreted the persecution as a sign that the end of the world was imminent. This **apocalyptic** perspective is also reflected in the later chapters of the Book of Daniel, which describe the toppling of Antiochus from his throne.

The Hasmonean Family

In 167 BCE, a family of priests known as the Hasmoneans mounted a successful uprising against Antiochus and Hellenized Jews. One member named Judah and his brothers coordinated a band of fighters whose guerrilla-style warfare proved unexpectedly effective. Judah's prowess as a fighter and leader earned him the nickname "Maccabee" ("the Hammer"), from which the revolt as a whole derives its name. The Maccabeans recaptured the Temple, purged it of foreign idols and impure animals, and rededicated it to its rightful deity in 164 BCE. It is this rededication that is recalled by the annual Hanukkah holiday (see Practice box).

Establishing themselves as client kings of the Seleucids, the Hasmoneans ruled from 164 to 63 BCE in precarious semi-independence during a time of profound sectarian discord and civil war. Eventually many of them willingly adopted Hellenistic culture. In 63 BCE, however, the Roman general Pompey secured Jerusalem and made the state a vassal of Rome, bringing Jewish self-rule to an end.

A Variety of Judaisms

An astonishing variety of Jewish groups emerged during the Hasmonean period. Then as now, there were competing views about who was a Jew, what it meant to be a Jew, and how Jews should relate to non-Jews. Because of this diversity, it is more accurate to refer to "Judaisms" than "Judaism" in the Second Temple period.

Sadducees and Pharisees

The Sadducees came primarily from the wealthy upper echelons of society. They made up most of the membership of the Sanhedrin, the local Jewish council, and were responsible for the running of the Temple, in particular the sacrificial system. Considering the Torah to be the only authoritative text, they demanded a narrow, literal interpretation of it and focused on cultic worship as Jews' primary obligation.

By contrast, the Pharisees sought to apply Halakhah to everyday life—that is, to ensure that daily lives were lived in accordance with the Torah. In contrast to the Sadducees, the Pharisees tended to interpret the scriptural text broadly. They had a social conscience; practiced almsgiving, prayer, and fasting; and believed in the resurrection and future day of judgment. For them, the entire Tanakh was sacred and worthy of study.

Among their concerns were the Torah's instructions regarding matters such as food purity, Sabbath observance, and family issues. For example, the Decalogue called on Jews to keep the Sabbath day holy. But what did that mean in practical terms? If it meant refraining from work on the Sabbath, how did one define "work"? The Pharisees not only formulated answers to such questions but established rules and instructions to help Jews observe the Law. In time, these teachings attained the status of divinely revealed law and came to be known as the Oral Law or Oral Torah.

Essenes

The Essenes are generally held to have been the authors of the Dead Sea Scrolls, a collection of texts produced between the second and first centuries BCE that were discovered in 1947. These manuscripts shed light on the worldview of the Essenes—a monastic community of meticulously observant priests. They also include the earliest manuscripts of nearly every book of the Hebrew Bible.

Practice
Hanukkah

Hanukkah, the festival of lights, commemorates the return of the Temple to the Jews by Judah the Maccabee and his brothers. According to the legend, when the Temple was purified, only one vial of oil could be found to light the seven-branched oil lamp called the **menorah**. This amount of oil should have run out after one day, but—miraculously—it lasted for eight days. For this reason Hanukkah is celebrated by lighting a candle on a special menorah for eight consecutive days and eating foods cooked in oil, such as potato latkes (pancakes) and *sufganiot* (doughnuts filled with jam or caramel).

Like the Pharisees, the Essenes sought to apply the Bible to daily life, but in a much more rigorous manner. They established their community at Qumran in the Judean desert after expressing disapproval of the way the Hasmoneans were running the Temple cult. They held an apocalyptic worldview, believing that the world was under the control of evil forces and that God would soon intervene to defeat the powers of darkness. The Essenes thought of themselves as the new children of Israel, biding their time until the day when, with God's help, they would take back the Promised Land from the corrupt leadership of Hellenized Jews.

Zealots

The Zealots did not exist as an organized group until well into the first century CE. In contrast to the Sadducees, the Zealots vehemently refused to cooperate with Rome, and they encouraged their fellow Jews to engage in violent rebellion. The result was the First Jewish Revolt (66–73 CE), in the course of which most of Jerusalem, including the Temple, was destroyed and much of the Jewish population was either killed or forced into slavery.

Other Visions of the Future

Further expressions of diversity can be seen in the varied expectations for the future held by Jews in this period. Some hoped for a messiah who would lead them out from under Roman oppression. Until the end of Judean monarchic rule in 586 BCE, the term *mashiach*, "anointed one," had referred exclusively to the current Hebrew king. But by Hellenistic times the idea of an "anointed" king had moved out of the world of current possibility and into the realm of anticipation: now the *mashiach* was the ideal future king whom God would empower to defeat Israel's enemies. The Essenes awaited two messiahs: one a king and one a priest.

Not all expectations centered on a messiah, however. Some Jews hoped for a new covenant between God and his people; others, a new era of justice and equality. There were also some who

Practice
Purim

Purim is a joyful minor holiday that falls around March. The Book of Esther tells how the Jews of Persia were saved from the evil plot of a Persian official named Haman, who sought to exterminate them. Esther, a wise and beautiful Jewish woman, and her uncle Mordecai together prevented the destruction of the Jews. Since the holiday celebrates deliverance from a physical threat, it focuses on material rather than spiritual things. When the Book of Esther is read in the synagogue, members of the congregation use noise-makers or bang pots and pans to drown out every mention of Haman's name. There is also a festive meal, at which guests are expected to drink enough wine to be unable to distinguish between "Blessed be Mordecai" and "Cursed be Haman." Finally, there are costume parties and gifts of food, especially *hamantashen*, cookies (traditionally filled with poppy seeds) that are supposed to resemble the ears of Haman.

looked forward to a time when Jerusalem would become central to the world and all peoples would worship God at Mount **Zion**. The range of thought regarding the future is similarly broad among modern Jews.

Points of Consensus

Diversity of expectations notwithstanding, a degree of consensus did exist concerning certain fundamental factors of the tradition. The majority of Jews, regardless of sect, believed in:

1. The oneness of God. By the Second Temple period, Judaism was a monotheistic tradition centered on the idea of a single, all-powerful creator God.
2. The authority and sacred nature of the Torah.
3. The special status of Israel as the chosen "people of God." Who exactly was included in the "people of God" was a point of contention (as it continues to be in the modern state of Israel). But there was a general belief in both a "people of God" and a "land of God."
4. The status of the Temple in Jerusalem as the place where God and his people met.

Finally, it is important to note that most Jews in late antiquity did not belong to any of the sects discussed here. They simply continued to observe the aspects of the Torah law that their parents, and their parents' parents before them, had observed.

⊕ Enter the Romans (63 BCE)

In time, conflicts among the Hasmonean leaders led to a bloody civil war. In 63 BCE the Roman general Pompey was called to Judea to settle the rivalry among the various contenders for the Hasmonean throne. Instead, he took control of the land. Thus began approximately four centuries of repressive Roman rule over Judea.

Herod the Great

In 37 BCE the Romans put an end to the Hasmonean dynasty by naming Herod the Great king of Israel. Herod's governance style was one of self-indulgence, brutality, and deception, yet he was one of the most successful leaders in all of Jewish history, cleverly balancing Roman and Jewish interests. Nevertheless, because he was not of Judean descent—his ancestors were Idumeans, converts to Judaism who inhabited the territory just south of Judea—many Jews did not accept his rule as legitimate.

Although Herod was devoted to Rome and Hellenistic culture, he made many advances on behalf of Judean culture and religion. While he built many impressive public structures, including temples, aqueducts, and theaters, his most famous project was the renovation of the Temple in Jerusalem. He replaced what had been a rather modest building built more than four centuries prior with a stunningly beautiful structure on a much-enlarged site.

The Rabbinic Period (70–700 CE)

In 70 CE the Romans destroyed the Second Temple, which was never rebuilt. Among the only groups to survive were the Pharisees; by the second century CE, however, those who would have been called Pharisees in an earlier time were referred to as **rabbis** (from *rav*, "teacher" in Hebrew).

The Pharisees' oral tradition likewise survived and was developed further under the rabbis, who added their own interpretations to those they inherited. According to rabbinic tradition, God gave Moses the Oral Torah and the written version at the same time. Finally, the Oral Torah was written down and codified around the year 220 CE by Judah haNasi ("Judah the Prince") and in this written form is called the **Mishnah**.

The interpretations developed by the **rabbinic movement** have defined Jewish belief and practice for the past 2,000 years. The teachers and religious leaders who helped to steer Jewish communities after the loss of the Temple replaced sacrificial worship—which was never practiced again—with liturgical prayer and a new emphasis on ethical behavior.

Synagogues (a term drawn from the Greek for "gathering together") already existed while the Temple still stood, but they gained in importance once it was gone. Communal gathering places in which Jews met to read the Torah, to pray, and to study, by the first century CE synagogues were scattered across the Roman Empire. By the end of the first century CE, most Jews were living outside Judea. The total Jewish population was probably between 5 and 6 million, and Jewish communities could be found in every major city of the Roman Empire.

The Talmud and Women

The fact that texts and interpretations, rather than a particular place, became the focus of Judaism helped isolated Jewish communities maintain a sense of unity. Because of the centrality of Torah study to Judaism, literacy rates tended to be higher among Jewish males than among their non-Jewish counterparts. If most Jewish boys learned to read, however, it seems that girls and women were generally excluded from Torah study on the grounds that women's primary domain

This model of Jerusalem in Herod's day (the late first century BCE), including the refurbished Second Temple (above; scale 1:50), was constructed in the 1960s and is now located at the Israel Museum in Jerusalem (© Vladimir Khirman/Alamy).

A woman deep in prayer on the women's side of the Western Wall. Also visible are some of the many prayer requests that, by tradition, the faithful have placed in the cracks (© Michele Murray).

was the home. The limiting of Torah study to males was not unusual for the era in which the rabbis were writing (between roughly the second and sixth centuries CE).

The foundational literature of rabbinic Judaism reflects the interests and concerns of the male rabbis. Women largely were excluded from the rabbinic hierarchies of achievement and exempted from the rituals and activities considered most meritorious, such as the study of Torah and the performance of *mitzvot* ("commandments," the plural of **mitzvah**). Women were typically expected to fulfill only those commandments that were negative ("You shall not . . .") and did not have to be performed at a specific time. While rabbinic Halakhah gave women more freedom and protection than biblical law did, and the rabbis made it possible for some women to inherit, control, and dispose of property, the status of most women—in particular wives and unmarried minor daughters—was clearly subordinate to that of men in all areas of life: judicial, religious, sexual, and economic.

What may be surprising is that the rabbis outlined a set of laws (based on Exodus 21:10) according to which a wife is entitled to three things from her husband: food, clothing, and "marital rights" (i.e., sexual relations). The Talmud specifies how often a man must provide sex for his wife based on his profession, since what he does for a living will affect how long he will be away from her and how physically tired he will be (BT, Ketubbot 5:6). If a husband does not fulfill his duty, he must divorce his wife so that she can find a different husband to meet her sexual needs. Given the period in which the Talmud was composed, this acknowledgment of women's sexual needs seems rather progressive. On the other hand, these laws may have been based on the idea that women's sexuality is so passive that they are not capable of asking for sex or perhaps are not capable of controlling their sexuality and therefore have to be satisfied. The same laws, by prohibiting men from taking vows of abstinence, increased the likelihood that Jews would obey what the rabbis of the Talmudic period considered the first mitzvah (commandment) in the Bible: "Be fruitful and multiply, and fill the earth. . . ." (Genesis 1:28).

And yet, nonrabbinic evidence (such as inscriptions) demonstrates that some women did achieve positions of prestige and influence. Some even served as heads of synagogues, particularly in the Greco-Roman Diaspora, and others were patrons and benefactors of both civic and religious institutions. While it is true that these women would have belonged to the elite and so would have had opportunities that most women would not, they remind us of how important it is to differentiate between the idealized life of the Jewish woman that the rabbis prescribed and the realities of the lives that Jewish women actually lived in antiquity. It was—alas—the idealized image, not the flesh and blood reality, that would determine the norms, roles, and expectations for Jewish women in subsequent centuries.

Another Clash with Rome

The last major Jewish revolt against Roman rule took place between 132 and 135 CE. It is associated with a messianic figure named Shimon Bar Kosiba, who was called by his supporters Bar Cochba ("son of the Star") but was known to his critics as Bar Koziba ("son of the Lie" or "Liar"). The revolt was likely prompted by the emperor Hadrian's plan to establish a Roman city on the remains of Jerusalem and a temple to Jupiter on what had been the site of the Temple. The revolt failed miserably. Those Jews who had been living in Jerusalem were driven out and faced death if they tried to return. It was at this time that the Romans renamed Judea—a Roman province since 6 CE—"Syria-Palestina." Until the establishment of the state of Israel in 1948, Judaism would be mainly a religion of the Diaspora.

Rabbi Hillel

Rabbi Hillel was a popular teacher who was active between 30 BCE and 10 CE, and hence was an older contemporary of Jesus of Nazareth. He was a humble woodworker who became the leader of a religious school (**yeshiva**) and was renowned for his piety. According to a famous story, an impertinent non-Jew once came to Hillel and said that he would convert to Judaism if the rabbi could recite all of the Torah while standing on one foot. Hillel reportedly told him: "What is hateful to you, do not do to your neighbor: that is the entire Torah. The rest is commentary; go and learn it!" Whereas Hillel was said to have been lenient in his interpretation of the Torah, his compatriot and rival, Rabbi Shammai, took a stricter, more literal view. More than 300 arguments between the House of Hillel and the House of Shammai are recorded in the Talmud, and in most cases it was Hillel's interpretation that the rabbinic scholars followed.

Focus

Mishnah and Gemarah: The Talmud

The written version of the Oral Torah, the Mishnah, is divided into six "orders," each of which deals with a particular sphere of life and the laws that govern it, although some also address other subjects. The names of the orders reveal their central topics: Seeds (laws of agriculture), Appointed Seasons (laws governing festivals, fast days, and the Sabbath), Women (laws governing marriage, divorce, betrothal, and adultery, as well as vows), Damages (civil and criminal law, and the most commonly read section of the Mishnah, the "Sayings of the Fathers," a collection of ethical maxims), Holy Things (Temple-related matters such as sacrifices, ritual slaughter, and the priesthood rituals), and Purities (issues of ritual purity and impurity).

The writing of the Mishnah in the early third century CE did not mark the end of rabbinic commentary, however. Over the next few centuries, rabbis in both Babylonia and the land of Israel continued to study and interpret traditional teachings, including the Mishnah. Their commentaries, called **Gemarah** (from an Aramaic root that means "teaching"), were transmitted orally from teacher to student, just as the Oral Law had been. The Gemarah contains both Halakhah (legal material) and **Aggadah** (narrative material). Aggadah includes historical material, biblical commentaries, philosophy, theology, and wisdom literature.

Eventually, this commentary also was written down. The Gemarah produced in Palestine was put into writing in the early fifth century and in that form is called the Palestinian (or Jerusalem) Talmud. The Gemarah produced by Babylonian rabbis was written down about a century later, and it was this "Babylonian Talmud" that gained predominance in the Jewish world; consequently, any general reference to "the Talmud" is understood to refer to this latter collection. Both Talmuds are compendia of law, interpretation, and argument that offer what may be described as a "slice of life" from the rabbinic academies of the time, since the discussions they present (in stream-of-consciousness fashion) often go round and round before reaching a conclusion.

Two Main Rabbinic Centers: Palestine and Babylonia

After the Bar Kochba revolt, Judaism developed under the guidance of the rabbis, the successors of the priestly leaders of the previous period. There were two main centers of development: the Galilee region of northern Palestine and Babylonia, which was now ruled by the Parthians. Relations between Palestinian Jews and the Romans eventually calmed, and the Jews were granted the same treatment as other minorities in the empire, with the extra privilege of exemption from pagan cultic observances. Roman leaders recognized the Jewish patriarch, a descendant of Rabbi Hillel, as the central political leader of the Jewish community. But the situation for Jews deteriorated as the third century progressed, primarily because of a general decline in economic and political circumstances across the Roman Empire that left Palestine relatively impoverished.

In general, conditions were better for Babylonian Jews in that era. When the Persian Sassanids replaced the Parthians in 226 CE, Jews experienced some persecution as a result of the Sassanids' efforts to promote their own religion (Zoroastrianism), but by the middle of the century the Persian rulers were allowing the Jews extensive autonomy under their communal leader in exile.

Intellectual activity flourished in Babylonian academies that rivaled and eventually surpassed in prestige the rabbinic schools of Palestine, thriving as centers of Jewish scholarship until the eleventh century.

The Rise of Christianity

When the Roman emperor Constantine I gave Christians the liberty to practice their faith in 313, he began a process that led to Christianity's becoming the official religion of the Roman Empire in 380. Henceforth all inhabitants of the Byzantine Empire would be expected to follow the Christian faith. This did not bode well for Jews.

Christian attitudes toward Jews had been shaped by the fact that Christianity had begun as a Jewish sect. Jesus was Jewish, as were his earliest disciples, but his message had had only modest success among Jews. By the end of the second century, most new Christians were Gentiles (non-Jews). In time, as Christian leaders sought to differentiate their movement from Judaism, tensions developed, especially with certain Gentiles who identified themselves as Christians but chose to adopt Jewish practices such as circumcision, observe Jewish dietary laws, and attend synagogue. Since these "Judaizers" were undermining Christian efforts at differentiation, Christian leaders such as Paul sought to dissuade them. In his letter to the Galatians (c. 50 CE), for example, he urged Gentile Christians not to tie themselves to "a yoke of slavery" (5:1) by observing Jewish law. Other Christians argued that their movement had superseded Judaism. In response to Christians in Syria, who were still attending synagogue services in the fourth century, the bishop of Antioch, John Chrysostom, preached some of the most vehement anti-Jewish sermons in Christian history, condemning the synagogue as "a whorehouse and a theatre . . . a den of thieves and a haunt of wild animals" (*Against the Judaizers* 1.3). Although this rhetoric was directed at Christian Judaizers, it would eventually be repurposed for use against Jews.

Other early Christian literature, such as the Gospel of Matthew, explicitly blamed the Jews for the death of Jesus (e.g., 24:26); this charge would be recycled in later centuries whenever tensions between Jews and Christians were high. The same gospel contains a diatribe against Jewish leaders that has unfortunately been influential in the formation of anti-Jewish attitudes: "Woe to you scribes and Pharisees, hypocrites! for you are like whitewashed tombs, which outwardly appear beautiful, but within they are full of dead men's bones and all uncleanness. . . . You serpents, you brood of vipers, how are you to escape being sentenced to hell?" (23:27, 32).

By the early fifth century the continuing vitality of Judaism was seen by some as contrary to Christian interests. Now the Roman Empire introduced laws restricting Jewish religious and commercial activities. Jews were forbidden to hold public office, build new synagogues, or marry Christians. They were also prohibited from owning Christian slaves. At a time when slavery was an integral part of the agricultural system, this injunction meant that Jews had no hope of competing economically with Christian farmers (Efron et al. 2009: 134). It also represented a first step in the alienation of Jews from the land, a process that by the Middle Ages would transform them into an almost entirely urban people.

Certain Christian leaders favored banning Judaism entirely and presenting Jews with the choice that the Romans had given Christians themselves in the third century CE: renunciation of their faith or death. The church's approach, formulated in the fifth century by Augustine of Hippo in his *City of God* and later accepted by Pope Gregory I (r. 590–604), was devastating for Jews. Augustine wished Jews to serve as an example of the consequences of not accepting Jesus as messiah. To that

Focus

The Jewish Calendar

The Gregorian calendar, used in the Western world, is based on the solar year of 365.25 days. The Jewish calendar is a lunar calendar, based on 12 months of 29.5 days. Since this adds up to 354 days for a lunar year—about 11 days less than are in a solar year—any given date in the lunar calendar will move backward each year by 11 days. In order to ensure that holidays and festivals consistently fall around the same time of the year, the Jewish calendar adds a thirteenth "leap month" on a fixed schedule of 7 years out of every 19. Today the astronomical calculations are made by experts, and festival dates and leap months are established far in advance.

According to the Gregorian calendar, a new day begins at midnight—the first moment of the morning. By contrast, the Jewish day begins at nightfall, defined as the time when at least three stars can be seen in one glimpse of the sky. Thus the Sabbath begins at nightfall on Friday evening and ends at nightfall on Saturday. This is in accordance with the description of the first day of creation in Genesis 1:5—"And there was evening and there was morning, the first day"—in which evening precedes the day.

end, he proposed that Jews not be eradicated, but rather allowed to live in suffering. To justify his position, Augustine quoted Psalms 59:11, in which David, the ancient king of the Israelites, says of his enemies: "Do not destroy them, lest my people forget."

⊕ Jewish Life under Islam: Seventh to Twelfth Century

Islam emerged in the early seventh century and would soon have a deep impact on Jewish history. Within a few decades, Islamic forces had seized Palestine and Egypt from the Christian Byzantine Empire and Persia from the Persian Empire, and by the end of that century most of the world's Jews resided in a unified Islamic empire encompassing territory from the Iberian Peninsula in the west to India in the east. As a consequence, Jews in Palestine, Egypt, and Spain were liberated from the injustice and oppression they had known under antagonistic Christian rulers. Muslims considered Judaism and Christianity their partners in monotheism and respected them for possessing, as did Islam, a divinely revealed book. Thus Jews and Christians living under Islam were defined as *dhimmis* ("protected peoples") and guaranteed protection of their lives and property, as well as the right to practice their religion, as long as they paid special taxes and adhered to certain rules stipulated in a document called the Pact of Umar.

For Jews, life under Muslim rule was considerably better than it had been under Christian Rome. Without the complicated history shared by Christianity and Judaism, Jewish–Muslim relations were less fraught with tension. In addition, Muslims understood that with Jews they shared not only belief in a single god, but opposition to the use of images in the worship of Yahweh/Allah. Hence they tended to be less suspicious of Jews than of Christians, whose doctrine of the Trinity and pervasive use of crucifixes overtly contradicted Islamic principles.

The period of European decline often called the "Dark Ages," from the seventh to the thirteenth century, was a time of great advances for Islam. And since the majority of the world's Jews lived in the Islamic empire, they benefited from its prosperity. By the end of the eighth century, more Jews in the Muslim world were active in urban trade and commerce than in agriculture. Arabic, originally the language of a small tribal population, was now the language of a vast culture, and it replaced Aramaic as the Jewish lingua franca.

The Gaonic Period

In 750 CE the Abbasid dynasty overthrew the Umayyads, and as a result the capital of the Muslim caliphate moved from Damascus to Baghdad. The main rabbinic academies likewise moved to Baghdad, where they attracted Jewish students from all over the Muslim world. They also attracted letters from rabbis seeking advice from the academies' leaders, the **Gaonim**, on problematic cases involving matters that ranged from divorce and inheritance to commercial affairs. The answers to the rabbis' questions, called **responsa**, reflected the Gaonim's interpretations of Talmudic laws and provided the foundation for later legal and philosophical developments.

The main opposition to the Gaonim came from the **Karaites** ("scripturalists"), a movement founded in Iraq in the eighth century by Anan ben David. Rejecting the principle that the rabbinic interpretations of the Oral Torah/Talmud had the status of divinely revealed truth and arguing that the Tanakh was the exclusive source of legal authority, Ben David encouraged individual Jews to interpret the (written) Torah for themselves, and to favor the plain meaning of the words in their context over the creative explanations of the rabbis. Because of its emphasis on individual interpretation, the Karaite movement was characterized by division and disunity. Nevertheless, it enjoyed significant popular support, and its impact on the rabbinic world was important: the Karaites were the first Jews to make an intensive study of Hebrew grammar and the manuscript traditions of the Bible, and they influenced the codification of the Hebrew text in the tenth century. Although the rabbinic tradition eventually prevailed, largely because the Muslim authorities recognized the rabbis as the official representatives of Judaism, small communities of Karaites still exist today in Israel, Turkey, and elsewhere in the Diaspora.

Maimonides

By the beginning of the eleventh century, Iraq no longer dominated the Muslim world. At the same time the influence of the Gaonim was waning, and instability in Babylonia prompted many Jews to leave for more promising lands.

Some Babylonian Jews headed to Spain, where Jewish culture was blossoming under the Umayyads. But that period too came to an end in the twelfth century, when a puritanical Muslim sect took power and banned both Judaism and Christianity. Many Jews fled Spain as a result.

Among the latter was the family of a judge named Maimon. His son, Moses ben Maimon, better known as **Moses Maimonides** (1135–1204), would become one of the most famous Jewish philosophers and legal scholars of the Islamic age, identified in religious texts as "Rambam" (R-M-B-M, the acronym of "Rabbi Moses ben Maimon").

Focus

Ashkenazim, Sephardim, and Mizrahim

Over time, three distinct Jewish cultural traditions took shape. The oldest by far originated in Babylonia with the exiles who did not return to Judea in the sixth century BCE—the first members of the Diaspora. These Jews, and all the others whose ancestors remained in the general region of the Middle East, eventually came to be known as **Mizrahim** (from the Hebrew meaning "East"). Since many Mizrahi Jews come from Arab countries, the language most closely associated with them is Arabic, but some speak languages such as Persian and Kurdish. Other Jews made their way west to Europe. Those who settled on the Iberian Peninsula (modern Spain and Portugal) came to be known as **Sephardim** (from the Hebrew for "Spain"), while those who turned north toward France and Germany became the **Ashkenazim** (from the Hebrew for "Germany"). From the eighth century until the fifteenth, the Sephardic communities fared significantly better under the

Muslim rulers of Al-Andalus than did the Ashkenazic communities of Christian-dominated Europe.

These two groups are distinct from one another in language, food, and certain religious rituals. **Ladino** (a blend of medieval Spanish and Hebrew that is written in Hebrew characters) is traditionally associated with Sephardic Jews, while Yiddish (which is German-based, with influences from Hebrew and other languages, and written in Hebrew characters) is the lingua franca of the Ashkenazic community. At Passover Sephardic Jews eat rice, corn, and beans—all of which comply with the Passover prohibition on foods made with yeast (such as bread)—but Ashkenazic Jews avoid such foods because when they are cooked they rise and expand just as leavened foods do. In addition to lighting two candles on Sabbath eve, Sephardic Jews light candles in honor of family members who have died. Mizrahi Jews tend to follow Sephardic religious practices.

As an adult, Maimonides ultimately established himself in Egypt—a central hub of Jewish life, at that time under the control of the renowned Salah al-Din (Saladin). Jews were generally treated well at his court, and Maimonides became the personal physician to a high official.

Maimonides was a prolific writer, producing the 14-volume code of Jewish law called **Mishneh Torah** as well as treatises on medicine and logic, but his most important work was philosophical. *The Guide of the Perplexed*, originally written in Arabic, was directed to Jews "perplexed" by the challenges of living in a cosmopolitan and philosophically sophisticated environment that tested their faith. Using Greek philosophy, Maimonides sought to diminish the tension between faith and knowledge and emphasized that learning ought not to undermine faith. He believed that all the biblical commandments were rational, and he argued against the literal interpretation of scripture (see Document box).

Medieval Jewish thought was deeply influenced by Islam. Muslim writers and thinkers had translated the scientific and philosophical works of Greeks such as Plato and Aristotle into Arabic—works that emphasized rational thought and human reason over revelation. Muslims considered Greek philosophy to be part of their culture and did not see it as alien or threatening to the revelatory foundation of Islam. Jewish intellectuals such as Maimonides, inspired by Muslim thinkers to undertake the challenge of connecting philosophy to religion, in turn influenced Jewish thought in Christian Europe.

Document

From Maimonides, *Guide of the Perplexed: On Image* (tzelem) *and Likeness* (demut)

People have thought that in the Hebrew language *image* [*tzelem*] denotes the shape and configuration of a thing. This supposition led them to the pure doctrine of the corporeality of God, on account of His saying: "Let us make man in our image, after our likeness" (Gen. 1:26). . . . [They] deemed that if they abandoned this belief, they would give the lie to the biblical text. . . .

As for the term *likeness* (*demut*), . . . it too signifies likeness in respect of a notion. For the Scriptural dictum, "I am like a pelican in the wilderness" (Ps. 102:7), does not signify that its author resembled the pelican with regard to its wings and feathers, but that

his sadness was like that of the bird. . . . Now man possesses as his proprium something in him that is very strange as it is not found in anything else that exists under the sphere of the moon, namely, intellectual apprehension. In the exercise of this, no sense, no part of the body, none of the extremities are used; and therefore this apprehension was likened to the apprehension of the Deity. . . . It was because of this something, I mean because of the divine intellect conjoined with man, that it is said of the latter that he is "in the image of God and in His likeness" (Gen. 1:26–7), not that God, may He be exalted, is a body and possesses a shape. (Twersky 1972: 246–247)

⊕ Jews in the Christian World: Seventh to Fifteenth Century

Christian Europe between the seventh and twelfth centuries was largely a feudal agricultural society in which peasants farmed land owned by the wealthy in exchange for their protection. Jews, however, belonged mainly to the urban merchant class and relied on government for protection. Jewish intellectual life flourished in France and Germany, but elsewhere in Europe Jews faced undercurrents of hostility that at times surged into waves of persecution, expulsion, or both.

Perhaps the most infamous expulsion was the one ordered by the Christian monarchs of Spain, Ferdinand and Isabella, in 1492. Having finally taken the last Muslim stronghold, they completed their "reconquest" by commanding that the Jewish population either convert to Christianity or leave the country that had been their home for centuries. Of the tens of thousands who left, most sought refuge in the Ottoman Turkish Empire. There they were welcomed by Sultan Bayazid II, who recognized the potential value of the refugees, many of whom were highly skilled. To this day, some Turkish Jews still speak Ladino.

The Spanish Inquisition

In order to avoid expulsion, other Spanish Jews did convert to Christianity, but some of these "Conversos" (and their descendants) would continue to practice Jewish rites in secret. They were not the first to do so. As early as 1481, Ferdinand and Isabella had petitioned the pope for permission to establish an inquisition to root out and punish such heresy. Known for its ruthlessness, the Spanish Inquisition established tribunals in many cities with the goal of finding and executing those Conversos (also referred to as Marranos, "swine") who had not abandoned all Jewish traditions. More than 13,000 Conversos were put on trial during the first 12 years of the Spanish Inquisition.

The Kabbalah

Perhaps in response to the pain of expulsion, many Jews took a renewed interest in mysticism, particularly the tradition known as **Kabbalah** (from the Hebrew meaning "to receive"). Although Kabbalah itself appears to date from the twelfth century, some of its teachings are said to have been passed from teacher to student beginning as far back as Moses, and perhaps earlier. Certainly the biblical Book of Ezekiel abounds in prophecies and mystical visions of the divine, and there is a long tradition of literature recounting visionary ascents into the heavenly palaces of the divine. In the Jewish mystical tradition, the devout can experience direct revelation of God, usually through meditation or ecstatic prayer. This tradition developed in new ways in the Middle Ages, influenced in part by the Islamic mystical tradition of Sufism.

Kabbalists refer to God as the *Ayn Sof* ("Without End" or "Infinite"), for God is considered to be beyond thought, beyond form, and beyond gender—in effect, the unknowable creator. What *can* be known about God are the aspects of his being that connect the created world with its unknowable divine source, and through which the powers of the Ayn Sof flow, revealing him to the world. Kabbalists call these aspects—of which there are 10—*Sefirot*, which literally means "numbers" but is usually translated as "emanations" or "channels" of God's creative energy and power. The Sefirot are *Keter*/Crown, *Hokhmah*/Wisdom, *Binah*/Understanding, *Hesed*/Lovingkindness, *Gevurah*/Might, *Tiferet*/Beauty, *Hod*/Splendor, *Netzakh*/Victory, *Yesod*/Foundation, and *Malkhut*/Sovereignty. Each is an aspect of the Ayn Sof that radiates from the divine sphere into the created, material realm, and each one is interlinked with the others. Kabbalists seek not only to understand the Sefirot and their interrelations, but also (through the Kabbalists' own actions, thoughts, and words) to modify these interrelations.

But why should humans intervene in such divine matters? And how can they possibly do so? The most authoritative Kabbalah text, a commentary on the five books of Moses called the Zohar ("splendor" or "radiance"), explains that at the beginning of creation, the powers of the Sefirot were perfectly in balance, but this balance was disturbed when Adam and Eve disobeyed God by eating the forbidden fruit. According to the Zohar, the Torah was given to Israel to provide a way of restoring the Sefirot to their original harmony. Each time a Jew fulfills a commandment, a small positive shift occurs that helps to bring the Sefirot into balanced alignment. Likewise, every time a commandment is not fulfilled, the Sefirot are pushed into further disarray. When perfect balance is achieved, the divine powers will flow unhindered, just as they did at the beginning of creation.

Isaac Luria

An enormously influential later scholar of the Kabbalah was **Isaac Luria** (1534–1572), who was born in Jerusalem and moved to the northern Palestinian city of Safed in 1569. Although he died just three years later, at the age of 38, he and his disciples transformed the city into the center of Jewish mysticism that it remains to this day.

Map 4.1 Expulsion and Migration of Jews from Europe, c. 1000–1500 CE

Source: I.R. al Faruqi and D.E. Sopher, Historical Atlas of the Religions of the World (New York: Macmillan, 1974): 148–9.

One important component of Lurianic mysticism is the concept of *tikkun* ("mending" or "restoration"). The basis of this idea is Luria's understanding of how the universe was created. First, since the Ayn Sof was everywhere, he had to contract himself in order to make room for the world. Luria interpreted this *tzimtzum* ("contraction") as a type of divine exile. Next, divine light surged from God into the empty space, taking the form of the 10 Sefirot as well as the first man: Adam Kadmon ("primal man"). Out of the eyes, nose, and mouth of Adam Kadmon the light streamed, and this created vessels that held the light. But the vessels were unable to contain such divine power, and so they exploded into luminous fragments that became trapped in the created world. In this way, thought Luria, evil entered creation.

Like the authors of the Zohar, Luria held that Jews had the capacity to reverse this dismal situation, for the divine sparks longed to be liberated from their material abode and returned to their original state; through prayer, study, and the performance of mitzvot, Jews could assist in the process of "restoring the world," or *tikkun olam*. For Jews struggling with the aftermath of the expulsion from Spain, the idea that individual religious acts made a difference was empowering. At the same time, the concept of the Ayn Sof's fragmentation, resulting in the introduction of evil into the world, offered a way of understanding the Jews' suffering.

Eastern Europe

For centuries, Ashkenazic Jews had tended to live in their own (largely urban) communities, somewhat separate from the Christian mainstream of European life. By the early 1500s, however, many places were beginning to enforce segregation. Among them was the Republic of Venice, which called its Jewish quarter the "ghetto." Meanwhile, persecution was pushing many Jews farther east. Poland welcomed them, and several areas of eastern Europe became home to a vibrant Ashkenazic culture.

In 1648, however, a revolt against the Polish nobles by Ukrainian peasants brought this peaceful period to an end. Jews, who had developed ties with the nobility through their commercial activities, were also targeted by the rebels. This prompted many Ashkenazim to leave Poland and move west, back into the regions their ancestors had fled.

Hasidism

In the mid-eighteenth century, in southeastern Poland, a movement emerged to counter the scholarly rabbinic leaders who dismissed uneducated Jews as incapable of knowing God. The charismatic founder of **Hasidism** (from the Hebrew word for "piety"), Israel ben Eliezer (1698–1760), came to be known as the **Baal Shem Tov** ("Master of the good name") or "Besht" (an acronym). An itinerant healer and teacher, the Besht encouraged his fellow Jews to worship God with joy and delight, from the heart rather than the head. The little that is known about his personal life comes from the stories of his disciples, who claimed that he had supernatural powers, including the ability to heal illness and even revive the dead. Today the movement continues to flourish in certain Jewish communities. Hasidic men in particular are easily identified by their long black coats, black hats, and substantial beards and sidelocks.

In keeping with the Besht's emphasis on deep religious feeling rather than scholarship, Hasidic leaders are not rabbinic scholars but charismatic individuals known as Tzaddikim ("righteous men") whose authority is based on what are believed to be their supernatural powers; Hasidic teaching goes so far as to assert that "whatever God does, it is also within the capacity of the tzaddik to do" (Efron et al. 2009: 264). Hasidim believe that through a personal relationship with a **Tzaddik** it is possible for an ordinary person to attain attachment to God. Thus the relationship between a Tzaddik and his disciples tends to be very close, and Hasidim address their Tzaddikim by the Yiddish title "Rebbe" instead of the more formal "Rabbi."

With the passage of time, many subgroups developed within the Hasidic tradition. The largest and best known today is Chabad, founded by Rebbe Shneur Zalman (1745–1813) and widely known as Chabad–Lubavitch. Chabad's adherents, often referred to as Lubavitchers, follow many Lurianic traditions. For example, they attribute human suffering to the fragmentation of the Ayn Sof, and their prayer book follows the same arrangement as Luria's. In 1940 the community fled wartime Europe and set up a synagogue in New York. Menachem Mendel Schneerson (1902–1994), who assumed the group's leadership in 1951, significantly expanded its international activities and founded a worldwide organization that aims to reach out to Jews and, in so doing, hasten the coming of the Messianic Age. In fact, some of his followers believed Schneerson was the Jewish messiah (although he denied it). All Lubavitcher homes displayed his portrait, followers regularly sought his blessing, and some devotees still consider him the messiah. The reverence with which he was treated by his followers led many Jewish critics, from both the right and the left, to decry what they saw as the personality cult that had developed around him. Despite the criticism and the fact that no successor has yet emerged to replace Schneerson, Chabad continues to grow: it now claims more than 200,000 adherents, and up to a million Jews attend Chabad services at least once a year.

A poster in Jerusalem shows the "Lubavitcher Rebbe," the late Menachem Mendel Schneerson (1902–1994), and proclaims, "The King, the Messiah Lives!" (© Michele Murray).

⊕ The Modern Period

Haskalah: The Jewish Enlightenment

In the eighteenth century, European philosophers articulated a radical program for freedom of individual thought, arguing that individuals should be able to judge for themselves what was right and wrong. As the Enlightenment swept western Europe, Jews benefited from its emphasis on reason, tolerance, and material progress. Restrictions were lifted, the walls that surrounded many ghettos fell, and Jews were freed to live where they wished. Some countries gave Jews citizenship, which opened up opportunities for them to vote, attend universities, and choose their own occupations.

It was in response to these developments that the **Haskalah** (Jewish Enlightenment) was launched. As doors began opening for Jews, Haskalah leaders advocated a restructuring of Jewish education to devote less time to the Talmud and more to subjects such as modern languages and practical skills, which would help Jews integrate (without assimilating) into European society. The philosopher Moses Mendelssohn (1729–1786) recognized that, after so many years behind ghetto walls, his fellow German Jews had become inward-looking and segregated from the rest of society. Encouraging them to speak German rather than Yiddish, he urged them to be Jews at home and Germans on the street. The "new Jew" would be both a committed adherent of Judaism and a full participant in modern culture.

Modern Branches of Judaism

The adaptation of traditional Jewish thought and practice to the modern world laid the foundation for the emergence of what we know today as the Reform, Orthodox, Conservative, Reconstructionist, and Humanistic branches of Judaism. Each of these movements originated in an effort to reconcile centuries-old traditions with the new ways of thinking and living promoted by the European Enlightenment.

Reform

Reform Judaism began with the goal of making Jewish practice meaningful for Jews living in eighteenth-century Germany. Its pioneers explicitly supported Enlightenment ideals and drew attention to their compatibility with Judaism. The father of the Reform branch was Israel Jacobson (1768–1828), who in 1815 opened his Berlin home for worship services with sermons by other leaders of the movement. Three years later the Hamburg Temple was established for Sabbath services that used the everyday German of the community rather than Hebrew and eliminated the traditional references to the hoped-for restoration of the Temple in Jerusalem. Reform synagogues did not have a meaningful presence in Germany until the 1830s, however, and a German-language prayer book was not introduced until 1848.

The spiritual leader of the Reform movement was Abraham Geiger (1810–1874), a scholar who argued that Judaism had been adapting to its surroundings throughout history, and hence reform was natural to it. Geiger argued that the Hebrew Bible reflected the concerns and perspectives of postbiblical Jewish movements. He also demonstrated the connections among Judaism, Christianity, and Islam.

Today Reform Jews do not generally observe the dietary laws (see Practice box), although growing numbers are now becoming more observant. They understand Judaism to be a flexible, living religion that remains relevant because it evolves as the realities of human life change. Reform encourages interfaith dialogue. It also allows women to serve as rabbis; it was a Reform seminary that ordained Sally Priesand, the first female rabbi in North America, in 1972.

Orthodox Judaism

The spread of Reform Judaism stimulated the establishment of the Orthodox branch, a traditionalist reaction spearheaded by Samson Raphael Hirsch (1808–1888). Hirsch sought to prove that traditional Judaism was compatible with modernity, and he promoted the application of Torah in all aspects of everyday life.

Orthodox Jews believe that the Hebrew Bible is the revealed word of God, and understand the Mishnah and Talmud to be written forms of Oral Law that originated with Moses; they follow rabbinic Halakhah and observe the laws of Torah. While the more liberal Orthodox Jews participate to some degree in non-Jewish society, the most conservative, the **Haredim**, tend to live and work in segregated communities, and every part of their lives is governed by Halakhah. The Hasidim are a subgroup of the Haredim.

In April 2013, while attending the monthly women's prayer service at the Western Wall, this woman was arrested for wearing a tallit (prayer shawl), which the Haredi community insists is reserved for men. Four other women were also detained (AP Photo/Michal Fattal).

Conservative

The third branch of Judaism was founded by Zacharias Frankel (1801–1875) as "Positive-Historical Judaism." An attempt to find middle ground between rigid Orthodox Judaism and the radical liberalism of Reform Judaism, it eventually developed into what is known today as Conservative Judaism. Frankel argued that core teachings such as the oneness of God had been divinely revealed but also acknowledged that Judaism had developed within history, and therefore that its traditions were open to moderate reinterpretation and modification. Conservatives interpret the text more literally than Reform Jews do, but more liberally than the Orthodox, though typically they do follow the dietary laws. Since they are not Orthodox, however, they also allow for some restructuring in order to stay relevant in modern times. Conservative synagogues vary in their attitudes toward women's roles: more liberal congregations allow female rabbis and full female participation in synagogue services, whereas more traditional ones do not.

Reconstructionism

Whereas the Reform, Orthodox, and Conservative movements all originated in Germany, the Reconstructionist movement began in the United States. Its founder, Mordechai Kaplan (1881–1983), began his career as an Orthodox rabbi but soon grew uncomfortable with Orthodoxy. He then obtained a teaching position at the Jewish Theological Seminary (a Conservative institution in New York City) and in 1922 established a Reconstructionist synagogue called the Society for the Advancement of Judaism. Kaplan called for the synagogue to be a social and cultural center (rather than a religious one), and he introduced the idea of the Jewish community center—an institution that has become a regular part of the North American Jewish environment. He also argued that the scriptures had not been divinely revealed but created by the Jewish people themselves; the traditions existed for the people, not the other way around, and so could be modified. As an example, in 1922 Kaplan conducted the world's first bat mitzvah for his daughter Judith: this ceremonial equivalent to the **bar mitzvah** for boys is now practiced regularly not only by Reconstructionists, but by Reform and Conservative Jews as well. Thus Kaplan's influence is felt well beyond the movement he established.

Since Reconstructionism developed primarily out of the Conservative movement, it preserved a number of traditional features of Judaism, such as the dietary laws and the custom of wearing the **kippah** (skullcap) for men, as well as a significant amount of Hebrew in the liturgy. As a consequence, its practice resembles that of Conservative Judaism, although the two traditions are clearly distinguished by Reconstructionism's rejection of the idea of the Jews as the chosen people, its gender-neutral prayer book, and the fact that some of its adherents may well describe themselves as atheists. What matters to Reconstructionists more than individual faith is active participation in a community and the effort to honor Jewish history by retaining meaningful symbols and customs.

Humanistic Judaism

The American rabbi Sherwin Wine (1929–2007) took Kaplan's ideas several steps further, removing God from the picture altogether. Wine initially served as a rabbi in a Reform synagogue, but as his belief in the existence of God waned, he looked for a more congenial community. Finding none, in 1963 he established a secular congregation called the Birmingham Temple, which continues today with some 400 members in Farmington Hills, Michigan. In 1969 this congregation united with several like-minded others to form the Society for Humanistic Judaism (SHJ), which

Practice

Dietary Laws

Food is an essential part of Jewish observance. Jewish dietary laws (*kashrut*) stipulate the foods that are acceptable to eat and those that must be avoided, as well as how to cook the acceptable foods and the types of food that can be eaten together in the same meal. Food is considered **kosher** if it is "fit" or "proper" in accordance with Jewish law.

Leviticus 11 and Deuteronomy 14:2–21 instruct that, among land animals, only those that have split hooves and chew their own cud are acceptable (thus cows and goats can be eaten, but pigs and rabbits cannot). Among sea creatures, only those with both scales and fins are permitted; thus, mussels and crustaceans such as shrimp are prohibited. Among birds, the chicken, turkey, goose, and duck are acceptable, but birds of prey such as the vulture, owl, and hawk are not. The products of nonacceptable animals are likewise considered unkosher (except for honey, which is understood to derive from flowers rather than bees, which fall into the forbidden category of "winged swarming things").

Even a permitted meat must be prepared and cooked correctly to qualify as kosher. For example, an animal that has died a natural death is not to be eaten; only animals that have been slaughtered in accordance with the Law are acceptable. There are also rules about how food is to be eaten. For example, meat must not be consumed at the same time as dairy. This stipulation is drawn from an instruction that appears twice in the Torah: "You shall not boil a kid in its mother's milk" (Exodus 23:19 and Deuteronomy 14:21). Some Jews consider it so important to keep meat and dairy separate that they have not only two sets of dishes and cutlery (one for meat, one for dairy), but two sinks and two dishwashers.

Kosher manufacturers use various symbols to inform consumers of their products' status. One of the most common is a capital U (for "Union of Orthodox Jewish Congregations") inside a circle, which indicates that a body of rabbis has inspected the plant at which the product was prepared and deemed it to be kosher.

now includes congregations across North America. According to the society's website, its goal is "to foster a positive Jewish identity, intellectual integrity, and ethical behavior."

Over the years Wine developed a new liturgy, in both Hebrew and English, which makes no reference to God. Humanistic Jews welcome everyone to participate in their services, regardless of gender, sexual orientation, or religious background. From the perspective of Humanists, Jewish identity is largely a personal decision. Not surprisingly, Humanist rabbis will officiate at marriages between Jews and non-Jews.

The Modern Synagogue

The synagogue is at the heart of the Jewish religious community: it is a place for prayer and study of sacred texts, a venue for communal worship, and a place to learn. It also functions as a center for social interaction and charitable activity. Orthodox and Hasidic Jews typically use the Yiddish term "Shul" (from the German for "school") to refer to the synagogue and emphasize its role as an intellectual hub. Whereas Conservative Jews tend to use the term "synagogue," Reform Jews call their local place of assembly a "temple" because in their view it has definitively replaced the Temple in Jerusalem.

The Holy Ark (or Ark of the Covenant) in which the Torah scrolls are kept symbolizes the place where the tablets given to Moses were stored. Once the scrolls have been opened, a pointer is used to aid in the reading; often in the shape of a hand, it is called a *yad* ("hand" in Hebrew). Human hands never touch the parchment, since sweat contains acids that could damage it. The scrolls are stored in a fabric cover that may be ornately decorated with silver or gold.

Prayer Services

Jewish prayers take two forms: preset (typically from the ancient period) and spontaneous (created on the spot by the individual Jew). Prayer services revolve around the former type. Three times a day, in the evening, morning, and afternoon, practicing Jews pray in communal worship services that correspond to the three daily sacrifices performed at the Temple in Jerusalem. Prayers are also recited during mundane activities, such as getting up in the morning and before washing one's hands, as well as before and after eating.

Every Sabbath morning service includes readings from the Torah and the Prophets. The Torah has 54 sections, each of which is read and studied for a week, so that the entire Torah is covered in an annual cycle. Every section is further divided into seven parts, all of which are read during the Sabbath morning service. The only other days when the Torah is read are Monday and Thursday.

The *yad* ("hand" in Hebrew) is a pointer that tapers into the shape of a closed hand with an index finger extended. Often quite ornate and made of silver, it is used to guide the reader of the Torah scrolls in a synagogue service (Jim Havey/Alamy Stock Photo).

Tradition teaches that it is better to pray in a group than alone. Thus in Orthodox practice at least 10 adult males are needed to make up a quorum for public prayer; this group of 10 is called a **minyan** ("number" in Hebrew). Certain Conservative synagogues allow women to be part of the minyan, and Reform Judaism does not require a minyan at all.

In most Conservative and Orthodox synagogues, males wear the skullcap known as a kippah in Hebrew and a **yarmulke** in Yiddish. The **tallit** is a fringed prayer shawl typically worn by men during the morning prayers (the only time it is worn in the evening is on Yom Kippur). The tallit fulfills the commandment to the Israelites to "make fringes on the corners of their garments throughout their generations and to put a blue cord on the fringe at each corner" so that they will "remember all the commandments of the Lord and do them" (Numbers 15:37–41). Likewise, for weekday morning prayer men put on **tefillin** (or **phylacteries**), small black leather boxes containing words of scripture from Exodus and Deuteronomy, which are tied to the forehead and upper arm in literal fulfillment of the instruction in the Shema to "bind them [these words] as a sign on your hand, fix them as an emblem on your forehead." Traditionally, only men have worn the tallit and tefillin, but in modern times some Conservative and Reform women have begun wearing them as well.

Practice

The High Holidays

The High Holidays, also called the High Holy Days or Days of Awe, encompass 10 days that usually fall in September or October. The first day, **Rosh Hashanah**, is considered the Jewish New Year: on it God is said to open the "Book of Life" in which he will inscribe the individual's fate for the year on the Day of Atonement, **Yom Kippur**. This is the time of the year when Jews are supposed to examine their consciences. Historically, it was also the only time when the divine name of God was pronounced—by the high priest before the Ark in the Jerusalem Temple's most sacred place, the Holy of Holies—in order to atone for the sins of the people. Apples dipped in honey are customarily eaten at Rosh Hashanah as an expression of the hope for a "sweet" new year.

Nowadays Yom Kippur is spent at the synagogue in prayer and supplication, asking for God's forgiveness. Fasting—from sundown on the evening of Yom Kippur until the following nightfall—is compulsory for all adults except pregnant women, the elderly, and the ill. Although God is understood to forgive sins against himself, a person who has been wronged must be asked for forgiveness. The liturgy during the High Holy Days makes frequent references to the many ways in which human beings hurt each other, both in speech and in action. The time between Rosh Hashanah and Yom Kippur is meant to be devoted to contemplative reflection on one's own words and behavior. Yet these "days of penitence" should not be sad, because Jews are supposed to have confidence in the power of repentance and the mercy of God.

Most members of the Jewish community mark Yom Kippur to some degree, and many attend synagogue even if they do not go again for the rest of the year. At intervals throughout the service, the shofar (usually a ram's horn) is sounded. This tradition has been ascribed many symbolic meanings, including serving as a "wake-up" call to reflect on one's sins and the need for repentance, a summons to war against evil inclinations, and a reminder of the ram that God told Abraham to sacrifice instead of his son Isaac. Whatever the interpretation, the plaintive sound of the shofar is one of the most stirring aspects of Yom Kippur.

Document

The Shema

Among the prayers recited by Jews daily, the oldest and most highly revered is the **Shema** *(from its first word, meaning "hear"). The first section (reprinted here) comes from Deuteronomy 6:4–9 and is followed by sections from Deuteronomy 11:13–21 and Numbers 15:37–41.*

Hear, O Israel: The Lord is our God, the Lord alone. You shall love the Lord your God with all your heart, and with all your soul, and with all your might. Keep these words that I am commanding you today in your heart. Recite them to your children and talk about them when you are at home and when you are away, when you lie down and when you rise. Bind them as a sign on your hand, fix them as an emblem on your forehead, and write them on the doorposts of your house and on your gates.

As this storefront display in Jerusalem shows, the kippah (skullcap; literally "dome" in Hebrew) can be a colorful and creative vehicle for personal expression, including expressions of support for favorite sports teams (© Michele Murray).

In Reform and Conservative synagogues, all members of the congregation sit together, but Orthodox men are not permitted to pray in the presence of women, lest they be distracted from their prayers. Thus Orthodox women sit in their own section at the back or side of the room, or in a balcony. Language is another area of difference. In Orthodox and many Conservative synagogues, every part of the service is in Hebrew, but Reform services in North America are conducted mainly in English—although the use of Hebrew has been increasing in the last decade or so.

Anti-Semitism

In the aftermath of the Enlightenment, the nineteenth century seemed to offer Jews the opportunity to participate more fully in western European culture and society. But a new debate arose over what came to be known as "the Jewish Question." In an 1843 essay, a German Protestant theologian named Bruno Bauer claimed that Jews as a group were scheming against the rest of the world, and that they were to blame for the hostility they encountered in modern society because they refused to abandon their ancestral culture. Underpinning these accusations was the long-standing Christian view of Jews as "Christ-killers." In fact, European society was undergoing major changes in the later 1800s, and with those changes came severe tensions. Workers were beginning to demand more rights, while middle-class shopkeepers and skilled workers were watching the growth of department stores and factories with mounting concern. Competition among England, France, and Germany was increasing, and nationalism and racism added to the tensions leading up to the outbreak of the First World War.

At a time of anxiety and division, politicians used opposition to Jews to bring disparate social groups together. In central and western Europe, parties from across the political spectrum exploited anxieties to gain votes and popular support. No matter how illogical and contradictory the charges, Jews were to blame, whether for Marxism, liberalism, communism, or rampant capitalism. Even when they were not blamed for the unsettling shifts in European society, Jews were said to be undeserving of the benefits of emancipation.

Political parties were established specifically to promote anti-Semitism; Jews were openly derided in cartoons, posters, and pamphlets all over Europe. Germany produced more of this propaganda than any other country, and the organizations that distributed it were located at the very center of society. In this way anti-Semitic attitudes were made respectable.

The central difference between ancient anti-Judaism and modern anti-Semitism was the racial dimension associated with the latter. In the modern world, Jews were publicly attacked for being racially "other": whereas ancient writers had focused on Jews' religious practices and customs, nineteenth-century propaganda portrayed them as racially alien. Even when they converted to Christianity, they remained racially tainted.

The German writer credited with coining the term "anti-Semitism" was Wilhelm Marr (1819–1904). Noting that Jewish financial investors emerged from the economic depression of 1873 in better shape than non-Jewish investors, he suggested that the problem was not that Jews lacked connection with European society, but rather that they were so well integrated that they were taking over. These views were promoted at the First International Anti-Semites' Congress held in Dresden in 1882.

The Dreyfus Affair

In France, hostility toward the changes brought about by the Revolution of 1789 was reflected in increasingly anti-Semitic attitudes. French Jews, who had been granted legal equality in 1791, came to be seen as symbols of all that was wrong with postrevolutionary France, and anti-Semitism served as a rallying point for the discontented. In 1894 a Jewish army officer named Alfred Dreyfus (1859–1935) was falsely accused of spying for Germany based on forged documents and a military cover-up. The "Dreyfus Affair" was motivated by overt anti-Semitism. Four years after Dreyfus was found guilty and sentenced to life imprisonment, his cause was taken up by the novelist Émile Zola, who charged ("J'accuse!") the French army with having hidden the truth of the situation. The army tried Dreyfus again, and again he was found guilty, but this time under "extenuating circumstances" (Efron et al. 2009: 378). In 1899, after the details of the army cover-up were made public, he was pardoned, and eventually he was awarded the Legion of Honor.

The Russian Context

In tsarist Russia, both church and state labeled Jews outsiders in Russian society and enemies of Christianity. Jews became targets of violent persecutions called pogroms, in which their houses were burned, their businesses ransacked, and they themselves were beaten, tortured, and killed. Although the government did not organize these pogroms, it did nothing to stop them. Russia's most lasting contribution to modern anti-Semitism, however, was *The Protocols of the Elders of Zion*, a fiction created by the Russian secret police in the late 1890s that purported to be the minutes of a meeting at which members of a Jewish conspiracy had discussed a secret plan for global domination. The *Protocols* enjoyed widespread distribution in western Europe, especially in the years after the First World War, and was published in the United States by the automobile entrepreneur Henry Ford. Although it was exposed as fraudulent not long after its composition, the document resonated with anti-Semites around the world and is still in circulation today.

Zionism

The pogroms and poverty faced by Jews in eastern Europe and the growth of political and racial anti-Semitism in western Europe triggered the development of the movement called **Zionism**, which sought to return Jews to the ancient land of Israel to establish a nation there. The idea was not new: the words of the Passover Seder, "Next year in Jerusalem," indicate an enduring desire for return to the ancient homeland, whether in the present or in some future messianic age. Zion is the biblical name of a hilltop in Jerusalem that is described as God's dwelling place and is known today as the Temple Mount. In ancient times the name "Zion" had a variety of associations and could be used to refer to the land around Jerusalem, the people, or their religious and political traditions.

Jewish Nationalism

Zionism as a political movement was formally established by the Austro-Hungarian journalist and playwright Theodor Herzl (1860–1904). Herzl had become persuaded that a Zionist movement was necessary during the Dreyfus Affair and the resulting rise in anti-Jewish sentiment. In August 1897 he spearheaded the first Zionist Congress, held in Basel, Switzerland. Out of that meeting came a platform calling for a Jewish national home in what was then Ottoman-controlled Palestine and insisting that the future state would have to be recognized by international law. It would be half a century before that state—Israel—was established, by which time the need for it could no longer be disputed.

⊕ The Holocaust (1933–1945)

Of all the adversities that the Jewish people have experienced in their long history, the most shattering took place between 1933 and 1945 under Adolf Hitler's National Socialist German Workers' Party, better known as the Nazis. By the end of the Second World War at least 6 million Jews were dead, and the vibrant Ashkenazic and Sephardic cultures established on European soil over the previous millennia had been all but eradicated. Now widely known as the **Holocaust** (from the Greek meaning "whole" and "burnt"), the Nazi program of genocide is referred to in Hebrew as the **Shoah** ("catastrophe").

The Rise of Hitler

In the grim economic conditions that followed Germany's defeat in 1918, the Nazi Party attracted enthusiastic popular support. Hitler placed the blame for Germany's defeat squarely on the Jews. In the account of his life and thought entitled *Mein Kampf* ("My Struggle"; 1925), Hitler tells how, as a young man, he learned of a Jewish conspiracy to infiltrate German politics in order to destroy the "Aryan" world. "Aryan" was in fact a linguistic term referring to the Indo-European family of languages, but it had already been given a racial meaning and used to argue for the supremacy of so-called Aryans over people of Semitic stock ("Semitic" too originally referred to a group of languages, including Hebrew, Arabic, and Aramaic). Hitler associated "Aryan" with purity and "Semitic" with impurity. His goal was first to reveal the threat that the Jews posed to Aryans, and then to destroy that threat.

When Hitler became chancellor of Germany in January 1933, he enacted legislation to overturn the emancipation of Germany's Jews, eliminate them from public life, and divest them of their citizenship. On March 11, Jewish-owned department stores in Braunschweig were ransacked, and two days later all Jewish lawyers in Breslau were expelled from court. On April 1, the government orchestrated a day-long boycott of Jewish-owned stores and businesses, during which Hitler's soldiers, the Stormtroopers, stood in the streets with signs advising "Germans" not to enter shops owned by Jews and wrote *Jude* ("Jew") across those establishments' windows, often accompanied by a Star of David (the six-pointed star that served as a Jewish symbol). New discriminatory laws were introduced almost daily thereafter, and on May 10, books written by Jews were publicly burned at universities across the country (Efron et al. 2009: 377–8).

Some Jews began planning to leave the country, but as yet there was no widespread panic: of the roughly 525,000 Jews in Germany in 1933, only 37,000 left in that year (Efron et al. 2009: 378). Those who remained hoped that the wave of persecution would subside. Given *Mein Kampf*'s references to Jews as "cockroaches," "maggots," and *Untermenschen* ("subhumans"), they hoped in vain.

A new phase in Hitler's offensive against the Jews was introduced in September 1935, when the Nuremberg Laws revoked Jews' German citizenship, deprived them of legal and economic rights, and prohibited marriage between Jews and people of allegedly "pure" Nordic blood. On October 20, 1935, the *New York Times* reported that a Jewish doctor named Hans Serelman, who had transfused his own blood to save the life of a non-Jew, had been charged with "race defilement" and sent to a concentration camp for seven months (Gilbert 1985: 50).

Jewish businesses were taken over by members of the Aryan "master race" in two stages. From 1933 to 1938 Jews could "voluntarily" transfer their businesses; after November 1938 they were compelled to hand them over. Again, many Jews left Germany, but many others stayed. Although the Nazis also targeted gays and lesbians, Roma (Gypsy) people, communists, and the disabled, Germany's hardships were blamed on the Jews alone.

The first burning of a synagogue took place in Munich on June 9, 1938; afterward, more than 2,000 Jews were incarcerated throughout Germany. In October approximately 17,000 Polish Jews were expelled from German territory; Poland then refused them entry, leaving them in a no-man's-land. Barely a week later, on November 6, 17-year-old Hershel Grynszpan, whose parents had been among the deported Polish Jews, assassinated the third secretary at the German embassy in Paris. In response, Hitler ordered that free rein be given to "spontaneous" anti-Jewish demonstrations, and on the night of November 9 a series of riots took place that came to be known as *Kristallnacht*, the "Night of Broken Glass." More than 1,000 synagogues were plundered and some 300 burned as Jewish homes and businesses were destroyed by Stormtroopers and ordinary German citizens. Ninety-one Jews were killed, and approximately 26,000 were rounded up and placed in concentration camps (Efron et al. 2009: 384).

The MS St. Louis

Thousands of Jews left Germany over the months that followed. In May 1939, the German passenger ship *St. Louis* left Hamburg for Cuba with 936 Jews aboard seeking asylum. Although all had paid $150 for a tourist visa, on their arrival the Cuban government refused them entry unless they paid an additional fee of $500 each—money that most of them did not have. Captain Gustav Schröder, the ship's non-Jewish commander, hoped that the United States would accept his passengers, but ultimately it too refused, having enacted quotas on immigrants from eastern and southern Europe in 1924.

A group of academics and clergy in Canada tried to persuade Prime Minister Mackenzie King to offer the passengers sanctuary. But Canadian immigration officials and cabinet ministers opposed to Jewish immigration persuaded King not to intervene. Among the officials was Frederick Charles Blair, director of the Immigration Branch, who argued that Canada "had already done too much for the Jews" and that "the line must be drawn somewhere" (Abella and Troper 1991: 8, 64).

Thus the ship returned to Europe, docking at Antwerp, Belgium, in June 1939. The United Kingdom, France, Belgium, and Holland granted the passengers refuge, but in 1940 Germany invaded Belgium and France, putting the lives of all the Jews in those countries in jeopardy. Of the 936 refugees who returned to Europe, it is estimated that 227 were killed in concentration camps (Thomas and Witts 1974: 135–217). Calling the refusal to accept passengers from the ship "an absolute moral failure," Canadian Prime Minister Justin Trudeau officially apologized on November 7, 2018, in the House of Commons for the 1939 government decision to turn away the *St. Louis*.

The Second World War

The Second World War began on September 1, 1939, when German forces invaded Poland. By the end of September Poland's Jews were being herded into ghettos surrounded by fences or walls that were locked from the outside by German guards. Overcrowding led to rampant disease, which, along with starvation, killed many inhabitants.

In Germany the enactment of anti-Semitic laws continued. Jews increasingly were moved into separate apartment buildings; Germans writing doctoral dissertations were permitted to quote

Jews only when unavoidable, and Jewish authors had to be listed in a separate bibliography. In November 1939, all Polish Jews over the age of 10 were ordered to wear a yellow badge in the shape of the Star of David, and on September 1, 1941, German Jews were required to follow suit.

The Death Camps

To facilitate what they called the "final solution to the Jewish problem," the Nazis built a network of large-scale death camps in Poland. The gassing of Jews began at the Chelmno camp in December 1941. One after another, groups of Jewish and Roma prisoners were placed in a sealed van and driven away to be gassed by the exhaust fumes that were channeled back into the compartment where they were held. The first camp to use gas chambers was Belzec, in southeastern Poland, in March 1942. But the largest extermination camp was Auschwitz-Birkenau, where more than 1 million Jews as well as tens of thousands of Roma, Poles, and Soviet prisoners of war were killed using a cyanide-based insecticide. Up to 7,000 Jews were gassed each day at Auschwitz-Birkenau alone. When it became clear that the Allied forces were advancing on Poland in the winter of 1944, prisoners were removed from the Polish camps and sent to Germany both by train and on foot; such "death marches" killed approximately 250,000 prisoners. British and American forces liberated the rest of the camps between April and May 1945 (Efron et al. 2009: 385–405).

During the two-minute siren that sounds throughout Israel on Holocaust Memorial Day, people cease whatever they are doing—including driving—to stand at attention and honor those who died during the Holocaust (© Reuters/Corbis).

Interview

Rabbi Shlomo Bistritzky, Chief Rabbi of Hamburg, Germany

When the new Jewish school in Hamburg, Germany, opened in 2007, there was considerable fanfare and media attention. Local journalists came, took photos, and wrote articles. It was an event! Given Germany's World War II history, such occurrences today garner much attention. Rabbi Shlomo Bistritzky, in fact, wishes that this were not the case.

Nazi atrocities carried out during the Holocaust decimated Hamburg's Jewish population and destroyed most of its Jewish institutions. In 1938, prior to the Second World War, the city's Jewish population was between 20,000 and 25,000, organized into a robust community with numerous Jewish-owned and Jewish-run businesses. Today there are approximately 8,000 Jews living in Hamburg. Multiple *stolpersteine* (German for "stumbling stones") commemorate Jewish (and other) victims of the Holocaust throughout the city.

Chief rabbi of Hamburg since 2012, Rabbi Bistritzky is a member of the Chabad-Lubavitch movement. He was born and raised in Israel but has lived in Hamburg with his wife and eight children for the past 14 years. He was sent from Israel as a *shaliach* ("ambassador") of the Lubavitcher movement to help reestablish Jewish life in Hamburg. One of Rabbi Bistritzky's goals is for Jewish life in the city to be lived as normally as possible. "In New York, when a new Jewish school opens, there is no fanfare or media coverage," he said. "I'd like Jewish life in Hamburg to be the same: just a regular part of life in the city."

In fact, Rabbi Bistritzky's grandfather, Yehuda Bistritzky, was born in Hamburg and was 12 years old when he fled the city in 1938 because of the Nazis. This meant, of course, that Yehuda's studies at the Hamburg Talmud Torah School were interrupted. The family was able to escape to Rotterdam and eventually settled in New York.

Shlomo Bistritzky. (Courtesy of Shlomo Bistritzky)

When, in 2007, Rabbi Shlomo Bistritzky reopened the school—in the same building it had occupied prior to the war—it was a poignant moment for the family. Twelve children were registered as students, and one of them was Rabbi Bistritzky's daughter. Yehuda Bistritzky called his granddaughter on her first day of school. He told her that while he had not been able to complete his studies there, he was profoundly pleased that she would be able to do so. Today, there are 160 children in the school, and the Jewish community of Hamburg is growing.

In 2012, Rabbi Bistritzky's grandfather, despite being 87 years old and having sworn that he would never step foot in Germany again, attended his grandson's installation as the chief rabbi of Hamburg. "This is the best response to the Holocaust," he declared.

For Rabbi Bistritzky, being chief rabbi and working to reestablish Jewish life in Hamburg are extraordinarily meaningful. When asked what message he would like to share with non-Jews, his response was to quote from the Mishnah: "Do not judge your fellow until you have stood in his place" (*Pirkei Avot* 2:5). "It is easy to make quick judgments of others," he said, "but if you do not fully understand another person's life, you should not judge that person." Respect for others is key, he added, and that includes respect for other people's religious traditions. "The

diversity within Judaism is not well understood; often non-Jews judge Orthodox Jews, for example, based on their own backgrounds rather than truly understanding Orthodox Judaism," he noted. "It is difficult to understand a tradition to which one does not belong personally. Rather than judging, I wish there to be respect." Rabbi Bistritzky endeavors to follow this precept himself and has cultivated positive, respectful relationships with leaders of Christian and Muslim communities in Germany.

While much work remains to be done before Jewish life is once again considered a regular part of Hamburg, many affirmative steps have already been taken in that direction. Rabbi Bistritzky is optimistic about the future.

The State of Israel

When the horrors perpetrated against the Jews of Europe came to light, the United Nations voted to create a Jewish state in Palestine. The decision gave hope to Jews around the world. Yet it created a new refugee problem for the indigenous Arab people of Palestine, many of whom would be forced out of their homes. The original UN plan partitioned the land between the Jews and the Arabs, with Jerusalem to be administered by a UN Trusteeship Council for the first decade, after which the city's fate would be negotiated. Neither the Palestinian Arab community nor the Arab League accepted the partition plan, and Jewish leaders themselves had reservations about it, although they accepted it because the need for a Jewish homeland was so great.

The Jewish state of Israel came into being on May 14, 1948, and was attacked the following day by Egypt, Jordan, Syria, and Iraq. This was the start of decades of battle between Israel and the Palestinians, as well as neighboring Arab countries. While peace treaties have been signed with Egypt and Jordan, and some of the territory that Israelis gained in later conflicts has been given back, the region continues to be extremely volatile. Most residents, whether Israeli or Palestinian, now support a two-state solution, but negotiating the boundaries of these states continues to be inordinately difficult.

In 1950 the Israeli government adopted the Law of Return, which granted "every Jew . . . the right to immigrate to the country." The Israel Central Bureau of Statistics put the country's 2013 population at approximately 8 million, of whom perhaps 75 percent are Jews and just over 20 percent Arabs. In the early years of the state's existence most Jewish Israelis were of European Ashkenazi descent, but now the majority are of Middle Eastern origin (termed "Mizrachi" since the 1990s). Just over a million Israeli Jews are immigrants from the former Soviet Union, and they now have their own political parties and Russian-language media. Another 130,000 are Beta Israel ("House of Israel")—Ethiopian Jews, many of whom were evacuated to Israel by the Israeli government between the late 1970s and 1991. Although the process of integration has not been

Focus

Holocaust Memorial Day

Holocaust Memorial Day, or Yom HaShoah, was inaugurated in 1953. It falls on the twenty-seventh day of the Hebrew month of Nisan (usually in March or April). In Israel, Yom HaShoah begins at sundown with a state ceremony at Yad Vashem, Israel's official Holocaust memorial in Jerusalem. The national flag is lowered to half-mast, the president and prime minister deliver speeches, Holocaust survivors light six torches symbolizing the 6 million who died, and the chief rabbis recite prayers. At 10 o'clock the next morning sirens are sounded throughout Israel for two minutes, during which people cease whatever they are doing and stand in silent tribute to the dead. Ceremonies and services are held at schools, military bases, and other community institutions. Places of public entertainment are closed by law, television broadcasters air Holocaust-related documentaries and talk shows, and subdued songs are played on the radio.

Idan Raichel is an Israeli singer-songwriter and musician whose group, the Idan Raichel Project, sings in Amharic, Arabic, Spanish, and Swahili, as well as Hebrew (AP Photo/Dan Balilty/CP).

Map 4.2 Jewish Populations Around the World

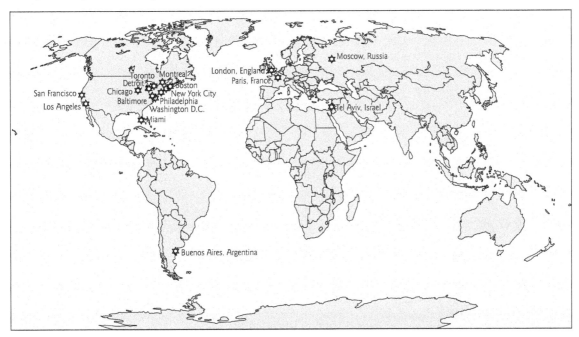

easy, especially for older people, the community now has a strong presence in Israeli society—a presence that is reflected in the fact that popular entertainers such as the Idan Raichel Project now include songs in the Ethiopian language, Amharic, in their repertoire.

⊕ Life-Cycle Events

How Jews Deal with Death

Jews consider death to be a natural part of the life cycle. If possible, members of the immediate family should maintain a constant presence in the room of a dying person. The reasoning behind this custom is that we do not enter the world alone, and therefore we ought not to depart it alone. Jewish customs associated with the bereavement process allow mourners to express their grief and facilitate their return to regular life. Friends and relatives outside the deceased person's immediate family are expected to comfort them and provide for their needs.

Jewish law and tradition require that the body be buried as soon as possible after death, preferably within 24 hours. Members of the local burial society wash and dry the body while reciting prayers and psalms, and then wrap it in a simple white shroud. Candles, symbolic of the soul, are lit and placed at the head of the body, and an attendant is hired to stand by and read psalms continuously; Psalm 91, which refers to God taking humans "under the shelter of his wings," is considered particularly appropriate.

No consolation visits are made before the funeral, and there is no public viewing of the body. The deceased is simply buried in the ground, in accordance with Genesis 3:19: "You are dust, and to dust you shall return." The corpse is not embalmed, and if a coffin is used, it is expected to be simple, made out of plain wood. But coffins are rare in Israel; in most cases the body is simply lowered into the ground on a stretcher or a bed of reeds. After the burial, the children of the deceased (in Orthodox families, only the sons) recite the Kaddish, a prayer that is part of every synagogue service, but that since the Middle Ages has also been used as a mourner's prayer. Intriguingly, it does not mention death or loss but instead praises the name of God.

After the funeral, members of the bereaved family "sit shiva" (from the Hebrew for "seven") for seven days, during which they receive visitors, whose primary duty is to listen: Jewish tradition encourages them to remain silent until the bereaved person speaks. Especially at this time, family and friends will cook and drop off food so that the mourners will be free to focus on their grief. Mourners do not go to work during that week, and all mirrors in the home are covered to reinforce the idea that they need not keep up appearances. After the first week the mourners return to work but do not participate in social activities.

One month after the death, the standard mourning period is considered complete. A brief memorial service is held, during which a few words are spoken about the deceased and Kaddish is recited; then mourners may return to a full schedule of work and social life. Children of the deceased, however, recite the Kaddish every day for a year. In the Orthodox context, sons are expected to attend synagogue every day to recite the Kaddish, and social restrictions remain in force for both sons and daughters for the entire year.

By the first anniversary of the death the mourners are expected to return to living a full life. Widows may remarry after 90 days—the minimum time required to determine the paternity of a child born soon after the death of the husband—but widowers are to wait until three festivals pass, or about seven months. The shorter time period for women probably reflects their vulnerability without husbands in ancient times.

Marriage

Marriage in Judaism is regarded as a natural and highly desirable state for human beings. Indeed, as we have seen, the rabbis held "Be fruitful and multiply . . ." to be Yahweh's first mitzvah; thus, everyone is encouraged to marry and raise children. Sexual relations within the sanctified bounds of marriage are encouraged both for reproduction and for the pleasure they bring to the couple.

Jewish marriages are occasions for happy celebration in a framework of religious seriousness and sanctity. A wedding can take place almost anywhere: in a home, a synagogue, a hotel, or outdoors. A rabbi is present in a legal capacity, to make sure that the marriage contract, the *ketubah*, is properly prepared and the appropriate procedures followed. The early rabbis introduced this contract mainly to protect the economic rights of wives. To provide for a woman in the event of divorce or widowhood, it would stipulate a "bride price" to be paid to her from the husband's estate. The contract also established the dowry (such as bedding and linens) that the bride's family would provide to help the young couple set up a home. Today the dowry and bride-price customs are no longer observed, and the ketubah does not have much official power in North America, since the legal obligations of spouses are set by law. However, traditional Jews continue to sign a ketubah written in Aramaic (the lingua franca in the era when the ketubah was created), while liberal Jews sign a modern version of it.

For the marriage ceremony, the couple stands under a *chuppah*, a wedding canopy supported by four poles that may be either free-standing or held by family or friends. At Orthodox and

Document

The Kaddish Prayer

Reader: Hallowed and enhanced may He be throughout the world of His own creation. May He cause His sovereignty soon to be accepted, during our life and the life of all Israel. And let us say: Amen.

Congregation and Reader: May He be praised throughout all time.

Reader: Glorified and celebrated, lauded and worshiped, acclaimed and honored, extolled and exalted may the Holy One be, praised beyond all song and psalm, beyond all tributes that mortals can utter. And let us say: Amen.

May the prayers and praise of the whole House of Israel be accepted by our Father in Heaven. And let us say: Amen.

Let there be abundant peace from Heaven, with life's goodness for us and for all the people Israel. And let us say: Amen.

He who brings peace to His universe will bring peace to us and to all the people Israel. And let us say: Amen.

Conservative weddings, the bride and her family circle the groom under the chuppah several times; this custom derives from the instruction in Jeremiah 31:22 that "a woman shall court a man," which the rabbis interpreted to mean that she should "go around" him.

Traditionally the ring is placed on the index finger of the bride's right hand, where it can be seen by the official witnesses to the wedding, and moved to the third finger of the left hand after the ceremony. The rabbi, **cantor**, or friends then recite seven blessings, which include a blessing over a cup of wine and expressions of hope for the future happiness of the couple; then the bride and groom drink from the cup.

The conclusion of the wedding comes with one of the best-known rituals associated with Jewish weddings: the breaking of the glass. At Orthodox and some Conservative weddings the glass is broken under the foot of the groom, while at Reform, Reconstructionist, and Humanistic weddings both of the newlyweds typically step on a glass wrapped in a napkin. The sound of the shattering glass is greeted with joyful shouts of "Mazel tov!" ("Congratulations!"). The glass-breaking ritual has multiple interpretations: some understand it to be a reminder of the destruction of the Jewish Temple—and the realization that even in happy times one must be aware that life also brings sadness and pain—while others suggest that it reminds the couple how fragile life and love are. At Orthodox and some Conservative weddings, the newlyweds spend a few minutes alone after the ceremony, sharing some bread and wine, before joining their family and friends at the reception.

Divorce

Divorce is mentioned several times in the Bible (particularly in Deuteronomy 24:1–4), and Judaism accepts it as a legal institution. The Bible gives the power of divorce to the husband, and even today a divorce must be initiated by him. The husband presents the divorce decree, called a *get*, to the wife. Obtaining a divorce was traditionally rather easy under Jewish law; on the other hand, no woman

Many Jewish homes have a mezuzah ("doorpost") affixed beside the front entrance as a reminder of God's presence and commandments. Inside the decorative container is a piece of rolled parchment with handwritten verses from the Shema prayer. Religiously observant Jews touch the mezuzah and then kiss their fingers as they pass through the doorway (© Pascal Deloche/ Godong/Corbis).

can be divorced against her will, as mutual consent is required. In practice, divorce is strongly discouraged, and this is one reason that in North America divorce rates are lower among Jews than in the general population.

The text of the get often stipulates a financial settlement and provisions for the return of property that rightfully belongs to the wife. Among nonreligious and many liberal Jews, civil divorce is deemed sufficient, but Orthodox and certain Conservative Jews must obtain a get if either party wishes to remarry; however, it is not provided until the civil divorce is completed.

⊕ Recent Developments

In the course of its history, Judaism became the foundation for two other major monotheistic religions. Christianity and Islam, like Judaism, are referred to as "Abrahamic traditions" because they too trace their spiritual lineage back to the biblical Abraham. Judaism is by far the smallest of the three, with only 1 to 2 percent of the adherents that Christianity and Islam have. In total, there are approximately 14 million Jews in the world, the vast majority of whom live in either the United States or Israel, each of which is home to roughly 6 million Jews. There are about 1.5 million Jews in Europe (including more than 100,000 in Germany), 400,000 in Latin America, and 375,000 in Canada.

The Jewish Bloodline

One issue of concern in Jewish communities today is patrilineal versus matrilineal descent. According to Halakhah, it is the mother's status as a Jew that determines the status of her children: to be a Jew by birth, one must be born to a Jewish mother. Orthodox and Conservative Jews accept a child as Jewish only if the mother is Jewish by either birth or conversion in an Orthodox or Conservative synagogue. Reform and Reconstructionist Jews do not consider the Halakhic rules binding. They accept a child as Jewish if either parent is Jewish, as long as the child is raised as a Jew and adopts a Jewish identity. Because different branches of Judaism follow different conversion processes, conversions performed by more liberal denominations are not accepted by rigorously observant groups.

Attitudes Toward Gays and Lesbians

Traditionally, male homosexual intercourse was considered unacceptable (based on Leviticus 18:22; 20:13), and this is still the Orthodox position. The Reform and Reconstructionist branches, however, advocate full equality and accept both same-sex marriage and ordination of gays and

Women in the Traditions

An Influential Jewish Leader

One of the most influential rabbis in the United States today is female. Rabbi Sharon Brous, co-founder along with Melissa Balaban of IKAR (the Hebrew word for "essence") and currently based in Los Angeles, California, has drawn both Jews formerly disconnected from Judaism and non-Jews into a vibrant community that cares deeply about social justice and seeks to make a positive difference in the world. Rabbi Brous led a prayer during President Obama's second inaugural prayer service, and her TED Talk, "Reclaiming Religion," has been viewed by more than 1 million people and translated into 14 languages.

Rabbi Brous has written and spoken out against the flourishing of racism and violence in America since the election of Donald J. Trump as US president; she also has addressed the concomitant increase in anti-Semitism.

Indeed, Jewish community centers in 33 US states and two Canadian provinces have altogether received over 100 bomb threats since Trump's election. On October 27, 2018, 11 people were murdered at the Tree of Life Synagogue in Pittsburgh. Jewish cemeteries, furthermore, have been the targets of vandalism. In an encouraging show of interfaith support, Muslim-American activists Linda Sarsour and Tarek El-Messidi began a fundraising effort to help pay for the repair of toppled headstones in a St. Louis Jewish cemetery. The goal was to raise $20,000, but close to seven times that amount was provided by donors. In Philadelphia, members of the Ahmadiyya Muslim Community USA group—a Muslim-American organization—visited a Jewish cemetery that had experienced vandalism and assisted in the cleanup efforts.

Rabbi Sharon Brous. (Courtesy of Sharon Brous)

lesbians as rabbis. The Conservative branch's Committee on Jewish Law and Standards took the same view as the Orthodox branch until recently but since 2006 has recognized multiple positions in support of its pluralistic philosophy. One position upholds the Orthodox view, but another is significantly more relaxed regarding homosexual relationships, although it continues to regard certain sexual acts as prohibited.

The Hebrew Bible makes no reference to lesbianism, and rabbinic tradition considers it a minor offense—an example of immoral behavior, but nowhere near as serious a transgression as male homosexuality. This reflects the androcentric perspective of rabbinic law, which defines a sexual act as penetration by the male member; hence, sexual activity between women cannot violate the law.

Gender Equality: A Distance Yet to Go

Finally, extraordinary strides have been taken in recent decades toward full gender egalitarianism. The Conservative, Reform, and Reconstructionist branches now ordain women to the rabbinate and allow full female participation in synagogue worship. Orthodox women, by contrast, cannot become rabbis, do not count as members of a minyan, and cannot be called to read from the Torah in synagogue services. Yet increasing numbers are studying Torah with other women—an activity formerly limited to males. As Jewish feminists point out, gender equality means that gendered traditions, images, regulations, rites, and rituals deeply embedded in Judaism must be re-created in the spirit of gender equality. This process of transformation is underway in all branches of Judaism but is far from finished.

⊕ Summary

In this chapter you have learned about the development of Judaism from its sacred beginnings as recorded in the Bible through its varied expressions during the Second Temple period to the innovations introduced in late antiquity by the rabbis. The importance of both oral and written texts has been discussed, as have the diverse types of literature produced through the centuries by Jewish communities. You have also learned about the history of the Jewish people and their resilience in difficult times. Finally, you have seen how the challenges of the Enlightenment and modernity were reflected in the development of the multiple, frequently incompatible, approaches to Jewish law, practice, and identity that are manifest in the various branches of Judaism that exist today.

Sacred Texts

Religion	Text	Composition/ Compilation	Compilation/ Revision	Use
Judaism	Hebrew Bible (Tanakh): 24 books organized in three sections: Teaching or Law (Torah), the Prophets (*Nevi'im*), and Writings (*Ketuvim*)	Written in the first millennium BCE	Canon fixed sometime between 200 BCE and 100 CE	Doctrinal, inspirational, educational, liturgical
	Mishnah	Teachings of rabbis in the land of Israel between 100 BCE and 220 CE	Compiled by Rabbi Judah the Prince c. 220 CE	One of the foundations of Jewish law; the object of ongoing study
	Babylonian Talmud	Teachings of rabbis in the land of Israel and in Babylonia between 100 BCE and 500 BCE	Compiled in Babylonia in 6th century CE	Another foundation of the Law; also the object of ongoing study
	Zohar	Mystical teachings of various rabbis	Composed/edited in the 13th century	Study, inspiration, contemplation

Sites

Jerusalem

Within Jerusalem's boundaries are monuments sacred to all three Abrahamic faiths. It was this city that, according to the Bible, King David made his capital, and in which his son Solomon built the First Temple. It became a center of worship for Christians with the construction of the Church of the Holy Sepulchre (begun in 326). In 637 it became part of the new Islamic world; the Muslim shrine known as the Dome of the Rock was completed on the Temple Mount in 691.

The city's status remains one of the most contentious issues in the Israeli–Palestinian conflict. During the 1948 war, West Jerusalem was among the areas captured and later annexed by Israel, while East Jerusalem, including the Old City, was captured by Jordan. Israel subsequently annexed East Jerusalem after the 1967 Six-Day War, and although Israelis call the city Israel's "undivided capital," the international community considers East Jerusalem to be Palestinian territory held under military occupation. On May 14, 2018, the US government opened its embassy in Jerusalem.

The Western Wall

The Western Wall (*kotel* in Hebrew) is the last remnant of Herod's temple, and since antiquity Jews have gathered before it to mourn on the ninth day of the month of Av—the day on which, according to legend, both the First and Second Temples were destroyed. In 1967, the wall area was designated an open-air synagogue, and since then it has been sex-segregated, with men praying on the left and women on the right.

Aleppo, Syria

Aleppo was once one of Judaism's most important intellectual and spiritual centers. After 1948, Jews in Syria were banned from government employment and political office, and were virtually forbidden to leave the country (for fear they would immigrate to Israel, and in hope that their presence in Syria would prevent Israel from attacking it). When the travel restriction was finally lifted in 1992, an estimated 4,000 Jews left immediately, and by 2011 the Jewish population had fallen to no more than 150.

Discussion Questions

1. Explain how Jewish identity can be based on religious, ethnic, or cultural elements—or any combination of them.

2. In what ways is the theme of exile from their homeland reflected in Jewish literature?

3. How did the Enlightenment affect Jews living in Europe?

4. What is anti-Semitism, and how does it differ from anti-Judaism? What were some of the circumstances in Europe in the nineteenth and early twentieth centuries that gave rise to anti-Semitism?

5. Describe the life-cycle rituals that provide a "framework of meaning" for Jews as they pass through different stages of their lives.

6.   What are some of the religious traditions that Jewish women today are challenging?

7.   How do different Jewish rituals and practices reflect the importance that Judaism attributes to its historic past?

Glossary

Aggadah Anecdotal or narrative material in the Talmud; see also **Halakhah**.

apocalyptic Refers to the belief that the world is under the control of evil forces, but that God will intervene and defeat the powers of darkness at the end of time; from "apocalypse," a Greek term meaning "unveiling" (the Latin equivalent is "revelation"). Apocalyptic literature flourished in the Hellenistic era.

Ashkenazim Jews of central and eastern European ancestry, as distinguished from Sephardim and Mizrahim.

Baal Shem Tov "Master of the good name"; Rabbi Israel ben Eliezer (1698–1760), the founder of Hasidism; also known as "the Besht" (an acronym).

bar mitzvah "Son of the commandment"; the title given to a 13-year-old boy when he is initiated into adult ritual responsibilities; some branches of Judaism also celebrate a bat mitzvah for girls.

bris The Yiddish form of the Hebrew *brit*. "Treaty" or, most commonly, "covenant." The special relationship between God and the Jewish people. *Bris milah* is the covenant of circumcision.

cantor The liturgical specialist who leads the musical chants in synagogue services; *hazzan* in Hebrew.

covenant The special relationship or treaty between God and the Jewish people.

Diaspora A collective term for Jews living outside the land of ancient Israel; from the Greek meaning "dispersal." The Diaspora began with the Babylonian Exile, from which not all Jews returned to Judea.

Exile The deportation of Jewish leaders from Jerusalem to Mesopotamia by the conquering Babylonians in 586 BCE; disrupting local Israelite political, ritual, and agricultural institutions, it marked the transition from Israelite religion to Judaism.

Exodus The migration of Hebrews from Egypt under the leadership of Moses, understood in later Hebrew thought as marking the birth of the Israelite nation.

Gaonim The senior rabbinical authorities in Mesopotamia under Persian and Muslim rule; singular "Gaon."

Gemarah The body of Aramaic commentary attached to the Hebrew text of the Mishnah, which together make up the Talmud (both the Jerusalem and the Babylonian versions).

Haggadah The liturgy for the ritual Passover dinner.

Halakhah Material in the Talmud of a legal nature; see also **Aggadah**.

Haredim A rigorously observant subgroup of Orthodox Judaism.

Hasidism Movement founded in eastern Europe by the eighteenth-century mystic known as the Baal Shem Tov. Today the movement encompasses many subgroups, each of which has its own charismatic leader. The Hasidim ("pious ones") make up a significant part of Orthodox Judaism.

Haskalah The Jewish Enlightenment.

Hebrew Bible The sacred canon of Jewish texts, known to Jews as the Tanakh and to Christians as the Old Testament.

Holocaust The mass murder of approximately 6 million European Jews by the Nazi regime of Adolf Hitler during the Second World War; from the Greek words meaning "whole" and "burnt." The Hebrew term is Shoah ("catastrophe").

Israelites The biblical people of Israel.

Kabbalah The medieval Jewish mystical tradition; its central text is a commentary on scripture called the Zohar, which is thought to have been written by Moses of León (d. 1305) but is attributed to Rabbi Shimon bar Yohai, a famous second-century rabbinic mystic and wonder-worker.

Karaites "Scripturalists"; an eighth-century antirabbinic movement that rejected the Talmud, taking only the Bible as authoritative.

kippah "Dome" or "cap"; the Hebrew word for the skullcap that Jewish men wear; see also **yarmulke**.

kosher Term for food that is ritually acceptable, indicating that all rabbinic regulations regarding animal slaughter and the like have been observed in its preparation.

Ladino A language composed mainly of old Spanish and Hebrew, spoken by some Sephardic Jews.

Luria, Isaac (1534–1572) Influential Kabbalah scholar.

Maimonides, Moses (1135–1204) Latinized name of Moses ben Maimon, one of the most famous Jewish philosophers and legal scholars of the Islamic age, identified in religious texts as "Rambam" (from R-M-B-M, the acronym of "Rabbi Moses ben Maimon").

menorah The seven-branched oil lamp that has been a Jewish symbol since ancient times, well before the widespread adoption of the six-pointed star; the nine-branched menorah used at Hanukkah is sometimes called a *hannukiah*.

messiah From the Hebrew *Mashiach*, "anointed [one]." The Greek translation is "Christos," from which the English term "Christ" is derived.

minyan The quorum of 10 required for a prayer service. In more rigorously observant synagogues, only adult males count toward this quota; in more liberal synagogues adult women may also participate in the minyan.

Mishnah The Oral Law—inherited from Pharisaism and ascribed to Moses—written down and codified by topic; edited by Rabbi Judah haNasi around 220 CE, it has an authority paralleling that of the written Torah.

Mishneh Torah A topically arranged code of Jewish law written in the twelfth century by Maimonides.

mitzvah A commandment (plural "mitzvot"); in the Roman era, the rabbinic movement identified exactly 613 specific commandments contained within the Torah.

Mizrahim Jews of Middle Eastern ancestry, as distinguished from Ashkenazim and Sephardim.

mohel A ritual circumciser.

Passover A major spring festival that began as a celebration of agricultural rebirth but came to commemorate the supposed liberation of the Israelites from slavery in Egypt under Moses's leadership.

Pentateuch The Greek name for the first five books of the Hebrew Bible, ascribed by tradition to Moses but regarded by modern scholars as the product of several centuries of later literary activity.

phylacteries The usual English term for **tefillin**.

Purim Literally "lots"; the holiday commemorating the escape of the Jews of Persia from an evil plot of a Persian official named Haman, as described in the Book of Esther. Haman used a lottery system to determine the date for the destruction of the Jews—hence the name of this holiday.

rabbi Literally "teacher," but by the second century CE the official title of an expert on the interpretation of Torah;

once priestly sacrifices had ended with the destruction of the Temple in 70 CE, the rabbi became the scholarly and spiritual leader of a Jewish congregation.

rabbinic movement Legal teachers and leaders who inherited the teachings of the Pharisees and became the dominant voices in Judaism after the destruction of the Temple in 70 CE.

responsa From the Latin for "answers"; accumulated rulings on issues of legal interpretation issued by rabbinical authorities in response to questions from rabbis.

Rosh Hashanah The new year festival, generally falling in September; the day when God is said to open the Book of Life in which he will inscribe an individual's fate for the year on Yom Kippur.

Sabbath The seventh day of the week, observed since ancient times as a day of rest from ordinary activity.

Seder "Order"; the term used for the ritual Passover dinner celebrated in the home; the six divisions of the Mishnah are also called orders or seders.

Sephardim Jews of Spanish–Portuguese ancestry, as distinguished from Ashkenazim and Mizrahim.

Shavuot A one-day festival (two days in the Diaspora, except for Reform and Reconstructionist Jews) in late May or early June that celebrates the revelation of the Torah by God to Moses on Mount Sinai; also known as the Festival of Weeks for the seven weeks that separate the second day of Passover and the day before Shavuot.

Shema, the The oldest and most sacred fixed daily prayer in Judaism, found in Deuteronomy 6:4–9 and 11:13–21, as well as Numbers 15:37–41. "Shema" ("Hear") is its first word.

Shoah "Catastrophe"; the Hebrew term for the Holocaust.

Simchat Bat "Joy of a daughter"; the naming ceremony for girls that more liberal branches of Judaism have adopted as an equivalent to the bris ceremony conducted for boys.

Sukkot The Feast of "Tabernacles" or "Booths"; probably named for the temporary shelters that were constructed by farmers in autumn to protect their ripening crops and later given a historical interpretation commemorating the wanderings of the Israelites in the wilderness after the Exodus.

synagogue From the Greek for "gathering together"; the local place of assembly for congregational worship, which became central to the tradition after the destruction of the Jerusalem Temple.

tallit A shawl with fringes at the corners, worn for prayer; usually white with blue stripes.

Tanakh The entire Hebrew Bible, consisting of Torah (Law), Nevi'im (Prophets), and Ketuvim (Sacred Writings); the name is an acronym of the initial letters of those three terms.

tefillin Small black leather boxes containing parchment scrolls on which the words of four paragraphs from the Torah are written, tied to the forehead and upper arm by leather thongs. See **phylacteries**.

Tetragrammaton "Four-letter" word; the personal name of the Jewish deity, consisting of the four Hebrew letters *yod*, *hay*, *vav*, *hay* (YHWH); conventionally written as "Yahweh."

tikkun olam "Restoration of the world"; the Kabbalistic concept, introduced by Isaac Luria, that the world can be restored through prayer, study, meditation, and the observance of commandments.

Tzaddik "Righteous person"; a title conveying the Hasidic ideal for a teacher or spiritual leader; plural "Tzaddikim."

yarmulke The Yiddish word for the kippah or skullcap worn by Orthodox males.

yeshiva A traditional school for the study of the scriptures and Jewish law.

Yiddish The language spoken by many central and eastern European Jews in recent centuries; although it is written in Hebrew characters and contains some words derived from Hebrew, it is essentially German in its structure and vocabulary.

Yom Kippur The "Day of Atonement," dedicated to solemn reflection and examination of one's conduct; falls 10 days after Rosh Hashanah, usually in September.

Zion In biblical times, the hill in Jerusalem where the Temple stood as God's dwelling place; by extension, the land of the Israelites; in modern times, the goal of Jewish migration and nation-state settlement (Zionism).

Zionism The modern movement, initiated by Theodor Herzl in 1897, for a Jewish nation-state in the ancient land of Israel.

Further Reading

Abella, Irving, and Harold Troper. 1991. *None Is Too Many: Canada and the Jews of Europe 1933–1948*. Toronto: Lester Publishing. An eye-opening must-read for Canadians.

Ausubel, Nathan, ed. 1961. *A Treasury of Jewish Folklore: The Stories, Legends, Humor, Wisdom and Folk Songs of the Jewish People*. New York: Crown Publishers. A collection offering a sense of the Jewish penchant for storytelling.

Baskin, Judith, ed. 1999. *Jewish Women in Historical Perspective*. Detroit: Wayne State University Press. A collection of insightful research.

Berlin, Adele, and Marc Zvi Brettler, eds. 2004. *The Jewish Study Bible*. Oxford: Oxford University Press. The best translation of the Hebrew scriptures currently available.

Biale, Rachel. 1984. *Women and Jewish Law: The Essential Texts, Their History and Their Relevance for Today*. New York: Schocken Books. An excellent source of insight into issues of concern to observant Jewish women.

Brooten, Bernadette J. 1982. *Women Leaders in the Ancient Synagogue: Inscriptional Evidence and Background Issues*. Chico, CA: Scholars Press. Groundbreaking research findings that argue against the long-standing assumption that women could not have held leadership roles in the Judaism of late antiquity.

Cohen, Martin S., and Michael Katz, eds. 2012. *The Observant Life: The Wisdom of Conservative Judaism for Contemporary Jews*. New York: Rabbinical Assembly. A thorough and accessible source for everything about Conservative Judaism.

De Lange, Nicholas. 2003. *Judaism*. 2nd ed. Oxford: Oxford University Press. An accessible overview of Jewish history.

Diamant, Anita. 1997. *The Red Tent*. New York: Wyatt Books for St. Martin's Press. A historical novel that centers on a minor female character in the Book of Genesis and provides a fascinating glimpse into what life might have been like for girls and women in the time of the ancient Israelites.

Diamant, Anita, and Howard Cooper. 1991. *Living a Jewish Life: Jewish Traditions, Customs and Values for Today's Families*. New York: HarperCollins. An easy-to-read guide written from a liberal perspective.

Goldstein, Elyse. 1998. *ReVisions: Seeing Torah Through a Feminist Lens*. Toronto: Key Porter Books. An insightful, accessible analysis of biblical writings by a female Reform rabbi.

Goldstein, Elyse, ed. 2009. *New Jewish Feminism: Probing the Past, Forging the Future*. Woodstock, VT: Jewish Lights. An excellent anthology of feminist writings from a variety of denominational perspectives.

Greenberg, Irving. 1988. *The Jewish Way: Living the Holidays*. New York: Simon & Schuster. A comprehensive exploration of Judaism through an examination of its holy days.

Magness, Jodi. 2012. *The Archaeology of the Holy Land: From the Destruction of Solomon's Temple to the Muslim Conquest*. Cambridge: Cambridge University Press. A lucid, engaging overview of the archaeology of ancient Palestine by a specialist.

Plaskow, Judith. 1991. *Standing Again at Sinai: Judaism from a Feminist Perspective*. New York: Harper One. A classic of Jewish feminism.

Scholem, Gershom G. 1974. *Kabbalah*. Jerusalem: Keter. A survey of the medieval mystical tradition by one of its most respected modern interpreters.

Spiegelman, Art. 1986–1992. *Maus I and II*. New York: Pantheon Books. A powerful graphic novel that tells the story of Spiegelman's father, a survivor of the Holocaust.

Steinsaltz, A. 1989. *The Talmud, the Steinsaltz Edition: A Reference Guide*. The "go-to" source for understanding the Talmud.

Wiesel, Elie. 1960. *Night*. New York: Bantam. A short, compelling memoir by a writer who, as a teenager, survived the concentration camps at Auschwitz, Buna, and Buchenwald.

Recommended Websites

http://www.centuryone.com/hstjrslm.html
A chronological history of Jerusalem.

http://www.ushmm.com
The website of the United States Holocaust Memorial Museum.

http://www.idanraichelproject.com/en/
The website of Idan Raichel's group, which performs in multiple languages, including Arabic, Amharic, and Swahili as well as Hebrew and has been described by the *Boston Globe* as providing a "window into the young, tolerant, multi-ethnic Israel taking shape away from the headlines."

http://www.jbooks.com
The Online Jewish Book Community.

http://www.jewishfilm.com
A website that publishes an annual list of films concerning Jewish themes and issues.

http://www.tikkun.org
The website for *Tikkun Magazine*, an excellent source of articles on politics, religion, and creating a meaningful life from a progressive Jewish perspective.

http://jwa.org
A comprehensive archive of Jewish women's issues.

http://www.myjewishlearning.com
A site offering useful information on Jewish life.

http://www.jewishvirtuallibrary.org
A vast collection of information and resources, with more than 13,000 entries and 6,000 photos.

References

Abella, Irving, and Harold Troper. 1991. *None Is Too Many: Canada and the Jews of Europe 1933–1948*. Toronto: Lester Publishing.

Efron, John, Steven Weitzman, Matthias Lehmann, and Joshua Holo. 2009. *The Jews: A History*. Upper Saddle River, NJ: Pearson Education.

Gilbert, Martin. 1985. *The Holocaust: A History of the Jews of Europe During the Second World War*. New York: Holt, Rinehart and Winston.

Hallo, William W., ed. 2003. *The Context of Scripture*, Vol. 2: Monumental Inscriptions from the Biblical World. Leiden: Brill.

Thomas, Gordon, and Max Morgan-Witts. 1974. *Voyage of the Damned*. London: Hodder & Stoughton.

Twersky, Isadore. 1972. *A Maimonides Reader*. New York: Behrman House.

5

Christian Traditions

Wendy L. Fletcher

Traditions at a Glance

Numbers

There are about 2.2 billion Christians around the world.

Distribution

Christians constitute the majority of the population in Europe and the Americas, Oceania, sub-Saharan Africa, Russia, and the Philippines, and nearly a quarter of the population of Asia.

Founders and Leaders

Christianity was founded by the followers of Jesus of Nazareth, called the **Christ**, on the basis of his teachings and resurrection. Among the early founders, the Apostles Peter and Paul were especially important.

Deity

Christians worship one deity, called "God" or "Lord."

Authoritative Texts

The Christian Bible consists of the Old Testament (the Hebrew Bible) and the New Testament. The Roman Catholic and Orthodox churches include as part of the Old Testament a number of books from the Septuagint (the Greek translation of the Hebrew Bible) that Protestants set apart as apocrypha.

Noteworthy Teachings

According to the doctrine of the Trinity, the one God exists in three persons, as Father, Son, and Holy Spirit. Jesus, the second person of the Trinity, is truly God as well as truly man, and his resurrection is the sign that those who believe in him will have eternal life. The authority of the church has been passed down from the apostles.

In this chapter you will learn about:

- The development of Christianity from the beginnings of the Jesus movement through the Greco-Roman period to the modern era
- Christian literature, including the Gospels, Paul, and theological writings from different periods of Christian history
- Issues relating to church structure, including governance, authority, and the relationship between church and state
- The debate over "right belief," which occupied the first several councils of the church, concluding with the Council of Chalcedon in 451 CE
- How Christians use outward expressions, such as liturgy, art, and architecture, to express their faith and theological beliefs
- The changing role of women in the church
- How Christianity has adapted to the challenges of the modern era

From its beginnings as a small movement within Palestinian Judaism, Christianity has grown to become the world's largest religion. Comprising more than 25,000 distinct denominational groups, whose ethnic and cultural diversity reflect their wide geographic distribution, today's Christianity is a study in complexity and adaptation. This is not a new thing. From the beginning, Christianity has evolved through negotiation of differences in belief, practice, and ecclesiastical form.

Christ in Majesty: detail of a thirteenth-century mosaic in Hagia Sophia, Istanbul (© Cultura Creative (RF)/Alamy).

Christians profess the faith commitment that Jesus of Nazareth was the Son of God, both human and divine; that he died on a cross for the sins of all; and that he was resurrected two days later, demonstrating the power of God over death. From these propositions an "**atonement theology**" was developed, according to which Jesus's suffering and death atoned for the sins of the world and reconciled humanity with God, thus assuring the possibility of what Christians call salvation: going home to God after death. What that faith commitment means and how it is expressed vary widely depending on time, place, sociopolitical context, theological perspective, and cultural–ethnic identity.

⊕ Origins

There is very little that we can say definitively about the historical Jesus. However, it is generally agreed that he was born in Palestine around the year 3 BCE, was raised as a Jew in an Aramaic-speaking family, and began his public ministry around the age of 30. From the **Gospels** written after his death, it seems he was an itinerant teacher in the prophetic tradition of his day. Accompanied by a growing group of followers, he moved from place to place, teaching and preaching, healing, casting out demons, and on occasion raising the dead. At the age of about 33, he was arrested by the Romans and sentenced to death by crucifixion. The nature of his crime is unclear. Pontius Pilate, the Roman official who presided over his trial, found him guilty of nothing. But those who had handed him over to Pilate insisted he be put to death for the blasphemy of claiming to be the Son of God. What distinguished Jesus from other prophetic leaders of his time was his followers' claim that, two days after his execution, he rose from the dead and commissioned them to carry on his work.

The broader story of Jesus's life as recorded in scripture situates him as a figure of historical import immediately through the narratives that describe his birth. He is said to have been conceived by a young woman named Mary through the intervention of God. Her betrothed, Joseph, was instructed by an angelic being to continue in his commitment to her, which he did, raising Jesus as his own son. Jesus then, after a short sojourn with his parents in Egypt to escape a violent king who had pledged to wipe out all young male children of the Israelite people for fear that a messiah had been born who would grow up to challenge secular political authority, was raised in Nazareth as the son of a carpenter. At the age of 12 he is reported to have stood up in the Temple and exhorted the community in a way that set the course for his adult work. Leaving home roughly around the age of 30, he spent three years traveling the countryside sharing his message about the free forgiveness and love of God. His preaching and teaching drew large crowds and often violent antagonism from the religious establishment. As well as large crowds, Jesus gathered a group of disciples, or committed followers, who went with him to learn more closely from him. As he traveled and taught, many people flocked to him asking for a miraculous intervention—healing, casting out of demons, and sometime even resurrection after death. These requests reflected the worldview of the day that such things were not only possible but in some ways normative.

Jesus was not the only itinerant teacher and prophet known for enacting miracles. Throughout his travels he consistently shared a prophetic message that critiqued the religious establishment of his day, stressing that access to God was immediate and possible for all, that the Kingdom of God was not a future state but had already arrived, and that all persons of faith could know the love and mercy of God now. This was disconcerting to the religion of which he was a part, as a highly evolved sacrificial and religious system had developed to mediate the presence of God in the world for religious adherents.

Eventually the political establishment of the day found Jesus's messages too controversial to be sustained, and his time of teaching and acting in the world ended with his execution by the Roman government of the day. The story of Christianity really begins with the experience that his disciples had after his death. The people who had lived most closely with Jesus and followed him to the end witnessed his resurrection and then devoted their lives to sharing that experience more broadly. Sharing the good news of Jesus's resurrection was what, in fact, the Jesus movement was all about.

The main sources of information on Jesus are the four Gospels of Matthew, Mark, Luke, and John, and the **Pauline Epistles** (a series of letters written by the Apostle **Paul** to various early Christian communities). The first Gospel, Mark, was likely written at least 30 years after Jesus's death, and overlapping themes, words, and phrases indicate that it served as the basis for Matthew and Luke. As a consequence, these three books are known as the **Synoptic** Gospels (from the Greek *syn*, "together," and *optic*, "seen"). Although they were named after three followers of Jesus, their actual authors are not known. They were written not to record an actual life, but to sustain and inform a later generation of Christian believers. Nevertheless, scholars agree that some of the material they contain does go back to Jesus of Nazareth, including sayings, **parables** (simple stories illustrating a moral or spiritual lesson), and accounts of his miracles, as well as stories of his death and resurrection. The fact that the sayings and parables recur, often in differing contexts, in Matthew and Luke has led scholars to hypothesize that both drew on a single earlier source referred to as Q (from *Quelle*, German for "source").

Compared with these narratives, the Gospel of John is a major theological essay proclaiming Jesus's identity as messiah and savior. The opening passage makes the author's purpose clear: "In the beginning," he writes (recalling the opening words of the Hebrew Bible) "was the **logos**, and the logos was with God, and the logos was God; all things were made through him" (John 1:1). This logos is the "word" with a capital W, used by John to declare Jesus the **incarnation** of that divine Word: "The logos became flesh and dwelt among us, full of grace and truth; we have beheld his glory, glory as of the only Son from the Father" (John 1:14). As John's Gospel unfolds, Jesus and his followers are continually challenged by Jewish opponents, and Jesus prophesies that his followers will be expelled from synagogues. These details draw attention to Christianity's origins as a movement within Judaism. For John, the true inheritors of Abraham's faith are those who believe that the Word became flesh in Jesus, that the risen Jesus lives among them, and that it is their mission to declare those beliefs to the world.

The Gospels' authors selected certain teachings and events from the life of Jesus to give the early Christian community a context in which to understand the events they professed to have experienced. They took particular care to situate Jesus amid conflict and tell stories that foreshadowed his death and resurrection.

The Pauline Epistles discuss issues of theology, practice, and discipline. Paul (d. c. 65) had a profound influence on the shape that early Christian life took. He never met the historical Jesus; in fact, earlier in his life he had persecuted Christians on behalf of the Pharisees. But one day on the road to Damascus he was overcome with an experience of the risen Christ, which led him to believe that Jesus was the messiah that many Jews had been waiting for, the Son of God who had been raised from the dead to extend to all the promises that God had first made to Israel.

Not all the epistles called Pauline are believed to have been written by Paul. The undisputed letters—Romans, 1 and 2 Corinthians, Galatians, Philippians, 1 Thessalonians, and

Timeline

c. 3 BCE	Birth of Jesus
c. 30 CE	Death of Jesus
c. 65	Death of Paul
312	Constantine's vision of the cross
325	First Council of Nicaea
c. 384	Augustine's conversion experience
529	Benedict establishes monastery
842	Iconoclast controversy ends
862	Cyril and Methodius preach in Moravia
c. 1033	Birth of Anselm (d. 1109)
1054	Break between Rome and Constantinople
1095	Urban II calls for the First Crusade
c. 1225	Birth of Thomas Aquinas, author of *Summa Theologiae* (d. 1274)
1517	Luther posts his 95 Theses
1534	Henry VIII proclaims himself head of the Church of England
1536	Calvin publishes *Institutes*
1563	Council of Trent concludes
1738	John Wesley's conversion experience
1781	Immanuel Kant publishes *Critique of Pure Reason*
1830	*Book of Mormon* published
1859	Charles Darwin's *On the Origin of Species* published
1870	First Vatican Council concludes
1910	Publication of *The Fundamentals*
1944	Florence Li Tim-Oi becomes the first woman ordained as a priest in the Anglican Church
1948	First assembly of the World Council of Churches
1965	Second Vatican Council concludes
1980	Roman Catholic Archbishop Oscar Romero killed in El Salvador
1982	"Baptism, Eucharist and Ministry" (BEM) document published
1984	Archbishop Desmond Tutu is awarded the Nobel Peace Prize for his role in opposing apartheid in South Africa
1988	United Church of Canada declares that homosexuality in itself is not an impediment to ordination
1992	Porvoo Common Statement is signed, facilitating cooperation between a number of Lutheran and Anglican churches
2013	Benedict XVI becomes the first pope in 600 years to resign
2015	Libby Lane is consecrated bishop of Stockport, the first woman consecrated as a bishop in the Church of England

Philemon—emphasize Paul's understanding of Jesus as the Jewish messiah whose death and resurrection were ordained by God. By contrast, the disputed epistles—Ephesians, Colossians, 2 Thessalonians, and the Pastorals (1 and 2 Timothy and Titus)—focus on life in the church and the church's place in the larger world, and were most likely written by followers of Paul. Contemporary with the Gospels, they testify to the institutionalization of beliefs, practices, and emerging leadership structures. Whereas Paul believed the end of the world to be imminent, the later letters suggest a longer, less urgent perspective.

The Epistles give clear instructions as to the shape that a Christian life should take. Paul did not write a systematic treatise on his thought; rather, he wrote to the congregations he had founded to instruct and admonish them. Since these letters address conflicts related to Paul's teachings, we know that opinions regarding the meaning of Jesus's life, death, and resurrection varied. Although Paul's beliefs became normative, it seems that this early period was marked by disagreements over Jesus's message and intentions, as well as differences in both ethics and religious practices.

Internal Conflicts in the Early Church

It took approximately four centuries for Christianity to become an organized religion in its own right. The process involved fundamental questions of identity, authority, belief, and organizational structure. For example, was the Jesus movement only for Jews, or could it accommodate Gentiles?

An Easter procession along the Via Dolorosa in Jerusalem, where Jesus is said to have carried the cross to his crucifixion (GALI TIBBON/AFP/Getty Images).

Practice

Christian Sacraments

From the beginning, members of the Christian community gathered regularly for worship, prayer, and instruction from community leaders. The rituals that they called "**sacraments**" also developed very early on. A sacrament is defined as an outward and visible sign of an inward and spiritual grace—something in the physical world that demonstrates the love and action of God. All Christians accept the sacraments of **baptism** (the rite of initiation) and the **Eucharist** (which commemorates the last meal that Jesus shared with his disciples before his death)

as essential, but the Roman Catholic and Anglican churches also recognize five more: ordination (the setting apart of some individuals for particular work or positions of authority), unction (the anointing of people who are sick or dying), confirmation (the public confession of faith by adults who were baptized as infants or children), marriage, and penance (the confession of sins and receiving of forgiveness). Most sacraments must be administered by an ordained minister, and each church has its own laws regulating them.

Jesus of Nazareth probably conceived of himself as an emissary sent to Israel alone (Matthew 10:6; Mark 7:19–29). But his reinterpretation of the Torah resulted in a radical reformulation of the idea that God's covenant applied only to Jews. Paul dramatically expanded Jesus's teachings by interpreting them as part of a universalizing plan whereby membership in the community of the faithful would depend not on adherence to laws, but on faith in Jesus (Romans 3:21–31). In Matthew (28:19) Jesus commands his disciples to baptize Gentiles and teach them what he taught; in Acts (1:6–9) they are commissioned to be his witnesses "to the ends of the earth." A movement that began with a message directed solely to Israel expanded to embrace all the earth's peoples as potential followers.

A second question concerned whether, if Gentiles were to be included, they should conform to Jewish norms regarding circumcision, food, and ritual purity. Eventually Gentiles were forbidden to adopt the markers of Jewish identity. Perhaps it is not surprising that a movement that explicitly separated itself from Judaism has, tragically, often been actively hostile to Jews.

⊕ Relations Between Church and Society

The religious climate of the age into which Jesus was born was, to a significant degree, otherworldly and escapist. Greco-Roman religion was an amalgam of beliefs and cults from many lands and stages of cultural development. Religious practice was largely unorganized, and people were free to worship the gods they chose. However, at the head of the pagan pantheon stood the state gods of Rome, most notably the emperor himself. The imperial cult made loyalty to the empire a primary social and religious duty.

As monotheists, Jews and Christians could not acknowledge any god but theirs. Thus they refused to offer sacrifices to the emperor, and it was this refusal, above all, that led to their persecution, particularly after 250, when the emperor Decius ordered that all inhabitants of the empire prove they had made the required sacrifices. Some Christians converted to paganism, others went into hiding, and still others were **martyred**. Seven years later, in 257, the emperor Valerian ordered first the deportation and then the execution of many Christian clergy. The result was a serious loss of leadership for the young church.

Valerian's death was followed by 40 years of peace during which Christianity, though technically illegal, was tolerated. This made possible a consolidation of the church's organization, and regular meetings of regional leaders promoted greater unity, although one last great persecution was launched in 298 by the emperor Diocletian.

Constantine

The external fortunes of Christianity changed significantly in 312, after the emperor of the western segment of the Roman Empire, **Constantine** (C. 272–337), won a major battle at a bridge over the Tiber. According to legend, he had seen a cross symbol over his head before the battle and taken this as a portent of victory. With the realization of that victory, Constantine confirmed his loyalty to the Christian God. Although he was not baptized until shortly before his death, Constantine's policies became increasingly favorable to Christians. Beginning in 313, he exempted North African clergy from taxation and used imperial money to enlarge churches, laying the foundation for the accumulation of vast ecclesiastical fortunes. As well, he gave bishops the same power as magistrates, and a significant number of Christians were appointed to upper-level posts in his administration.

A member of the Westboro Baptist Church, a Kansas-based independent Baptist group that is notorious for its protests against homosexuals and Jews, pickets a Jewish high school for girls in Los Angeles (Todd Bigelow/Aurora Photos/GetStock).

Between 320 and 330 Constantine thrust the church to the forefront of public life, guaranteed religious toleration, and forbade both the erection and the worship of statues of himself, thus undermining the political function of the pagan religious system. Later Constantine declared that the church had the right to emancipate slaves belonging to Christians and empowered its bishops to exercise juridical authority in disputes among its adherents.

With Constantine Christianity began its journey from persecuted sect to power-holder in Western culture. No longer did affiliation with Christianity come with a negative stigma; now it promised status and opportunity. Membership expanded accordingly, with troubling implications for a community that until then had been characterized by its capacity for self-sacrifice. In retrospect, many have asked what it meant for Christianity to become a partner of the state rather than a humble servant of the world.

⊕ Authority in the Early Church

Portrait medallion of Constantine the Great, c. 320. The Chi Rho symbol (☧) on his headdress is one of the earliest symbols of the cross used by Christians. It represents Christ by overlaying the Greek letters for ch (X) and r (P). (The Art Archive/Shutterstock)

The earliest Christian worship was conducted in the privacy of the household. Although there were public spaces dedicated to religious expression—temples for pagans and synagogues for Jews—devotional activity was still largely centered in the home. It was only when Christianity grew large enough to move into the public realm that formal authority structures began to develop.

From the beginning, to be a follower of Jesus was to live out God's commandment to love one's neighbor as oneself. This concrete expression of an internal faith was called ministry. Baptism signaled the Christian's entry into the ministry of Christ himself; thus, joining the community of Christians meant living a life of self-giving love. During the lifetimes of the **apostles** (those who had seen the risen Christ and received his commission to continue his work), ministry was largely a matter of **charism**, a spiritual gift that surfaced in the context of the local community. By the end of the first century, however, the need for a more structured system of ministry and a recognized chain of authority was evident.

The early Christians believed that the end-times and "Second Coming" of Jesus were imminent, and they lived accordingly. However, a broader vision was required once it became clear that Jesus was not returning in the expected time frame, especially as the numbers of Christians continued to grow. Together, the external threat of persecution and the internal threat of theological division made it essential for the early Christians to standardize their institutional structures, as well as their doctrine.

The foundational office was the **episcopacy** (literally, "oversight"). As the 12 disciples (the list of names varies slightly between the Gospels and the Book of Acts) became traveling evangelists, carrying the good news of his resurrection from one place to the next, they appointed local people to oversee the nascent communities of believers. These local leaders, or *episcopoi*, were what the early church came to call **bishops**. Although there is no record of formal ordination, this was the beginning of the church's structure of authority. The role of the bishop was to preach the Word, preside at sacraments, and administer discipline, providing oversight for the continuity and unity of the church.

As the numbers of Christians and Christian communities grew, individual *episcopoi* found that they needed to delegate the authority to administer sacraments to others. Those others, who were appointed for their particular spiritual gifts, were known as **presbyters** (literally, "elders"). Over time, the role of presbyter evolved to become the role of the priest as we understand it today. A third office that dates from the earliest days of the church is that of the **deacon** (from Greek *diakonia*, "service"). The deacon's work supported that of the bishops and often took the form of service to the poor and the destitute.

Centralized Authority

With regional expansion, it became necessary to decide how authorities in different parts of the Christian world should relate to one another. Five major episcopal areas, or **sees**, developed—Rome, Constantinople, Alexandria, Antioch, and Jerusalem—whose authority reflected both their place in the development of the church and the administrative structure of the Roman Empire. From the time of the emperor Justinian I (r. 527–565), the eastern sees generally accepted this division of authority; however, Rome insisted on its own primacy from very early on. Conflict was particularly intense between Rome and Constantinople. Both theological and institutional, it eventually led to a permanent schism between eastern and western Christianity.

In the east, a system of oversight developed in which the secular emperor was invested with both secular and religious authority. This led to the concept of a single society in which the sacred and the secular lived in harmony, guided by the Holy Spirit and presided over by an emperor who was the earthly counterpart of the divine monarch, God. In the ancient eastern church, the term "pope" was reserved for the bishop of Alexandria, but today it applies to all Orthodox priests.

Over time, the bishop of Rome, whom we identify today as the **pope**, the head of the western (Roman Catholic) church, assumed primary authority over all churches in the west. Rome's claim to primary authority in western Christianity was accepted on the grounds that its bishop was the direct successor of **Peter**, the "prince of apostles," who was said to have arrived in Rome as early

St. Peter's Basilica is said to sit on the burial site of St. Peter. Its square was designed by the great Baroque sculptor and architect Gian Lorenzo Bernini between 1656 and 1667 (© Günter Lenz/imagebroker/Corbis).

as the year 42. Although there is little or no evidence to support that tradition, we do know that when Paul wrote his epistle to the Romans, around the year 58, there was already a large Christian community in the city.

The model of church–state relations that developed in the west in this period was strikingly different from its eastern counterpart. In the west a fundamental dualism between sacred and secular set the stage for constant antagonism between religious leaders and secular princes.

Women in Ministry

As the center of Christianity shifted from the private household to the public square, the place of women in the church also shifted. Women held significant authority in the household, and some were the heads of their households. Thus gatherings of early Christians were sometimes presided over by the female head of the house in which they met. As the church became more deeply embedded in the public world, however, the roles that women could fill in and for it were increasingly restricted, and the function of presiding over worship gatherings was lost.

In the Gospels we see Jesus welcoming women as followers. Paul wrote about the equality of all before God, including male and female, and his letters indicate that women as well as men performed diaconal (service) roles for the early community. Individual women were also acknowledged as prophets and identified as co-preachers with men in the work of evangelization (Acts 2:17–18). Yet by the end of the Apostolic Age, the letters known as the Pastoral Epistles were admonishing women to be silent in church. And as the three orders of ministry (bishop, priest, deacon) developed, women were excluded from all of them. Only two lesser offices were open to women: those of **widow** and **deaconess**.

The order of widows originated in response to the needs of poor women in the community whose husbands had died. Because the church supported them, only a limited number of women were granted the official designation of widow. To qualify for it, a woman had to be at least 60 years of age, have no other means of support, have had only one husband, and be known for her domesticity, compassion, and abstinence from sexual activity. In return for support, the widows lived lives of contemplation and intercession, praying for the church.

Although they too took their title from the concept of *diakonia*, deaconesses were not female equivalents of deacons, and it was only over time that their role developed into an ecclesiastical office. Different regions had different practices, but it is known that by the third century women (like men) were ordained through the laying on of hands during the service of the Eucharist. Beyond this, we know only that deaconesses helped to prepare female candidates for baptism, visited sick women and children, and prayed for the suffering, as well as the church. By the sixth century the office of deaconess had died out almost entirely, and the idea of women in ordained ministry would not surface again until the nineteenth century.

Ecclesiastical Virgins

In the third and fourth centuries several upper-class Christian women—some widowed, some never married—used their wealth to establish spiritual communities of female relatives and friends, orphaned girls, and poor women. The *mater familias* was the head of the household, setting the schedule for common prayer and determining what kinds of charitable work the women would perform. These women voluntarily withdrew from society, and their consecration to the religious life was informal, but their asceticism was often rigorous.

⊕ The Development of Orthodoxy

By the end of the second century the church was developing an institutional form, but it did not yet have a clearly defined system of doctrine and belief. Passions ran high for centuries as church leaders and theologians disputed what would eventually become the church's normative theological positions, including its **Christology** (understanding of who Jesus was). Early controversies were addressed through the compilation of "Rules of Faith" based on bishops' teachings, the establishment of a scriptural canon, and the use of councils to settle disputes.

The Scriptural Canon

To preserve its legitimacy as the successor to the church of the apostles, the early church decided to recognize as **scripture** only writings that were associated with an apostle and "orthodox in doctrine" (although **orthodoxy** itself was still in the process of being defined). Eventually, 27 books were recognized as constituting the official **canon** of **New Testament** scriptures. From the fourth century in the west and the fifth in the east, there was a general consensus on the canon. As well, both traditions considered the sacred texts of the Jewish people—in the form of the Greek translation known as the Septuagint—authoritative.

Councils of the Church

Very early in the church's history, bishops began to meet in councils known as synods to discuss common problems and work out solutions. Four councils held between 325 and 451 are called "ecumenical" ("worldwide") because they were accepted by both the eastern and western branches of Christianity.

The Council of Nicaea, 325

The first significant agreements as to the nature of Christ were reached at the **Council of Nicaea**, convened by Emperor Constantine in 325. **Athanasius** and **Arius** represented the opposing sides of a debate over whether Jesus was of the same substance (*homoousious*) as God the Father or of similar substance (*homoiousious*). The debate was resolved in favor of the Athanasians, and a statement of belief was formulated that came to be called the **Nicene Creed**. This creed as primary among other **creeds** became the foundational articulation of Christian theology in the western church.

The Councils of Antioch, 341, and Constantinople, 381

Although it had seemed that the question of Jesus's nature had been settled at Nicaea, debates continued to rage, particularly in the eastern churches. The Council of Antioch was a non-ecumenical meeting summoned in an attempt to reverse the decision made at Nicaea and produce a creedal statement more reflective of the Arian position, but the result was further division in the eastern churches. Four decades later, the Council of Constantinople also failed to resolve the matter.

The Council of Ephesus, 431 CE

The Council of Ephesus was convened in response to a theological movement called **Nestorianism**, which was eventually declared a **heresy** (a belief or practice contrary to the accepted doctrine

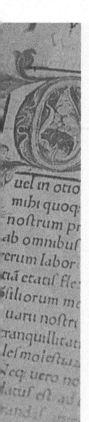

Document

The Nicene Creed

The Nicene Creed affirms the humanity and the divinity of Jesus in one person, as the second person of the Trinity. It expresses the understanding of his nature that is shared by all Christian traditions. However, the text was modified more than once after the Council of Nicaea, and the version that follows includes three words—"and the Son"—that have never been accepted by the eastern churches. At issue is the nature of the relationship of the Holy Spirit to the Father and the Son (see also p. 193).

We believe in one God, the Father almighty, maker of heaven and earth, and of all things visible and invisible; and in one Lord Jesus Christ, the only-begotten Son of God, begotten of the Father before all worlds, God of God, light of light, very God of very God, begotten not made, being of one substance with the Father, by whom all things were made, who for us men and for our salvation came down from heaven, and was incarnate by the Holy Spirit of the Virgin Mary, and was made man, and was crucified for us under Pontius Pilate. He suffered and was buried, and the third day he rose again according to the scriptures, and ascended into heaven, and sits on the right hand of the Father, and he shall come again with glory to judge both the living and the dead; whose kingdom shall have no end. And we believe in the Holy Spirit, the Lord and giver of life, who proceeds from the Father *and the Son*, who with the Father and Son together is worshipped and glorified, who spoke by the prophets. And we believe in one holy catholic and apostolic church. We acknowledge one baptism for the remission of sins. And we look for the resurrection of the dead, and the life of the world to come.

---

of the church). Nestorius and his followers argued that the incarnate Christ had two natures, one fully divine (Christ) and one fully human (Jesus), and that the human Mary—the mother of the human Jesus—could not be the mother of God (the divine Christ). The Council of Ephesus decided against Nestorius, and Mary was affirmed as **Theotokos** ("God bearer").

The Council of Chalcedon, 451 CE

Disputes over the nature of Jesus were finally resolved at the **Council of Chalcedon**, which was convened in response to the argument that Christ had two natures (human and divine) before the incarnation but only one divine nature after it. This view was a variation on a position known as **monophysitism**, according to which Christ had only one nature (divine). The Council of Chalcedon affirmed the decisions of both Nicaea and Ephesus and adopted as orthodoxy for both branches the position known as **dyophysitism**, according to which the two natures of Jesus, human and divine, are united in the second person of the Trinity. Although monophysitism persisted in breakaway branches such as the Coptic Church, the dyophysite belief affirmed at Chalcedon became normative thereafter.

Other Early Heresies

Nestorianism was not the only movement defined as heretical. Among the others were Gnosticism and Pelagianism.

Focus

Christianity in Egypt, Ethiopia, and Armenia

The indigenous Christians of Egypt, the Copts, believe that their faith was taken to Egypt by the Gospel writer Mark, and that their ancestors were pioneers in the development of monasticism (see p. 200). After the Islamic conquest in the seventh century, Egyptians who remained Christian were a minority, but a significant one. The Copts have retained a sense of cultural pride as "original" Egyptians.

By the fourth century, Coptic influence had extended to Ethiopia. A few centuries later, Ethiopia gave asylum to Muslim immigrants but remained Christian, recognizing the authority of the Coptic **patriarch** in Cairo and maintaining its own priests and monks in Jerusalem. The Ethiopian Church has remained essentially Coptic, though it has been formally independent of Cairo since the mid-twentieth century.

In Armenia, legend traces the introduction of Christianity to the missionary activity of the Apostles Thaddeus and Bartholomew. Armenian Christians maintain that their king Tiridates III, who was baptized around 301, was the first ruler anywhere to establish Christianity as a state religion.

One of 11 rock-hewn churches on UNESCO'S World Heritage list, Bieta Ghiorghis (St. George's House) in Lalibela, Ethiopia, was carved from volcanic rock in the thirteenth century. It is an important pilgrimage site for members of the Ethiopian Orthodox Tewahedo Church (© Philippe Lissac/Godong/Corbis).

Gnosticism (from *gnosis*, "knowledge") was a worldview that influenced many ancient religions, including Christianity. Based on a radical dualism that gave priority to reason and spirit over the physical, Gnosticism took Neoplatonic metaphysics as its point of departure for interpreting the relationship between God the Father and Jesus the Son. Gnostics separated God the creator from God the supreme being, positing that the creator was a lower being, or "demiurge." This idea contradicted the developing Christian orthodoxy of the **Trinity**, which conceived of God as three co-equal persons of one divine substance: Father, Son, and Holy Spirit. Among the texts generally considered Gnostic gospels today is the "Gospel of Mary," an incomplete document, discovered in 1896, recounting a conversation with Jesus that a female disciple had in a vision, and the opposition she encountered when she told some male disciples about it.

The heresy of **Pelagianism** centered on the concept of **original sin**, the teaching that the sin of the first humans, Adam and Eve—their disobedience of God's command not to eat of the Tree of Knowledge of Good and Evil—was passed down to all their descendants, and that for this reason no human being could live a moral life without God's grace. The British theologian Pelagius (354–c. 420) argued that humans were not so tainted as to be unable to choose the good of their own free will. His opponents, most notably Augustine of Hippo, declared him a heretic on the grounds that he attributed too much autonomous agency to humans and required too little dependence on God's grace.

Key Figures in Early Church Development

The theology and structures of the early church were significantly shaped by two key figures. The theology of Augustine influenced the intellectual tradition, and Gregory the Great was determinative in molding leadership and church practices.

St Augustine of Hippo

The theologian who argued against Pelagius was **Augustine** (354–430), bishop of Hippo Regius in North Africa and author of (among other works) *The City of God* and *De Trinitate*. Augustine's thought in the areas of original sin, grace, suffering, and just war shaped the emerging scholastic tradition, which would reach its full flower in the thirteenth century with Thomas Aquinas.

Gregory the Great

The papacy of Gregory the Great (540–604) was a watershed in the development of the western church. In a sense, Gregory embodied the transitional character of the late sixth century, drawing on the traditions of late antiquity while heralding the Rome-centered clerical culture of the medieval West. His letters reveal efforts to strengthen Christian authority over secular rulers, to establish bishops as leaders of Christian communities at every level, to eradicate the superstition and idolatry retained from antiquity, and to bolster the authority of Rome by promoting the cults of St. Peter and St. Paul.

Gregory's measures did not constitute a master strategy to achieve Roman supremacy, but his strong stance against temporal authority, his assertion of Roman authority against Byzantium (the tradition of the four eastern sees), his internal consolidation of the bureaucracy, and his careful oversight of internal church life served as foundations for the medieval papacy.

Map 5.1 The Spread of Christianity

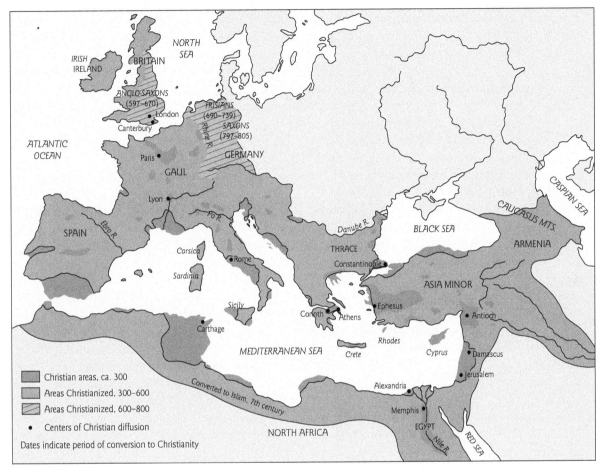

NORTH SEA

IRISH IRELAND   BRITAIN

ANGLO-SAXONS (597–670)

London
Canterbury

FRISIANS (690–739)
SAXONS (797–805)

ATLANTIC OCEAN

Paris   GERMANY

GAUL

Lyon

Po R.

SPAIN   Ebro R.

Corsica

Rome

Sardinia

Danube R.   BLACK SEA

THRACE

Constantinople

CAUCASUS MTS.   CASPIAN SEA

ARMENIA

ASIA MINOR

Sicily   Corinth   Athens   Ephesus

Antioch

Carthage   Rhodes   Cyprus   Damascus

MEDITERRANEAN SEA   Crete

Jerusalem

Converted to Islam, 7th century

Alexandria

Memphis

NORTH AFRICA   EGYPT

Nile R.   RED SEA

Christian areas, ca. 300
Areas Christianized, 300–600
Areas Christianized, 600–800
• Centers of Christian diffusion
Dates indicate period of conversion to Christianity

Relations Between East and West

Although the Council of Chalcedon upheld a non-Arian Christology, the Arian controversy persisted, leading to a schism between Rome and Constantinople that lasted from 486 to 518. After the breach was closed, the bishops of Rome were under the thumb of Byzantium, deprived of the liberty they had enjoyed during the schism.

The Lombard invasion of Italy in 586 served to limit Byzantium's control of Rome, but it also inaugurated a long period during which the Roman church had to negotiate power with secular rulers from the north and west. This meant that by the early seventh century the western church was less stable than its eastern counterpart and had not developed its infrastructure, theology, art, institutions, and social mission to the degree that the eastern church had.

Constantinople and Rome

After Chalcedon, Greek and Latin Christianity grew further apart. The underlying reasons probably had more to do with politics and cultural differences than religious conflicts, but once again a theological formulation provided a rallying point. At issue was the word *filioque* (Latin, "and the son"). Did the Holy Spirit "proceed" from God the Father alone, as the original Nicene Creed had it, and as the Greek church continued to hold, or from the Father "and the Son," as the Latin church came to maintain in the ninth century? Photius, the patriarch of Constantinople, in 867 denounced the insertion of *filioque* into the creed. For the next two decades, one party in Constantinople repudiated the term and condemned the pope, while another supported the term and condemned Photius. Behind the theological concerns lay the basic issue of authority, for Rome had added *filioque* to the creed without the consent of a universal church council. In so doing, Rome had staked not only its claim to be the center of authority against the Greek view of it as just one among five equally important patriarchates, but also the Roman notion of papal authority against the Greek notion of authority as vested in councils of bishops. The final break between the two sides is conventionally dated to 1054, though it was in the making before then, and attempts were made after that date to heal it.

The *filioque* was not the only issue that separated the Orthodox and Roman traditions. In addition, the Orthodox tradition venerated icons (see p. 203), permitted married clergy, used languages other than Latin in Bible readings and **liturgy**, and—most important—refused to recognize the Roman pontiff as supreme.

Eastern-Rite Catholic Churches

Rome's efforts to recruit new adherents among Eastern Orthodox Christians led to the formation of new churches that, even though they were aligned with Rome, retained important elements of the eastern tradition, from the use of local languages (rather than Latin) to immersion baptism. These churches also continued to have married priests, although their higher ecclesiastical officers were generally celibate. Since most of the eastern Catholic churches had Orthodox roots, most of them continue to have Orthodox counterparts today. The exception is the Maronite Church of Lebanon, which has been part of the Roman Catholic world since its founding in the fifth century.

⊕ Practice

Worship Spaces

Because Christianity began as a small movement, private dwellings were the logical places to gather for worship. Such gatherings usually took place in the larger homes of the group's wealthiest members, although poorer urban Christians met on the upper levels of multifamily dwelling spaces. This kind of domestic worship continued well into the Constantinian era, but from that time on the worship spaces used by Christians became more diverse.

From the mid-second century, some houses used for Christian worship were remodeled to accommodate as many as 75 people in a single room. This type of building is known as a house church (*domus ecclesiae*). As well, rooms known as baptisteries provided space for full-immersion baptism rituals. The house church at Dura Europos in Syria, built in the third century, is the earliest known example.

Constantine's pro-Christian initiatives led to the construction of much larger and grander worship spaces called basilicas. Constantine had several of these buildings—in the shape of long rectangles with side aisles—constructed as spaces for Christian worship, usually adorned with wall paintings and gilded mosaics.

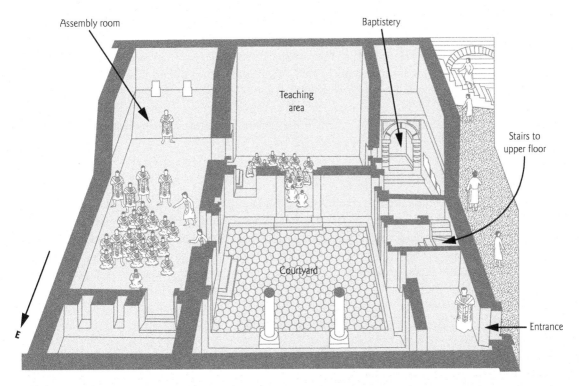

Diagram of the house church at Dura-Europos, Syria.

Source: Adapted from www.deeperstudy.com/link/dura_church.html.

The earliest records suggest that two rituals with their roots in Judaism were critical to the identity of the first communities: baptism, the rite of initiation into the Christian community, and the Eucharist, the shared symbolic meal, which became part of the weekly worship life of the community.

Baptism

In the Jewish world of the first century, there were several rituals involving the use of water. Some were designed to wash away impurities and restore the worshiper to fitness for contact with God. In Jewish communities outside Palestine, conversion to Judaism required a water bath, along with instruction and male circumcision, and although the early Christians abandoned the latter, they retained the ideas of instruction and immersion in water as a symbolic purification in preparation for initiation into the faith.

In the Synoptic Gospels, the story of Jesus's baptism by his cousin, a holy man known as John the Baptist, is generally understood to signal the beginning of his public ministry. Early Christians developed their baptism ritual in keeping with the story of Jesus's own baptism. It is in the act of baptism that the Christian life begins and the path of discipleship is undertaken.

The Eucharist

We know that the early Christians usually gathered for a shared meal at which scripture was read, prayers were offered, and the consecrated bread and wine of the Eucharist were distributed. This structure was modeled on that of Jewish gatherings for prayer and worship.

The idea of the Eucharist drew on the Synoptic Gospels' accounts of the night before Jesus was arrested. At supper with his friends, he took bread, gave thanks to God, blessed the bread, broke it, and shared it with them. He then took a cup of wine, gave thanks, blessed it, and also shared it. As Jesus shared the wine and bread, he said, "Do this in memory of me." This ritual act of remembering Jesus's life and death became central to Christian life and worship. The Synoptic Gospels reflect the assumption that the "Last Supper" was a Passover meal, although it does not follow the pattern of a seder. Over time, the form of the Eucharist became fairly predictable, and that form was then established as liturgical practice.

Early Christian Art

The earliest art of the Christian community reflects the influence of classical Greco-Roman models. Most of what has survived is funerary art: sarcophagi (coffins) decorated with scenes from Jesus's life, biblical stories, and images of the deceased; statues representing Jesus as the Good Shepherd carrying a lamb across his shoulders; wall and funerary plaque inscriptions with Christian symbols; portraits of the deceased with their arms raised in prayer; representations of early Christian martyrs; and scenes depicting both the Last Supper and the symbolic heavenly banquet at which Jesus's followers would gather after the Second Coming. These symbols suggest the frame of meaning that early Christians placed around their practice.

The Rise of Monasticism

In time, many churches became substantial landowners and bishops became influential patrons, often interceding with the state on behalf of individuals. From the third century forward, some Christians became concerned about the implications of this worldly activity. Could the church fill that role without losing some of its moral agency and independence?

Such questions contributed to the rise of the monastic movement. The idea of living under an ascetic discipline was not unique to Christianity: in the Jewish tradition, the Essenes were ascetics with a rigorous communal lifestyle, and the Theraputae practiced a severe discipline. Pagan religious traditions had their own versions of ascetic discipline, with many philosophers embracing solitude and a strictly celibate life.

External societal factors also contributed to the rise of monasticism. As the Roman Empire fragmented, social, political, and economic chaos combined with serious epidemics to create a climate of instability that called for new ways of both surviving and living in community. Among them were two streams of monastic life: **anchoritic** and **cenobitic**.

Anchoritic and Cenobitic Monasticism

The term "anchorite" refers to hermits, people who devote their lives to silence, prayer, and (sometimes) mortification of the flesh. The first significant Christian anchorite was Anthony of Egypt (251–356), who at the age of 18 gave up all his possessions and retired to the desert, where he attracted disciples who joined him in the ascetic life.

Thousands of others, including some women, followed suit. Through a life of silence, refusal of attachments (both material and spiritual), continual prayer, and self-supporting work, the Desert Fathers and Desert Mothers (as they became known) sought to move more deeply into communion with God.

A fourth-century mosaic in the basilica of Santa Pudenziana in Rome shows Jesus teaching the apostles in the heavenly Jerusalem (© jozef sedmak/Alamy).

"Cenobitic" means "communal." The founder of cenobitic monasticism is understood to be St. Pachomius (290–346), a pagan who converted to Christianity and lived for a time as a hermit but felt himself drawn toward community life. He built a monastery, or community house, and many came to join him there. By the time of his death the movement or "order" he had founded included nine monasteries and two nunneries. These large communities supported themselves by practicing a variety of trades and occupations, and they became models for the religious communities to follow.

Communal monasticism developed further in the east under the influence of St. Basil, bishop of Caesarea (358–384), and in the west under St. Benedict of Nursia in Italy (480–550). Basil wrote a rule (code of discipline) that still forms the basis of eastern monasticism. Basilian monasteries tended to be small (containing no more than 40 people), and all property was held in common. No excesses of asceticism were allowed, local bishops maintained control over orders in their area, and each Basilian community was expected to be of service to the larger community around it.

More than a century later, Benedict began his commitment to the ascetic life as a hermit, but after 12 monks had gathered around him, he developed the prototype for western monastic life. **Benedict's Rule** was grounded in the principle that the community's central activity was the divine office, the devotional services held at specified hours throughout the day and the night. As in the east, all possessions were held in common, and moderation and balance were key aspects of the religious life.

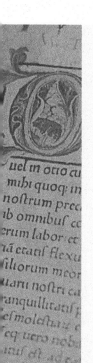

Document
The Desert Fathers and Mothers

Although the Desert Fathers and Mothers lived mainly as recluses, they would share their wisdom with pilgrims who sought them out, often in the form of anecdotal stories designed to help the petitioners find their own way forward.

Someone asked Abba [Father] Anthony, "What must one do in order to please God?" The old man replied, "Pay attention to what I tell you: whoever you may be, always have God before your eyes; whatever you do, do it according to the testimony of the holy Scriptures; in whatever place you live, do not easily leave it. Keep these three precepts and you will be saved." (Anthony the Great in Ward 1975: 2)

One of the old men said, "When Saint Basil came to the monastery one day, he said to the abbot, after the customary exhortation, 'Have you a brother here who is obedient?' The other replied, 'They are all your servants, master, and strive for their salvation.' But he repeated, 'Have you a brother who is really obedient?' Then the abbot led a brother to him and Saint Basil used him to serve during the meal. When the meal was ended, the brother brought him some water for rinsing his hands and Saint Basil said to him, 'When I enter the sanctuary, come, that I may ordain you deacon.' When this was done, he ordained him priest and took him with him to the bishop's palace because of his obedience." (Basil the Great in Ward 1975: 39–40)

⊕ Eastern Orthodoxy

The eastern Mediterranean was comparatively stable and prosperous in the seventh and eighth centuries, and thus was more conducive to intellectual life than its western counterpart, which was still struggling after the barbarian invasions. Byzantium lasted more than 1,000 years after Constantine. Even the slow but steady spread of the Ottoman Turks, who took control of Constantinople in 1453, did not mean the end of the Greek church. Formally tolerated under Islam, though forbidden to proselytize, Orthodox Christians became a self-governing religious community, with the patriarch as their civil ruler.

Christianizing the Slavs

Eastern Orthodoxy was carried from Byzantium to various peoples in eastern Europe. Orthodox missionaries to the Slavic peoples made significant headway in the ninth century. Language played an important part in the success of the Orthodox missionaries, who used local vernaculars rather than Greek; this encouraged the development of independent local churches with a strong sense of national identity. The missionary effort was pioneered by two brothers, Cyril (826–869) and Methodius (C. 815–885). In 862 they traveled to Moravia (today's Czech Republic), where they preached in the vernacular and translated the Bible and liturgy into Slavonic. When a new alphabet (based on the Greek) was later created for Slavic languages such as Bulgarian, Serbian, Ukrainian, and Russian, it was named Cyrillic in Cyril's honor. Romania was Christian from the fourth

Practice

Worship in the Greek Church

Many Christians celebrate the eve of **Easter** with a vigil service in which members of the congregation pass a flame symbolizing Jesus's resurrection from candle to candle. The ceremony is particularly spectacular at the Greek Orthodox Church of the Holy Sepulchre in Jerusalem. Hundreds of worshipers, each carrying a candle, pack the church's rotunda. A priest is ritually searched to ensure that he is not carrying any matches. He then enters the chamber at the center of the rotunda—the traditional site of Jesus's tomb. After a time he extends his arm from the chamber holding a miraculously burning taper. The people closest to him light their candles from his and then share the fire with others, so that within moments the vast rotunda is a sea of flame. Outside the church, the fire is carried by runners to Orthodox congregations elsewhere. This ritual symbolizes the spreading of the Easter light and the gospel message.

century on and adopted the Latin alphabet, but its church was eventually brought into the Eastern Orthodox orbit during a period of Bulgarian rule. Other parts of eastern Europe were converted by Roman Catholic missionaries, who instituted a Latin liturgy and more centralized church control. Thus the languages of mainly Catholic peoples such as the Croats, Slovenes, Czechs, Slovaks, Poles, Lithuanians, and Hungarians use the Latin alphabet.

The early center of Russian Orthodoxy was Kiev, in Ukraine, whose pagan people were forcibly converted to Christianity following the marriage of their ruler Vladimir to the sister of the Byzantine emperor around the year 987. It was only after Kiev fell to Mongol invaders in 1237 that Moscow replaced it as the center of Russian religion and politics.

Byzantine Art

The influence of the Byzantine imperial tradition can be seen in images of Jesus. After Constantine made Christianity mainstream, Jesus began to appear in art not as the young shepherd of the early centuries, but as a distinguished older man dressed in the robes of a king or a judge. It was also around this time that he began to be depicted with a halo representing the radiance of the sun. (Third- to seventh-century Sasanian kings were also portrayed with halos, and similar imagery was used throughout Asia in representations of the Buddha.) By the sixth century, Byzantine mosaics were showing Christ enthroned in heaven as the ruler of creation.

Icons in the Orthodox Church

The Orthodox churches developed a distinctive form of portraiture for depicting religious figures. An **icon** (from the Greek for "image") might be an entirely two-dimensional painting, often on a piece of wood, or it might be overlaid in low relief, in wood or precious metal, and ornamented with jewels. While the robes clothing the figure were generally executed in relief, the hands and face were typically two-dimensional, so that the parts of the image representing flesh appeared to exist on a different plane from the material world around them. Nevertheless, in the seventh and eighth centuries these images became the subject of a heated dispute known as the iconoclastic controversy.

A shop selling religious icons in Monastiraki, Athens (© Mike Kemp/In Pictures/Corbis).

Pitting a faction called the iconoclasts ("icon breakers") against one called the iconodules ("icon worshipers"), the controversy served in part as a vehicle for other antagonisms (political, regional, etc.). But points of principle were also at stake, and Byzantine intellectuals engaged in serious theological discussions concerning the role of images in worship. In the end the Second Council of Nicaea in 787 decided that icons were permissible as long as the faithful did not actually worship them.

Some historians wonder whether the dispute might also have reflected the success of Islam, which rejects any kind of iconography, since the iconoclastic movement seems to have been particularly strong in the regions bordering Syria. In any event, the opponents of the iconoclasts prevailed, and eastern Christendom retained its distinctive tradition. In Orthodox sanctuaries today, a massive screen in front of the altar holds a row of large icons. Smaller icons are hung in private homes.

⊕ Medieval Christianity

Decline and Expansion

The first widespread decline in Christian influence began about the year 600 and continued until the mid-tenth century. Internally, the western church was weakened by poor leadership and corruption. External factors included the decline of the Roman Empire, the ensuing sociopolitical and economic turmoil, and Islam's rise to power across Europe and around the Mediterranean.

After only three centuries, Islam was as geographically widespread as Christianity and was the official faith of states much more powerful than many that professed to be Christian. And then the tide turned. Near the end of the tenth century, the invasions that had racked western Europe for 500 years ceased, even though Muslim populations were well established on the Iberian Peninsula. The resulting stability was conducive to urban growth, the development of commerce and wealth, and the emergence of modern states.

Between 950 and 1050 CE, Christianity made the greatest geographic advances in its history. Scandinavia, which had been a passionate enemy of Christianity, was converted. Czechs, Poles, and Hungarians were Christianized, and Sicily and northern Spain were "recovered" from Islam. For a while, Christians coexisted with Muslims, Jews, and paganism. By 1350, however, most of Europe had converted to Christianity.

In western Europe, nations were emerging from feudalism. In 911 Germanic tribal princes elected a king, in 987 feudal princes chose a king of France, and in 1066 William the Conqueror began establishing a strong state in England. Across territories previously conquered by Islam, political power shifted from Muslim to Christian rulers.

The Crusades

After the Arab Muslims captured Jerusalem in 637, the Christians who lived there were tolerated, and Christian pilgrims were still allowed to visit. In 1071, however, the city was captured by the Seljuq Turks, who were less accommodating than the Arabs had been. The Byzantine emperors appealed to the west for help, and in 1095 Pope Urban II proclaimed the first of what would become a series of "crusades" to liberate the holy places of Palestine. Participation was framed as a sacred pilgrimage and encouraged by promises that those who died in the attempt to free the Holy Land would be honored as martyrs. At the same time, the prospects of worldly adventure and profit encouraged peasants and nobles alike to "take up the cross."

In all, the **Crusades** spanned nearly four centuries, but the most significant period of their activity ended in 1204, when crusaders attacked the Christian city of Constantinople, plundering it and placing a ruler from Flanders on the throne. Although the Byzantines recaptured the city in 1261, relations between western and eastern Christians did not recover.

Punishing Heresy

Beginning in the thirteenth century, the church undertook the task of discovering and punishing Christians whose views differed from church teaching. Until the twelfth century the punishment for heresy was **excommunication** (exclusion from participation in the Christian community), but by the early thirteenth century the church had access to state power and was increasingly turning to it to enforce its decisions.

The first Inquisition was established in 1232 after Emperor Frederick II entrusted the hunt for heretics to state officials. Pope Gregory IX, fearing Frederick's ambitions, claimed this responsibility for the church and appointed papal inquisitors to search for heretics. If accused heretics did not confess and do penance, they were put on trial. In this, the inquisitor was assisted by a jury, and evidence was heard from at least two witnesses. (The famous Spanish Inquisition had a different character, as it was established by the state specifically to investigate Jewish and Muslim converts to Christianity. Its grand inquisitor, Tomás de Torquemada, ordered more than 2,000 executions and was a major force behind the expulsion of the Jews and Muslims from Spain in 1492.) Penalties for those found guilty ranged from confiscation of goods to imprisonment to execution; those sentenced to death were handed over to secular authorities and burned at the stake.

The Development of Papal Authority

Innocent III

After several weak predecessors, Innocent III (C. 1160–1216) asserted the authority of the papacy over secular princes and promoted the development of ecclesiastical government. The papacy became a consultative focal point for the church, maintaining communication with churchmen all over Europe, Byzantium, and Russia.

By the later Middle Ages, however, the pope and the councils of the church were competing for power. A contest with secular authorities also arose as councils allowed opportunities for secular challenges to papal authority. Some of the strongest claims for papal authority in the temporal realm were made by Pope Boniface VIII (1235–1303), who in 1302, in the bull *Unam Sanctam*, proclaimed it "absolutely necessary for salvation that every human creature be subject to the Roman pontiff."

During this period the monarchs of Europe were competing for power, and the kings of both England and France decreed that church revenues in their countries should be used to support their respective governments (and help pay for their wars against one another). Boniface tried to prevent such appropriations, but both Philip IV of France and Edward I of England asserted their higher authority to exact tax from the church. Philip prohibited the export of gold, silver, precious stones, or food from France to the Papal States, which cut off major revenue sources for the papacy. In 1297 the papacy decreed that kings could tax the church in an emergency.

The Avignon Papacy

Boniface's successor, Clement V, had the papal court moved to Avignon in southern France. The Avignon period continued for 67 years, during which papal administration was increasingly influenced by the French crown.

Finally, in 1377, Pope Gregory XI returned the papacy to Rome. On his death, however, division emerged between his successor, Urban VI, and the cardinals, who established a second line of popes in Avignon while Urban remained in Rome. Although the church considered them illegitimate, the Avignon pope and his successor remained in power until 1398, when the latter lost the support of the French king. This "western schism" was not officially brought to an end until 1417, at the Council of Constance.

The Conciliar Movement

The Avignon years gave rise to a critique of papal authority in the church. A theologian named Marsilius of Padua (1290–1343) held that the pope could teach salvation but had no right to command obedience. He argued that power flowed from God to the people and from the people to the king in the realm of worldly affairs, and from the people to the pope with reference to spiritual matters. With Marsilius we see the kernel of medieval conciliar theory, according to which the councils of the church represented the people and the popes depended on the councils for their power. In the old model, God invested both spiritual and worldly authority in the pope, who in turn invested worldly power in the secular ruler; then the two of them, each in his own sphere, ruled the people.

It was the Council of Constance that declared the council itself the supreme authority within the church. It then used its new power to demonstrate conciliar authority over the papacy, deposing the competing popes and electing a single successor. The Constance council also decreed that a new council should be called within 5 to 7 years and every 10 years thereafter.

The conciliar theory provided for a broader sharing of power. However, the theory was never fully developed as a working model of power-sharing and accountability, and by the mid-fifteenth century the movement had been crushed by a revived papal monarchy. Nevertheless, the Council of Constance would influence both the development of representative governments in emerging nation-states and the thinking of religious reformers, both inside and outside the Catholic Church.

Reason and Revelation: Scholasticism and Mysticism

The most critical intellectual issue of the Middle Ages was framed as an epistemological question: How do we know what we know? That question was answered by two competing (or complementary) perspectives: scholasticism and mysticism.

Scholasticism

Scholasticism was the product of an effort to reconcile the philosophy of ancient Greece and, later, Rome with Christian theology. This method of philosophical and theological speculation came to characterize medieval learning.

Institutionally, scholasticism is defined as the teaching of the clergy in the "schools"—that is, the emerging universities of Paris, Bologna, and Oxford, where theology was a central part of the curriculum. Intellectually, scholasticism is defined in terms of its assumptions and goals. For the scholastics, faith and reason were mutually confirming, and by the fifth century Augustine was describing theology as "faith seeking understanding."

John Scotus Erigena, who was born in Ireland around 810 and taught in Paris, expanded on Augustine's understanding of the relationship between reason and scriptural revelation. For Erigena, scripture was the source of authority, but it was the duty of reason to examine and expound it. While scholastic teaching was initially based on the reading of scripture in an effort to arrive at a rational grasp of its meaning, in time it developed a dialectical structure in which a proposition of doctrine was stated and then objections to it were raised and systematically addressed.

Some two centuries later, **Anselm** (C. 1033–1109) moved away from the principle of scriptural authority, asserting that faith itself has a kind of rationality. One of the formulations for which he is famous is the statement "I believe so that I may understand." The most tantalizing of the medieval proofs for the existence of God is Anselm's **ontological argument**. Unlike later proofs that infer God's existence from inspection of the universe, Anselm's argument finds it implied in the very idea of God.

Thomas Aquinas

The tradition on which the early scholastics relied was based on the thought of Plato and dominated by abstract ideas. In the twelfth century, however, Latin Christianity discovered the thought of Plato's contemporary Aristotle, who had developed a model of rational argument that provided more scope for examination of the material world. The greatest of the Aristotelian scholastics was the **Dominican** thinker **Thomas Aquinas** (1225–1274).

In writings such as the *Summa Theologiae* ("Summation of Theology"), Aquinas sharpened the distinction between reason and faith. Although he believed some Christian doctrines, such as those of the Trinity and the incarnation of God in Christ, to lie beyond reason in the realm of faith (though that did not mean they were contrary to reason), he thought others, such as the existence of God, were provable by reason. Aquinas identified five "ways" of proving God's existence, most of which involved describing some feature of the material world and arguing that such a world could not exist without a God. For example, in his second proof he argued that the pattern of cause and effect necessarily implies the existence of a "First Cause" that itself is uncaused, and that that First Cause must be God.

Because the new rational approach was based on logic rather than faith, its exponents were sometimes suspect in the eyes of church authorities. Nevertheless, it was used to explore the key theological questions of the age: How can reason be present in the soul? What is the right relationship between reason and revelation? What is the basis of knowledge?

Mysticism

While scholasticism sparked discussion of the limits of reason in matters of faith, the late Middle Ages also saw a remarkable flowering of mysticism.

Mysticism is a specific tradition that emphasizes the certainty of profound personal experience. Typically, mystics are certain of God not because of some logical proof but because they have experienced a moment of intense, vivid awareness. One characteristic of that experience is a sense of union with the divine through a temporary dissolving of the barriers that normally separate humans from God, granting new perspectives to the mystic. Medieval mysticism was part of a long tradition of cultivation of the interior life, or "spirituality," in which the heart or conscience opens itself to the divine through prayer and contemplation. For many Christians, spirituality reflects the action of the Holy Spirit on the soul. Christian spirituality had roots in the Jewish tradition, was cultivated by the Desert Fathers and Mothers, and was central to the monastic life.

In medieval Europe, one of the most notable mystics was the German Dominican Johannes ("Meister") Eckhart (c. 1260–1327). Eckhart believed that although human beings are created in the image of God, our divine nature is obscured because our life is finite. However, the mind of the spiritual person permits actualization of the divine nature that the soul contains. Eckhart's mysticism sought to dissolve distinctions between self and God.

Whereas Eckhart sought to identify the self with the image of God, the French Cistercian **Bernard of Clairvaux** likened the awareness of God to the awareness of one's beloved. Like the ecstasy of love, this union is fleeting, but no less intensely experienced: "To lose yourself so that you are as though you were not, to be unaware of yourself and emptied of yourself, to be, as it were, brought to nothing—this pertains to heavenly exchanges, not to human affection" (O'Brien 1964: 122).

Female Mystics

A striking feature of late medieval mysticism was the scope it afforded women. Although they were forbidden to participate fully in clerical activities and were limited to supporting roles even in female religious orders, there was no limit to the experiential depth that women could attain in their devotion.

Hildegard of Bingen (1098–1179) was a Benedictine abbess, writer, and musician who was also involved in politics and diplomacy. Feudal nobles as well as clergy sought her advice. When she became an abbess in 1141, she had a vision of tongues of flame from the heavens settling on her, and over the next 10 years she wrote a book of visions entitled *Scivias* ("Know the ways [of God]").

Catherine of Siena (1347–1380 or 1333–1380) in Italy was a member of a Dominican lay order. Actively involved in the religious politics of the day, her *Dialogue* records her mystical visions.

Finally, the English mystic Julian of Norwich (C. 1342–C. 1413) was 30 when she experienced a series of visions during a severe illness. After two decades of reflection, she wrote an analysis of those visions in her *Showings, or Sixteen Revelations of Divine Love*. To Julian, evil was a distortion, introduced by the human will, that served to reveal the divine love of God all the more clearly.

Medieval Religious Communities: Monastic and Mendicant Orders

Monastic Orders

Monastic communities developed a highly structured religious discipline. Monks (male) and **nuns** (female) were required to take vows of poverty, chastity, and obedience; to stay within the physical precincts of the community; and to follow its rule.

Monks played an important part in both the Greek and Latin traditions. Technically, since monasticism had begun as an alternative to established religion, monks were laymen rather than priests, but they followed a demanding schedule of prayer and worship. A distinction was drawn between "religious" (or "regular") clergy, who followed a monastic rule, and "secular" clergy, who worked in the world. In the Greek church (though not the Roman), secular clergy were permitted to marry;

Document
Julian of Norwich

Julian has attracted new attention in recent years, as she speaks to the anxiety so prevalent in the world today. Her revelations assured her that all that is created is known, loved, and held by God. The following text uses the image of the hazelnut to express this understanding.

And at the same time I saw this corporeal sight, our Lord showed me a spiritual sight of his familiar love. I saw that he is to us everything which is good and comforting in our help. He is our clothing, for he is that love which wraps and enfolds us, embraces us and guides us, surrounds us for his love, which is so tender that he may never desert us. And so in this sight I saw truly that he is everything which is good, as I understand. And in this he showed me something small, no bigger than a hazelnut, lying in the palm of his hand, and I perceived that it was as round as a ball. I looked at it and thought: What can this be? And I was given this general answer: It is everything which is made. . . . In this little thing I saw three properties. The first is that God made it, the second that he loves it, the third is that God preserves it. It is that God is the Creator and the lover and the protector. (Colledge and Walsh 1978: 130–131)

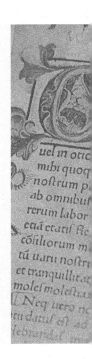

members of the ecclesiastical hierarchy were always celibate, however. The insistence that priests be celibate became stronger in the Middle Ages. Rationales included the spiritual benefit of surmounting worldly desires and the practical benefit of freedom from the responsibilities of marriage and parenthood. In addition, since it made a hereditary priesthood impossible, celibacy worked against the tendency for institutional influence to become concentrated in particular families.

Cluniac Fathers

Founded in 910, the monastery at Cluny in France became the center of a movement to bring Benedictine monastic institutions under the control of religious rather than secular authorities. Cluny under the leadership of the **Cluniac Fathers** became a center of revitalization that inspired other efforts at renewal. Nevertheless, within a century of its founding Cluny itself had grown rich and begun to abandon the rigorous simplicity that Benedict had called for.

Cistercians

In response to the changes at Cluny, an austere new order was founded at Cîteaux, north of Cluny, in 1098. The **Cistercians** wore simple undyed wool habits, ate no meat, and worshiped in sparsely decorated churches. By 1100 there were 500 Cistercian abbeys. One group of Cistercians in particular became known for their rule of silence. The Cistercians of the Strict Observance, or Trappists, were founded in the 1600s at the monastery of La Trappe in Normandy. The best-known Trappist of the twentieth century was the mystic Thomas Merton (1915–1968), who explored Asian spirituality, especially Zen Buddhism, and was active in social protest in the 1960s. Other Cistercians helped to found spiritual orders of knights such as the Knights Templar, the Knights of St. John, and the Teutonic Order. Their members made pilgrimages to the Holy Land and took as their biblical model the Maccabees, the Jewish patriots of the second century BCE.

Carthusians

Founded in 1084, the austere **Carthusian** order (named after its base at La Grande Chartreuse in France) demanded a vow of silence from its members. Like the Benedictine abbey of Fécamp near the English Channel, the Chartreuse abbey supported itself in part by making and selling a famous drink—in this instance, the brilliant green liqueur that gave its name to the color chartreuse.

Mendicant Orders

The monastic response to the secular world had been to withdraw from it, but with urban growth some monastics felt compelled to respond to the needs of the urban poor. Thus a new type of religious order emerged whose members—called **friars**, from the Latin *frater* ("brother")—dedicated themselves to pastoral work. These **mendicants** either worked or begged for their living, and were not bound to a particular convent.

Franciscans

Francis of Assisi (1182–1226) was the son of a wealthy cloth merchant in central Italy, but a serious illness in his 20s led him to rethink his life. On a pilgrimage to Rome, he was so moved by the beggars outside St. Peter's Basilica that he exchanged clothes with one of them and spent the day begging for alms. When he returned to Assisi, he dedicated his life to serving the poor. Gradually attracting a small group of like-minded companions, he established a monastic rule emphasizing poverty, which received papal approval in 1209. Within a few years, his friend Clara of Assisi had formed a **Franciscan** women's order known as the Poor Clares. An offshoot of the Franciscans called the Capuchins drew up their own rule in 1529 and are still known today for their soup kitchens, which offer free meals in impoverished neighborhoods.

In 1224 Francis experienced a vision of an angel from whom he received the "stigmata," wounds in his own body that replicated those suffered by Christ on the cross. Proclaimed a saint in 1228—just two years after his death—he became the subject of many legends, including one in which he preached to a flock of birds, telling them how fortunate they were that God provided for them.

Dominicans

In 1216–1217 a priest from northern Spain named Dominic Guzmán received a papal mandate to establish a preaching order dedicated to combating the "Albigensian heresy." (Named for the city of Albi in southwestern France, Albigensianism was a dualistic doctrine, not unlike **Manichaeism**, centered on a view of existence as a struggle between light and darkness, and highly critical of Roman Catholicism.) Dominicans such as Aquinas rapidly established their influence as itinerant preachers of doctrine in university towns such as Paris.

Founded in 1929 by Capuchin friars, the Capuchin Soup Kitchen in Detroit now serves 2,000 people a day in some of the city's poorest neighborhoods. In 1997 the friars founded a farm that in 2011 harvested nearly 7,000 pounds of produce for the soup kitchen (© Jim West/Alamy).

Carmelites

The hermits of Mount Carmel were organized in Palestine in 1154, during the Crusades, and given a rule by the patriarch of Jerusalem. As the numbers of crusaders in the Holy Land declined, the **Carmelites** established themselves in Europe and England, where they were termed "White Friars."

Women in Medieval Catholicism

The tradition of women participating in a consecrated religious life had roots in the early church, but its most significant period of development was the Middle Ages. In response to women's requests for direction on how to order a common religious life, local bishops would write rules ("canons") for them. Communities of "canonesses" were characterized by their diversity, lack of formal structure, and relative autonomy.

Nuns

The rules governing female monastic communities paralleled those for male communities. Normally, each woman entering the convent was required to furnish a dowry and relinquish all private property. Nuns lived together under one roof and took vows of poverty, continence, and obedience that reflected a permanent commitment to the religious life. The formal consecration ended with the vow to live always as the bride of Christ.

Over time, it became common for women's communities to separate themselves entirely from the world; by the thirteenth century, the male hierarchy of the church had imposed this "cloistering" on all women's communities, over which powerful **abbesses** presided. In addition to making and enforcing the convent's laws, the abbess was responsible for its landholdings and so played a significant role in the feudal system. She administered the financial affairs of the estate and also oversaw the lives of the tenants who farmed it.

Nevertheless, the power of the female monastic community declined by the later Middle Ages. Secular princes anxious to limit the autonomy of the church claimed an interest in church-owned lands. Furthermore, since no woman could be ordained, even an abbess was by definition a layperson and therefore forbidden to exercise authority over a male cleric, however junior. Increased strictures around cloistering also meant that abbesses could not leave their convents to conduct business.

Beguines and Beghards

Beguines were unconsecrated women who lived a freer type of communal religious life than their monastic counterparts. They did not live under the authority of local bishops and did not follow any of the traditional monastic rules, but came together in small groups, mainly in urban environments, to live in poverty, celibacy, prayer, and service, after the model of the gospel. This new style of religious life also attracted some men, known as **Beghards**, though in smaller numbers.

A number of Beguines are known for their writings in the tradition of love mysticism. Among them are Mechthild of Magdeburg in Saxony (1207–1297) and Hadjewich, a Beguine from Flanders who wrote many letters as well as poems and accounts of visions. A common theme in their work is the ecstatic union of the soul with God. A third notable female mystic who is widely thought to have been a Beguine was Marguerite Porete, who was burned at the stake for heresy in 1310. Though condemned by church authorities, her book *The Mirror of Simple Souls* influenced Christian mystics for centuries.

Document

Mechthild of Magdeburg, "Of the Nine Choirs and How They Sing"

The nine orders or "choirs" of angels were a standard part of the religious imagery of Mechthild's day. The idea of a hierarchy of angels had been well established since the fifth century.

Now listen, my love. Hear with spiritual ears what the nine choirs sing.

    We praise You, O Lord.

    For you have sought us in your humility,

Saved us by your compassion,
Honoured us by your humanity,
Led us by your gentleness,
Ordered us by your wisdom,
Protected us by your power,
Sanctified us by your holiness,
Illumined us by your intimacy,
Raised us by your love. (Madigan 1998: 138)

Sainthood

The expansion of Christianity into Africa, Asia, and eastern Europe was facilitated by its emphasis on the miraculous power of **saints**. Over the centuries the church developed criteria for sainthood (including the performance of attested miracles), a canonical list of saints, and a rigorous procedure for screening candidates. The first person to be declared a saint was the German bishop Ulrich of Augsburg, in 993.

    The saints came to be regarded as beings possessed of a special merit or virtue who could be approached by believers who wanted them to intercede with God on their behalf. By praying to certain saints or making pilgrimages to their shrines, one might win release from punishment in the next existence, a state named "purgatory" by the Christians of this era. Particular saints came to be associated with specific conditions or occupations. St. Christopher, for example, who was said to have carried the child Jesus across a dangerous river, is one of several patron saints of travelers, and St. Cecilia is the patron of musicians because she is said to have sung to God on her deathbed.

The Virgin Mary

Preeminent among the saints was **Mary**, the virgin chosen by God to become the mother of Jesus. By the later Middle Ages it was thought that someone so close to Christ must share in his redeeming work, and that she would be willing to plead with her son on behalf of sinners. The resulting increase in devotion to Mary reflected a broader theological shift toward a greater concern with the humanity of Jesus.

    In Latin Europe, artistic depictions of Mary followed a particular set of conventions. Although some of them can be traced to the cult of the pre-Christian goddess Isis, Mary's role was not limited to that of the devoted young mother. She was also the mature woman who grieved at the martyrdom of her adult son and the model of purity and incorruptibility, devotion and fidelity, sorrow and compassion.

Worship in the Medieval Church

Liturgical reforms in the early medieval period limited the opportunities for ordinary people to participate in worship. Portions of the liturgy that had been spoken in the vernacular were increasingly performed in Latin, and the rules governing the Eucharist were tightened to require confession and penitence before the sacrament could be received. This meant that priests could take communion frequently, but laypeople perhaps only once a year. In addition, only the clergy were allowed to receive the wine (the blood of Christ); laypeople were given only the bread (the body).

Church music also became less accessible to the average person. Gregorian chant or plainsong had been easy for congregations to learn, but as musical forms became more complex, participation was increasingly restricted to formal choirs made up of monks and clergy.

Church architecture contributed to the distancing of laypeople. Between the nave (the main body of the church, where the worshipers gathered) and the altar, another section of seats (the chancel) was added for the choir, and by the later medieval period, worshipers' view of the altar had been further obstructed by screens erected between the nave and the chancel. Finally, the altar was pushed up against the wall so that instead of standing behind it, facing the people, while celebrating the Eucharist, the priest now turned his back on them. This change had a theological basis: now the priest was offering the sacrifice on behalf of the people rather than presiding at the Eucharistic banquet of the whole people of God.

⊕ The Early Modern Era

Humanism

The fourteenth century marks the divide between medieval and early modern Europe. During this century, Western culture began to rediscover the philosophy, science, art, and poetry of Greek and Roman antiquity. Among the consequences of this revival of interest was a renewed emphasis on life in this world, the celebration of beauty, and the capacity of human beings to govern themselves. This put the humanists in conflict with a church that had traditionally understood itself to be the primary interpreter and mediator of human experience.

Much of the groundwork for later reformers was laid by **Erasmus** (1466–1536). An Augustinian priest from Rotterdam in the Netherlands, he was critical of the church's abuses and called for demanding new standards of scholarship in theology, based on new translations of the original sources.

In itself, **humanism** posed no real threat to the church, but the external force of humanism was met with a push toward reform from within the church itself. Together, these external and internal forces for change led to the schism within western Christianity that came to be known as the Protestant Reformation.

The Protestant Reformation in Continental Europe

The English Reformation, though not unrelated to the reforming activity on the continent, was uniquely linked to the British political context; therefore, it will be discussed separately (see "The English Reformation").

In the early sixteenth century, the church was Europe's largest landholder. Clergy played more than one role in society, not only dispensing the sacraments, but providing medical care and education. The religious enthusiasm of the laity was reflected in pilgrimages, ostentatious public devotions, and huge investments in the church through paid funeral **masses** and the purchase of **indulgences** (releases from the time that the soul was required to spend in purgatory). In Germany, while many German clergymen were penniless and ill-educated, bishops often came from very affluent families and used their ecclesiastical positions to reinforce their wealth, social status, and political power. At the same time, this period was one of unprecedented advances in lay literacy, which reformers such as **Martin Luther** promoted by translating the scriptures into vernacular languages. The combination of a changing intellectual world, rising dissatisfaction with inequalities within the church, and the ability of ordinary people to directly access scripture (a development facilitated by the invention of the printing press) set the stage for the Reformation.

Martin Luther (1483–1546)

Widely considered to be the father of the Protestant Reformation, Luther was the son of a German miner. He became an Augustinian friar in 1505, and in 1512 was made a doctor of theology and professor of scripture at the University of Wittenberg.

Luther struggled with the theological issues of salvation. In the complex system of clerical mediation between God and sinner, he feared that he would not be found worthy, until a sudden revelation convinced him that humans are justified (set right with God) only by faith, which itself is a gift of God's grace; there are no "works" we can do to earn that justification. From this point forward, Luther argued that if a person has faith, then he or she is assured of salvation.

In October 1517 Luther posted a list of "95 Theses" against indulgences on the door of the church at Wittenberg. This public protest eventually led to his excommunication and emergence as the primary agent of the Protestant Reformation, a schism that split the church into many differing groups, among them one named for Luther himself.

Although Luther's core doctrine was justification by faith alone, through grace alone, the Lutheran tradition also emphasizes the idea of the priesthood of all believers, whereby all have direct access to God without mediation by a priest. This notion led to the development of a church that was much less dependent than its Catholic counterpart on ministers, particularly bishops.

Jean Calvin (1509–1564)

Jean Calvin represents the second stage of the Reformation. A French Protestant theologian who had been trained as a lawyer, he soon found himself unwelcome in Catholic France and so took refuge in Geneva between 1536 and 1538. Although his first attempt to establish his version of Christianity in Geneva failed, in 1541 he returned and became the undisputed master of the Genevan Reformation.

This bronze statue by Johann Gottfried Schadow, erected in Wittenberg's town square in 1821, was the first public monument to Luther (© typo-graphics/iStockphoto).

Like Luther, Calvin attributed primary authority to scripture rather than clergy, and affirmed the justification of the sinner by faith alone. Where Calvin differed from Luther was in his theology of sin and salvation. He believed that since the fall of Adam, no human had been able to freely choose faith and thereby realize his own salvation: only God could bring that about, and even before the creation he had predestined some of his creatures for damnation and some for salvation. (By contrast, Luther believed that the death and resurrection of Christ made the gift of faith by grace available to all.) Calvin's notion of **predestination** emphasized the omnipotence of God. After his death, his teachings were developed in a number of emerging Protestant traditions.

Calvin's Geneva reflected his vision of a reform community, with regular preaching, religious instruction for adults and children, and close church regulation of the business and moral life of the community. In effect, it was a **theocracy**, a state ruled by God through religious authorities. The Genevans hoped to convert France, but in 1562 the first in a series of "Wars of Religion" broke out between French Roman Catholics and Protestants (Huguenots) who were heavily influenced by Calvin. Facing persecution in the seventeenth and eighteenth centuries, the Huguenots sought refuge in Protestant lands throughout Europe and as far afield as the present-day United States and South Africa. As we will see, a variety of denominations, usually identified as "Reformed" or "Presbyterian," resulted from this diaspora.

Ulrich Zwingli (1484–1531)

The father of the Swiss Reformation, **Ulrich Zwingli**, was ordained a Roman Catholic priest in 1506. Inspired by Luther, Zwingli argued that the gospel is the sole basis of truth and in so doing rejected the authority of the pope. Until 1522 he accepted the traditional Roman Catholic view of the Eucharist as a ritual of **transubstantiation**, in which the bread and wine become the literal body and blood of Jesus. But by 1524 he was arguing that the Eucharist was strictly symbolic. This stance made union with other Protestant churches impossible, as most accepted the idea of the real presence of Christ in the bread and wine in some form.

Sixteenth-Century Protestant Denominations

The Reformation was marked by division. Many early reformers were no less authoritarian than the church they had rejected, and their competition for adherents led to confusion. Denominational fragmentation has continued to the present day. In continental Europe, two main theological directions emerged in the sixteenth century—Lutheran and Calvinist—although there were also several more radical movements.

Lutherans

Lutheranism flourished in Germany and Scandinavia. Stressing the authority of scripture and the guidance of the Holy Spirit, it allowed ample scope for rational argument, but it also encouraged personal piety. Images of God as friend and companion are just as frequent in Lutheran hymns as images of God as warrior or judge.

In worship and ecclesiastical organization, Lutherans departed in only some respects from the Roman church. They retained a Eucharist-like sacrament, although they celebrated it in the vernacular and held that Christ's body was present along with the bread and wine but was not produced out of them. Lutheran priests continued to be governed by bishops but were permitted to marry. In recent years, women have been ordained as Lutheran priests.

In most parts of Germany and Scandinavia, Lutheran Christianity became the state religion. The **Evangelical** Church, as it is called in Germany, is dominant in the north of the country, while Catholicism is stronger in the south (to this day, Germany provides basic funding for both churches out of tax revenues). Lutheranism was carried to North America by Germans, who settled in places such as Pennsylvania, Ohio, Missouri, and Ontario, and by Scandinavians, most of whom settled in Minnesota and Wisconsin.

Reformed Churches

In the mid-1500s reformers in and around Switzerland departed from Luther's position on several points. While Zwingli in Zürich disputed Luther's Eucharistic theology, Martin Bucer in Strasbourg promoted a more active role for laypeople as ministers, elders, deacons, and teachers. From Geneva the ideas of the Swiss Reformation spread to France, the Netherlands, Hungary, England, and Scotland. In the Netherlands and Hungary, the Calvinist churches are known as **Reformed churches**.

In England the Reformed tradition is called "Presbyterian" because it is governed by lay elders or "presbyters"; for the same reason, the established Church of Scotland is termed Presbyterian. Reformed churches do not have bishops; instead, the presbyters corporately perform the tasks of a bishop. Presbyterians from England and Scotland settled in North America, New Zealand, and Australia. Dutch Reformed settlers carried their tradition to South Africa, New York, and Michigan. In the nineteenth and twentieth centuries, Presbyterian missionaries reached many parts of Asia and Africa, but in most cases the churches they founded remained small. The Presbyterians did become a sizable minority in Korea, however.

Anabaptists

The "Radical Reformation" rejected the broader Protestant movements' affiliations with secular power. Groups such as the Anabaptists shunned politics, military service, and even the taking of oaths. Believing that baptism should be actively sought on the basis of mature personal commitment, the Anabaptists practiced adult rather than infant baptism. Essentially anti-establishment in orientation, the Anabaptist movement emerged in the 1520s when some of the more radical followers of Zwingli began administering adult baptism in defiance of Zwingli himself. A decade later, in Münster, Germany, Anabaptist efforts to establish the Kingdom of God by force prompted a crackdown by both Catholic and Protestant authorities.

Thereafter a former Dutch priest named Menno Simons led the movement into a largely otherworldly and nonviolent path. Since there was no chance of removing the authorities, he urged his followers to remove themselves from society. Some of his followers—the Mennonites—settled in the Netherlands. As the movement spread eastward, however, persecution led some to leave Europe altogether.

Mennonites who migrated to the Americas settled mainly in Pennsylvania, where they came to be known as Pennsylvania Dutch. Today most Mennonites are fully part of the modern world, though branches such as the Old Order Amish continue to live a strictly traditional life, using only the simple tools of a century ago because they associate modern technology with the moral temptations and corruption of the secular world.

Unitarians

Unitarians took their name from their understanding of God as a single person rather than the three persons of the Trinity. Among the first to express this view was the German Martin Cellarius (1499–1564), but Unitarian communities also emerged in Poland and Hungary. In England, John Biddle began to publish Unitarian tracts in 1652, and a Unitarian congregation was organized in London in 1773–1774. In the United States, William Ellery Channing preached a sermon in 1819 that American Unitarians have taken as a kind of denominational manifesto.

In North America, Unitarianism has appealed mainly to people of a humanist and rationalist bent. Because of its minimal creedal demands (from early on, some Unitarians even dispensed with the idea of a divinity), it has become the denomination of choice for many Jewish–Christian couples.

Women and the Continental Reformation

Although the reformers did not see women as equal to men, their emphasis on the individual believer's direct relationship with God had considerable significance for women. One of the more consequential reform arguments was against celibacy. In the course of the Reformation, many convents and monasteries were closed, and although most nuns did not renounce their vocations, some did leave and marry. Martin Luther himself married a former nun, Katherine Von Bora, and together they made their home a center for the new movement. In addition, Luther's commitment to the principle that ordinary people should have unmediated access to scripture led him to advocate public education for girls as well as boys.

The Counter-Reformation

The Protestant Reformation stimulated reform from within the Roman Catholic Church, which led to its revitalization as an institution. This phenomenon is known as the Counter-Reformation. From the mid-1500s to the Thirty Years' War (1618–1648), the reforming church was reinvigorated by the development of new religious orders, the Council of Trent, and a renewed sense of spirituality.

The defining religious order of the Counter-Reformation was the Society of Jesus (better known as the Jesuits). Its founder, Ignatius Loyola (1491–1563), was a knight from a noble Spanish family who had had a conversion experience after being wounded in battle. After several years as a hermit, in 1534 he joined with six companions to form the Society of Jesus. Characterized by a rigorous discipline that reflected Loyola's military background, the Jesuits became the spearhead of the missionary forces that carried Christianity to both the Americas and Asia.

The Council of Trent (1545–1563) was the first ecumenical council to be convened since the Council of Constance. Over the course of 18 years, it laid the foundations for renewal of both the discipline and the spiritual life of the church. It would be three centuries before another council was convened. Thus Trent was a watershed that marked the beginning of early modern Roman Catholicism.

Counter-Reformation Mysticism

During the Counter-Reformation many religious orders experienced a revitalization of spiritual life. The most notable figures in this renewal were the Spanish mystics Teresa of Avila (1515–1582) and John of the Cross (1542–1591).

Educated by Augustinian nuns, Teresa of Avila entered a Carmelite convent in 1535. Her personal experience of God fired her with reforming zeal to establish several houses within her order. Teresa wrote extensively about her religious experience. All her teachings were grounded in intense personal experience of revelation in which she experienced the immediacy of God's presence in a physical as well as a spiritual sense. Significantly, her writings (especially *The Way of Perfection* and *The Interior Castle*) were received with enthusiasm, even though her time was one of extreme repression for women.

Teresa's primary themes were self-knowledge, the need for awareness of one's weakness and vulnerability, the reality of God's presence, and the certainty of forgiveness and transformation through Christ. For Teresa mysticism was not an escape from reality. Rather, the experience of divine illumination set humanity free to live for God and others. From suffering came compassion, and through prayer the person who practiced looking inward would be transfigured, released to live a life of active love.

John of the Cross was also a Carmelite, and with Teresa he founded a reform order called the Discalced ("Barefoot") Carmelites. He is best known for the beauty of his writings, which are considered the apex of Spanish mystical literature. Like Teresa, John experienced the movement toward God as a journey of many stages. His most famous poem, "The Dark Night of the Soul," describes the stage when the soul, longing for God, becomes disoriented and loses its way. As he later explained in a commentary on the poem, this part of the journey is painful and can last for years, but it is a necessary stage on the way to union with God.

The English Reformation

The relationship of the English Reformation to the Continental Reformation was complex. England had been acquainted with Christianity since the fourth century, and by the seventh century it was fully embedded in the Roman ecclesiastical system. However, it was predisposed to embrace the principles behind the continental Reformation.

Document

Mysticism

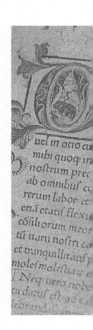

The first passage comes from Teresa of Avila's "The Interior Castle," while the second is drawn from John of the Cross's commentary on the poem "The Dark Night of the Soul."

Now let us come to imaginative visions, for they say the devil meddles more in these than in the ones mentioned, and it must be so. But when these imaginative visions are from our Lord, they in some way seem to me more beneficial because they are in greater conformity with our nature. I'm excluding from that comparison the visions the Lord shows in the last dwelling place. No other visions are comparable to these. (Teresa of Avila in Madigan 1998: 250)

However greatly the soul itself labours, it cannot actively purify itself so as to be in the least degree prepared for the Divine union of perfection of love, if God takes not its hand and purges it not in that dark fire. (John of the Cross 1990: 22)

A century and a half before Luther posted his 95 Theses, John Wycliffe (1320–1384) had written against indulgences as well as the wealth and power of the papacy. He also advocated the use of the vernacular in both scripture and worship, and promoted an early translation of the Bible into the language of ordinary people. Even though possession of a translated Bible could lead to a death sentence, many copies were made between the 1380s and 1530s, when Wycliffe's version was superseded by a new translation, from the original Hebrew and Greek, that had the benefit of being produced using the printing press (as did Luther's German Bible). The main author of that work was William Tyndale (1492–1536). Having left the still-Catholic England of Henry VIII in the 1520s for the continent, Tyndale was arrested in the Netherlands and put to death as a heretic before he could complete his translation. Yet just three years later, Henry himself authorized a different English translation. What had changed?

The English Reformation was as much political as it was theological. When the continental Reformation began, Henry VIII defended the papacy, put his name on an anti-Lutheran tract, sentenced priests with reform sympathies to death, and, through Lord Chancellor Sir Thomas More, actively suppressed Protestant heresies. But things changed when Henry needed a divorce from his wife, Catherine of Aragon, so that he could marry Anne Boleyn, who herself was significantly influenced by Protestant thinking. The pope's refusal to grant the divorce eventually led to a schism between England and Rome. The Church of England was established as an autonomous entity, no longer subject to the authority of the bishop of Rome, in 1534.

The concept of church–state relations that developed in England was different from the concept that prevailed in Roman Catholic lands. In England, Henry declared himself the head of the church as well as the head of state. This model was based on the idea that temporal and spiritual authority were united in the person of the monarch. Religion in this system was "established" as the official religion of the state, and any changes to it would have to be passed into law by the country's parliament.

To demonstrate his authority in ecclesiastical matters (and appropriate the church's wealth for the crown), Henry suppressed the monasteries. Smaller monasteries were dissolved and their properties confiscated. Then, after an act of Parliament transferred all monastic possessions to the crown, the larger monasteries began to dissolve themselves, with the last house surrendering in 1540.

England remained Protestant under Henry's young son, Edward VI, but with the succession of Edward's half-sister Mary I (r. 1553–1558) it once again became officially Catholic. The contest for power was violent. Not until Elizabeth I (r. 1558–1603) negotiated what came to be known as the Elizabethan Settlement did the situation begin to stabilize. The Act of Supremacy (1559) reestablished the English church's independence from Rome and made Elizabeth the "Supreme Governor of the Church of England." It also reestablished the liturgy contained in the *Book of Common Prayer* as the standard for the new church.

Puritans

The Puritans embraced a more extreme purification of the church along Calvinist lines. They were never a majority in the English church, but they held considerable economic and political power. They condemned all forms of church ornamentation, the elaborate robes worn by clergy, and the use of organ music while calling for an emphasis on preaching rather than sacraments and strict observance of Sunday as the Sabbath. As well, Puritans insisted on the Calvinist principle of predestination. Their most problematic commitment, however, was their insistence, following Calvin, that the state should be subject to the church. This would eventually lead to charges of treason against the Puritans.

Quakers

Also significantly at odds with the established Church of England was the Religious Society of Friends, better known as the Quakers, a sect based on the principles and practices of George Fox (1624–1691). Coming of age during the upheaval of the English Civil War, Fox developed a pacifist approach to life as a Christian. Opposing the established religion, he traveled the countryside as a dissenting (non–Church of England) preacher advocating a Christianity stripped of nonessential trappings, including clergy, ceremonial rites, church buildings, and special holy days.

The name "Quaker" referred to the Friends' tendency to tremble when overflowing with the spirit within. Friends worshiped together without paid clergy and sat in silence during worship unless the spirit moved a member to speak. They refused to pay tithes to support the established church, to take legal oaths (because one should always tell the truth), and to serve in the military (because we should love our enemies). Embracing simplicity and love of neighbor, the Quakers cultivated a practical mysticism in which union with God was meaningful only insofar as it furthered the goal of service to others.

Congregationalists

The Congregational churches trace their roots to "separatist" clergy in the time of Elizabeth I, but they did not become a significant force in England until the mid-1600s. Doctrinally, there is little to distinguish Congregationalism from Presbyterian Calvinism. Where they differ is in their form of governance. Carrying the notion of the priesthood of all believers to its logical conclusion, Congregationalists reject the idea of elders and accord every congregation the authority to manage its own theological and institutional affairs; for them, the only higher power is God.

In England, Congregational churches formed a union in 1832 and were active in political and missionary causes throughout the nineteenth century. But the tradition's stronghold was Massachusetts, where Congregationalists founded Harvard University in 1636 in order not "to leave an illiterate ministry to the churches, when our present ministers shall lie in the dust." Yale University (1701) was also founded by Congregationalists.

Baptists

Like the Anabaptists on the continent, the English Baptists practiced the baptism of mature believers rather than infants. But they were much more intimately connected with the Puritans than with the Anabaptists. By the 1640s, the English Baptist movement had two branches. Calvinist, or "Particular," Baptists reserved redemption for a particular sector of humanity, whereas "General" Baptists proclaimed a general redemption for humanity.

The first Baptist churches in the United States were established as early as 1639, but the Baptist presence remained small until the revival movement of 1740–1743 known as the Great Awakening. Though the Baptists were not among its principal protagonists, they made massive numerical gains in its wake. They positioned themselves to become the largest American Protestant denomination partly through their successful appeal to the black population; by the mid-1950s, two out of every three African American Christians were Baptists.

Worship and the Protestant Reformation

Protestant reformers such as Luther, Zwingli, and Calvin all called for less mediation by clergy in order to give the faithful more direct access to God. Although each denomination developed its own new worship forms, all emphasized the use of the vernacular. New forms of music were designed for full congregational participation, the frequency of Communion increased, and in the Lutheran and Anglican traditions clergy and congregation alike shared in both the bread and the wine. Worship spaces were reconfigured, especially in the traditions influenced by Calvin, putting clergy and people together in a less hierarchical arrangement. Some traditions placed their altars away from the wall; others introduced a movable Communion table. These changes were designed to communicate that all the baptized have direct access to God, without mediation by clergy.

⊕ The Modern Era

The Enlightenment

By the end of the eighteenth century Christianity was no longer at the center of Western civilization, and the ties between church and state had been significantly loosened. The intellectual movement responsible for those changes is generally known as the Enlightenment.

A crucial early moment in the Enlightenment came in 1543, when the Polish astronomer Nicolaus Copernicus proposed that the universe revolved around the sun rather than the earth. Half a century later, the Italian mathematician Galileo Galilei confirmed that theory through observation. The church responded by adding Copernicus's book to its list of prohibited writings and, in 1633, bringing Galileo to trial before the Inquisition. Found guilty of heresy, he was forced to "abjure, curse, and detest" his supposed errors and lived the rest of his life under house arrest.

Deism

The growing importance of science was reflected in the rise of Deism, a philosophical position that gained a considerable following in England in the seventeenth and eighteenth centuries. Recognizing that the universe manifests regular patterns or "laws of nature," the Deists envisioned it as the product of a divine intelligence or designer. They saw their creator God as a divine clockmaker who assembled the universe and then left it to run on its own. This idea is known as the **teleological argument**, or argument from design.

The English philosopher William Paley offered the following example of the teleological argument from design for the existence of God in his *Natural Theology* (1802). If we found a watch on a desert island, we would not need to have seen any other watch in order to posit the existence of a maker; the watch would not even have to work perfectly, nor would we have to understand the function of every part. The same is true of the universe as evidence for God: even if the creation is imperfect or not fully comprehensible, humans can still reasonably posit the existence of a perfect creator deity.

Philosophy: Kant and Schleiermacher

At the same time, Enlightenment philosophers such the German Immanuel Kant were questioning Christian claims for the existence of a transcendent being. According to Kant, Thomas Aquinas's argument for God as the First Cause cannot be proved. But what Kant showed to be in principle unprovable is by the same token not disprovable. Whereas earlier thinkers sought to prove the existence of the transcendent itself, many philosophers of religion since Kant have focused instead on experience and feeling—that is, the human response to the transcendent. In the early nineteenth century, philosopher Friedrich Schleiermacher characterized religion as an "intuitive sense of absolute dependence": if we cannot prove the existence of what we intuitively feel that we depend on, at least we can describe that intuition.

Schleiermacher also contributed to a "subjective" understanding of Christ's atonement. In the traditional Christian understanding, it is through Christ's sacrifice that humanity is saved and restored to its proper relationship with God, but for Schleiermacher Jesus functions as a moral example, an embodiment of human awareness of God; salvation comes first as a change in spiritual awareness, and then atonement follows as a divine–human reconciliation.

Evolution

At the beginning of the nineteenth century, scientists held that every species on earth had been created by God with specific characteristics. This view was challenged by Charles Darwin, whose theory of evolution proposed that new types of organisms were not created by a deity but developed over time through a process he called natural selection. Darwin's *On the Origin of Species* was published in 1859, more than 20 years after he had worked out the basics of his theory. Having studied theology, Darwin was well aware of the resistance his theory would encounter. He needed not merely to make a credible case for evolution, but to refute the basic tenets of biological creationism. He also knew that natural selection was antithetical to the teleological argument from design. If the natural world was completely self-regulating, there was no need for a supervising deity.

Because of Darwin, modern Christian theologians have tended to locate human distinctiveness not in a special physical creation, but in a unique intellectual and spiritual capacity for transcendence. For religious thinkers persuaded by Darwin's discoveries, what matters is not so much where we came from as where we are going.

Sociopolitical Context

Following the Enlightenment, social, political, and economic revolutions precipitated a fundamental shift in the relationship between church and society, which in turn meant significant internal changes within Christianity. The French Revolution (1789) represents a watershed between the past and modern political systems. The violent overthrow of the French monarchy left the church without a partner in political power. Meanwhile, the American Revolution allowed the fledgling United States to establish itself as a sovereign nation, without an established church. From that point on, religion would be a choice. Running parallel to these political revolutions was the economic revolution whereby a land-based economy became a money-based one. This shift precipitated several other changes that also affected the role of the churches in society.

Anti-evolution literature for sale in 1925 in Dayton, Tennessee—the site of the famous "monkey trial" in which John Scopes was convicted of violating a Tennessee law that prohibited the teaching of evolution in state-funded schools. The conviction was later overturned, but only on technical grounds, and the law remained in place until 1967. The creation-versus-evolution debate continues to rage, particularly where school curricula are concerned (© AP Photo/CP).

Rural-to-urban migration and the breakdown of the extended family helped displace the church from its position as the focal point of community and social norms. The exploitation of the industrial working class led to the development of labor unions, which became this group's primary champions, reducing workers' reliance on the churches. At the same time, organized religion increasingly became the preserve of the emerging middle class. All these contextual changes contributed to the declining significance of Christianity in Western culture.

Evangelical Great Awakenings

In the face of that decline, Christianity paradoxically experienced several waves of revival in the early years of the modern era. The first "Great Awakening" swept Protestant Europe and British America in the 1730s and 1740s. Focusing mainly on believers, it summoned them to participate actively in proclaiming the Word of God. The second Great Awakening, beginning around 1800, focused instead on bringing nonbelievers to Christ. Many significant missionary organizations trace their origins to this time.

The third Great Awakening spanned the period from 1858 to 1914. In 1858, after two centuries of self-imposed isolation, Japan allowed the first Christian missionary of modern times to enter the country, and the publication of David Livingstone's *Missionary Travels and Researches in South Africa* fueled enthusiasm for global mission work. The principle of the priesthood of all believers summoned all Christians to become active agents of God's saving work. This time the emphasis was on social engagement, whether through religious education, distribution of the Bible, or social reform. Both the movement for women's suffrage and the modern ecumenical movement had their roots in this period.

John Wesley (1703–1791)

The primary catalyst of the first Great Awakening was John Wesley. Ordained an Anglican priest at the age of 25, he formed a small study group that was nicknamed the "Methodists" for their methodical pursuit of holiness. Wesley spent some time in the mission field in Georgia in 1735, but on the return voyage his life was changed by an encounter with a group of German Moravians. They reflected a lively and heartfelt faith that Wesley had not experienced in the Anglican world.

Back in England, Wesley had a transformative religious experience that he described as a moment when his heart "was strangely warmed." From then on it was his mission to summon lukewarm believers to an engaged experience with the living Christ. Wesley's theology reflected his Anglican heritage in that (like Luther) he rejected the Calvinist theory of predestination in favor of the Arminian view that all who believed would be saved by grace. Unlike Luther, however, Wesley also believed that all who had been saved by faith would become progressively more holy. According to this notion of "sanctification," the transfiguration of the heart by the saving grace of God would be reflected in one's works.

Wesley had not intended to break with the Church of England, but his new way of preaching and teaching was not welcome within his Anglican tradition. In his commitment to theology as experience, Wesley developed a new expression of Christianity that became known as Methodism. Giving priority to preaching of the Word and lay involvement, the Methodists emphasized engagement with the world as the place where the Kingdom of God was to be made real. The notion of progressive sanctification became central to the denomination.

Jonathan Edwards (1703–1758)

Edwards was an American-born revivalist preacher from Puritan Calvinist roots who sparked enthusiasm for the gospel throughout the thirteen colonies. An itinerant preacher, like most in the revivalist mode, he inspired new enthusiasm for his faith through his dramatic and emotional style. Where Edwards and Wesley differed was in their primary theological commitment. While Wesley was an Arminian, Edwards was grounded in the Calvinist assumptions that only some were predestined to be saved, and that God alone knew who they were. He made a major contribution to American revivalism through both his preaching and his writings, which inspired thousands to pursue a missionary vocation.

Women and Revivalism

In emphasizing the ministry of all the baptized, the Great Awakenings allowed women to participate more actively in their churches. Although the majority of revivalist preachers were men, most of the people who attended their meetings were women, and once the visiting preachers had moved on, it was those same women who found new ways to live their faith. This openness to the revival experience was reinforced by the prevailing gender assumption that while men toiled in the corrupt public world, women made the private world of the family a haven of virtue.

Led mainly by middle-class women who could afford time away from their household responsibilities, voluntary associations were formed that promoted the development of Sunday Schools and missionary societies (which sent both male and female missionaries into the field), supported the paid employment of single laywomen in various church contexts, and maintained connections with other women's groups. These activities laid the groundwork for the recognition of women's right to vote in church councils and, eventually, be ordained. As the women of the revival era learned the skills required for organization building, fundraising, and so on, their churches gradually became accustomed to the idea of women in leadership roles.

Missions

From its beginnings, Christianity has been a missionary religion. What was new in the era of the Great Awakenings was that now the missionary organizations included Protestants as well as Catholics. Although the mission societies reflected their varied denominational traditions, they shared a strong adherence to the exclusive claims of Christianity; a tendency to see the religions of missionized people as the work of the "Devil"; and an emphasis on conversion and the distribution of Bibles, with little social outreach.

By the third Great Awakening, both Protestant and Catholic missionaries were also actively promoting the Christianization of their own societies. This led various colonial churches to work with governments on projects of cultural assimilation. Conversion to Christianity and cultural assimilation were often presented to new immigrants as one and the same thing. As well, in places such as the United States, Canada, and Australia, the colonial churches collaborated with government to promote the assimilation of Indigenous people. The most disturbing examples of this collaboration were the residential school systems in which governments paid the churches to strip Indigenous children of their culture and assimilate them to European norms. Together, the loss of culture and the abuse suffered by those children have harmed several generations of Indigenous people.

Theological Controversies and Denominational Splitting

The development of historical biblical criticism and "modernist" theology led to increased splitting of denominations and the creation of new traditions. Three schools of thought shaped the drama of denominational splitting: liberalism, evangelicalism, and fundamentalism.

The term "modernist" was first used to refer to a group of Roman Catholic theologians who, in the late nineteenth century, adopted a critical and skeptical attitude toward traditional Christian doctrines, especially with reference to Christology and salvation. This movement fostered a positive attitude toward radical biblical criticism and stressed the ethical rather than the doctrinal dimensions of faith. The term migrated into American Protestantism fairly rapidly. By the turn of the twentieth century, mainstream Protestant denominations were increasingly influenced by "modernist attitudes," as reflected in a rethinking of the doctrine of creation; an emphasis on God's presence in creation rather than his transcendence; and a shift in atonement theology toward Schleiermacher's view, in which the emphasis is less on Christ's sacrifice as the means to human salvation and more on the moral example he set for humanity ("What would Jesus do?").

Focus

Black Elk (1863–1950)

In the United States, some now argue that the harm done by Christianity in the process of colonization means that it has no value for Indigenous people today. Yet there have been Aboriginal leaders who have believed that Indigenous wisdom and Christian belief are complementary. An Oglala Lakota man by the name of Black Elk is perhaps the most significant example. During a childhood illness he experienced a vision that led him to become a healer. As an adult he was converted to Christianity by Roman Catholic missionaries but continued to receive visions that confirmed the experience of his youth, and in time he came to see parallels between Lakota and Christian teachings. Thus the "Great Spirit" or Creator of the Lakota tradition was analogous to the creator God of the Christian Trinity, and the traditional pipe given to the Lakota people was a way of knowing God before the arrival of Christianity. Black Elk believed that the path of all creation, known as the "Red Road" in Lakota teaching, led to the Christ he had met when he was converted to Christianity. Today his visions and theology continue to play a significant role in conversations between Indigenous elders and Christian theologians.

Historical Biblical Criticism

In the nineteenth century the Bible came to be studied as a historical document. Historical criticism is a method of biblical interpretation in which understanding the true meaning of a biblical passage requires knowledge not of Christian doctrine but rather of the historical and social conditions in which it was composed. Many scholars saw historical criticism as the enemy of Christianity, as it undermined the "absolute truth" claims of Christian doctrine and appeared to make faith conditional on historical circumstance.

Yet many theologians saw in history a means of freeing Christianity from developments that, in their view, Jesus never intended. They used historical methods to write biographies of him that were free of Christian dogma. When the German theologian and humanist Albert Schweitzer (1875–1965) noticed that these "lives" coincidentally affirmed the values of Jesus's biographers, he condemned what he called "the Quest for the Historical Jesus" based on modern notions while himself constructing a Jesus, based on the Gospels, who thought the end-time was coming within the current generation. The historical quest was largely abandoned until after the Second World War, when new archaeological discoveries began to shed new light on the Judaism of Jesus's day. In 1985, 150 scholars formed the Jesus Seminar to study the sayings and deeds attributed to Jesus and debate whether they had originated with Jesus or had been attributed to him by later followers. Like the earlier questers, they have been criticized for "discovering" a Jesus who conforms to the ideals of liberal democracy.

Reactions to Modernism

Evangelicalism

Reactions against modernist theology were expressed in two primary forms: evangelicalism and fundamentalism. Evangelical Protestants' position is reflected in their emphasis on the necessity of personal conversion, the goal of personal sanctification, and the preeminence of scripture and

preaching (the ministry of the Word). In the twentieth century, evangelicalism influenced many Protestant denominations but was most significant among the Reformed churches.

Fundamentalism

The term "**fundamentalism**" derives from "The Fundamentals," a series of 12 tracts by eminent evangelical leaders that were widely distributed in the English-speaking world beginning in 1909. In reaction against historical criticism and the theory of evolution, fundamentalists sponsored a series of Bible conferences at which they developed a statement of belief based on what came to be known as the "Five Points" or "Fundamentals": the inerrancy of scripture, the divinity of Jesus Christ, the virgin birth, the substitutionary theory of the atonement (the idea that Christ died in our place and in so doing paid the debt we owe God for our sins), and the physical resurrection and Second Coming of Christ. Fundamentalism affected a variety of denominations, inspiring theological conflicts so intense that they led to denominational splitting.

Focus

Aimee Semple McPherson (1890–1944)

Spirit-based movements such as Pentecostalism have been more likely than more mainstream denominations to offer women opportunities as preachers and leaders. This unusual openness stems from the idea that if God has given someone a gift for a particular kind of ministry, then the church should affirm that gift.

Aimee Semple McPherson was an important example of this phenomenon. Born in Ontario and converted to Pentecostalism in her teens, she followed her passion for preaching all the way to Los Angeles, where she became the most famous evangelist of her generation. Unlike other early Pentecostals, she quickly realized the potential of modern media as vehicles for evangelization. She became renowned both for her preaching and for the healings that were reported to take place at her revival meetings. Eventually she built a large church that was filled by the thousands for every worship service. She also founded a Pentecostal denomination known as the Four Square Gospel Church, which still exists today. The media-based ministry that she pioneered served as a prototype for later forms of North American Pentecostalism.

Aimee Semple McPherson prays enthusiastically with her congregation at Tom Noonan's Chinatown mission in New York in 1933 (© Hulton-Deutsch Collection/ Corbis).

Practice

Speaking in Tongues

The renewal movement that gave rise to Pentecostalism was led by an American evangelist named Charles Parham, who taught that speaking in tongues was evidence of the "baptism of the spirit" described in Acts. This practice, known as "glossolalia," arose in the context of early Christian worship and was accepted by the believers of that generation as evidence of the presence of God. The purpose, as expressed in worship, was sometimes prophetic or instructive, but often was simply a sign of the perceived presence of the Holy Spirit. One of Parham's students, an African American pastor named William J. Seymour (1870–1922), adapted his message to be inclusive across racial and gender lines and began preaching the imminent return of Jesus to mixed-race crowds in Los Angeles in 1906. The popularity of Seymour's "Azusa Street Revival" sparked similar gatherings across the United States and around the world. Speaking in tongues, divine healing, and prophecy were interpreted as signs that God was with the community. Many new denominations were born from this renewal movement, including the Assemblies of God, the Pentecostal Fellowship, and the Church of God.

Pentecostalism

Pentecostalism should not be confused with fundamentalism; it has more in common with the **Holiness** movement of the nineteenth century. It takes its name from an episode in the Book of Acts in which the Holy Spirit visits a gathering of the apostles and some others on the Feast of the **Pentecost** (the fiftieth day after Easter) and bestows on them the gift of **glossolalia**, or "speaking in tongues."

Of the more than 2 billion Christians in the world today, more than one-quarter are Pentecostal or "charismatic." While many Latin Americans, Native Americans, Africans, and Asians say that Pentecostal interpretations of Christianity are more in keeping with their cultural worldviews than other forms of Christianity, current studies indicate that the single most important reason for the growth of Pentecostalism is the experience of divine healing—a significant attraction in places where access to health care is difficult for most people. A second attraction is the fact that most Pentecostal churches (unlike the historic colonial churches) offer their congregations help with everyday problems.

The Social Gospel

Early in the twentieth century, an American Baptist minister named Walter Rauschenbusch (1861–1918) argued that Christianity is by nature revolutionary, that realizing the Kingdom of God is a matter not of getting to heaven but of transforming life on earth into the harmony of heaven. He focused on social sin rather than individual sin, with particular attention to religious bigotry, graft, and the corruption of justice as a perversion of God's intention. This way of approaching the relationship of the gospel to the world captured the imagination of Christians across theological and denominational lines and inspired a new emphasis on social engagement in a wide range of Christian communities.

THE HOLY TRINITY

DOROTHY DAY

HE RAISES THE POOR/THE PRINCES OF HIS FROM THE DUST AND/PEOPLE HE GIVES THE LIFTS THE NEEDY/BARREN WOMAN A FROM THE ASH HEAP/HOME MAKING HER TO MAKE THEM SIT/THE JOYOUS MOTHER WITH PRINCES WITH/OF CHILDREN

The social activist Dorothy Day (1887–1980), cofounder of the Catholic Worker movement. A convert to Roman Catholicism, Day is currently under consideration for canonization (© Brian Nicholas Tsai).

Theological Diversity in the Modern/Postmodern Era

Particularly in North America, liberal theologians developed new forms of theological expression. These included the application of existential philosophy to theology, as in the work of Paul Tillich (1886–1995); the development, by Alfred North Whitehead (1861–1947), Charles Hartshorne (1897–2000), and others, of process theology, which draws on physics to argue for a God who is in some respects changeable, existing in ongoing relationship with the unfolding universe; and the rise of liberation theologies focused on the particular concerns of oppressed groups, including women, Indigenous people, African Americans, and, in Latin America, the poor and politically violated.

In response to this explosion of liberal theologies, an opposing "neo-orthodoxy" emerged in the interwar years. Its primary architect was Karl Barth (1886–1968), who emphasized the transcendence of God and the inability of human beings to work out their own salvation. Barth's radical doctrine of sin and grace found resonance among the Reformed churches in particular.

The Changing Place of Women

Even today, only a minority of Christians belong to a church that allows women to participate fully in leadership roles. More than half of the world's Christian population is Roman Catholic, another significant segment is Eastern Orthodox, and yet another is conservative Protestant. With minor variations, women in these churches do not have full ecclesiastical voting rights and are not eligible for ordination. Although most historic colonial or mainline Protestant denominations, as well as some evangelical churches, do ordain women today, some of them have had difficulty expanding the roles that women can play. For example, it wasn't until 2014 that the Church of England voted overwhelmingly to open the House of Bishops to women.

The refusal of the Roman Catholic and Eastern Orthodox churches, some conservative evangelical denominations, and some Indigenous denominations in Africa, Asia, and Latin America to ordain women at all can be traced back to the early church, though in some cases it also reflects current views on gender. Both Roman Catholic and Orthodox theologians have argued that women cannot represent Christ because Christ was male.

Twentieth-Century Movements for Social Change

In the twentieth century, Christians played an active part in several grassroots movements for social change, including the anti-apartheid movement in South Africa, the grassroots *Comunidades de Base* movement in Latin America, and the civil rights movement in the United States.

However, in each case there were Christians on both sides of the debate. While some demanded an end to injustice and oppression, particularly of the poor, others defended the status quo.

In South Africa, the Afrikaners who justified the seizure of land from black South Africans were generally members of the Dutch Reformed Church. They argued that they had been chosen by God to administer South Africa and prevent the mixing of races through intermarriage. South African Anglicans for the most part opposed apartheid, and black Anglican clergy such as Desmond Tutu became high-profile political figures. However, individual church members disagreed over the tactics to use in these campaigns, and some Anglicans of European descent vigorously opposed their church's involvement in politics. Methodism quickly became an overwhelmingly black denomination with a strong anti-apartheid stance, which cost it support among those who feared the power of the apartheid state. The Roman Catholic Church in South Africa opposed apartheid as well, although a group calling itself the South African Catholic Defense League condemned the church's political involvement and denounced school integration.

In Latin America the Roman Catholic Church was an agent both of change and of resistance to change. As the official church of Spain in the colonial era, it allied itself with the state in regimes of control and repression, but with decolonization the church–state relationship shifted. When economic crises from the 1960s to the 1990s permitted the rise of military dictatorships, the poor faced crushing poverty and extreme violations of human rights. Although some local church leaders stood with the military regimes, most positioned themselves in solidarity with the poor and suffering. In 1968, the second conference of Latin American bishops generated three important documents. Entitled "Justice," "Peace," and "Poverty of the Church," they shattered the centuries-old alliance between the church, the military, and the wealthy. The key words that emerged as blueprints for the future were "liberation" and "participation." The church pledged to participate in the dynamic action of an awakened community in resistance to the forces that oppressed and denied life. This consciousness raising was reflected in the *Communidades de Base*. Offering Bible study, prayer, and fellowship in the poorest *barrios* and slums, these communities became focal points of resistance and renewal, and expressions of the church's theological commitment to the dignity of all human beings. Many church leaders paid with their lives for their commitment to the poor. The most notable example was Bishop Oscar Romero of El Salvador, who became a recognized leader of the nonviolent resistance to the military

Bishop Barbara Harris of the Episcopal Diocese of Massachusetts at her ordination as the first female bishop in the Anglican Communion, in 1989 (© Reuters/Corbis).

Women in the Traditions

The Mothers' Union

As part of the voluntary movements spearheaded by women in the late nineteenth century, the Mothers' Union was begun within the Church of England. Originally birthed in England in the face of emergent industrialization, this organization was framed around protection of the family and family values. However, as the various traumas of the twentieth century unfolded and the Anglican Communion spread globally, most notably in Africa, this organization rose to prominence as a force for social reconstruction. In several countries where social dislocation, civil war, the AIDS pandemic, and other challenges confronted local society, the Mothers' Union organized resources to reclaim and redevelop communities by building bridges across the horrors of tribal genocides in Rwanda and Burundi, caring for orphans in Uganda, advocating for AIDS medications in South Africa, lobbying for the rights of women and girls, speaking against human trafficking, and working for health care and an end to poverty in local communities everywhere. Committed to the well-being of the next generation, members of the Mothers' Union also run various initiatives such as literacy projects, development initiatives, and church-building and microfinance initiatives. Currently the Union comprises over 1.3 million members in Africa alone.

dictatorship of the day. His assassination, while presiding at worship in March 1980, inspired many others to take up the defense of the human rights of political resistors and the poor.

In the United States, the civil rights movement was largely driven by the black churches. Historically, through the era of slavery and beyond, black churches had served as focal points for communal life and empowerment. Thus, when the time came for resistance to white repression, the black clergy played a pivotal role in gathering the community and providing both inspiration and strategy. Most notable of all was the Reverend Dr. Martin Luther King, Jr. (1929–1968), a Baptist pastor whose skills as an orator and insistence on nonviolence made him the movement's principal spokesman until he was murdered at the age of 39. The Christian principle that all people are made in the image of God animated social action in a world where a significant proportion of the population was not accorded the most basic human rights.

Vatican II

The election of Pope John XXIII in 1958 sparked significant change in the Roman Catholic Church. Though already in his late 70s, the new pope had a fearless openness to change. Calling for *aggiornamento* ("updating"), John XXIII convoked the Second Vatican Council, which met from 1962 to 1965.

The changes set in motion at the council ushered in a new era for Catholicism. Latin was replaced by the vernacular as the language of the mass, and the priest now turned to face the congregation (although the doctrine of transubstantiation was retained). Whereas the First Vatican Council (1869–1870) had emphasized the monarchical aspect of the pope's role, Vatican II emphasized the more collegial nature of his work in council with the bishops. Efforts were also made to improve relations both with other Christians and with people of other religions, especially Jews.

A major breach developed in the church shortly after the council, in 1968, when John's successor, Pope Paul VI, in his encyclical *Humanae Vitae* ("On Human Life") prohibited the use of artificial birth control. The gap between the church's official stand on sexuality and the actual practice of the faithful has only widened in the intervening decades. Many Catholics have ceased to follow some of the teachings they consider out of date. At the same time *Humanae Vitae* intensified the theological tension between the reform-minded and traditionalist wings in the church's hierarchy.

⊕ The Church of Rome Today

More than 50 years after Vatican II, its agenda still has not been completed, and pressing problems remain. The numbers of candidates for the priesthood are in serious decline. A variety of factors have contributed to this trend, most notably rising secularism in Western culture generally and an increasing disinclination to choose celibacy as a way of life. The challenges to the church's authority and credibility resulting from a tide of sexual abuse charges may also be affecting the numbers of men offering themselves for leadership as clergy. The sexual abuse of children by religious professionals is not solely a phenomenon of the modern era or of the Roman Catholic Church. However, in recent years the latter has been shaken by widespread sexual abuse cases involving priests. Criminal trials have received significant media attention in Canada, the United States, and Ireland in particular, and thousands of civil lawsuits have been filed against the church seeking compensation. Restitution payments made between 1950 and 2012 have been estimated at more than $3 billion. As a consequence, eight dioceses in the United States declared bankruptcy between 2004 and 2011, and by 2013 another five had filed for bankruptcy protection. Even more significant than the financial implications of these cases are the challenges that they have posed to the credibility and authority of the church.

In February 2013 Pope Benedict XVI became the first pope since 1415 to resign from the papal office. At the age of 86, he said he no longer had the physical strength to perform his duties adequately. His successor, Cardinal Jorge Bergoglio of Argentina, who took the name Francis I, is the first pope from the global South and is well known for his commitment to social justice and his solidarity with the poor and migrants. His election has sparked hope that positive change within the church is not only possible but imminent.

⊕ Recent Developments

For several decades the mainline denominations in Europe and North America have been declining, even as Christianity grows rapidly in the global South. In response, the traditional churches have been reevaluating the forms and structures of their worship and organizational life. Meanwhile, new groups such as the Emergent Church Movement have been experimenting with innovative forms of urban monastic community, house churches, and participation in environmental and social projects as an expression of faith. Although continuing immigration from Asia and the global South is likely to slow the decline to some degree, it will also inevitably lead to changes in church life in the next generation.

Ecumenism

By the middle of the twentieth century, a generation of leaders who had grown up with interdenominationalism had moved into positions of responsibility in their own churches. The time was ripe for worldwide collaboration, and in 1948 the World Council of Churches was formed, with

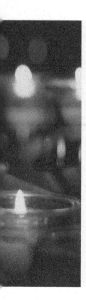

Practice

Indigenization of Christian Liturgy

Christian liturgy is understood to reflect the particular culture in which it develops. Thus as cultures evolve over time, so do their liturgies. And as new communities adopt Christianity, they adapt the liturgies they have been given to reflect their own culture, taking key aspects of the faith and integrating them into local life in a reciprocal conversation between history and the present. This basic process of adaptation, or indigenization, can be seen at work today in several places. In Africa, for instance, historic colonial denominations are adapting their liturgies to include traditional local songs and drumming. In Canada, Indigenous Anglicans in various parts of the country have developed services in their own languages, incorporating traditional musical forms and words. And in New Zealand, the Anglican Church has developed a prayer book that contains worship services in English, Polynesian, and Maori, with content that reflects the symbol systems of all three cultures.

representation from most major Protestant and Orthodox bodies. **Ecumenism** (from the Greek meaning "inhabited world") offered a climate of mutual acceptance and common purpose, although Protestants agreed to continue disagreeing on issues such as Eucharistic theology. In the United States, a merger of multiple Protestant denominations in 1961 produced the United Church of Christ.

Among the most significant advances have been the theological agreements reached between various churches. In 1982 the Faith and Order Commission of the World Council of Churches produced a document entitled "Baptism, Eucharist and Ministry" that reflects a significant degree of consensus on these issues while identifying areas of ongoing difference

Rome's move into ecumenism is associated primarily with the papacy of John XXIII. A permanent Secretariat for the Promotion of Christian Unity was established in 1960, and rapprochement with other Christians was an important item at Vatican II. By the end of the 1960s, Protestant and Catholic institutions for the study of theology and the training of clergy were making collaborative arrangements, while their students were attending the same lectures and reading the same books.

Fission and Fusion

Reflecting the explosion of theological diversity and the rapid global expansion of Christianity, historic colonial denominations seeded new churches that developed in their own ways. There are now more than 20,000 distinct denominational families in the world, most of which have come into being in the last century (Barrett, Currian, and Johnson 2001). Perhaps ironically, the ecumenical movement has contributed to further division when complicated union negotiations have left some parties behind.

Currently, as we have noted, the single largest Christian denomination in the world is Roman Catholicism and the fastest-growing dimension of Christianity is Pentecostalism (not as a denomination in itself but as a way of being Christian). These two factors have led the demographer Philip Jenkins to conclude that eventually only two basic forms of Christianity will remain: Roman Catholicism and Pentecostalism.

Interview

Three "Millennials" on Christianity

The following interview was conducted with three millennials: two sisters raised in a Protestant family in Canada (born 1992 and 1993) and one young man raised in the Roman Catholic school system in Ireland (born 1994).

Q: Were you raised in the church?
Sisters 1 and 2: We were, with two clergy parents.
Young Man: No, but I was raised in the Roman Catholic school system.

Q: Are you currently a part of a Christian community?
Sisters 1 and 2: No.
Young man: No way!

Q: Why?
Sister 1: I feel a strong desire to be part of a worshiping community, but not one like the one I was raised in. It was too much about ritual. I want something with more emotion, more about God. My parents also raised me in a very leftist mode of Christian practice. That didn't make sense to me then and doesn't now. The fascism of the left limits my choices as a woman and a mother.
Sister 2: The ritual of the church feels dead to me. I would be a part of a community if it was more free form, more about reflection and ideas.
Young Man: The church is ridiculous. It has no place in the world I inhabit.

Q: Do you believe in God?
Sisters 1 and 2: Yes.
Young Man: Absolutely not. I am in control of my life. I choose. I decide. I don't hand over control of my life to an old man in the sky.

Q: Do you believe God has a plan for your life?
Sisters 1 and 2: Yes.

Young Man: If God does not exist, God cannot have a plan for my life.

Q: What does God look like? Where is God?
Sister 1: God is everywhere. God is right here. God is never far from any of us.
Sister 2: God is not a person. God is energy. God is everywhere.
Young Man: I told you—God does not exist.

Q: What does God want for the world?
Sister 1: Love. God is about love. Not judgment and harm. Not violence and exclusion in the name of religion. Love.
Sister 2: I really don't know.
Young Man: Your question is nonsensical. The question is, What do I want for my life, and what will I contribute to the world?

Millennials interpret their world. (John Thompson Photography)

Together, the rapid expansion of Christianity in the global South and its rapid decline in the global North and West have reshaped the face of Christian missions. In prior centuries, European and North American denominations sent missionaries to the Far East and the global South, but today the largest numbers of missionaries are being sent from Africa, Latin America, and Korea to convert the largely de-Christianized societies of Europe and North America (Jenkins 2007: 214–220).

Christianity and Pluralism

By the beginning of the third millennium, diversity had become part of the national fabric not only of societies built on immigration, like the United States, but also of European societies in which until recently the great majority of citizens had shared a common cultural background, including the Christian faith.

One of the great opportunities and challenges of this generation is the fact that Christians now live side by side with people of many faiths. Opportunities abound for people of differing religious commitments to work together for the well-being of local and global communities. Of course, religious diversity can fuel division and violence. Yet traditional commitments to compassion, love of one's neighbor, and mutual respect impel Christian communities, in their best moments, toward new ways of authentically Christian living in partnership with non-Christian neighbors. To learn this discipline well will be one of the most significant projects for Christians in the next centuries.

Table 4.1 Professing Christians Worldwide, 2011

Total Christians as percent of world population: 33%	
Affiliated Christians (church members)	**2,187,138,999**
Church attenders	1,523,229,000
Evangelicals	965,400,000*
Pentecostals/Charismatics/Neocharismatics	612,472,000
Membership by six ecclesiastical megablocs	
Roman Catholic	1,160,880,000
Protestant	426,450,000
Independent	378,281,000
Orthodox	271,316,000
Anglican	87,520,000
Marginal Christian	35,539,000

* Includes Great Commission Christians

Source: Adapted from Johnson, Barrett, and Crossing 2011: 28–9.

Focus

The Major Branches of Christianity

Christianity has seven major branches comprising 156 distinct traditions and more than 21,000 denominations.

1. Orthodox

Greek
Russian
Syrian
Bulgarian, Serbian, Romanian (offshoots: Monophysites such as Nestorians and Coptic Christians)
Armenians

2. Roman Catholic

3. Catholic (Non-Roman or Eastern)

Old Catholic
Russian and Ukrainian

4. Protestant

Sixteenth century

Lutheran
Reformed (Presbyterian)
Anabaptist

Seventeenth and eighteenth centuries

Pietist
Congregationalist
Baptist
Methodist

Nineteenth century

Holiness Churches
Salvationists

Twentieth century

Pentecostal
Uniting Churches

5. Anglican (from the sixteenth century)

6. Nonwhite Indigenous Protestant (from the seventeenth century, but mainly the nineteenth and twentieth)

7. Marginal Protestant

Unitarian
Mormon
Jehovah's Witnesses

Source: Adapted from Barrett 1982: 34–45.

 Summary

This short overview has suggested both the complexity and the consistency of Christianity. Originating as a Jewish reform movement, it grew to spread throughout the globe, incorporating philosophical perspectives that produced diverse schools of theology and a wide range of ecclesiastical forms and practices. Today it continues to expand, but rather than looking back to Europe, it now looks to the global South as the location of its most pressing concern. As it carries the gospel of Jesus Christ into the future, it will fashion its next becoming with the tools it has honed in the workshop of negotiated difference.

Sites

Jerusalem

Jerusalem, a holy city for all three Abrahamic traditions, is sacred to Christians as the place where Jesus died. Tradition holds that he carried the cross along the Via Dolorosa to the hill where he was to be crucified.

St. Peter's Basilica

A late Renaissance church in Vatican City that is one of the most sacred places in the Roman Catholic tradition, St. Peter's is said to sit on the burial site of St Peter—the disciple said to have been martyred, along with Paul, during the persecution of 64. It serves as a pilgrimage site for Catholics from around the world.

Wittenberg, Germany

It was on the doors of what is now All Saints' Lutheran Church in Wittenberg that Luther nailed his 95 Theses. Today the church houses Luther's tomb.

Sacred Texts

Religion	Text	Composition/Compilation	Compilation/ Revision	Use
Christianity	Old Testament (Genesis, Exodus, Leviticus, Numbers, Deuteronomy, Joshua, Judges, Ruth, 1 Samuel, 2 Samuel, 1 Kings, 2 Kings, 1 Chronicles, 2 Chronicles, Ezra, Nehemiah, Esther, Job, Psalms, Proverbs, Ecclesiastes, Song of Solomon, Isaiah, Jeremiah, Lamentations, Ezekiel, Daniel, Hosea, Joel, Amos, Obadiah, Jonah, Micah, Nahum, Habakkuk, Zephaniah, Haggai, Zechariah, Malachi)	Composed by various individuals and schools from approximately 625 BCE to the 1st century BCE	Individual books and sections revised from the 6th to 1st century BCE. At the Council of Yavne (70–90 CE) these writings were brought together and the canon reached final form. However, later writings suggest that debates were ongoing as to which texts belonged in the canon.	Doctrinal, ritual, inspirational, educational
	New Testament: undisputed Pauline Epistles (1 Thessalonians, Galatians, Philippians, 1 Corinthians, 2 Corinthians, Romans, Philemon)	Composed between approximately 51 and 63 CE, over the course of Paul's career in Ephesus, Corinth, Philippi, Macedonia, and Rome		Doctrinal, ritual, inspirational, educational
	New Testament: disputed Pauline Epistles (2 Thessalonians, Colossians, Ephesians)	Composed in Macedonia and Asia Minor between approximately 60 and 85 CE. Scholars doubt that they were actually written by Paul.		Doctrinal, ritual, inspirational, educational
	New Testament: Pastoral Epistles (1 Timothy, 2 Timothy, Titus)	Composed in Asia Minor and perhaps Crete between approximately 90 and 140 CE. These letters are named after the people to whom they were addressed and traditionally attributed to Paul, but their actual authors are unknown.		Doctrinal, ritual, inspirational, educational

Sacred Texts (Continued)

Religion	Text	Composition/Compilation	Compilation/Revision	Use
Christianity	New Testament: additional epistolary writings (1 Peter, 2 Peter, James, Jude, 1 John, 2 John, 3 John)	Composed in Asia Minor and Rome between 64 and 150, and attributed to the disciples after whom the texts are named. Their real authors are unknown.		Doctrinal, ritual, inspirational, educational
	New Testament: Hebrews	Composed in either Rome or Alexandria in 63 CE by an anonymous author		Doctrinal, ritual, inspirational, educational
	New Testament: Synoptic Gospels (Matthew, Mark, Luke)	Composed in Antioch, southern Syria or possibly Galilee, and Ephesus between 65 and 85 CE; attributed to the disciples for whom they are named, but their actual authors are unknown.		Doctrinal, ritual, inspirational, educational
	New Testament: Gospel of John	Composed in Ephesus or possibly Alexandria in 90 CE and traditionally attributed to Jesus's disciple John, son of Zebedee; actual author unknown.		Doctrinal, ritual, inspirational, educational
	New Testament: Acts of the Apostles	Composed in western Asia Minor, perhaps Ephesus, between 85 and 140 CE; attributed to Luke the Evangelist, the same disciple named as the author of the Gospel of Luke; the actual author is unknown.		Doctrinal, ritual, inspirational, educational
	New Testament: Revelation	Dated to between 64 and 96 CE and traditionally attributed to John the Evangelist, writing on the Greek island of Patmos, but the actual author is unknown.		Doctrinal, ritual, inspirational, educational

Discussion Questions

1. How has local culture shaped Christian thought and practice?

2. How did the shift from private to public worship affect Christianity?

3. What are some examples of changes in Christian thinking that reflect the changing world in which Christianity has existed?

4. In what contexts has Christianity been a reform movement? How has it served as a stabilizing influence within society?

5. Even though Christians suffered persecution in their own early days, they have acted as persecutors in other contexts. Discuss.

6. What factors have influenced the place of women in Christianity?

7. How do you imagine the future of Christianity will unfold, based on its past?

Glossary

abbesses Powerful nuns who oversaw the lands owned by their communities.

anchoritic monasticism The form of monasticism practiced by the Desert Fathers and Mothers, who withdrew from society.

Anselm Eleventh-century Archbishop of Canterbury and originator of the ontological argument for the existence of God.

apostles The early followers of Jesus who witnessed his return as the risen Lord and were sent out into the world to proclaim him.

Aquinas, Thomas Dominican theologian considered the greatest of the scholastics, author of the *Summa Theologiae*.

Arius The early theologian who argued (against Athanasius) that Jesus was of like substance with God rather than the same substance.

Athanasius The bishop of Alexandria who argued (against Arius) that Jesus was of the same substance as God.

atonement Christ's restoration of humanity to a right relationship with God, variously interpreted as divine victory over demonic power, satisfaction of divine justice, or demonstration of a moral example.

Augustine Bishop of Hippo Regius in North Africa, whose writings shaped much of the theological tradition of western Christianity.

baptism The ritual of initiation into the Christian faith; one of the two key sacraments.

Beghards, Beguines Lay men and women, respectively, who lived together in semimonastic communities that were usually not under the authority of a local bishop.

Benedict's Rule The prototype for western monastic life, written in the sixth century by St. Benedict.

Bernard of Clairvaux Twelfth-century founder of a Cistercian monastery at Clairvaux.

bishop The supervising priest of an ecclesiastical district called a diocese.

Calvin, Jean The French Protestant theologian who is seen as the father of the Reformed churches.

canon A standard; a scriptural canon is the list of books acknowledged as scripture. Canon law is the accumulated body of church regulations and discipline.

Carmelites An ascetic monastic order of hermits established on Mount Carmel in Palestine.

Carthusians A monastic order that demanded a vow of silence and considerable austerity from its members.

cenobitic monasticism The form of monasticism practiced by religious people who live in community with one another.

charism A spiritual gift such as preaching, healing, speaking in tongues (glossolalia), and prophesying. Movements that emphasize such gifts are described as "charismatic."

Christ From *Christos*, the Greek translation of the Hebrew *mashiach* (messiah), "anointed one."

Christology A theory of who Jesus was, by nature and in substance.

Cistercians An austere monastic order founded in France in 1098.

City of God, The Work by Augustine of Hippo that articulated a vision for the relationship between sacred and secular in the age of the decline of the Roman Empire.

Cluniac Fathers An order, founded in 910, at the center of a movement to reform monasticism by bringing its institutions under the control of religious rather than secular authorities.

Constantine The first Christian emperor of Rome, who convened the Council of Nicaea in 325 CE.

Council of Chalcedon The fifth-century church council at which the controversies over the nature of Jesus's humanity and divinity were finally resolved.

Council of Nicaea The fourth-century church council, convened by Constantine, that formally established many beliefs about Christ.

creeds Brief formal statements of doctrinal belief, often recited in unison by congregations.

Crusades A series of military actions (1095–late 1200s) undertaken by European Christians to drive Islam out of the Holy Land.

deacon From Greek *diakonia*, meaning "service"; the third order of (male) ministry in the early church.

deaconess The female counterpart of the deacon's office in the early church, devoted to serving women and children in the community.

Dominicans A mendicant preaching order formed in the early 1200s to combat the "Albigensian heresy."

dyophysitism The belief that the two natures of Jesus, human and divine, are united in the second person of the Trinity; affirmed at both Nicaea and Ephesus and proclaimed as orthodoxy for both the western and eastern Christian churches.

Easter The festival, held in March or April, celebrating the resurrection of Jesus.

ecumenism The movement for reunion or collaboration between previously separate branches of Christianity.

episcopacy Literally, "oversight"; the foundational office of authority in early Christianity; see also **bishop**.

Erasmus The humanist thinker who laid the groundwork for Reformation theologians such as Luther.

Eucharist The sacramental meal of bread and wine that recalls Jesus's last supper before his crucifixion; a standard part of Christian worship.

evangelical A term used to describe a type of Protestantism that crosses denominations, incorporating key identifiers such as an emphasis on preaching and scripture.

excommunication Formal censure or expulsion from a church, particularly the Roman Catholic Church, for doctrinal error or moral misconduct.

Franciscans Mendicant order whose monks live by a rule based on the life and example of St. Francis of Assisi.

friar A member of a mendicant order such as the Carmelites, Dominicans, or Franciscans.

fundamentalism A twentieth-century reaction to modernity, originally among Protestants who maintained the infallibility of scripture and doctrine.

glossolalia Speaking in "tongues"; a distinguishing feature of charismatic groups such as Pentecostals, in which people who feel filled with the spirit begin speaking in what they believe is a special heavenly language.

Gnosticism A worldview based on a radical dualism that prioritized reason and spirit over the physical.

gospel "Good news" (*evangelion* in Greek); the news of redemption that the Hebrew prophets had promised. The Gospels are the accounts of Jesus's life attributed to his disciples Mark, Matthew, Luke, and John.

heresy A belief or practice that is contrary to the accepted orthodoxy.

Holiness Churches Protestant churches that believe their members have already received "holiness" (spiritual perfection) as a gift from God.

humanism The intellectual movement that is seen as a necessary precursor of the Protestant Reformation.

icon From the Greek for "image"; a distinctive Byzantine form of portraiture used to depict Jesus, Mary, and the saints.

incarnation The embodiment of the divine in human form; the Christian teaching that God became human in the person of Jesus.

indulgences Releases from time in purgatory.

liturgy A prescribed form for public worship.

logos "Word" in the sense of eternal divine intelligence and purpose.

Luther, Martin The father of the Protestant Reformation.

Manichaeism An intensely dualistic religion, founded in the third century.

martyrs Christians who have died for their faith.

Mary The mother of Jesus; a major saint, deeply venerated by Roman Catholics in particular.

mass The Roman Catholic name for the Eucharist.

mendicant orders Monastic orders that, instead of withdrawing from the world and living predominantly in closed communities, dedicate themselves to pastoral work, serving the people; examples include Carmelites, Dominicans, and Franciscans.

monophysitism The belief that Christ had only one nature, either divine or a synthesis of divine and human; abandoned in favor of dyophysitism, which is the classical teaching of the church.

mysticism The pursuit of intensely experienced spiritual union with the divine.

Nestorianism The position that there was one (divine) nature in Christ and it was separate from the human Jesus.

New Testament The collection of 27 books—the Gospels, Acts of the Apostles, the epistles, and Revelation—written by various authors in the first and early second centuries and determined to be authoritative for the early Christian church.

Nicene Creed The statement of faith agreed on at the Council of Nicaea.

nuns Women living a common life under vows in a monastic community.

ontological argument Anselm's argument for the existence of God based not on observation but on the logic that such a being must necessarily exist.

original sin The idea that human beings are inherently sinful because our earliest ancestors, Adam and Eve, chose to disobey God.

orthodoxy Literally, the "straight way," meaning correct belief; in any church, the accepted doctrine.

parables Simple stories told to illustrate a lesson.

patriarchs In the early church, the five bishops who held primacy of authority by geographical region: Rome, Constantinople, Alexandria, Antioch, and Jerusalem. Today the term refers to those bishops in the Eastern Orthodox churches who preside over specific geographical regions and/or historical forms of the churches.

Paul, St. The Jewish convert to Christianity (originally known as Saul of Tarsus) who founded a number of Christian communities and wrote them letters of instruction and guidance.

Pauline Epistles Letters attributed to Paul in the New Testament.

Pelagianism A heresy according to which human nature was not so tainted by original sin as to be incapable of choosing good or evil without divine assistance.

Pentecost The fiftieth day after Easter, commemorated as the dramatic occasion when Jesus's followers experienced the presence of the Holy Spirit.

Pentecostals Modern Protestant groups that emphasize glossolalia as a sign of the presence of the Holy Spirit and hence of the individual's holiness or spiritual perfection.

Peter, St. The "prince of apostles" who was said to have been the first bishop of Rome.

pope The head of the Roman Catholic Church.

predestination The notion that God anticipates or controls human actions and foreordains every individual to either salvation or damnation.

presbyter Literally, "elder"; a key office that developed in the post-apostolic period.

Reformed Churches Churches that are Calvinist in doctrine and often Presbyterian in governance.

sacrament A ritual action seen as signifying divine grace. The most widely accepted sacraments are baptism and the Eucharist, although the Catholic and Anglican churches also recognize five others.

saints People recognized by the church for their faith and virtue.

scriptures The holy writings of Christianity, consisting of the Hebrew Bible in Greek translation (the Septuagint), which Christians call the "Old Testament," and the "New Testament" accounts of Jesus's life and the early years of the Christian community.

see One of the five major episcopal areas: Rome, Constantinople, Alexandria, Antioch, and Jerusalem.

Synoptic Gospels The Gospels of Matthew, Mark, and Luke, called "synoptic" ("seen together") because of their many overlapping stories and themes.

teleological argument From Greek *telos*, "end" or "purpose"; an argument inferring the existence of God from the perception of purpose or design in the universe.

theocracy A state in which all of society is controlled by the church or religious leaders.

Theotokos Title for Mary as "God bearer."

transubstantiation The view, held mainly by Roman Catholics, that during the mass the bread and wine of the Eucharist become the literal body and blood of Jesus.

Trinity The doctrine that God exists in three "persons" or manifestations: as Father, as Son, and as Holy Spirit.

widows The earliest known order for women in Christianity, originally a response to the social problem of providing support for poor widows in the community.

Zwingli, Ulrich The father of the Swiss Reformation.

Further Reading

Beilby, James, ed. 2009. *The Historic Jesus: Five Views.* Downers Grove, IL: IVP Academic. The presentation of five scholars' views of the historic Jesus.

Bettenson, Henry S., and Chris Maunder, eds. 1999. *Documents of the Christian Church.* 3rd ed. London: Oxford University Press. A book that is strong on the early church and Anglicanism.

Cross, F. L., and E. A. Livingstone, eds. 2005. *The Oxford Dictionary of the Christian Church.* 3rd ed. New York: Oxford University Press. The best general one-volume reference handbook.

Ehrman, Bart. 2011. *The New Testament: An Historical Introduction to Early Christian Writings.* New York and Toronto: Oxford University Press. An overview of the Christian scriptures in their historical, social, and literary contexts within the Greco-Roman world.

Farmer, David Hugh. 2004. *The Oxford Dictionary of Saints.* New York: Oxford University Press. A comprehensive guide.

Hastings, Adrian. 2000. *A World History of Christianity.* Grand Rapids, MI: Eerdmans. A detailed history including Orthodox, Asian, African, Latin American, and North American Christianity.

Holder, Arthur, ed. 2005. *Blackwell Companion to Christian Spirituality.* Oxford, UK: Blackwell. A work including essays by various scholars, each of whom represents a different perspective on Christian spirituality and its forms.

Jenkins, Philip. 2007. *The Next Christendom: The Coming of Global Christianity.* New York: Oxford University Press. A work that explores the implications of the shift in Christianity's center of gravity from Europe and North America to South America, Africa, and Asia.

Kraemer, Ross. 1998. *Maenads, Martyrs, Matrons, Monastics: A Sourcebook on Women's Religions in the Greco-Roman World.* Philadelphia: Fortress Press. A collection of primary texts relating to women's religion in antiquity.

MacCulloch, Diarmaid. 2010. *Christianity: The First Three Thousand Years.* New York: Viking Adult. A large recent work by a noted Reformation historian.

McGinn, Bernard. 2006. *The Essential Writings of Christian Mysticism.* New York: Modern Library. A wide-ranging anthology.

McManners, John. 2002. *The Oxford Illustrated History of Christianity.* Oxford: Oxford University Press. A comprehensive volume detailing the development of Christianity.

Murray, Peter, and Linda Murray. 1998. *The Oxford Companion to Christian Art and Architecture.* New York: Oxford University Press. An illustrated guide.

Sakenfeld, Katharine Doob. 2009. *New Interpreter's Dictionary of the Bible.* 5 vols. Nashville, TN: Abingdon. A good reference work on biblical topics.

Schussler-Fiorenza, Elisabeth. 1994. *In Memory of Her: A Feminist Theological Reconstruction of Christian Origins.* New York: Crossroad. A classic work exploring the role of women in the development of Christianity.

Skinner Keller, Rosemary, and Rosemary Radford Ruether. 2006. *Encyclopedia of Women and Religion in North America.* 3 vols. Bloomington: Indiana University Press. A three-volume collection of essays on women's religious experience in North America, past and present.

White, James. 2001. *Introduction to Christian Worship.* 3rd ed. Nashville, TN: Abingdon. A work examining the liturgical history of the Christian church.

Wilson-Dickson, Andrew. 1997. *The Story of Christian Music: From Gregorian Chant to Black Gospel: An Authoritative Illustrated Guide to All the Major Traditions of Music for Worship.* Oxford: Lion Publishing. A work tracing the development of Christian worship music.

Recommended Websites

http://www.ccel.org
A site providing links to many classic Christian texts.

http://www.newadvent.org
A Catholic site with links to many primary texts from the time of the early church.

http://biblos.com
A tool for Bible study, containing many different translations of the Bible.

http://www.christianity.com
A comprehensive source of articles, videos, and audio resources on Christian history, theology, and living, as well as Bible study tools.

http://www.ncccusa.org
The site of the National Council of Churches USA.

http://www.oikoumene.org
The site of the World Council of Churches.

http://www.religionfacts.com/christianity/index.htm
A wide-ranging source of information on Christianity as well as other religions.

http://www.vatican.va/phome_en.htm
The English-language version of the official Vatican site.

http://virtualreligion.net/forum/index.html
The site of the Jesus Seminar.

http://www.wicc.org
The site of the Women's Inter-Church Council of Canada.

http://www.worldevangelicals.org
The site of a global association of evangelical Christians.

References

Barrett, David B. 1982. *World Christian Encyclopedia: A Comparative Survey of Churches and Religions in the Modern World.* Oxford: Oxford University Press.

Barrett, David B., George T. Currian, and Todd M. Johnson. 2001. *World Christian Encyclopedia: A Comparative Survey of Churches and Religions in the Modern World.* 2nd ed. 2 vols. Oxford: Oxford University Press.

Colledge, Edmund, and James Walsh, ed. and trans. 1978. *Julian of Norwich: Showings.* Western Classics of Spirituality. New York: Paulist Press.

Jenkins, Philip. 2007. *The Next Christendom: The Coming of Global Christianity.* New York: Oxford University Press.

John of the Cross. 1990. *The Dark Night of the Soul.* Trans. E. Allison Peers. Ed. P. Silverio de Santa Teresa, C.D. New York: Doubleday.

Johnson, Todd M., David B. Barrett, and Peter F. Crossing. 2011. "Christianity 2011: Martyrs and the Resurgence of Religion." *International Bulletin of Missionary Research* 35, no. 1: 28–29.

Madigan, Shawn, ed. 1998. *Mystics, Visionaries and Prophets: A Historical Anthology of Women's Spiritual Writings.* Minneapolis: Fortress Press.

O'Brien, Elmer. 1964. *Varieties of Mystic Experience.* New York: Holt, Rinehart and Winston.

Ward, Benedicta, ed. and trans. 1975. *The Sayings of the Desert Fathers.* Trappist, KY: Cistercian Publications.

Note

My appreciation to Harry O. Maier for his assistance with the preparation of the New Testament materials. I am also grateful to have been able to incorporate portions of the late Willard Oxtoby's original chapter here.

6 Muslim Traditions

Amir Hussain

Traditions at a Glance

Numbers

There are approximately 1.6 billion Muslims around the world, including more than 1 million in Canada, nearly 3 million in Great Britain, and 6 to 7 million in the United States.

Distribution

Although Islam originated in Arabia, the largest Muslim populations today are in Indonesia, Pakistan, India, and Bangladesh. Muslims are the second-largest religious community, after Christians, in many Western countries, including Canada, Great Britain, France, and Germany.

Principal Historical Periods

Key moments in Islamic history include the lifetime of the Prophet Muhammad, from 570 to 632; the time of the four caliphs, from 632 to 661; and the Umayyad and 'Abbasid caliphates, which lasted from 661 to 750 and 750 to 1258, respectively. Finally, the Ottoman caliphate lasted from 1517 to 1924.

Founder and Principal Leaders

There are two major branches of Islam: Sunni and Shi'a. All Muslims place authority in Muhammad as the last prophet, but the Shi'a give special authority after Muhammad to his son-in-law 'Ali and 'Ali's descendants (the Imams).

Deity

Allah is Arabic for "the God" and is cognate with the Hebrew *'Eloh*, "deity." Muslims believe Allah to be the same God worshiped by Christians, Jews, and other monotheists.

Authoritative Texts

The essential text is the Qur'an (literally, "The Recitation"), believed to have been revealed by God to Muhammad between 610 and 632 CE. Second in importance are the sayings of Muhammad, known collectively as the **hadith** (literally, "narrative").

Noteworthy Doctrines

Islam, like Judaism and Christianity, is based on ethical monotheism. Its prophetic tradition begins with the first human being (Adam) and ends with the Prophet Muhammad. Muslims believe that the first place of worship dedicated to the one true God is the Ka'ba in Mecca, built by Abraham and his son Ishmael.

In this chapter you will learn about:

- The Arabian environment in which Islam emerged
- The biography of Muhammad and its importance to Muslims
- The story of the Qur'an and its role in Islam
- The basic religious practices of Islam
- The distinctions within Islam, including the Sunni–Shi'a split and the mystical tradition (Sufism)
- The development of Islamic law (*shari'ah*), philosophy, and theology
- Contemporary issues facing Muslim communities in North America

Before the terrorist attacks of September 2001, many instructors would begin their courses on Islam with standard historical introductions to the life of Muhammad and the beginnings of Islam.

 An imam at the Imamzadeh Helal-ebne Ali Shrine in Kashan, Iran (© ZUMA Press, Inc./Alamy Stock Photo).

Their students often knew little about Islam or the religious lives of Muslims before signing up, and even for Muslim students, such a course was often their first formal introduction to their faith. After 9/11, however, some instructors found that students were coming in with preconceptions about Islam that came from the popular media and were at odds with Muslims' own understandings of their faith. As a result, those instructors decided that they had to begin with a crash course on media literacy, underlining how TV news in particular privileges the controversial and provocative over the thoughtful and accurate. How many of us come to the study of Islam with our minds already made up, convinced either that it is a religion of peace that can help modern Western society or that it is a religion of violence and intolerance, incapable of coexisting with that society?

"Islam" means "submission" in Arabic: the name signifies the commitment to live in total submission to God. A person who professes Islam is called a Muslim, meaning "one who submits to God." An older term, rarely used today, is "Mohammedan," which misleadingly—and to Muslims offensively—suggests that Muslims worship the Prophet Muhammad himself.

The Qur'an, the Islamic scripture, presents Islam as the universal and primordial faith of all the prophets from Adam to Muhammad, and of all those who have faith in the one sovereign Lord, creator, and sustainer of all things. According to the Qur'an, Islam is God's eternal way for the universe.

Who is a Muslim? Inanimate things, plants and animals, and even the angels are all *muslims* to God by nature or instinct. Only human *islam* is an *islam* of choice. Human beings may accept or reject God, but on the Day of Judgment they will be either rewarded for their faith or punished for their rejection of it.

Most Muslims are born into Muslim families. But one can also become a Muslim simply by repeating before two Muslim witnesses the **shahadah**, or profession of faith: "I bear witness that there is no god except God, and I bear witness that Muhammad is the messenger of God." Anyone who does this becomes a Muslim, with all the rights and responsibilities that this new identity entails.

⊕ Beginnings

Pre-Islamic Arabia

The Qur'an refers to Arab history before Islam as the age of "foolishness" or "ignorance." The term designates not so much a lack of knowledge as it does a lack of moral consciousness. The Arabs before Islam (like the ancient Hebrews) did not believe in an afterlife. Since time would spare no one, they believed that humans ought to make the most of this life while they could. Arab society was thus focused on earthly accomplishments and pleasures, praising the man who made a good name for his tribe while drowning his existential sorrows in wine, women, and sentimental verse.

The Arabs before Islam recognized Allah (Arabic for "the God") as the supreme creator god, but they worshiped many other deities as well, including a god named Hubal ("vapor"), who may originally have been a rain god, and three goddesses who were said to be the daughters of Allah (one of them may have been a version of the Greco-Roman goddess of love Aphrodite or Venus). Although the three goddesses were worshiped as intermediaries who might bring devotees closer to their father (see Q. 39:3), the Qur'an repudiates them as mere "names which you [the Arabs] and your fathers named; God sent down no authority concerning them" (Q. 53:20–3).

Arabs shared the general Semitic idea of a sacred place (*haram*) where no living thing—plant, animal, or human—could be harmed. For the people of Mecca (Makkah) and most of Arabia, the chief *haram* was the shrine called the Ka'ba, an ancient square building that contained many idols or images of gods and goddesses (among them some figures that may represent Jesus and his virgin

Timeline

622 CE	Muhammad's *hijrah* from Mecca to Medina
632	Muhammad dies; leadership passes to the caliph
642	Birth of al-Hasan al-Basri, early Sufi ascetic (d. 728)
661	Damascus established as capital of Umayyad caliphate
680	Death of Husayn at Karbala, commemorated as martyrdom by Shi'as
711	Arab armies reach Spain
762	Baghdad established as 'Abbasid capital
801	Death of Rabi'a al-'Adawiyah of Basra, a famous female Sufi
1058	Birth of al-Ghazali, theological synthesizer of faith and reason (d. 1111)
1071	Seljuq Turks defeat Byzantines in eastern Anatolia
1165	Birth of Ibn 'Arabi, philosopher of the mystical unity of being (d. 1240)
1207	Birth of Jalal al-Din Rumi, Persian mystical poet (d. 1273)
1258	Baghdad falls to Mongol invaders
1492	Christian forces take Granada, the last Muslim stronghold in Spain
1529	Ottoman Turks reach Vienna (again in 1683)
1602	Muslims officially expelled from Spain
1703	Birth of Ibn 'Abd al-Wahhab, leader of traditionalist revival in Arabia (d. 1792)
1924	Atatürk, Turkish modernizer and secularizer, abolishes the caliphate
1930	Muhammad Iqbal proposes a Muslim state in India
1947	Pakistan established as an Islamic state
1979	Ayatollah Khomeini establishes revolutionary Islamic regime in Iran
2001	Osama bin Laden (d. 2011) launches terrorist attacks on America
2006	Orhan Pamuk becomes the second Muslim (after Naguib Mahfouz in 1988) to win the Nobel Prize for Literature
2010	Islamic scholars at the Mardin Conference in Turkey issue a ruling against terrorism
2011	The "Arab Spring," during which the governments of Tunisia, Egypt, Yemen, and Libya are overthrown; Tawakkul Karman, a leader of the movement in Yemen, becomes the second Muslim woman (after Shirin Ebadi in 2003) to win the Nobel Peace Prize
2018	Ilhan Omar and Rashida Tlaib become the first Muslim women elected to Congress in the United States
2019	Mahershala Ali, an American Muslim, wins his second Academy Award for Best Supporting Actor

mother Mary) and still contains an unusual black stone (perhaps a meteorite) that has been revered since pre-Islamic times. The Ka'ba was believed to have been built by the biblical patriarch Abraham and his son Ishmael (Isaac's brother), who had settled with his mother, Hagar, in the valley of Makkah (Q. 14:37). Before Islam, then, the Ka'ba was already a major pilgrimage site.

During the *hajj,* as many as 500,000 pilgrims gather in the inner courtyard of the Great Mosque of Mecca and circumambulate the Ka'ba. Outside the courtyard but still within the mosque there may be almost 2 million more pilgrims. (© Jamal Nasrallah/epa/Corbis).

When Islam emerged in the seventh century CE, Arabia was bordered to the west by the Christian Byzantine Empire and to the east by the Zoroastrian Sasanian Persian Empire. The city of Mecca, some 40 miles inland from the Red Sea, was dominated mainly by the Quraysh tribe, but it was open to many cultural and religious influences, including those of the Jewish and Christian communities that had been present in the territory for centuries. Mecca also attracted desert hermits who practiced holiness and healing, as well as a group of Meccan Arabs known as *hanifs* ("pious ones"), who shared the ethical monotheism of Judaism and Christianity.

The Life of Muhammad (570–632 CE)

Muhammad was born into the Quraysh tribe around the year 570. His father died before his birth and his mother a few years later. In the tribal society of pre-Islamic Arabia, to be without a family was to be on the margins of society, but the orphaned Muhammad was taken in first by his paternal grandfather, 'Abd al-Muttalib, and later by his uncle Abu Talib.

The young Muhammad worked with his uncle in the caravan trade. By his mid-20s, however, he was employed as a merchant for a rich widow named Khadijah, and when she proposed marriage to him, he accepted. He was called al-Amin ("the faithful" or "trustworthy"), and early biographies describe him as a contemplative, honest, and mild-mannered young man. Once a year, during the month of **Ramadan**, Muhammad spent days in seclusion in a cave a short distance from Mecca.

Tradition reports that it was during one of those retreats that he received the call to prophethood and the first revelation of the Qur'an.

As Muhammad was sitting one night in his retreat, an angel—later identified as Gabriel (Jibril in Arabic)—appeared. Taking hold of him, the angel commanded, "Recite [or read]!" Muhammad answered, "I cannot read." After repeating the command a second and third time, the angel continued: "Recite in the name of your Lord who created, created the human being from a blood clot. Recite, for your Lord is most magnanimous—who taught by the pen, taught the human being that which s/he did not know" (Q. 96:1–5). Shivering with fear, Muhammad ran home and asked the people of his household to protect him. Khadijah was the first to believe his story of the encounter with Gabriel, but his young cousin 'Ali (the son of Abu Talib) also supported him.

After this event, the angel returned to him often, saying, "O Muhammad, I am Gabriel, and you are the Messenger of God." Eventually, Khadijah took Muhammad to her cousin, a learned Christian named Waraqah ibn Nawfal, who declared him to be the Prophet for the Arabs, chosen by God to deliver a sacred law to his people just as Moses had to the Jews.

The idea of a prophet was not unfamiliar to the Meccans, but for 12 years most of them resisted Muhammad's message. They did not want to abandon the gods of their ancestors, and they feared the implications of the new faith both for their way of life and for the status of the Ka'ba, which as a pilgrimage center brought significant income to their city. Muhammad's message was not only religious but also moral and social. He instructed the Meccans to give alms, care for the orphaned, feed the hungry, and assist the oppressed, and he warned of impending doom on the day of the last judgment. The first to accept the new faith, after Khadijah, were his cousin (and future son-in-law) 'Ali ibn Abu Talib, his slave Zayd ibn Harithah (whom he later freed and adopted), and his faithful companion Abu Bakr.

Like Jesus and his disciples, Muhammad and his followers were often vilified. Around 615, one group of Muslims faced such severe persecution from the Meccans that the Prophet advised them to migrate across the Red Sea to Christian Abyssinia (Ethiopia), where they were well received. And in 619 the Prophet himself was left without support or protection when both his wife and his uncle died. Although he later entered into a number of polygamous marriages (as was the custom in his society), the loss of Khadijah must have been particularly hard: they had been married for almost half his life, she was the mother of their four daughters, and she had been the first person to believe in him. But the death of Abu Talib, his protector and surrogate father, must have been almost equally hard. It was soon after these losses that Muhammad experienced what came to be known as the "night journey," during which he traveled from Mecca to Jerusalem on his horse Buraq in the course of a single night, and the *mi'raj*, a miraculous ascent to heaven, where he met some of the earlier prophets and was granted an audience with God. For the Muslims, these miraculous events confirmed that their Prophet still had the support of God. Even so, it would be another three years before he found a place for the Muslims to establish their own community, free of the persecution they had suffered in Mecca.

The First Muslim Community

Finally, in 622, an invitation was offered by the city of Yathrib, about 250 miles north of Mecca. The migration (*hijrah*) to Yathrib, which thereafter came to be known as "the city of the Prophet" or Medina ("the city"), marked the beginning of community life under Islam, and thus of Islamic history. In Medina Muhammad established the first Islamic commonwealth, a theocracy led by a prophet who was believed to be guided by a divine scripture.

Medina's social structure was far more diverse than Mecca's, for it included a substantial Jewish community as well as two feuding Arab tribes who kept the city in a continuous state of civil strife. Muhammad succeeded in welding these disparate elements into a cohesive social unit. In a brief constitutional document known as the covenant of Medina, he stipulated that all the people of the city should form a single Muslim commonwealth. Jews were granted full religious freedom and equality with the Muslims, on condition that they avoid any action against the state.

The Qur'an's worldview is closely akin to the prophetic view of history laid out in the Hebrew Bible. The Prophet expected the Jews of Medina, recognizing this kinship, to be natural allies, and he adopted several Jewish practices, including the fast of the Day of Atonement (Yom Kippur). But the Medinan Jews rejected both Muhammad's claim to be a prophet and the Qur'an's claim to be a sacred book. The resulting tension is reflected in the Qur'an's treatment of the Jews. Some references are clearly positive—for example, "Among the People of the Book are an upright community who recite God's revelations in the night, prostrate themselves in adoration, believing in God and the Last Day . . ." these are of the righteous . . ." (Q. 3:113–115). Others are just as clearly negative: "Take not the Jews and Christians for friends" (Q. 5:51). Increasingly, Islam began to distinguish itself from Judaism, so that the fast of Ramadan soon took precedence over the Yom Kippur fast, and the *qiblah* (direction of prayer) was changed from Jerusalem to the Ka'ba in Mecca.

The Conversion of Mecca

The Muslims who had fled Mecca for Medina had left all their property behind; thus, to support themselves, they began raiding the caravans of Meccan traders. In 624, when the Meccans sent an army of roughly 1,000 to Medina to stop the raids, they were met at the well of Badr by a 300-man detachment of Muslims. Though poorly equipped and far outnumbered, the Muslims inflicted a crushing defeat on the Meccans. Thus the Battle of Badr is celebrated in the Qur'an as a miraculous proof of the truth of Islam: "You [Muhammad] did not shoot the first arrow when you did shoot it; rather God shot it" (Q. 8:17). To avenge their defeat, the Meccans met the Muslims the following year by Mount Uhud, not far from Medina, and this time they prevailed. Following that battle, the Jews were expelled from Medina on the grounds that they had formed alliances with the Meccans against the Muslims. But the real reason may have been that the Muslim state sought to free itself of external influences at a critical stage in its development.

Meanwhile, the Muslims continued to raid the caravans of the Quraysh, and before long they learned that the Meccans were planning to attack Medina itself. On the advice of Salman the Persian, a former slave, the Prophet had a trench dug around the city to prevent the Meccan cavalry from entering. Thus when the Quraysh and their allies tried to invade Medina in 627, they failed. The Battle of the Trench marked a tipping point, and in 628 the Meccans sought a truce. Two years later, when the Quraysh breached the truce, the Prophet set out for Mecca at the head of a large army. But there was no need to fight. When the Muslims arrived, the Meccans surrendered to them and accepted Islam en masse.

Whenever an individual or tribe accepted Islam, all hostilities were to cease. Therefore the Prophet granted amnesty to all in the city. He attributed the victory solely to God, as prescribed in the Qur'an: "When support from God comes, and victory, and you see people enter into the religion of God in throngs, proclaim the praise of your Lord . . ." (Q. 110). He returned to Medina, where he died two years later, in 632.

Muhammad was always known as the "Messenger of God" rather than as a ruler or military leader, but in fact he was all of these. He waged war and made peace. He laid the foundations of a community (**ummah**) based on Islamic principles. He established Islam in Arabia and sent expeditions to Syria. Within 80 years the Muslims would administer the largest empire the world had ever known, stretching from the southern borders of France through North Africa and the Middle East into Central Asia and India.

No one could have foreseen that future at the time of his death. The majority of Muslims—the **Sunni**, meaning those who follow the *sunnah* (traditions) of the Prophet—believed that he had not even designated a successor or specified how one should be chosen. But a minority community, known as the **Shi'a** (from the Arabic meaning "party"), believed that Muhammad had in fact appointed his cousin and son-in-law 'Ali to succeed him. Muhammad's death therefore precipitated a crisis that would grow into a permanent ideological rift.

A *khalifah* is one who represents or acts on behalf of another. After Muhammad's death, his close companion Abu Bakr became the *khalifat rasul Allah*—the "successor" or "representative" of the Messenger of God—and Abu Bakr's successor, 'Umar ibn al-Khattab, was at first referred to as the "successor of the successor of the Messenger of God."

From the beginning, the institution of the caliphate had a worldly dimension as well as a religious one. As a successor of the Prophet, the **caliph** was a religious leader, but as the chief or administrative head of the community, he was also the *amir*, or commander, of the Muslims. Perhaps conscious of this temporal role, 'Umar is said to have chosen the title "commander of the faithful." Nevertheless, the caliph continued to function as the religious leader ("imam") of the community. In all, four caliphs ruled from 632 to 661. From 661 to 750, the Muslim world was ruled by a hereditary dynasty known as the Umayyads, who in turn were defeated by the 'Abbasid dynasty, which ruled from 750 to 1258.

⊕ Foundations

Prophets and Messengers

According to the Qur'an, God operates through prophets and messengers who convey God's will in revealed scriptures and seek to establish God's law in their communities. From the Islamic perspective, therefore, human history is prophetic history. Tradition maintains that from the time of Adam to the time of Muhammad, God sent 124,000 prophets into the world to remind people of every community of their obligations to the one Lord and warn them against disobedience. Among the 25 prophets whom the Qur'an names are the biblical figures Abraham, Moses, David, Solomon, Elijah, John the Baptist, and Jesus. Islamic tradition distinguishes between prophets and messengers. A prophet is one who conveys a message from God to a specific people at a specific time. A messenger is sent to a specific community, but the message he delivers is a universally binding sacred law (*shari'ah*). The Torah given to Moses was an example of the latter: though delivered to the ancient Hebrews, it was binding on all who knew it, Hebrews and others, until the arrival of the next revelation—the gospel of Jesus. In other words, every messenger is a prophet, but not every prophet is a messenger. Among the messenger-prophets, five—Noah, Abraham, Moses, Jesus, and Muhammad—are called "prophets of power" (Q. 46:35), because their revelations were universally binding.

Abraham

In the Qur'an, it is the innate reasoning capacity of Abraham—Ibrahim in Arabic—that leads him away from the Hebrews' tradition of idol worship and toward the knowledge of God. Even as a youth he recognizes that idols *cannot* hear the supplications of their worshipers and therefore can do them neither good nor harm.

The Qur'an records that one night, gazing at the full moon, Abraham thought that it must be God. But he changed his mind when he saw it set. He then gazed at the bright sun and thought that, since it was so much larger, it must be the real God. But that night the sun too set, leading

Abraham to declare: "I turn my face to the One who originated the heavens and the earth. . . . I am not one of the Associators [those who associate other things or beings with God]" (Q. 6:77–79).

Jesus

Muslims believe that all the major prophets' claims to have been sent by God are supported by evidentiary miracles. The Qur'an presents Jesus as a miracle in himself. His virgin birth and his ability to heal the sick, feed the hungry, and even raise the dead all affirm God's creative and life-giving power against those who deny the reality of the resurrection and life to come. Furthermore, he performed his miracles at a time when Greek medicine, science, and philosophy were challenging the sovereignty of God as the sole creator and Lord of the universe. The miracles of Jesus therefore assert God's power over human learning and wisdom.

The Qur'an presents Jesus as delivering this message to the children of Israel: "God is surely my Lord and your Lord. Worship him, therefore; this is the straight way" (Q. 3:51). For Muslims, Jesus was a world-renouncing ascetic, a wandering prophet of stern piety but deep compassion

Document

From the Qur'an: Abraham Destroys the Idols

When [Abraham] said to his father and his people, "What are these idols that you so fervently worship?" they said, "We found our fathers worshipping them."

He said, "Both you and your fathers are in manifest error." They said, "Have you come to us with the truth, or are you one of those who jest?"

He said, "Your Lord is indeed the Lord of the heavens and the earth, for your Lord originated them; and to this I am one of those who bear witness. By God, I shall confound your idols as soon as you turn your backs."

He thus destroyed them utterly except for the chief one, so that the people might turn to it [for petition].

They said, "Who did this to our gods? He is surely a wrongdoer."

Some said, "We heard a youth called Abraham speaking of them."

Others said, "Bring him here in the sight of the people, so that they may all witness."

They said, "Did you do this to our gods, O Abraham?"

He said, "No, it was their chief who did it. Question them—if they could speak."

The people then turned on one another, saying, "Indeed you are the wrongdoers!" Then they bowed their heads in humiliation, saying, "You know well, [O Abraham], that these do not speak."

He [Abraham] said, "Would you then worship instead of God a thing that can do you neither good nor harm? Shame on you and on what you worship instead of God; do you not reason?"

They said, "Burn him and stand up for your gods, if you would do anything."

We [God] said, "O fire, be coolness and peace for Abraham."

They wished evil for him, but We turned them into utter losers. And We delivered him and Lot to a land that We blessed for all beings. We also granted him Isaac and Jacob as added favour, and We made them both righteous. We made them all leaders guiding others by our command. We inspired them to do good deeds, perform regular worship, and give the obligatory alms; and they were true worshippers of Us alone. (Q. 21:51–73) for the poor, suffering, and oppressed. Although the Qur'an categorically denies that Jesus is the divine Son of God (Q. 5:116, 19:34–35, and 5:17 and 72), it sees his role as extending far beyond his earthly existence, insisting that he did not die, but was lifted up to heaven by God (Q. 4:157–158) and will return at the end of time to kill the Antichrist and establish true Islam on earth.

Each prophet prepares for and supports the prophet to come after him. Thus Jesus in the Qur'an announces the coming of Muhammad: "O children of Israel, I am the messenger of God to you, confirming the Torah that was before me, and announcing a messenger who shall come after me whose name is Ahmad [Muhammad]" (Q. 61:6).

Muhammad

For Muslims, Muhammad is the "Prophet of the end of time." Just as the sacred book that he received from God, the Qur'an, is God's final revelation for humanity, confirming and supplanting all previous revelations (see Q. 5:48), so Muhammad himself is "the seal of the prophets," and his life-example (*sunnah*) is the prophetic model that will guide history until it comes to an end on the Day of Judgment.

For the early Muslims, whatever the Prophet said or did was on God's behalf and by his command; therefore, obedience to the *sunnah* of the Prophet was the same as obedience to God. When the Qur'an says that God sent his Messenger with "the Book and wisdom" (Q. 62:2), Muslims understand "the Book" to be the Qur'an and the "wisdom" to be the *sunnah*. Thus Muslims believe the Prophet's actions and sayings to be no less divinely inspired than the Qur'an itself.

To show their respect for Muhammad, Muslims speak (or write) the phrase "peace [and blessings of God] be upon him" every time his name or title is mentioned. In writing, the formula is often abbreviated as PBUH. When the prophets as a group, culminating in Muhammad, are mentioned, the formula changes to "peace be on them all."

The Qur'an

The *ayahs* (verses) and **surahs** (chapters) that make up the Qur'an were revealed to Muhammad by the angel Gabriel over a period of 23 years. The Prophet's role as transmitter is reflected in the Qur'an's characteristic phrasing: God ("We") instructs the Prophet ("you") to "say" something to the people (that is, to deliver a particular message to them). Yet the first instruction, as we have seen, was the command that Muhammad himself "recite" or "read." The term "Qur'an" is derived from the same root: q–r–', meaning "to read" or "recite."

The Qur'an is nearly as long as the New Testament. Its contents range from short verses on a single theme or idea to fairly lengthy chapters. The early Meccan *surahs* are generally brief admonitions, while the later ones are didactic tales of earlier prophets and their communities. Through stories, parables, and exhortations, the Qur'an aims to create an *ummah*, a "community" united by faith. The *surahs* revealed in Medina are fewer but longer, presenting didactic arguments, discourses, and legal pronouncements, often in response to situations arising in the life of the community.

The Status of the Qur'an

Muslims believe that the Qur'an contains the eternal Word of God. In fact, there is a theological parallel with Christian understandings of Jesus, who in the prologue to John's Gospel is proclaimed to be the eternal Word of God made incarnate at a certain moment in history. For Christians Christ is the Word of God made flesh, while for Muslims the Qur'an is the Word of God made into a book.

Muslims understand the Qur'an to have been revealed specifically in Arabic—the language of its first audience. Hence any translation is considered an interpretation, not the Qur'an itself. Even in places where few if any Muslims speak the language, the Qur'an is always recited in Arabic. Of course, each passage is usually followed by a translation in the appropriate language.

The words of the Qur'an are spoken in a newborn's ear as a blessing. They are also recited to seal a marriage contract or a business deal, to celebrate a successful venture, or to give solace. They are broadcast daily on radio and television throughout the Muslim world, and in the form of calligraphy they have also been a central motif in Islamic art.

Compiling the Qur'an

When the Prophet died in 632, there were many people who had committed the Qur'an to memory, but the only physical records of it were fragments written on stones, bones, palm leaves, and animal parchment. In some cases the same material existed in several versions, and certain words or phrases could be read in more than one way. These variants came to be identified with specific readers through the generations of Muslim scholars. Tradition maintains that the verses within each *surah* were arranged by the Prophet at Gabriel's instruction, but that the order of the *surahs* in relation to one another—roughly in decreasing order of length—was fixed by the committee appointed to compile an official version. When it was completed, within 20 years of the Prophet's death, one of the first copies was given to Hafsah, one of his widows.

Qur'anic Commentary (Tafsir)

The term for commentary on the Qur'an, **tafsir**, means "unveiling" or elucidating the meaning of a text. Any such interpretation is based on one of three authoritative sources: the Qur'an itself, the Prophetic *hadith*, and the opinions of the Prophet's Companions and their successors. Like the Qur'an and the *hadith*, the earliest commentaries were transmitted orally, but by the tenth century Qur'anic interpretation had become a science with several ancillary fields of study. Since every legal or theological school and religious or political movement in Muslim history has looked to the Qur'an as its primary support, a wide range of interpretations has emerged over time.

The Qur'an's Concept of God

The Qur'an speaks of the deity as the one and only God, creator, sustainer, judge, and sovereign Lord over all creation. For Muslims, it is a sin to associate any other being with God.

As we noted earlier, "Allah" is not the name of a particular deity: it means "the God," "the Lord of all beings" (Q. 1:2) who demands faith and worship from all rational creatures. It was used in the same sense by the pagan Arabs before Islam and is still used in that sense by Arab Jews and Christians today.

Islamic theology holds that God's essence is unknowable, inconceivable, and above all categories of time, space, form, and number. Materiality and temporality cannot be attributed to God. Nor can any gender, although references to God use masculine pronouns, verbs, and adjectives. God is known through the attributes known as the "most beautiful names" (sometimes translated as "wonderful names"): "God is God other than whom there is no god, knower of the unknown and the visible. God is the All-merciful, the Compassionate. God is God other than whom there is no god, the King, the Holy One, Peace, the Faithful, the Guardian, the Majestic, the Compeller, the Lofty One" (Q. 59:22–23).

Faith and Action

Righteousness in the Qur'an has several components. In addition to faith in God, God's angels, books, prophets, and the Last Judgment, it includes good works: Muslims should give of their wealth to orphans and the needy, and for the ransoming of slaves and war captives. Righteousness also includes steadfastness in times of misfortune and war, and integrity in one's dealings with others.

Because all men and women are part of one humanity, they are all equal before God, regardless of race, color, or social status. They may surpass one another only in righteousness: "Humankind, We have created you all of one male and one female and made you different peoples and tribes in order that you may know one another. Surely, the noblest of you in God's sight is the one who is most aware of God" (Q. 49:13).

The Arabic word *iman* means faith, trust, and a personal sense of well-being in God's providential care, mercy, and justice. On this level of inner personal commitment, *iman* is a deeper level of *islam*: total surrender of the human will and destiny to the will of God. The opposite of *iman* is **kufr**: knowing the truth but willfully denying or obscuring it. The Qur'an also makes an important distinction between Islam and faith. Islam is a religious, social, and legal institution, while faith, *iman*, is an inner conviction whose sincerity God alone can judge, a commitment to a way of life. This is described beautifully in the Qur'an (49:14), in an episode in which the Bedouin come to Muhammad and say, "We have faith." Muhammad responds: "Do not say that you have faith, rather, say that you have submitted [you have *islam*], for faith has not yet entered your hearts." When asked, "What is faith?" the Prophet is said to have answered, "Faith is seventy-odd branches, the highest of which is to say 'There is no god except God' and the lowest is to remove a harmful object from the road." In short, faith is a comprehensive framework of worship and moral conduct.

Above Islam and *iman* stands *ihsan* (doing good or creating beauty). On the level of human interrelations, *ihsan* is a concrete manifestation of both Islam and *iman*. On the level of the Muslim's personal relationship with God, *ihsan* constitutes the highest form of worship, expressed in this *hadith*: "*Ihsan* is to worship God as though you see God, for even if you do not see God, God sees you."

⊕ Practice

The Five Pillars of Islam

Individual faith and institutional Islam converge in the worship of God and service to others. According to tradition, the Prophet himself said that Islam was built on five "pillars." With the exception of the first (the *shahadah*, the profession of faith), these pillars are all rites of worship:

- to declare, or bear witness, that there is no god except God, and that Muhammad is the Messenger of God;
- to establish regular worship;
- to pay the **zakat** alms;
- to observe the fast of Ramadan; and
- to perform the **hajj** (pilgrimage to Mecca) once in one's life.

These are the foundations of Islam as a religious system of faith and social responsibility, worship, and piety. Each one has both an outer or public obligatory dimension and an inner or private voluntary dimension.

Bearing Witness

The first pillar is the *shahadah*: "I bear witness that there is no god except God, and I bear witness that Muhammad is the Messenger of God." The first part, affirming the oneness of God, expresses the primordial state of faith in which every child is born. The Prophet is said to have declared, "Every child is born in this original state of faith; then his parents turn him into a Jew, Christian, or Zoroastrian, and if they are Muslims, into a Muslim." The second part, affirming Muhammad's role as messenger, signifies acceptance of his claim to prophethood, and hence the truth of his message.

Prayer

The obligatory prayers (*salat*) are distinguished from voluntary meditations and personal prayers (which may be offered at any time) in that they must be performed five times in a day and night: at dawn, at noon, in mid-afternoon, at sunset, and after dark. The *salat* were the first Islamic rituals and must always be preceded by a cleansing ritual that includes washing the face, rinsing the mouth and nostrils, washing the hands and forearms to the elbows, passing one's wet hands over the head, and washing the feet to the heels.

Five times a day—on radio and television, through loudspeakers, and from high minarets—the melodious voice of a **mu'adhdhin** chants the call to prayer. Whether praying alone at home or at the mosque, as a member of the congregation, every Muslim is always conscious of countless other men

Women in Fez, Morocco, perform ablutions at the Zawiya (shrine) of Moulay Idris II, who ruled Morocco from 807 to 828 (© Charles O. Cecil/Alamy).

and women engaged in the same act of worship at the same time. Each phrase of the call to prayer is repeated at least twice for emphasis: "God is greater. I bear witness that there is no god except God, and I bear witness that Muhammad is the Messenger of God. Hasten to the prayers! Hasten to success (or prosperity)! (Shi'as add: Hasten to the best action!). God is greater. There is no god except God."

The prayers consist of cycles or units called *rak'ahs*, which incorporate bowing, kneeling, and prostration. The dawn prayers consist of two cycles, the noon and mid-afternoon prayers of four each, the sunset prayers of three, and the night prayers of four. Apart from some moments of contemplation and personal supplication at the end of the *salat*, these prayers are fixed formulas consisting largely of passages from the Qur'an, especially the opening *surah* (*al-Fatihah*):

> In the name of God, the All-merciful, the Compassionate:

> Praise be to God, the All-merciful, the Compassionate, King of the Day of Judgment. You alone do we worship, and to you alone do we turn for help. Guide us to the straight way, the way of those upon whom you have bestowed your grace, not those who have incurred your wrath, nor those who have gone astray. (Q. 1:1–7)

Known as the **Fatihah**, this prayer is repeated in every *rak'ah*—at least 17 times in every 24-hour period.

Unlike Judaism and Christianity, Islam has no Sabbath specified for rest, but Friday is the day designated for congregational assembly and prayers. On Friday the first two *rak'ahs* of the noon prayers are replaced by two short sermons, followed by two *rak'ahs*. The place of worship is called the *masjid* ("place of prostration in prayer") or *jami'* (literally, "gatherer"). The English term "mosque" is derived from *masjid*. Other congregational prayers are performed on the first days of the two major festivals, **'Id al-Fitr** and 'Id al-Adha, which mark the end of Ramadan and the *hajj* pilgrimage, respectively.

Faithful Muslims see all things, good or evil, as contingent on God's will. Hence many preface any statement about hopes for the future with the phrase *in-sha' Allah*, "if God wills."

Almsgiving

The third pillar reflects the close relationship between worship of God and service to the needy. Traditionally, all adult Muslims who had wealth were expected to "give alms" through payment of an obligatory tax called the *zakat*. Offering alms in this way served to purify the donor, purging him of greed and attachment to material possessions.

The *zakat* obligation was 2.5 percent of the value of all one's wealth (savings, financial gains of any kind, livestock, agricultural produce, real estate, etc.). During the early centuries of Islam, when the community was controlled by a central authority, the *zakat* revenues were kept in a central treasury and disbursed for public projects, education, care of orphans and the needy, and the ransoming of Muslim war captives. Now the Muslim world is divided into nation-states, most of which collect some form of income tax, and the *zakat* obligation has become largely voluntary. However, Muslims are also expected to practice voluntary almsgiving (**sadaqah**). The Qur'an calls *sadaqah* a loan given to God, which will be repaid on the Day of Resurrection (Q. 57:11).

The Ramadan Fast

The fourth pillar of Islam is the fast of Ramadan, which extends from daybreak till sundown each day for a month. Named for the month in which the Qur'an was revealed to the Prophet, the Ramadan fast requires complete abstention from food, drink, smoking, and sexual relations. The fast is broken at sunset, and another light meal is eaten at the end of the night, just before

Practice

A Muslim Ritual: The Call to Prayer

It is Friday afternoon, a few minutes before the start of the weekly congregational prayer. In this mosque in Southern California, perhaps 1,000 men and 100 women are gathered; the difference in numbers reflects the fact that this prayer is obligatory for men but optional for women. A young man walks to the front of the men's section (the women are seated in a second-floor gallery), raises his hands to his ears, and begins the call to prayer: "*Allahu akbar*, God is greater. . . ." When he has finished, the people behind him line up in rows and wait for the imam—the person who will lead the prayer—to begin.

Were this service in a different location, the call to prayer might already have been sounded in the traditional way, broadcast from minarets (towers) beside the mosque. But there are no minarets here, as the mostly non-Muslim neighbors wanted the building to "fit in" with its surroundings. Nor does this mosque have the characteristic dome; instead, it is a two-story building that looks more like a school than a mosque. In this nontraditional context, the function of the call to prayer has changed. Instead of being broadcast outside to let the community know that it is time to pray, the call is broadcast inside to those already assembled for prayer. This is one of the ways in which this congregation has adapted to its surroundings.

the next day's fast begins at dawn. Since, as the Qur'an notes, "God desires ease for you, not hardship" (Q. 2:185), children, the sick, travelers, and women who are pregnant, nursing, or menstruating are exempted from the fast, either altogether or until they are able to make up the missed days.

Before Islam, the Arabs followed a lunar calendar in which the year consisted of only 354 days. To keep festivals and sacred months in their proper seasons, they (like the Jews) added an extra month every three years. The Qur'an abolished this custom, allowing Islamic festivals to rotate throughout the year. When Ramadan comes in the summer, abstaining from water in particular

Focus

Beginning the Fast

Ms. Becker teaches fourth grade in a public elementary school. Eleven of the school's pupils are Muslim, and one of them is in Ms. Becker's class. This year, seven of the Muslim students have decided that they will fast during Ramadan. Some of them have fasted before, but for the nine-year-old in Ms. Becker's class this will be the first time.

There is no set age at which Muslim children are expected to begin observing the fast. It may be as early as eight or nine, or as late as adolescence. In certain Muslim cultures, girls begin at an earlier age than boys, who are usually exempted on the grounds that they "aren't strong enough." While their non-Muslim classmates have lunch, those who are fasting gather in Ms. Becker's classroom to work quietly on school projects. They are also excused from their physical education classes and instead do a writing assignment about physical fitness. In this way, a public school accommodates the needs of its Muslim students.

can be a real hardship, especially in hot climates. But when it comes in winter, as it did in the 1990s in the Northern Hemisphere, it can be relatively tolerable.

Ramadan ends with a three-day festival called 'Id al-Fitr. Children receive gifts and wear brightly colored new clothes, people visit the graves of loved ones, and special sweet dishes are distributed to the poor. Before the first breakfast after the long fast, the head of the household gives special alms on behalf of the family. Those who are exempted from fasting because of old age or chronic illness must feed a poor person for every day they miss.

The fast becomes a true act of worship when a person shares God's bounty with those who have no food with which to break their fast. True fasting also means abstaining from gossip, lying, or anger, and turning the heart and mind to God in devotional prayer and meditation.

The Pilgrimage to Mecca

The fifth pillar of Islam is the *hajj* pilgrimage, instituted by Abraham at God's command after he and his son Ishmael were ordered to build the Ka'ba. Thus most of its ritual elements are understood to reenact the experiences of Abraham, whom the Qur'an declares to be the first true Muslim.

Before the pilgrims reach Mecca, they exchange their regular clothes for two pieces of white linen, symbolic of the shrouds in which Muslims are wrapped for burial. With this act they enter the state of consecration required to enter the city. The Great Mosque is the world's largest, covering more than 88 acres of land that features in the Abrahamic narrative, and the first ritual, the "lesser *hajj*," is performed there: after circumambulating the Ka'ba seven times, pilgrims run seven times between the two small hills (al-Safa and al-Marwa) contained within the mosque's walls. This part of the ritual recalls how Hagar, the mother of Abraham's son Ishmael, is said to have run between these hills in search of water for her dying child. After the seventh run, water gushed out by the child's feet, and Hagar contained it with sand. According to tradition, the place is marked by the well of Zamzam ("the contained water"). Its water is considered holy, and pilgrims often take some of it home for family and friends.

The *hajj* proper begins on the eighth of Dhu al-Hijjah, the twelfth month of the Islamic calendar, when throngs of pilgrims set out for the plain of 'Arafat, about 13 miles east of Mecca, on which stands the Mount of Mercy (Jabal al-Rahmah). As the sun passes the noon meridian, all the pilgrims gather for the central rite of the pilgrimage: standing till sunset on the Mount of Mercy as though standing before God on Judgment Day. At sundown the pilgrims leave 'Arafat for Muzdalifah, a sacred spot a short distance along the road back to Mecca. There they observe the combined sunset and evening prayers and gather pebbles for the ritual throwing of stones at Mina the next day.

Tradition says that it was as Abraham was on his way from 'Arafat to Mina that God commanded him to sacrifice that which was dearest to him—his son Ishmael. Satan whispered to him three times, tempting him to disobey God's command. Abraham responded by hurling stones to drive him away. Thus pilgrims gather early in the morning at a spot called al-'Aqabah, meaning the "hard" or "steep road," to throw seven stones at a pillar representing Satan. Three other pillars in Mina representing the three temptations are also stoned.

Following the stoning ritual, the head of each pilgrim family or group offers a blood sacrifice—a lamb, goat, cow, or camel—to symbolize the animal sent from heaven with which God ransomed Abraham's son (Q. 27:107). Part of the meat is eaten by the pilgrims, and the rest is distributed to the poor. Then, to mark the end of their state of consecration, pilgrims clip a minimum of three hairs from their heads (some shave their heads completely). The *hajj* ends with a final circumambulation of the Ka'ba and the completion of the rites of the lesser *hajj* ('*umrah*) for those who have not done so.

Tradition asserts that Muslims return from a sincerely performed *hajj* free of all sin, as on the day when they were born. Thus the *hajj* represents a form of resurrection or rebirth, and its

Pilgrims throw stones at one of the pillars representing Satan. This ritual is a key part of the *hajj* pilgrimage (© AP Photo/Hassan Ammar/CP).

completion marks a new stage in one's life. Every pilgrim is henceforth distinguished by the title *hajjah* or *hajji* before her or his name.

Religious Sciences

The "religious sciences" were part of a comprehensive cultural package—including theology, philosophy, literature, and science—that developed as Islam expanded far beyond the religio-political framework of its Arabian homeland. Cosmopolitan, pluralistic Islamic cultural centers like Baghdad, Cordoba, and Cairo offered ideal settings for intellectual growth.

Islam is a religion more of action than of abstract speculation about right belief. Hence the first and most important of the religious sciences, Islamic law, stresses that the essence of faith is right living. For Muslims, inner submission to the will of God means living within the framework of divine law, the *shari'ah*.

Sources of Shari'ah (Islamic Law): The Qur'an and the Sunnah

The Qur'an and the *shari'ah* are concerned with relationships among individuals in society and between individuals and God. The most intimate human relationship is the one between husband

and wife; the second is the relationship between parent and child. The circle then broadens to include the extended family, the tribe, the *ummah*, and the world.

Islam has no priesthood. Every Muslim is responsible both for his or her own morality and for the morality of the entire *ummah*: "Let there be of you a community that calls to the good, enjoins honorable conduct, and dissuades from evil conduct" (Q. 3:104).

The Qur'an places kindness and respect for parents next in importance to the worship of God. These are followed by caring for the poor and needy. But renunciation of material possessions is no more desirable than total attachment to them. Rather, the Qur'an enjoins the faithful to "seek amidst that which God has given you, the last abode, but do not forget your portion of the present world" (Q. 28:77). In short, the Qur'an is primarily concerned with moral issues in actual situations. It is not a legal manual: of its 6,236 verses, no more than 200 are explicitly legislative.

The life-example of the Prophet includes not only his actions and sayings but also his tacit consent. His actions are reported in anecdotes about events he participated in or situations to which he reacted. In cases in which he expressed neither approval nor objection, his silence is taken to signify consent. Thus the *sunnah* of consent became a normative source of Islamic law.

Accounts of the Prophet's *hadith*s must go back to an eyewitness. The *hadith* literature is the most important component of *sunnah* because it is the most direct expression of his judgments regarding the community's conduct.

To qualify as a *hadith*, a text must be accompanied by its chain of transmission, beginning with the compiler or last transmitter and going back to the Prophet. The aim of *hadith* study is to ascertain the authenticity of a particular text by establishing the completeness of the chain of its transmission and the veracity of its transmitters.

There are six canonical *hadith* collections. The earliest and most important collectors were Muhammad ibn Isma'il al-Bukhari (810–870) and Muslim ibn al-Hajjaj al-Nisaburi (c. 817–875). As their names suggest, the former came from the city of Bukhara in Central Asia and the latter from Nishapur in northeastern Iran. Although they did not know one another, both spent many years traveling across the Muslim world in search of *hadith*s. The fact that their independent quests produced very similar results suggests that a unified *hadith* tradition was already well established by this time.

Both men are said to have collected hundreds of thousands of *hadith*s, out of which each selected about 3,000, discounting repetitions. Their two collections, *Sahih* (literally, "sound") *al-Bukhari* and *Sahih Muslim*, soon achieved canonical status, second in authority only to the Qur'an. Within less than half a century, four other collections had been produced. It's worth noting that their compilers also came from Central Asia and Iran. Each of these collections is entitled simply *Sunan* (the plural of *sunnah*). As legal manuals, all six collections are organized topically, beginning with the laws governing worship and continuing with the laws regulating social, political, and economic life.

The Scope of Islamic Law

The *shari'ah* is sacred law, "the law of God." It consists of the maxims, admonitions, and legal sanctions and prohibitions enshrined in the Qur'an and explained, elaborated, and realized in the Prophetic tradition.

Shari'ah originally signified the way to a source of water. Metaphorically it came to mean the way to the good in this world and the next. It is "the straight way" that leads the faithful to paradise in the hereafter. Muslims believe the *shari'ah* to be God's plan for the ordering of human society. Within the framework of the divine law, human actions range from those that are absolutely obligatory and will bring rewards on the Day of Judgment to those that are absolutely forbidden and will bring harsh punishment. Actions are classified into five categories:

- lawful (**halal**), and therefore obligatory;
- commendable, and therefore recommended;
- neutral, and therefore permitted;
- reprehensible, and therefore disliked; and
- unlawful (**haram**), and therefore forbidden.

These categories govern all human actions. The correctness of an action and the intention that lies behind it together determine its consequences for the person who performs it.

Jurisprudence

Jurisprudence, or *fiqh*, is the theoretical and systematic aspect of Islamic law, consisting of the interpretation and codification of the *shari'ah*. Islamic jurisprudence is based on four sources, of which the Qur'an and *sunnah* are primary. The two secondary sources are the personal reasoning (**ijtihad**) of the scholars and the general consensus (**ijma'**) of the community. There are four major schools of Sunni Islamic law (Hanafi, Maliki, Shafi'i, and Hanbali), which differ in the degree of emphasis or acceptance that they give to each source.

The legal scholars who founded these various schools of thought used personal reasoning to deduce from the Qur'an and *sunnah* the laws that would become the foundations of their thinking. *Ijtihad* represents a scholar's best effort in this endeavor, which is based on reasoning from analogous situations in the past; thus, modern software piracy would be considered analogous to theft.

Finally, the principle of consensus (*ijma'*) is meant to ensure the continuing authenticity and truth of the three other sources. In the broadest sense, it refers to the community's acceptance of applied *shari'ah*. More narrowly, it has encouraged an active exchange of ideas among the various schools, at least during the formative period of Islamic law. Consensus has remained the final arbiter of truth and error, expressed in the Prophet's declaration that "my community will not agree on an error."

Yet even this important principle has been the subject of debate and dissension. Among the questions at issue are whether the consensus of earlier generations is binding on the present one, and whether the necessary consensus can be reached by scholars alone, without the participation of the community at large.

Early Jurisprudence

The Qur'an calls on Muslims to choose a number of individuals to dedicate themselves to the acquisition of religious knowledge so that they can provide instruction when the people ask for it (Q. 9:122). The need for such a group was felt from the beginning of the tradition, when some pilgrims visiting Mecca from Medina accepted Islam and on returning took with them some Muslims with the necessary knowledge to teach the Medinans. As Islam spread across Arabia, the Prophet sent governors with special religious knowledge to administer the new Muslim communities and instruct their people in Islam.

Among those governors was Mu'adh ibn Jabal. Before sending him to Yemen, the Prophet is said to have asked him how he would deal with the People of the Book (Jews and Christians), who made up the majority of the region's population. Mu'adh supposedly answered that he would deal with them in accordance with the Book of God and the *sunnah* of his Prophet. Muhammad then asked what would happen if he did not find the answer to a problem in either of the two sources. Mu'adh is said to have answered, "I would then use my reason, and would spare no effort."

This pious tale no doubt was invoked to bestow on a developing discipline an aura of Prophetic blessing and authority. Nevertheless, the anecdote aptly illustrates the development of Islamic law in its early stages. A number of the Companions were known for their ability to deduce judgments from Qur'anic principles, together with the actions and instructions of the Prophet.

As the Muslim domains expanded, the need for a uniform body of religious law was filled for a time by Muslims of the first and second generations (the Companions and their successors), who laid the foundations for subsequent legal traditions. Until the eighth century, these traditions were centered in western Arabia, particularly in Medina and Mecca, and Iraq, especially in Kufah and Basrah. It was in these centers that the "living tradition" of jurisprudence was transformed from an oral to a written science, with an ever-growing body of literature.

The End of *Ijtihad*

The Prophet is reported to have declared that "the best generation is my generation, then the one that follows it, and then the one that follows that." The idea that Muslim society grew increasingly corrupt after the normative period of the first four "rightly guided" caliphs was widely held. Yet there continued to be people who modeled their lives on the examples of scholars, jurists, and *hadith* collectors of that formative period.

With the establishment of the major Sunni legal schools by the tenth century, there was a sort of undeclared consensus that the gate of *ijtihad* had closed. This did not mean that the development of Islamic legal thinking ceased altogether, but it did mean that no new legal systems would henceforth be tolerated. In fact, the process of exclusion had already begun through the awarding of political patronage to some schools and the denial of it to others. From this time on, only the experts in religious law (*muftis*) of each city or country were empowered to issue legal opinions (**fatwas**) in accordance with the principles of their respective legal schools. Various collections of famous *fatwas* have served as manuals for less able or less creative *muftis*.

Ja'fari (Shi'i) Law

The Shi'i legal and religious system is named after the man regarded as its founder, Ja'far al-Sadiq (c. 700–765). The sixth in the line of Imams that began with 'Ali—the cousin and son-in-law of the Prophet whom the Shi'a believed to be his only legitimate successor—Ja'far was revered as a descendant of the Prophet's family and, with his father Muhammad al-Baqir (the fifth Imam), was among the leading scholars of Medina. They left no written works, but a rich oral tradition of their teachings was codified in the tenth and eleventh centuries as the foundation of the legal system that governs **Imami** or **Twelver** Shi'ism (see Focus box). In the Ja'fari school, Twelver Shi'ism embraces the Shi'i legal school closest to Sunni orthodoxy.

Focus

The Twelfth Imam

According to the Shi'i doctrine of *imamah*, the Prophet appointed 'Ali as his vice-regent. 'Ali in turn appointed his son Hasan to succeed him as Imam, and Hasan appointed his brother Husayn. Thereafter, each Imam designated his successor, usually his eldest son.

Mainstream Shi'as believe that the line of imams descended from Husayn continued until 874, when the twelfth Imam, the four-year-old Muhammad ibn Hasan al-'Askari, disappeared; it is for this reason that they are also known as "Twelvers." They maintain that he went into hiding ("occultation") but continued to communicate with his followers until

941, when he entered a new phase—known as the "greater occultation"—that will continue until the end of the world. At that time, before the Day of Resurrection, he will return as the **Mahdi**, "the rightly guided one," who with Jesus will establish universal justice and true Islam on earth. In short, Twelver Shi'ism understands the *sunnah* to include not only the life-example of the Prophet and his generation, but the life-examples of the twelve Imams—the men they believe to be his rightful successors. Hence for Twelvers the period of the *sunnah* extends over three centuries, until the end of the "lesser occultation" of the twelfth Imam in 941.

In contrast to Sunni legal schools, which developed first a science of jurisprudence and then a canonical *hadith* tradition to buttress it, the Ja'fari school based its legal system on a vast body of *hadith* centered on the traditions of the Imams descended from 'Ali. The first of what would become four collections of Imami *hadith* was compiled by Muhammad al-Kulayni (d. 941); entitled "The Sufficient," it resembles Sunni *hadith* collections in that it begins with the fundamentals of doctrine and worship and then addresses ancillary legal matters.

Where it diverges from the Sunni model is in the section dealing with the imamate. The essential point of difference is the Shi'i belief that the imam is the proof or argument of God to his human creatures, and hence the world cannot be without one, whether he be present and active in the community or hidden from human perception (see Focus box on "The Twelfth Imam").

Taqlid means following the personal reasoning (*ijtihad*) of a particular jurist. For the Sunni, it means following the founder of one of the recognized legal schools, which implies strict adherence to a traditional system with no room for innovation. For the Shi'a, the absence of the imam makes *taqlid* of a living jurist a legal necessity. This emphasis has had the same effect on the Shi'i community that the closing of the gate of *ijtihad* has had on the Sunni. The development of courageous and sensitive new approaches to the interpretation and application of the *shari'ah* is therefore imperative in both communities today.

Islamic Philosophy and Theology

Within Islam, an important subset of the religious sciences consisted of the "rational" sciences of philosophy and theology. Theology is discourse about God, but also about human free will and predestination, moral and religious obligations, and the return to God on the Day of Resurrection for the final judgment. Insofar as theology addresses human faith and conduct, it is part of the science of *fiqh*, jurisprudence.

In time, however, Islamic theology also came to address more philosophical questions about the existence of God, creation, and the problems of evil and suffering. In these areas it reflects the influence of Hellenistic philosophy, the principles and rationalistic methodology of which it adopted.

The rapid spread of Islam into Syria and Mesopotamia brought Muslims into contact with people of other faiths, including Hellenized Jews and Christians. By the mid-eighth century, interest in Greek philosophy, science, and medicine was increasing, and Arabic translations of Greek works began to appear.

The quest for knowledge reached its peak in the next century under the caliph al-Ma'mun (r. 813–833), whose "House of Wisdom" in Baghdad was the first institution of higher learning not only in the Islamic world but anywhere in the West. Christian scholars had already translated many Greek medical, philosophical, and theological treatises into Syriac, but the House of Wisdom, which featured an impressive library of Greek manuscripts, provided additional support for their work. Smaller centers of philosophical and medical studies in Syria and Iran also made notable contributions.

The Early Period

Early Islamic philosophy was strongly influenced by Greek thinkers. Two figures stand out in this period. The first was the Iraqi theologian-philosopher Abu Yusuf Ya'qub al-Kindi (d. 870), who used philosophical principles and methods of reasoning to defend fundamental Islamic teachings such as the existence and oneness of God, the creation of the universe out of nothing, and the necessity of prophets. In his argument for the latter, Al-Kindi distinguished between the philosopher, who acquires his knowledge through rational investigation, and the prophet, who receives his knowledge through divine revelation.

In sharp contrast to al-Kindi, the Iranian Abu Bakr Zakariyah al-Razi (c. 865–926) argued that the universe evolved from primal matter, floating gas atoms in an absolute void. The universe came into being when God imposed order on the primeval chaos, but it will return to chaos at some distant point in the future, because matter will revert to its primeval state.

The Flowering of Islamic Philosophy

Abu Nasr al-Farabi (c. 878–950) was not only a great philosopher but an important musician and musical theorist. According to his Platonic system, God is pure intellect and the highest good. From God's self-knowledge or contemplation emanated the first intellect, which generated the heavenly spheres, and a second intellect, which then repeated the process. Each subsequent intellect generated another sphere and another intellect.

Al-Farabi agreed with al-Kindi that a prophet has intellect capable of receiving philosophical verities and without mental exertion. He then communicates these truths to the masses, who are incapable of comprehending them on the philosophical level.

The self-taught genius Ibn Sina (known in Latin as Avicenna, 980–1037), born in Bukhara, Central Asia, mastered the religious sciences at the age of 10 and by 18 had become a leading physician, philosopher, and astronomer. Ibn Sina built on al-Farabi's ideas to produce a comprehensive system of mystical philosophy and theology. He developed al-Farabi's theory of emanations, placing it in a more precise logical and philosophical framework. Although he affirmed the prophethood of Muhammad, the revelation of the Qur'an, and the immortality of the soul, he rejected the Qur'anic traditions of the resurrection of the body, the reward of paradise, and the punishment of hell.

According to a widely accepted Prophetic tradition, at the beginning of every century God raises a scholar to renew the faith of the Muslim community. For the sixth Islamic century, that scholar was Abu Hamid Muhammad al-Ghazali (1058–1111) of Tus, in Iran. His work went far beyond theology and philosophy to encompass mysticism and all the religious sciences.

As a professor of theology and law in Baghdad, al-Ghazali defended mainstream Sunni Islam against the innovations of the theologians and the heresies of the philosophers. But in 1095 he suffered a psychological crisis and gave up teaching. After a long quest, he determined in his most important work, *The Revivification of the Religious Sciences*, that one cannot attain true knowledge through either the senses or the rational sciences, but only through a divine light that God casts into one's heart.

Ibn Rushd (known in Latin as Averroës, 1126–1198), who was born in Cordoba, Spain, came from a long line of jurists and was himself a noted scholar of Islamic law. His legal training decisively influenced his philosophy. Ibn Rushd essentially shared his Eastern predecessors' belief in the primacy of philosophy over religion. In his famous double-truth theory, however, he argued that both were valid ways of arriving at truth; the difference was that philosophy was the way of the intellectual elite, while religion was the way of the masses.

The great thirteenth-century philosopher-mystic Ibn 'Arabi is discussed later, in the context of Sufism. He was followed by a more empirical philosopher, the Tunisian-born 'Abd al-Rahman Ibn Khaldun (1332–1406). Through his extensive travels and his work as a jurist and political theorist, Ibn Khaldun gained insight into the workings both of nations and of political and religious institutions. This led him to write a universal history that is most notable for its introduction, in which he presents the first social philosophy of history in the Western world.

Islamic philosophy had a lasting influence on medieval and Renaissance thought in Europe. Among the Europeans who were influenced by Ibn Rushd in particular was the great medieval Catholic philosopher and theologian Thomas Aquinas. It is impossible to properly understand Aquinas's thought without appreciating its roots in the Muslim philosophy of Ibn Rushd and the Jewish philosophy of Maimonides.

⊕ Variations of Islam

Shi'ism

As we have seen, for Sunnis an "imam" is someone who serves as the leader of prayer at the mosque. For Shi'as, however, "imam" is also the title of the one individual divinely mandated to lead the Muslim community because he is descended from the Prophet's cousin, son-in-law, and rightful successor 'Ali.

Devotion to the family of the Prophet has always been a central characteristic of Shi'ism. Its source is a *hadith* according to which the Prophet, on his way back from Mecca to Medina, stopped at a place called Ghadir Khumm, took 'Ali by the hand, and made the following declaration: "O people, hear my words, and let him who is present inform him who is absent: Anyone of whom I am the master, 'Ali, too, is his master. O God, be a friend to those who befriend him and an enemy to those who show hostility to him, support those who support him and abandon those who desert him." On the basis of this and other sayings in which they believe the Prophet directly or indirectly designated 'Ali as his successor, Shi'i scholars constructed an elaborate legal and theological system supporting the doctrine of *imamah*, according to which the source of all legitimate authority is the imam.

Ashura

In the year 680 the Prophet's grandson Husayn ('Ali's son) was leading an uprising against the Umayyad caliph Yazid when he was killed in battle at Karbala in Iraq. The anniversary of his death has become a focal point for the Shi'i community's hopes and frustrations, messianic expectations, and highly eschatological view of history.

"Ashura," as the anniversary came to be known, is still commemorated by Shi'as around the world. Blending sorrow, blessing, and mystery, it has inspired a rich devotional literature and is observed by the Shi'a as a day of suffering and martyrdom that is marked by devotional activities that include solemn processions, public readings, and passion plays. The Sunni community commemorates Ashura with a day of fasting.

In the Iranian city of Isfahan, actors perform a *tazieh*, or "passion play," reenacting the events surrounding the death of Husayn at Karbala in 680. This is part of the Shi'a commemoration of Ashura (© CAREN FIROUZ/Reuters/Corbis).

Divisions Within Shi'ism

The Shi'a share a general allegiance to the right of 'Ali and his descendants to authority in the Muslim community after Muhammad. But "Shi'ism" is a broad term that covers a variety of religio-political movements, sects, and ideologies.

The majority of Shi'as accepted the line of Husaynid imams down to Ja'far al-Sadiq, the legal scholar who was sixth in the succession. But a major schism occurred when Ja'far's oldest son and successor, Isma'il, predeceased him. Ja'far then appointed a younger son, Musa al-Kazim, as his own successor. The Shi'a who accepted this appointment and went on to revere Musa as the seventh Imam eventually came to be known as Imamis or Twelvers (see Focus box on "The Twelfth Imam").

Others, though, considered the appointment irregular and insisted that the seventh imam should be Isma'il's son Ahmad. For this reason they came to be known as **Isma'ilis** or "**Seveners**." The largest faction, called the Nizaris, carried on the line of imams through Ahmad and his descendants down to the present. Over the centuries Isma'ili philosophers and theologians developed the doctrine of the divine mandate of the imam into an esoteric system of prophetology. The Isma'ilis have played conspicuous intellectual and political roles in Muslim history.

For centuries they lived as an obscure sect in Iran, Syria, East Africa, and the Indian subcontinent. Since 1818 their leader, or imam, has been known as the Agha Khan, an Indo-Iranian title signifying nobility. The third Agha Khan (1877–1957) initiated a movement for reconciliation with the larger Muslim community, and efforts to resolve differences have continued under his Harvard-educated successor, Karim Agha Khan (b. 1936). In modern times Isma'ilis have migrated in large numbers to the West. Prosperous and well organized, they now number roughly 15 million and are the best-integrated Muslim community in the West.

Sufism: The Mystical Tradition

The early Muslim mystics were said to wear a garment of coarse wool over their bare skin in emulation of Jesus, who is represented in Islamic hagiography as a model of ascetic piety. For this reason they became known as Sufis (from the Arabic meaning "wool").

Asceticism was only one element in the development of Sufism, however. At least as important was the Islamic tradition of devotional piety. Since the ultimate purpose of all creation is to worship God and sing his praises (Q. 17:44 and 51:56), the pious are urged to "remember God much" (Q. 33:41). The Prophet's night vigils and other devotions (Q. 73:1–8), embellished by hagiographical tradition, have served as a living example for pious Muslims across the centuries. *Hadith* traditions, particularly the "divine sayings" in which the speaker is God, have also provided a rich source of mystical piety. Above all, the *mi'raj*—the Prophet's miraculous journey to heaven—has been a guide for mystics on their own spiritual ascent to God. One early champion of the ascetic movement was a theologian and *hadith* collector named al-Hasan al-Basri, who was born in Medina in 642 and lived through both the crises and the rise to glory of the Muslim *ummah*. Hasan once likened the world to a snake: soft to the touch, but full of venom.

The early ascetics were sometimes called weepers, for the tears they shed in fear of God's punishment and in yearning for God's reward. Significantly, the movement emerged in areas of mixed populations, where other forms of asceticism had existed for centuries—places such as Kufa and Basra in Iraq (long the home of eastern Christian asceticism); northeastern Iran, particularly the region of Balkh (an ancient center of Buddhist asceticism, now part of Afghanistan); and Egypt (the home of Christian monasticism as well as Gnostic asceticism).

Asceticism for its own sake, however, was frowned on by many advocates of mystical piety. Among the critics was the sixth Imam, Ja'far al-Sadiq, who argued that when God bestows a favor on a servant, God wishes to see that favor manifested in the servant's clothing and way of life. Ja'far's grandfather 'Ali Zayn al-'Abidin is said to have argued that God should be worshiped not out of fear of hell or desire for paradise, but in humble gratitude for the gift of the capacity to worship God.

What transformed ascetic piety into mysticism was the all-consuming love of the divine exemplified by an early female mystic named Rabi'a al-'Adawiyah of Basra (c. 713–801). Born into a poor family, Rabi'a was orphaned and sold into slavery as a

The Agha Khan, spiritual leader of the world's 15 million Isma'ili Muslims, addresses the Canadian Parliament in February 2014 (Photo by Jason Ransom. Source: © Office of the Prime Minister, 2014).

child, but her master was so impressed with her piety that he set her free. She lived the rest of her life in mystical contemplation, loving God with no motive other than love itself: "My Lord, if I worship you in fear of the fire, burn me in hell. If I worship you in desire for paradise, deprive me of it. But if I worship you in love of you, then deprive me not of your eternal beauty" (Smith 1928).

Mystics of all religious traditions have used the language of erotic love to express their love for God. Rabi'a was perhaps the first to introduce this language into Islamic mysticism. She loved God with both the love of passion and the devotional love of the worshipful servant for her Lord. A more controversial tradition within Sufism pursued absolute union with God. Among the proponents of this ecstatic or "intoxicated" Sufism was Husayn ibn Mansur al-Hallaj (c. 858–922), whose identification with the divine was so intense as to suggest that he made no distinction between God and himself. For this apparent blasphemy he was executed by the 'Abbasid authorities.

Al-Hallaj had traveled widely, studying with the best-known Sufi masters of his time. But eventually he broke away from his teachers and embarked on a long quest for self-realization. This journey began when he went to see his teacher and, when asked who was at the door, answered, "I, the absolute divine truth"—calling himself by one of the 99 "wonderful names" of God. His teacher reprimanded him and warned against such apparent blasphemy. At its core, al-Hallaj's message was moral and intensely spiritual, but it was interpreted as suggesting that God can take the form of a human person (as Christians believe of Jesus)—a deeply shocking claim for most Muslims of his time. Whereas a less extreme predecessor, Bayazid Bistami, had preached annihilation of the mystic in God, al-Hallaj preached total identification of the lover with the beloved:

Document

Rabi'a al-'Adawiyah

When Rabi'a's fellow Sufis urged her to marry, she consented in principle, but only on the condition that the prospective husband—a devout man named Hasan—answer four questions. In the end she remained unmarried, free to devote all her thoughts to God.

"What will the Judge of the world say when I die? That I have come forth from the world a Muslim, or an unbeliever?"

Hasan answered, "This is among the hidden things known only to God. . . ."

Then she said, "When I am put in the grave and Munkar and Nakir [the angels who question the dead] question me, shall I be able to answer them [satisfactorily] or not?" He replied, "This is also hidden."

"When people are assembled at the Resurrection and the books are distributed, shall I be given mine in my right hand or my left?" . . . "This also is among the hidden things."

Finally she asked, "When mankind is summoned (at the Judgment), some to Paradise and some to Hell, in which group shall I be?" He answered, "This too is hidden, and none knows what is hidden save God—His is the glory and the majesty."

Then she said to him, "Since this is so, and I have these four questions with which to concern myself, how should I need a husband, with whom to be occupied?" (Smith 1928: 11)

> I am He whom I love, and He whom I love is I.
> We are two spirits dwelling in one body.
> If thou seest me, you see Him; and if thou seest Him, you see us both. (Nicholson 1931: 210–238)

After eight years in prison, al-Hallaj danced to the gallows, where he begged his executioners to "kill me, O my trusted friends, for in my death is my life, and in my life is my death."

The Development of Sufism

The mystical life is a spiritual journey to God. The novice who wishes to embark on such an arduous journey must be guided by a master who becomes his or her spiritual parent. But as Sufism grew, many well-recognized masters attracted too many disciples to allow for a one-to-one relationship. By the eleventh century, therefore, the ideas of the masters were being recorded and transmitted in writing. Perhaps the greatest work of the period was al-Ghazali's *Revivification of the Religious Sciences*.

Roughly half a century after al-Ghazali, Shihab al-Din Suhrawardi (c. 1155–1191) became known as the great master of illumination. Drawing on a verse in the Qur'an (24:35) that speaks of God as the light of the heavens and the earth, he described a cosmos of light and darkness populated by countless angelic spirits.

The most important Sufi master of the thirteenth century was Muhyi al-Din Ibn 'Arabi (1165–1240), who was born and educated in Muslim Spain and traveled widely in the Middle East before finally settling in Damascus. The central theme of his numerous writings is the "unity of being." According to Ibn 'Arabi, God's essence remains in "blind obscurity" but is manifested in the creation through an eternal process of self-disclosure. Thus even as human beings need God for their very existence, God also needs them in order to be known. Ibn 'Arabi's doctrine of the unity of being had many implications, among them the idea that if God alone really is, then all ways ultimately lead to God. This means that all the world's religions are in reality one.

Rumi

The most creative poet of the Persian language was Jalal al-Din Rumi (1207–1273). Rumi was born in Balkh, Afghanistan, but as a child fled with his parents from the advancing Mongols. At last they settled in the city of Konya in central Anatolia (Turkey), a region that had been part of the Roman Empire.

In 1244 Rumi met a wandering Sufi named Shams of Tabriz. The two men developed a relationship so intimate that Rumi neglected his teaching duties because he could not bear to be separated from his friend. Yet in the end Shams disappeared, leaving Rumi to pour out his soul in heart-rending verses expressing his love for the "Sun" ("Shams" means "sun" in Arabic) of Tabriz.

Rumi's masterpiece is his *Mathnawi* ("Couplets"), a collection whose opening verses evoke the haunting melodies of the reed flute lamenting its separation from its reed bed. In stories, lyrical couplets, and at times even coarse tales of sexual impropriety, the *Mathnawi* depicts the longing of the human soul for God.

Sufi Orders and Saints

By the thirteenth century a number of Sufi fraternities were becoming institutionalized as religious orders, usually under the leadership of a famous **shaykh** ("master"). The validity of a *shaykh*'s claim to leadership depended on his or her spiritual genealogy, which had to lead back in an unbroken chain from the *shaykh*'s own master to an authority such as 'Ali, a Companion of the Prophet, or one of his successors. The *shaykh*s are similar to saints of the Catholic Church in that the faithful pray to them for assistance and ascribe miracles to them, although they are recognized through popular acclaim rather than official canonization.

Devotional Practices

Although Sufis also perform the five daily prayers, their most characteristic practice is a ritual called the **dhikr** ("remembrance") of God, which may be private or congregational. The latter type of the ritual is usually held before the dawn or evening prayers. It consists of the repetition of the name of Allah, or the *shahadah*, "There is no god except God" (*la ilaha illa Allah*). The *dhikr* is often accompanied by special bodily movements and, in some Sufi orders, by elaborate breathing techniques. Often the performance of the *dhikr* is what distinguishes the various Sufi orders from one another. In some popular orders it is a highly emotional ritual intended to stir devotees into a state of frenzy. By contrast, in the sober Naqshbandi order the *dhikr* is silent, an inward prayer of the heart.

Another distinctly Sufi practice is the *sama'* ("hearing" or "audition"), in which devotees simply listen to the hypnotic chanting of mystical poetry, accompanied by various musical instruments.

Document

Jalal al-Din Rumi, *Diwan*, Ghazal no. 1826

If anyone asks you about *houris* [heavenly beings], show your face and say, "Like this."

If anyone speaks to you about the moon, rise up beyond the roof and say, "Like this."

When someone looks for a fairy princess, show your face to him.

When someone talks of musk, let loose your tresses and say, "Like this."

If someone says to you, "How do clouds part from the moon?"

Undo your robe, button by button, and say, "Like this."

If he asks you about the Messiah, "How could he bring the dead to life?"

Kiss my lips before him and say, "Like this."

When someone says, "Tell me, what does it mean to be killed by love?"

Show my soul to him and say, "Like this."

If someone in concern asks you about my state,

Show him your eyebrow, bent over double, and say, "Like this."

The spirit breaks away from the body, then again it enters within.

Come, show the deniers, enter the house and say, "Like this."

In whatever direction you hear the complaint of a lover,

That is my story, all of it, by God, like this.

I am the house of every angel, my breast has turned blue like the sky—

Lift up your eyes and look with joy at heaven, like this.

I told the secret of union with the Beloved to the east wind alone.

Then, through the purity of its own mystery, the east wind whispered, "Like this."

Those are blind who say, "How can the servant reach God?"

Place the candle of purity in the hand of each and say, "Like this."

I said, "How can the fragrance of Joseph go from one city to the next?"

The fragrance of God blew from the world of his Essence and said, "Like this."

I said, "How can the fragrance of Joseph give sight back to the blind?"

Your breeze came and gave light to my eye: "Like this."

Perhaps Shams al-Din in Tabriz will show his generosity, and in his kindness display his good faith, like this. (Chittick 2000: 89–90)

As instrumental music is not allowed in the mosque, *sama'* sessions are usually held in a nearby hall or at the shrine of a famous *shaykh*.

Music and dance are vital elements of devotional life for members of the Mevlevi (Mawlawi) order, named after Mawlana ("our master") Rumi. As practiced by the Mevlevis—also known as the "Whirling Dervishes"—dance symbolizes the perfect motion of the stars, while the melodies that accompany the chanting echo the melodies of the heavenly spheres.

Sufism has always shown an amazing capacity for self-reform and regeneration. It was the Sufis who preserved Islamic learning and spirituality after 1258, when Baghdad fell to Mongol invaders,

Dervishes at the Dervish Festival in Konya, Turkey (© Bruno Morandi/Robert Harding World Imagery/Corbis).

and Sufis who carried Islam to Africa and Asia. Today in the West it is often Sufi piety that attracts non-Muslims to Islam.

Women and Sufism

Women have played an important role in the Sufi tradition, often serving as role models and teachers for men as well as women. This may help to explain part of the historical tension between orthodox Islam and Sufism. One of the most beloved stories about Rabi'a has her roaming the streets of Basra carrying a bucket of water and a flaming torch, ready to put out the fires of hell and set fire to the gardens of paradise so that people will worship God out of love alone.

The Sufi tradition provided a rare outlet for Muslim women to be recognized as leaders. After Rabi'a, Sufi women could serve as *shaykahs* for mixed congregations, even though they were barred from the role of imam in such groups (women did serve as imams for other women, however). It's also worth noting that the shrines of Sufi saints, male or female, tend to attract more women than men, inverting the usual gender breakdown at mosques. It isn't hard to imagine how some men could feel threatened by a public space in which women are the dominant presence. Thus they might categorize Sufism as "un-Islamic," not because of its doctrines, but because of the power and privilege it accords to women.

Sufi women in Srinagar, Kashmir, pray outside the shrine of their order's founder, Shaikh Abdul Qadir Jilani, on the anniversary of his death (ROUF BHAT/AFP/Getty Images).

⊕ The Spread of Islam

Islam, like Christianity, is a missionary religion. Muslims believe that their faith is intended for all humankind, and that the Qur'an confirms the scriptures that preceded it, notably the Torah and the Gospels. From the beginning, they interacted with people of other faiths, particularly Christians and Jews. As a religio-political power, therefore, Islam had to regulate its relations with non-Muslim citizens.

As People of the Book, Jews and Christians living in Muslim lands were free to practice their faith as long as they paid a tax that also guaranteed them physical and economic protection and exemption from military service. Legally such communities came to be known as **dhimmis** ("protected people"). The same designation was later extended to other communities with sacred scriptures, including Zoroastrians in Iran and Hindus in India.

In its first century Islam spread through conquest and military occupation. Much of the Byzantine and Roman world and all of the Sasanian Persian domains came under Umayyad rule. In later centuries, politico-military regimes continued to contribute to Islam's dominance, especially in regions under Arab, Iranian, or Turkish rule.

Over time, however, the influence of mystics, teachers, and traders has reached farther and endured longer than the power of caliphs and conquerors. It was mainly through the efforts of individual Muslims that Islam spread to China, Southeast Asia, and East and West Africa. In modern times, migration and missionary activity have carried Islam to the Western Hemisphere as well.

North Africa

After conquering Syria, Egypt, and Iran, the Muslims moved into North Africa in the second half of the seventh century. Before that time North Africa had been first an important Roman province and then an equally important home of Latin Christianity. With its Indigenous Berber, Phoenician, Roman, and Byzantine populations, the region has always maintained a distinct religious and cultural identity that reflects its ancient diversity.

The Umayyads established their capital in Damascus in 661. With the shift of the capital to Baghdad under the 'Abbasids in 762, the main orientation of the eastern Islamic domains became more Persian than Arab, more Asian than Mediterranean. Meanwhile, the center of Arab Islamic culture shifted from Syria to the western Mediterranean: to Qayrawan in what is today Tunisia and to Cordoba in Spain, which rivaled Baghdad and Cairo in its cultural splendor. North African mystics, religious scholars, and philosophers were all instrumental in this achievement, and in the nineteenth and twentieth centuries, North African Sufi masters in particular played a crucial role in the struggle for independence, mobilizing resistance to the colonial regimes in Libya (Italian) and Algeria (French). Despite the deep influence of the French language and secular culture in the region, North African popular piety still reflects its classical Islamic heritage.

Map 6.1 Language and Culture in the Spread of Islam

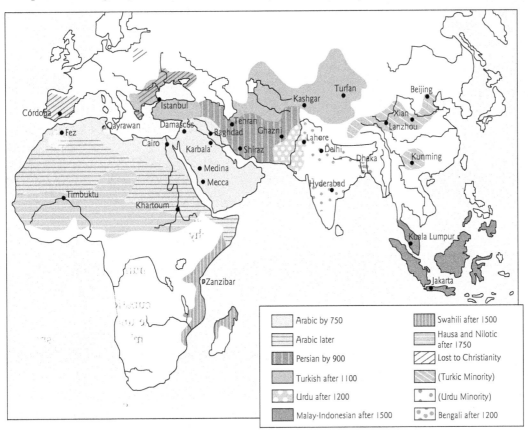

Arabic by 750		Swahili after 1500	
Arabic later		Hausa and Nilotic after 1750	
Persian by 900		Lost to Christianity	
Turkish after 1100		(Turkic Minority)	
Urdu after 1200		(Urdu Minority)	
Malay-Indonesian after 1500		Bengali after 1200	

Spain

When Arab forces arrived on the Iberian Peninsula in 711, Jews who had lived there for centuries were facing harsh restrictions imposed by rulers recently converted to Christianity. They welcomed the Arabs as liberators.

With astonishing speed, Umayyad forces conquered al-Andalus, as they called southern Spain, and laid the foundations for an extraordinary culture. Arab men married local women, and a mixed but harmonious society developed that was Arab in language and expression and Arabo-Hispanic in spirit. Muslims, Christians, and Jews lived together in mutual tolerance for centuries before fanatical forces on all sides stifled one of the most creative experiments in interfaith living in human history.

Arab Spain produced some of the world's greatest minds, including not only Ibn 'Arabi and Ibn Rushd but the jurist and writer Ibn Hazm (994–1064) and the mystic-philosopher Ibn Masarrah (d. 931). Students came from as far away as Scotland to study Islamic theology, philosophy, and science in Cordoba and Toledo. It was in these centers of higher learning that the European Renaissance was conceived, and the great universities in which it was nurtured were inspired by their Arabo-Hispanic counterparts.

In Muslim Spain the Jews enjoyed a golden age of philosophy and science, mysticism, and general prosperity. Jewish scholars, court physicians, and administrators occupied high state offices and served

The Mosque–Cathedral of Cordoba began as a Visigoth church, was transformed into a medieval Muslim mosque, and is now a Catholic cathedral. Spanish Muslims have been lobbying the Spanish government and the Vatican to be allowed to perform prayers inside its walls (© Bettina Strenske/Alamy).

as political and cultural liaisons between Islamic Spain and the rest of Europe. Arab learning penetrated deep into western Europe and contributed directly to the rise of the West. In addition to symbiotic creativity, however, the 900-year history of Arab Spain (711–1609) included the tensions and conflicts typical of any multireligious, multicultural society ruled by a minority regime. In the end, Islamic faith and civilization were driven out of Spain and failed to establish themselves anywhere else in Europe.

Sub-Saharan Africa

Islam may have arrived in sub-Saharan Africa as early as the eighth century, spread first by traders and then on a much larger scale by preachers. Finally jurists established the new faith in the region as a religious and legal system. Sufi orders played an important part both in the spread of Islam and in its use as a motivation and framework for social and political reform.

To compete with traditional African religion, Muslim prayers had to show themselves to be no less potent than Indigenous rain-making prayers or rituals. In the fourteenth century, the Moroccan Muslim traveler Ibn Battutah wrote a vivid account of the efforts of Muslim converts in the Mali Empire of West Africa to adapt their new faith to local traditions.

In East Africa Islam spread along the coast, carried mainly by mariners from Arabia and the Persian Gulf trading in commodities and slaves. From the sixteenth century on, after Portuguese navigators rounded the southern cape of Africa, the cultural and political development of East African Islam was directly affected by European colonialism as well.

Unlike the populations of Syria, Iraq, Egypt, and North Africa, the peoples of East Africa did not adopt the Arabic language. But so much Arabic vocabulary penetrated the local languages that at least one-third of the Swahili vocabulary today is Arabic, and until recently most of the major African languages were written in the Arabic script.

An important element of East African society has been the Khoja community. Including both Sevener (Isma'ili) and Twelver (Imami) Shi'as, the Khojas emigrated from India to Africa in the mid-1800s. They have on the whole been successful businesspeople, with Western education and close relationships with Europe and North America. These relationships have been strengthened by the migration of many Khojas to Britain, the United States, and Canada.

Central Asia and Iran

Before the arrival of Islam, Central Asia had been a cosmopolitan culture in which Buddhism, Gnosticism, Judaism, and Christianity existed side by side in mutual tolerance with the Zoroastrianism of its Iranian rulers. The Arab conquest took more than a century, from 649 to 752.

In Iran itself, Persian culture flourished under the Samanid dynasty in the ninth and tenth centuries, as did *hadith* collectors, historians, philosophers, and religious scholars working in Arabic. Important centers of learning developed in the cities of Bukhara and Samarkand (in what is now Uzbekistan). While the Buyids promoted Shi'i Islam in the region that is now Iraq, the Samanids established the Sunni tradition in Central Asia. Among the great Sunni minds of tenth- and eleventh-century Central Asia were the philosopher Ibn Sina, the theologian al-Maturidi, the historian of religion Abu Rayhan al-Biruni, and the famous Persian poet Ferdowsi. In this intellectual environment, Islam was spread by persuasion rather than propaganda and war.

Early in the eleventh century, however, the Karakhanid Mongols conquered both Iran and Central Asia. The devastating consequences of the conquest were compounded by the loss of trade revenues when the traditional caravan routes were abandoned in favor of sea travel to India and China. Central Asia never recovered from the resulting decline in its culture and prosperity.

The Turks

As Turkic tribal populations from Central Asia moved into the Middle East, they were converted to Islam mainly by Sufi missionaries. Mahmud of Ghazna in Afghanistan (r. 998–1030) and his successors, the Ghaznavids, extended Muslim power in northern India. Mahmud was the first person to be called "sultan," a term that until then had referred to the authority of the state. Another Turkic family, the Seljuqs, prevailed in Iran and the territories located farther west a generation after Mahmud. After defeating the Byzantines in eastern Anatolia (modern Turkey) in 1071, the Seljuqs ruled over the region until they were conquered by the Mongols in 1243.

In 1299 Osman I took over the caliphate from the 'Abbasids, establishing a dynasty that endured until 1924. Having absorbed former Seljuq territory in eastern Anatolia and taken western Anatolia from the Byzantines, his descendants, known as the Ottomans, reached the height of their power in the sixteenth century, occupying the Balkans as far north as Vienna, the Levant (the Syro-Palestinian region), and all of North Africa except Morocco. So vast was their empire that until the nineteenth century Christian Europe thought of Islamic culture as primarily Turkish.

As their imperial emblem the Ottomans adopted the crescent, an ancient symbol that the Byzantines had also used. Conspicuous on the Turkish flag, the crescent thus came to be seen by Europeans, and eventually by Muslims themselves, as the symbol of Islam. Turkic languages still prevail across much of the Central Asian territory that was ruled by the Soviet Union for most of the twentieth century, and from Azerbaijan to Uzbekistan and Turkmenistan, a dominant element of the population is Turkic. The same is true of Chinese Central Asia.

China

The first written references to Islam in China do not appear until the seventeenth century, although the minaret of the mosque in Guangzhou (Canton) and inscriptions in the province of Fujian suggest that maritime trade with the Islamic world may have been under way as early as the eighth century. From the beginning, Persian and Arab merchants were allowed to trade freely so long as they complied with Chinese rules. But it was not until the thirteenth century that Muslim traders began settling in China in numbers large enough to support the establishment of mosques. Muslim communities prospered under the Mongol (1206–1368) and Ming (1368–1644) emperors. With the decline of the overland trade with Central Asia in the 1600s, however, Chinese Muslims were virtually cut off from the rest of the Muslim *ummah*.

Unlike Buddhism centuries earlier, Islam never came to be seen as culturally Chinese. The Uighurs—the Muslim population of Xinjiang (Chinese Turkestan), in the far northwest—are an identifiable minority in Chinese society, distinguished by their Turkic language as well as their religion. Yet even the Chinese-speaking Muslims in the eastern cities of China are set apart by their avoidance of pork—a staple of the Chinese diet. The presence of *halal* (ritually acceptable) restaurants and butcher shops is a sure sign of a Muslim neighborhood.

Chinese Muslims experienced their share of repression under the Communist regime, particularly during the Cultural Revolution of 1966–1976. Although the overall situation for Muslims has improved since then, Uighur demands for independence have been severely suppressed, and Uighur nationalists are often called "terrorists." Today there are approximately 50 million Muslims in China. Like other religious communities in contemporary China, they face an uncertain future, but their ethnic base in the country's Central Asian interior is not likely to disappear anytime soon.

The Great Mosque of Guangzhou, known as the Memorial of the Holy Prophet, is among the earliest mosques in China (dbimages/Alamy Stock Photo).

South Asia

Islam arrived early in India, carried by traders and Arab settlers. Umayyad armies began moving into the region in the early eighth century, and since then Islam has become an integral part of Indian life and culture.

The Muslim conquest of India was a long process. In the second half of the tenth century the city of Ghazni, in what is today Afghanistan, became the base from which the armies of the sultan Mahmud of Ghazna and his successors advanced over the Khyber Pass onto the North Indian Plain. By the fourteenth century all but the far south had come under Muslim rule.

For the Muslim rulers of India, who came from Iran and Central Asia, maintaining and expanding their power over a large Hindu population meant continuous warfare. For Hindus, the Muslim regime was undoubtedly repressive, yet Indian Islam nevertheless developed a unique and rich religious and intellectual culture.

India represented something new in the history of Islam's territorial expansion. For the first time, the majority of the conquered population did not convert to the new faith. In ancient Arabia Islam had been able to suppress and supplant polytheism, but in India it had to coexist with a culture that remained largely polytheistic. At the same time Islam also represented something new to India. In a land where people often had multiple religious allegiances and community boundaries were fluid, Islam's exclusive devotion to the one God and its clear delineation of community membership represented a dramatically different way of life.

Today, India, Pakistan, and Bangladesh together have the largest Muslim population in the world. The Muslims of India alone number between 100 and 120 million. Even so, they are a minority whose future appears bleak in the face of rising Hindu nationalism.

Southeast Asia

When Islam arrived in Southeast Asia, the region was home to a wide variety of languages and cultures, and its religious life had been strongly influenced by the Hindu and Buddhist traditions. There is no evidence for the presence of Islam in Southeast Asia before the tenth century. But Yemeni traders are reported to have sailed into the islands of the Malay archipelago before the time of the Prophet, and this suggests that the Malay people may have been exposed to Islam at an early date. Muslim communities in small states ruled by sultans were widely reported by the thirteenth century, and scattered evidence from Chinese and Portuguese travelers, as well as passing references by Ibn Battutah, indicate that Islam had spread widely in Southeast Asia by the 1400s. Two centuries later, when British and Dutch trading companies arrived in the region, Islam was the dominant religion and culture of the Malay archipelago.

Some of the states that emerged in the fifteenth century gained considerable prominence both culturally and economically, and Muslim religious scholars from India were attracted to them. In an effort to expand and strengthen his realm, the sultan Iskandar Muda of Acheh (r. 1607–1636) became the first Muslim ruler in Southeast Asia to establish alliances with European powers. Acheh also produced noteworthy Islamic legal scholarship, which is still used in the Malay world today.

In Southeast Asia even more than elsewhere, Sufi orders played a crucial part in the process of Islamization. They were also prominent in later political and social struggles for reform and liberation. In the late nineteenth and early twentieth centuries, reform movements in the Middle East inspired similar movements in Indonesia and other countries of the region. Today Islam is the majority religion in Malaysia, Brunei, and Indonesia (the largest Muslim country in the world today, with more than 200 million Muslims), and there are Muslim minorities in all the other countries of Southeast Asia. Today Southeast Asia can claim at least one-third of the world's Muslims.

⊕ Cultural Expressions

Islamic Architecture

The functions of the mosque include both prayer and other community activities. Early mosques functioned as treasuries, where financial records were kept and law courts and educational centers were located. In time these activities moved into their own buildings, but the functions of public assembly and prayer continued to dictate the architectural form of mosques, which is also reflected in two other structures with religious functions: the *madrasah*, or religious school, and the tomb or mausoleum.

Every mosque includes four essential features: a fountain for washing; a large area for kneeling and prostration in prayer; a pulpit from which the leader of Friday noon worship delivers the sermon; and an imageless niche in the wall closest to Mecca, indicating the direction of prayer. Not part of the earliest mosques in Arabia but characteristic of Islam in many other places is the minaret, the tower from which the call to prayer is delivered.

Architect Gulzar Haider designed the mosque of the Islamic Society of North America, built in 1982 in Indiana, with no external domes. Instead, Haider constructed three "veiled" domes inside the mosque, which blends into the surrounding American landscape. (Martin Nguyen & Kiran Tahir)

Focus

Mohamed Zakariya

Mohamed Zakariya (b. 1942) is the most celebrated Islamic calligrapher in the United States. Born in California, he saw Islamic calligraphy for the first time in the window of an Armenian carpet store. While traveling in Morocco in his late teens, he became fascinated with Islam and Islamic calligraphy. On his return to the United States he converted to Islam.

Later he made other journeys to North Africa and the Middle East, and spent some time studying manuscripts in the British Museum in London. After studying with the Egyptian calligrapher Abdussalam Ali-Nour, Zakariya in 1984 became a student of the Turkish master calligrapher Hasan Celebi. In 1988 he received his diploma from Celebi at the Research Center for Islamic History, Art and Culture in Istanbul, the first American to achieve this honor.

He received his second diploma, in the *ta'lik* script, from the master calligrapher Ali Alparslan in 1997.

Zakariya's work has been displayed in various museums and galleries, and is in a number of private collections. He was the artist commissioned by the United States Postal Service to design its Eid stamp, which made its debut on September 1, 2001.

In addition to teaching calligraphy according to the Ottoman method, Zakariya writes contemporary instructional material and translates classic texts. In 2009, he was commissioned by US president Barack Obama to create a piece of calligraphy that was presented to King Abdulaziz of Saudi Arabia. Mohamed Zakariya's work shows that American Islam has become an integral part of the Muslim world. Now students from that world travel to the United States to study with an American master of an ancient Islamic art.

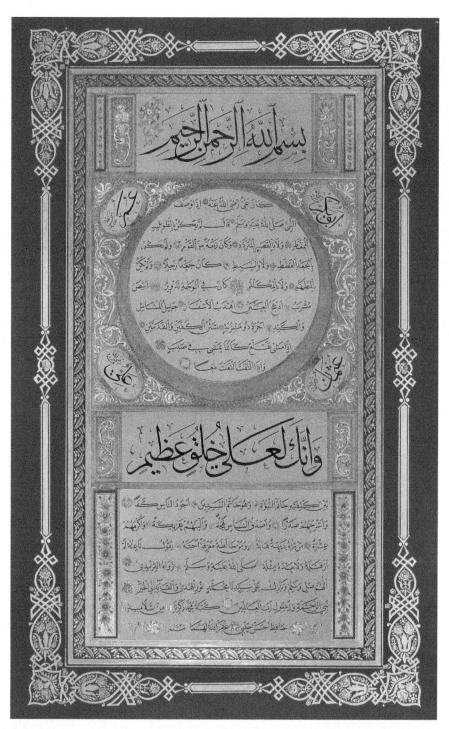

A modern *hilye* (calligraphic description) of the Prophet by Mohamed Zakariya. The top line reads "In the name of God. Universally Merciful. Specifically Merciful," and the circular section is surrounded by the names of the first four caliphs (courtesy of Mohamed Zakariya).

Islamic Art

Islamic art is rich, elaborate, and even exuberant. Three elements are particularly distinctive: calligraphy (the decorative use of script and units of text), geometrical decoration (particularly the interlaced motifs called arabesques in the West), and floral designs (especially common in Iran).

All three are more abstract than pictorial and therefore point beyond themselves in a way that pictorial images may not. Design using these elements captures the viewer's attention and directs it to the larger structure on which the decoration appears, whether a page of the Qur'an, a prayer rug, or the tiled entrance of a mosque. Religious content is most obvious in the decorative use of calligraphy in mosques, where the texts used are often passages from the Qur'an, but even the craft items sold in bazaars are often adorned with some of the 99 "wonderful names" of God.

Three-dimensional sculpture is prohibited in Islam, but the two-dimensional representation of living creatures is highly developed. Some Persian carpets include animals in garden scenes. Persian and Indian manuscripts are illustrated with miniature paintings of rulers and legendary heroes. Among Iranian Shi'a, portraits of 'Ali are a focus of popular piety. While representations of the Prophet himself are avoided, his legendary steed Buraq is portrayed in popular art as a winged horse with a human head—a motif that has become common on trucks and buses in Afghanistan and Pakistan.

⊕ Toward the Modern World

Islam and Modernity

Throughout the history of Islam, many Muslims have sought to reform the rest of the *ummah*. An external impetus has been Muslim interaction with western Christendom. The first major Western challenges to Muslim power were the Crusades. Determined to liberate Jerusalem from Muslim domination, the armies of the First Crusade captured the Holy City in 1099 after massacring its Jewish and Muslim inhabitants. For nearly two centuries, Frankish Christian kingdoms existed side by side with Muslim states along the eastern Mediterranean, sometimes peacefully, but most often at war.

In the end most of the crusaders returned home, and those who remained were assimilated into the larger Muslim society. But the spirit of the Crusades lived on, as did the distorted images of Islam and Muslims that the crusaders took home with them. The equally distorted images of Christianity and western Christendom that the crusaders left in Muslim lands have also lived on and have been reinforced and embellished in response to Western imperialism.

Premodern Reform Movements

Common to all Muslim reform movements has been the call to return to pristine *islam*, the *islam* of the Prophet's society and the normative period of his "rightly guided" successors. Among those who have championed this cause was the religious scholar Ibn Taymiyyah (1263–1328), a jurist who waged a relentless campaign against Shi'ism, Sufism, and the blind imitation of established legal traditions while fighting to revive the practice of *ijtihad*. Perhaps his most famous *fatwa* (religious legal opinion) was one that allowed Muslims in the city of Mardin (in what is now Turkey) to wage war against the occupying Mongols, even though the latter had converted to Islam after their conquest of Baghdad. In so doing, Ibn Taymiyyah contradicted the standard teaching that Muslims should not wage war against Muslim rulers. The "Mardin *fatwa*" would exert a powerful influence on subsequent reform movements.

Some four centuries later, Ibn Taymiyyah's ideas became the basis of an uncompromising revivalist movement that, significantly, began in the highlands of Arabia, the birthplace of Islam. The founder of the Wahhabi movement, Muhammad Ibn 'Abd al-Wahhab (1703–1792), allied himself with Muhammad 'Al Sa'ud, a local tribal prince, on the understanding that the prince would exercise political power to protect the nascent movement, which would hold religious authority. This arrangement continues today: the kingdom of Saudi Arabia is a Wahhabi state, ruled by the descendants of 'Al Sa'ud.

The Wahhabis preached a strictly egalitarian Islam based on a direct relationship between the worshiper and God. They repudiated the widely cherished hope that the Prophet and other divinely favored individuals would intercede with God on behalf of the pious. The Wahhabis regarded the veneration of saints, including the Prophet, as a form of idolatry and even called for the destruction of the sacred black stone of the Ka'ba, on the grounds that it stood as an idol between faithful Muslims and their Lord.

At the beginning of the nineteenth century (1801–1804), the Wahhabis waged a violent campaign aimed at purging Muslim society of what they considered un Islamic beliefs and practices. They destroyed the Prophet's tomb in Medina and leveled the graves of his Companions. They attacked the Shi'a's sacred cities of Najaf and Karbala, massacred their inhabitants, and demolished the shrines of 'Ali and his son Husayn. They also went on a rampage in Arab cities, desecrating the tombs of Sufi saints and destroying their shrines.

The basic ideals of Wahhabism have appealed to many revivalists and played an especially significant role in provoking reform efforts within eighteenth- and nineteenth-century Sufism. In recent years, extremist groups influenced by Wahhabi ideology, including Al-Qaeda, the Taliban, and the Islamic State of Iraq and Syria (ISIS), have transformed the internal struggle to "purify" Islam into an external war against all perceived enemies, Muslim and non-Muslim alike.

Modern Revivalism and Reform

As the British Empire extended its rule in India and European influence in the Muslim world grew, Muslim thinkers became resentful of the political inertia into which the *ummah* had apparently fallen. Even so, many parts of the Islamic world did experience intellectual, religious, and cultural renewals in the nineteenth century.

In the Middle East, the Arab renaissance was to a large degree stimulated by developments in the West. Undermined first by the Protestant Reformation and then by the Enlightenment, Western religious faith and institutions were giving way to secularism and romantic nationalism—ideas that were attractive to many Muslims. As a consequence, nationalistic identities came to compete with Islamic identities and in some cases even to supersede them.

Africa

In Africa, meanwhile, a number of Sufi movements arose in the nineteenth century, partly in response to Wahhabi criticisms and partly in reaction against European colonial encroachment on Muslim domains. Several of them succeeded in establishing their own states for some period of time, including the movement led by Usman ('Uthman) dan Fodio, which produced the Sokoto caliphate (1809–1903) in Nigeria; the Sanusi movement (1837–1969) led by Muhammad al-Sanusi in Libya; and the Mahdi rebellion (1881–1889) led by Muhammad Ahmad al-Mahdi in Sudan. Common to all these movements was an activist ideology of *jihad* (Arabic for "struggle"), a concept that has two components. Inner *jihad* is the struggle to make oneself more Islamic, while outer *jihad* is the struggle to make one's society more Islamic.

These Sufi movements exerted a lasting influence on most subsequent reformers. In North Africa in particular, Sufi *shaykh*s and religious scholars helped to preserve their countries' religious, linguistic, and cultural identity while in some cases spearheading struggles for independence from French and Italian colonial rule. In the nineteenth century, for example, the Sufi *shaykh* Abdelkader ('Abd al-Qadir) played an important political role in the long campaign for Algeria's independence. King Muhammad V of Morocco, who negotiated his country's independence from France in 1956, was himself a *shaykh* and a "venerable descendant" of the Prophet. And the grandson of al-Sanusi, Idris I, ruled Libya as king from independence in 1951 until he was overthrown in a coup led by Muammar Gaddafi in 1969.

The al-Sanusi movement in Libya promoted reform and Muslim unity across North and West Africa. By contrast, al-Mahdi in Sudan saw himself as God's representative on earth and set out to establish a social and political order modeled on that of the Prophet. He believed the Ottoman–Egyptian occupation of Sudan to be un-Islamic and waged *jihad* against it. In 1885 he triumphed over Egyptian forces and established an Islamic state based on strict application of the *shari'ah* law. Although al-Mahdi himself died within a few months, the regime lasted until 1889, when it was overthrown by British and Egyptian forces.

The Indian Subcontinent

The Mughal dynasty founded by Babur in 1526 reached its peak under his grandson Akbar (r. 1556–1605). With its decline in the seventeenth century, demands for reform along traditional lines intensified. One of the strongest voices was that of Ahmad Sirhindi (1564–1624), who called for a return to the *shari'ah*, regarded Sufis as deviants, and condemned Ibn 'Arabi in particular as an infidel.

The most important Islamic reform movement on the subcontinent was begun by Shah Wali Allah of Delhi (1702–1762). Although he was a disciple of Ibn 'Abd al-Wahhab, he was a Sufi himself, and instead of rejecting Sufism he sought to reform it. He also sought to reconcile Shi'a–Sunni differences, which had been (and sometimes are still) a source of serious friction. His grandson Ahmad Barelwi transformed that program into a *jihad* against British rule and the Sikhs. In 1826 he established an Islamic state based on the *shari'ah* and adopted the old caliphal title "commander of the faithful." At the opposite end of the spectrum of reaction to British rule was Sayyid Ahmad Khan (1817–1898). Like all reformers, Khan called for modern *ijtihad*, or rethinking of the Islamic heritage, but unlike most of them he rejected *hadith* tradition as a legitimate basis for modern Islamic living. He founded the Aligarh Muhammadan College (later renamed Aligarh Muslim University), where he attempted to apply his ideas in a modern Western-style program of education.

The career of Mirza Ghulam Ahmad (1835–1908) reflects the social and religious diversity of the Punjab in the 1880s—a time of various movements for renewal of Hindu and Muslim identity, as well as growing emphasis on self-definition among Sikhs. The author of several volumes of commentary on the Qur'an, in 1889 he accepted from his followers the homage reserved for a prophet. Ahmadis, as they are known, have also revered him as the *mujaddid* ("renewer") who ushered in the fourteenth century of Islam, the Mahdi of Shi'i expectation, the tenth incarnation of the Hindu deity Vishnu, and the returning messiah of Christianity (they also maintain that Jesus did not die in Palestine but went to Afghanistan, in search of the 10 lost tribes of Israel, and was buried in Srinagar, Kashmir).

The Ahmadi movement has spread widely. Including 4 million adherents in Pakistan, Ahmadis now total at least 10 million, or 1 percent of the world's Muslims. As early as 1891, orthodox

Muslim authorities rejected Ghulam Ahmad's claim to prophethood, and in Pakistan (where the Ahmadis relocated their base in 1947) they have been prohibited from calling themselves Muslims or using Islamic vocabulary in their worship and preaching. Thus Ahmadiyah's future may lie in its diaspora. Missions have been notably successful in lands such as West Africa, the Caribbean, and North America. Mahershala Ali, the Academy Award–winning actor, is an Ahmadi Muslim.

The ideas of Sayyid Ahmad Khan and his fellows culminated in the philosophy of Muhammad Iqbal (1876–1938), the greatest Muslim thinker of modern India. Central to Iqbal's work is the idea of an inner spirit that moves human civilization. Iqbal argued that Western science and philosophy were rightfully part of the Islamic heritage and should be integrated into a fresh "reconstruction of religious thought in Islam" (a phrase that serves as the title of his only major work in English, published in the 1930s). A poet as well as a philosopher, Iqbal frequently repeated this call for a rethinking of Islamic faith and civilization in his verse.

⊕ Recent Developments

Twentieth-Century Secularism

Many of the early Muslim reformers were at once liberal modernists and traditional thinkers. For this reason they are known as *salafis*, reformers who sought to emulate the example of "the pious forebears." But the ideal of equilibrium between tradition and modernity disappeared by the 1920s. Thereafter, Islamic reform meant one of three things: revivalism, reasoned defense (apologetics), or secularism.

Following the Ottoman defeat in the First World War, a young army officer named Mustafa Kemal Ataturk (1881–1938) launched a movement for national liberation. As the first president of the new Republic of Turkey (1923), he abolished the caliphate, transforming what had been a traditional Islamic domain into a modern secular state. Although for centuries the caliphate had been a shadowy office without any power, it had nevertheless embodied the only hope for a viable pan-Islamic state. Its disappearance had far-reaching consequences for Islamic political thought.

Ataturk banned Sufi orders, dissolved Islamic religious institutions, replaced the Arabic alphabet (in which Turkish had traditionally been written) with the Latin, and mounted a nationwide campaign for literacy in the new script. His express aim was to Westernize the Turkish republic. He encouraged the adoption of Western-style clothing and even banned the fez—the brimless conical red hat that, like all traditional Muslim headgear, allowed the faithful to touch their foreheads to the ground during prayer. Though Ataturk's ideology has remained the official state policy in Turkey, his program largely failed. Islamic faith and practice remain strong among the people of Turkey, and the country has experienced its own powerful revivalist movements. The most recent of these is the Hizmet ("service") movement, led by Fetullah Gulen, who has lived in the United States since 1999. The Hizmet movement has been in tension with the government of Turkish president Recep Tayyip Erdogan, which blamed the movement for an attempted coup in 2016.

Twentieth-Century Islamic Revivalism

Islamic reform movements in general seemed to diminish after the First World War and the breakup of the Ottoman Empire. Despite their differences, the various reform movements of the nineteenth century shared a dynamic spirit of progress. The premature stifling of that spirit may have reflected the lack of a coherent program of reform on which postcolonial Muslim thinkers could build. In any event, the liberal reform movements of the nineteenth century were transformed into traditional revivalist movements in the twentieth.

On the eve of Ataturk's abolition of the caliphate in 1924, Muhammad Rashid Rida published an important treatise on the imamate, or supreme caliphate, in which he argued for the establishment of an Islamic state that would be ruled by a council of jurists or religious scholars. Such a state would recognize nationalistic sentiments and aspirations, but would subordinate them to the religio-political interests of the larger community. Rida's Islamic revivalism and Arab nationalism came to represent two major trends in twentieth-century Muslim thinking, and his plan for a council of jurists would be implemented in Iran following the revolution of 1978–1979.

Contemporary Revivalist Movements

It remains the ideal of Islamic reform to establish a transnational Islamic caliphate. Yet the reality has been a proliferation of local movements reflecting local needs and ideas.

Common to most revivalist movements after 1950 was the ideal of an all-inclusive and self-sufficient Islamic order. This ideal had its roots in the Society of Muslim Brothers (*Jam'iyat al-Ikhwan al-Muslimin*, also known as the Muslim Brotherhood), founded in 1928 by an Egyptian schoolteacher named Hasan al-Banna. The aim of this society was to establish a network of Islamic social, economic, and political institutions through which the total Islamization of society might in time be achieved. Working through institutions such as schools, banks, cooperatives, and clinics, the Muslim Brotherhood penetrated all levels of Egyptian society.

The political and militaristic aspects of revivalism also had their beginnings in the Muslim Brothers, particularly after the assassination of the generally peaceful al-Banna in 1949. He was succeeded by hardline leaders who advocated active *jihad* against the Egyptian state system, which they regarded as un-Islamic. Among the products of this ideology were the young officers, led by Gamal Abdel Nasser, behind the 1952 socialist revolution that abolished monarchical rule in Egypt.

A charismatic proponent of Arab nationalism in the 1950s and 1960s, Nasser nevertheless clashed with the Muslim Brothers, and in the mid-1960s he imprisoned, exiled, or executed most of their leaders. Among the latter was Sayyid Qutb, who has been claimed as an inspiration by modern Islamist groups. As a theoretician, he influenced Islamist ideology; as an activist, he provided younger militants with a model of martyrdom to emulate.

Following the Arab defeat in the six-day Arab–Israeli war of June 1967 and Nasser's death three years later, the Muslim Brothers were suppressed under Egyptian president Anwar Sadat and his successor Hosni Mubarak and superseded by more powerful revivalist movements, some of which advocated the use of violence. Although the Brotherhood spread in other Arab countries, it was more influential on the level of ideology than on that of social action until the "Arab Spring" of 2011.

A similar organization, the *Jama'at-i Islami* (Islamic Society), was established in 1941 by Mawlana Sayyid Abu al-A'la Mawdudi. Like al-Banna, Mawdudi was committed to pan-Islamic unity, but (also like al-Banna) he concentrated his efforts on his own community—in this case the Muslims of India and (after 1947) Pakistan. The influence of both organizations spread far beyond their original homes.

While most contemporary revivalist movements, including the two noted here, have been open to modern science and technology, they have rejected many Western values and practices—including capitalist democracy, women's liberation, and the free mixing of the sexes—as decadent. Therefore, unlike the nineteenth-century reformers who looked to the West for ideas and models, contemporary revivalists have insisted on finding Islamic alternatives. Mawdudi, for example, wishing to distinguish his Islamic state model from Western democracies, described it as a "theo-democracy" based on the broad Qur'anic principle of consultation and the *shari'ah* law.

State Islam and the Islamic Revolution

Following a coup in 1969, Gaafar Mohamed el-Nimeiri made *shari'ah* the law in Sudan. The result was a bloody conflict between the Muslim north and the generally Christian south that has reduced a formerly rich agricultural country to famine; although South Sudan became an independent republic in 2011, violent clashes continue along the border that separates the two states. Similarly, in Pakistan, which for three decades had been a constitutionally Islamic but modern state, the 1977 introduction of *shari'ah* by General Mohammad Zia-ul-Haq led to violent social and political conflict.

In almost every Muslim country there is at least one revivalist movement advocating some form of Islamic state. In Malaysia and Indonesia, the governments themselves espouse Islamic national policies in order to silence extremist demands for radical reform. Nevertheless, in most Muslim countries tensions continue to run high between Islamic movements made up of educated middle-class men and women and despotic regimes determined to hold on to power at any cost.

On December 19, 2010, a Tunisian named Mohamed Bouazizi set himself on fire to protest police and government corruption that made it impossible for him to sell fruits and vegetables from a cart without paying bribes to officials. His self-immolation sparked widespread protests, which led to the overthrow of the Tunisian president. These dramatic events in turn sparked protests in Algeria and Egypt. The largest coordinated protests began in Cairo in late January 2011. On February 11, Egyptian president Hosni Mubarak stepped down, and in 2012 Mohammed Morsi of the Muslim Brotherhood was announced as the new Egyptian president. He served for almost exactly a year before being removed by the Egyptian military on July 3, 2013. Among the other countries swept up in the "Arab Spring" were Syria, Yemen, Bahrain, and Libya. On March 18, 2011, the UN Security Council authorized a resolution to protect civilians under attack in Libya, and the following day the first Western air strike was launched against the military regime of Muammar Gaddafi. He was killed in October 2011, and a new assembly was elected in July 2012. As of 2019, the violence triggered in Syria by the Arab Spring continues, exacerbated by the self-proclaimed "Islamic State" (ISIS).

In such highly charged social and political conditions, religion serves as a powerful moral, social, and spiritual expression of discontent—not only for Islamic activists, but for a broad spectrum of the community. It was on precisely such mass discontent that Imam Ruhollah Khomeini (1901–1989) and his fellow Shi'i *mullahs* (religio-legal functionaries) built the Islamic Republic of Iran, in which social, political, economic, and religious life are all controlled by a religious hierarchy under a supreme ayatollah (*ayat Allah*, "sign of God").

Throughout the long period of secular Shi'i rule in Iran (1501–1979), the authority of the religious *'ulama'* ('scholars') operated in more or less continuous tension with the secular authorities. This tension was greatly increased during the reign of the US-supported Shah Mohammad Reza Pahlavi, who sought to Westernize the country and obscure its Islamic identity by emphasizing its pre-Islamic cultural past. In 1963, during the Muharram observances of Husayn's martyrdom, matters came to a head when the shah's dreaded secret police ruthlessly put down mass demonstrations led by the *'ulama'*. Khomeini, already a prominent religious leader, was sent into exile, where he elaborated his theory that the jurist should have all-embracing authority in the community. In 1979 Khomeini returned to Iran at the head of the Islamic Revolution. The Islamic republic he founded has had a turbulent history, including an eight-year war with Iraq (1980–1988), out of which it emerged greatly weakened but still intact. Prodemocracy protests and challenges to the authority of the *'ulama'* came to international attention with the controversy that surrounded the 2009 election and the protests that erupted in March 2011.

Islam in Western Europe

The Islamic presence in western Europe began with the establishment of Umayyad rule in southern Spain in 711. Commercial, political, and cultural relations were initiated with both Latin and Byzantine states, but medieval Europe would not tolerate a permanent Muslim community on its soil. The campaign to drive the Muslims out of Spain succeeded in 1492 with the conquest of Granada. As a result, the Muslim presence in western Europe today is a relatively recent phenomenon.

In the twentieth century some Muslims migrated to Europe from various colonies as students, visitors, and merchants. Many also went as menial laborers and factory workers, especially after 1945. The majority of these postwar immigrants were men ranging in age from their teens to their 40s.

The ethnic makeup of the Muslim communities in Europe was largely determined by colonial ties. Muslims from the French colonies in North Africa, for example, went to France. Indian and, later, Pakistani and Bangladeshi Muslims tended to go to Britain. Those from Turkey and the former Soviet Turkic republics went to Germany and the Netherlands, while Bosnians went to Austria. These patterns, established early in the twentieth century, have continued despite many restrictions.

Muslim communities in Europe tend to reflect ethnic and linguistic rather than sectarian affiliations. In recent years hundreds of mosques and cultural centers have been established in Europe, and Muslim communities have become a dynamic religious and intellectual force in European society. France and Britain no longer confine Muslims to the status of "guest workers," as most other European countries do. Yet even in those two countries, the long histories of European racism, ethnocentrism, and colonialism have ensured that many Muslims continue to be treated as second-class citizens. This has created serious problems.

After the Islamic Revolution of 1978–1979, many Iranians immigrated to Europe, adding yet another layer of ethnic and religious diversity to European Muslim society. The 15-year Lebanese Civil War of 1975–1990, as well as disturbances in other Arab countries, including the Gulf War of 1991, also sent many political and economic refugees to the West. Meanwhile, intermarriage and conversion have infused new blood into Western Muslim communities.

Today, many Muslims born in Europe to foreign-born parents have assimilated into European society and culture. However, most European countries have taken steps to limit immigration from Muslim-majority countries, and since the mid-1980s some of them have repatriated some of their Muslim immigrants. Such actions may have been prompted in part by economic considerations, but also perhaps by nationalistic fear that Muslim immigrants might alter the social and ethnic character of these countries. In 2009, for example, Swiss citizens supported a ban on minarets for new mosques—even though only 4 of the approximately 150 mosques and Islamic centers in Switzerland have minarets. Across Europe there have been anti-immigrant and xenophobic policies enacted, as well as a rise of far-right political parties in response to migrants and refugees entering Europe. At the same time, European discrimination against ethnic minorities and the Islamic awakening precipitated by the Iranian Revolution have made Muslims more aware of their own religious and cultural identity.

Islam in North America

When the first Muslims arrived on American shores is a matter of conjecture. Suggestions that Muslims from Spain and West Africa may have sailed to America before Columbus should not be discounted, although they have not been proven. Scattered records point to the presence of Muslims in Spanish America before 1550, and it is very likely that the Inquisition drove many to flee to America soon after 1492.

In the sixteenth and seventeenth centuries, hundreds of thousands of Africans were taken as slaves to the Spanish, Portuguese, and British colonies in the Americas. Although the majority were from West Africa, Muslims made up at least 20 percent of the total. And among the slaves taken from Senegal, Nigeria, and western Sudan, the majority were Muslims, many of whom were well educated in Arabic and the religious sciences. Some were able to preserve their faith and heritage, and some tried to maintain contact with Muslims in their home areas, but many others were quickly absorbed into American society, adopting their masters' religious affiliations and even their family names.

Islamic customs and ideas can still be traced in the African American community, and today efforts are under way to reconstruct the story behind them. Beginning in the late 1800s, African Americans made conscious efforts to recover their Islamic heritage. In the early 1930s, when Elijah Muhammad (born Elijah Poole, 1897–1975) founded the Nation of Islam in America (see "New Religions and Movements" in this text), he saw Islam as a religion of black people only, misrepresenting the universalistic and nonracial nature of Islam. But his sons and successors, after traveling in the Muslim world and observing the international and multiracial character of the *hajj* pilgrimage, have moved closer to classical Islam. African American Muslims sometimes refer to themselves as Bilalians, after Bilal, an African Companion of the Prophet. Islam continues to be the fastest-growing religion in America, particularly among African Americans.

Before the revival of Islam in the African American community early in the twentieth century, small numbers of Muslims traveled to Canada and the United States, mainly from Syria and Lebanon. These early immigrants were largely uneducated men who intended only to work in North America for a few years and then return home, but many married local women and were soon completely assimilated.

The first Muslim missionary in America was Muhammad Alexander Webb, a jeweler, newspaper editor, and diplomat who converted to Islam in 1888 while traveling in India. On his return, Webb created an Islamic propaganda movement, wrote three books on Islam, and founded a periodical entitled *The Muslim World* (not to be confused with the academic journal of the same name). He traveled widely to spread his new faith and established Islamic study circles known as Muslim brotherhoods in many northeastern and midwestern American cities. With his death in 1916, however, his movement died as well.

The numbers of Muslim immigrants to North America increased markedly during the twentieth century. Most were of South Asian origin. Many were students who later chose to stay or well-educated professionals hoping to find better opportunities. But others came to escape persecution in their homelands on account of their religious or political activities. Interestingly, many recent newcomers who arrived as staunch anti-Western revivalists soon forgot their hostility and adapted to North American life.

Although these and other religiously committed Muslim immigrants may have moderated their political convictions, they retained their religious zeal, which they put to good use in the service both of their own community and of the society at large. They have played a crucial role in preserving the Islamic identity of fellow immigrants and promoting a better understanding of Islam through media activities and academic meetings.

The first mosque in the United States was built in 1915 by Albanian Muslims in Maine; another followed in Connecticut in 1919. Other mosques were established in the 1920s and 1930s in South Dakota and Iowa. In 1928, Polish Tatars built a mosque in Brooklyn, New York, which is still in use. The first Canadian mosque was built in Edmonton, Alberta, in 1938.

The exact numbers of Muslims in North America are unclear. The 2011 National Household Survey in Canada counted over 1 million Muslims, making Islam the second-largest religion in the country. The United States has not had a religious census since 1936, but its Muslim population today is estimated at between 6 and 7 million. Whatever the numbers may be, Islam is no longer an exotic rarity in North America: it is the faith of many people's coworkers and neighbors.

Issues of gender equality and sexual diversity are rarely discussed in the largest North American Muslim political and religious organizations (such as the Islamic Society of North America), partly because those groups tend to emphasize traditional interpretations of Islam, and partly because they have been preoccupied with matters such as community building, immigration policy, discrimination, and (to some extent) foreign policy. But as the size of their constituencies has grown, and the range of perspectives within those constituencies has increased, there has been growing pressure to address issues involving gender and sexuality.

Diasporic communities in large urban centers tend to become more open to questions about traditional religious and cultural ideas as they become more deeply rooted (or "assimilated") in their new societies. As contact with the "host" community intensifies, those who question traditional ideas are likely to have much easier access to information and networks of like-minded people than their counterparts in the home country. Some will "exit" their communities of origin and seek full assimilation to the dominant society, but in large communities particularly, some will remain connected and mobilize their challenges to traditionalism from within.

In general, Muslims born and raised in North America are more open to diversity than those born abroad, especially if their communities are not sufficiently homogeneous to support their own separate social institutions (such as schools). The likelihood of dissent is further amplified in North America by relatively high levels of education. In general, higher education increases openness to diversity, as well as to equity claims by women and sexual minorities. The fact that Muslim minorities in North America are less economically marginalized than those in Europe also reduces the likelihood of strict adherence to religious belief.

On the other hand, the great majority of Muslims in Canada and the United States are still relatively recent immigrants from places where social norms regarding gender and sexuality are starkly conservative, and the mosques and Islamic centers to which new immigrants become attached are almost invariably conservative on moral questions. Groups seeking to challenge conservative ideas are developing, as we shall see later, but LGBTQ Muslims in particular continue to face condemnation from mainstream Muslim society.

Marriage and the Family

Marriage under Islam is essentially a contractual relationship negotiated between the prospective husband and the woman's father or guardian. But the Qur'an emphasizes that the true contract is between the husband and the wife, based on mutual consent: the woman's father or guardian is expected to act on her behalf and, ideally, in her interest. Divorce is allowed, but only as a last resort after every effort has been made to save the marriage.

The Qur'an allows polygyny, or simultaneous marriage to more than one wife. But it places two significant restrictions on such marriages. First, it limits to four the number of wives that a man can have at one time (before Islam the number was unlimited). Second, it demands strict justice and equality in a man's material and emotional support for his wives. If this is not possible, the Qur'an stipulates, "then only one" is allowed. The Qur'an also warns that a man "cannot act equitably among [his] wives however much [he] tr[ies]" (Q. 4:3 and 129). As a result, the vast majority of Muslim marriages are monogamous.

Even more significantly, the Qur'an changed the nature of polygyny from an entitlement to a social responsibility. The verses dealing with this subject open with a proviso: "If you [men] are afraid that you would not act justly towards the orphans [in your care], then marry what seems good to you of women: two, three, or four" (Q. 4:3). This statement may be interpreted in two ways. It may mean that a man could marry the widowed mother of orphans in order to provide a family for them. It may also mean that a man could marry two, three, or four orphan girls after they attained marriageable age, again to provide a home and family for them. In either case, marriage to more than one wife was explicitly allowed as a way of providing for female orphans and widows in a traditional society beset with continuous warfare, where a woman could find love and security only in her own home.

Adultery, Fornication, and "Family Honor"

The Qur'an (17:32) is explicit in condemning adultery: "And do not come close to adultery—it is truly a shameful deed and an evil way." The punishment provided in the Qur'an (24:2) for adulterers (married men or women who have sex with someone other than their spouse) or fornicators (unmarried women or men who have sex with anyone) is 100 lashes. Since the illicit act had to be witnessed by four reliable eyewitnesses, such cases were rarely prosecuted.

Yet there have been cases, especially in recent times, in which adultery and fornication have been punished by law, and in some places the penalty has been capital punishment by stoning. Among those places is Iran, which according to Amnesty International has carried out six such executions since 2006. The scriptural source used to justify stoning is not the Qur'an but the *hadith* literature. Many activists, both Muslim and non-Muslim, have sought to end this barbaric practice.

Another barbaric practice that has attracted attention in recent years is the murder of family members by their relatives, ostensibly to preserve the family's "honor"; the victims in such cases are almost always young women or girls who are perceived to have brought shame on the family by disobeying male authority. In Canada, the 2009 Shafia case was a horrific example of such a practice in which a father, his second wife in a polygamous marriage, and their son murdered the family's three teenaged daughters (Zainab, Sahar, and Geeti Shafia), as well as the husband's first wife (Rona Mohammed). The three perpetrators were convicted in 2012 and sentenced to life imprisonment. There is nothing in the Qur'an that calls for the taking of an innocent life. The thinking behind such killings is rooted not in religion but in honor/shame culture.

War, Terrorism, and Violence

Many hoped that the end of the Cold War in 1989 and the moves made in the 1990s toward ending the long and bitter conflict between Israelis and Palestinians might allow for better relations between the Western and Muslim worlds in general. But the Israeli–Palestinian conflict has only deepened, and new conflicts have emerged in recent years.

Women in the Traditions

Women's Rights in Muslim Traditions

Of all the social and political issues that are currently being debated within the Muslim community, perhaps the most important is the question of women's rights. The Qur'an (9:71) makes it clear that men and women have the same religious duties and obligations: "The Believers, men and women, are protectors one of another: they enjoin what is just, and forbid what is evil: they observe regular prayers, practice regular charity, and obey God and God's Messenger." Another example can be found in *surah* 33, verse 35:

> For Muslim men and women, for believing men and women, for devout men and women, for true men and women, for men and women who are patient and constant, for men and women who humble themselves, for men and women who give in charity, for men and women who fast (and deny themselves), for men and women who guard their chastity, and for men and women who engage much in God's praise, for them God has prepared forgiveness and great reward.

The Qur'an allows women to acquire property through bequest, inheritance, or bride dowry and dispose of it as they please. These rights may well be inadequate in the modern world, but they point to a recognition of women's human dignity that until recently was denied in many societies. In general, Islamic law and social custom have tended either to restrict the rights of women laid out in the Qur'an or to render them virtually inoperative. Although women as well as men are supposed to receive education, some Islamic societies (such as that of Afghanistan under the Taliban) deny women education and employment opportunities.

As for the **hijab**, or veil, the Qur'an does not refer to it at all. It merely demands that women avoid wearing jewelry and dress modestly; in the next verse it also demands modesty of males. The *hadith* tradition indicates that most Muslim communities adopted the practice of veiling during the time of the caliphate, probably under the influence of eastern Christian and ancient Greek customs. An extreme extension of the practice, which may also be attributable to non-Arab influences, is the seclusion of women. Under the South Asian system of *purdah*, for instance, women are not only veiled but isolated from men. And seclusion became a hallmark of Turkish life under the *harim* system of the Ottoman aristocracy. In Afghanistan, the *burqa* covers the entire body; even the woman's eyes are obscured by a screen.

In the twenty-first century, the *hijab* has become a powerful—and powerfully ambiguous—symbol, widely condemned (especially by non-Muslims) as a limitation on women's rights but often defended by Muslim women themselves as a freely chosen affirmation of their Islamic identity. The question at issue is to what extent women can be excluded from public life. Around the world, social and economic conditions increasingly demand equal participation and rights for women and men alike.

In March 2005 Professor Amina Wadud led a mixed-gender Muslim prayer service in New York City—an event that broke at least three Islamic conventions. Traditionally, women have led prayer only among other women or within their own families; some of the women attending the service had their hair uncovered; and men and women were not separated (the only time such mixing of genders during worship is accepted by all Muslims is during the pilgrimage to Mecca, when men and women circumambulate the Ka'ba and pray together). Events similar to the New York prayer service have since been held in several North American cities.

Muslim women's activists in some mainstream Muslim organizations have challenged male leaders to adopt more inclusive language and develop policies to encourage women's participation. They are also becoming more vocal in their engagement with Western feminism. Although their positions sometimes diverge from those of Western feminists, controversies over issues such as veiling have created significant openings for Muslim women to engage in political debate in their own religious communities.

Sajda Khalil ties a *hijab* for Mikaela Valenzuela on National Hijab Day at the University of Toronto (Photo by Lucas Oleniuk/Toronto Star via Getty Images).

One major political development in the shaping of these relations was the Iranian Revolution of 1979. Four decades later, the prospect of an Iran with nuclear weapons has only increased tensions between the Islamic regime and the West, especially with the administration of President Donald Trump in the United States. A second development can also be traced to 1979, when the Soviet Union invaded Afghanistan. Muslims from around the world volunteered to fight with the Afghans for their liberation, and the United States contributed heavily to their training. Called *mujahidin* (the word is derived from *jihad*), these soldiers were seen at this time—before the end of the Cold War—as "freedom fighters" by much of the world, including then–American president Ronald Reagan. Among the other contributors to Afghanistan's "holy war" was Osama bin Laden,

Interview

Dr. Aminah Beverly (McCloud) Al-Deen, African American Muslim Scholar and Activist

Dr. Aminah Al-Deen is a professor of Islamic studies in the Department of Religious Studies at DePaul University in Chicago. She began teaching there as a graduate student instructor in 1990 and was promoted to a tenure-track assistant professor in 1993. That same year, she founded the Islam in America Archives at the Richardson Library at DePaul University, which collects the work of American Islamic scholars. As an associate professor in 1995, she organized the first of several "Islam in America" conferences at the university, and as a full professor in 2003, she began to write the courses that in 2006 became the foundation of the nation's first undergraduate baccalaureate program in Islamic world studies. A former editor-in-chief of the *Journal of Islamic Law and Culture*, she has published numerous books, including *African American Islam, Transnational Muslims in American Society, Questions of Faith, An Introduction to Islam in the 21st Century*, and *History of Arab Americans: Exploring Diverse Roots*. She has also written two manuscripts entitled *Islamic Ethics in the 21st Century* for graduate schools in Abu Dhabi.

Photo courtesy of Dr. Aminah Beverly (McCloud) Al-Deen.

Al-Deen is a senior Fulbright Scholar, an advisory board member of the Institute for Social and Policy Understanding, a board member of the American Islamic College, and an executive board member of the Inner-City Muslim Action Network. She also ran a 10-week "Exploring Muslim Cultures" program in the city of Chicago, which included 22 lectures, 10 events, and three exhibits that engaged 60,000 Chicago high school students and their social studies teachers. For this program, she was able to turn her DePaul University students into docents. It was one of the many ways in which Al-Deen has showcased her activism as well as her scholarship. A 2004 article about her in the *New York Times* ran under a headline that summed up her work: "An Islamic Scholar with the Dual Role of Activist."

As an African American Muslim woman, she has been outspoken about her support for both Indigenous American Muslims in general, and African American Muslims in particular. During Ramadan in 2013, she spoke poignantly about the Trayvon Martin trial, in which the killer of an unarmed African American teenager was found not guilty:

> As Americans of various ethnicities and ages poured into the streets either to support

or decry the verdict, Muslim Americans remain focused on Egypt, Syria and Turkey while living in America. Ramadan is a time for reflection and I am terribly sad to report that many American Muslims are not either Muslim in their sensibilities or American in their understandings of the need to stand up for justice or against injustice. There is little that has to do with this place of our sustenance that even moves us unless the issue is us. Our organizations only cry out for alliance with others over our own personal issues Egypt, Syria and Turkey or *shari'ah* bans, not that which affects this society, our society at its core—justice, prejudice, voting rights, healthcare. Yet all of the apologists among us want other Americans to consider Muslims, American.

We could have vigorously discussed the merits of the case, the potential slippery slopes of either verdict. We could have discussed what this case means for the history of race relations in this country. We could have discussed the potential outcome of "stand your ground," what constitutes a "threat" to which the response is lethal force, or the refusal of a police department to arrest a user of lethal force until facts could be obtained.

Are we so limited that we can only think of our own yet expect others to ignore our singleness of mind and come to our aid when needed? Are we that selfish? Of course, we need to lament and assist other Muslims but we have been so selective and Allah demands that we provide assistance to the orphan, stand up for what is just! Or at least inquire. To ignore this watershed case because the victim is a black boy and not an American Muslim or a Muslim child overseas is an injustice to our own souls. (McCloud 2013)

In 2017, she was appalled that the reports of slavery and slave markets being reintroduced in Libya had not become an issue of concern for American Muslims. In an interview for this text, she declared, "The Muslim world is in bad shape. Re-creating it here in the United States isn't going to help us. This is why we see African American Muslims pulling away from immigrant Muslim communities. They do not want to see reproductions of a bad story." She sees her home as a "third space," a safe space where Muslims who are frustrated with their mosque communities can meet. In her home, they can speak freely without the "strictures that the mosque community is putting on people—gender segregation, clothing, what you say, and if you say it with the correct number of Qur'anic references recited in a particular style of Arabic."

Al-Deen is one of the key Muslim scholar/activists in America today, one who constantly challenges us to look at the hard issues of race and class that often divide us as Americans.

the son of a wealthy Saudi Arabian family who created Al-Qaeda ("the base") to help fund and train *mujahidin*. The Soviet troops were withdrawn in 1988, but Al-Qaeda was not disbanded. In 1996 bin Laden issued a *fatwa* calling for the overthrow of the Saudi government and the removal of US forces from Arabia, and in 1998 he declared war against Americans generally. A series of terrorist actions followed, including the attacks on the United States on September 11, 2001. In response, the United States and its allies went to war, first in Afghanistan and then in Iraq.

Muslims around the world have repeatedly condemned terrorist activity. Muslim leaders have pointed out that suicide bombings violate Islam's prohibitions on both suicide and the killing of civilians in war, and in March 2005, on the first anniversary of the 2004 Al-Qaeda train bombing in Madrid, Spanish clerics issued a *fatwa* against bin Laden himself. Even so, it would be another seven years before he was tracked down and killed by US forces.

An important reference point in discussions of martyrdom is the Mardin Conference, held in March 2010 in the city that was at issue in Ibn Taymiyyah's famous fourteenth-century *fatwa* legitimizing the use of violence against unjust Muslim rulers. Because many modern terrorists (among them bin Laden) have used this *fatwa* to justify their actions, the Mardin Conference brought together 15 senior Islamic scholars from across the Muslim world to discuss the context in which it was issued some 700 years earlier.

In condoning violence against authoritarian rulers in order to reestablish true Islamic rule, Ibn Taymiyyah broke with the teachings of his own conservative school. As the scholars who met at Mardin pointed out, however, his *fatwa* was issued in a very particular historical context, in the aftermath of the Mongol conquest and the devastation of Baghdad (the seat of Islamic authority at the time). They concluded that "anyone who seeks support from this *fatwa* for killing Muslims or non-Muslims has erred in his interpretation." They also stated that "it is not for a Muslim individual or a group to announce and declare war or engage in combative *jihad* . . . on their own."

Unfortunately, extremists seem impervious to mainstream Muslim opinion. Muslims can accomplish much in the West if they work with their non-Muslim neighbors to promote justice and moral consciousness. But many non-Muslims see "Islam" and "the West" as mutually exclusive realities and do not recognize their shared heritage. If future generations are to remain active as Muslims in pluralistic Western societies, it is more important than ever to reexamine old images and ideas.

Anti-US graffiti on the wall of the former US embassy in the Iranian capital, Tehran, in 2008 (© Roberto Fumagalli/Alamy).

⊕ Summary

A major development in the history of Islam is now under way in the West. Muslims who, through migration, have moved from majority to minority status are being spurred to define the priorities of their faith. Their decisions about what to pass on to their Western-born children will shape the contours of Islam in the twenty-first century and beyond. At the same time, the Western emphasis on open discussion calls on Muslims from different cultural and regional backgrounds to think

Sites

Mecca, Saudi Arabia

Mecca is the original home of the Prophet Muhammad as well as the site of the Ka'ba, the focal point of the annual *hajj* (pilgrimage), when more than 2 million Muslims visit the city over a period of about 10 days. Mecca is permanently closed to non-Muslims.

Medina, Saudi Arabia

Medina is the home of the first Muslim community and the place where Muhammad was buried. Unlike Mecca, it is open to non-Muslims. The Prophet's Mosque, where he and his first two successors are buried, was originally quite simple but is now one of the largest mosques in the world.

Al-Azhar University, Cairo

The oldest university in the Western world and an important center of Sunni learning, Al-Azhar was transformed into a modern institution in 1961, when (under the direction of Egypt's President Nasser) it opened a faculty for women.

Karbala, Iraq

Karbala is home of the shrine of Imam Husayn (the third Imam), who was killed there in 680. It is of special importance to the Shi'a, who during their daily prayers touch their heads to a small disk of clay made from the soil of Karbala. Since 2004, hundreds of innocent worshipers have been killed in suicide bombings near the shrine.

Cordoba, Spain

The city at the heart of the *convivencia* ("shared life") in medieval Spain, Cordoba was described by a tenth-century Benedictine nun as "the ornament of the world."

Istanbul, Turkey

The Byzantine city of Constantinople was renamed Istanbul after its capture by the Turks in 1453. The capital of the Ottoman Turkish Empire and the center of the sultan's power, it is the site of many imperial buildings, including the Topkapi Palace (the principal residence of the sultans from 1465 to 1856) and its successor, the Western-influenced Dolmabahce Palace.

Haram al-Sharif, Jerusalem

Located in the ancient city of Jerusalem, Haram al-Sharif (the "Noble Sanctuary," known to Jews and Christians as the Temple Mount) contains two sacred buildings: the Masjid al-Aqsa—the "farthest mosque," where Muhammad is said to have prayed before ascending to heaven, and the Dome of the Rock, a sanctuary built on the spot from which tradition says the ascent began.

Sacred Texts

Variation	Text	Composition/ Compilation	Compilation/Revision	Use
Sunni and Shiʻa	Qurʼan	Revelations received by Muhammad between 610 and 632 CE	Authoritative codex produced between 644 and 656 CE	Doctrinal, ritual, inspirational, educational
Sunni and Shiʻa	*Hadith*	Sayings of Muhammad and his early Companions collected during their lifetimes	Earliest authoritative collection produced by al-Bukhari (d. 870 CE)	Doctrinal, ritual, inspirational, educational
Shiʻa only	*Nahj al-Balagha* ("The peak of eloquence")	Sayings and sermons of ʻAli, the first Shiʻi Imam	Collected by Al-Radi (d. 1015)	Doctrinal, ritual, inspirational, educational
Ismaʼili Shiʻa only	*Ginans* (hymns of praise and worship of God)	Collection begun by Pir Nur in the 12th century	Composition and collection continued until the beginning of the 20th century	Doctrinal, ritual, inspirational, educational

clearly about what they do and do not share. Muslims living in the West will use Western technology and democratic institutions to help their brothers and sisters revitalize the Muslim communities in their countries of origin, as well as the rest of the Muslim *ummah*. The potential of modern tools of communication to contribute to this process became clear during the Arab Spring of 2011. The year 2017 saw the rise of Muslims in North American popular media, with Mahershala Ali winning an Academy Award, Kumail Nanjiani achieving the breakout romantic comedy of the summer in *The Big Sick*, and Aziz Ansari winning a number of Emmy awards for *Master of None*. Ali would win a second Academy Award in 2019.

Discussion Questions

1. What is the significance of the *hijra* in Muslim history? Why is it so important to Muslims?

2. Write a brief biography of the Prophet highlighting two events in his life that are particularly significant to Muslims. In your answer, explain why those events are so central to the tradition.

3. What is the Qurʼan? What do Muslims understand it to be?

4. Discuss the differences between Sunni and Shiʻa Islam. What are the two primary groups within the Shiʻa?

5. Outline the development of Sufism, the mystical dimension of Islam.

6. What are the Five Pillars of Islam?

7. What are some of the issues raised by feminist interpretations of the Qurʼan and the Muslim tradition?

Glossary

caliph From the Arabic *khalifah* ("one who represents or acts on behalf of another"). The caliph was the Prophet's successor as the head of the Muslim community; the position became institutionalized in the form of the caliphate, which lasted from 632 to 1924.

dhikr "Remembering" God's name; a chant used in Sufi devotional exercises, sometimes while devotees dance in a circle.

dhimmis "Protected people"; non-Muslim religious minorities (specifically Jews and Christians, as "People of the Book") accorded tolerated status in Islamic society.

Fatihah The short opening surah of the Qur'an, recited at least 17 times every day.

fatwa A ruling issued by a traditional religio-legal authority.

fiqh Jurisprudence, or the theoretical principles underpinning the specific regulations contained in the *shari'ah*.

hadith The body of texts reporting Muhammad's words and example, taken by Muslims as a foundation for conduct and doctrine; a *hadith* is an individual unit of the literature.

hajj The annual pilgrimage to Mecca.

halal Ritually acceptable; the term is most often used in the context of the slaughter of animals for meat, but also refers generally to Muslim dietary regulations.

haram "Forbidden"; a term used especially in reference to actions but similar in its connotations to "taboo."

hijab A woman's veil or head covering.

hijrah The Prophet's migration from Mecca to establish a community in Medina in 622 CE. In dates, the abbreviation AH stands for "year of the *hijrah*" (the starting point of the Islamic dating system).

'Id al-Fitr The holiday celebrating the end of the Ramadan fast; the festival traditionally begins following the sighting of the new moon.

ijma' The consensus of religio-legal scholars and one of the two secondary principles used in jurisprudence; some legal schools give it more weight than others.

ijtihad Personal reasoning applied to the development of legal opinions.

Imamis ("Twelvers") Shi'a who recognize 12 imams as legitimate heirs to the Prophet's authority; the last, in occultation since 874, is expected to return some day as the Mahdi.

Isma'ilis ("Seveners") Shi'a who recognize only seven imams; the name comes from the last of them, Isma'il, whose lineage continues to the present in the Agha Khan.

jihad Struggle in defense of the faith; some jihads are military, waged in response to threats to the community's security or welfare, while others are spiritual, waged to improve moral conduct in society.

kufr Rejecting belief; implies lack of gratitude for God's grace.

Mahdi The Shi'i twelfth Imam, understood in his role as the "rightly guided one" who will emerge from hiding at some unspecified future date to restore righteousness and order to the world.

mi'raj The Prophet's miraculous journey to heaven.

mu'adhdhin The person who calls people to prayer.

qiblah The direction of prayer, marked in mosques by a niche inside the wall nearest Mecca.

Ramadan The month throughout which Muslims fast during daylight hours.

sadaqah Alms given voluntarily, in addition to the required zakat.

salat The prescribed daily prayers, said five times during the day.

shahadah The Muslim profession of faith in God as the only god, and in Muhammad as God's Prophet.

shari'ah The specific regulations of Islamic law (jurisprudence, or theoretical discussion of the law, is *fiqh*).

shaykh The Arabic term for a senior master, especially in Sufism.

Shi'a From the Arabic meaning "party"; Muslims who trace succession to the Prophet's authority through the line of imams descended from 'Ali. The term is also used for the smaller of the two main divisions of Islam, accounting for about one-sixth of all Muslims today. "Shi'i" is the adjective form.

sunnah The "life-example" of Muhammad's words and deeds, based mainly on the *hadith* literature; the primary source of guidance for Muslims.

Sunni Muslims who trace succession to the Prophet's authority through the caliphate, which lasted until the twentieth century. The term also denotes the larger of the two main divisions of Islam, accounting for about five-sixths of all Muslims today.

surah A chapter of the Qur'an; there are 114 in all, arranged mainly in decreasing order of length except for the first (the *Fatihah*).

tafsir Commentary on the Qur'an.

taqlid Following the *ijtihad* or legal opinion of a particular jurist.

ummah The Muslim community.

zakat The prescribed welfare tax, amounting to 2.5 percent of each Muslim's accumulated wealth, collected by central treasuries in earlier times but now donated to charities independently of state governments; see also **sadaqah**.

Further Reading

Ahmed, Leila. 1992. *Women and Gender in Islam: Historical Roots of a Modern Debate*. New Haven, CT: Yale University Press. A frequently cited contribution on this topic.

Alvi, Sajida Sultana, Homa Hoodfar, and Sheila McDonough, eds. 2003. *The Muslim Veil in North America: Issues and Debates*. Toronto: Women's Press. A good collection of essays about the issues surrounding *hijab*.

Coulson, N. G. 1964. *A History of Islamic Law*. Edinburgh: Edinburgh University Press. A work that traces the development of Islamic jurisprudence from its inception in the ninth century through its shifts in response to the influence of modern Western legal systems.

Dodds, Jerrilyn D., María Rosa Menocal, and Abigail Krasner Balbale, eds. 2008. *The Arts of Intimacy: Christians, Jews, and Muslims in the Making of Castilian Culture*. New Haven, CT: Yale University Press. A beautifully illustrated book that looks at the *convivencia* ("shared life") between Muslims, Christians, and Jews in medieval Spain.

The Encyclopedia of Islam, rev. ed. 1963–. Leiden: E. J. Brill. A vast and technical but authoritative compendium first published in four volumes between 1913 and 1938. Entries appear under Arabic headwords, sometimes in unfamiliar transliterations, and so pose a challenge for the beginner.

Esposito, John, ed. 2009. *The Oxford Encyclopedia of the Islamic World*. New York: Oxford University Press. An indispensable reference.

Grabar, Oleg. 1973. *The Formation of Islamic Art*. New Haven, CT: Yale University Press. A work concentrating on Islamic art in the Middle East in the early Islamic centuries.

Haddad, Yvonne Y., and Jane I. Smith, eds. 1994. *Muslim Communities in North America*. Albany: State University of New York Press. An examination of Islamic tradition and identity in the modern Western diaspora.

Mottahedeh, Roy. 2002. *The Mantle of the Prophet: Religion and Politics in Iran*. Oxford: Oneworld. One of the best single-volume studies of the events leading up to the Iranian Revolution.

Peters, Francis E. 1994. *A Reader on Islam*. Princeton, NJ: Princeton University Press. An anthology of historical source readings.

Qureshi, Emran, and Michael A. Sells, eds. 2003. *The New Crusades: Constructing the Muslim Enemy*. New York: Columbia. An excellent collection of essays on Western representations of Islam and Muslim lives.

Safi, Omid, ed. 2003. *Progressive Muslims: On Justice, Gender and Pluralism*. Oxford: Oneworld. A collection of essays by Muslim scholars of Islam on contemporary topics.

Schimmel, Annemarie. 1975. *Mystical Dimensions of Islam*. Chapel Hill: University of North Carolina Press. A survey of Sufism by one of its most respected Western interpreters.

Taylor, Jennifer Maytorena. 2009. *New Muslim Cool* [documentary film]. Seventh Art Releasing. http://www.7thart.com. The story of Hamza Perez, a Puerto Rican–American hip hop artist who converted to Islam.

Watt, W. Montgomery. 1962. *Islamic Philosophy and Theology*. Edinburgh: Edinburgh University Press. A masterly survey of Muslim religious intellectuals, especially in the first six centuries of Islam.

Recommended Websites

http://www.uga.edu/islam

The best academic site for the study of Islam, presented by Professor Alan Godlas of the University of Georgia.

http://www.cie.org/index.aspx

The website of the Council on Islamic Education, offering useful resources for teachers.

http://acommonword.com

The website of an interfaith initiative supported by a wide range of Muslim scholars and leaders.

http://www.msawest.net/islam

An excellent selection of resources on Islam, including searchable translations of both the Qur'an and the hadith literature, presented by the Muslim Students Association.

References

Chittick, William C. 2000. *Sufism: A Beginner's Guide*. Oxford: Oneworld.

McCloud, Aminah. 2013. "Some Ramadan thoughts on the 'Americanness' of some American Muslim organization," available at https://www.alimprogram.org/articles/some-ramadan-thoughts-on-the-americanness-of-some-american-muslim-organizations/

Nicholson, Reynold A. 1931. "Mysticism." In *The Legacy of Islam*, ed. T. Arnold and Alfred Guillaume, 210–238. London: Oxford University Press.

Smith, Margaret. 1928. *Rabi'a the Mystic*. Cambridge: Cambridge University Press.

7 Hindu Traditions

Vasudha Narayanan

Traditions at a Glance

Numbers

There are approximately 1 billion Hindus around the world.

Distribution

Most Hindus live in India, with large numbers in other regions of South Asia, as well as the United States, Canada, Australia, western Europe, and many parts of Southeast Asia.

Principal Historical Periods

The first key period in the history of Hinduism was the Indus Valley civilization, which lasted from about 3000 to 1500 BCE. The Vedas were probably composed between 1500 BCE and 600 BCE, but these time periods are contested. The epics and the *Puranas* were composed between 500 BCE and 1000 CE. Between 600 and 1700 CE, notable devotional poetry was produced in local languages, and major temples were built in South and Southeast Asia. From the thirteenth to the eighteenth century, northern India was under Muslim rule, before the British colonial period began in the mid-1700s, lasting until 1947.

Founders and Leaders

Important figures include Shankara, Ramanuja, Madhva, Vallabha, Ramananda, Chaitanya, Swaminarayan, Ramakrishna, and Vivekananda. Among the hundreds of teachers who have attracted followings in the last century alone are Aurobindo, Ramana Maharishi, Maharishi Mahesh Yogi, Sathya Sai Baba, Anandamayi Ma, and Ma Amritananda Mayi.

Deities

Hindu philosophy recognizes a supreme being (the ineffable Brahman) who is not limited by gender and number and who may take countless forms; classical rhetoric typically refers to 330 million. Some sectarian traditions identify the supreme deity as Vishnu, some as Shiva, and some as a form of the Goddess. The supreme being may be understood as male, female, androgynous, or beyond gender. There are also many local deities.

Authoritative Texts

The Vedas are technically considered the most authoritative texts, although the epics (the *Ramayana* and the *Mahabharata*, including the *Bhagavad Gita*), the *Puranas*, and several works in regional languages have also been very important.

Noteworthy Teachings

Hindus in general recognize a supreme being, variously conceived—personal for some, impersonal for others. Most think of the human soul as immortal and believe that when it reaches liberation it will be freed from the shackles of karma and rebirth. Specific teachings vary depending on sectarian tradition, region, and community.

In this chapter you will learn about:

- The history of the Hindu traditions in South Asia
- The diversity of Hindu traditions and the common threads they share
- Significant texts, both in Sanskrit and in vernacular languages
- Major philosophical traditions and religious teachers
- The importance of devotion (*bhakti*)
- The significance of temples in South and Southeast Asia and North America
- The place of the performing arts in the Hindu traditions

The Vishram Ghat, Mathura (Himanshu Khagta/Getty Images).

The earliest compositions in the Hindu tradition are the **Vedas**, four collections of hymns and texts that are said to have been "revealed" to *rishis* (visionaries or seers) through both sight and sound; thus, the sacred words are called *shruti* ("that which is heard"). This dual emphasis on seeing and hearing the sacred is characteristic of all Hindu traditions.

When Hindus go on a pilgrimage or visit a temple, they seek an experience known as a *darshana*: to see and be seen by a particular deity or **guru**. But Hindus also believe in the importance of reciting or singing prayers aloud. Reading from ancient texts, telling or dancing stories of the gods, chanting prayers, singing devotional songs, or meditating on a holy **mantra**—these are just some of the ways in which Hindus actively live their tradition through its sacred words. In short, Hindus experience the divine through both sight and sound. Although sacred texts have been important over Hinduism's history, for most Hindus the primary source of knowledge about their traditions has been performance: rituals, recitations, music, dance, and theater.

Hinduism is characterized by diversity. While some texts and some deities are widely accepted, there is no single text, deity, or teacher that *all* Hindus consider supremely authoritative. Similarly, there are many local deities who may or may not be identified with pan-Indian gods. The Hindu tradition is in fact many traditions encompassing hundreds of communities and sectarian movements, each of which has its own hallowed canon, its own sacred place, and its own concept of the supreme deity.

"Hinduism"

The term "Hinduism" is frequently used as a shorthand for diverse philosophies, arts, branches of knowledge, and practices associated with people and communities that have some connection with the Indian subcontinent and do not explicitly self-identify with another religious tradition. While a lot of the Hindu tradition springs from the Vedas, knowledge of the Vedas is not required to qualify as Hindu; there are probably millions of people in India who have never heard of them. Yet all those people would be considered Hindu as long they did not belong to a faith tradition that explicitly denied the exalted status of the Vedas. For many Hindus, plurality of beliefs and practices is a way of life.

The word "Hinduism," like "India" itself, is derived from "Sind": the name of the region—now in Pakistan—around the river Sindhu (Indus). To the British colonizers of India in the eighteenth and nineteenth centuries, "Hinduism" meant the religion of those Indians—the majority—who were not Muslims, although a few smaller groups, including Jainas, Parsis, Christians, Jews, and sometimes Sikhs, were also recognized. As a term for a religious identity, "Hinduism" did not become popular until the nineteenth century.

There are approximately one billion Hindus in the world today. Yet when they are asked about their religious identity, those from India are more likely to refer to their caste or community than to Hinduism. Under Indian law, the term "Hindu" applies not only to members of a Hindu "denomination" such as Vira Shaiva or Brahmo Samaj, but also to "any other person domiciled in the territories to which [the Hindu Family Act] extends who is *not a Muslim, Christian, Parsi, or Jew* by religion" (emphasis added). In effect, India's legal system considers anyone who does not profess to be a member of one of the specified religions to be Hindu. Thus, while we can make some generalizations about the tradition and trace some important lines of historical continuity, we must keep in mind their limitations.

The very concept of religion in the Western, post-Enlightenment sense is only loosely applicable to the Hindu tradition. Some Hindus think the Sanskrit word **dharma** comes close to "religion" in that it refers to righteousness, justice, faith, duty, and religious and social obligation, but it does not cover everything that is sacred for Hindus. Many things—from astrology to music and dance, from phonetics to plants—may be essential to an individual Hindu's practice of religion. Therefore this discussion will include a number of features not usually covered by the term "religion" in the Western world.

⊕ Origins

In the early twentieth century, Hinduism was believed to have grown from a fusion of the indigenous religions of the Indus Valley with the faith of an Indo-European people usually thought to have migrated there sometime between 1750 and 1500 BCE. More recently, however, some scholars have argued that the Indo-Europeans ("Aryans") originated in other parts of Asia, while others suggest that the subcontinent itself was their original homeland.

The Harappa Culture

In 1926 excavations revealed the remains of several large towns on the banks of the Indus River in what is now Pakistan. Two of these towns, known today as Mohenjo Daro ("Mound of the Dead") and Harappa, are more than 300 miles apart. Yet archaeological evidence suggests similarities in the cultures found across the entire northwestern part of the subcontinent. Although that overall culture is still widely identified with the Indus Valley, some scholars now call it the Harappa culture because it extends well beyond the Indus basin itself.

It is generally believed that the towns were in existence by about 2750 BCE. Inscriptions on carved seals show that there was a written language, although no reading of it is universally accepted. Clearly the Harappans were impressive builders. At Mohenjo Daro there is a huge swimming pool–like structure, surrounded by porticos and flights of stairs, that scholars believe was designed for religious rituals of some sort. In addition, some houses appear to have included a room with a fire altar, and there are carvings of what looks like a mother goddess that may have been used for offerings of incense. Excavations around the Indus River have uncovered seals showing a man seated in a position that resembles a **yoga** posture, wearing a headdress that suggests he could be a prototype of the god who came to be known as Shiva. Other seals show a horned figure emerging from a *pipal* tree, in front of which stand seven figures with long braids who have been tentatively identified as either holy men or goddesses.

What might have brought the Indus Valley civilization to an end? Some think it was the arrival of the Indo-Europeans around 1750 BCE. Others suggest that flooding, drying of the river, or changes in crop-growing patterns that had adverse effects might have driven the people farther east. Whatever the answer, the fragmentary evidence found in the Indus Valley suggests that some features of Hinduism may have originated well before 1750 BCE.

We know even less of the early history in other parts of the subcontinent. Nevertheless, scholars have noticed correspondences between sites that were inhabited 4,000 or 5,000 years ago and sites that are of religious significance today. It seems likely that at least some elements of Hinduism as we know it have been present for as long as five millennia.

The Indo-Europeans

The language of the Vedas is an early form of Sanskrit, a member of the language family known as Indo-European (or "Indo-Aryan"). Western scholars in the nineteenth century noted similarities

Timeline

c. 3300–1900 BCE	Evidence of Indus Valley civilization (early to mature phases)
c. 1750?–1500	Earliest Vedic compositions
c. 600	Production of *Upanishads*
c. 500	Production of Hindu epics begins
326	Alexander the Great comes to the northwest border of India
c. 272	Accession of King Ashoka
c. 200	First contacts with Southeast Asia
c. 200 BCE–200 CE	Composition of *Bhagavad Gita*
c. 200 CE	Compilation of *Laws of Manu* and *Natya Sastra* completed
c. 500	Beginnings of tantric tradition
c. 700–900	Lives of Alvars and Nayanmars, Tamil *bhakti* poets
c. 700–800	Emergence of Shankara's *advaita* Vedanta
c. 1008–1023	Mahmud of Ghazni raids kingdoms in India several times, strips temples of their wealth; Somnath Temple in Gujarat destroyed
1017	Traditional birthdate of Ramanuja, Vaishnava philosopher (d. 1137)
1100–1150	Angkor Wat built in Cambodia
c. 1400	Major endowments at Tirumala–Tirupati temple
1486	Birth of Chaitanya, Bengali Vaishnava *bhakti* leader (d. 1583)
c. 1543	Birth of Tulsidas, North Indian *bhakti* poet (d. 1623)
1757	British rule established in Calcutta
1828	Ram Mohan Roy founds Brahmo Samaj
1836	Birth of Ramakrishna Paramahamsa (d. 1886)
1875	Dayananda Sarasvati founds Arya Samaj
1893	Vivekananda attends World's Parliament of Religions in Chicago
1905–1906	Vedanta Temple built in San Francisco
1926	Birth of Sathya Sai Baba
1947	Partition of India and Pakistan on religious lines, resulting in almost a million deaths
1959	Maharishi Mahesh Yogi brings Transcendental Meditation to America and Europe
1965	A. C. Bhaktivedanta Swami Prabhupada, founder of ISKCON, sails to America
1977	Hindu temples consecrated in New York and Pittsburgh
2005	Major earthquake levels historic temples in Durbar Square, Kathmandu
2014	Pro-Hindu Bharatiya Janata Party coalition forms government in India

Map 7.1 Hinduism

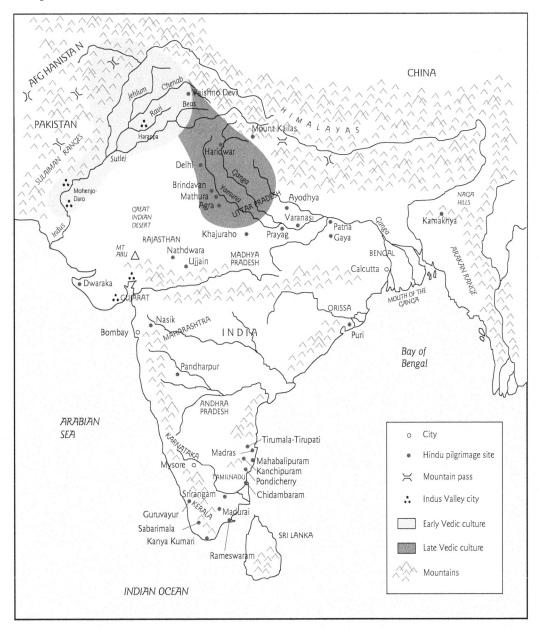

Source: Adapted from Nielsen et al. 1993: 85.

between some Indian and European languages in both grammar and vocabulary. Based on this evidence, many scholars believe that the Indo-Europeans originated in Central Asia and that their migration to the subcontinent began around 2000 BCE. Others think they originated in the region of modern Turkey and began spreading out from there as much as 4,000 years earlier.

Yet another school of thought holds that Indo-Europeans originated on the Indian subcontinent itself. Proponents of this theory base their arguments on astronomical data and evidence concerning a great river that they identify as the legendary Sarasvati. According to the ancient Hindu text known as the *Rig Veda*, the Sarasvati had five Aryan tribes living on its banks, yet geological evidence shows that it was dry by the time the Aryans were supposed to have entered India (c. 1750 BCE). If the Aryans were actually there before the Sarasvati dried up, their dates must be pushed back at least as far as the time of the Harappan civilization.

None of the evidence is conclusive, and some theories on the origins of the Indo-Europeans have been motivated by political, racial, religious, and nationalist agendas. What we do know is that the Indo-Europeans composed many poems and, eventually, manuals on rituals and philosophy. They committed these traditions to memory and passed them from generation to generation orally.

The Vedas

The Vedas (from the Sanskrit for "knowledge") are the works collectively known as *shruti* ("that which was heard"). The Vedic *rishis* "saw" the mantras and transmitted them to their disciples, starting an oral tradition that has continued to the present.

Traditionally regarded as revealed scripture, the Vedas are now generally thought to have been composed between roughly 1500 BCE (possibly 1750 BCE) and 600 BCE. There are four Vedic collections: *Rig*, *Sama*, *Yajur*, and *Atharva*. Each of these consists of four sections: hymns (*Samhitas*; the earliest parts), directions for the performance of sacred rituals (**Brahmanas**), "compositions for the forest" (*Aranyakas*), and philosophical works called the **Upanishads** ("sitting near [the teacher]").

The earliest section of the *Rig Veda* contains 1,028 hymns. The hymns of the *Sama Veda* and *Yajur Veda* are largely borrowed from the *Rig*, and the *Sama Veda* was meant to be sung. The *Upanishads* are the most recent sections of each collection, composed around 600 BCE. The *Atharva Veda* differs from the other three in that it includes material used for purposes other than sacrificial rituals, such as incantations and remedies to ward off illness and evil spirits; one verse (7.38) refers to the use of herbs to make a lover return, and another (7.50) requests luck in gambling. Although for Hindus "Vedas" denotes the whole corpus, some Western scholars have used "Veda" only for the hymns portion of each collection.

The Status of the Vedas

Almost all educated Hindus would describe the Vedas as their most sacred texts, yet most would be hard pressed to describe their contents. The Vedas are not books that people keep in their homes. A few Vedic hymns are recited regularly, and the philosophical sections have often been commented on, but the rest of the contents are known only to a handful of ritual specialists and Sanskrit scholars. The Vedas are particularly significant to the brahmins—the class that historically considered itself the "highest" in Hindu society—who reserved for themselves the authority to teach them. Though members of two other classes were technically "allowed" to study the Vedas, in time this privilege was lost, or in some cases, abandoned.

Historically, the Vedas were treated as "revealed" scripture, though the source of the revelation was not necessarily considered to be a deity. All medieval schools agreed that the Vedas have a transcendental aspect and an authoritative nature. Where they differed was on the question of their origin. The Nyaya ("logic") school of philosophy believed that the Vedas were composed by God, but others, such as the Mimamsa and Vedanta schools, held that they are eternal, coeval with God.

As the supreme source of knowledge, the Vedas have served as manuals of ritual for all Hindu traditions, and some sections have been passed down without major changes for more than 2,000 years. Interpretations have not been static, however. In every generation, specialists have worked to make the texts' messages relevant to the particular time and place.

The highest honor that can be given to any Hindu religious text is to describe it as another "Veda." Among the works that have been accorded this title are the epic **Mahabharata**; Bharata's *Natya Sastra*, a treatise on dance and performance composed around the beginning of the Common Era; and a number of Tamil-language compositions from South India, especially the *Tiruvaymoli* ("sacred utterance") of Nammalvar (ninth century) and the *Periya Puranam* (twelfth century), a collection of the life stories of saints who were devotees of Shiva. These texts made no attempt either to imitate the Vedas or to comment on them. They are called "Vedas" only because they reflect the wisdom which adherents believe to be embodied in the original Vedas, and making their eternal truth relevant to a new place and time.

The Vedic Hymns

The figures who were to become the principal Hindu deities—goddesses like Lakshmi and gods like Narayana (Vishnu)—are rarely mentioned in the *samhitas*; only the later Vedic hymns address them directly. Rather, the earliest hymns of the Vedas speak of deities who were later superseded, and many of the stories they allude to would not be familiar to most Hindus today.

Indra, for instance, was a warrior god who battled other cosmic powers. Agni was the god of fire who served as a messenger, carrying to the deities the offerings that humans placed in the sacrificial fire for them. Soma was the name of a god identified with the moon, but also of a plant-based elixir used for ritual purposes. Sarasvati was a goddess described in the *Rig Veda* as beautiful and fortunate, the inspirer of noble thoughts. By the time the *Brahmanas* were composed, Sarasvati had taken over the attributes formerly associated with the goddess Vac ("speech"). Now Sarasvati is viewed as speech incarnate, the power of the word, and the mother of the Vedas.

The early hymns typically offer praise to the gods; thus, the river Indus is praised for giving cattle, children, horses, and food. But many of them also include petitions—not for salvation or eternal bliss (in fact, the idea of an afterlife is rarely mentioned), but for a good and happy life on this earth.

One of the dominant features of Vedic religious life was the ritual sacrifice, typically performed using fire. Whether they took the form of simple domestic affairs or elaborate community events, these sacrifices were conducted by ritual specialists and priests. A connection was understood to exist between the rituals and the maintenance of cosmic and earthly order, or *rta*: truth and justice, the rightness of things that makes harmony and peace possible on earth and in the heavens. A number of hymns composed around 1000 BCE speculate on the origins of life. "The Creation Hymn" (see Document box) expresses wonder at the creation of the universe from nothing and suggests that perhaps no one knows how it all came to be.

Another account, however, describes how the universe itself was created through the cosmic sacrifice of the primeval man (*Purusha*). This account, the "Hymn to the Supreme Person," has figured continuously in the Hindu tradition for some 3,000 years. Straining to capture infinity in

Document

The Creation Hymn, *Rig Veda* 10.129

There was neither non-existence nor existence then; there was neither the realm of space nor the sky which is beyond. What stirred? Where? In whose protection? Was there water, bottomlessly deep?

There was neither death nor immortality then. There was no distinguishing sign of night nor of day. That one breathed, windless, by its own impulse. Other than that there was nothing beyond.

Darkness was hidden by darkness in the beginning; with no distinguishing sign, all this was water. The life force that was covered with emptiness, that one arose through the power of heat.

Desire came upon that one in the beginning; that was the first seed of mind. Poets seeking in their heart with wisdom found the bond of existence in non-existence.

Their cord was extended across. Was there below? Was there above? There were seed-placers; there were powers. There was impulse beneath; there was giving-forth above.

Who really knows? Who will here proclaim it? Whence was it produced? Whence is this creation? The gods came afterwards, with the creation of this universe. Who then knows whence it has arisen?

Whence this creation has arisen—perhaps it formed itself, or perhaps it did not—the one who looks down on it, in the highest heaven, only he knows—or perhaps he does not know. (Doniger O'Flaherty 1981: 25–26)

words, the composer uses the notion of "a thousand" to evoke what cannot be measured or perhaps even imagined:

> The cosmic person has a thousand heads
> a thousand eyes and feet
> It covers the earth on all sides
> and extends ten finger-lengths beyond
> The cosmic person is everything
> all that has been and will be. . . . (1–2)

Various elements of the universe are said to have arisen from this sacrifice:

> From his mind came the moon
> from his eye, the sun
> Indra and Agni from his mouth
> the wind came from his breath.
> From his navel came space
> from his head, the sky
> from his feet, earth;
> from his ears, the four directions
> thus the worlds were created. (13–14)

In this context an idea is introduced that would change forever the religious and social framework of the Hindu tradition:

> From his mouth came the priestly class
> from his arms, the rulers.
> The producers came from his legs;
> from his feet came the servant class. (12)

Thus the origins of the four classes (*varnas*) of Hindu society are traced to the initial cosmic sacrifice. Although this verse is the first explicit reference to what came to be called the caste system, it is likely that the stratification of society had taken place long before the *Rig Veda* was composed.

The Upanishads

By the time of the *Aranyakas* and *Upanishads*, in the seventh and sixth centuries BCE, the early Vedic emphasis on placating the gods through ritual sacrifice had given way to critical philosophical inquiry. This period, around the time of Shakyamuni Buddha and the Jaina teacher Mahavira, was one of questioning authoritarian structures. Yet the *Upanishads* do not totally reject the early hymns and sacrificial rituals. Instead, they rethink and reformulate them. Thus some rituals are interpreted allegorically, and the symbolic structures of the sacrifices are analyzed in some detail. Most of the *Upanishads* take the form of conversations—between a teacher and a student, between a husband and wife, or between fellow philosophers.

Karma and Samsara

It is in the *Upanishads* that we find the earliest discussions of several concepts central to the later Hindu tradition, among them the concept of **karma**. The literal meaning of "karma" is "action," especially ritual action, but in these texts the word eventually comes to refer to the rewards and punishments attached to various actions. It is understood that this system of cause and effect may require several lifetimes to work out. Thus the concept of karma implies a continuing cycle of death and rebirth or reincarnation called **samsara**. To achieve liberation (**moksha**) from this cycle, according to the *Upanishads*, requires the attainment of a transforming wisdom. Those who acquire that wisdom become immortal.

A frequent theme of the *Upanishads* is the quest for a unifying truth. This "higher" knowledge is clearly distinguished from the "lower" knowledge that can be conceptualized and expressed in words. Its nature cannot be taught; it can only be evoked, as in this question posed by the seeker in the *Mundaka Upanishad*: "What is it that, being known, all else becomes known?" (1.1.3). The *Brihadaranyaka Upanishad* of the *Yajur Veda* reflects the quest for enlightenment in these lines:

> Lead me from the unreal to reality
> Lead me from darkness to light
> Lead me from death to immortality
> Om, let there be peace, peace, peace.

Significantly, in works from later centuries the "higher wisdom" is not connected with any Vedic or book learning or conceptual knowledge. It is only through the experience of enlightenment that one is freed from the birth-and-death cycle.

Atman and Brahman

At the heart of that higher wisdom is experiential knowledge of the relationship between the human soul (**Atman**) and the Supreme Being (**Brahman**). Brahman pervades and at the same time transcends not only human thought but the universe itself. To know Brahman is to enter a new state of consciousness. The *Taittiriya Upanishad* associates Brahman with existence or truth, knowledge, infinity, consciousness, and bliss; elsewhere Brahman is described as the hidden, inner controller of the human soul.

Many passages of the *Upanishads* discuss the relationship between Atman and Brahman, but invariably they suggest rather than specify the connection between the two. In a famous passage of the *Chandogya Upanishad*, a father has his son dissolve salt in water and tells him that Brahman and Atman are united in the same way. The father ends this lesson with a famous dictum—*tat tvam*

Stone shrine (c. 1500 CE), modeled after a wooden processional chariot, in the Vitthala (Vishnu) temple complex in Hampi, northern Karnataka. The two elephants pulling the chariot date from a later time (© Vasudha Narayanan).

asi ("you are that")—in which "that" refers to Brahman and "you" to Atman. More than 1,000 years later, philosophers were still differing in their interpretations of this passage.

Women in the Vedas

Ghosa, Apala, and Lopamudra are all female poets named in the early part of the Vedas. The *Upanishads* also identify a number of women who participated in the quest for ultimate truth and sought salvific knowledge in both domestic and public forums. In the *Brihadaranyaka Upanishad*, for instance, Maitreyi, the wife of the sage Yajnavalkya, questions him in depth about the nature of reality, and a woman philosopher named Gargi Vachaknavi challenges a scholar with the same name in a public debate. When he does not answer to her satisfaction, Gargi presses her question, and eventually she pronounces a judgment about him to her fellow philosophers, saying that he is indeed wise. Apparently Gargi and Maitreyi were honored and respected for their wisdom, as were dozens of other women whose names appear in the *Upanishads* and elsewhere in the Vedas.

These women were possibly among the teachers through whom the sacred knowledge was transmitted. While the fathers of the teachers listed in the *Upanishads* are frequently named, in some cases the teachers are identified as the sons of particular women. In the *Brihadaranyaka Upanishad* (VI.5.1) roughly 45 teachers are listed with their mothers' names instead of their fathers'. So, while it is clear that a male spiritual lineage was generally accepted in the early centuries of the Hindu tradition (after all, it is the male teachers who are named), it is possible that some teachers received spiritual instruction from their mothers as well.

Document

How Many Gods Are There?

Vidagdha Shakalyah asked: "Yajnavalkya, how many gods are there?"

He answered . . . in line with the formulaic [mantra], ". . . three hundred and three, and three and three thousand."

"Yes, but Yajnavalkya, how many gods are there, really?"

"Thirty-three."

"Yes, but really, how many gods are there, Yajnavalkya?"

"Six."

"Yes, but really, how many gods are there, Yajnavalkya?"

"Three." . . .

"Yes, but really, how many gods are there, Yajnavalkya?"

"One and a half."

"Yes, but really, how many gods are there, Yajnavalkya?"

"One."

"Yes, but who are those three hundred and three and three thousand and three?"

"They are but the powers of the gods; there are only thirty-three gods." (*Brihadaranyaka Upanishad* 3.9.1–2; trans. Vasudha Narayanan)

⊕ Classical Hinduism

The literature that was composed after the Vedas, starting around 500 BCE, was recognized to be of human origin and was loosely called **smrti** ("that which is remembered"). Though theoretically less authoritative than the "revealed" shruti, this material was still considered inspired, and it has played a far more important role in the lives of Hindus. Several kinds of text are classified as *smrti*: epics (*itihasas*), ancient stories (**Puranas**), and codes of law and ethics (*dharmashastras*).

For many Hindus the phrase "sacred books" refers specifically to the **Ramayana** ("Story of Rama") and the *Mahabharata* ("Great [Epic of] India" or "Great [Sons of] Bharata"). The best-known works in the Hindu tradition, these epic tales invariably constitute children's first and most lasting encounter with Hindu scripture.

The *Ramayana*

The *Ramayana* has been memorized, recited, sung, and performed on stage, often in dance, for 2,500 years. Its hero is the young prince Rama, whose father, Dasaratha, has decided to abdicate in favor of his son. On the eve of the coronation, however, a heartbroken Dasaratha is forced to exile Rama because of an earlier promise made to one of his wives. Rama accepts this order cheerfully and leaves for the forest, accompanied by his beautiful wife, Sita, and his half-brother Lakshmana, who both refuse to be separated from him. Bharata, the brother who has now been named king, returns from a trip to discover that Rama has gone into exile and his father has died of grief. He finds Rama and begs him to return, but Rama refuses because he feels he must respect his father's decision to banish him. He asks Bharata to rule as his regent.

While in the forest, Sita is captured by Ravana, the demon king of Lanka. Rama sets out to search for her with the aid of his brother and a group of monkeys led by Hanuman, a monkey with divine ancestry. It is Hanuman who finds Sita and reports her whereabouts to Rama, who, with the monkeys' help, goes to war with Ravana. After a long battle, Rama kills Ravana and is reunited with Sita. They eventually return to the capital and are crowned. Rama is considered the ideal son, husband, and king, and in later centuries he came to be seen as an incarnation of Vishnu. Sita too has been idealized both for her own qualities and for her relationship with her husband. In a sequel to the *Ramayana*, however, Rama's subjects become suspicious about Sita's virtue following her captivity by Ravana. Because there is no way to prove her innocence, and possibly because he does not want to create a legal precedent for excusing a wife who has slept outside her husband's home, Rama banishes his own wife, who by now is pregnant.

The exiled Sita gives birth to twin sons. Some years later, the twins prepare to meet Rama in battle, and it is then that Sita tells them that he is their father. There is a brief reunion. Rama asks Sita to prove her innocence in public by undergoing some ordeal, but Sita refuses and asks Mother Earth to take her back. She is then swallowed up by the ground.

Many Hindus have considered Sita the ideal wife because she follows her husband to the forest. Others see her as a model of strength and virtue in her own right. She complies with her husband as he does with her; their love is one worthy of emulation. Yet she is also a woman who stands her ground when her husband asks her to prove her virtue. On one occasion, in Lanka, she acquiesces to his request, but the second time he makes it she gently but firmly refuses and so rules out any possibility of reunion. The tale has sometimes been retold from Sita's viewpoint under the title *Sitayana*. Temples dedicated to Rama and Sita are found in many parts of the world.

The *Mahabharata* and the *Bhagavad Gita*

With approximately 100,000 verses, the *Mahabharata* is said to be the longest poem in the world. It is not found in many homes, but many people own copies of an extract from it called the **Bhagavad Gita**.

The *Mahabharata* is the story of the great struggle among the descendants of a king named Bharata. The main part of the story concerns a war between two families, the Pandavas and the Kauravas. Though they are cousins, the Kauravas try to cheat the Pandavas out of their share of the kingdom and will not accept peace. A battle ensues in which all the major kingdoms are forced to take sides. Krishna, by this time considered to be an incarnation of the god Vishnu, is on the side of the Pandavas. He refuses to fight directly in the battle but agrees to serve as charioteer for the warrior Arjuna, who would come to be seen as representing the human soul in quest of liberation.

Just as the war is about to begin, Arjuna, who has won several battles, puts down his bow and asks Krishna whether it is correct to take up arms against one's own kin. Krishna replies that it is correct to fight for what is right; peaceful means must be tried to resolve a conflict, but if they fail one must fight for righteousness ("dharma"). The conversation between Arjuna and Krishna, which unfolds across 18 chapters, constitutes the *Bhagavad Gita*.

The *Gita* teaches both loving devotion to Krishna and the importance of selfless action. It was probably written sometime between 200 BCE and 200 CE, and for centuries people learned it by heart. In verses that are still recited at Hindu funerals, Krishna describes the soul as existing beyond the reach of the mind and the senses, unaffected by physical nature. Just as human beings exchange old clothes for new ones, so the human soul discards one body and puts on another again and again through the ages, until it acquires the knowledge that will free it forever from the cycle of birth and death.

Thus Arjuna is told not to grieve at what is about to take place, but he is also warned that if he does not fight for righteousness, he will be guilty of moral cowardice and will have to face the consequences of quitting at a time when it was his duty (dharma) to protect the people by waging a just war.

Krishna also makes several statements about himself in the *Gita* that mark an important shift in Hindu theology. The *Upanishads* present the Supreme Being, Brahman, as beyond human conceptualization, but in the *Gita* Krishna speaks of himself as both a personal god, one so filled with love for human beings that he will incarnate himself to protect them, and the ultimate deity, the creator, maintainer, and destroyer of the universe.

The Three Ways to Liberation

In the course of the *Gita*, Krishna describes three ways to liberation from the cycle of birth and death: the way of action, the way of knowledge, and the way of devotion. Some Hindus, however, would argue that they are three aspects of the same way. Each way (*marga*) is also a discipline (*yoga*).

The way of action (*karma yoga*) is the path of unselfish duty, performed neither in fear of punishment nor in hope of reward. To expect a reward will lead to bondage and unhappiness, since even if we do receive it, we will not be satisfied for long. Soon that goal will be replaced with another, leading to further action—and further accumulation of karma, which only leads to further rebirth. Other books of the time taught that even the "good" karma acquired by performing good deeds is ultimately bad, because to enjoy it we must be reborn. Therefore Krishna urges Arjuna to act without attachment to the consequences.

Document

From the *Bhagavad Gita*

On the immortality of the soul:

Our bodies are known to end, but the embodied self
    is enduring, indestructible, and immeasurable;
    therefore, Arjuna, fight the battle!

He who thinks this self a killer and he who thinks
    it killed, both fail to understand it does not kill,
    nor is it killed.

It is not born, it does not die; having been, it will never
    not be; unborn, enduring, constant, and primor-
    dial, it is not killed when the body is killed. . . .

As a man discards worn-out clothes to put on new
    and different ones, so the embodied self discards
    its worn-out bodies to take on other new ones.

Weapons do not cut it, fire does not burn it, waters
    do not wet it, wind does not wither it. It cannot
    be cut or burned; it cannot be wet or withered; it
    is enduring, all-pervasive, fixed, immovable, and
    timeless. . . .

On the way of action:

Be intent on action, not on the fruits of action; avoid
    attraction to the fruits and attachment to inaction!

Perform actions, firm in discipline, relinquishing at-
    tachment; be impartial to failure and success—
    this equanimity is called discipline. . . .

When he shows no preference in fortune or misfor-
    tune and neither exults nor hates, his insight is
    sure. . . .

On the mystery and purpose of avatara or incarnation:

Whenever sacred duty decays and chaos prevails,
    then, I create myself, Arjuna.

To protect men of virtue and destroy men who do
    evil to set the standard of sacred duty, I appear
    in age after age. . . .

On the nature of God and the way of devotion:

Always glorifying me, striving, firm in their vows,
    paying me homage with devotion, they worship
    me, always disciplined. . . .

I am the universal father, mother, granter of all,
    grandfather, object of knowledge, purifier, holy
    syllable OM, threefold sacred love.

I am the way, sustainer, lord, witness, shelter, refuge,
    friend, source, dissolution, stability, treasure,
    and unchanging seed.

I am heat that withholds and sends down the rains;
    I am immortality and death; both being and
    non-being am I. . . .

The leaf or flower or fruit or water that he offers with
    devotion, I take from the man of self-restraint in
    response to his devotion.

Whatever you do—what you take, what you offer,
    what you give, what penances you perform—do
    as an offering to me, Arjuna!

You will be freed from the bonds of action, from the
    fruit of fortune and misfortune; armed with the
    discipline of renunciation, yourself liberated,
    you will join me. . . .

Keep me in your mind and devotion, sacrifice to me,
    bow to me, discipline yourself toward me, and
    you will reach me! (Miller 1986: 32–87)

Krishna also explains the second path to liberation, the way of knowledge (*jnana yoga*), through
which we may achieve a transforming wisdom that also destroys our past karma. True knowledge
is insight into the real nature of the universe. Later philosophers said that when we hear scripture,
ask questions, clarify doubts, and eventually meditate on this knowledge, we achieve liberation.

The third way—the one emphasized most throughout the *Gita*—is the way of devotion (*bhakti yoga*). If there is a general amnesty offered to those who sin, it is through devotion. Ultimately, Krishna promises that he will forgive all our sins if we surrender and devote ourselves to him (*Gita* 18:66).

The Deities of Classical Hinduism

The period of the Gupta Empire (c. 320–540) was one of great cultural and scholarly activity. Contact with Greek and Roman trade missions from the Mediterranean increased, and coastal towns flourished, particularly in southern India. Meanwhile, Hindus, Jainas, and Buddhists all composed poems and plays that reveal a great deal about the religious life of the time.

Hinduism had not been dormant during the previous seven centuries, but it had been overshadowed to some degree by Buddhism. Now, under the Guptas, Buddhist influences receded and Hindu sectarian traditions became popular. Eventually, some Hindu texts would even assimilate the Buddha as an incarnation of Vishnu.

Precisely when the transition occurred is not clear, but from the Gupta era onward three deities become increasingly prominent: Vishnu, Shiva, and Shiva's consort, variously known as Parvati, Durga, Devi, or simply "the Goddess." Devotees who give primacy to Vishnu are termed Vaishnavas; those who focus on Shiva are termed Shaivas; and some followers of the Goddess are called Shaktas, in reference to her role as the *shakti* ("power") of her divine consort.

Starting around 300 BCE and continuing until roughly 1000 CE, texts called the *Puranas* (from the Sanskrit for "old") retold the "old tales" of the Hindu tradition, shifting the emphasis away from the major Vedic gods and goddesses in favor of other deities. As these gods moved to the forefront, the Hindu tradition as we know it today crystallized.

Vishnu

Vishnu ("the all-pervasive one") is portrayed as coming to earth in various forms, animal and human, to rid the world of evil and establish dharma or righteousness. In the first of these incarnations (**avataras**) he appears as a fish who saves Manu, the primeval man. This story was originally part of the Vedic literature but is expanded in the *Puranas*.

While bathing in a lake, Manu finds a small fish in his hand. The fish speaks to him and asks him to take it home and put it in a jar. The next day it has expanded to fill the jar. Now Manu is asked to put the fish into a lake, which it outgrows, then into a river, and finally into the ocean. The fish, who is really Vishnu, then tells Manu that a great flood is coming, and that he must build a boat and put his family in it, along with the seven sages, or *rishis*, and "the seeds of all the animals." Manu does as he is told, and when the flood sweeps the earth, those on the ship survive. This story is strongly reminiscent of flood myths in other religious traditions.

Eventually, Hindus believe that Vishnu will have 10 incarnations in the present cycle of creation. Nine are said to have taken place already, and the tenth is expected to occur at the end of this age. Some of the earliest carvings in India, in the Udayagiri caves of Madhya Pradesh, dated to around 400 CE, depict Vishnu's second and third incarnations, as a tortoise and as a boar who saved the earth goddess Bhu. His seventh incarnation was Rama, the hero of the epic, and according to some narratives the ninth was Krishna, whom we have already met in the *Bhagavad Gita*. The *Puranas* tell many stories about Krishna: the delightful infant, the mischievous toddler who steals

The Hindola Torana at Gyaraspur, Madhya Pradesh, dates from the tenth or eleventh century and was probably a gateway to a temple. The 10 incarnations of Vishnu are carved on the pillars. Gyaraspur is near the famous Buddhist Sanchi stupa and Udayagiri, the site of a fifth-century Gupta-era temple complex (© Vasudha Narayanan).

the butter he loves, and the youth who steals the hearts of the cowherd girls and dances away the moonlit nights in their company. Some of the later *Puranas* celebrate the love of Krishna and his beloved Radha.

In many other incarnations Vishnu is accompanied by his consort Sri (Lakshmi), the goddess of good fortune, who blesses her worshipers not only with wealth but, eventually, with liberation. All stores display pictures of her, and so do most homes.

Shiva

Like Vishnu, Shiva emerged as a great god in the post-Upanishadic era. Unlike Vishnu, however, he does not reveal himself sequentially, in a series of incarnations. Instead, Shiva expresses the manifold aspects of his power by appearing simultaneously in paradoxical roles: as creator and

Vishnu in his boar incarnation, saving the earth goddess Bhu from the demon Hiranyaksha. This depiction was found in the Udayagiri caves, Madhya Pradesh, India, and dates to c. 401 CE (© Vasudha Narayanan).

destroyer, exuberant dancer and austere yogi. The wedding portrait of Shiva and his divine consort, Parvati, is an important part of his tradition, and his creative energy is often represented in the symbolic form of a **linga**, an upright stone shaft placed in a receptacle, *yoni*, that symbolizes the womb. Stories of Shiva and his local manifestations—for instance, as Sundaresvara in the city of Madurai—are popular throughout India.

The Goddess

The great Goddess also appears in multiple forms, although the lines between them are not always clearly defined. Though many goddesses appear in the Vedas, none of them are conceived as all-powerful. Likewise, the epics and the early *Puranas* honor many consort goddesses, but no supreme female deity. It is only in the later *Puranas* that we begin to see explicit references to worship of a goddess as the ultimate power, the creator of the universe, and the redeemer of human beings. In these stories she is sometimes considered to be the *shakti*, or power, of Shiva, but often her independence from the male deity is emphasized.

The most familiar manifestation of the Goddess is as Parvati, the wife of Shiva. Durga is her warrior aspect, represented iconographically with a smiling countenance and a handful of weapons. As Kali, the Goddess is fierce and wild, a dark, disheveled figure who wears a garland of skulls, yet even in this manifestation, her devotees call her "mother." In addition there are countless local goddesses with distinctive names and histories. Festivals like the autumn celebration of **Navaratri** ("nine nights") are dedicated to the Goddess, and millions of Hindus offer her devotions every day.

An image of the Hindu goddess Sarasvati outside the Indonesian embassy in Washington, DC. Indonesia is the country with the largest Muslim population (© Vasudha Narayanan).

Sarasvati

In the *Puranas* the Vedic goddess Sarasvati becomes the goddess of learning. Although she is the consort of a creator god named **Brahma** (a minor deity, not to be confused with Brahman), portraits usually depict her alone, without any male god. In these representations she is a beautiful young woman, radiant with wisdom, sitting gracefully on a rock beside a river. She has four hands; two of them hold a stringed musical instrument called a *vina*, another holds a string of beads, and the last holds a manuscript. The *vina* symbolizes music and the manuscript learning, while the beads signify the counting and recitation of holy names, which is thought to lead to transformative knowledge. All these themes would eventually coalesce to form the composite picture of Sarasvati as the patron goddess of arts and education, music and letters.

Other Popular Deities

Ganesha, the elephant-headed son of Shiva and Parvati, is probably the most beloved of all the Hindu gods. He removes obstacles and hindrances, and no new project or venture begins without a prayer to him. Murugan, another son of Shiva, is popular among Tamil-speaking people in India, Sri Lanka, Malaysia, and Canada. And the monkey god Hanuman, a model devotee of Rama and Sita, is everyone's protector.

In South India, Vishnu, Shiva, and Devi are frequently known by local names. Thus Vishnu is known in the Tirupati hills and Srirangam as Venkateshwara ("Lord of the Venkata hill") or Ranganatha ("Lord of the stage"). Each manifestation has both a unique personality and a mythical history that links it with a particular place. Sri or Lakshmi is called the mother of all

A Ganesha image for the digital age shows the dynamism of the Hindu tradition (© Vasudha Narayanan).

creation, who bestows wisdom and salvation and is grace incarnate. Many teachers have composed hymns celebrating her compassion and wisdom.

The Hindu "Trinity"

In the symbolism of *trimurti* ("three forms"), the gods Brahma, Vishnu, and Shiva either coalesce into one form with three faces or are represented as equal. This has sometimes been interpreted as implying a polytheistic belief in three gods: Brahma the creator, Vishnu the preserver, and Shiva the destroyer. It is true that the *trimurti* concept brings together the three great functions of a supreme god and distributes them among three distinct deities. But this interpretation is misleading in two ways.

First, it suggests that Hindus give equal importance to all three gods, when in practice most focus their devotions on a single supreme deity (whether Shiva, Vishnu, the Goddess, or a local deity who may be unknown in other parts of India) and consider the other deities secondary. Furthermore, Brahma is not worshiped as a supreme deity. Though portrayed in mythology as the creator god, he is only the agent of the supreme deity who created him; that deity, at whose pleasure Brahma creates the universe, may be Vishnu, Shiva, or the Goddess, depending on the worshiper's sect.

Second, the "polytheistic" interpretation of *trimurti* suggests that creation, preservation, and destruction are functions that can be performed separately. But in fact these functions are seen as three parts of an integrated process for which one particular supreme god is responsible. In this context, destruction is neither unplanned nor final; rather, it is simply one phase in the ongoing evolution and devolution of the universe. The cycle of creation will continue as long as there are souls caught up in the wheel of life and death. It is in this sense that devotees of Shiva, Vishnu, or the Goddess see their chosen deity as the creator, maintainer, and destroyer of the universe.

Ages of Time

The *Puranas* refer to the cosmic cycles of creation and destruction as the days and nights of Brahma. Each day of Brahma contains approximately 4,320 million earthly years, and the nights of Brahma are equally long. A year of Brahma is made up of 360 such days, and Brahma lives for 100 years. Each cycle therefore amounts to 311,040,000 million earthly years, at the end of which the entire cosmos is drawn into the body of Vishnu or Shiva (depending on which *Purana* one is reading), where it remains until another Brahma is evolved.

Each day of Brahma contains 14 secondary cycles of creation and destruction called *manavantaras*, each of which lasts 306,720,000 years. During the long intervals between *manavantaras*, the world is re-created and a new Manu, or primeval man, appears and once again begins the human race.

Each *manavantara* in turn contains 71 great eons (*maha yugas*), each of which is divided into four eons (*yugas*). A single eon is the basic cycle. The golden age (*krta yuga*) lasts 1,728,000 earthly years. During this time dharma, or righteousness, is envisioned as a bull standing firmly on all four legs. The Treta age is shorter, 1,296,000 earthly years; dharma is then on three legs. The Dvapara age lasts half as long as the golden age; thus, for 864,000 earthly years dharma hops on two legs. Finally, during the *kali yuga*, the worst of all possible ages, dharma is reduced to one leg. This age lasts for 432,000 earthly years, during which the world becomes progressively worse. It is in this degenerate *kali yuga*—which, according to traditional Hindu reckoning, began around 3102 BCE—that we live today.

There is a steady decline in morality, life span, and human satisfaction throughout the *yugas*. At the end of the *kali yuga*—which is still a long time off—there will be no righteousness, no virtue, no justice. When the world ends, seven scorching suns will dry up the oceans, torrential rains will fall, and eventually the cosmos will be absorbed into Vishnu until the next cycle of creation begins. The *Puranas* deal with astronomical units of time; the age of the earth itself is infinitesimally small in relation to the eons of time that the universe goes through. Individual beings may end their own cycles of birth and death by attaining *moksha*, but this has no effect on the cycles of creation and destruction of the universe.

Temple architecture sometimes reflects the Puranic cycles of time. At the great Vishnu temple of Angkor Wat in Cambodia, for instance, the causeways and passages were designed so that their measurements (when calculated in the units used in the building of the temple) represent the numbers of years in various cycles of time.

Caste and the *Laws of Manu*

"Caste" is a shorthand for the thousands of social and occupational divisions that have developed from the simple fourfold structure laid out in the "Hymn to the Supreme Person": priests, rulers, merchants, and servants. There are more than 1,000 *jatis* ("birth groups") in India, and people routinely identify themselves by their *jati*. Ritual practices, dietary rules, and sometimes dialects differ between castes, and intercaste marriage is rare.

By the early Common Era, many treatises had been written regarding the nature of righteousness, moral duty, and law. These *dharmashastras* became the foundations of later Hindu laws. The most famous is the *Manava Dharmashastra* ("Laws of Manu"), which probably dates from around the first century. These "laws" were probably codified around the first century, for they reflect the social norms of that time; in them, the caste system is firmly in place, and women have slipped to an inferior position from the relatively high status they enjoyed in the period of the Vedas. When reading this text, it is important to understand that in many parts of India the rules it laid down were not followed strictly. It is also important to take its pronouncements on women with a grain of salt.

The *dharmashastras* set out the roles and duties of the four principal castes that make up Hindu society: **brahmins** (priests), **kshatriyas** (rulers, warriors), **vaishyas** (merchants), and **shudras** (servants). The brahmins were (and are still) the priestly class, the only group in Hindu society supposedly authorized to teach the Vedas. Although not all members of the brahmin community were priests, all enjoyed the power and prestige associated with spiritual learning.

The dharma of the kshatriya class, which was permitted to study the Vedas but not to teach them, was to protect the people and the country. In the Hindu tradition, lines of descent are all-important. Thus many kings sought to confirm their legitimacy by tracing their ancestry to the primeval progenitors of humanity—either the sun or the moon—and even usurpers of thrones invoked divine antecedents. Later Hindu rituals explicitly emphasized kshatriya families' divine connections. The *Laws of Manu* describe in detail the duties of a king. He must strive to conquer his senses, for only those who have conquered their own senses can lead or control others, and he must shun not only the vices of pleasure—hunting, gambling, drinking, women—but also the vices of wrath, such as violence, envy, and slander.

The dharma of the vaishya (mercantile) class made them responsible for most commercial transactions, as well as agriculture. The power of wealth and economic decisions lay with the vaishyas, who were likewise permitted only to study the Vedas.

The duty of the last class mentioned formally in the *dharmashastras*, the shudras, was to serve the other classes; they would not be permitted to accumulate wealth even if they had the opportunity to do so. As the *Laws of Manu* put it, "The seniority of brahmins comes from sacred knowledge, that of kshatriyas from valor, vaishyas from wealth, and shudras, only from old age."

In practice, however, the caste system was far more complex and flexible than the *dharmashastras* suggest. For example, the Vellalas of South India wielded considerable economic and political power, even though the brahmins considered them shudras. They were wealthy landowners, and the *dharmashastra* prohibitions do not seem to have had any effect on their fortunes.

Although they emphasized the importance of marrying within one's own class, the *dharmashastras* recognized that mixed marriages did take place, and so they listed the kind of subcastes that could emerge from various permutations. A marriage was generally acceptable if the male partner was of a higher caste, but if the woman's caste was higher, their offspring were considered to be of a lower caste than either parent.

Also part of India's social fabric were various "out-castes": groups officially excluded from the caste system either because they originated in mixed marriages in the distant past or, more often, because they were associated with occupations deemed polluting, such as dealing with corpses or working with animal hides.

Until the nineteenth century, caste was only one factor among the many considered in the judicial process and in society itself. Legal cases were decided with reference to the immediate circumstances, and local customs were no less important than written texts—sometimes more so. It was India's British colonial rulers who, assuming that the caste laws were binding, attributed a new authority to them.

The caste system is such a strong social force in India that even non-Hindu communities such as the Christians, Jainas, and Sikhs have been influenced by it. In Southeast Asia, on the other hand, the caste system bears little resemblance to the Indian model: although inscriptions after the eighth century show that brahmins were honored, the rest of society seems to have been organized in different ways, and the king sometimes awarded specific caste status to various groups. The caste system still functions to a limited extent in some diasporas but has been significantly diluted among Hindus in North America.

The Stages and Goals of Life

The dharma texts of the classical period recognized four stages of life (*ashramas*) for males from the three higher classes in society. First, during studenthood, a boy was to remain celibate and concentrate on learning. Education was to be provided for all those who desired it, and families were to support students. Although the early epics suggest that girls could also become students, it is likely that this right had been withdrawn by the time the *Laws of Manu* were codified.

In the next stage the young man was to repay his debts to society and his forefathers, as well as his spiritual debt to the gods, by marrying and earning a living to support his family and other students. It was the householder's duty to work and lead a conjugal life with his partner in dharma. Few men went beyond these two stages, and it is likely that most people never had the opportunity to study at all.

Nevertheless, the *Laws of Manu* describes two more stages. When a man's children had grown and become householders themselves, he and his wife could retire to the forest and live a simple life. Finally, in the last stage, an elderly man would renounce the material world altogether and take up the ascetic life of the *samnyasin*. His former personality was now dead; he owned nothing, relied on food given as alms, and spent the rest of his days seeking enlightenment and cultivating detachment from life. This kind of formal renunciation became rare with the increasing popularity of the *Bhagavad Gita*, which stresses controlled engagement with the world.

The literature of the period just before the beginning of the Common Era also recognized a number of aims for which human beings strive. These are seen as neither good nor bad in themselves, but may become immoral if they are pursued at an inappropriate time of life or with inappropriate intensity. The aims are dharma, the discharging of one's duties; *artha*, prosperity and power; *kama*, sensual pleasure of many types, including sexual pleasure and the appreciation of beauty; and finally *moksha*, or liberation from the cycle of birth and death. The last was sometimes seen as belonging to a different category, but texts like the *Gita* make it clear that humans may strive for liberation even in daily work as long as they act without attachment.

Attitudes Toward Women

The Hindu scriptures were written by men, and many of their statements about women's position in society may seem contradictory, alternately honoring, respecting, and even venerating women, but also scorning them. The *Laws of Manu* make it only too clear that by the early Common Era women no longer enjoyed the relatively high status suggested in the Vedas. Although the text states that a wife is the goddess of fortune and auspiciousness (*Manu* 9.26) and that only if women are honored will the gods be pleased (*Manu* 3.56), it also declares: "Though destitute of virtue, or seeking pleasure elsewhere, or devoid of good qualities, a husband must be constantly worshiped as a god by a faithful wife" (*Manu* 5.154). Male commentators through the centuries have quoted such statements approvingly.

Negative statements on women, and the weight given to them by later commentators, did much to shape Western notions of Hindu women. As influential as *Manu* has been in some communities and at certain times, however, the views it presents cannot be considered prescriptive or normative. In fact, *Manu*'s dictates were not necessarily followed. As we will see, medieval women were more than dutiful wives: they composed poetry, endowed temples, gave religious advice, and wrote scholarly works, including commentary on scripture. Far from being ostracized or condemned, those women were respected, honored, and in some cases even venerated. Despite *Manu* and its proponents, many women of some socioeconomic groups enjoyed both religious and financial independence and made substantial contributions to literature and the fine arts.

Some of the contradictions in Hindu thinking about women can be traced to the concept of auspiciousness. "Auspiciousness" refers primarily to prosperity in this life—above all, wealth and progeny. Thus cattle, elephants, kings, and married women with the potential to bear children are all auspicious, as are birth and marriage rituals, because they are associated with the goals of dharma, *artha*, and *kama*. There is also a second level of auspiciousness, however, that is related to the fourth and ultimate human goal of *moksha*. The two levels of auspiciousness have been implicit in Hindu religious literature and rituals. In many contexts, women have auspiciousness in different degrees, which determines the degree of their acceptance in society.

The ideal is the *sumangali*, the married woman who is a full partner in dharma, *artha*, and *kama*, through whom children are born and wealth and religious merit are accumulated. Only a married woman may be called *Srimati* ("the one with *sri*," or auspiciousness). Traditionally, a Hindu wife's dharma included not only loyalty to her husband in life but fidelity to his memory after his death. While some of these notions are still adhered to in Hindu life, a woman's position in society depends on a variety of factors, including religious culture.

⊕ Schools and Communities of Theology

Vedanta

Six schools of "philosophy" are recognized within the Hindu tradition—Samkhya, Nyaya, Vaisheshika, Mimamsa, Yoga, and Vedanta—and elements of all six can be seen in modern Hinduism. Although popularly called "philosophies," these traditions are closer to theological schools, as they build on many Hindu texts. Yoga has attracted a wide popular following in recent years, but as a philosophical school Vedanta is by far the most important. Although the term "Vedanta" ("end of the Vedas") traditionally denoted the *Upanishads*, in popular usage it more often refers to systems of thought based on a coherent interpretation of the *Upanishads*, *Bhagavad Gita*, and *Brahma Sutras* (roughly 500 aphorisms summarizing the teachings of those texts).

An important early interpreter of Vedanta was Shankara (active. c. 800). For him, reality was nondual (**advaita**): the only reality is Brahman, and this reality cannot be described because it is without attributes. Brahman and Atman (the human soul) are identical; Shankara interpreted the Upanishadic phrase "you are that" literally and upheld the unity of what most people perceived as two distinct entities. Under the influence of *maya* (often translated as "illusion") we believe we are different from Brahman, but when the illusion is dispelled, the soul is liberated by the realization of its true nature. Liberation therefore is the removal of ignorance and the dispelling of illusion through transforming knowledge. We can achieve liberation while still embodied; those who attain that goal act without binding desire and help others to achieve liberation. But final release will come only after the death of the body.

Shankara also posited three levels of reality. He recognized that humans believe life to be real but pointed out that when we are asleep we also believe that what happens in our dreams is real. Only on waking do we discover that what we dreamt was not real. So too in this cycle of life and death do we believe that everything we experience is real. And it is—until we are liberated and wake up to the truth. With the transformative knowledge spoken of in the *Upanishads*, we recognize that we are in reality Brahman and are liberated from the cycle of life and death. But that cycle goes on for the other souls still caught in the snares of *maya*.

Shankara's philosophy was criticized by later philosophers such as Ramanuja and Madhva. One of their principal objections involved the status of *maya*. If *maya* is real, then there are *two* realities, Brahman and *maya*; if *maya* is unreal, it cannot be the cause of the cosmic delusion attributed to it. Shankara himself circumvented this objection, however, by saying that *maya* is indescribable, neither real nor unreal, and his followers would say that in the ultimate state of liberation, which is totally ineffable, such criticisms are not valid in any case.

The most significant interpreter of theistic Vedanta for the Sri Vaishnava community—devotees of Vishnu and his consorts—in South India was Ramanuja (traditionally 1017–1137), who emphasized that devotion to Vishnu leads to ultimate liberation. He challenged Shankara's interpretation of scripture, especially regarding *maya*, and his belief that the supreme reality (Brahman) is without attributes. For Ramanuja, Vishnu (whose name means "all-pervasive") was immanent throughout the universe, pervading all souls and material substances, but also transcending them. Thus from one viewpoint there is a single reality, Brahman, but from another viewpoint Brahman is qualified by souls and matter. Since the human soul is the body and the servant of Brahman, who (according to Ramanuja) is also the supreme deity Vishnu, liberation is portrayed not as the realization that the soul and Brahman are the same, but rather as the intuitive, joyful realization of the soul's relationship with the Lord.

Sri Vaishnavas differ from other Hindus in that they hold sacred not only Sanskrit texts such as the Vedas and *Gita*, but also the Tamil compositions of the **Alvars**, 12 South Indian poet-saints who lived between the eighth and tenth centuries CE. Specifically, the Sri Vaishnavas call the *Tiruvaymoli* of Nammalvar the "Tamil Veda" and refer to their scriptural heritage as dual Vedic theology. They also revere Ramanuja, whose image is found in many of their temples.

The philosopher Madhva (c. 1199–1278) was unique in classifying some souls as eternally bound. For him there were different grades of enjoyment and bliss even in liberation. He was also explicitly dualistic, holding that the human soul and Brahman are ultimately separate, not identical in any way.

The temple tower at Tirukoshtiyur, Tamilnadu. One of the 108 places sung about by the Alvars, this temple was made famous by Ramanuja in the eleventh century CE. After being given a secret mantra that would grant salvation, he is said to have climbed the tower and shouted the mantra aloud so that all the devotees in the area could receive the grace of Vishnu (© Vasudha Narayanan).

Yoga

Historically, "yoga" has had many meanings, but in general it is the physical and mental discipline through which practitioners "yoke" their spirit to the divine. Its origins are obscure, though (as we saw) some scholars have suggested that seals from the Harappan culture portray a man sitting in what looks like a yogic position.

For many Hindus the classic yoga text is a collection of short, aphoristic fragments from the early Common Era called the *Yoga Sutras*, attributed to Patanjali, who is said to have lived in the second century BCE. It's likely that yoga had been an important feature of religious life in India for centuries before the text was written.

Patanjali's yoga was a system of moral, mental, and physical discipline and meditation with a particular object, either physical or mental, as the "single point" of focus. It is described as having eight "limbs" or disciplines. The first of these, *yama*, consists of restraints: avoidance of violence, falsehood, stealing, sexual activity, and avarice. The second, *niyama*, consists of positive practices such as purity (internal and external), equanimity, asceticism, the theoretical study of yoga, and the effort to make God the focus of one's activities. In addition, Patanjali recommended bodily postures and breathing techniques. A crucial aspect of yoga practice is learning to detach the mind from external sensory stimuli. Perfection in concentration (*dharana*) and meditation (*dhyana*) lead to *samadhi*: absorption into and union with the divine, culminating in emancipation from the cycle of life and death.

Although Patanjali's yoga is widely considered the classical form, there are numerous variations. "Yoga" can mean many forms of meditation or practice, or any path that leads to final emancipation. Thus in the *Bhagavad Gita* the way of action is called *karma yoga* and the way of devotion is *bhakti yoga*. In some interpretations, the eight "limbs" of classical yoga are not present; *bhakti yoga* simply comes to mean *bhakti marga*, the way of devotion. In this context yoga becomes a way of self-abnegation, in which the worshiper seeks union with the Supreme Being through passionate devotion. However, few religious teachers have regarded Patanjali's yoga as a separate path to liberation.

Tantra

The term **tantra** refers to a body of ritual practices and the texts interpreting them; it may be derived from a word meaning "to stretch" or "expand." Tantra appears to be independent of the Vedic tradition, having gained importance in both the Hindu and Buddhist traditions around the fifth century. The Shaiva, Shakta, and Vaishnava communities all have their own tantric texts.

Tantra is difficult to define because of its esoteric nature, its regional and sectarian variations, and its mingling with other systems of philosophy and practice. In general, tantric systems have four components: *jnana* (knowledge of the deities and divine powers), *yoga* (practice), *kriya* (practice and rituals), and *charya* (conduct and behavior). Shaivas, Shaktas, and Vaishnavas have all incorporated elements of tantra into their own practice. For example, when an image of a deity is installed in a temple, a large geometric drawing (*yantra* or *mandala*) representing deities and the cosmos is drawn on the floor and used as an object of meditation and ritual. Worship of the deities in temples is to a large extent based on tantric texts and practices. The use of *mantras*—words or short, formulaic phrases that are said to have transformational potency—is also important in the practice of tantra.

Some forms of tantric yoga center on the *shakti*, or power, of the Goddess, which is said to lie coiled like a serpent at the base of the spine. When awakened, this power rises through six chakras, or "wheels," within the body to reach the final chakra (under the skull) known as the thousand-petal lotus. The ultimate aim is to allow this power to unite with the divine being in the thousand-petal lotus. When this union is achieved, the practitioner is granted visions and psychic powers that eventually lead to liberation (*moksha*).

There are many types of tantrism, but the main division is between "left-" and "right-handed" schools. As the left hand is considered inauspicious, the term "left-handed" was applied to tantrism involving the ritual performance of activities forbidden in everyday life, such as drinking liquor, eating fish and meat, and having sexual intercourse with a partner other than one's spouse. "Right-handed" tantrism is more conservative.

Hinduism in Southeast Asia

Hindu culture today is associated almost exclusively with the Indian peninsula, but until the fourteenth century, Hindu influences were strong across Southeast Asia. Extensive trade links between the two regions were established by the second century CE, and cultural connections were widespread. Many Sanskrit inscriptions and thousands of icons and sculptures portraying Hindu deities including Shiva, Brahma, Vishnu, and Ganesha indicate that Hinduism was pervasive in Cambodia, Thailand, Laos, Vietnam, Java, Indonesia, and Bali. One of the largest Hindu temples in the world is Angkor Wat, built and dedicated to Vishnu in the twelfth century, and kings and queens of Cambodia had names reminiscent of Indian–Hindu royalty, including Jayavarman, Indravarman, and Indira-lakshmi.

Even so, Hindu traditions in Southeast Asia have distinctive local characteristics. The Khmer people of Cambodia, for instance, have emphasized some stories that have not been so important in India. And although temples in Cambodia, Laos, and Indonesia are often similar to their Indian counterparts in their basic design, they are strikingly different in effect.

Knowledge of Indian Vaishnava texts, including the two epics, was historically widespread among the elite, and carvings of Vishnu in various incarnations can be found in temples across Southeast Asia. The Prambanan temple near Yogyakarta, Indonesia, is one of many in the region whose walls are carved with scenes from the *Ramayana* and the *Puranas*. It also has shrines for Brahma and Vishnu, although the main shrine is dedicated to Shiva. In fact, most of the temples in Southeast Asia were home to more than one deity.

Even though Hinduism had largely been displaced by Buddhism by the fifteenth century in Southeast Asia and is not widely practiced today except in Bali and among descendants of Indian

A carving of Vishnu reclining on a snake called Ananta, surrounded by Shiva *lingas*, from Cambodia's Kbal Spean River (© Vasudha Narayanan).

immigrants, cultural traditions associated with it linger. Dances based on stories from the *Ramayana* are part of almost every cultural event, and names of Indian origin are still common in Indonesia, Thailand, and Cambodia.

South Indian Devotion (*Bhakti*)

The standard portrait of Vedic and classical Hinduism is based on the culture of the northern part of the Indian subcontinent. But South India had a flourishing cultural life of its own by 400 BCE and possibly earlier. It was here that an entirely new type of Hindu devotion known as **bhakti** emerged and spread throughout India.

A sophisticated body of literature in the Tamil language existed 2,000 years ago. Its earliest components were a number of poems on secular themes that fall into two groups: one dealing with the outer world of warfare and honor, the other with the inner world of love and romance.

Religious literature began to flourish in South India after the fifth century, with several poems addressed to Vishnu, Shiva, and Murugan (the son of Shiva and Parvati). The *bhakti* movement began when poet-devotees of Vishnu and Shiva began singing the praises of their deities not in formal Sanskrit but in Tamil—the mother tongue of the people, the language of intimacy and powerful emotion. This represented a major shift in Hindu culture.

Women in the Traditions

The Songs of Andal

Andal ("she who rules") was an eighth-century Alvar who is worshiped in many South Indian temples dedicated to Vishnu. Her passionate poetry is not only recited and sung by the Vaishnava community today but broadcast over every radio station in Tamilnadu and Karnataka in the month of December. Tradition says that she refused to marry and longed for union with Vishnu—a wish that her biographers claim was fulfilled. Thus, in her life as well as her work, Andal represents a radical alternative to Manu's view of women and their role in society and religion. Icons of Andal can be found in major South Indian Hindu temples across North America, *as well as in many other parts of the world*. The following is an excerpt from one of her many poems.

A thousand elephants circle,
as Narana, Lord of virtues,
walks in front of me.
Golden jars brim with water;

Festive flags and pennants fly through this
  town,
eager to welcome him—
I saw this in a dream, my friend!
Drums beat happy sounds; conches were
  blown.
Under the canopy strung heavy with
  pearls,
Madhusudha, my love, filled with virtue,
came and clasped the palm of my hand
I saw this in a dream, my friend!
Those with eloquent mouths recited the
  good Vedas,
With mantras they placed
the green leaves and the grass in a circle.
The lord, strong as a raging elephant,
softly held my hand as we circled the fire.
I saw this in a dream, my friend! (*Nachchi-yar Tirumoli* 1.1, 1.6–7; trans. Vasudha Narayanan)

By the twelfth century, 75 of these devotees had been recognized as saints: 63 devotees of Shiva known as the Nayanmars ("masters") and 12 devotees of Vishnu known as the Alvars ("those 'immersed deep' in the love of Vishnu"). Composed between the seventh and ninth centuries, the vernacular songs of the Alvars were introduced into the temple liturgy as early as the tenth century, challenging orthodox claims that Sanskrit was the exclusive vehicle for revelation and theological communication. Moreover, brahmin theologians honored their authors as ideal devotees. This was extraordinarily significant, for some of the Alvars came from what was deemed to be lower-caste (perhaps even out-caste) backgrounds, and one of them—Andal—was a woman. Selections from their works, collected in the eleventh century as the *Sacred Collect of Four Thousand Verses*, are recited daily by the Sri Vaishnava community, which considers them the Tamil equivalents of the Sanskrit Vedas.

The poems of the Alvars follow the literary conventions of earlier Tamil poetry, incorporating the symbolism of the *akam* and *puram* poems. Vishnu is seen as a lover and a king, accessible and remote, gracious and grand. In their songs of devotion, the Alvars sought from Vishnu both the embrace of the beloved and the protection of the king. Many incidents from the *Ramayana*, *Mahabharata*, and *Puranas* made their way into the Alvars' songs, along with some stories not found in any of these sources. Above all, the poets focused on the supremacy of Vishnu–Narayana, emphasizing how his incarnation as Rama or Krishna and his presence in the temple show his desire to save all beings.

Many of the Tamil saints, both Vaishnava and Shaiva, traveled all over South India and parts of the north, visiting temples in which their chosen deity was enshrined. In this way pilgrimage became an important part of the Hindu tradition. Eventually, 108 sites came to be known as sacred places where Vishnu abides, and the number was even higher for the Shaivas in Tamilnadu. The Virasaivas, a sect in Karnataka, rejected temple worship as well as the caste system and ritual sacrifice, and expressed their devotion to Shiva by wearing a small linga.

North Indian *Bhakti*

North Indian *bhakti* resembled its southern counterpart both in its use of vernacular languages and in the fact that it was open to people of every caste, but it differed in the focus of its devotion. Whereas South Indian *bhakti* was generally addressed to either Vishnu or Shiva, the object of devotion in the north was often Rama or Krishna (*avataras* of Vishnu), and sometimes the divine being without a form. An early exponent of Krishna devotion was the twelfth-century poet Jayadeva, whose Sanskrit work *Gita Govinda* ("Song of the Cowherd") extols the love of Radha and Krishna; it also contains a reference to the Buddha as an incarnation of Krishna–Vishnu, filled with compassion.

The sometimes synergistic relationship that developed between Hindus and Muslims in northern India (see Focus box on "Hindu–Muslim Relations") was reflected in the delightful, sometimes poignant works composed in the vernacular by poet-singers of the Sant ("holy person" or "truth") tradition. Emphasizing the *nirguna* ("without attributes") Brahman of the *Upanishads*, the Sants held the divinity to be without form. Hence their worship had nothing to do with physical images, and—unlike the Tamil poet-saints, who traveled from temple to temple precisely in order to express their devotion to local manifestations of their chosen deity—they expressed their devotion either in poetry or in silent meditation. They also rejected distinctions between religious communities. Among the most important Sant poets was Kabir (1440–1518?), who is said to have been both Hindu and Muslim.

Document

From the *Tiruvaymoli*

Although philosophical texts say that the soul is beyond gender, devotional poets have often used the language of human love to express their feelings for the divine. In the following extract from the Tiruvaymoli—*the ninth-century masterpiece that is considered to be a "fifth Veda"—the poet Nammalvar speaks in the voice of a young girl who longs for Vishnu as she would for a human lover (the indented lines refer to various incarnations of Vishnu).*

Where do I go from here?
I can't stand the soft bells, the gentle breeze,

the dark water-lily, darkness that conquers day,
dulcet notes, jasmines, the refreshing air.
The Lord, my beguiling one,
   who creates, bores through,
   swallows and spews this earth,
   who measures here and beyond,
does not come.
Why should I live? (*Tiruvaymoli* 9.9.2; trans. Vasudha Narayanan)

With the spread of the North Indian *bhakti* movement, powerful devotional works in vernacular languages made the classic teachings accessible to everyone. Two important figures in this movement were Surdas and Tulsidas. Surdas (c. 1483–1563) was a blind singer and poet whose Hindi compositions celebrate Radha's devotion to the youthful Krishna as a model of *bhakti*. Tulsidas (1543?–1623) is perhaps best known for his *Lake of the Deeds of Rama*, a Hindi retelling of the *Ramayana* that many people still quote and that formed the basis for a blockbuster TV serial in the 1980s.

An important figure in the North Indian *bhakti* movement was the Bengali theologian Chaitanya (1486–1583), who took the religious name Krishna-Chaitanya, "he whose consciousness is Krishna." Like his contemporaries who emphasized *bhakti*, he maintained that human beings in the present degenerate age cannot fulfill all the requirements of religious action and duty; therefore, the only way to liberation is through trusting devotion to a gracious deity.

For Chaitanya, however, the ultimate goal was not liberation from attachment in the traditional sense but rather the active enjoyment of his intense love of Krishna. Chaitanya is said to have led people through the streets, singing about his Lord and urging others to join him in chanting Krishna's names. Chaitanya's movement was revived in the 1800s and eventually led to the formation of the International Society for Krishna Consciousness (ISKCON)—better known as the Hare Krishna movement (see Chapter 13). Both the Hare Krishnas' theology, which locates divine grace in Krishna, and their practice, which is centered on devotional chanting, can be traced directly to Chaitanya.

Colonialism and Beyond

The Portuguese explorer Vasco da Gama (1469–1524) landed in the Indian city of Calicut in 1498, opening the way for European traders, missionaries, and, eventually, rulers. Before long, the Dutch, English, and French were also traveling to India and establishing settlements there. Early European

Focus

Hindu–Muslim Relations

Islam arrived in India around the middle of the eighth century CE. In southern India the first Muslims were seafaring Arab traders who visited the region's many ports on their way to and from Southeast Asia. Over time, a minority Muslim population was established that became well integrated into the larger society.

Early encounters in northern India took a more hostile form. The invasions led by Mahmud of Ghazni (971–1030) and Muhammad of Ghor (1150–1206) paved the way for the installation of Ghor's general Qutbuddin Aibak as the first Muslim ruler in northern India. The plundering and destruction of sacred Hindu monuments such as the Somnath temple in Gujarat in 1025 have long been a part of the Hindu collective memory. At the same time, the synergy made possible by the confluence of cultural influences from the Middle East and India gave rise to extraordinary innovations in all the arts.

The period of Mughal rule, from the early sixteenth century to the early eighteenth, was characterized by a growing sense of "Hindu" identity in North India (although "Hindu" was not yet the standard term that it would become under the British). There was also growing antagonism against Muslim rulers, especially Aurangzeb, the last Mughal emperor, who imposed severe hardships on large segments of the population. It was in this political climate that several leaders emerged to fight for Hindus' religious and political freedom. Notable among them was Shivaji (c. 1630–1680), from what is now Maharashtra. A hero of national proportions, he is credited with developing the concept of self-rule for Hindus.

research into Indian languages, especially Sanskrit, led to the historical reconstruction of the movements of the Indo-European people from Central Asia and pioneered the theory of a common Indo-European ancestry. This was the first glimpse that Hindus received of their pre-Vedic history.

In time, the foreign powers became involved in local politics. As the Mughal Empire disintegrated in the early eighteenth century, many chieftains enlisted English or French help in their efforts to acquire land. Eventually large parts of the Indian subcontinent were loosely united under British control. In the past, most rulers, whether Hindu or Muslim, had accepted a large degree of local autonomy, but the British—despite their policy of "religious neutrality"—did not recognize the importance of local tradition or practice. At the same time, foreign missionaries were severely critical not only of what they called Hindu "idolatry," but of the caste system and practices such as *sati* (self-immolation of widows on their husbands' funeral pyres). The foreigners were not the only ones to call for change, however—some Hindu intellectuals were equally convinced of the need for reform. Among the most important of these figures were Ram Mohan Roy; Dayananda Saraswati; and Ramakrishna Paramahamsa.

The Brahmo Samaj

Ram Mohan Roy (1772–1833) was born into an orthodox brahmin family in western Bengal. Roy believed that if Hindus could read their own scriptures they would recognize that practices such as *sati* were not part of the classic tradition. Therefore he translated extracts from Sanskrit texts into

Document

From Mirabai, Caturvedi no. 27

Mirabai (1450?–1547) was a Rajput princess in Gujarat. A devotee of Krishna, she wrote passionate poetry about her love for him.

Sister, I had a dream that I wed
the Lord of those who live in need:
Five hundred sixty thousand people came
and the Lord of Braj was the groom.

In dream they set up a wedding arch;
in dream he grasped my hand;
in dream he led me around the wedding fire
and I became unshakably his bride.
Mira's been granted her mountain-lifting Lord:
from living past lives, a prize. (Hawley and Juergensmeyer 1988: 137)

Bengali and English and distributed them for free. In 1828 he established a society to hold regular discussions on the nature of Brahman as it is presented in the *Upanishads*. This organization, the Brahmo Samaj ("congregation of Brahman"), emphasized monotheism, rationalism, humanism, and social reform. A pioneer in the area of women's rights, including the right to education, Roy fought to abolish *sati* and child marriage. He also founded a number of periodicals and educational institutions.

The Arya Samaj

The Arya Samaj was established in 1875 by Dayananda Saraswati (1824–1883). Dayananda believed that the Vedas had literally been revealed by God, and that the vision they presented could be revived by stripping away later human accretions such as votive rituals and social customs and teaching young people about their true Vedic heritage. To that end, he founded many educational institutions.

Dayananda also believed that the Vedic teachings were not at variance with science or reason. He rejected the notion of a personal savior god; in fact, he rejected any anthropomorphic vision of the divine and believed that the human soul is in some way coeval with the deity. In his view, the ideal was not renunciation but a full, active life of service to other humans; working to uplift humanity would promote the welfare of both the body and the soul.

The Ramakrishna Movement

Ramakrishna Paramahamsa (1836–1886; born Gadadhar Chatterjee) was a Bengali raised in the Vaishnava *bhakti* tradition, cultivating ecstatic trance experiences. In his early 20s he was employed as a priest at a temple to the goddess Kali, and by his account he experienced the Divine Mother as an ocean of love. From the age of 25 he took instruction in tantra as well as Vedanta. He concluded that all religions lead in the same direction and that all are equally true.

Following his death, his disciples in Calcutta formed the Ramakrishna Mission to spread his eclectic ideas. Among them was Swami Vivekananda (Narendranath Datta, 1862–1902), who believed that Western science could help India make material progress, while Indian spirituality could help the West along the path to enlightenment. As a Hindu participant in the 1893 World's Parliament of Religions in Chicago, and later as a lecturer in America and Europe, he presented an interpretation of Shankara's nondualist (*advaita*) Vedanta in which Brahman is the only reality. As a consequence of the attention he attracted, it was this philosophy that the West generally came to consider the definitive form of Hinduism.

Under Vivekananda's leadership, the movement established a monastic order and a philanthropic mission, both dedicated to humanitarian service. In keeping with Ramakrishna's ecumenical vision, it encouraged nonsectarian worship. It also ignored caste distinctions, founding hundreds of educational and medical institutions that were open to all. The introduction of a Hindu presence in these fields was significant because until then most of India's new schools and hospitals had been run by Christian missionaries.

The monastic wing of the movement maintains that renunciation promotes spiritual growth. Unlike other monastic orders, however, it insists that its members not withdraw from the world but live in and for it, giving humanitarian service to others.

The Struggle for India's Independence

Hindus and Muslims came together to fight for independence from British colonial rule. The earliest eruption was India's First War of Independence, known in Europe as the "Sepoy Mutiny" of 1857. The struggle would continue for another 90 years. Of the many leaders, Hindu and Muslim, who contributed to the achievement of independence in 1947, undoubtedly the best known is the one to whom Rabindranath Tagore, India's famed poet and Nobel laureate, gave the title "Mahatma" ("great soul"): Mohandas Karamchand Gandhi (1869–1948).

Born in Gujarat and trained as a barrister in England, Gandhi practiced law in South Africa from 1893 to 1915. It was in response to the racial discrimination faced by the Indian minority there that he began experimenting with civil disobedience and passive resistance as vehicles for protest. After his return to India, where he became the leader of the Indian National Congress in 1921, he combined the techniques he had developed in South Africa with practices drawn from India's Hindu and Jaina religious traditions and applied them to the campaign for India's freedom.

In particular, Gandhi emphasized the principle of nonviolence (*ahimsa*) and developed a strategy of nonviolent resistance called *satyagraha* ("truth-force"). Also borrowed from religious observances was his practice of fasting, which he used both for "self-purification" and as a psychological weapon. Gandhi's fasts drew attention to social injustices and the atrocities perpetrated by the British authorities. Faced with brutality, he refused to retaliate, saying that "an eye for an eye makes the world blind." Another major influence was the *Bhagavad Gita*, which he understood as an allegory of the conflict between good and evil within human beings. It remained his guide throughout his life.

In addition to his political work, Gandhi promoted social reform, especially with respect to the people then known as "untouchables." He gave the generic name *Harijan* ("children of God") to out-caste communities such as the Dalits. Although out-castes today reject the name as patronizing, it drew attention to the discrimination built into the traditional structure of Hindu society.

Gandhi's efforts to promote peace between Muslims and Hindus in the context of the struggle for independence were less successful. Some scholars hold that the British followed a "divide and rule" policy that amplified underlying tensions between Hindus and Muslims. Conflict over issues such as leadership and electoral representation eventually led the Muslims to demand their own independent state in the northwest, where they appeared to form the majority of the population. The name of the new country, Pakistan, means "land of the pure" but is also an acronym representing the regions it comprises: Punjab, Afghania, Kashmir, Sindh, and Baluchistan.

In the violence that accompanied the partition, some 12 million people were displaced and 1 million killed—representing a major failure for Gandhi. A few months after the partition, on January 30, 1948, he was assassinated by a Hindu incensed by what he perceived as Gandhi's support for the Muslim cause. Since then, Gandhi's influence has been felt in many parts of the world, but perhaps most notably in the US civil rights movement under the leadership of Martin Luther King, Jr.

Independence and the Secular State

Although India is a secular state, personal and/or family law differs depending on the religious tradition that the individual belongs to. *Dharmashastra* prescriptions were flexible, and Hindus did not consider them "laws" in the Western sense; nevertheless, they became the framework for "Hindu" law under the British. In an effort to accommodate the different religions, the British and later the Indian government upheld the traditional legal structures of Islam, Christianity, and Zoroastrianism. Thus how people marry, divorce, adopt children, inherit property, and engage in other activities all depends on their religious affiliation. Legislation was passed in the 1950s to codify the Hindu laws regarding marriage, succession, and so on, but the fact that the new laws did not reflect the diversity of the Hindu traditions led to further tensions between Hindus and Muslims because the laws in the other traditions were not codified. Despite calls for a uniform civil code with the same laws for all citizens, the different legal regimes remain in effect today.

Contemporary Religious Leaders

For more than 2,000 years Hindus have venerated holy men and women. The *Taittiriya Upanishad* exhorts a student to think of his **acharya** (religious instructor) as a god, and there have been countless other gurus, ascetics, mediums, storytellers, and **sadhus** ("holy men") who have commanded both obedience and veneration. For many Hindus, religious experience is mediated by someone they believe to be in some way divine.

Followers of Sri Sathya Sai Baba (Sathya Narayan Raju; 1926–2011), a charismatic teacher from Andhra Pradesh in the south, believe him to be an *avatara*. The heads of the monasteries established by Shankara in the eighth century continue to exercise considerable influence in some Hindu communities, as do a number of intellectual Vedantic commentators whose interpretations of the ancient scriptures show the dynamic and adaptable nature of the Hindu tradition.

All *acharyas* are gurus, but not all gurus are *acharyas*. Gurus, unlike *acharyas*, are not necessarily connected to any sectarian tradition, and they tend to emphasize "universal" and humanist messages, stressing the divinity in all human beings and encouraging their followers to transcend caste and community distinctions. Another difference is that whereas *acharyas* are almost invariably male, many women have been gurus. An example is Ma Amritananda Mayi ("Ammachi"; b. 1953), the leader of a movement that sponsors an international network of charitable, humanitarian, educational, and medical institutions. Known as the "hugging guru," she is one of the most popular religious leaders in the world today.

Many charismatic teachers are called *swami* ("master") by their followers. Others take their titles from the ancient Vedic "seers" known as *rishis*. An example is the founder of the Transcendental Meditation movement, Maharishi ("great seer") Mahesh Yogi (1911?–2008), who has been one of the most influential teachers in the Western world.

⊕ Practices, Rituals, and Arts

Many Hindus are fond of the dictum that "Hinduism is not a religion, it is a way of life." While most know very little about the texts, beliefs, and philosophies of their tradition, they have generally observed the practices all their lives. Performances of various kinds—music and dance, drama and enactments of devotional poetry—are just as important as rituals, since it is through them that most Hindus learn the stories of the epics and *Puranas*.

Temple Worship

It is not clear when temples began to figure in Hindu worship. The Vedic literature says nothing about temples, although the Harappa civilization does appear to have set some buildings apart for worship. South India has a number of temples that have survived from about the fifth century CE, but in the north many older temples were destroyed by either invaders or Muslim rulers. However, cave carvings depicting incarnations of Vishnu and icons of Shiva suggest that worship at public shrines was established by the early fifth century. Some temples to Shiva and Vishnu in Southeast Asia may date from the same period.

Deities in Hindu temples are treated like kings and queens. The **murtis**—variously translated as "idols," "icons," "forms," or "objects to be worshiped"—are given ritual baths, adorned, carried in processions, and honored with all the marks of hospitality offered to royal guests, including music and dance to entertain them. This treatment reflects the fact that for many Hindus *murtis* are not symbols but the deities themselves, fully present and accessible, representing direct analogues to Vishnu's incarnations as Rama or Krishna. The presence of a deity in the temple does not detract from his or her presence in heaven, immanence in the world, or presence in a human soul. The deity is always complete and whole, no matter how many forms he or she may be manifest in at any given time.

Others, however, believe that the image in a temple is only a symbol of a higher reality. This does not prevent adherents of Shankara's nondual Vedanta from flocking to shrines to express their devotion—even though they believe it is transforming wisdom, not *bhakti*, that leads to liberation. And some sects reject images altogether.

A temple is seen as having a correlation to the universe itself and to the body of divine beings; for Sri Vaishnavas, the temple is heaven on earth. In South India, even a single glimpse of a temple tower is said to be enough to destroy one's sins.

Generally, in Hinduism, there is no congregational prayer. Rather, the priest prays on behalf of the devotees; presents offerings of fruit, flowers, or coconut to the deity; and then gives back some of those blessed objects to the devotees. The food thus presented is now considered **prasada** ("divine favor"), a gift from the deity. In some temples devotees must buy the *prasada*, but in others

The strings of flowers sold outside temples may be worn by devotees themselves or presented to the deities inside (© Vasudha Narayanan).

it is provided at no charge, drawing on endowments made in the past. Patrons frequently earmark their donations for particular charitable purposes or functions in the temple, and records of their donations are inscribed on stones in the temple walls. Such inscriptions are an important source of information about the past. For example, an inscription in Tirumala-Tirupati (Tiruvenkatam) says that in the year 966 a woman called Samavai donated two parcels of land and ordered that the revenues derived from them be used to celebrate festivals and consecrate a silver processional image of Vishnu (known here as Venkateshwara). The fact that she was able to make such donations suggests a certain independence both of lifestyle and of income.

Some of the largest Shiva and Vishnu temples are found in the region of the Khmer Empire, which stretched from modern Cambodia to parts of Thailand and Laos. Although there are striking similarities between these structures and Indian temples, the Khmer temples have their own architectural idiom. Shiva temples are shaped like mountains; the large mountain-temples at Bakheng

Angkor Wat in northern Cambodia was built by King Suryavarman II in honor of Vishnu. Its unusual three-level structure may indicate a connection with South India, which also has a handful of three-storied Vishnu temples (© Vasudha Narayanan).

and Bakong in the Siem Reap area of Cambodia, for instance, look more like the Buddhist temple of Borubodur in Indonesia than their counterparts in India. The large Vishnu temple of Angkor Wat in Cambodia, like many temples in India, is situated and built according to astronomical calculations: the sun rises directly behind the central tower at the time of the spring and autumn equinoxes.

Sculptural and Pictorial Symbolism

The Naga

One of the earliest symbols in the Hindu tradition may be the *naga* (serpent). In many towns and villages there are sacred trees surrounded with small stone images of intertwined snakes. Women worship at these open-air shrines when they want to make a wish regarding a matter such as childbirth. *Nagas* are also important in the iconography of Shiva and Vishnu, and Cambodian narratives trace the origins of the kingdom to the union of a *naga* princess and a Hindu prince from India.

The Dance of Shiva

Shiva is often portrayed as a cosmic dancer known as Nataraja, the king of the dance. In this form Shiva is the archetype of both the dancer and the ascetic, symbolizing mastery over universal energy on the one hand and absolute inner tranquility on the other.

In the classic Nataraja representation, Shiva has four hands. One of the right hands holds an hourglass-shaped drum, symbolizing sound—both speech and the divine truth heard through revelation. The other right hand is making a gesture that grants fearlessness to devotees. One of the left hands holds a flame, symbolizing the destruction of the world at the end of time. The feet grant salvation and are worshiped to obtain union with Shiva. The left foot, representing the refuge of the devotee, is raised, signifying liberation. The other left hand points to this foot.

Dancing through the creation and destruction of the cosmos, Shiva–Nataraja is the master of both the fierce, violent dance that gives rise to energy and the gentle, lyrical dance representing tenderness and grace. The entire universe shakes when he dances; Krishna sings for him, the snake around his neck sways, and drops of the Ganga River, which he holds in his hair, fall to the earth.

The Linga

In temples, Shiva is usually represented by a *linga*. Although *linga* is generally translated as "phallus," Hindus do not normally think of it as a physical object. Rather, it symbolizes the spiritual potential in all of creation, and specifically the creative energies of Shiva. The union of the *yoni* and *linga* is a reminder that male and female forces are united in generating the universe. Although Shiva is characterized as the "destroyer" in some literature, it is his creative role that is represented in the temple.

Erotic Sculpture

People from other cultures have often been shocked by Hindu temple sculptures celebrating *kama*, sensual love. Probably the most famous examples are found at Khajuraho (c. 1000 CE) in Madhya Pradesh and Konarak (c. 1250), in the eastern coastal state of Orissa. While some art historians have suggested that such scenes illustrate passages from various myths and texts such as the *Puranas*, or are symbols of fertility, others have speculated that the sculptures may have been intended to serve an educational purpose for young men who as students were isolated from society, preparing them for adult life in a world where spouses were expected to be partners in *kama* as well as dharma.

Forehead Marks

Perhaps the most common visual sign of Hindu culture is the forehead mark, especially the red dot (*bindi*) traditionally worn by married women. At the simplest level, *bindis* are decorative: unmarried and Christian women wear them as well, and in recent years, the traditional dot of red powder has been largely replaced by stickers in many shapes and colors. Yet the *bindi*'s value is more than cosmetic: married women see it as a symbol of their role in society.

In many parts of India, male ascetics and temple priests also wear forehead marks. As with many elements of Hinduism, the meaning of such marks depends on the gender, marital status,

The dancing Shiva (© Vasudha Narayanan).

and sect of the person wearing it; the occasion; and, occasionally, his or her caste. Marks denoting affiliation to a particular deity may be made with white clay, sandalwood paste, flower petals, or ash. In general, followers of Vishnu, Krishna, and Lakshmi wear vertical marks; worshipers of Shiva and Parvati wear horizontal or slightly curved crescent marks made of ash or other substances, with a red dot in the middle; and a combination of dots and crescents usually indicates allegiance to the Goddess (Devi) in one of her many manifestations.

Domestic Worship

One of the most significant ways in which Hindus express their devotion to a deity or a spiritual teacher is through rituals (**puja**) performed in the home. Many households set aside some space for a shrine to hold small images of the revered figure. Daily puja typically consists of simple acts in which all family members can take part, such as lighting oil lamps and incense sticks, reciting prayers, or offering food to the deity.

Significantly, a number of domestic rituals are specific to the women of the household. In many parts of India, women gather on certain days of the year to celebrate the Goddess by fasting and feasting, and then perform "auspiciousness" rituals for the happiness of the entire family. Other women's rituals are found only in certain geographic regions. In the south, for example, women will often gather before a major family celebration (such as a wedding) to ask for the blessing of female ancestors who have had the good fortune to die before their husbands and therefore have preserved their status as *sumangalis*, or "auspicious women." And in the north, during some domestic festivals such as Navaratri (see later section), prepubescent girls are venerated by older women as temporary manifestations of the Goddess.

In the home as in the temple, by speaking a prayer or singing a hymn, worshipers link themselves with the devotional community extending through time. Thus in Sri Vaishnava worship, devotees who recite a verse of Andal's are to some extent participating in her own devotion.

Ayurvedic Medicine

Medicine made great progress in the Hindu world in the first millennium. One of the most important systems was called **Ayurveda**: the *veda* (knowledge) of enhancing life. In this system, the physician promotes both longevity and quality of life. The prototype is a deity called Dhanavantari, sometimes identified as an incarnation of Vishnu. The South Indian parallel to Ayurveda is the Tamil system called Siddha.

Ayurveda is considered to be an ancillary to the Vedas. An early compendium on healing by a physician named Charaka (c. third century BCE) says that every human being should have three desires: the will to live, the drive for prosperity, and an aspiration to reach the world beyond. As with many other subjects, treatises on healing and medicine are often framed as conversations between two sages or between a god and a sage.

Both Charaka and the surgeon Sushruta claimed that their theories had been transmitted to them by the gods. They understood illness as a lack of balance among three elements: air, phlegm, and bile. This analytic approach recalls Greek and Chinese medical theories of roughly the same period. The *Sushruta Samhita* begins by declaring that the physician's aim is "to cure the diseases of the sick, to protect the healthy, to prolong life," while the *Charaka Samhita* includes a detailed statement of the ethics required of a physician. In these respects, the ancient roots of Ayurvedic medicine seem strikingly modern.

The Annual Festival Cycle

In the Hindu tradition there is a festival of some kind almost every month of the year. The most popular are the birthdays of Rama, Krishna, and Ganesha; their precise dates vary from year to year with the lunar calendar, but they always fall within the same periods.

Some festivals have been specific to certain regions. **Holi**, for instance, is a North Indian festival celebrated in March or April with bonfires to enact the destruction of evil and exuberant throwing of colored powder to symbolize the vibrant colors of spring. It is now popular all over the world, with tens of thousands of people—not all of them Hindu—joining in the celebrations. It commemorates Vishnu's incarnation as a man-lion in order to save the life of his devotee Prahlada as well as his incarnation as Krishna.

Vishnu's fifth incarnation, as a dwarf-brahmin, is celebrated in the state of Kerala in a late summer festival called Onam. Other festivals, like Navaratri and **Deepavali** (known as Diwali in some areas), are more or less pan-Hindu. A detailed discussion of Navaratri will give us an idea of the variations in observance that can be seen across different communities.

Practice

The Significance of Food

The Hindu tradition is preoccupied with food: not just what kind of food is eaten, where, and when, but how it is prepared, who prepares it, who has the right to be offered it first, and who may be given the leftovers. Certain dates and lunar phases require either feasting or fasting, and there are different types of fast: some demand abstention from all food, others only from grain or rice. According to some texts, liberation can be attained simply by observing the right kinds of fast.

Contrary to a common Western stereotype, most Hindus are not vegetarians. The strictest vegetarians are generally the Vaishnavas, who are found all over India. In addition, most brahmins are vegetarian—except in Bengal, Orissa, and Kashmir. In the West, members of ISKCON not only abstain from meat, fish, and fowl, but also avoid vegetables such as onions and garlic, which are thought to have negative properties.

These dietary prohibitions and habits are based on the idea that food reflects the general qualities of nature: purity, energy, and inertia. Pure foods such as dairy products and many vegetables are thought to foster spiritual inclinations. By contrast, meat, poultry, and onions are believed to give rise to passion and action, while stale food and liquor are seen as encouraging sloth. Thus a strict vegetarian diet is prescribed for those who seek to cultivate spiritual tranquility and avoid passion.

Weddings, funerals, ancestral rites, and birthdays require the use of auspicious spices such as turmeric. What one feeds the forefathers is different from what one feeds the gods and human beings; life-promoting rituals call for different foods than do rituals associated with death, and the latter must not include nontraditional ingredients such as potatoes and red pepper (both of which were introduced to India by Europeans). Various regional traditions also rely on different foods to rectify imbalances of "cold" and "heat" in the body.

In addition, the nature of a given food is thought to be influenced by the inherent qualities of the person who cooks it. For this reason it was common even in the mid-twentieth century for strictly observant Hindus to eat only food prepared by people of their own caste.

Beyond the practicalities of use or avoidance, food appears in Hindu thought as an important symbol of spiritual experience.

Navaratri

The festival of Navaratri ("nine nights") begins on the new moon that appears between September 15 and October 14 and is celebrated all over India, but in different ways and for different reasons. In Tamilnadu it is largely a celebration of womanhood. Exquisite dolls representing the goddesses Sarasvati, Lakshmi, and Durga are arranged in elaborate tableaux depicting scenes from the epics and *Puranas*. Every evening, women and children dressed in bright silks visit one another, admire the dolls, play musical instruments, and sing classical songs in praise of one or another of the goddesses. On the last two days—a special countrywide holiday—large pictures of Lakshmi and Sarasvati, draped with garlands of fresh flowers, are placed in front of the display of dolls and worshiped.

In West Bengal, the festival commemorates the goddess Durga's killing of the buffalo-demon Mahisa. Local communities make extravagant statues of Durga for her spirit to inhabit; then, after nine nights, they immerse the statues in water to symbolize her return to the formless state.

A Holi celebration in Jaipur (© Jonathan Irish/National Geographic Society/Corbis).

In Gujarat, Navaratri is celebrated with two special dances. In the circular dance called *garbha*, a sacred lamp is kept in the center of the circle as a manifestation of the Goddess. The second dance, called *dandiya*, is performed with sticks and recalls the dance that Krishna is said to have performed.

According to some traditions, it was during the same 9 nights and 10 days that Rama battled Ravana. In Ramnagar, Varanasi, on the river Ganga, people act out the story of the *Ramayana*, with little boys in the parts of Rama and his brothers, and on the tenth day celebrate Rama's victory.

Some Hindus believe that it was on the ninth day of Navaratri that Arjuna found the weapons he had hidden a year before and paid respect to them before entering battle. Because of this story, the last two days of the festival, dedicated to Lakshmi and Sarasvati, celebrate the importance of weapons and machines in life: cars and buses are draped with garlands, while computers and typewriters are blessed with sacred powders. On the ninth day South Indians honor Sarasvati, the patron of learning and music. Musical instruments, writing devices, and textbooks are placed in front of her image, to be blessed by her for the rest of the year.

In many parts of India, the last day of the festival is dedicated to Lakshmi. This is a time for fresh starts—to begin new ventures and acquire new knowledge—and to honor traditional teachers. On the last days of Navaratri, the fortune of learning, the wealth of wisdom, and the joy of music are said to be given by the grace of the goddesses. While most Indians do celebrate Navaratri, then, it is in different ways and for different reasons.

Deepavali

Deepa means "lamp" and *vali* means "necklace" or "row." Thus Deepavali (or Diwali) means "necklace of lights." It is celebrated at the time of the new moon between October 15 and November 14. Hindu families all over the world decorate their houses with lights, set off firecrackers, and wear new clothes. In some parts of India, Deepavali marks the beginning of a new year, but that is only one of several reasons for the festival. As in the case of Navaratri, the significance of Deepavali varies from region to region.

In South India, for instance, the festival celebrates the dawn when Krishna is said to have killed Narakasura, a demon from the netherworld, thus ensuring the victory of light over darkness. In North India, Deepavali marks the return of Rama to Ayodhya and his coronation. And in Gujarat it is the beginning of the new year, when new account books are opened and new clothes are worn. Presents are exchanged in some communities, and it is generally a time of feasting. In Tamilnadu, people say that the river Ganga itself is present in all the waters on Deepavali day. They get up at three or four in the morning for a special purifying bath, and members of some communities greet one another by asking, "Have you had a bath in the river Ganga?" Whatever the local customs may be, the celebrations are always family-centered.

Life-Cycle Rites

Every culture has its rites of passage: rituals that mark the transitions from one stage of life to another. In some of the *dharmashastras* the discussion of the life-cycle sacraments begins with the birth of a child. In others the first sacrament is marriage, for it is in this context that each new life is expected to begin.

Two factors are important to note in discussing life-cycle rites. First, not all are pan-Hindu, and even those that are do not necessarily have the same importance in all communities. Some of the rites discussed here are practiced only by the "upper" castes and higher economic classes. Second, many important rites, especially those involving girls or women, are not discussed in the classical texts—possibly because those texts were written by men. It may also be that some of these rites developed after the texts were written. We will discuss the normative *dharmashastra* sacraments first and then look at a few rites of passage with more localized importance.

Certain kinds of people, animals, rituals, smells, sounds, and foods are considered auspicious in that they are thought to bring about good fortune and a good quality of existence. Auspicious times are chosen for the performance of all sacraments; these times depend on the horoscope of the person concerned, which is cast at birth.

Birth Rituals

The cycle of sacraments (*samskaras*; literally, "perfecting") begins before birth. The time of conception, the rituals administered to a pregnant woman, and her behavior during pregnancy are all thought to condition the personality of the child. The *Upanishads* describe specific rituals to be followed to produce a learned daughter or a heroic son (though in later times daughters were rarely desired).

At the moment of birth, care is taken to note the exact time in order to ensure an accurate horoscope. In the first ceremony performed after the birth, the father prays for the intellectual well-being of the child and longevity for himself and the child: "May we see a hundred autumns, may we hear a hundred autumns."

Weddings

According to the *dharmashastras*, a man is born with debts to the sages, the gods, and the ancestors. His wife helps him repay these debts, and without her a man cannot fully perform his religious obligations.

Before a wedding can be arranged, the parents of the prospective bride must find a suitable bridegroom; for this they used to rely on the help of friends and extended family, but today the

Practice

Initiation Rituals

The upper classes have generally been called "twice-born," in reference to the initiatory rite in which young men are spiritually reborn as sons of their religious teachers (whether a similar initiation was performed for girls in the early Vedic era is unclear). This rite, the **upanayana**, marks a boy's initiation into studenthood—the first of the four stages in life. It takes two days to complete. On the first day, the boy is bathed in water into which the essence of all the sacred waters has been invoked through the recitation of verses from the Vedas. This ritual is called "peace brought on the waters," and it ends with repeated requests for *shanti* (peace): for the individual, the soul, the body, the divine beings, the family, the community, and the entire earth. On the second day the boy is given a sacred "thread," or cord, to wear over his left shoulder. Some think it represents an upper garment that the student would wear when he was fit to perform a sacrifice; others, that it symbolizes an umbilical cord connecting the boy to his teacher—the spiritual parent through whom he will be reborn. The boy is now taught how to thank the earth for his food and ask divine beings to bless it. Then comes the actual imparting of the sacred teaching. As the boy sits with his father, a sacred mantra is given to him that he will be expected to chant 108 times in succession, three times each day. Although it is very short—"I meditate on the brilliance of the sun; may it illumine my mind"—this *Gayatri*, or sun mantra, is considered the most important of all mantras and has become popular among many sections of Hindu society. The boy is then taken outside and shown the sun, the source of light, knowledge, and immortality. He must twine his fingers in a particular way to ward off the harmful rays while looking directly at its heart.

search is often conducted through the Internet and social media. Ideally, he will come from the same geographic region, speak the same language, and belong to the same community, though he must belong to a different clan. He should be compatible with the bride in education, looks, age, and outlook, and the two families should be of similar socioeconomic status.

When a potential husband is found, the families sometimes compare the young people's horoscopes, not only to assess compatibility and character, but also to balance the ups and downs in their future lives. When the horoscopes are compatible, the young people (and their families) meet to decide whether they like each other. Obviously, arranged marriages are less common today than in earlier centuries. Now that men and women increasingly study and work together, a couple may meet and decide to get married with or without their families' approval. Such marriages often cross boundaries of caste, community, and even language and geography.

To be legally binding, the marriage ceremony must include several basic features: an exchange of flower garlands, the gift of the girl by her parents, the clasping of hands, *sapta padi* (taking seven steps together around fire, the eternal witness), and the giving of a symbol of "auspiciousness" to the bride. Some weddings include lavish exchanges of presents with friends and extended family members. At particular moments the couple's close relatives have active roles to play, but the guests are free to come and go as they please. The ceremony itself lasts several hours. Often the couple sits on a platform near a fire, to which offerings are made. The bride's father quotes from the *Ramayana*, reciting the words spoken by Sita's father as he gives her in marriage to Rama: "This is Sita, my daughter; she will be your partner in dharma."

In many communities, though not all, the groom's family then presents the bride with a "gift of auspiciousness"—a gold necklace, a string of black beads, or a simple yellow thread carrying the insignia of the particular god that the family worships—that she will wear for the duration of her marriage. There is no equivalent symbol for the groom.

In the central rite of the wedding, the bride and groom take seven steps around the fire together as he recites a series of verses from the Vedas, concluding as follows: "You have taken seven steps with me; be my friend. We who have taken seven steps together have become companions. I have attained your friendship; I shall not forsake that friendship. Do not discard our relationship." It is worth noting that these passages refer to the wife as the husband's partner in dharma and his companion in love.

Funeral Rites

Except for infants and ascetics (who may be buried), cremation by fire is the final sacrament in most communities. No fire is to be lit or tended in the house where the death occurred until the cremation fire has been lit, and the family of the deceased is considered to live in a state of pollution for a period that varies from 12 days to almost a year. Although each religious community (Shaiva, Vaishnava, etc.) has its own list of scriptures to recite from on such occasions, most funeral rituals will also include portions of the Vedas and the *Bhagavad Gita*.

The rituals are usually performed by the eldest son of the deceased. For the first few days the spirit of the deceased is considered a *preta* (ghost). To quench the thirst resulting from the body's fiery cremation, the spirit is offered water, as well as balls of rice for sustenance. Some of these rituals go back to the earliest Vedic times, when the dead were thought to need food for the journey to the afterlife on the far side of the moon.

After the designated period of time, the injunctions relating to pollution are lifted in an "adoption of auspiciousness" ceremony. On every new-moon day, the departed soul is offered food in the form of libations with sesame seeds and water. After a year, the anniversary of the death is marked with further ceremonies, and the family is then freed of all constraints.

Women's Rituals

Most women's rituals are domestic, undertaken for the welfare of the family and earthly happiness, but a few are intended solely for personal liberation. Many practices—worship at home shrines or temples, pilgrimages, the singing of devotional songs—are similar to those undertaken by men, but some are unique to married women whose husbands are alive. Underlying many of these rites is the notion that women are powerful and that the rites they perform have potency. Though many women's rituals share certain features, they are marked by considerable differences among communities, castes, and regions.

Calendrical Rituals

Many traditional women's rituals are no longer practiced today, but a number of votive rituals are still observed on particular days. These rituals involve the welfare of others—whether the husband and children, the extended family, or the community. Although Sanskrit manuals say that performing these rites will enable a woman to attain final liberation from the cycle of birth and death, most participants ask only for more worldly rewards, such as marriage or a long life for their husbands.

After prayers to the family deity, the women may distribute emblems of auspiciousness such as betel leaves, bananas, coconuts, or turmeric. The rituals may take anywhere between a few minutes and five days to complete, with periods of fasting alternating with communal eating.

In South India married women were traditionally enjoined to stay celibate during the month of Adi (approximately July 15–August 14). During this time women of some castes carry special pots of water and other ritual items to the temples of local goddesses and perform rites in their honor for the benefit of the entire family. Others cook rice and milk dishes in the temples of the local goddesses and distribute the food. In the temple of Draupadi Amman, women and men alike enter a trance state and walk over hot coals in a ceremony called "walking on flowers."

In North India many women's rites focus on the welfare of male relatives. In late summer, for example, girls tie a protective cord around the wrists of their brothers. And in October–November, women undertake two fasts for the well-being of their husbands, as well as one for the health of their sons. These daytime fasts are broken only after the moon rises.

Karva Chauth is a North Indian festival celebrating married women's devotion to their husbands. Participants observe a daylong fast from sunrise to moonrise during which they pray for their husbands' well-being (REUTERS/ Ajay Verma).

Women's Life-Cycle Rituals

In the upper castes the standard life-cycle rituals associated with childhood, marriage, and death are much the same for both sexes. There are many other sacraments associated with women, however, that have not received scriptural ratification. Some of these rites are specific to certain regions and communities.

In the past, for instance, many communities would celebrate a young girl's first menstrual period, since this "blossoming" meant that she was ready for marriage. Today urban communities tend to consider this tradition old-fashioned, but it is still practiced in rural areas. The girl is showered with gifts of money or clothing by her family, and the ritual celebration often resembles a mini-wedding.

Special rituals may also attend pregnancy, especially the first. In a popular South Indian ritual, the pregnant woman is dressed in a silk sari, and women of all ages slip bangles onto her arm. In earlier days a bangle-seller was invited and the woman's parents gave all the guests glass bracelets that were supposed to safeguard them from evil spirits.

In another rite the expectant mother's hair is adorned with flowers to enhance the natural radiance that is often said to accompany pregnancy. In the Hindu tradition women often wear flowers in their hair, but normally only a bride's hair is completely woven with flowers. Rituals such as these acknowledge the importance of a woman's body and celebrate its life-bearing potential.

Women, Reproduction, and Childbirth

With a few exceptions, most Hindu communities have traditionally regarded menstruation as physically polluting. Menstruating women were excluded from everyday life, and even though strict segregation is no longer widespread, vestiges of the old attitudes remain. Most communities still do not permit menstruating women to attend a place of worship or participate in any religious ritual. Virtually all Hindu women take a purifying ritual bath on the fourth day of their cycle, but many of these observances are discarded when Hindus migrate to other countries.

The same concept of pollution extends to childbirth. Even though the birth of a child is a happy and auspicious occasion, it is thought to render the entire family ritually impure. For several days after the birth, the family cannot go to a temple or celebrate an auspicious event.

Of all the technological innovations developed in recent years, those associated with reproduction tend to be among the most controversial. Yet Hindus generally appear to be quite accepting of intervention in this area. In the case of assisted reproduction, this is probably not surprising: the traditional teachings have always emphasized that reproduction is a primary duty. Thus many Hindus today accept artificial insemination, although for most couples the husband is the only acceptable donor.

The ethical considerations become more complex when contraception and gender selection are concerned. For thousands of years, male children have been more welcome than females, largely because of the traditional understanding of duty to the ancestors: in a patriarchal, patrilineal society, sons would continue the family line and could be counted on to look after their parents in old age, whereas daughters would need costly dowries and would be of benefit only to their husbands' families. Although Indian law forbids the use of sonograms and amniocentesis for the purpose of sex selection, the ratio of female to male births has dropped significantly in recent years.

The *dharmashastra* texts maintain that the unborn fetus has life; according to popular belief and stories from the *Puranas*, it is even capable of hearing and learning from the conversations that take place around it. Nevertheless, abortions are legal in India and are accepted without any strong dissent from religious leaders or prolonged editorial, legislative, or judicial debate. Thus it appears that some teachings of the dharma texts do not have any compelling authority for Hindus today.

The Performing Arts

The performing arts are central to the practice and transmission of the Hindu traditions. The knowledge related to music and dance was considered to be an ancillary branch of the Vedas. A treatise on theater and dance called the *Natya Sastra* is attributed to a legendary sage named Bharata but was said to have originated with the creator god Brahma, who took the reading text from the *Rig Veda*, the music from the *Sama Veda*, gestures and makeup from the *Yajur Veda*, and emotional acting from the *Atharava Veda* and combined them to create the fifth Veda.

Dancing the *garbha* during Navaratri celebrations in Mumbai (© DIVYAKANT SOLANKI/epa/Corbis).

Acting, music, and dance have even been considered ways to liberation. Classical Indian dance requires total control of the body—the same control that is central to the physical discipline of yoga. Theoretically speaking, all dance is divine, but many dances are explicitly devotional in tone. This is particularly true of Bharata Natyam, the classical dance form of South India. While the dancer expresses the human soul's longing for union with the Lord in passionate terms, the audience may also participate in the divine joy of movement, whether that of the dancer, of Krishna with his cowherd friends, or of Shiva Nataraja, the King of the Dance, and through this participation attain the frame of mind that leads to liberation.

Sanskrit texts such as the *Natya Sastra* usually make a distinction between classical and folk dance, but sometimes the boundaries between them have been fluid, and both forms have derived inspiration from each other. A striking example of singing and dancing that occurs in public (though originally performed in the home) is the *garbha* dance of Gujarat, in which women and young girls celebrate the Mother Goddess by dancing around a *garbha*, a clay pot holding a lamp. *Garbha* means "womb," the source of all creative energy; it is the Mother Goddess who is understood to be present in the lamp inside the clay pot. It seems that when the focus is on *moksha* (liberation), rather than dharma (issues of righteousness), women have more freedom to take part in public activities. The androcentric controls imposed on the public activities of women are simply bypassed in contexts in which the focus is on the potential for liberation that is inherent in all human beings; thus, even though society may disapprove of a woman who has rejected marriage, the women poets who rejected marriage in favor of union with their deity are venerated.

To study dance forms such as Bharata Natyam, Manipuri, Kathak, Kathakali, or Kuchipudi—classical forms from different regions of India—is not only to learn a fine art. Through them dancers (and audiences) learn the stories of the Hindu gods as well as about their physical appearance, their insignia, and their demeanor. The dances offer insight into the allegorical structures of Hindu devotional songs, in which the love between the deity and the human being is often portrayed as the love between a man and a woman. Whether in India or in places such as Fiji, Trinidad, or South Africa, the classical dances introduce new generations to the world of Hinduism.

The ostensible reason for the "revelation" of the treatise on dance was to make the Vedas accessible to *all* human beings. However, it is interesting to note that after the fifteenth century (and possibly earlier), the only women who sang and danced in public seem to have been courtesans. This was apparently not the case in earlier times; even as late as the twelfth century, sculptures of women dancers, perhaps royalty, adorned the niches of the Belur temple in Karnataka. The apparent prohibition against women from "decent families" dancing in public may have come from a gradual coalescence of the conservative attitudes explicit in many Hindu texts and Islamic mores, as well as the puritanical perspectives of Christian missionaries from Europe.

As for sound, it has been part of Hindu worship since the time of the Vedas. The holy word *om*, which is chanted at the beginning and end of all Hindu and Jaina prayers and recitations of scripture, and is central to Buddhist practice as well, is perceived to be filled with power. It is understood to have three sounds, *a–u–m*, with the diphthong *au* producing an *o* sound. The sound of *om*, which begins deep in the body and ends at the lips, is considered auspicious. Its history in the Hindu tradition is ancient; the *Mandukya Upanishad* discusses its meaning and power. Hindu philosophers and sectarian communities all agree that *om* is the most sacred sound.

Yet that sound does not have a particular meaning. Almost every Hindu community has speculated about the meaning of *om*. Some say it represents the supreme reality or Brahman. Many philosophers have believed that *om* was present at the beginning of the manifest universe and that it contains the essence of true knowledge. Some say that its three sounds represent the three worlds: earth, atmosphere, and heaven. Others say that they represent the essence of the three Vedas (Rig, Yajur, and Sama). According to followers of the nondualist philosopher Shankara, the three sounds *a*, *u*, and *m* have the following experiential meanings:

- *A* stands for the world that we see when we are awake, the person who is experiencing it, and the waking experience.
- *U* stands for the dream world, the dreamer, and the dream experience.
- *M* represents the sleep world, the sleeper, and the sleep experience.

These three states we experience on this earth, while a fourth, unspoken syllable represents the state of liberation.

Some Vaishnava devotees, on the other hand, say that *a* represents Vishnu, *u* denotes the human being, and *m* denotes the relationship between the two. Other Vaishnavas say that the sounds represent Vishnu, Sri, and the devotee. In a sense, then, the sound of *om* is a whole greater than the sum of its parts, exceeding in significance the many meanings attributed to it.

Music, too, has been perceived as sacred in both origin and function since the time of the *Sama Veda*. Knowledge of the nature of sound and its proper expression has therefore been considered to be religious knowledge. The Vedas specify the different pitches and tones in which the verses are meant to be recited. The exalted status of the *Sama Veda* is in part a reflection of the melodious sounds produced when it is sung according to the instructions.

Classical music was largely religious in nature. Treatises on music refer to a divine line of teachers, frequently beginning with the deities Shiva and Parvati, and honor Sarasvati as the patron goddess of the fine arts. Some later *Puranas* say that Vishnu and Sri are manifested as Nada Brahman or the Supreme Being in the form of sound.

When properly controlled and articulated, sound itself is said to induce a religious experience. Thus the sound of a hymn is considered no less important than the words. *Nadopasana*, meditation through sound, became a popular religious practice. The Alvars composed their poems to be sung and danced, and many devotional poet-composers addressed their songs to the deities.

⊕ Recent Developments
Global Hinduism, Interaction, and Adaptation

Hinduism is a global religion in at least three ways. There are sizable numbers of Hindus in almost every part of the world who trace their roots to the Indian subcontinent; people in various countries have accepted Hindu teachers, doctrines, beliefs, or practices; and Hindu ideas and practices have been separated from the name "Hindu" and have become part of cultures outside India. An example of the last point can be seen in the United States. Since the New England Transcendentalists of the early nineteenth century, generations of Americans have engaged with ideas, philosophies, and practices rooted in Hindu traditions without identifying them as such; instead, ideas such as reincarnation and practices such as meditation and yoga have been described as "spiritual" or "universal."

One could say that Hinduism comes in both brand-name and generic forms. It is rare to find a generic Hindu in India; everyone belongs to a particular caste, community, and sectarian group, all of which are further subdivided along linguistic and geographic lines.

The Hindu Diaspora

There have been at least three major waves of Hindu migration to places outside the Indian subcontinent. The first was a gradual process that took place over several centuries in the first millennium and probably involved very small groups of influential elites who carried Hindu ideas and practices to Southeast Asia. The second major migration was the movement of workers (primarily indentured) seeking employment in the nineteenth century. The third large wave began in the second half of the twentieth century and has been more varied in its composition. The watershed year in the United States was 1965, when immigration laws were relaxed to allow skilled, educated professionals such as engineers, physicians, and, later, software professionals to enter the country. Since 1965 diasporic communities in Europe and the Americas have also received political refugees and members of second diasporas (descendants of earlier immigrants from India who are now immigrating themselves).

Interview

Sri Dushyanth Sridhar

Sri Dushyanth Sridhar (b. 1986) has degrees in engineering and chemistry but has become a popular exponent of Hindu texts, organizing religious tours and giving religious discourses all over the world as well as on television. He reaches out to young Hindus and incorporates into his speeches allusions to popular culture such as Harry Potter. He also uses social media to promote Hindu teachings and the works of Sri Vaishnava teachers such as Vedanta Desika and Ramanuja. The following is excerpted from a longer interview.

Dushyanth Sridhar.

On shifting focus after a career as a consultant in a major company:
Right from a very young age, due to my parents' initiative, I was able to learn the Sanskrit hymns and the Tamil verses. Knowledge which is restricted to a certain class is useless. Until and unless it is made digestible and enjoyable to the masses, that knowledge will remain in a cage. So that's how I started rendering public lectures, which is often characterized as *upanyasams* ("lectures").

On the moral imperative of religious discourses:
Religious discourses, religious lectures are all close to an *upanyasam*. A lecture may have a PowerPoint presentation or standing before a podium. But in the *upanyasam*, the person who speaks is regarded as Vyasa [the legendary author of the epic *Mahabharata*], the incarnation of the Lord. So the lecturer should first practice and then preach. In the *upanyasam*, if I say you need to respect your parents, it should rather be a value that I should have practiced first; only then that I become eligible to preach. So *upanyasam* is not narrating stories; it is interspersed with anecdotes from personal life so that it makes society better.

On making the Hindu texts accessible to the masses:
I not only go to the metro cities such as Bangalore, Chennai, and others which are some of the biggest cities in India and even in the world, I also go to [the smaller] towns of Tamil Nadu.

On making Hindu stories accessible to youth:
When I talk about the great friendship that existed between Krishna and Sudama, I refer to Harry Potter and his friends Hermione and Ron. They stayed with him all through his life, even those phases

Continued

which were very turbulent. So when I look at Harry, it reminds me of Hari [another name of Vishnu], the Lord and potter. Vedanta says my Lord is the potter who makes the mud into pots [a popular analogy in Vedanta philosophy]. He is the material and the ancillary cause. If Harry Potter can bring death to the evil Voldemort, to me, Hari [Vishnu] brings death to the internal enemy we face such as anger, lust, and so on. So everything modern is ancient, and everything ancient is modern; nothing changes. If we say we are in the modern times, imagine 1,000 years later. To me nothing is new. Nothing is old. Everything is constant.

On the eligibility to learn scriptures:

Dushyanth Sridhar mused on the importance placed in texts on the eligibility to learn. He asked how we can use the texts without "diluting them, yet make an impact on the masses?" Traditionally, the gender and caste of devotees had a bearing on one's eligibility to learn. And yet, men and women from all castes and sectors of life attend his talks.

Probably the preceptors of those [the past] age never thought that [we] will come to this stage when everything is accessible with just a single click. So we should take all steps to make sure that the knowledge reaches all sections of the society.

In this digital age, it is tough for traditional scholars to protect the meanings of the *rahasyams*. When everything is available in just one click, it is high time that teachers find newer ways to reach out the meaning of the *rahasyas* so that people still have belief in it. So how do we do it? We can work with the masses to make them eligible for the criteria [mentioned by the scriptures].

On the challenges facing Hinduism:

Dushyanth Sridhar listed several challenges, including not knowing Sanskrit and the languages of the texts, relying on subjective translations, misunderstanding Hinduism as having "many gods," past social evils such as sati, and social hierarchies. Sensitive to social justice but cognizant of texts that espouse hierarchies, he spoke eloquently about internal reform, quoting Ramanuja as an example.

We need to understand that we have had intelligent reformers in our own society who have done a lot. The simplest example I can give is about a person whose one thousandth year we are celebrating now—Ramanuja. Ramanuja was very service-oriented; he worked for the masses.

Dushyanth Sridhar gave a detailed example of how Ramanuja reinterpreted a Sanskrit statement theologically to imply that anyone with devotion to Vishnu would achieve salvation and then concluded:

Ramanuja says your caste doesn't matter; what matters is your interest and your dedication. So this caste hierarchy system has already been worked upon by one of the preceptors who says that wherever you are born, however you are born, you are entitled [to] salvation and we should respect [others].

Temples in the Diaspora

Perhaps the most noticeable feature of global Hindu communities is the tremendous amount of time, money, and energy they devote to the building of temples. Since the 1970s in particular, Hindu immigrants to North America have been transforming their new homes into sacred places.

Places of worship were established as early as 1906 in the San Francisco area, but the first truly ambitious attempt to reproduce the traditional architecture and atmosphere of a Vaishnava sacred place came in 1976 with the construction of the Sri Venkateshwara temple in Penn Hills, a suburb of Pittsburgh, Pennsylvania. (Since then, other Venkateshwara temples or shrines have been established in many parts of the United States and Canada.) The Penn Hills temple enshrines a manifestation of Vishnu as Venkateshwara, Lord of the hill in the South Indian state of Andhra Pradesh known as Venkata ("that which can burn sins"). The Penn Hills temple was built with the help, backing, and blessing of one of the oldest, richest, and most popular temples in India, the Venkateshwara temple at Tiruvenkatam. Devotees celebrate the significance of having Venkateshwara dwelling on American soil with his consort Sri (known locally as Padmavati, "the lady of the lotus").

Drawing on Puranic lore, the Penn Hills devotees think of their temple's physical location—at the confluence of three rivers, one of them subterranean—as recalling the sacred place in India where the rivers Ganga and Yamuna meet the underground Sarasvati.

The particular place from which Hindu immigrants come has an influence on the kinds of temples they build. In Canada, Australia, and parts of Europe such as France and Switzerland, the large numbers of Tamil-speaking immigrants, among them political refugees from Sri Lanka, are reflected in an emphasis on Tamil deities. People from other parts of India as well as second-diaspora Hindus from Guyana, Trinidad, and South Africa have also built temples in the Toronto area, making this one of the most diverse areas of Hindu worship in the world.

North American temples do their best to replicate the traditional pattern of activities—the morning wake-up prayers, the offering of food to the deity, worship, and the recitation of prayers at specific points of the day—but community participation tends to be limited to weekends, since many devotees must travel significant distances to worship. Although a few seasonal festivals, such as Navaratri and Deepavali, are celebrated at the traditional times, for the most part temples try to plan big events around the North American holiday calendar. Thus in the United States most of the

Focus

Yoga in North America

Since it was introduced to the West in the late nineteenth century, yoga has become one of the most popular activities among middle-class Americans, especially women. Today some 6 to 18 million people in the United States report that they either practice or plan to practice yoga. The fact that Americans spend as much as $27 billion a year on yoga-related products suggests that commodification has played an important part in the popularization process.

Is yoga Hindu? Certainly its roots are in traditions that eventually came to be called Hindu. Yet some consider it to be independent of any religious framework—that is, if yoga deepens practitioners' spirituality, it is only in a generic way. Practicing yoga outside the religio-spiritual context does not make one Hindu.

To appreciate how different "American yoga" is from "Indian yoga," recall that Patanjali's yoga centered on moral discipline and meditation; although

he recommended the kinds of bodily postures and breathing techniques that are at the core of American yoga, for Patanjali these were just two aspects of a much more complex discipline. According to him, perfection in concentration and meditation lead to *samadhi*, the final state of absorption into and union with the Supreme Being or higher consciousness. Anyone who reaches this stage is well on the way to emancipation from the cycle of life and death.

Obviously, the scope of the yoga taught in North American church basements and fitness centers is much more limited. The kinds of yoga that have become popular since the 1970s focus mainly on physical well-being and stress reduction. The same is true of popular gurus such as Maharishi Mahesh Yogi and Deepak Chopra: they do not connect their teachings with any specific "religion," and they say that the techniques they advocate are compatible with any religious tradition.

major festivals are scheduled to take advantage of the long weekends between Memorial Day (in May) and Labor Day (in September).

In addition to serving as places of worship, temples in the diaspora serve as community centers, with regular newsletters and website updates that provide "outreach." They also help to educate the diaspora-born in their ancestral traditions through language and religion classes, lectures, study circles, classical music and dance lessons, and summer camps. In addition, perhaps because many of their founding trustees have been physicians, temples in Canada, the United States, and Australia frequently organize events such as blood drives and health screenings. In the home country, temples do not serve any of these functions.

Hinduism and the Environment

The history of environmental activism in India is sometimes traced back as far as the late fifteenth century, when a guru named Jambho—inspired by the pastoral life of Krishna the cowherd—taught his followers to minimize harm to the natural world. The community he established took the name Bishnoi, after his 29 (*bish-noi*) most important teachings, which included everything from vegetarianism to water conservation and the protection of trees. Based in Rajasthan, the Bishnoi have followed those teachings for more than 500 years.

Today, growing numbers of Hindu leaders and institutions are drawing on the classic texts to encourage eco-activism. Billboards at the Venkateshwara temple in Tirumala-Tirupati, for instance, proclaim that "trees, when protected, protect us," and temple authorities draw attention to a line from the *Matsya Purana* in which the goddess Parvati declares that "one tree is equal to ten sons." In a culture where sons are so highly prized, this statement is striking. The Tirumala-Tirupati temple also maintains a large nursery in which tree saplings are grown to be given as *prasada* to pilgrims, who are encouraged to plant them at home. Many environmental activists take inspiration from a section of the *Yajur Veda* known as the *Song of Peace*: "May there be peace in the skies, peace in the atmosphere, peace on earth, peace in the waters. May the healing plants and trees bring peace; may there be peace [on and from] the world, the deity. May there be peace in the world, peace on peace. May that peace come to me!" (*Yajur Veda* 36.17).

Other Challenges

There are many other challenges that Hindus face today in terms of both their relationship to other religious traditions and issues of identity and representation.

Internal Challenges

Internal challenges faced by modern Hindus involve the abuse and misuse of ideas and practices connected with the tradition's larger sociocultural system by human beings for personal gain, wealth, or power. An immediate example is the caste system. Although more characteristic of South Asia and not necessarily an integral part of global Hinduism, the caste system has given rise to prejudice and discrimination. Not only is this illegal, but the Indian government has worked hard in the last few decades to establish extremely large quotas for castes and communities that have faced discrimination historically.

Gender inequality—again associated more with the larger ethos of the subcontinent than with just one religion—also stands out as an internal challenge, especially when it manifests itself in social aberrations such as the demanding of dowries at weddings. Hindus from practically every area and almost all communities are working to address these issues.

The Return to "Traditional" Values and the Rise of Intolerance

As in many other religious traditions, some sectors of the Hindu tradition are alarmed by what they think of as "Western" influences. Members of these groups may deride Hindus who celebrate St. Valentine's Day or harass young unmarried girls who date. Some groups encourage a return to a mythical "golden" past when Hindu dharma is said to have ruled. These groups may sometimes be empowered by people or political parties in power that seek to create dissension between religious communities.

Relationships Between Religious Communities

The present politics of dividing and divided religious groups is the historical legacy of the Muslim conquest of parts of northern India and colonial rule. The challenge that faces India—and one that is not rightly considered "Hindu"—is the creation of a pluralistic society in which people are at peace with one another. At the grassroots level, as seen in personal friendships and networks, people of all religious traditions seem to be more aware of and sensitive to other faiths than they are in many other parts of the world. However, as the partition of the subcontinent showed, these links can be fragile and easily exploited by political interests.

Of the several issues that trouble contemporary Hindus in this sphere, a few are particularly pressing. Many of these issues arise from the Indian understanding of "secularism," which is seen not as a clear separation between church and state (a definition accepted by many Western nations), but as a system in which all religious traditions are treated equally and the state gives their adherents equal opportunities. However, as noted earlier, India has no uniform civil code, and this has been a source of some tension between communities. Furthermore, perceptions that members of the "minority" religions of India are given special preferences, protections, and subsidies (e.g., for the *hajj* pilgrimage) have provoked considerable concern among Hindus and led to the empowerment of the Hindutva political party.

Issues of Identity and Representation

While the colonial era saw the beginning of a systematic study of India and Hinduism through Western intellectual lenses, a considerable number of these accounts were either critical, Orientalist, or riddled with misrepresentations. The translation of subtle concepts and sophisticated ideas into English also caused problems. For example, many accounts depicted Hindus as polytheistic, idolatrous, "phallus" worshipers, and so on. Several of these stereotypes have persisted, despite sensitive work in the last several decades. Some accounts have presented exotica such as "left-handed" tantric adherents as "real Hinduism," whether to increase missionary activity or to gain television ratings. Furthermore, given the impoverishment of the subcontinent by colonial rulers and the decades it took for India to become self-sufficient in terms of food resources, India—and Hinduism—also became associated with poverty on the one hand and an otherworldly "spirituality" on the other. The latter was due in part to the many gurus who came to the West, where they taught meditation and yoga as "universal" practices. In time, however, yoga has become disengaged from the Hindu religious framework and is now often seen as just one more destressing mechanism. School textbooks in the diaspora, many Hindus argue, still adhere to many of these stereotypes. Many Hindus point out that while western media and textbooks still associate Hinduism with negative stereotypes, popular ideas and practices like yoga become disconnected with the parent tradition.

Hindus also struggle with issues of caste discrimination and untouchability. While many of these problems are nonexistent in urban areas in the subcontinent and the diaspora, India is a vast country, and, as in many other traditions, intolerance in the name of religion can be seen there. In all these cases, what is at stake is the representation of Hindus and Hinduism, and because there is a diversity of voices speaking for Hinduism, the issues have become very complex.

Summary

Through music, dance, stories, rituals, and celebrations, through architecture and literature, the Hindu traditions continue to be practiced and transmitted all over the world. The dynamism of these traditions is unmistakable. Scholars continue to interpret Vedanta. People still experience possession by deities, situate their homes in auspicious directions, and choose astrologically correct times for weddings. Ancient manuscripts are still being restored and edited, and new technologies are making the literature accessible to virtually everyone; the tradition confining the sacred word to particular castes is gone forever. In short, Hinduism continues to adapt to the world around it.

Sites

Kamakhya, Assam

Kamakhya is one of the most important sites where the power of the Goddess is said to be felt. The temple is dedicated to the goddess Kamakhya, a form of Shakti/Parvati/Durga.

Badrinath, Uttaranchal

One of 108 places sacred to the Sri Vaishnava community, Badrinath is located high in the Himalayas, with a temple of Vishnu in the form of the sages Nara and Narayana.

Srirangam, Tamilnadu

Srirangam is an island temple town where Vishnu, here called Ranganatha ("Lord of the stage"), reclines on the serpent Ananta ("infinity"). It is celebrated in the poems of the Alvars.

Madurai, Tamilnadu

Madurai is a large city that is home to dozens of temples, including a famous complex dedicated to Meenakshi (a local form of Parvati) and Sundaresvara (Shiva).

Tirumala-Tirupati (also known as Tiruvenkatam), Andhra Pradesh

One of the most important pilgrimage sites in India, Tirumala-Tirupati is dedicated to Venkateshwara (Vishnu).

Puri, Orissa

Puri is the site of a famous festival celebrating Lord Jagannath (a form of Vishnu) and his siblings, during which his image is rolled through the streets on a huge chariot. This event is the source of the English word "juggernaut."

Varanasi, Uttar Pradesh

Also known as Banaras, Varanasi is one of the holiest cities in India, located on the river Ganga. After cremation, many Hindus' ashes are brought here to be ritually submerged in the waters.

Mount Kailas, Tibet

A peak in the Himalayan range, Mount Kailas is said to be the abode of Lord Shiva. It is sacred to Jainas and Buddhists as well as Hindus.

Sacred Texts

Religion (Sect)	Text(s)	Composition/Compilation	Compilation/Revision	Use
Hinduism	Vedas (Sanskrit)	Composed between c. 1500 and 600 BCE		Considered the most authoritative of all texts. Parts of the Vedas were used in both domestic and temple rituals.
	Upanishads: the last section of the Vedas, focusing on philosophy (Sanskrit)	c. 6th century BCE	Used by most Vedanta philosophers in or as the subject of commentaries. The commentarial tradition continues today.	Philosophical
	Ramayana (Sanskrit)	Very approximately, c. 5th century BCE–1st century CE	Periodically rendered in local languages. Tulsidas's *Ramcharitmanas* in Hindi is very important.	Doctrinal, ritual, performative, inspirational, devotional, narrative, educational
	Mahabharata (Sanskrit)	c. 5th century BCE–2nd century CE		Doctrinal, ritual, narrative, performative, inspirational, devotional, educational
	Bhagavad Gita (part of the *Mahabharata*; Sanskrit)	c. 2nd century BCE–2nd century CE	Extensive tradition of commentary	Doctrinal, ritual, performative, devotional, inspirational, narrative, educational
	Puranas (Sanskrit)	1st millennium CE	Often re-created in local languages.	Doctrinal, ritual, devotional, narrative, inspirational, educational
Vaishnava, (specifically Gaudiya and ISKCON)	*Bhagavata Purana* (Sanskrit)	c. 1st millennium CE		Doctrinal, ritual, devotional, narrative, inspirational, educational
	Dharmasutras, followed by the *Dharmashastras*. Many texts, of which the *Manava Dharmashastra* ("Laws of Manu") is the most important (Sanskrit).	*Dharmasutras* composed in the 1st millennium BCE; *dharmashastras* in the 1st millennium CE	Extensive tradition of commentary. Medathithi (c. 9th–11th centuries CE?) commented on *Manu*.	Ritual, moral, and legal prescriptions on all aspects of life (personal, domestic, public); discussions of right behavior
	Yoga Sutras of Patanjali	c. 200 BCE–300 CE	Commentarial tradition	Classical philosophical text for yoga
Vaishnava (Tamil)	*Nalayira Divya Prabandham* ("Sacred Collect of Four Thousand Verses") by the Alvars (Tamil)	c. 8–10th centuries CE; said to have been "revealed" in 11th century	Extensive commentarial tradition	Doctrinal, ritual, performative, devotional, inspirational, narrative, educational
Shaiva (Tamil)	Tirumurai	c. 8th–12th centuries		Devotional, philosophical
Vaishnava	Poems of Surdas (Hindi/ Braj Bhasha)	16th century		Doctrinal, ritual, performative, devotional, inspirational, narrative, educational
Vaishnava (Marathi)	*Dnyaneshwari* or *Jnaneswari*	Composed by Dnyaneshwar, c. 13th century		Doctrinal, devotional, educational

Discussion Questions

1. What is the origin of the word "Hindu"? What elements of the Harappa culture suggest connections with Hindu traditions?

2. Why are the *Ramayana* and *Mahabharata* central to Hinduism?

3. What role do sacred texts play in Hinduism?

4. Identify some of the deities, major and minor, that Hindus worship. How is it that Hindus describe themselves as monotheistic?

5. Who or what is Brahman? What is the relationship between Brahman and deities such as Vishnu, Shiva, and the Goddess?

6. What is *bhakti*? What role does it play in Hinduism?

7. What are the three ways to liberation discussed in the *Bhagavad Gita*?

8. Describe some of the distinctive features of Hinduism as it developed in Southeast Asia.

9. What is the role of the performing arts in Hinduism?

10. What are the primary ways in which women historically contributed to various Hindu traditions?

Glossary

acharya The leading teacher of a sect or the head of a monastery.

advaita Shankara's school of philosophy, which holds that there is only one ultimate reality, the indescribable Brahman, with which the Atman or self is identical.

Alvars Twelve devotional poets whose works are central to the South Indian *bhakti* tradition.

artha Prosperity; one of the three classical aims in life.

ashramas The four stages in the life of an upper-class male: student, householder, forest-dweller, and ascetic.

Atman The individual self, held by Upanishadic and Vedantic thought to be identical to Brahman, the world-soul.

avatara A "descent" or incarnation of a deity in earthly form.

Ayurveda A system of traditional medicine, understood as a teaching transmitted from the sages.

Bhagavad Gita A section of the *Mahabharata* epic recounting a conversation between Krishna and the warrior Arjuna, in which Krishna explains the nature of God and the human soul.

bhakti Loving devotion to a deity seen as a gracious being who enters the world for the benefit of humans.

Brahma The creator god; not to be confused with Brahman.

Brahman The world-soul, sometimes understood in impersonal terms; not to be confused with Brahma.

Brahmanas Texts regarding ritual.

brahmin A member of the priestly class.

darshana Seeing and being seen by the deity (in the temple) or by a holy teacher; the experience of beholding with faith.

Deepavali (Diwali) Festival of light in October–November, when lamps are lit.

dharma Religious and social duty, including both righteousness and faith.

guru A spiritual teacher.

Holi Spring festival celebrated by throwing brightly colored water or powder.

jnana Knowledge; along with action and devotion, one of the three avenues to liberation explained in the *Bhagavad Gita*.

kama Sensual (not merely sexual) pleasure; one of the three classical aims of life.

karma Action, seen as both good and bad, as it is believed to determine the quality of rebirth in future lives.

kshatriya A member of the warrior class in ancient Hindu society.

linga A conical or cylindrical stone column symbolizing the creative energies of the god Shiva.

Mahabharata A very long epic poem, one section of which is the *Bhagavad Gita*.

mantra An expression of one or more syllables, chanted repeatedly as a focus of concentration in devotion.

moksha Liberation from the cycle of birth and death; one of the three classical aims in life.

murti A form or personification in which divinity is manifested.

Navaratri "Nine nights"; an autumn festival honoring the Goddess.

om A syllable chanted in meditation, interpreted as representing ultimate reality, or the universe, or the relationship of the devotee to the deity.

prasada A gift from the deity, especially food that has been presented to the god's temple image, blessed, and returned to the devotee.

puja Ritual household worship of the deity, commonly involving oil lamps, incense, prayers, and food offerings.

Puranas "Old tales"; stories about deities that became important after the Vedic period.

Ramayana An epic recounting the life of Lord Rama, an incarnation of the god Vishnu.

rishi A seer; the composers of the ancient Vedic hymns are considered *rishis*.

sadhu A holy man.

samnyasin A religious ascetic; one who has reached the last of the four stages of life for a Hindu male; see *ashramas*.

samsara The continuing cycle of rebirths.

sati The self-sacrifice of a widow who throws herself onto her deceased husband's funeral pyre.

shruti "What is heard"; the sacred literature of the Vedic and Upanishadic periods, recited orally by the brahmin priests for many centuries before it was written down.

shudra A member of the lowest of the four major classes, usually translated as "servant," though some groups within the shudra class could be quite prosperous.

smrti "What is remembered"; a body of ancient Hindu literature, including the epics, *Puranas*, and law codes, formed after the *shruti* and passed down in written form.

tantra An esoteric school outside the Vedic and brahminical tradition, which emerged around the fifth century and centered on a number of controversial ritual practices, some of them sexual.

upanayana The initiation of a young brahmin boy into ritual responsibility, in which he is given a cord to wear over his left shoulder and a mantra to recite and is sent to beg for food for the day.

Upanishads Philosophical texts in the form of reported conversations on the theory of the Vedic ritual and the nature of knowledge, composed around the sixth century BCE.

vaishya A member of the third or mercantile class in the ancient fourfold class structure.

Vedas The four collections of hymns and ritual texts that constitute the oldest and most highly respected Hindu sacred literature.

yoga A practice and discipline that may involve a philosophical system and mental concentration as well as physical postures and exercises.

Further Reading

Bryant, Edwin. 2003. *The Quest for the Origins of Vedic Culture: The Indo-Aryan Migration Debate*. New York: Oxford University Press. A balanced and thorough discussion of a controversial topic.

Bryant, Edwin, ed. 2007. *Krishna: A Sourcebook*. New York: Oxford University Press. A good introduction to one of the most important deities in the Hindu tradition from a variety of sectarian and regional perspectives.

Bryant, Edwin, and Maria Eckstrand. 2004. *The Hare Krishna Movement: The Postcharismatic Fate of a Religious Transplant*. New York: Columbia University Press. An eclectic collection of essays on the International Society for Krishna Consciousness.

Chapple, Christopher, and Mary Evelyn Tucker, eds. 2000. *Hinduism and Ecology: The Intersection of Earth, Sky, and Water*. Cambridge, MA: Center for the Study of World Religions, Harvard Divinity School. Part of an important series in which various traditions address current environmental issues.

Coward, Harold. 2005. *Human Rights and the World's Major Religions, Vol. 4: The Hindu Tradition*. Westport, CT: Praeger. A good introduction to an important topic.

Dalmia, Vasudha, and Heinrich von Steitencron, eds. 1995. *Representing Hinduism: The Construction of Religious Traditions and National Identity*. New Delhi: Sage. A good set of essays discussing whether Hinduism is one or many traditions.

Doniger O'Flaherty, Wendy, ed. and trans. 1988. *Textual Sources for the Study of Hinduism*. Manchester, UK: Manchester University Press. A good sourcebook, in a rather compressed format, covering the main phases of the Hindu tradition.

Eck, Diana L. 1981. *Darsan: Seeing the Divine Image in India*. Chambersburg, PA: Anima Books. A brief but authoritative work on the significance of coming into the presence of the deity.

Embree, Ainslie T., ed. 1988. *Sources of Indian Tradition*. 2nd ed. 2 vols. New York: Columbia University Press. A work that expands on the first edition edited by de Bary but drops a few items in the process.

Erndl, Kathleen M. 1993. *Victory to the Mother: The Hindu Goddess of Northwest India in Myth, Ritual, and Symbol*. New York: Oxford University Press. A well-focused book on one region.

Findly, Ellison B. 1985. "Gargi at the King's Court: Women and Philosophic Innovation in Ancient India." In *Women, Religion and Social Change*, ed. Yvonne Y. Haddad and Ellison B. Findly, 37–58. Albany: State University of New York Press. An article that shows that intellectual activity was not entirely limited to males.

González-Reimann, Luis. 2009. "Cosmic Cycles, Cosmology and Cosmography." In *Brill's Encyclopedia of Hinduism*, ed. Knut Jacobsen, Helene Basu, Angelika Malinar, and Vasudha Narayanan, 1:411–428. Leiden: Brill. A good introduction to time, space, and the cosmos in Hinduism.

Hawley, John S., and Donna M. Wulff. 1982. *The Divine Consort: Radha and the Goddesses of India*. Berkeley Religious Studies Series. Berkeley: University of California Press. Another useful work on feminine aspects of the Hindu tradition.

Hawley, John S., and Donna M. Wulff. 1996. *Devi: Goddesses of India*. Berkeley: University of California Press. An expansion on the theme of Hawley and Wulff's previous work.

Jacobsen, Knut, Helene Basu, Angelika Malinar, and Vasudha Narayanan, eds. 2009–2014. *Brill's Encyclopedia of Hinduism*. 6 vols. Leiden: Brill. An excellent and comprehensive resource on the Hindu traditions.

Leslie, Julia, ed. 1991. *Roles and Rituals for Hindu Women*. London: Pinter. A coherent set of essays on the subject.

Lopez, Donald S., Jr., ed. 1995. *Religions of India in Practice*. Princeton, NJ: Princeton University Press. A sourcebook containing a fine range of material that is strong on ritual.

Marglin, Frédérique, and John B. Carman, eds. 1985. *Purity and Auspiciousness in Indian Society*. Leiden: E. J. Brill. A useful collection in an anthropological series.

Miller, Barbara Stoler, trans. 1977. *Love Song of the Dark Lord: Jayadeva's Gitagovinda*. New York: Columbia University Press. An important *bhakti* text.

Miller, Barbara Stoler, trans. 1986. *The Bhagavad Gita: Krishna's Counsel in Time of War*. New York: Columbia University Press. A good translation that is accessible to undergraduates.

Mittal, Sushil, and Gene Thursby, eds. 2004. *The Hindu World*. New York: Routledge. Fairly comprehensive coverage of Hinduism, using Sanskrit terms, concepts, and categories.

Narayan, R. K. 1972. *Ramayana: A Shortened Modern Prose Version of the Indian Epic*. New York: Viking. A useful point of access to this classic.

Narayanan, Vasudha. 1994. *The Vernacular Veda: Revelation, Recitation, and Ritual Practice*. Columbia: University of South Carolina Press. A work that addresses the ritual use of the *Tiruvaymoli* among India's scheduled castes as well as brahmins.

Narayanan, Vasudha. 1996. "'One Tree Is Equal to Ten Sons': Hindu Responses to the Problems of Ecology, Population, and Consumption." *Journal of the American Academy of Religion* 65: 291–332. A discussion of some classic resources for addressing concerns of today.

Nelson, Lance E., ed. 1998. *Purifying the Earthly Body of God: Religion and Ecology in Hindu India*. Albany: State University of New York Press. One of the earliest and best collections of essays on an important topic.

Orr, Leslie C. 2000. *Donors, Devotees, and Daughters of God: Temple Women in Medieval Tamilnadu*. New York: Oxford University Press. A useful corrective to prescriptive male writings in Sanskrit on Hindu women.

Patton, Laurie L., ed. 2002. *Jewels of Authority: Women and Text in the Hindu Tradition*. New York: Oxford University Press. A wide-ranging collection of essays on Hindu and Buddhist women's relationship to sacred texts and mantras.

Pechilis, Karen, ed. 2004. *The Graceful Guru: Hindu Female Gurus in India and the United States*. New York: Oxford University Press. A good set of essays on women gurus, with an excellent introduction by the editor.

Rajagopalachari, Chakravarti. 1953. *Mahabharata*. Bombay: Bharatiya Vidya Bhavan. A sampling from this vast epic.

Sweetman, Will. 2003. *Mapping Hinduism: "Hinduism" and the Study of Indian Religions, 1600–1776*. Halle, Germany: Franckesche Stiftungen.

Tharu, Susie, and K. Lalita. 1991. *Women Writing in India: 600 BC to the Present*. New York: Feminist Press. A must-read for all those interested in hearing women's voices from the past. Includes literature not necessarily perceived to be religious or Hindu.

Waghorne, Joanne P., Norman Cutler, and Vasudha Narayanan, eds. 1985. *Gods of Flesh, Gods of Stone: The Embodiment of Divinity in India*. New York: Columbia University Press. An exploration of the range of forms in which Hindus see deity manifested.

Williams, Raymond Brady, ed. 1992. *A Sacred Thread: Modern Transmission of Hindu Traditions in India and Abroad*. Chambersburg, PA: Anima. A good description of the Hindu diaspora in the 1970s and 1980s.

Wujastyk, Dominik, trans. 1998. *The Roots of Ayurveda: Selections from Sanskrit Medical Writings*. Delhi: Penguin. A useful work on the relationship between traditional Indian medicine and religion.

Zimmer, Heinrich. 1946. *Myths and Symbols in Indian Art and Civilization*. New York: Pantheon. A classic study, still often cited.

Recommended Websites

http://www.sacred-texts.com/hin/index.htm
A website offering free online translations (mostly from the late nineteenth to early twentieth century) of the Vedas, epics, *Puranas*, *Yoga Sutras*, smrti literature, etc.

http://www.sscnet.ucla.edu/southasia
A site with very good links for South Asian culture, religions, and history.

http://www.harappa.com/har/har0.html
A collection of many links to various aspects of the Indus civilization.

http://www.wabashcenter.wabash.edu/resources/result_browse.aspx?topic=569&pid=361
A meta-site with links to many useful resources, including course syllabi.

http://www.columbia.edu/itc/mealac/pritchett/00 generallinks/index.html
A good site with links to many resources on South Asia.

http://virtualvillage.wesleyan.edu
An on-the-ground look at a "virtual village" in North India.

http://www.veda.harekrsna.cz/encyclopedia/index.htm
A site offering links to articles on various topics in Hinduism from an ISKCON perspective.

http://www.sathyasai.org
The official site of Sri Sathya Sai Baba, maintained by his devotees.

http://prapatti.com
A site presenting texts and MP3 audios of several Tamil and Sanskrit Vaishnava prayers.

http://www.hindupedia.com/en/Main_Page
An online encyclopedia offering "a traditional perspective" on the Hindu religion and way of life.

http://www.hinduismtoday.com
The website of a popular magazine based in Hawaii and rooted in the classical Shaiva tradition that offers articles of interest to Hindus all over the world.

References

Doniger O'Flaherty, Wendy, ed. and trans. 1981. *The Rig Veda: An Anthology, One Hundred and Eight Hymns*. Harmondsworth, UK: Penguin.

Hawley, John S., and Mark Juergensmeyer, trans. 1988. *Songs of the Saints of India*. New York: Oxford University Press.

Miller, Barbara Stoler, trans. 1986. *The Bhagavad-Gita: Krishna's Counsel in Time of War*. New York: Columbia University Press.

Nielsen, Niels C., Norvin Hein, Frank E. Reynolds, Alan L. Miller, Samuel E. Karff, eds. 1993. *Religions of the World*, 3rd edition. New York: Bedford/St. Martin's.

8 Sikh Traditions

Pashaura Singh

Traditions at a Glance

Numbers

There are 25 million Sikhs around the world.

Distribution

Sikhs are primarily found in northern India, especially Punjab, Haryana, and Delhi, with minorities in other provinces of India and many other countries, including Canada, the United States (especially California), and Britain.

Founders and Leaders

The tradition was founded by Guru Nanak around 1500 CE and developed by a succession of nine other inspired teachers, the last of whom, Guru Gobind Singh, died in 1708.

Deity

The supreme being is considered to be one and without form. Guru Nanak referred to the deity as Akal Purakh ("Timeless Person"), Kartar ("Creator"), and Nirankar ("Formless"), among many other names.

Authoritative Texts

The Adi Granth (also known as Guru Granth Sahib) is a compilation of divinely inspired hymns by six gurus, 15 poet-saints, and 15 Sikh bards; the Dasam Granth, a collection of hymns made in the time of the tenth guru, is also revered as a secondary scripture.

Noteworthy Teachings

Sikhism teaches that there is one supreme reality, which is never incarnated. In addition to reverence for the gurus and the sacred scriptures, Sikhs emphasize egalitarianism, tolerance, service to others, and righteous life in this world as the way to ultimate liberation from the cycle of rebirth.

In this chapter you will learn about:

- The origins of Sikhism, the Sikh Panth, and the 10 gurus
- Sikh–Mughal conflict and the creation of the Khalsa
- Sikh teachings and sacred scriptures
- Sikh reform movements and variations in modern Sikhism
- Sikh social norms, culture, and institutions of doctrinal authority
- The Sikh diaspora and recent developments in the tradition

"Sikh" is a Punjabi word meaning "disciple." People who identify themselves as Sikhs are disciples of **Akal Purakh** ("Timeless Being," God), the 10 Sikh **gurus**, and the sacred scripture called the **Adi Granth** ("Original Book"). The youngest of India's Indigenous religions, Sikhism emerged in the Punjab approximately five centuries ago and quickly distinguished itself from the region's other religious traditions by its preference for active engagement with the world rather than ascetic renunciation.

Today the global Sikh population numbers approximately 25 million, of whom more than 20 million live in India, mainly in Punjab. Sikhs make up only about 2 percent of the country's 1 billion people, but their contributions to its political and economic life are significant. The rest of the world's Sikhs are part of a global diaspora that includes substantial communities in Southeast Asia, Australia, New Zealand, East Africa, Britain, and North America.

 Entering the Darbar Sahib (Golden Temple) in Amritsar (Ashok Sinha/Getty Images).

⊕ Overview

The religious environment of the fifteenth-century Punjab was suffused with the thought of the North Indian **Sants**. The founder of Sikhism, Guru Nanak (1469–1539), shared both the mystic and the iconoclastic tendencies of these "poet-saints." Nevertheless, he declared his independence from the prevailing thought forms and sought to kindle the fire of independence in his disciples.

Timeline

1469	Birth of Guru Nanak, the founder of the Sikh tradition
1499	Guru Nanak underwent his mystical experience
1519	Establishment of the first Sikh community at Kartarpur
1539	Guru Nanak succeeded by Guru Angad
1577	Guru Ram Das established town of Ramdaspur (Amritsar)
1604	Adi Granth compiled under Guru Arjan's supervision
1606	Guru Arjan martyred on the orders of Emperor Jahangir
1675	Guru Tegh Bahadur martyred on the orders of Emperor Aurangzeb
1699	Guru Gobind Singh organized the Khalsa
1708	Death of Guru Gobind Singh ends succession of human gurus; from now on the guru is the scripture, known as Guru Granth Sahib
1765	Sikhs capture Lahore
1799	Punjab united under Maharaja Ranjit Singh
1849	Annexation of the Punjab by the British
1865	Publication of the first printed edition of the Guru Granth Sahib
1873	Singh Sabha movement is established
1892	Singh Sabha establishes Khalsa College in Amritsar
1920	Shiromani Gurdwara Prabandhak Committee (SGPC) established
1925	Sikh Gurdwara Act gives SGPC legal authority over all gurdwaras
1947	Punjab partitioned between India and Pakistan
1973	Sikh Akali Dal party passes Anandpur Sahib Resolution, demanding greater autonomy for all Indian states; relations with the central government become increasingly strained
1984	Indian army attacks the Golden Temple and other gurdwaras in the Punjab
1999	Sikhs celebrate tricentenary of the Khalsa
2004	Manmohan Singh elected first Sikh prime minister of India
2008	Tricentenary celebration of the installation of Guru Granth Sahib as guru
2010	Tricentenary celebration of Sikh rule established by Banda Singh Bahadur
2012	Indian Parliament passes Anand Marriage (Amendment) Act to register Sikh marriages
2016	Indian Parliament amends 1925 Sikh Gurdwara Act, denying Sehajdhari Sikhs the right to vote in SGPC elections
2017	350th anniversary celebration of birth of Guru Gobind Singh at Patna Sahib
2019	550th anniversary celebration of Guru Nanak's birth

The foundation of the Sikh tradition was Nanak's belief in the possibility of achieving spiritual liberation in a single lifetime through meditation on the divine Name (**nam**), the constant presence of Akal Purakh in the heart, and the living of an ethical life in the world. The interaction of this belief with two environmental factors—the rural base of Punjabi society and the historical circumstances of the period during which Nanak's successors built on the foundations he laid—determined the historical development of Sikhism.

The name "Punjab" ("five waters") refers to the five tributaries of the Indus River that define the region. Historically, it was a geographical crossroads where the cultures of the Middle East, Central Asia, and India met and through which a series of Muslim invaders made forays into the subcontinent.

Sufi Islam had become established in the Punjab by the eleventh century. By the fifteenth century the Buddhists had disappeared from the region, although a few Jaina ascetics remained. There were also three distinct Hindu communities, devoted to Shiva, Vishnu, and the Goddess, along with a cluster of tantra-influenced yogic sects known collectively as the Nath tradition. This diverse religious universe required the Sikhs to define themselves in an ongoing process of interaction and debate.

Guru Nanak

Guru Nanak was born in 1469 to an upper-caste professional family at Talwandi (Nankana Sahib), not far from what is now Lahore, Pakistan. By then the Punjab had been under Muslim control for more than 200 years. When the Mughal emperor Babur (1483–1530) came to power in 1526, Nanak had already established a community of his followers in the village of Kartarpur. For the next two centuries the Sikh tradition evolved in the historical context of the Mughal regime.

Guru Nanak's Mystical Experience

Much of what we know about Guru Nanak comes from stories that began circulating orally during his lifetime. His life may be divided into three distinct phases: an early contemplative period, a mystic enlightenment followed by years of pilgrimage, and a conclusion during which he established the first Sikh community.

Employed as a steward by a Muslim nobleman, the young Nanak spent the beginning and end of each day absorbed in meditation and devotional singing (**kirtan**). Early one morning, while he was bathing in a river, he disappeared. Three days later he stepped out of the water and proclaimed: "There is no Hindu, there is no Muslim."

The significance of this statement becomes clear in the context of a religious culture divided between the Islamic and Hindu traditions. Nanak emphasized the common humanity underlying the external divisions. After his immersion in the waters—a metaphor of dissolution, transformation, and spiritual perfection—Nanak was ready to proclaim a new vision. One of his own hymns describes his experience: "I was a minstrel out of work; the Lord assigned me the task of singing the Divine Word day and night. He summoned me to his Court and bestowed on me the robe of honour for singing his praises. On me he bestowed the Divine Nectar (**amrit**) in a cup, the nectar of his true and holy Name" (M1, *Var Majh* 27, Adi Granth/AG 150).[1]

This hymn marked the beginning of Nanak's ministry to preach the message of the divine Name. He was then 30 years of age, had been married for more than a decade, and was the father of two young sons. Yet he left his family to travel to both Hindu and Muslim places of pilgrimage, where he tested his ideas in debate with the leaders of different religious persuasions.

Map 8.1 The Punjab

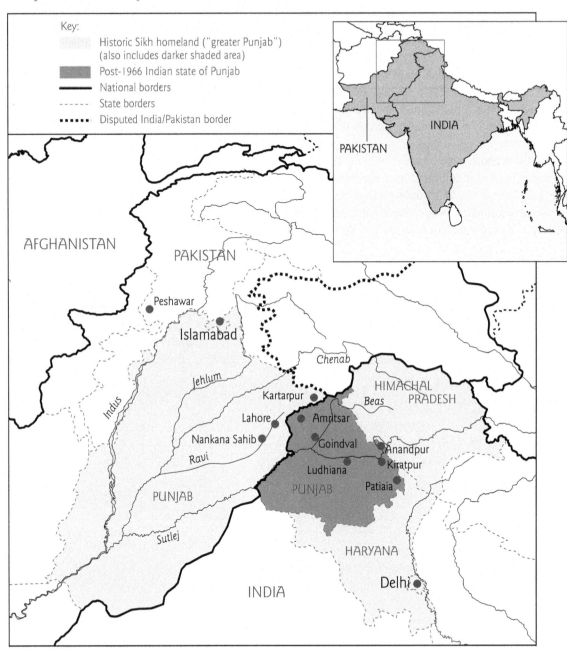

Key:
- Historic Sikh homeland ("greater Punjab") (also includes darker shaded area)
- Post-1966 Indian state of Punjab
- National borders
- State borders
- Disputed India/Pakistan border

Source: Adapted from Nesbitt 2005: 9.

Foundation of the Sikh Panth

At the end of his travels, Guru Nanak founded the village of Kartarpur in Punjab in 1519. There he lived for the rest of his life as the spiritual guide of a new religious community. His charisma won him many disciples, who received the message of liberation through hymns that became central to Sikh congregational worship. The Kartarpur community formed the nucleus of the Nanak-**Panth**

("Path of Nanak"). Nanak called for a decisive break with existing religions and laid the groundwork for a new, rational model of human behavior based on divine authority.

The authenticity and power of Guru Nanak's message derived from his personal experience of divine reality, which gave him a perspective from which to interpret and assess existing traditions. He understood his work to be divinely commissioned, and he demanded obedience of his followers as an ethical duty.

Some of the 974 hymns of Guru Nanak that are preserved in the Adi Granth contrast the beliefs and practices of other traditions with those of his own. At the same time he recognized "true Hindus" and "true Muslims" and invited them to follow his path of inner spirituality based on ethical values. Understanding that they would grasp his message more easily if it was expressed in the language of their own religious heritage, he reached out to them using concepts from their respective traditions (see Document box).

Guru Nanak's belief that "one should live on what one has earned through hard work and share with others the fruit of one's exertion" (AG 1245) was reflected in the Kartarpur community. Members supported themselves through agricultural work and shared what they earned

A *dhadhi,* a traditional singer and musician who specializes in martial ballads, plays a *sarangi* outside the Darbar Sahib in Amritsar (© Andrea Magugliani/Alamy).

Document

Guru Nanak Speaks to Muslims and Hindus

To Muslims:

Make mercy your mosque and devotion your prayer
    mat, Righteousness your Qur'an;
Meekness your circumcising, goodness your fasting;
    For thus the true Muslim expresses his faith.
Make good works your Ka'bah, take truth your Pir
    Compassion your creed and your prayer.
Let service to God be the beads which you tell
    And God will exalt you to glory.
    (M1, *Var Majh,* AG 140–1)

To Hindus:

Make compassion the cotton, contentment the thread,
    Continence the knot, and truth the twist.
This is the sacred thread of the soul,
    If you possess it, O Brahmin, then place it on me.
It does not break or become soiled with filth.
    This can neither be burnt, nor lost.
Blessed are the mortals, O Nanak,
    Who wear such a thread round their neck.
    (M1, *Var Asa,* AG 471)

through the institution of the **langar**, the communal meal that is offered to everyone attending the **gurdwara** (the Sikh place of worship) and is prepared as a community service by members of the congregation (*sangat*). As established by Guru Nanak, the *langar* tradition requires people of all castes and conditions to sit side-by-side in status-free rows—female next to male, socially high next to socially low, ritually pure next to ritually impure—and share the same food. This was the first practical expression of the guru's mission to reform society. Promoting community service, egalitarianism, and belonging, the *langar* marked a major step in the definition of a distinctive Sikh identity.

Finally, before his death in 1539, Guru Nanak created the institution of the guru. Bypassing his own son Sri Chand, an ascetic who had renounced the life in the world that Sikhism embraced, he chose his disciple Lehna as his successor, renamed him Angad ("my own limb"), and bowed before him, becoming a disciple himself. In this act of humility, Guru Nanak clearly asserted the primacy of the message over the messenger, gave the office of guru charismatic authority, and established that the guru is "one," whatever form the occupant of the office might take.

The 10 Gurus

The 62 couplets or stanzas composed by Guru Angad throw light on the historical situation of the Panth during the period of his leadership and mark the doctrinal boundaries of the Sikh faith as interpreted in strict conformity with Guru Nanak's message. Guru Angad also refined the **Gurmukhi** ("from the guru's mouth") script in which the guru's hymns were recorded (the original script was a version of the business shorthand that Guru Nanak had used as a young man). The use of this script signaled the early Sikhs' rejection of the authority attributed to Sanskrit, Arabic, and Persian by scholars of the period while reinforcing the Sikhs' distinct identity. In fact, language has been the single most important factor in the preservation of the Sikh cultural heritage. The idea that spiritual truth could be inscribed in their own language was empowering for Punjabis.

Document

Guru Nanak on Women

Guru Nanak spoke out against the inferior position assigned to women in Punjabi society, as the following verse from his Asa Ki Var *("Ballad in the Asa mode") shows. Note that the guru often addressed himself in his writings.*

From women born, shaped in the womb,
To woman betrothed and wed;
We are bound to women by ties of affection,
On women man's future depends.
If one woman dies he seeks another;
With a woman he orders his life.

Why then should one speak evil of women,
They who give birth to kings?
Women also are born from women;
    None takes birth except from a woman.
Only the True One [Akal Purakh/God], Nanak
    needs no help from a woman.
Blessed are they, both men and women,
    Who endlessly praise their Lord.
Blessed are they in the True One's court,
    There shall their faces shine
(M1, *Var Asa*, AG 473; McLeod 1997: 241–242)

Langar at a gurdwara in Siliguri, India (© RUPAK DE CHOWDHURI/Reuters/Corbis).

The third guru, Amar Das (1479–1574), introduced institutional innovations that strengthened the unity of the Panth. In addition to founding the town of Goindval, he established two annual festivals (Divali and Baisakhi) that provided regular opportunities for the growing community to get together; introduced a system of 22 *manjis* (seats of authority) as bases for missionaries seeking converts; and oversaw the preparation of the Goindval **pothis** ("volumes"), the initial collections of the compositions of the first three gurus and some of the medieval poet-saints. As the geographical base of the Panth expanded, missionaries needed copies of the **bani** ("divine Word") that they could carry with them, and growing numbers of Sikhs needed a common frame of reference for communal worship. Thus Guru Amar Das had scribes make copies of the hymns for distribution.

The reforms that Guru Amar Das instituted regarding women were perhaps even more significant. He abolished both the wearing of the veil and the practice of **sati**, permitted widows to remarry, appointed women as missionaries (roughly half of the original 22 *manjis* were held by women), and gave all Sikh women equal rights with men to conduct prayers and other congregational ceremonies.

These early steps speak of the practical wisdom of the second- and third-generation Sikhs, who had to find ways to convey Guru Nanak's message without the benefit of direct emotional experience. In every religious tradition, translation into a standard written form and objectification in rituals and ceremonies become imperative as the gap separating new converts from the founder and original disciples widens.

The fourth guru, Ram Das (1534–1581), established the town that would come to be known as Amritsar ("nectar of immortality") and ordered the construction of a large pool there. The fact that the Panth undertook such complex projects suggests the support that Guru Nanak's message soon attracted. Guru Ram Das also contributed 679 new hymns to Sikh scripture and expanded the number of melodies (*ragas*) specified for their singing. The musicality and emotional appeal of his hymns had a tremendous impact, and the liturgical requirement to sing as well as recite the sacred Word contributed significantly to Sikhs' self-image as a distinct community.

It was the fifth guru, Arjan (1563–1606), who built the Darbar Sahib ("Divine Court," also known as the Golden Temple) in Amritsar; surrounded by the sacred pool, it remains the central symbol of the Sikh faith to this day. He also organized the scriptural corpus he had inherited into the Adi Granth, the definitive statement of Sikhism.

By the mid-seventeenth century, a Persian author was able to comment that "there were not many cities in the inhabited countries where some Sikhs were not to be found." So significant was the growth of Sikhism that it attracted the attention of the Mughal authorities. The fact that, ethnically, the majority of Sikhs were Jats—agriculturalists with distinctly martial cultural traditions—would play a significant role in the community's relationship with those authorities.

Rise of Sikh–Mughal Conflict

To a large extent, the peaceful growth of the Panth throughout the sixteenth century can be attributed to the liberal policy of Emperor Akbar (r. 1556–1605). Within eight months of Akbar's death, however, Guru Arjan himself was dead, executed by order of the new emperor, Jahangir (r. 1605–1628). This "first martyrdom" became the decisive factor in the crystallization of the Sikh Panth, pushing the community in the direction of separatism and militancy.

The sixth guru, Hargobind (1595–1644), signaled this new direction when, at his investiture, he donned two swords, one symbolizing temporal and the other spiritual authority. Another

Document

Bhai Gurdas on the Gursikh

Arising at the ambrosial hour the **Gursikh** bathes in the sacred pool.

Having chanted the Guru's divine Words his thoughts then turn to the *dharamsala*.

Proceeding there he joins the fellowship and hears with love the Guru's sacred words (*gurbani*).

All doubts are driven far away as devotedly he serves his fellow Gursikhs.

By honest labour he performs duty's calling, and from what it yields distributes food.

Giving it first to other Gursikhs and then feeding himself upon what remains.

Light has shown in the dark age of the Kaliyug, the Guru a disciple and the disciple a Guru.

This is the highway which the *Gurmukh* (one oriented toward the Guru) treads!

(*Varan Bhai Gurdas* 40:11; McLeod 2003: 33)

Bathing in the Pool of Nectar (© Raghu Rai/Magnum Photos).

symbol of temporal authority was Hargobind's construction, facing the Darbar Sahib, of the Akal Takhat ("Throne of the Timeless Being"), the first of an eventual five "thrones" of religious authority. Under his leadership the Panth took up arms to defend itself against Mughal hostility. But this new martial orientation did not mean that the Sikhs had abandoned their spiritual base.

Relations with the Mughal authorities eased under the seventh and eighth gurus, Har Rai (1630–1661) and Harkrishan (1655–1664), although both gurus kept a regular force of horsemen. But the increasing strength of Sikhism under the ninth guru once again attracted Mughal attention in the 1670s. Guru Tegh Bahadur (1621–1675) encouraged the Sikhs to be fearless in their pursuit of a just society: "He who holds none in fear, nor is afraid of anyone, is acknowledged as a man of true wisdom" (AG 1427). In so doing, he posed a direct challenge to Emperor Aurangzeb (r. 1658–1707), who had imposed Islamic laws and taxes, and ordered the replacement of Hindu temples with mosques. Guru Tegh Bahadur was summoned to Delhi, and when he refused to embrace Islam he was publicly executed on November 11, 1675. If the martyrdom of Guru Arjan had helped to bring the Panth together, this second martyrdom helped to make human rights and freedom of conscience central to its identity.

Creation of the Khalsa

Tradition holds that the Sikhs who were present at Guru Tegh Bahadur's execution concealed their identity for fear of meeting a similar fate. For this reason the tenth guru, Gobind Singh, resolved to impose on Sikhs an outward form that would make them instantly recognizable. On **Baisakhi**

Day 1699 he created the **Khalsa** ("pure"), an order of loyal Sikhs bound by a common identity and discipline (***rahit***). The nucleus of the new order were the "Cherished Five" (***Panj Piare***), who were the first to respond to his call for volunteers. To this day, the Khalsa initiation ceremony follows the same pattern: initiates drink sweet "nectar" (*amrit*) that has been stirred with a two-edged sword and sanctified by the recitation of five prayers.

The Khalsa

Three aspects of the Khalsa are particularly significant. First, in undergoing the *amrit* ceremony, the Khalsa initiates were "reborn" as spiritual children of Guru Gobind Singh and his wife, Sahib Kaur, and given new surnames: *Singh* ("lion") for men and *Kaur* ("princess") for women. This collective identity gave Khalsa members a powerful sense of belonging. Second, the guru himself received the nectar of the double-edged sword from the hands of the Cherished Five. In so doing, he symbolically transferred his spiritual authority to them, paving the way for the termination of the office he occupied as a human guru.

Finally, it was at the inauguration of the Khalsa that Guru Gobind Singh delivered the nucleus of what would become the order's *rahit* ("code of conduct"). To ensure that Khalsa members would never seek to conceal their identity as Sikhs, he made five physical symbols mandatory:

1. *Kes*: unshorn hair, symbolizing spirituality and saintliness
2. *Kangha*: a wooden comb, signifying order and discipline in life
3. *Kirpan*: a miniature sword, symbolizing divine grace, dignity, and courage
4. *Kara*: a steel "wrist-ring," signifying responsibility and allegiance to the guru
5. *Kachh*: a pair of short breeches, symbolizing moral restraint

Known (from their Punjabi names) as the **Five Ks** (***Panj Kakke***), these outward symbols of the divine Word imply a direct correlation between *bani* ("divine utterance") and *bana* ("Khalsa dress"). Every morning, in putting on those symbols (as well as the turban, in the case of male Sikhs) while reciting prayers, Khalsa Sikhs dress themselves in the Word of God; their minds are purified and inspired, and their bodies are girded to do battle with the day's temptations. Four sins are specifically prohibited: cutting the hair, using tobacco (an injunction later expanded to include all intoxicants), committing adultery, and eating meat that has not come from an animal killed with a single blow.

The launch of the Khalsa was the culmination of Sikhism's formative period, but it was only one of the major reforms instituted by Guru Gobind Singh. After adding a collection of the works of Guru Tegh Bahadur to the Adi Granth, he closed the Sikh canon, and before his death in 1708 he brought to an end the succession of human gurus. Thereafter, the authority of the guru would be invested not in an individual but in the scripture (Guru-Granth) and the corporate community (Guru-Panth).

⊕ Crystallization

The term "crystallization" comes from Wilfred Cantwell Smith, who identified several stages in the development of a religious tradition. The process begins with the vision of a mystic whose preaching attracts followers and continues with the organization of a community, the positing of an intellectual ideal of that community, and the development of its institutions. Smith maintains that in the case of Sikhism the last two stages were reached under the fifth guru, Arjan, and the tenth, Gobind Singh. Of course the crystallization process continues as the community responds to changing conditions.

The Sacred Scriptures

The Adi Granth is the primary scripture of the Sikhs, comprising the hymns of the first five gurus and the ninth, plus material by additional bards and poets ranging historically from the twelfth century to the seventeenth. The standard text contains 1,430 pages, and every copy has exactly the same material on each page.

The second sacred collection, the **Dasam Granth**, dates from the 1690s and is attributed to the tenth (*dasam*) guru, Gobind Singh. Eighteenth-century revisions added his *Zafarnama* ("Letter

Document

From the Sacred Writings of the Sikhs

Guru Nanak exalts the divine Name:

If in this life I should live to eternity, nourished by nothing save air;

If I should dwell in the darkest of dungeons, sense never resting in sleep;

Yet must your glory transcend all my striving; no words can encompass the Name.

> (*Refrain*) He who is truly the Spirit Eternal, immanent, blissful serene;
> Only by grace can we learn of our Master, only by grace can we tell.

If I were slain and my body dismembered, pressed in a hand-mill and ground;

If I were burnt in a fire all-consuming, mingled with ashes and dust;

Yet must your glory transcend all my striving, no words can encompass the Name.

If as a bird I could soar to the heavens, a hundred such realms in my reach;

If I could change so that none might perceive me and live without food, without drink;

Yet must your glory transcend all my striving; no words can encompass the Name.

If I could read with the eye of intelligence paper of infinite weight;

If I could with the winds everlasting, pens dipped in oceans of ink;

Yet must your glory transcend all my striving; no words can encompass the Name (M1, *Siri Ragu 2*, AG 14–15; McLeod 1984: 41)

The following passage, in which the tenth guru, Gobind Singh, praises the sword, is often repeated at Sikh functions and now serves as the anthem of the Khalsa:

Reverently I salute the Sword with affection and devotion.

Grant, I pray, your divine assistance that this book may be brought to completion.

Thee I invoke, All-conquering Sword, Destroyer of evil, Ornament of the brave.

Powerful your arm and radiant your glory, your splendour as dazzling as the brightness of the sun.

Joy of the devout and Scourge of the wicked, Vanquisher of sin, I seek your protection.

Hail to the world's Creator and Sustainer, my invincible Protector of the Sword!

(*Bachitar Natak*, Dasam Granth, 39; McLeod 1984: 58)

of Victory"; see the section on "Justice") and fixed the sequence of its contents, which include de-votional texts, autobiographical works, miscellaneous writings, mythical narratives, and popular anecdotes.

The third category of sacred literature consists of works by Bhai ("Brother") Gurdas (c. 1558–1637) and Bhai Nand Lal Goya (1633–1715), which are officially approved for singing in the gurd-wara. This last category is made up of three distinct genres. The *janam-sakhis* ("life narratives") date from the late sixteenth century but are based on earlier oral traditions. The *rahit-namas* ("man-uals of code of conduct") provide rare insight into the evolution of the Khalsa code in the eighteenth and nineteenth centuries. And the *gur-bilas* ("splendour of the guru") literature praises the mighty deeds of the two great warrior gurus, Hargobind and Gobind Singh, in particular.

Finally, it is important to emphasize that the Adi Granth is inextricably embedded in Sikh daily life. It is not merely to be read and understood, but to be interiorized, practiced, and lived.

Sikh Doctrine

The primary source of Sikh doctrine is the Adi Granth. Its first words are Guru Nanak's invoca-tion of One God (1-*Oankar*) in the **Mul Mantar** ("Seed Formula"). This succinct expression of the nature of the ultimate reality is the fundamental statement of Sikh belief: "There is One ("1") Su-preme Being, the Eternal Reality, the Creator, without fear and devoid of enmity, immortal, never incarnated, self-existent, known by grace through the Guru. The Eternal One, from the beginning, through all time, present now, the Everlasting Reality" (AG 1).

By beginning with "One" (the original Punjabi text uses the numeral rather than the word), Guru Nanak emphasized the singularity of the divine; as he put it in a later hymn, the Supreme Being has "no relatives, no mother, no father, no wife, no son, no rival who may become a po-tential contender" (AG 597). At the same time he drew attention to the unity of Akal Purakh, the Eternal One, the source and the goal of all that exists. The Mul Mantar illuminates the Sikh understanding of ultimate reality as being at once transcendent and immanent, a personal God of grace for his humblest devotee. The vital expression of the One is through the many, through the

Document

Bhai Gurdas on External Religious Observance

If bathing at *tiraths* ["pilgrimage centers"] procures liberation, frogs, for sure, must be saved;
And likewise the banyan, with dangling tresses, if growing hair long sets one free.
If the need can be served by roaming unclad the deer of the forest must surely be pious;
So too the ass which rolls in the dust if limbs smeared with ashes can purchase salvation.

Saved are the cattle, mute in the fields, if silence pro-duces deliverance.
Only the Guru can bring us salvation; only the Guru can set a man free. (*Varan Bhai Gurdas*, 36:14; McLeod 1984: 67)

infinite plurality of creation. This understanding of the One distinguishes the Sikh interpretation of monotheism from its Abrahamic counterparts. The gurus fiercely opposed any anthropomorphic conception of the divine. Nevertheless, Akal Purakh watches over the universe as lovingly as any parent. Simultaneously "Father, Mother, Friend, and Brother" (AG 268), God is without gender.

In general, then, Sikhs worship a transcendent, nonincarnate, universal God who is nevertheless partly embodied in the divine Name (*nam*) as well as the collective Words (*bani*) and persons of the gurus. Only through personal experience can he be truly known.

Creation

According to Guru Nanak's cosmology hymn, the universe was brought into being by the divine order, will, or command (**hukam**). This *hukam* is an all-embracing principle, a revelation of the nature of God:

> For endless eons, there was only darkness.
> Nothing except the divine order existed.
> No day or night, no moon or sun.
> The Creator alone was absorbed in a primal
>   state of contemplation . . .
> When the Creator so willed, creation came
>   into being . . .
> The Un-manifest One revealed itself in the
>   Creation.
>   (AG 1035–1036)

In Sikh cosmology, the world is divinely inspired, the place that gives human beings the opportunity to perform their duty and achieve union with Akal Purakh.

The Value of Human Life

For Guru Nanak, human life was worth a "diamond," but its value dropped to a "farthing" if a person did not realize his or her true spiritual nature (AG 156): "One is blessed with the rarest opportunity of the human birth through the grace of the Guru. One's mind and body become dyed deep red (with the love of the divine Name) if one is able to win the approval of the True Guru" (AG 751).

For Guru Arjan, the human being was the epitome of creation: "All other creation is subject to you, O man/woman! You reign supreme on this earth" (AG 374). Like Guru Nanak, he emphasized the opportunity that human life offers: "Precious this life you receive as a human, with it the chance to find the Lord" (AG 15). But those who seek the divine beloved while participating in the delights of the world are rare.

Karam, Sansar, and Divine Grace

The notions of **karam** (karma, "action," the principle of moral cause and effect) and *sansar* (samsara, "reincarnation") are fundamental to all religious traditions originating in India. In Sikh doctrine, however, karam is not an inexorable, impersonal law. Rather, it is subject to the "divine order" (*hukam*), an all-embracing higher principle that is the sum total of all divinely instituted laws. Thus karam can be overridden in the name of justice by Akal Purakh's omnipotent grace.

Divine Revelation

Guru Nanak used three key terms to describe the nature of divine revelation: *nam* ("divine Name"), **shabad** ("divine Word"), and *guru* ("divine Preceptor"). *Nam* refers to the divine presence that is manifest everywhere, though most people fail to perceive it because of the self-centered desire for personal gratification. Because this self-centeredness (**haumai**, meaning "I, I" or "me, mine") separates us from Akal Purakh, we continue to suffer within the cycle of rebirth. Yet Akal Purakh takes pity on human suffering, and therefore he reveals himself through the guru in the form of the *shabad*, the utterance that awakens those capable of hearing it to the reality of the divine Name that is immanent in everything.

Remembering the Divine Name

Under the influence of *haumai*, humans become so attached to worldly pleasures that they forget the divine Name and waste their lives in evil and suffering. To achieve spiritual liberation, we must transcend that influence by adopting the strictly interior discipline of **nam-simaran**, "remembering the divine Name." There are three levels to this discipline: repetition of a sacred word (usually *Vahiguru*, "Praise to the Eternal Guru"), devotional singing, and meditation on the nature of Akal Purakh. The first and third levels are undertaken in private, while the second is a public, communal activity. As *nam-simaran* gradually brings practitioners into harmony with the divine order (*hukam*), blissful equanimity grows until the spirit reaches the "realm of Truth" and attains mystical union with Akal Purakh.

The primacy of divine grace over personal effort is fundamental to Guru Nanak's theology. Yet personal effort is imperative: "With your own hands carve out your own destiny" (AG 474). By teaching his followers to see their own "free" will as part of Akal Purakh's will, Guru Nanak encouraged them to create their own destinies. The necessity of balance between meditative worship and righteous life in the world is summed up in the triple commandment to earn one's living through honest labor, adore the divine Name, and share the fruits of one's labor with others.

Four Notions of Guruship

In Indic traditions the guru is a human teacher who communicates divine knowledge and guides disciples along the path to liberation. In Sikhism, however, the term encompasses four types of spiritual authority: the divine guru, the personal guru, Guru-Granth, and Guru-Panth.

God as Guru

Guru Nanak used the term "guru" to refer to Akal Purakh himself, to the voice of Akal Purakh, and to the Word, the Truth of Akal Purakh. In this view, to experience the eternal guru is to experience divine guidance. Guru Nanak himself acknowledged Akal Purakh as his guru: "He who is the infinite, supreme God is the Guru whom Nanak has met" (AG 599). In Sikh usage, therefore, the guru is the voice of Akal Purakh, mystically uttered within the human heart, mind, and soul (*man*). Akal Purakh is often characterized as *Nirankar*, "the One without Form," and Guru Arjan explicitly stated that he is not to be anthropomorphized: "Do not believe that he is in the form of a human being" (AG 895).

Sikhs evoke the absolute knowledge and power of the divine Name by chanting "*Vahiguru! Vahiguru!*" ("Hail the Guru"). The sound vibrations of this phrase are believed to be supremely powerful. In addition, Sikh scripture often uses Hindu and Muslim names for God. Hindu names such as Ram, Hari, and Govind and Muslim names such as Allah, Karim, and Sahib express different aspects of Akal Purakh, as Guru Nanak recognized (AG 1168). And Guru Arjan provided a comprehensive list of the names from various contemporary religious traditions associated with different attributes of God (AG 1083). In the Sikh context, however, these names acquire meaning only when they are viewed through the lens of the Mul Mantar. Most important, the "truth of the Name" is a reality that lies beyond any name.

The Teacher as Guru

The personal guru is the channel through which the voice of Akal Purakh becomes audible. Nanak became the embodiment of the eternal guru only when he received the divine Word and conveyed it to his disciples. The same voice spoke through each of his successors. In keeping with the theory of spiritual succession known as "the unity of the office of the guru," there was no difference between the founder and his successors: all represented the same fire, passed from one torch to the next. Similarly, in the Adi Granth, the compositions of six individual gurus are all signed "Nanak."

The Scripture as Guru

Sikhs normally refer to the Adi Granth as the Guru Granth Sahib ("Honorable Scripture Guru"). In so doing, they acknowledge their faith in it as the successor to Guru Gobind Singh, with the same status, authority, and functions as any of the 10 personal gurus. The perennial source of divine guidance for Sikhs, it is treated with the most profound respect.

The Community as Guru

The phrase "Guru-Panth" is used in two senses: as "the Panth *of* the Guru," it means the Sikh community; as "the Panth *as* the Guru," it refers to the idea that the guru is mystically present in the congregation. Although the Khalsa has always claimed to speak authoritatively on behalf of the whole Panth, at times non-Khalsa Sikhs have interpreted the Guru-Panth doctrine as conferring authority on the broader community. In practice, consensus is achieved by following democratic traditions.

Sikh Ethics

The Adi Granth opens with a composition of Guru Nanak's known as the *Japji*. In it the guru asks how Truth is to be attained and answers thus: "Submit to the divine Order (*hukam*), walk in its way" (AG 1). In other words, Truth is attained not by intellectual effort, but by personal commitment. To know Truth, one must live it. Indeed, truthful conduct is at the heart of Guru Nanak's message. The aim of cultivating wisdom, contentment, justice, humility, truthfulness, temperance, love, forgiveness, charity, purity, and reverence of Akal Purakh promotes socially responsible living, hard work, and sharing.

The Panj Piare (Cherished Five) take part in a procession to celebrate the 347th birth anniversary of Guru Gobind Singh, in Bhopal, India, on January 16, 2013 (© SANJEEV GUPTA/epa/Corbis).

Service

To Sikhs, the key to a righteous life is the rendering of service to others. Such service must be voluntary and undertaken without any desire for self-glorification. Nor should those who give aid sit in judgment on those who receive it. The Sikh Prayer (*Ardas*, "Petition") emphasizes the importance of "seeing but not judging." The ideals are social equality and human brotherhood. Therefore discrimination based on caste or gender is expressly rejected. The gurus also emphasized the importance of optimism in the face of adversity.

Justice

Guru Nanak regarded the violation of human rights as a serious moral offense: "To deprive others of their rights must be avoided as scrupulously as Muslims avoid the pork and the Hindus consider beef as a taboo" (AG 141). The use of force is permitted, but only in defense of justice, and then only as a last resort. Guru Gobind Singh taught that peaceful negotiation must be tried first. A famous verse from the *Zafarnama* ("Letter of Victory")—a poem addressed to Emperor Aurangzeb after the latter, instead of negotiating, sent his forces against the Sikhs—makes this point explicitly: "When all other methods have been explored and all other means have been tried, . . . then may the sword be used." For the Khalsa, the quest for justice is the primary ethical duty.

Oneness of Humankind and Religion

Sikhism is committed to the ideal of universal brotherhood. In a celebrated passage from his *Akal Ustat* ("Praise of the Immortal One"), Guru Gobind Singh declares that "humankind is one, and all people belong to a single humanity": "The temple and the mosque are the same, so are the Hindu worship and Muslim prayer. All people are one; it is through error that they appear different. . . . Allah and Abhekh are the same, the Purana and the Qur'an are the same. They are all alike, all the creation of the One" (v. 86). To this day, Sikhs conclude their morning and evening prayers with the words "In thy will, O Lord, may peace and prosperity come to one and all."

⊕ Practice

Prayer

Devout Sikhs rise during the "ambrosial hours" (between 3 and 6 a.m.) and begin their daily routine with approximately an hour of devotions, beginning with meditation on the divine Name and continuing with recitation of five prayers, including Guru Nanak's *Japji* ("Honored Recitation") and Guru Gobind Singh's *Jap Sahib* ("Master Recitation"). Evening prayers are selected from a collection of hymns entitled *Sodar Rahiras* ("Supplication at That Door"), and the *Kirtan Sohila* ("Song of Praise") is recited before retiring for the night. Learnt by heart in childhood and recited from memory every day, these prayers are always available to provide guidance.

Congregational Worship

In every gurdwara a copy of the Guru Granth Sahib is ceremoniously installed each morning on a cushioned, canopied stand. All who enter the gurdwara are expected to cover their heads, remove their shoes, and bow before the sacred volume by touching their foreheads to the floor. Worshipers

Practice

Daily Liturgical Prayers

The Early Morning Order (3–6 a.m.)

1. *Japji* ("Honored Recitation")
2. *Jap Sahib* ("Master Recitation")
3. The 10 *Savayyas* ("10 Panegyrics")
4. *Benati Chaupai* ("Verses of Petition")
5. *Anand Sahib* ("Song of Bliss")

The Evening Prayer

Sodar Rahiras ("Supplication at That Door")

The Bedtime Prayer

Kirtan Sohila ("Song of Praise")

sit on the floor, and it is the Punjabi custom for men to sit on the right side of the hall and women on the left, but this is not mandatory.

Sikhism has no ordained priesthood. Instead, every gurdwara has a **granthi** ("reader") who, in addition to reading from the Guru Granth Sahib, takes care of the book and serves as custodian of the gurdwara. Although the office is also open to women, in practice most *granthis* are men.

Worship consists mainly of *kirtan*, led and accompanied by musicians playing harmoniums and *tabla* drums. Through *kirtan* the devotees attune themselves to the divine Word and vibrate in harmony with it. Many today believe that *kirtan* helps them cope with the obstacles that modern society puts in the way of spiritual life.

At some time during the service, either the *granthi* or a traditional Sikh scholar may deliver a homily based on a particular hymn or scriptural passage. Then all present will join in reciting the *Ardas* prayer. The Sikh understanding of the Adi Granth as living guru is most evident in the practice known as "taking the guru's Word" or "seeking a divine command," in which the Guru Granth Sahib is opened at random and the first hymn on the left-hand page is read aloud in its entirety (beginning on the previous page if necessary). In this way the congregation hears the Guru's **Vak** ("Saying") for that particular moment or occasion. Taken in the morning, the Vak serves as the inspiration for personal meditation throughout the day; taken in the evening, it brings the day to a close with a new perspective on its joys and sorrows. The reading of the Vak is followed by the distribution of **karah prashad**—a sweet, rich paste of flour, sugar, and butter that is "sanctified"

The *granthi* reads from the Guru Granth Sahib in Yuba City, California (AP Photo/Appeal-Democrat, David Bitton).

by the recitation of prayers during its preparation and by resting next to the scripture during the service, and represents the bestowal of divine blessings on those who receive it. At the end of congregational worship everyone shares in the *langar* meal prepared and served by volunteers as part of the community service expected of all Sikhs. This custom is a powerful reminder of the egalitarianism that is so central to Sikhism.

The Annual Festival Cycle

The most important festival is Baisakhi (Vaisakhi) Day, which usually falls on April 13. Celebrated throughout India as New Year's Day, it has been considered the birthday of the Sikh community ever since the institution of the Khalsa on Baisakhi Day in 1699. Sikhs also celebrate the autumn festival of lights, Divali, as the day when Guru Hargobind was released from prison. These two seasonal festivals were introduced by the third guru, Amar Das, and Guru Gobind Singh added a third: Hola Mahalla, the day after the Hindu festival of Holi (March–April), which is celebrated with military exercises and various athletic and literary contests.

The anniversaries of the births and deaths of the gurus are marked by the "unbroken reading" of the entire Sikh scripture by a team of readers over a period of roughly 48 hours. The birthdays of Guru Nanak (usually in November) and Guru Gobind Singh (December–January) and the martyrdom days of Guru Arjan (May–June) and Guru Tegh Bahadur (November–December) in particular are celebrated around the world.

The Golden Temple is illuminated to mark Divali (© MUNISH SHARMA/Reuters/Corbis).

Life-Cycle Rituals

At the center of every important life-cycle ritual is the Guru Granth Sahib.

Naming a Child

When a child is to be named, family members take the baby to the gurdwara and present *karah prashad* to the Guru Granth Sahib. After various prayers of thanks and a recitation of *Ardas*, the Guru Granth Sahib is opened at random, and the first letter of the first composition on the left-hand page is noted; then a name beginning with the same letter is chosen. In this way the child takes his or her identity from the guru's Word. A boy is given the second name *Singh* and a girl the second name *Kaur*. Then *amrit* is applied to the eyes and head, the infant is given a sip of the sweetened water to drink, and the first five stanzas of Guru Nanak's *Japji* are recited.

Marriage

"They are not said to be husband and wife, who merely sit together. Rather, they alone are called husband and wife who have one soul in two bodies" (AG 788). This proclamation of Guru Amar Das has become the basis of the Sikh view of marriage, which emphasizes the necessity of spiritual compatibility between spouses. In a traditional society in which the family is more important than the individual, the fact that Sikh marriages have traditionally been arranged is not inconsistent with that principle.

The bride and groom at a traditional Sikh wedding in Queens, New York. (Ira Berger/Alamy Stock Photo)

To be legal, a Sikh wedding must take place in the presence of the Guru Granth Sahib. The bride and groom circumambulate the sacred scripture four times, once for each of their four vows:

1. to lead an action-oriented life based on righteousness and never to shun obligations of family and society;
2. to maintain reverence and dignity between one another;
3. to keep enthusiasm for life alive in the face of adverse circumstances and to remain detached from worldly attachments; and
4. to cultivate a balanced approach in life, avoiding all extremes.

The circular movement around the scripture symbolizes the cycle of life in which there is no beginning and no end.

Khalsa Initiation

The Khalsa initiation ceremony (**amrit sanskar**) must also take place in the presence of the Guru Granth Sahib. There is no fixed age for initiation; candidates need only be willing and able to accept the Khalsa discipline. Five Khalsa Sikhs, representing the original Cherished Five, conduct the ceremony. Each recites from memory one of the five liturgical prayers while stirring the *amrit* with a double-edged sword.

The novices then drink the *amrit* five times so that their bodies are purified of five vices (lust, anger, greed, attachment, and pride), and five times the *amrit* is sprinkled on their eyes to transform their outlook on life. Finally, the *amrit* is poured on their heads five times, sanctifying their hair so that they will preserve its natural form and listen to the voice of conscience. At each stage of the ceremony, the initiates repeat the words *Vahiguru Ji Ka Khalsa! Vahiguru Ji Ki Fateh!* ("Khalsa belongs to the Wonderful Lord! Victory belongs to the Wonderful Lord!").

Document

On Religious Differences

Despite his militancy, Guru Gobind Singh shared Guru Nanak's conviction that religious boundaries are irrelevant to God.

There is no difference between a temple and a mosque, nor between the prayers of a Hindu and a Muslim. Though differences seem to mark and distinguish, all men/women are in reality the same. Gods and demons, celestial beings, men called Muslims and others called Hindus—such differences are trivial, inconsequential, the outward results of locality and dress. With eyes the same, the ears and body, all possessing a common form—all are in fact a single creation, the elements of nature in a uniform blend. Allah is the same as the God of the Hindus, Puran and Qur'an are the same. All are the same, none is separate; a single form, a single creation. (*Akal Ustat, Dasam Granth*, 19–20; McLeod 1984: 57)

Death

A dedicated Sikh welcomes death, for it means the perfecting of his or her union with Akal Purakh and final release from the cycle of rebirth. In India, the body of the deceased is bathed, dressed in new clothes, and placed on a pyre for cremation, after which the ashes are scattered in a nearby stream or river. In the diaspora, family and friends gather at a funeral home with the facilities for cremation. Following devotional singing and a eulogy, *Ardas* is offered by the *granthi*. Then the casket is taken to the cremation furnace, usually accompanied by family and friends. While the casket is burning, the congregation recites the late-evening prayer, *Kirtan Sohila*.

In addition, a reading of the entire scripture takes place either at home or in a gurdwara. At the conclusion of the reading, which may take up to 10 days to complete, the final prayers are offered in memory of the deceased.

⊕ Differentiation

Encounter with Modernity

The Khalsa spent most of its first century fighting the Mughals and Afghan invaders. Immediately after the death of Guru Gobind Singh, Khalsa Sikhs led by Banda Singh Bahadur took part in a civil war that ended in 1710 with the defeat of the Mughals and the establishment of Sikh rule in Punjab. Although the Mughals returned to power in 1716, in 1799 Ranjit Singh (1780–1839) succeeded in unifying the Punjab and declared himself maharaja. For the next four decades Sikhs enjoyed more settled political conditions, and with territorial expansion, people of different cultural and religious backgrounds were attracted into the faith.

Although the maharaja himself was a Khalsa Sikh, his rule was marked by religious diversity within the Panth. Khalsa members realized that they needed the support of those Sikhs who lived as members of the Nanak Panth but did not accept the Khalsa code of conduct. The Khalsa conceded the religious culture of these **Sehaj-dharis** ("gradualists") to be legitimate even though the latter revered Hindu as well as Sikh scriptures and in some cases even worshiped Hindu images.

Sikh Reform Movements

The successors of Maharaja Ranjit Singh could not withstand the advancing British forces. After two Anglo–Sikh wars in 1846 and 1849, the Sikh kingdom was annexed to the British Empire. It was in this context that three reform movements tried to restore a distinct spiritual identity to a people whose religious tradition was just one among a vast array of traditions that existed within colonial India.

The Nirankari movement sought to purge Sikhism of Hindu influences (especially image worship) and recall Sikhs to the worship of the "formless and invisible God" (*Nirankar*), while the Namdharis emphasized chanting of the divine Name. As the number of his followers grew, the Namdharis' leader, Baba Ram Singh, promoted boycotts as a form of nonviolent resistance to the British occupation of the Punjab. After more than 60 of them were executed without trial, the Namdharis came to be seen as political martyrs and forerunners of the twentieth-century Gandhian movement for the independence of India.

The third reform movement, the **Singh Sabha** ("Society of the Singhs"), was established in 1873 and sought to reaffirm Sikh identity in the face of two threats: the casual reversion to Hindu practices under Maharaja Ranjit Singh and the proselytizing efforts not only of the Hindu Arya Samaj, but of Christian missionaries. By the end of the nineteenth century the dominant wing of the Singh Sabha, the Tat ("Pure" or "True") Khalsa, had made the Khalsa tradition the standard of orthodoxy for all Sikhs.

In the twentieth century, the Tat Khalsa reformers contributed to two important legal changes. In 1909 they obtained legal recognition of the distinctive Sikh wedding ritual in the Anand Marriage Act (1909). Then in the 1920s they helped to reestablish direct Khalsa control of the major historical gurdwaras, many of which had fallen into the hands of corrupt "custodians" supported by the British. Inspired by the Tat Khalsa, the Akali movement of the 1920s secured British assent to the Sikh Gurdwara Act (1925), under which control of all gurdwaras passed to the Shiromani Gurdwara Prabandhak Committee (SGPC; "Chief Management Committee of Sikh Shrines"). The Akalis were the forerunners of the modern political party known as the Akali Dal ("army of the immortal").

The SGPC Rahit Manual

Control of the gurdwaras gave the SGPC enormous influence. By 1950 it was the central authority on all questions of religious discipline, and in that year it published the code of conduct called the *Sikh Rahit Maryada*.

Based on the teachings of the Guru Granth Sahib and supplemented with teachings from revered Sikh leaders, the *Sikh Rahit Maryada* enjoins Sikhs to cultivate a pure and pious inner spirituality (*bani*), to adopt the Five Ks as external signs of virtue, and to abstain from the four cardinal sins (hair-cutting, adultery, the use of intoxicants, and the consumption of improperly slaughtered animals). The manual encourages the worship of God and meditation on his name, Khalsa initiation, and attendance at divine services. It also calls on Sikhs to earn an honest living; to share selflessly with the less fortunate; to nurture virtues such as compassion, honesty, generosity, patience, perseverance, and humility; and to avoid superstition, idols, and images.

Not punitive in either intent or effect, the *Sikh Rahit Maryada* calls for tolerance of those who stray as well as the *Sehaj-dharis*, assuming that in time they will accept the full Khalsa discipline. The only code of conduct sanctioned by the Akal Takhat, the *Sikh Rahit Maryada* is distributed free of charge by the SGPC and is now available in Hindi and English for Sikhs living outside their historical homeland.

Variations in Modern Sikhism

The Sikh Panth has never been monolithic or homogeneous, and it continues to encompass a number of variations. The Khalsa itself includes a rigorously observant order called the Nihangs, who are ready to die for their faith at any time. Another group within the Khalsa, the Akhand Kirtani Jatha ("continuous singing of the Sikh scriptures"), follows a special discipline that includes a strictly vegetarian diet and requires that female members wear a small turban.

In recent years the Internet has allowed many groups to claim that they represent the "true" Panth. Of the 25 million Sikhs in the world today, only about 20 percent are orthodox **Amrit-dharis** ("initiates"). But many other Sikhs follow most of the Khalsa code even though they have not been initiated.

Many Sikhs (the majority of whom reside in the diaspora) cut their hair but still use the Khalsa names "Singh" and "Kaur" and do not consider themselves to be "lesser Sikhs" in any way. Finally, there are Khalsa Sikhs—especially in the diaspora—who have committed one or more of the four sins after initiation. Although they are known as "apostates," that designation is not necessarily permanent: Sikhism recognizes that people may change as they move through different stages in life, and their status within the Panth changes accordingly. In short, there is no single way of being a Sikh.

⊕ Cultural Expressions

Social Norms

Guru Nanak's successors shared his belief that the key to liberation lay not in ascetic renunciation but in the life of the householder. To understand family relationships within the tradition, we must look at the Sikh perspectives on caste and gender. Rejection of caste-based discrimination was a fundamental feature of Sikhism from the beginning, and the *Sikh Rahit Maryada* explicitly states that "no account should be taken of caste" in the selection of a marriage partner. In practice, however, most Sikhs still marry within their own group, though intercaste marriage is increasing among urban professionals.

In Punjabi society, marriage connects not just two individuals but, more important, two groups of kin. It is in this context that the concept of honor continues to play a significant role in family relationships.

The Role of Women

Despite their egalitarian principles, the Sikh gurus lived in a traditional patriarchal society, and its values were reflected in their ideas about women. Thus the ideal woman was defined by her conduct in the context of the family as a good daughter, sister, wife, and mother. However, the gurus also expected men to live up to the cultural norms of modesty and honor. There was no tolerance for premarital or extramarital sexual activity, and rape was regarded as a particularly serious violation for the dishonor and loss of social standing it brought to the families of both the perpetrator and the victim. Furthermore, the rules governing the Khalsa are clearly egalitarian in principle. Candidates for initiation cannot be accepted without their spouses; hence the proportions of male and female initiates are roughly equal. And Khalsa women wear all of the Five Ks.

A number of women are remembered for their contributions to the Panth, some but not all of them sisters, wives, or daughters of the gurus. Guru Nanak's older sister Nanaki supported his travels, while his wife, Sulakhani, raised their children during his long absences. Mata Khivi, the wife of the second guru, made important contributions to the development of the *langar* tradition. In 1705, when the forces of Guru Gobind Singh had abandoned him in battle, a brave woman named Mai Bhago persuaded them to return and fight. And after the guru's death in 1708, his wife Sundri organized the compilation of the Dasam Granth and issued a number of edicts to Sikh congregations.

In modern times, Bibi Jagir Kaur was twice elected president of the SGPC, in 1999 and 2004. Other exceptional women include the mystic Bibi Nihal Kaur; Bibi Balwant Kaur, who established a gurdwara and a women's group in honor of Bebe Nanaki in Birmingham, England; and Bibi Jasbir Kaur Khalsa, who devoted her life to the promotion of Sikh music and established a chair for its study at Punjabi University in Patiala, India. Female musicians often perform in the gurdwaras. Women have also played important roles in the Akhand Kirtani Jatha and the Healthy, Happy, Holy Organization (3HO; now known as Sikh Dharma).

It is true that most Sikh institutions are still dominated by men, and many Sikh women are still subject to patriarchal cultural assumptions. In this they differ little from their counterparts in India's other major religious communities. Even so, Sikh women have been asserting themselves with growing success in recent years.

Music

Sikhism is the only world religion in which the primary medium of the founder's message is song. In specifying the *ragas* to which the hymns were to be sung, Guru Nanak and his successors sought to promote harmony and balance in devotees' minds. Thus *ragas* likely to arouse passions were adapted to produce a gentler effect.

Art

The earliest known paintings of Guru Nanak appear in a *janam-sakhi* from the mid-1600s. The first examples of Sikh graphic art were illuminated scriptures produced in the late sixteenth century. Sikh scribes followed the Qur'anic tradition of decorating the margins and opening pages of a text with abstract designs and floral motifs. Both fine and applied arts flourished under the patronage

Women in the Traditions

In every major city of India with a significant Sikh population, Sikh women have organized themselves into clusters called Istari Satsang ("Spiritual Fellowship of Women") for devotional purposes. Normally, participants gather at historical gurdwaras in the afternoon to participate in devotional singing (*kirtan*) of scriptural hymns and to recite Guru Arjan's celebrated composition Sukhmani ("Pearl of Peace," AG 262–296) in unison, following the lead of the group leader. In some cases, they gather weekly or biweekly at individual houses by rotation to participate in devotional activities.

Sikh women have undoubtedly been empowered by Istari Satsang. Sikh women are actively involved in home-based worship, children's education, and community advancement projects. Under the guidance of Bibi Narinder Kaur, the so-called Bebe

Nanaki Istari Satsang was responsible for building a beautiful gurdwara in Model Town, Ludhiana, to celebrate the memory of Bebe Nanaki within the Sikh Panth. Active women's groups in New Delhi such as Mata Sahib Kaur Istari Satsang and Mata Gujar Kaur Istari Satsang have been named after famous Sikh women. These groups enthusiastically participate in the celebration of festivals related to the anniversaries of the Sikh gurus. Additionally, the idea and concept of Istari Satsang has already spread into diaspora gurdwaras. Gurdwara Sri Guru Nanak Satsang (Katong) in Singapore and Guru Ka Niwas Guru Gobind Singh Ji Wolverhampton in the United Kingdom have founded their own wings of Istari Satsang; these groups' participation in *Gurpurb* (celebrations around the anniversaries of the gurus) can be seen on YouTube.

Nineteen Eighty-Four, by the Singh Twins, 1998 (© The Singh Twins: www.singhtwins.co.uk).

of Maharaja Ranjit Singh. In addition, a distinctive architecture developed at his court. Murals and frescoes depicting major events from Sikh history can still be seen at historic gurdwaras, including the Darbar Sahib.

Two great Sikh artists emerged in the twentieth century. Sobha Singh (1901–1986) was skilled in Western oil painting, but he drew his themes from the romantic lore of the Punjab, the Indian epics, and the Sikh tradition; he is particularly well known for his portraits of the gurus. Kirpal Singh (1923–1990) specialized in realistic depictions of episodes from Sikh history, including appalling scenes of battle and martyrdom. A number of Sikh women have also made names as artists. Amrita Shergill (1911–1941) has been described as the Frida Kahlo of India. Raised largely in Europe, she studied art in Paris but returned to India in 1934 and explored village life in paintings that have been declared national art treasures. Arpana Caur (b. 1954) is a bold modern painter who addresses current issues and events directly. The Singh Twins, who were born in England in 1966, apply styles and techniques of the classic Indian miniature tradition to contemporary themes. Their painting *Nineteen Eighty-Four,* inspired by the storming of the Darbar Sahib, is a powerful reflection not only on the event itself but on the responses it evoked in the Sikh diaspora.[2]

Literature

A rich literary tradition began with the introduction of the Gurmukhi script. The *janam-sakhi* remained the dominant literary genre before the emergence of the twentieth-century novel. The impact of Sikh devotional literature is clear in the works of celebrated early modern authors such as Kahn Singh Nabha (1861–1938), the poet Bhai Vir Singh (1872–1957), and Mohan Singh Vaid (1881–1936), who wrote stories, novels, and plays as well as nonfiction. All three emphasized optimism, determination, faith, and love toward fellow human beings. Writers also played a leadership role in the Singh Sabha reform movement. Although much contemporary Punjabi literature reflects Western influences, Sikh devotional literature has continued to inspire more recent writers such as Harinder Singh Mehboob (1937–2010).

⊕ Interaction and Adaptation

Twentieth-Century India

Doctrinal Authority

By 1950, the SGPC had become the principal authority in both religious and political affairs for the worldwide Sikh community. Although it has often been challenged by Sikhs outside the Punjab, the SGPC claims to speak on behalf of the majority of Sikhs, and hence to represent the authority of the Guru-Panth.

Still, the ultimate authority is the Akal Takhat in Amritsar, which, in addition to issuing edicts on doctrine and practice, punishes violations of religious discipline and activities "prejudicial" to Sikh interests and recognizes individuals who have performed outstanding services for Sikhism.

The Partition of India

In 1947 the British withdrew from India, and the independent republics of India and Pakistan came into being. Most of the 2.5 million Sikhs living on the Pakistani side of the divided Punjab became refugees; though many settled in the new Indian state of Punjab, some moved on to major cities elsewhere in India.

Since 1976 India has defined itself as a secular state, and Article 25 of the Constitution guarantees freedom of religion. However, a subclause of the same article states that "persons professing the Sikh, Jaina, or Buddhist religion" fall within the general category of Hinduism. When the Constitution was drafted, the Sikh members of the Constituent Assembly refused to sign it because it did not recognize the Sikhs as a group with an independent identity. Since that time, both Sikh and Hindu politicians have deliberately stirred up popular resentment over the issue for political purposes.

In 2002 the National Commission to Review the Constitution recommended amending Article 25 to remove Sikhs, Jainas, and Buddhists from the "Hindu" category, but to date this has not been done.

"Operation Blue Star"

In 1973 the Akali Dal passed the Anandpur Sahib Resolution demanding greater autonomy for all the states of India. As a result, relations with the Indian government became strained, and in an apparent attempt to sow dissension in the Akali ranks, the Congress government encouraged the rise of a charismatic young militant named Jarnail Singh Bhindranvale (1947–1984). But this strategy backfired in the spring of 1984, when a group of armed radicals led by Bhindranvale decided to provoke a confrontation with the government by occupying the Akal Takhat building inside the Darbar Sahib complex. The government responded by sending in the army. The assault that followed—code-named "Operation Blue Star"—resulted in the deaths of many Sikhs, including Bhindranvale, as well as the destruction of the Akal Takhat and severe damage to the Darbar Sahib itself.

A few months later, on October 31, Indian prime minister Indira Gandhi was assassinated by her own Sikh bodyguards. For several days Hindu mobs in Delhi and elsewhere killed thousands of Sikhs. These events divided Sikhs around the world into two camps, liberal and fundamentalist.

In 2006, four years after Gurbaj Singh Multani was forbidden to wear a *kirpan* to his Montreal school, the Supreme Court of Canada ruled that the ban violated his charter right to freedom of religion (CP PHOTO/Fred Chartrand).

The Sikh Diaspora

Over the last century about 2 million Sikhs have left India. Wherever they have settled—in Singapore, Malaysia, Thailand, Hong Kong, Australia, New Zealand, East Africa, or the United Kingdom, as well as Canada and the United States—they have established their own places of worship. Today there are more than 500 gurdwaras in North America and the United Kingdom alone.

New cultural environments have required some adaptation. For example, congregational services in the diaspora are usually held on Sunday, not because it is the holy day—in India there is no specific day for worship—but because it is the only day when most Sikhs are free to attend.

Western societies have also presented Sikhs with serious challenges. Men who wear turbans have often faced discrimination from prospective employers, and Khalsa Sikhs have had to negotiate with various institutions for permission to wear the *kirpan*. At the same time, loss of fluency in the Punjabi language means that younger Sikhs are at risk of theological illiteracy. Members of the diaspora have made concerted efforts to revive interest in Sikh traditions by supporting "Sunday school" classes and youth camps. In addition, many Sikh families now worship at home as well as at the gurdwara.

White Sikhs

Around 1970, a number of yoga students in Toronto and Los Angeles were inspired by their teacher, a Sikh named Harbhajan Singh Puri (Yogi Bhajan), to convert to the Sikh faith and join 3HO. Eventually renamed Sikh Dharma, the organization has since established itself in various North American cities. All members—male and female—wear the same white turbans, tunics, and tight trousers, and for this reason they have come to be known as "White Sikhs." They live in communal houses, spending long hours in meditation and chanting as well as practicing yoga.

Although Punjabi Sikhs in general praise their strict Khalsa-style discipline, other aspects of the White Sikh culture are quite alien to them. In India, for instance, white clothing is normally a sign of mourning; only the Namdharis dress entirely in white. And the only Sikh women who wear turbans are members of the Akhand Kirtani Jatha. Finally, the concept of honor, which plays such an important role in Punjabi society, is irrelevant to the White Sikhs. Even in North America, therefore, the two groups have little to do with one another.

⊕ Recent Developments

Religious Pluralism

The fact that the Adi Granth includes works by non-Sikh poet-saints suggests that interfaith dialogue has always been integral to Sikhism. The coexistence of multiple religious worldviews, some of which may be incompatible, has always been a fact of life. But awareness of that fact has increased sharply with increasing urbanization, mass education, international migration, and advances in communications. Especially in democratic states that do not attempt to impose a single religion on their citizens, people of different faiths must learn how to live together in harmony.

Interfaith dialogue and interaction provide opportunities for spiritual reflection and growth. It is in this context that Sikhism emphasizes the importance of keeping an open mind while preserving the integrity of one's own tradition. The gurus strongly opposed any claim by any tradition to possession of the sole religious truth. Thus participants in interfaith dialogue must recognize that the religious commitments of others are no less absolute than their own and allow for disagreement on crucial points of doctrine. At the same time we must be willing to let the "other" become in some sense ourselves.

Political Militancy

Another issue confronting Sikhs around the world is the tendency to associate their tradition with violence. The use of warrior imagery to evoke the valor of the Sikhs has been standard since colonial times. Relatively little attention has been directed to the other, perhaps more demanding, dimensions of Sikhism. What is expected of Sikh warriors is not violence but militancy in the sense that they be prepared to take an active and passionate stand on behalf of their faith.

In Canada the association of Sikhism with violence was underlined by the 1985 bombing of Air India Flight 182, in which 329 people—most of them Canadian citizens—were killed. This happened in the highly volatile context of the 1984 assault on the Darbar Sahib. Nearly two decades passed before the two Vancouver men suspected of masterminding the attack, both of whom identified as Sikh, were brought to trial, and in the end they were acquitted. It took more than 20 years and several government inquiries for Canadians in general to recognize that the bombing was a Canadian tragedy, the result of a Canadian plot and the failure of Canadian security officials.

In India, separatist violence was contained within a decade, and the Akali Dal reasserted its right to work within the democratic system. In the long run, peaceful demonstrations and political engagement have proved more effective than violent struggle. In response to long-standing Sikh demands, the Indian Parliament in 2012 lifted the requirement that Sikh marriages be registered under the Hindu Marriage Act.

Sexuality and Bioethical Issues

The Adi Granth and the *Sikh Rahit Maryada* are silent on homosexuality. However, the official Sikh response to same-sex marriage has been negative, and the Akal Takhat has forbidden the performance of such marriages in the gurdwara. Since the Sikh ideal is the life of the householder, any sexual relationship that is not procreative and within the bounds of a marriage is opposed. Thus only heterosexual unions are officially accepted.

Interview

Simran Jeet Singh, *a Sikh educator and activist in the New York area, is working for change within the Sikh tradition and greater understanding of Sikhism outside the tradition.*

What is your understanding of the Sikh worldview?

My understanding of the Sikh worldview is a very simple one. I believe that Sikhi teaches us to live a life of love and that every practice and idea that we engage is centered on this core idea.

How do you present the Sikh worldview to your American audience?

When speaking to Western audiences, I present the Sikh worldview by introducing the theological principles of oneness and love. I try to explain the outlook of divine interconnectedness and presence, and I then connect that to the idea of recognition, remembrance, and, ultimately, love. I then gesture towards how these core principles translate into devotional actions, including service, justice, and activism.

How do you view your role as a Sikh activist to inform the general public to remove racial discrimination against the Sikhs and other minority communities?

I view myself as an educator and activist. I believe strongly that much of the discrimination that Sikhs and other minorities experience in modern America is the result of cultural and religious illiteracy. My aim is to help dispel that ignorance through education.

I also believe that discrimination is institutionalized and that we have to challenge the structures in our society in order to combat hate at its core. I try to bring such instances to light and help address structural discrimination in a way that is constructive and enduring.

Simran Jeet Singh.

As a practicing Sikh, are you excited to bring about a positive change within the Sikh tradition through new interpretations?

As a practicing Sikh, I feel blessed to have the opportunity to serve my community. My parents and mentors always taught me that the greatest way to express gratitude is to recognize one's privilege and to give back through *seva* ("self-less service"). This is what I am trying to do.

I understand that Sikh history is filled with people interpreting the teachings of our gurus and trying to live by those teachings as best as they can. From this perspective, I love being a part of this tradition and hope to contribute in whatever small way that I can.

Do you participate in interfaith dialogues to promote greater understanding outside the Sikh tradition?

I participate in interfaith dialogues for a number of reasons. One of these reasons is to help promote greater understanding of Sikhi among faith communities. I have grown spiritually from such encounters, so I personally enjoy such programs. I also believe that such conversations have incredible potential for building healthy communities. And I certainly believe that representation matters, especially in spaces where Sikhs have been historically excluded and underrepresented.

For centuries in Punjab, as elsewhere throughout the subcontinent, sons have tended to be preferred to daughters. The gurus explicitly prohibited female infanticide, and the *rahit-namas* include specific injunctions against it. Thus, although Sikhism does permit medical abortion when the mother's life is in danger, or in cases of incest or rape, it does not condone abortion for the purpose of sex selection. Nevertheless, in recent years the proportion of females to males in the Punjabi population has declined, apparently because, contrary to the Sikh principle of gender equality, female fetuses are being aborted.

Diaspora Sikhs are beginning to debate issues such as genetic engineering and the use of embryos in medical research. Advocates of organ donation often point to the example of Guru Tegh Bahadur, who sacrificed himself to defend the rights of Hindus. Many Sikhs believe that life begins at conception and therefore object to the use of embryos in research. On the other hand, some defend such research on the grounds that it will benefit humanity.

Environmental Issues

Guru Nanak himself spoke of the natural world with great tenderness: "Air is the Guru, water the Father and earth the mighty Mother of all. Day and night are the caring guardians, fondly nurturing all creation" (AG 8). Today environmental issues are becoming prominent both in the Punjab

A prayer vigil in memory of the six people who died when a gunman opened fire in a Sikh temple in Oak Creek, Wisconsin, in 2012 (© AP Photo/Appeal-Democrat, Nate Chute).

and in the diaspora. The celebration of Guru Har Rai's birthday in March has been fixed as "Sikh Environment Day." And in recent years the environmentalist Balbir Singh Seechewal has made it his mission to spread ecological awareness. He singlehandedly organized the restoration of the river associated with Guru Nanak's mystical experience, and he encourages congregations across the Punjab to plant trees in every available space.

Sikh Visibility

On September 15, 2001, an American Sikh became the first victim of the racial backlash that followed the 9/11 terrorist attacks. Balbir Singh Sodhi was shot dead in Phoenix, Arizona, by a self-described "patriot" who mistook him for a Muslim. On August 5, 2012, a gunman burst into the gurdwara in Oak Creek, Wisconsin, and opened fire, killing five men and one woman, and injuring three police officers before turning his gun on himself. It has been widely assumed that the killer, a white supremacist, thought the Sikhs were Muslims. Clearly, even today, too many people in the West simply do not know who Sikhs are.

Organizations such as the Canadian Sikh Coalition are working to raise awareness of Sikhism in Canada and elsewhere. In the United States, civil rights organizations such as the Sikh Coalition, the Sikh American Legal Defense and Education Fund (SALDEF), and Sikhs for Justice (SFJ) are providing legal aid to Sikhs and maintain dynamic information systems and extensive databases.

The situation is somewhat better in academic circles. Participants at the first North American conference on Sikh studies, held in 1976 at the University of California, Berkeley, generally felt that Sikhism was "the forgotten tradition" in North America. This is no longer the case. In the last two decades the scholarly literature on Sikhism has grown steadily, and the mistaken notion that Sikhism represents a synthesis of Hindu and Muslim ideals has been almost entirely abandoned. Today there are nine endowed chairs in Sikh studies in North America, and Sikhism is increasingly recognized in undergraduate academic programs.

⊕ Summary

The Sikh tradition has evolved in response to three fundamental factors: the ongoing tensions of the period in which the Panth evolved, when Punjab was governed by Mughal rulers and under constant threat of invasion from Afghanistan; the martial character of Punjabi society's rural base, which helped to bring the Panth into conflict with Mughal authorities and thus to shape its future direction; and, above all, the religious and cultural innovations of Guru Nanak and his successors.

The Sikh community has been engaged in renewal and redefinition throughout its history, and that engagement has only intensified in recent years. Today the question "Who is a Sikh?" is the subject of often-acrimonious online debate. Each generation of Sikhs has had to respond to that question in the light of new historical circumstances. Not surprisingly, diaspora Sikhs approach these issues from different perspectives, depending on the cultural and political contexts from which they come. In many cases they rediscover their identity through their interaction with other religious and ethnic communities. New challenges demand new responses, especially in a postmodern world where notions of self, gender, and authority are subject to constant questioning. Thus the process of Sikh identity formation is an ongoing phenomenon.

Sites

Patna, Bihar

The birthplace of Guru Gobind Singh and the site of the Takhat Sri Patna Sahib, Patna is one of the five seats of authority in the Sikh world.

Amritsar, Punjab

The holiest of all places for Sikhs, Amritsar was named for the "pool of nectar" that surrounds the Darbar Sahib. Facing the latter and connected to it by a causeway is the Akal Takhat, the most important of the five *takhats*.

Anandpur, Punjab

Anandpur is the birthplace of the Khalsa. The Takhat Sri Kesgarh Sahib stands on the spot where Guru Gobind Singh is said to have created the "Cherished Five" in 1699.

Talwandi Sabo, Punjab

Guru Gobind Singh stayed at Talwandi Sabo for several months around 1705, and it was there that he prepared the final version of the Adi Granth. This is also the site of the Takhat Sri Damdama Sahib.

Nanded, Maharashtra

Nanded is the site of the Takhat Sri Hazur Sahib, where Guru Gobind Singh installed the Adi Granth as the "Eternal Guru" shortly before his death in 1708.

Sacred Texts: Sikhism

Texts	Composition/Compilation	Compilation/Revision	Use
Adi Granth/Guru Granth Sahib; the primary scripture	First collection of Guru Nanak's hymns, compiled in the 1530s. This *pothi* ("sacred volume") was expanded by the succeeding gurus. A four-volume collection produced in 1570, under Guru Amar Das, came to be known as the Goindval Pothis.	The fifth guru, Arjan, produced a prototype of the Adi Granth in 1604. The tenth guru, Gobind Singh, added the works of his father and closed the canon in the 1680s. Before he died in 1708, he installed the Adi Granth as Guru Granth Sahib.	Worship, ceremony, life-cycle rituals; the central authority regarding both personal piety and the corporate identity of the Sikh community
Dasam Granth; the secondary scripture	First collection of works attributed to the tenth guru, Gobind Singh, dating to the 1690s	18th–19th centuries: subsequent collections added the *Zafarnama* of Guru Gobind Singh and fixed the sequence of compositions	Liturgy, both daily and in the Khalsa initiation ceremony

Discussion Questions

1. Do you think that Guru Nanak intended to establish a new religion, independent of Hindu and Muslim traditions? What is the evidence for your opinion in his works?
2. How did Sikhism evolve in response to changing historical circumstances during the time of the 10 gurus?
3. How did the martyrdoms of Guru Arjan and Guru Tegh Bahadur contribute to the emergence of militancy as a core tradition within the Panth?
4. How did modern Sikhism come into being? What role did the Singh Sabha play in defining Sikh doctrine and practice?
5. What is the role of the Guru Granth Sahib in Sikh life?
6. Why is the practice of *kirtan* central to Sikh congregational worship?
7. What role has the institution of the gurdwara played in the Sikh diaspora?

Glossary

Adi Granth Literally, "original book"; first compiled by Guru Arjan in 1604 and invested with supreme authority as the Guru Granth Sahib after the death of Guru Gobind Singh.

Akal Purakh "The One Beyond Time," God.

amrit "Divine nectar"; the Khalsa initiation nectar.

Amrit-dhari "Nectar-bearer"; an initiated member of the Khalsa.

amrit sanskar The formal ceremony initiating Sikhs into the Khalsa.

bani "Divine utterance"; the works of the gurus and the Bhagats ("holy people") recorded in the Adi Granth.

Baisakhi An Indian new year's holiday in mid-April, when Sikhs celebrate the birthday of the Khalsa.

Dasam Granth "The Book of the Tenth Guru"; the secondary Sikh scripture, attributed to Guru Gobind Singh.

Five Ks The *Panj Kakke*, or five marks of Khalsa identity: *kes* (uncut hair), *kangha* (wooden comb), *kirpan* (sword), *kara* (wrist ring), and *kachh* (short breeches).

granthi "Reader"; the reader and custodian of the Guru Granth Sahib who performs traditional rituals in the gurdwara.

gurdwara Literally, "Guru's door"; the Sikh place of worship.

Gurmukhi Literally, "from the guru's mouth"; the vernacular script in which the compositions of the gurus were first written down. It has since become the script of the Punjabi language.

gursikhs Literally, "disciples of the guru."

guru "Teacher"; either a spiritual person or the divine inner voice.

haumai "I-ness, my-ness"; self-centered pride.

hukam "Divine order," "will," or "command"; an all-embracing principle, the sum total of all divinely instituted laws; a revelation of the nature of God.

janam-sakhis "Birth testimonies"; traditional accounts of the life of Guru Nanak.

karah prashad A sweet pudding or paste of flour, sugar, and butter that is prepared in an iron (*karah*) bowl with prayers, placed in the presence of the Sikh scripture during worship, and then distributed in the congregation.

karam "Actions" or karma; the destiny or fate of an individual, generated in accordance with deeds performed in one's present and past existences.

Khalsa Literally, "pure"; an order of Sikhs bound by common identity and discipline.

kirtan The singing of hymns from the scriptures in worship.

langar The term for both the community kitchen and the meal that is prepared there and served to all present following services at the gurdwara.

Mul Mantar Literally, "Basic Formula"; the opening creedal statement of the Adi Granth, declaring the eternity and transcendence of God, the creator.

nam "The divine Name."

nam-simaran "Remembrance of the divine Name," especially the devotional practice of meditating on the divine Name.

Panj Kakke See **Five Ks**.

Panj Piare The "Cherished Five"; the first five Sikhs to be initiated as members of the Khalsa in 1699; five Sikhs in good standing chosen to represent a *sangat*.

Panth Literally, "path"; the Sikh community.

pothi Volume or book.

raga A series of five or six notes on which a melody is based.

rahit The code of conduct for the Khalsa.

sangat Congregation; group of devotees in Sikhism.

Sants Ascetic poets who believed divinity to exist beyond all forms or description.

sansar "Cycle of birth and death"; transmigration in Sikh terminology.

sati The immolation of a widow on her husband's funeral pyre.

Sehaj-dhari Literally, a "gradualist"; a Sikh who follows the teachings of the gurus but has not accepted the Khalsa discipline.

shabad Literally, "divine Word"; a hymn of the Adi Granth.

Singh Sabha Literally, "Society of Singhs"; a revival movement established in 1873 that redefined the norms of Sikh doctrine and practice.

Vak "Saying"; a passage from the Guru Granth Sahib that is chosen at random and read aloud to the congregation as the lesson of the day.

Further Reading

Dusenbery, Verne A. 2008. *Sikhs at Large: Religion, Culture, and Politics*. New Delhi: Oxford University Press. A collection of essays bringing together different perspectives on the cultural and political dimensions of the Sikh diaspora and of Sikhism as a global religion.

Fenech, Louis E. 2008. *The Darbar of the Sikh Gurus: The Court of God in the World of Men*. New Delhi: Oxford University Press. A work that traces the evolving nature of the court of the Sikh gurus in the broader historical context of Indo-Persian courtly tradition.

Grewal, J. S. 1991. *The New Cambridge History of India: The Sikhs of the Punjab*. Cambridge: Cambridge University Press. A classic chronological study of Sikh history from the tradition's beginnings to the present day.

Jakobsh, Doris R. 2012. *Sikhism*. Honolulu: University of Hawai'i Press. A comprehensive overview of Sikhism in its Indian context and as an increasingly global tradition.

Mandair, Arvind-pal S. 2010. *Religion and the Spectre of the West: Sikhism, India, Postcolonialism, and the Politics of Translation*. New York: Columbia University. A recent study of the Sikh tradition from a postcolonial perspective.

McLeod, W. H. 1984. *Textual Sources for the Study of Sikhism*. Manchester: Manchester University Press. An anthology of selections covering all aspects of Sikh belief, worship, and practice.

McLeod, W. H. 1999. *Sikhs and Sikhism*. New Delhi: Oxford University Press. An omnibus edition of four classic studies on the history and evolution of Sikhs and Sikhism by one of the world's leading scholars in the field.

McLeod, W. H. 2003. *The Sikhs of the Khalsa*. New Delhi: Oxford University Press. A study of how the *rahit*, or "Code of Conduct," came into being, how it developed in response to historical circumstances, and why it still retains an unchallenged hold over all who consider themselves Khalsa Sikhs.

Nesbitt, Eleanor. 2005. *Sikhism: A Very Short Introduction*. Oxford: Oxford University Press. An ethnographic introduction to Sikhism and its teachings, practices, rituals, and festivals.

Oberoi, Harjot. 1994. *Construction of Religious Boundaries*. New Delhi: Oxford University Press. A major reinterpretation of Sikh religion and society during the colonial period.

Singh, Harbans, ed. 1992–1998. *The Encyclopaedia of Sikhism*. 4 vols. Patiala, India: Punjabi University. A four-volume reference work covering Sikh life and letters, history and philosophy, customs and rituals, social and religious movements, art and architecture, and locales and shrines.

Singh, Nikky-Guninder Kaur. 2011. *Sikhism: An Introduction*. London and New York: I. B. Tauris. An introduction to Sikh religion and culture highlighting various issues related to doctrine, worship, ethics, art, architecture, and the diaspora.

Singh, Pashaura. 2006. *Life and Work of Guru Arjan: History, Memory and Biography in the Sikh Tradition*. New Delhi: Oxford University Press. A reconstruction of the life and work of the fifth guru, based on history, collective memory, tradition, and mythic representation.

Recommended Websites

http://www.columbia.edu/itc/mealac/pritchett/00generallinks/index.html

A good site with links to many resources on South Asia.

http://www.sikhs.org

The Sikhism Home Page, operated from Brampton, Ontario.

http://www.sikhnet.com

The SikhNet website, operated from Espanola, New Mexico.

http://www.sgpc.net

The website of the Shiromani Gurdwara Parbandhak Committee, Amritsar.

http://www.sikhchic.com

An online magazine offering a journey through the Sikh universe.

http://www.sikhcoalition.org

The website of a Sikh advocacy group in the United States.

http://www.saldef.org

The website of the Sikh American Legal Defense and Education Fund.

http://www.sikhsforjustice.org

The website of the human rights organization Sikhs for Justice.

References

McLeod, W. H. 1984. *Textual Sources for the Study of Sikhism*. Manchester, UK: Manchester University Press.

McLeod, W. H. 1997. *Sikhism*. London: Penguin Books.

McLeod, W. H. 2003. *The Sikhs of the Khalsa*. New Delhi: Oxford University Press.

Nesbitt, Eleanor. 2005. Sikhism: 8. Oxford: Oxford University Press.

Notes

This chapter is dedicated to the memory of my teacher, Professor Willard G. Oxtoby.

1. This reference means that the passage quoted comes from the twenty-seventh stanza of the ballad (*Var*) in the musical measure *Majh*, by Guru Nanak (M1), on page 150 of the Adi Granth (AG).

2. For a discussion of this work by the artists themselves, see http://www.sikhchic.com/article-detail.php?cat=21&id=747. *Nineteen Eighty-Four and the Via Dolorosa Project* (2009) is a semi-autobiographical documentary film in which the artists draw parallels with the Christian faith.

9 Jaina Traditions

Anne Vallely

Traditions at a Glance

Numbers

Estimates of the number of Jainas today range from 5 to 8 million worldwide.

Distribution

Jainas are primarily found in India, with smaller numbers in East Africa, England, and North America.

Principal Historical Periods

The traditional dates of the Mahavira are from 599 to 527 BCE. Around 310 BCE a split occurred in the Jaina community. One of the tradition's key texts, the *Kalpa Sutra*, was likely composed sometime in the second century BCE. The Svetambara and Digambara sects crystallized in the fifth century CE, with the Svetambara Sthanakvasi subsect emerging in the seventeenth century and the Svetambara Terapanthi subsect emerging in the eighteenth.

Founders and Leaders

Jainas revere the 24 Jinas, also known as the Tirthankaras: a series of "ford-builders" who achieved perfect enlightenment and serve as guides for other human beings. The most important are the two most recent, Parsavanath and Mahavira.

Deities

Jainism includes no deities in its philosophy. A few minor deities appear in popular practice, and some Jainas also worship Hindu deities such as Sri Lakshmi. Although the Tirthankaras are not gods, many Jainas revere their images.

Authoritative Texts

The earliest texts were lost long ago. The Svetambara sect reveres a collection called the *Agama*, consisting of various later treatises known as the *Angas*, as well as the *Kalpa Sutra*, which contains the life stories of the Tirthankaras. The Digambara sect believes that the original *Angas* were lost as well and focus instead on a set of texts called *Prakaranas* (treatises).

Noteworthy Teachings

Jainas believe that the soul is caught in karmic bondage as a result of violence, both intended and unintended, done to other beings. Nonviolence is the most important principle, in thought, word, and deed. Freed from karma, the soul attains crystal purity.

In this chapter you will learn about:

- The sociocultural context in which Jaina traditions emerged in northwestern India between the ninth and sixth centuries BCE
- The geographic spread of the early Jaina community and the concomitant rise of distinctive branches of belief and practice through the modern period
- The singularity of the soul in Jainism's intricate cosmology, which posits that the soul must free itself from the material world and that nonviolence is central to its liberation
- The rigorous demands of the idealized renouncer path, as well as the mainstream householder path and its relationship with the ideals of Jainism
- The central teachings, prayers, practices, and festivals that constitute the lifeblood of Jainism for its millions of adherents

A frail monk sits cross-legged on a bed, leaning against the wall for support as his followers enter the room. Everyone knows this is the last time they will gather for *darshana*—to pay homage to

Jaina pilgrims at a temple in the Jaisalmer Fort, Rajasthan (© Craig Lovell/Eagle Visions Photography/Alamy).

their guru and receive his blessing—for he has taken the vow of **sallekhana**, and the process is nearing its end. *Sallekhana* is the ritual death achieved at the end of a long fast. No Jaina is required to undertake such a fast; in fact, Jainas are expressly forbidden to cause harm to any living being, whether in thought, speech, or action. But the Jaina path is one of **renunciation**—of departure from life during life—and *sallekhana* is merely its logical end. Voluntary death is the most radical statement possible of detachment from the body and the world. A dispassionate death is a triumph for the eternal soul on its journey toward perfection.

⊕ Overview

Jainism confronts us with a simple yet extraordinary message: the path to happiness, truth, and self-realization is the path of restraint. Happiness is the product not of embracing the world but of disengaging from it. It is this emphasis on restraint that gives Jainism its distinctive ascetic character. And yet the Jaina community is well known for its business acumen, worldly success, and strong social identity—in other words, for its effective, dynamic engagement with the world.

Colossal rock-cut sculptures of the Tirthankaras at the Gwalior Fort in Madhya Pradesh (© Atlantide Phototravel/ Corbis).

Timeline

c. 850 BCE	Parsavanath, the 23rd Tirthankara
599–527	Traditional dates of Mahavira
4th century	Possible beginning of split within Jaina community with southward migration of one group
2nd century CE	Life of Umasvati, Digambara author of the *Tattvartha Sutra*
5th century	Construction of first Jaina temples
9th century	Life of Jinasena, Svetambara philosopher
10th century	Colossal statue of Bahubali erected in Shravanabelagola, Karnataka
11th century	Dilwara temple complex built in Rajasthan
12th century	Life of Hemachandra, Svetambara philosopher
15th century	Lonkashaha initiates reform in the Svetambara tradition
16th century	Banarsidass initiates reform in the Digambara tradition
17th century	Formation of Svetambara Sthanakvasi subsect
18th century	Formation of Svetambara Terapanthi subsect
20th century	Revitalization of the Bhattaraka tradition within the Digambara sect

Outsiders often perceive a paradoxical disjunction between Jainas' this-worldly achievements and their otherworldly ethos. But this seeming paradox reflects the principle that the power of renunciation lies not in opposing worldly power, but in transcending it. Conquering our attachment to the world is the most difficult of all battles, but for Jainas it is the only battle in which it is worth engaging. Such is the message of the **Jinas** ("victors" or "conquerors"), the 24 ascetic prophets—the most recent of whom was **Mahavira** (c. 599–527 BCE)—from whom Jainas take their name.

Jainism is a tradition that expresses itself ritually through the veneration and emulation of the Jinas (also known as "**Tirthankaras**"—builders of bridges across the ocean of birth and death, or *samsara*). The Jina is the highest expression of the Jaina ideal and the focus of the Jaina devotional apparatus. A commanding figure who could just as easily have been a worldly *chakravartin*—the ideal benevolent ruler—endowed with everything the world has to offer, the Jina "conquers" the world by turning his back on it. Indeed, the Jina is venerated in both his potentialities: as the regal *chakravartin*, and as the unadorned *Arhat* (perfected being) entirely detached from worldly concerns. World renouncer and world conqueror, though antithetical in their orientations, both trace their beginnings to the good karma accrued through a life of nonviolence. Restraint, self-discipline, and commitment not to harm are the starting points for the Jina and the *chakravartin* alike.

Jainas commonly express the essence of their tradition in three words: "*ahimsa paramo dharma*" ("nonviolence is the supreme path"). This is not to say that they seek to eradicate the violence of the world. In a universe where every life exists only at the expense of others, such a commitment would be futile. Rather, the Jaina commitment to nonviolence is a commitment to radical

Document

The Imperative of Nonviolence

The Acaranga Sutra, *or "Scripture of Correct Conduct," is the oldest and among the most important texts of the Svetambara tradition. Believed to contain the teachings of Mahavira, it focuses on the requirement of nonviolent action.*

All living beings love their life. For them happiness is desirable; unhappiness is not desirable. No living being likes to be killed. Every living being is desirous of life. (*Acaranga Sutra* 1:2:3; Jacobi and Muller 2001 [1895–1910])

noninterference. Jainas equate nonviolence with renunciation because it is only through the total cessation of activity that one can truly avoid harming others and, consequently, oneself.

Jainas believe that even the smallest forms of life possess an eternal soul (*jiva*), and none desire to be harmed. Yet their omnipresence means that we cannot perform any action without causing them harm. And in so doing, we harm ourselves, for every act of violence we perpetrate increases the negative karma attached to our souls. Lack of intention to commit harm is an important mitigating factor. But even unintended harm still increases karmic bondage—though the karma in question is less dark than the kind created when the harm is intended.

Jainism tells us that attachment to the world and to the worldly self comes at the expense of knowing the true Self that has nothing to do with this world. The true Self is fundamentally other. It is indifferent to worldly things, and as a result its presence is easy to ignore amid the endless distractions created by the demands of the body. Nevertheless, on very rare occasions our conscious minds may catch a glimpse of it. Jainas call this momentary awakening **samyak darshan** ("right faith" or "correct intuition" into the workings of the world), and it is the starting point of Jainism.

According to Jainas, there is only one path to emancipation: that of self-discipline and nonharm. Yet this singular path has led to a remarkable variety of Jaina communities. The most fundamental distinction is the one between the two Jaina sects: **Digambara** (naked or "sky-clad") and **Svetambara** (white-clad). The split occurred some 200 years after the death of Mahavira and was the product of enduring differences regarding ascetic practice, women's spiritual capacity, and the nature of the Jina, among other things.

Other issues that divide Jainas include the worship of images or idols and the use of "living beings" such as flowers, water, and fire in worship. Yet all Jainas share the commitment to renunciation and nonviolence. Renunciation is embodied by the "sky-clad" ascetics, but it is also present in the beliefs and practices of lay Jainas. Out of the diversity of Jaina expression emerges the unvarying message that nonviolence is the only path to liberation.

⊕ The Shramana Revolution

Jainism appeared on the historical scene sometime between the ninth and sixth centuries BCE as part of the same *shramana* ("world-renouncing") movement that gave rise to Buddhism. The later date is the more commonly accepted because the historicity of Mahavira (born Vardhamana

Map 9.1 Origin and Dispersion of Jainism

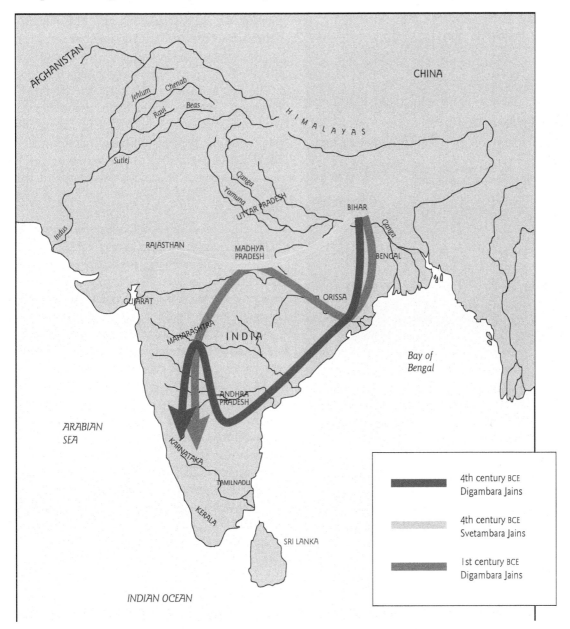

Today most Svetambara Jainas live in central and western India (Gujarat, Rajasthan, Madhya Pradesh, Uttar Pradesh) and most Digambara Jainas in the south, but communities of both sects can be found throughout the country, as well as abroad.

Perched on scaffolding constructed every 12 years for the Great Head Anointing Ceremony, Jainas bathe the colossal 57-foot Bahubali statue at Shravanabelagola in Karnataka with substances such as milk, sugarcane juice, saffron, sandalwood, and vermilion (© Frederic Soltan/ Sygma/Corbis).

Jnatrpura) has been widely established. The earlier date is associated with the life of the twenty-third Tirthankara, Parsavanath, for which the only evidence is the occasional scriptural reference.

The followers of Mahavira, like the followers of the Buddha, rejected the brahminical orthodoxy of the day. As their name implies, the "world renouncers" considered the brahmins' preoccupation with cosmic and social order to be fundamentally flawed. All the elements that went into maintaining that order—the hierarchical caste system, the elaborate liturgy, the rituals, and above all the cult of animal sacrifice—were anathema to the renouncers.

The *shramanas* also held similar views regarding the need for salvation from a meaningless cosmos. All regarded the cosmic order not as the creation of a transcendent god, but as a purposeless place of suffering that must be transcended. Finally, each *shramana* group claimed a unique insight into the attainment of **moksha** (liberation/nirvana). Despite their similarities, therefore, the various *shramana* groups developed as distinct traditions and even rivals.

Mahavira is said to have been born to a ruling family in the region of Nepal and northeastern India. Almost all that can be said with any certainty is that he was a historical personage whose teachings attracted both disciples and lay followers. Nevertheless, Jainas tell many tales of the teacher they call Mahavira, or "Great Hero," beginning with the miraculous transfer of his embryo from the womb of a brahmin woman named Devananda to that of Queen Trisala (which unequivocally established the supremacy of the kshatriya caste over the brahmins).

In any religion, the question of origins is often ambiguous. The ambiguities are multiplied in Jainism because, although Jainas have a strong sense of historical continuity, they also believe that we are embedded in a vast system of eternally recurring time that renders both myth and history ultimately meaningless.

Jainas believe that the cycles of generation and degeneration produce predictable patterns in social, moral, and physical life. Thus within each cycle there are periods that favor the emergence of Jinas who teach the path of liberation. Mahavira is merely the final Jina of the current degenerate time period. In the next cycle, which will be one of generation, another 24 Jinas will appear,

Focus

The Life of Mahavira in the *Kalpa Sutra*

Mahavira's Birth

[When] the Venerable Ascetic Mahavira was born, . . . [there] rained down on the palace of King Siddhartha one great shower of silver, gold, diamonds, clothes, ornaments, leaves, flowers, . . . sandal powder, and riches.

. . . [His parents] prepared plenty of food, drink, spices, and sweetmeats, invited their friends, relations, kinsmen. . . . His three names have thus been recorded: by his parents he was called Vardhamana; because he is devoid of love and hate, he is called sramana (i.e., Ascetic); because he stands fast in the midst of dangers and fears, patiently bears hardships and calamities, adheres to the chosen rules of penance, is wise, indifferent to pleasure and pain, rich in control . . . the name Venerable Ascetic Mahavira has been given him by the gods. (Jacobi 1884: 251–256)

Enlightenment

When the Venerable Ascetic Mahavira had become a Jina and Arhat, he was a Kevalin [liberated one],

omniscient and comprehending all objects; he knew and saw all conditions of the world, of gods, men, and demons: whence they came, whither they go, whether they are born as men or animals or become gods or hell beings, the ideas, the thoughts of their minds, the food, doings, desires, the open and secret deeds of all the living beings in the whole world; he, the Arhat for whom there is no secret, knew and saw all conditions of living beings in the world, what they thought, spoke, or did at any moment. (Jacobi 1884: 263–264)

Mahavira's Physical Death

In the fourth month of that rainy season . . . in the town of Papa . . . the Venerable Ascetic Mahavira died, went off, quitted the world, cut asunder the ties of birth, old age, and death; became a Siddha [a liberated being], a Buddha, a Mukta, a maker of the end (to all misery), finally liberated, freed from all pains. . . . [That night, the kings who had gathered there said]: "Since the light of intelligence is gone, let us make an illumination of material matter." (Jacobi 1884: 264–266)

---

preaching the same wisdom. And during the cycle of decline that will inevitably follow, yet another 24 will appear, and so on, in an unending cycle of decay and growth.

Jainas assert that Jainism—like the cosmos itself—has no point of origin. Just as the cosmos has always existed, so too has the struggle for liberation from it—as well as the truth about how to attain salvation. By declaring the cosmos to be eternal, Jainism directs our attention away from the question of origins to the more pressing issue of liberation from *samsara* (the cycle of birth and death).

Conveying the eternal message of liberation through restraint is an urgent task because it is accessible only to specific incarnations (human beings) residing in specific regions of the cosmos during specific time periods. Under any other conditions the message would not reach us. Thus we who have the good fortune to hear it must not squander our chance to learn from it how to escape.

A page from a fifteenth-century copy of the Kalpa Sutra, the devotional text narrating the lives of the Jinas (Indian. Mahavira Preaching at the Gunashilaka Shrine, Leaf from a Dispersed Jain Manuscript of the Kalpasutra, 15th century. Opaque watercolor and gold on paper, sheet: 4 1/2 x 11 3/8 in. [11.4 x 28.9 cm]. Brooklyn Museum, Gift of the Ernest Erickson Foundation, Inc., 86.227.48).

✪ The Early *Sangha*

Mahavira established Jainism as a community (*sangha*) made up of monks, nuns, laymen, and lay-women. His acceptance of women is noteworthy, since the *shramanas* generally regarded women as "objects of desire," to be avoided lest they distract male ascetics from their path. It is said that Mahavira's *sangha* grew to include 36,000 nuns and 14,000 monks, as well as 318,000 laywomen and 159,000 laymen (Jaini 1979: 37). The preponderance of nuns in comparison to monks has remained a distinguishing feature of Jainism.

At the age of 72, Mahavira is said to have "left his body" and attained *moksha*—a state of complete detachment from the world. Mahavira's disciples assumed leadership of the community, but within two centuries the once-cohesive *sangha* had begun to split into two discrete traditions. The precise causes of this divide remain unknown, but many sources suggest that the turning point came in the fourth century BCE, when one group moved south. Thereafter, as the two groups developed in isolation, each came to see the other as deviating from Mahavira's vision.

That the northern group had abandoned the principle of nudity was a particular abomination to the southerners, for whom nudity was among the most elemental expressions of nonattachment and nonviolence. The northerners argued that a simple garment had no bearing on spiritual progress. Nevertheless, the difference was so visible that it became the basis for the two groups' self-identification. Eventually, the northerners came to be known as the Svetambara ("white-clad") and the southerners as the Digambara ("sky-clad," or naked). The lay followers of both groups (including the fully clothed lay followers of the naked monks) likewise took on these names as markers of their religious identity.

This was not the only point of division, however. Another involved women's eligibility for full membership. The Digambaras' insistence on nudity meant that women were automatically disqualified from becoming full members, while the Svetambaras imposed no such condition and therefore did permit women to join them.

Both groups regard women's bodies as inferior to men's because they are weaker and therefore believe that the ascetic path is more difficult for women. For the Svetambaras, however, that obstacle is not insurmountable; they even maintain that the nineteenth Jina (Mallinath) was female. Digambaras vehemently disagree, arguing that asceticism requires a powerful, "adamantine" body (Jaini 1979: 39). They believe that rebirth in a male body is a prerequisite for full renunciation, but in the interim they permit women to lead a life of semi-renunciation.

Finally, the nature of the Jina's omniscience when embodied (that is, while in life) came to be a point of contention. According to the Digambaras, one who is omniscient must already have transcended bodily appetites and functions. Thus the Jina has no need of sleep or food, and instead of speaking communicates by a divine sound. The Svetambaras, by contrast, believe that all embodied beings are subject to bodily demands; therefore, the omniscient Jina eats, sleeps, and communicates as humans do.

Sacred Literature

The sacred literature of the Jainas was transmitted by Mahavira to his followers, but it is not believed to have originated with him. In our time cycle, the eternal teachings were first propounded by the Jina **Rsabha** and then transmitted anew by each succeeding prophet. Mahavira's teachings were committed to memory by his closest disciples, who then transmitted them orally to other disciples, who in turn passed them along down the generations. Thus the Jaina canon (*Agama*) for many years existed as a purely oral tradition.

The entire *Agama* has three main branches: the *Purva* ("the ancient"), concerned with metaphysics, cosmology, and philosophy; the *Anga* ("the limbs"), which includes discussion of **mendicant** conduct, doctrine, karma, and religious narratives; and the *Angabahya* ("ancillary limbs"), a subsidiary collection of commentaries on those topics, along with dialogues on matters such as astrology and the cycles of time.

The oral canon was faithfully preserved within the ascetic orders for more than 200 years. In the early fourth century BCE, however, northern India was struck by a devastating famine that is said to have continued for 12 years. The canon was nearly lost altogether as both the ascetics and the householders whom they depended on for sustenance struggled to survive.

From this point on, what happened to the *Agama* becomes unclear. Knowledge of the *Purvas*—the most ancient section, believed to date from the time of Parsavanath, in the ninth century BCE—was lost, although it is thought that much of their content was contained in the final section of the *Anga*, called the *Drstivada*. According to the Svetambaras, the *Drstivada* was also lost to memory, but its essence was preserved through a text contained within the *Angabahya*.

The Digambaras, however, claim that they managed to retain much of the *Drstivada* and put it in writing around the second century CE. This work, called the *Satkhandagama*, was the first Jaina scripture to be preserved in written form, and it is one of very few canonical works that the Digambaras recognize as authoritative. They reject the scriptures retained by the Svetambaras as inauthentic deviations from the original canon.

Document

From the *Bhaktamara Stotra*

The Bhaktamara Stotra is one of the most beloved Jaina texts. It is addressed to Adinatha—another name for Rsabha, the first Tirthankara.

In the fullness of faith
I bow
to the feet of the Jina,
shining as they reflect the gems in the crowns of the gods
who bow down in devotion,
illuminating the darkness
of oppressive sin,
a refuge in the beginning of time
for all souls

lost in the ocean of birth
. . .
Praising you
instantly destroys
the sinful karma that binds
embodied souls
to endless rebirth
just as the sun's rays
instantly shatter
the all-embracing
bee-black
endless dark night . . . (*Bhaktamara Stotra, Manatunga,* 1, 7; Cort 2005: 95–98)

In addition to the *Agamas*, vast collections of postcanonical writing were produced by the learned **acharyas** (mendicant scholars) of both sects, including Jinasena, Hemachandra, Kundakunda, Haribhadra, and Umasvati. These works are today among the most celebrated works of ancient and medieval Indian philosophy.

The dispute over the Svetambara and Digambara canons aside, the gulf between the two groups is not as wide as it may appear. Many fundamental ideas—on the nature of the soul, karma, nonviolence, and the cosmos—are common to both groups, as are many practices. The **Tattvartha Sutra** of Umasvati (second century CE) merits special note here. It is a comprehensive treatment of the fundamentals of the tradition and is cherished by both the Svetambara and the Digambara communities. Finally, the recent text *Saman Suttam* (1974)[1] is the first cross-sectarian effort to produce a concise summary of Jaina thought. The following section lays out the fundamentals of Jaina cosmology on which the two sects agree.

Cosmology

Jainas believe that the entire cosmos (*loka*) is made up of six eternal substances called *dravya*, and that knowledge of them is an important step toward self-perfection. These substances are classified in two broad categories: *jiva* (soul) and **ajiva** (nonsoul). *Jiva* is an eternal substance with consciousness. *Ajiva* is a substance without consciousness and consists of five types: *pudgala* (pure matter), *kala* (time), *dharma* (principle of motion), *adharma* (principle of rest), and *akash* (space). The latter four—all variants of *pudgala*—are "supportive" forms, without which existence would not be possible.

Pudgala is a concrete substance with the attributes of touch, taste, smell, and color. Although it has no special function, it is the basis of all matter and energy. All activities of the mind and body, including thought and speech, are considered to be *pudgala*. All worldly knowledge is acquired by means of *pudgala*—including the knowledge of how to free ourselves from it. Indeed, it is only through perception, which is also a form of *pudgala*, that we can know the cosmos and its contents.

Thus *pudgala* is not antithetical to *jiva*. It is neutral in this regard, although its natural tendency is to become attached both to other forms of matter and to *jiva*. This is an important point, because renouncers typically speak of matter in highly negative terms (e.g., referring to the world as vomit, or the body as a trap). Yet *pudgala* is *jiva*'s friend as well as its foe, for the worldly soul that seeks release from it is nevertheless utterly dependent on it.

The most fundamental existential problem, shared by all beings in the cosmos, is the fact that *jiva* and *ajiva* are thoroughly enmeshed. This is what prevents the soul from achieving bliss, which can be experienced only in a state of purity removed from all that is not-soul. Jainas assert that this state of entanglement is eternal, "without beginning," and that we are constantly exacerbating it, since every activity, mental as well as physical, causes vibrations that create ever more particles of binding karma. These karmic particles come in two types—auspicious ("good karma," called **punya**) and inauspicious ("bad karma," called **paap**)—but ultimately all forms of karma must be purged. The forces behind those karma-creating activities, and hence the root causes of our bondage, are the passions.

This is the quandary out of which the Jaina path of self-restraint offers a coherent way. By limiting—and eventually eliminating—the inflow of karma and cleansing the soul of the karmic particles that have become encrusted on it through eternity, we can eliminate the cause of the soul's suffering. The process of purging is called *nirjara*, and it is the purpose behind most Jaina practices. Normally, karma dissolves when (after giving pain or pleasure) it comes to fruition. But karma can be made to "ripen" and vanish prematurely through the practice of ascetic discipline.

⊕ Major Developments

As a tiny minority within India, Jainas have always been vulnerable to assimilation. How have they managed to differentiate themselves and thrive when other world-renouncing traditions have not? Paradoxically, the success of "otherworldly" Jainism likely owes much to its "this-worldly" understanding. The skills required to forge alliances with ruling elites and make inroads into established economic structures in the medieval period (fifth through seventeenth centuries) were developed in the first two centuries of its existence, when it enjoyed the patronage of the kshatriya rulers.

In the final centuries before the beginning of the Common Era, the fate of all the *shramana* groups depended on their ability to secure royal patronage. The sociopolitical "alliance" between the kshatriyas and *shramanas* was rooted in a shared ideological opposition to brahminic orthodoxy. The fact that Mahavira (like the Buddha) came from a kshatriya clan was a sign of the kshatriyas' ascent. The alliance was mutually beneficial: the *shramanas* prospered with the economic support of the kshatriyas, who gained popular support and legitimacy from the *shramanas*.

In the fourth century BCE, however, Emperor Ashoka converted to Buddhism, and the balance of power shifted. The Jainas slowly retreated from their original centers of power in eastern India (Magadha) toward the (then) more peripheral northwestern regions of Rajasthan, Gujarat, and Punjab, as well as into the southern areas of what are now Maharashtra and Karnataka. Nevertheless, the wealth and—more important—political skills that Jainas had acquired from serving (in legal positions, as advisors, etc.) at the various kshatriya courts gave them a worldly acumen that would serve them well long after their royal support had disappeared.

By the third century BCE, the once-unified Jaina community had begun to separate into the two groups that, centuries later, would become the Svetambaras and Digambaras. The split was reinforced by the geographical repositioning of the Svetambaras in the northwest and the Digambaras in the south. Yet Jainas of both sects managed to prosper in their new environments. Although their influence with local elites was always limited, their skills, especially in trade, enabled them to establish secure communities.

Jaina philosophy flourished over the following centuries. Among the *acharyas* who produced important treatises were the Digambaras Umasvati (the second-century author of the *Tattvartha Sutra*), his contemporary Kundakunda, and Haribhadra in the seventh century and the Svetambaras Jinasena in the ninth century and Hemachandra in the twelfth. Together, the philosophical works of the *acharyas* constitute an enormous and celebrated body of sacred literature.

The preservation of Jaina traditions through the medieval period can probably be attributed to the interdependence of Jaina householders and renouncers. Instead of establishing large monasteries, as the Buddhists did, the Jaina ascetics continued to rely for sustenance on householders, who likely served as unofficial enforcers of proper conduct. Although the Buddhist monasteries were supported by lay followers, the relationship between the two groups was never as close as the relationship between Jaina ascetics and householders, who provided mendicants with sustenance as often as three times a day. The latter played a central role in the perpetuation of Jaina tradition, and for that reason they may have been less vulnerable than their Buddhist counterparts to the rise of the Hindu *bhakti* movement. Furthermore, whereas the concentration of Buddhist monks and scriptures in large, wealthy monasteries made them easy targets for marauding armies, the Jainas were dispersed throughout society and had no property to plunder. Thus the decentralized nature of Jaina groups may have inadvertently contributed to their survival.

Reform

Idol veneration became an established feature of Jainism very early in its history (third century BCE), but the first Jaina temples did not appear until the early medieval period (c. fifth century CE). With time and growing affluence, the temples became sites not only of devotion but also of interaction between householders and the mendicants who gathered there.

Document
The Nature of the Self

Kundakunda was a celebrated second-century acharya *who composed several important texts, including the* Samayasara, *which focuses on the nature of the soul. Though revered by all Jainas, he is especially important to the Digambara tradition.*

The defining characteristic of the jiva is that it knows—that is its essence. Jiva and Jnana, self or knower and knowledge are not different, they are identical: the knower is essentially one with knowledge. (Kundakunda 1950: 232)

In Jainism, the care and management of temples is almost exclusively the responsibility of the laity. The general absence of settled, temple-based communities of mendicants today can be traced to a number of powerful reform movements that arose between the fifteenth and seventeenth centuries and effectively reinvigorated the tradition of ascetic discipline among both Svetambara and Digambara Jainas. The reformers saw a direct correlation between the proliferation of temples and what they considered to be a growing laxity on the part of many Jaina ascetics, who were gradually abandoning itinerancy for the relative comfort of a settled life in and around the temples.

The first in the Svetambara tradition to question the wealth and power of the *caityavasis* ("temple-dwelling renouncers") was a fifteenth-century lay reformer named Lonkashaha. He also challenged their deviation from the principle of restraint and criticized idol worship and temple building as contrary not only to the ethos of renunciation but also to the vow of nonviolence, given that the construction of idols and temples involved unnecessary violence to living beings. Lonkasha- ha's critique ended the institution of the *caityavasis* and gave rise to two influential Svetambara sects: Sthanakvasis (who oppose temple-based Jainism and reside in halls known as *sthanaks* on their peripatetic travels) and Terapanthis (reformers who oppose the use of *sthanaks* as well as temples).

Major changes took place in the Digambara tradition as well, initiated by the lay poet Banarsidass in the sixteenth century. Like Lonkashaha, Banarsidass criticized what he saw as the excessive ritualism and unnecessary violence (e.g., the use of flowers) associated with temple worship. At the same time he denounced a group of quasi-ascetic clerics called the *bhattarakas*. Analogous to the Svetambara *caityavasis* but with greater political clout, the *bhattarakas* served both as guardians of the temples and as intermediaries between the naked ascetics and the ruling elites—a role that, in addition to gaining them power and wealth, made them vulnerable to corruption.

The Digambaras responded to these critiques with sweeping reforms that led to the decline (though not the disappearance) of the *bhattarakas*. The revitalization sparked by the reformers' critiques put both the Svetambara and Digambara orders in positions of significant strength as they entered the modern period.

⊕ Practice

The importance that Jainism attaches to practice is one of its defining features. Correct practice (*samyak caritra*) constitutes one of the "Three Jewels" of Jainism, along with correct intuition (*samyak darshan*) and correct knowledge (*samyak jnana*). Although all three are fundamental, correct practice tends to overshadow the others because it is so conspicuous. Before we look at specific practices, however, it is important to grasp the special significance that the concept of practice has in Jainism and how it is grounded in Jaina metaphysics.

The Jaina emphasis on practice reflects an understanding of the world and human suffering as *real*—not illusory—and in need of active human intervention. This understanding stands in sharp contrast to that of Vedanta Hinduism and Buddhism, which essentially see the world and human suffering as products of thought and perception, and therefore focus on changing consciousness as the way to freedom. While Jainas recognize that lack of consciousness plays a key role in the problems of earthly existence, they also believe that the soul is physically (not just mentally) trapped, caught in karmic matter that must be dealt with physically through practices such as penance and fasting.

We have already described the Jaina view of the eternal soul (*jiva*) and matter (*ajiva*) as enmeshed in a labyrinthine web that will never be untangled without concrete action. Because this entrapment is real in a physical sense—not just an illusory state that can be dispelled through clearer thinking—Jaina belief holds that enlightenment hinges as much on practice as it does on worldview. Good intentions can never be enough; action must always be the foremost consideration. It is for this reason that renouncers follow an ascetic discipline designed to heighten their awareness of how they move their bodies in and through space—how they walk, sit, lie down, speak, collect alms, sleep, go to the toilet, and so on.

Jaina practice aims to purify the soul of the *pudgala* that clings to it. By shedding obstructive karma, the soul becomes free to manifest its true nature. Practices are of two types: defensive and offensive. In the process known as *samvara*, defensive strategies such as inculcating detachment and mindfulness are used to impede the accumulation of new karma, while the offensive practice of *nirjara* (purging) uses fasting, meditation, and various forms of physical discipline to "burn off" old karma.

The hallmarks of Jaina practice—ascetic discipline, dietary restrictions, fasting, **samayika** (the state of equanimity), **pratikramana** (the prayer of repentance), *sallekhana* (the fast to death), and Jina puja (worship of the Jinas)—are undertaken by both renouncers and householders with the aim of purification through the dual processes of *samvara* and *nirjara*. The main difference between the path of the renouncer and that of the householder lies in the degree of purification each permits; the renouncer's life is structured by a series of vows (**mahavratas**) that make it nearly impossible for new karma to develop.

Because renouncers are largely shielded from the risk of accumulating new karma, they can devote their time to whittling away their existing karmic load. Householders, immersed as they are in worldly activities—working, raising families, preparing food—are awash in karmic influences. Nevertheless, they can limit the influx of negative karma (*paap*) through lay practices (**anuvratas**) such as fasting or limiting possessions, travel, cosmetics, and so on; many women in particular undertake these exercises in restraint. What marks such activities as characteristically Jaina is that they all involve disengagement from the world. Even devotional activities (e.g., Jina puja) that outwardly resemble Hindu forms of worship are interpreted by Jainas as practices that foster worldly detachment.

Ideally, the lives of Jainas, whether renouncers or householders, are governed by a series of vows (*mahavratas* and *anuvratas*, respectively) that limit worldly engagement, discipline the body, and help the soul develop the tools it will need for its eventual liberation. Thus Jainism is unequivocally a renouncer tradition, even though the vast majority of Jainas at any given time have always been householders involved in worldly pursuits.

Jainism is a renouncer tradition because its defining framework is thoroughly ascetic in character. It creates and molds religious identity by asking the faithful to accept increasingly restrictive boundaries. The main difference between the *mahavratas* of the mendicants and the *anuvratas* of the householders is the degree to which they restrict worldly engagement.

Ascetic Practice

The *mahavratas* are five "great vows" accepted by everyone who takes up the life of a Jaina ascetic (*muni* or *sadhvi*): *ahimsa* (nonharm), *satya* (truthfulness), *asteya* (nonstealing), *brahmacharya* (celibacy), and *aparigraha* (nonpossession/nonattachment). In addition, the ascetic orders impose certain restrictions on themselves. Neither sect accepts individuals who are physically, emotionally, or mentally fragile. It is for this reason that the Digambara sect continues to claim that women are not suited for the ascetic life. "Femaleness"—determined as it is by karma—is seen as making the

A Jaina woman in New Delhi gives food to a nun. Jaina householders are very conscious of the strict dietary rules that govern the renouncers' lives and take care to ensure that all offerings have been rendered ajiv (without life) (© AP Photo/Manish Swarup/CP).

already challenging life of mendicancy impossible. The renouncer path is to be undertaken only by those who have both the spiritual desire and the physical fortitude for a life of denial.

By drawing the self back from worldly concerns, the vows create the conditions in which its true vitality and force can be unveiled. The first vow (*ahimsa*) is the weightiest of the five; for Jainas, it encompasses all the others. In effect, *ahimsa* forbids all involvement with the world and ensures that no action is undertaken spontaneously, without restraint. Because the vow of *ahimsa* is unconditional in its application, renouncers must be committed to causing no harm—through speech, action, or thought—even to "one-sensed" beings (invisible air-bodied beings, water, fire, and earth) and plants, insects, animals, and fellow human beings. Avoiding harm to human beings and animals is easy compared to avoiding harm to water, air, and other minute forms of life (all of which are equally endowed with an eternal soul); this is a monumental challenge and is the main reason behind the Jaina insistence on correct practice.

Munis and *sadhvis* are not permitted to prepare their own food, since even harvesting plants or boiling water inevitably causes harm to living beings. Thus the ascetics depend entirely on the generosity of householders, and even so they must be vigilant to maintain their vow of *ahimsa*. They are permitted only a small portion of the householder's "leftovers"; they cannot accept food

Document

From the *Acaranga Sutra* on Good Conduct

He who injures these (earth bodies) does not comprehend and renounce the sinful acts; he who does not injure these, comprehends and renounces the sinful acts. Knowing them, a wise man should not act sinfully towards the earth, nor cause others to act so, nor allow others to act so. He who knows these causes of sin relating to earth, is called a reward-knowing sage. Thus I say.

. . . the sage who walks the beaten track (to liberation), regards the world in a different way. "Knowing thus (the nature of) acts in all regards, he does not kill," he controls himself, he is not overbearing.

Comprehending that pleasure (and pain) are individual, advising kindness, he will not engage in any work in the whole world: keeping before him the one (great aim, liberation), and not turning aside, "living humbly, unattached to any creature." The rich in (control) who with a mind endowed with all penetration (recognizes) that a bad deed should not be done, will not go after it. What you acknowledge as righteousness, that you acknowledge as sagedom . . .; what you acknowledge as sagedom, that you acknowledge as righteousness. It is inconsistent with weak, sinning, sensual, ill-conducted house-inhabiting men. "A sage, acquiring sagedom, should subdue his body." "The heroes who look at everything with indifference, use mean and rough (food, &c.)." Such a man is said to have crossed the flood (of life), to be a sage, to have passed over (the samsara) to be liberated, to have ceased (from acts). Thus I say. (Jacobi 1884: 10–11, 46–47)

that has been prepared expressly for them, as this would implicate them in whatever violence that preparation entailed; and the food and water they receive in their alms bowls must already have been cooked, boiled, or peeled (in the case of fruits) to ensure that when it is consumed it is without life.

For Jainas, the path of renunciation is open to all, irrespective of caste, gender, or social position. But it is extremely demanding, and Jainas know that very few will ever be able to take it. The overwhelming majority who remain householders therefore accept, implicitly or explicitly, that a certain amount of violence will be a regular part of their lives. For these people, to support the renouncers is both a duty and an honor—one that carries the additional benefit of earning them merit or good karma. More important, it sustains a system in which the ideal of living without doing harm remains a genuine possibility for anyone with the requisite strength of character.

Focus

The *Mahavratas*

1. Nonviolence (*ahimsa*)
2. Truth (*satya*)
3. Nonstealing (*asteya*)
4. Chastity (*brahmacharya*)
5. Nonpossession/nonattachment (*aparigraha*)

The *mahavrata* of *ahimsa* prohibits outright many aspects of the renouncers' former householder lives, and no physical aspect of living escapes the call for restraint: eating, talking, sleeping, walking, defecating, urinating, thinking, even dreaming—all must be disciplined by the principle of nonharm. Renouncers must not walk on grass, for to do so would cause it harm; they must look carefully wherever they step to be sure they do not harm anything on the ground; they are forbidden from using electricity and flush toilets (which cause harm to fire-bodied and water-bodied beings, respectively); and their minds are subject to continuous self-censure as they try to eliminate anger, jealousy, greed, and desire. Negative or aggressive thoughts are believed to accrue bad karma in much the same way that stepping on an insect would.

The subsidiary vows of nonattachment, truthfulness, nonstealing, and celibacy reinforce the vow of *ahimsa*. The vows of truthfulness and nonstealing forbid false speech and the use of anything that has not been freely given. *Brahmacharya* is more than a vow of celibacy: it is a vow to renounce all desire. Even dreams of a "carnal" nature have the power to attract karma and therefore require penance. The vow of *aparigraha* entails the renunciation not only of all possessions (home, clothing, money, etc.), but of all attachments, whether to places, people, things, or ideas.

In addition to the actions to be avoided, there are six "obligatory actions" that renouncers are required to perform: equanimity (*samayika*), praise to the Jinas (Jina puja), homage to one's teachers, repentance, body-abandonment, and, finally, the more general pledge to renounce all transgressions.

The constraints imposed by the *mahavratas* and obligatory actions are seen as the means to achieve the sublime state of unconditional freedom, permanent bliss, and omniscience. Furthermore, each step toward self-realization is believed to bring benefits for the community as well as the individual. For Jainas, the renouncers embody a spiritual power that can work miracles—though of course they are not supposed to use their powers for "worldly" purposes.

Practice

Reflection: Meditation and Fasting

Whereas the *mahavratas* and *anuvratas* seek to discipline embodied activities, the practice of *samayika* seeks to halt them altogether. For 48 minutes a day, devotees practice meditation or reflection, cultivating indifference to the concerns of the body—attachments and aversions, sufferings and pleasures—so that they can "dwell in the soul." In the absence of distractions, the Self can experience and enjoy itself. Jainas believe that the practice of *samayika* offers a foretaste of the joy that final release will bring.

Closely connected in intent is fasting. The Jaina term for the practice, *upvas* (literally, "to be near

the soul"), underscores their belief that in order to get close to the soul we must get away from the demands of the body and ego. At the same time fasting is considered a highly effective means of eliminating karma.

Jaina fasts are legendarily long, frequent, and arduous. Laywomen, in particular, are celebrated for their heroic fasting, which is believed to benefit their families as well as themselves. The entire household gains social prestige from a woman's pious actions, and the auspicious karma created by fasting can bring karmic rewards for the family.

The path to the very highest levels of self-realization has 14 stages. Householders rarely rise above the fifth step and must fully renounce worldly life if they wish to go further. Even so, the householder path offers many opportunities for spiritual progress.

Householder Practice

The "small" or "lesser vows" (*anuvratas*) that govern lay life are normally taken without any formal ceremony. Modeled on the mendicant's *mahavratas*, they reflect the same aspiration to limit worldly engagement. They are identical in name and number to the *mahavratas*, but they are interpreted and applied more leniently.

For instance, the *ahimsa anuvrata* is not total. It prohibits the consumption of certain foods, as well as eating after dark (when injury to insects is more likely). But it accepts that harm to one-sensed beings is unavoidable for householders. The subsidiary vows work in a similar manner: truthfulness and nonstealing are emphasized in much the same way as they are for the *mahavratas*, but celibacy is redefined to mean chastity in marriage. Similarly, the *anuvrata* of *aparigraha* does not require householders to live without possessions. Instead, it demands that they scrutinize their psychological attachment to their possessions.

The *anuvratas* are seen as establishing a compromise between worldly existence and spiritual progress. They do not interfere with the householder's ability to lead a "normal" existence. Quite the contrary: Jainas have long been among the wealthiest, most literate, and most accomplished communities in India. And from the Jaina perspective, there is a direct connection between their socioeconomic success and their religious vows.

The Fast to Death

Jainas boast that whereas other traditions celebrate birth, they celebrate death. This statement can be traced to the *shramana* tradition, in which the highest goal was to escape embodied existence. A death that is "celebrated" is one that has been accepted voluntarily and with equanimity, indicating total detachment from the body and the world.

Although *sallekhana*, or the ritual fast that ends in death, is not the universal practice, it is not uncommon even among householders. To be able to "discard the body" without pain or fear and greet death with calmness and equanimity is to reap the ultimate reward of a life lived in accordance with Jaina principles.

In addition, *sallekhana* is believed to result in a powerful expulsion of bad karma while attracting the good karma required to ensure a good rebirth either in a heavenly realm or in a spiritually advanced human state. Jainas

A Digambara mendicant prays while fingering *mala* beads (Photo by Soltan Frederic/Sygma via Getty Images).

believe that at the moment of physical death, the soul will be instantaneously propelled into a new incarnation, determined by its karma. (A soul free of all karma, instead of being reborn, would ascend to the realm of liberation, but that is not possible in the current time cycle.)

In recent years, the practice of *sallekhana* has been at the center of media attention. In August 2015, in a Rajasthan high court ruling, *sallekhana* was equated with suicide, becoming a criminal offense for the first time ever in 155 years of Indian penal code jurisprudence. Jainas protested vociferously that the nonviolent, dispassionate, and voluntary death of *sallekhana* is the very antithesis of suicide, and that the high court ruling reflects ignorance of the ancient practice, as well as of the Jaina tradition in which it is rooted. Large-scale demonstrations were organized throughout India as well as in Jaina communities around the world. The practice was restored just two weeks later when, on August 31, the Supreme Court of India stayed the Rajasthan high court's judgment. A final Supreme Court judgment may be years away, so at present, the practice exists in a legal limbo.

Jaina Astrology

The complex and unique ways in which Jainas use astrological charts points to the role that Jainas believe external forces play in the process of self-realization. With no hope of assistance from a creator god, Jainas seeking liberation need to make use of all the assistance that is available. Astrology offers valuable insight into the manipulation of karma for both spiritual and worldly benefit.

Jainas' interest in astrology sheds light on their understanding of karma as something with positive as well as negative aspects. To the extent that astrology seeks to preempt misfortune and take advantage of opportunity, it also reminds us that Jaina renunciation is a matter not of flight from the world, but of a resolute fight to overcome it.

Jaina Worship

The objects of Jaina worship are the 24 perfected beings known as the Jinas. Temples are constructed to house icons of them, pilgrimages are made to places associated with them, and they are worshiped daily in prayer. Although four of the Jinas are especially revered (Mahavira, Parsavanath, Neminath, and Rsabha), all receive regular devotions.

The main Jaina festivals celebrate events in the lives of the Jinas, as do the exquisite miniature paintings for which the Jainas are known, while Jaina sculpture is devoted almost exclusively to portraits of the Jinas in meditation. Even among the Sthanakvasis and Terapanthis, who reject image worship, the Jinas are ubiquitous in narrative and prayer. Clearly, then, to be a Jaina is to worship the Jinas.

A lay Jaina worshiping at Palitana adopts the attire of an ascetic for the duration of the puja (© Francis Leroy/Hemis/Corbis).

Practice

Prayer: The *Namokar Mantra*

The central prayer in Jainism, the **Namokar Mantra** begins by proclaiming homage to the Jinas, then to all liberated beings, to *acharyas*, to religious leaders, and finally to all renouncers everywhere. There is no supplication in this prayer—only praise. Those most revered (the Jinas and liberated beings) are incapable of response, as they are beyond the world of give and take. Jainas recite the mantra to cultivate the ideals of detachment and nonviolence while also acknowledging its power to effect transformation through the inflow of good merit. Commonly recited before the start of any undertaking, it is equally revered by Svetambara and Digambara Jainas. Like so many prayers the world over, it can be recited collectively or privately.

Namo arihantanam	I bow to the *arihants* (Jinas).
Namo siddhanam	I bow to the *siddhas* (liberated souls).
Namo ayariyanam	I bow to the *acharyas* (mendicant leaders).
Namo uvajjhayanam	I bow to the mendicant teachers.
Namo loe savva sahunam	I bow to all mendicants everywhere.
Esopanncanamokkaro, savvapavappanasano Mangala na mca savvesim padamama havai mangalam	This fivefold mantra destroys all sins and obstacles and of all auspicious mantras is the first and foremost one.

And yet the Jinas are seen as profoundly absent. Having perfected themselves, they are indifferent to their worshipers, whose worldly concerns are literally "beneath them." The existence of a lively devotional cult within a tradition centered on renunciation of all attachments may seem paradoxical, but Jainas insist that the real purpose of devotion is self-transformation through surrender to the ideal that the Jina embody.

Puja assists devotees in two ways, helping them along the path of self-realization and at the same time bringing "worldly" benefits. The beneficent power of good karma, earned through devotional practice, makes a reciprocal relationship with a god unnecessary (see Cort 2001). It's important to add here that even though the devotional cult operates within its own nontheistic framework, Jainas also venerate gods and goddesses who are believed to reside in heavenly realms. These divinities (e.g., Padmavati, the female guardian deity of Parsavanath, or the Hindu god Ganesha) *are* believed to be capable of interceding on behalf of their followers, and Jainas do pray to them for assistance in worldly matters, but not for assistance along the path of liberation.

⊕ Expressive Dimensions

The Jaina community is rich in temples, festivals, art, and literature, as well as active philanthropy. How can a tradition dedicated to renunciation have such a robust culture? Although Jainas maintain that the path to freedom is one of restraint and withdrawal, to be a "good" Jaina does not require adoption of a mendicant's life, though this is unequivocally the ideal. The best that most Jainas can aim for is to live according to *samyak darshan* ("correct faith"). The life of a disciplined householder is perfectly respectable, as long as it is lived in a mindful manner.

What ignites the spark of spiritual awareness depends on the individual. For some it may be a powerful artistic experience; for others, a philosophical tract or participation in a public festival. Therefore all cultural expressions that inculcate *samyak darshan* are valued. Building a temple, creating a work of art, taking part in a festival—all help bring a community together in celebration of shared values. The tenth-century Digambara *acharya* Nemicandra praised "the great monks and *acharyas* who have established the celebration of festivals . . . due to which even the downtrodden and condemned people become religious" (cited in Jain 2008).

Festivals

The Jaina ritual calendar revolves around three major festivals, with many minor ones in between. The three are Divali, which coincides with the start of the new year in November–December; **Mahavira Jayanti** in spring; and, most important, Paryushana/Daslakshana in August–September.

Although it is common to think of Divali as a Hindu or even pan-Indian festival of light, many Jainas believe it began as a Jaina commemoration of Mahavira's liberation. For Jainas, the "light" that Divali celebrates is the light of omniscience. Yet Jaina celebrations of Divali do not differ much from those of their Hindu neighbors. Because Divali coincides with the new year, the Hindu goddess of wealth, Sri Lakshmi, is enthusiastically worshiped by all. And because the festival marks the start of a new financial year, members of the business community (of which Jainas constitute an important segment) are especially fervent in showing their appreciation of the goddess. Of course, the ascetics are never too far away to remind the Jainas that the greatest wealth is *moksha* itself.

Mahavira Jayanti is a joyous festival celebrating the birth of Lord Mahavira. Held in March–April, it is an occasion for great pageantry, with shops, streets, and temples all sumptuously decorated. Jainas enthusiastically undertake pilgrimages, listen to sermons, sing devotional hymns, and take part in pujas as well as ritual reenactments of the wondrous events associated with Mahavira's birth.

The most important of all Jaina festivals, however, is Paryushana/Daslakshana (the Svetambara

A devotee offers flowers at the Adinath Temple in Ranakpur, Rajasthan (© Boisvieux Christophe/Hemis/Corbis).

and Digambara names for the festival, respectively). It is celebrated at the end of the summer rainy season. The literal meaning of Paryushana is "abiding together"—a reference to the sustained interaction that takes place between householders and renouncers during the summer. Obliged to stay in one place, the renouncers must seek alms from the same local householders for several months, and the latter take advantage of this daily contact to seek the renouncers' advice on spiritual and worldly issues. With the end of the rains, the renouncers begin their wanderings again. Paryushana is the climax of a period of heightened religiosity. The end of the eight-day festival is a day of introspection, confession of sins, and fasting. The penultimate day is celebrated as the Day of Forgiveness, when Jainas seek to wipe the slate clean with one another and with the world itself by asking and offering forgiveness for all and reciting the *Micchami Dukkadam* prayer:

> We forgive all living beings
> We seek pardon from all living beings
> We are friendly towards all living beings,
> And we seek enmity with none.

Almost all Jaina cultural expressions (art, ritual, iconography) are tied in one way or another to the "five auspicious events" in the lives of the Jinas: conception, birth, renunciation, omniscience, and *moksha*. These five events are universally celebrated and are vividly represented in sculptures and miniature paintings, reenacted in theater and ritual, and described in narrative text. They are also closely associated with pilgrimages, since every *tirtha* (site of devotion) is linked with one or more of them.

⊕ Jainas among Others

Because Jainas have never made up more than a small proportion of the communities in which they live, the ability to interact with non-Jainas has been essential. Jainas themselves credit their adaptive success to their commitment to *ahimsa*: nonviolence in thought, speech, and deed makes for easy friendship. While Jainism unequivocally affirms the existence of truth, as well as its ultimate attainability, it also argues that those who have not reached enlightenment can never claim more than partial understanding. This perspective may very well foster—as Jainas claim it does—a general attitude of tolerance toward difference.

We have seen how Jainism's ethical principles—the restrictions it places on dietary practices, livelihoods, and so on—serve to keep the violence of worldly life at bay. Yet Jainism has never erected social fences to ensure religious purity. To have insisted on exclusion would likely have doomed a community so small and vulnerable. Instead, Jainas seek the closest possible integration with their neighbors, adopting local languages and customs while safeguarding their fundamental practices and beliefs.

Perhaps because of its emphasis on the solitary nature of the individual soul, Jainism is not inclined to question the "authenticity" of its followers. Thus Jainas rarely debate who is or is not a "true" Jaina. They do sometimes debate the question of "true" Jaina practices, however. Although the absorption of Hindu influences (e.g., theistic elements, ritual practices) into Jainism has gone on for a long time without causing much anxiety, these issues appear to be taking on increasing significance in the current climate of religious revival, as the symbolic boundaries between traditions are hardening.

⊕ Women

Since the time of Mahavira, the majority of those who have responded to Jainism's call have been women. This is highly unusual in the South Asian context, where asceticism is still closely associated with maleness.

Women embraced Jaina asceticism from the beginning, repudiating the "feminine" obligations of wife- and motherhood. Nuns' writings became part of the philosophical tradition, their roles were recognized in the narrative literature, and they were subject to almost all the same rules of ascetic discipline as monks.

Yet women were never considered equal to men. Although female scholar-ascetics are known, they are few in number. Furthermore, religious narratives are often ambivalent about gender, praising women for their piety and chastity but also condemning them as capricious and sexually predatory. While Digambara women are permitted to renounce marriage and motherhood for spiritual advancement, they are still not allowed to take the full vows, and their tradition holds that *moksha* is not achievable from within a female body. By contrast, Svetambaras do allow women full entry into mendicancy and do not consider the female body to be an obstacle to liberation. Yet even in the Svetambara sect, nuns are not equal to monks, and senior nuns are expected to demonstrate their ritually subordinate status by showing deference to junior monks.

Women in the Traditions

The ideals of womanhood within Jainism are similar to those of the other South Asian traditions in their linkage of female piety with modesty, patience, and chastity. But the capacity for spiritual independence is also a key feature of the Jaina feminine ideal, making the tradition distinctive in this regard. The most highly esteemed path within Jainism is that of world renunciation, and it is considered as accessible to women as it is to men. In practice, over three times as many Jaina women as men pursue this path, a pattern that was established during the time of Mahavira, when the female renouncer Chandanbala is said to have had 36,000 female disciples under her tutelage. But despite the historical presence of *sadhvis* (female renouncers) and their continued numerical strength, they have almost always held a subordinate place to the *munis* (male renouncers), reflecting the broader cultural norm of male dominance. Furthermore, religious narratives often contain ambivalent messages about women, extolling them for their piety and chastity but also aligning them closely with their bodies and sexuality. Indeed, the female body is at the center of the debate over spiritual liberation between Digambara and Svetambara Jainas. It is important to remember that these debates, and the ascetic ideal around which they revolve, rest upon the support of a committed and knowledgeable lay population who themselves are pursuing their own spiritual practices and are therefore in need of the example the mendicants embody. And it is mainly women who provide this support—most immediately by upholding the rules of lay–renouncer interaction and by providing the *sadhvis* and *munis* with their daily necessities, but also by being the primary keepers of the tradition. It is they who are responsible for the embodiment and transmission of religious ideals within the family, thereby ensuring the continuation of the Jaina tradition itself.

Nuns descend the steps of the major Jaina temple complex and pilgrimage site of Mount Shatrunjaya, Palitana, Gujarat (© Francis Leroy/Hemis/Corbis).

Nonetheless, the numerical strength of nuns may to some extent have offset the ideological bias in favor of monks. Nuns serve as role models and teachers in Jaina communities, and they are able to operate with considerable autonomy. For instance, although the female leader in the Terapanthi Svetambara order is formally subject to the ultimate authority of the male *acharya*, she has near-absolute control over its nearly 600 nuns.

Still, nuns constitute a tiny portion of the overall Jaina population. The vast majority of Jaina women (and men) live a "worldly" life that includes family, career, and community. Monks and nuns may be the religious heroes of Jainism, but they are utterly dependent on laywomen and -men for their existence. In defining itself as a fourfold community, Jainism explicitly acknowledges this dependence and hence the religious importance of the laity. Renouncers could not set themselves apart from the violence of worldly existence if it were not for the householders who shield them from it. Lay Jainas willingly act as buffers between renouncers and the world, enabling the heroic endeavors of the ascetics to bear fruit and in the process creating good karma for themselves. Importantly, it is mainly women who provide the daily necessities of life to mendicants of both sexes. This role is so significant that the entire Jaina infrastructure can be said to rest upon it.

Interview

Samani Suhasnidhi

Seven years ago, at the age of 24, Deepa Bohra underwent *diksha*, or initiation, into a Jaina mendicant order. All ties with her former life, including her "worldly" family and birth name, were severed. Now known as Samani Suyashnidhi ("Saminiji"), she considers her true family to be the Sthanakavasi Svetambara mendicant community with whom she lives, led by Dr. Shri Padamchandraji Maharaj Saheb, whom Samaniji affectionately calls her guru. Samaniji explains that although she was born into a religious family in which renunciation was not unknown, there was no expectation that she would pursue the renouncer path. She speaks of her deep affection and gratitude for her close-knit extended family and of how her duty to them was always her prime concern. She recalls, however, that when she was nine years old, her interest in the spiritual path was kindled by her aunt's decision to undergo *diksha*—but at that time it was but a slight stirring, and she kept it to herself. Outwardly, she immersed herself in her family life and her studies, but her interest in spirituality continued to grow steadily, and by the time she entered university, she was actively seeking a spiritual teacher (guru). Such a pursuit did not interfere with her worldly duties or ambitions, and she did not know what form her spiritual path would take until, during the *chaturmaas* season of 2008, she met Dr. Shri Padamchandraji Maharaj Saheb. According to Samaniji, it was as if his words awoke something in her that had long been dormant and communicated directly with her soul. She says, "I knew right away that I must renounce."

At that time, she was only 22 years old and was studying dentistry at Mysore University. Her guru advised her to finish her worldly studies and give herself the time to determine if the difficult

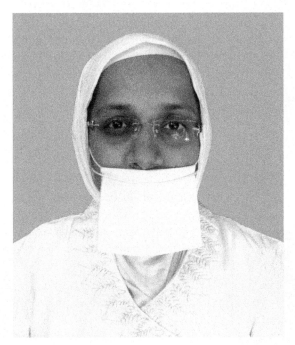

Samani Suhasnidhi. (By permission of Samani Suyashnidhi, Jr.)

path of renunciation was truly what she wanted. Her family too was adamant that she not be hasty in her decision. While they were proud of their daughter's spiritual resolve, their attachment to her made them ambivalent about her desire to renounce. Becoming a nun would mean a radical and permanent break with them and with all she had known. Samaniji diligently pursued her studies (receiving the university's Gold Medalist award) and continued to embrace her love of Indian dance and singing and to socialize with her university friends, who were unaware of her inner desire to renounce. Despite the appearance of worldly normalcy, her resolve to pursue the spiritual path never abated. At last her family relented, recognizing her intentions as genuine and heartfelt: they

Continued

granted her permission to renounce, as did Guru Padamchandraji Maharaj Saheb.

On May 15, 2010, in an elaborate initiation ritual, the person who had been Deepa Bohra effectively "died," as the name with which she had long been identified was discarded along with all her worldly belongings. Those duties that she had been so attentive in honoring were now abandoned. Her head was shaven, and she bid a final farewell to her family. While the day was an emotionally charged one for family members, who focused on the drama of her renunciation, Samaniji prefers to emphasize what was gained. She explains that her affection is no longer bound up with a select few but now encompasses all living beings. And her duties, which had been previously confined to the well-being of a single family, are now "directed to the spiritual upliftment of all human beings."

It is only through the efforts of laywomen that the institution of mendicancy exists: they are the ones who grow or purchase fruits and vegetables, who perform whatever preparation is necessary to make them acceptable as food (i.e., without life), and who follow the detailed rules that govern the offering. The sustenance they provide is the foundation that makes everything else possible.

⊕ Recent Developments

Jainism has been undergoing a profound revitalization over the last century. This renewal is evident in the growth of Jaina educational institutions, the wide dissemination of Jaina publications (including sacred texts), the emergence of nationwide Jaina organizations, rising numbers of mendicants, a revival of naked mendicancy in the Digambara sect, the birth of a strong and vocal diaspora Jainism, and the development of a more muscular political identity. All these changes have had the effect of creating a Jainism that is both more visible and more self-conscious, and whose followers are increasingly concerned with defining what is (and what isn't) "correct" Jaina belief and practice.

Twentieth-Century Reform Movements

The roots of these changes can be traced to India's turbulent colonial period (1857–1947), during which reform movements sought to modernize the Jaina tradition and give it a greater national presence alongside its Hindu, Muslim, and Christian counterparts. Reformers worked to move Jainism away from the conservative, defensive control of insular mendicants whose obsession with purity condemned Jaina teachings to public obscurity. They sought to have Jainism recognized as an essential part of India's national cultural heritage, integrated into its secular educational institutions, and they fought to combat the prejudice against those institutions within their own communities, which feared that secular education would endanger Jaina spiritual goals (Flügel 2005). Their successes were momentous: within a century Jainas would be among the most educated communities in India (with literacy levels second only to those of the tiny Parsi community), their cultural achievements would be recognized as part of India's national heritage, and their scriptures would be widely accessible.

Jaina Identity

The decades since Indian independence (1947) have witnessed simultaneous efforts to define more clearly the boundaries of Jaina identity and to gain recognition of Jainism as a world religion with universal appeal. Although these endeavors might seem contradictory—one constrictive and introverted, the other expansive and extroverted—both are fundamental characteristics of Jainism today. Indeed, the tension between those two poles is characteristic of identity politics in all world religions today.

Relationship with Hinduism

The effort to define Jaina identity took a more political turn after independence, focusing on the community's status as a minority vulnerable to the overwhelmingly dominant Hindu majority. This development was part of the trend toward pluralistic identity politics that can be seen in all religious and cultural traditions today. In the past, being "a follower of the Jina" was almost certainly not based on exclusion of non-Jaina ideas and practices; to the contrary, as we have seen, the Jaina community traditionally followed a strategy of "cautious integration." However, in an environment in which Hindu, Muslim, and Sikh nationalisms were finding increasingly frequent public expression, reform-minded Jainas rejected the treatment of Jainism as a sect of Hinduism under Indian law and began to seek recognition of their community as a discrete minority in India. In particular, they emphasized Jainism's fundamental differences from Hinduism, such as the fact that Jainas do not believe in any creator God and do not consider the Vedas to be sacred. Although some Jaina organizations saw no reason to upset the status quo, considering the social, cultural, and ideological commonalities between Jainas and Hindus more important than their differences, in January 2014 the reformers' campaign succeeded when the Supreme Court of India granted minority status to the Jaina community.

Jainism Around the World

Far less divisive have been contemporary efforts to establish Jainism as a world religion. The coexistence of expansive and constrictive tendencies is characteristic of all contemporary traditions; indeed, to be "modern" is to be simultaneously universal and distinctive, globally relevant and utterly singular. Interestingly, one factor that has bolstered both tendencies in Jainism has been the rise of the Jaina diaspora. There are now sizable Jaina communities in England, the United States, and Canada that are forging their own understandings of what constitutes Jainism. The kind of Jainism that is taking root outside India—removed from the immediate influence of the mendicant tradition—is contributing to significant new developments.

Outside India, for example, the renunciatory ethos becomes harder to sustain, and seemingly less important for Jaina religious identity. Although Jainas everywhere retain their philosophical commitment to the *ahimsa* principle, in diaspora communities it is often expressed in the "worldly" terms of animal rights, ecological health, and societal improvement; aspirations to self-purification and world transcendence seem to be less common. A similar shift is occurring with respect to dietary practices, which are no longer inextricably tied to the ideology of renunciation, although the connection with the *ahimsa* principle remains close. What seems to be occurring is a

Very few Jaina renouncers ever leave India, as most are not permitted to travel by any means other than foot. An exception is the Veerayatan order (established in 1973), which has relaxed many of the traditional rules in order to focus on social work. Here a Veerayatan sadhvi offers religious discourse to lay Jainas in the United Kingdom (© Gideon Mendel/Corbis).

redefinition of *ahimsa* and a decoupling of the previously inseparable relationship between *ahimsa* and renunciation.

Diaspora Jainas are far less inclined to describe Jainism as an ascetic, renunciatory ideology than as one that is progressive, environmentally responsible, egalitarian, nonsectarian, and scientifically avant-garde. In the same way, the cosmological dimensions of Jainism have been eclipsed by its ethical dimensions. This shift marks Jainism's universalizing aspirations: its message of *ahimsa* as a globally relevant principle establishes its credentials as a world religion.

Finally, Jainism's sectarian differences are less salient in the diaspora than in India, partly because the community's small numbers make it largely irrelevant. To identify oneself as "Jaina" is already to identify with a subcategory within the general category of "Indian," so for many Jainas (especially those of the second generation) additional identifiers carry little significance. The markers distinguishing the two Jaina sects may remain meaningful within families, but they are less important on the cultural or societal level. As a consequence, Jaina identity is increasingly emphasized, and this development in turn may play a role in the arena of identity politics in India.

⊕ Summary

This chapter has explored the historical roots of the Jaina path in ancient India, its flourishing over the past three millennia, and its emergence as a global tradition in the twentieth century. Its beginnings as a world-renouncing tradition have informed its social, cultural, and artistic development, so much so that even its tremendous worldly successes (in business and the professions) and its celebratory festivals have renunciatory dimensions. Jainism communicates a message of restraint, detachment, and nonviolence in all its expressions.

The Jaina community has undergone dramatic changes since the time of Mahavira, more than 2,500 years ago, but the centrality of *ahimsa* has remained constant. Though variously understood, it remains the foundation of all expressions of Jainism today, both in India and outside it. The resilience of Jaina teachings must be credited, at least in part, to their effectiveness; that they are now gaining attention well beyond the borders of the Jaina community is a testament to their enduring relevance.

Sites

Gwalior Fort, Madhya Pradesh

According to legend, the city of Gwalior was named for a Jaina saint named Gwalipa after he cured a Rajput chieftain of leprosy. The fort contains architectural treasures from several historic northern Indian kingdoms.

Shravanabelagola, Karnataka

Shravanabelagola is home of the colossal statue of the renouncer Bahubali (also known as Gomateshwara), a prince who, in the midst of a battle, gained sudden insight into the senselessness of violence and renounced all attachment to worldly existence. Digambaras believe he was the first person in our time cycle to attain *moksha*.

Sammet Shikarji, Jharkand

The "King of the Tirths," Sammet Shikarji is said to be the place where 20 of the 24 Jinas attained *moksha*. Located in a remote mountain range, the hilltop is covered with temples and shrines.

Rajasthan, India

Although Rajasthan is renowned as the ancient land of the Rajputs, Jainism has had a presence there for more than 2,000 years. The stunningly beautiful Dilwara temple complex near Mount Abu is a major Jaina pilgrimage center.

Palitana, Gujarat

Palitana is famous for the nearly 900 marble temples that sit on Shatrunjaya hill. Constructed over hundreds of years, beginning in the late tenth century, the complex remains a major pilgrimage center.

Jain Centre, Leicester, England

In 1979, the local Jaina community bought an old church in Leicester and transformed it into a temple with both Svetambara and Digambara idols imported from India.

Jain Center of Greater Boston

Established in 1973, the Jain Center of Greater Boston was the first such center in North America. Eight years later the community inaugurated a temple that now serves more than 300 families.

Sacred Texts

Religion (Sect)	Text(s)	Composition/Compilation	Compilation/Revision	Use
Jainism (Svetambara and Digambara)	*Purva Agama*	Ancient and timeless "universal truths" preached by all Jinas, from the first (Rsabha) to the last (Mahavira). Communicated to disciples by Jina Mahavira and transmitted orally until the 3rd century BCE, when the verbatim recitation of teachings was no longer possible. Both Svetambara and Digambara accept that all the *Purvas* were eventually lost.	Reconstructed by monks mainly between the 5th and 11th centuries CE. Commentaries and narratives added by scholar-monks.	Object of study for metaphysics, cosmology, and philosophy
Jainism (Svetambara)	*Anga Agama*	12 *Angas* compiled by the principal disciples of Mahavira. Svetambaras believe that the 12th *Anga*, called the *Drstivada*, contained the teachings of lost *Purvas*. All were transmitted orally until the 3rd century BCE.	Reconstructed by monks mainly between the 5th and 11th centuries CE. Commentaries and narratives added by scholar-monks.	Object of study for rules of mendicant conduct, stories of renouncers, karma
Jainism (Svetambara)	*Angabahya* (believed to contain the lost teachings of the *Purva* and *Anga Agamas*)	Compiled and orally transmitted by monks who succeeded the principal disciples of Mahavira. Contained the earliest commentaries on the *Purva* and *Anga*.	Reconstructed by monks mainly between the 5th and 11th centuries CE. Commentaries and narratives added by scholar-monks.	Object of study for specialized topics, story literature, etc.
Jainism (Digambara)	*Satkhandagama* (contains parts of *Drstivada* canon, said to mnemonically contain the lost teachings of the *Purva* and *Anga Agamas*)	Orally transmitted until 2nd century CE, when put in writing; the first Jaina scripture to be preserved in written form	No substantial revisions, though commentaries are common	Object of study for entire canon: metaphysics, cosmology, karma, and philosophy
Jainism (Digambara)	*Kasayaprabhrta* (text based on *Drstivada*)	Written by Yati Vrasabha based on compilations of Gunadhara, 1st–2nd century CE	No substantial revisions, though commentaries are common	Studied for philosophy of detachment
Jainism (Digambara)	*Nataktrayi* (*Samayasara*, *Pravanasara*, and *Pancastikaya*)	Written by Kundakunda between 1st century BCE and 2nd century CE	No substantial revisions, though commentaries are common	Object of study for mysticism, doctrine/philosophy, and ontology; the most sacred Digambara author and texts
Jainism (Svetambara and Digambara)	*Anuyogas* ("Expositions")	1st century BCE to 6th century CE		Object of study for philosophy, etc.

Sacred Texts *(Continued)*

Religion (Sect)	Text(s)	Composition/Compilation	Compilation/Revision	Use
Jainism (Svetambara and Digambara)	*Tattvartha Sutra*	Written by Umasvati in 2nd century CE	Many commentaries written by Svetambaras between 2nd and 8th centuries CE; the process of commenting continues	Object of study for doctrine, cosmology, ethics, philosophy, etc.
Jainism (Svetambara and Digambara)	*Bhaktamara Stotra*	Written by the *acharya* Mantunga in 3rd century CE		Devotion
Jainism (Svetambara)	*Kalpa Sutra* (lives of the Jinas, especially Parshvanath and Mahavira, and doctrine)	3rd century CE		Devotion and ritual during Paryushana
Jainism (Digambara)	*Adi Purana/ Mahapurana*	Written by the *acharya* Jinasena between 6th and 8th centuries CE		Object of study for life stories of Tirthankaras and all Digambara rituals

Discussion Questions

1. Lay (householder) Jainas are integral to the tradition, which has always recognized the centrality of their role. Explain.

2. What are some of the major differences between Svetambara and Digambara Jainism?

3. What are the main reasons believed to be responsible for the split that gave rise to the Svetambara and Digambara sects?

4. How are women understood in Jainism? What are some of the main differences between Svetambaras and Digambaras with regard to women?

5. Although Jainism envisions final liberation (*moksha*) as a purely spiritual state, it does not see the spiritual and the material in oppositional terms. Explain.

6. Nonviolence (*ahimsa*) informs every aspect of Jainism, from cosmology to dietary practices and devotional rituals. Elaborate.

7. How do Jainas understand their acts of devotion to beings (the Jinas) they believe to be removed from all worldly matters and unresponsive to their concerns?

8. What is the significance of "right faith" (*samyak darshan*) in Jainism?

9. How do Jainas understand the final state of liberation (*moksha*)?

10. What are some of the main ways in which expressions of Jainism in the diaspora differ from expressions in India today?

Glossary

acharya A mendicant scholar.

ajiva Nonsoul, nonconsciousness; also referred to as "matter" or "karma."

anuvratas Five vows modeled on the great vows of the renouncers but modified to make them practicable in lay life: nonviolence, truthfulness, nonstealing, nonattachment, and chastity.

Arhat A perfected, omniscient being (male or female) who teaches the Jaina dharma while embodied in the world and who upon death will attain *moksha*. All the Jinas were called *Arhats* during their final incarnation on earth.

chakravartin Universal monarch; one who governs the world ethically.

Digambaras Early Jaina sect with its own sacred scriptures; identified by male mendicants' practice of nudity.

Jina Literally, "conqueror"; an epithet for the 24 ascetic prophets who conquered the world of desire and suffering, and taught the path to eternal happiness; alternatively called Tirthankara.

jiva Eternal soul/consciousness; all living beings are endowed with *jiva*.

Mahavira Literally, "Great Hero"; epithet of the twenty-fourth and final Jina of our time cycle, born Vardhamana Jnatrpura in the sixth century BCE.

Mahavira Jayanti A joyous spring festival celebrating the birth of Mahavira.

mahavratas The five "great vows" adopted by renouncers: absolute nonviolence, truthfulness, nonstealing, nonattachment, and celibacy.

mendicants Jaina men and women who renounce all worldly attachments to seek self-realization (and eventually, *moksha*) by pursuing the difficult path of detachment and nonviolence. Male mendicants (monks) are called *sadhus* or *munis*, and female mendicants (nuns) are called *sadhvis*.

moksha The ultimate goal of the Jaina path: release from the cycle of birth and death; nirvana.

paap Karmic particles of an inauspicious nature ("bad karma").

pratikramana Ritual practice of repentance.

punya Karmic particles of an auspicious nature ("good karma").

renunciation The Jaina ideal: the giving up of all worldly attachments (family, friends, wealth, pride, etc.) in order to pursue the path of detachment and nonviolence. Though it is a powerful ideal for all Jainas, it is practiced fully only by mendicants; also referred to as *shramanism*.

Rsabha The first Tirthankara of our current time cycle; also called Adinath.

sallekhana A ritual fast to death undertaken voluntarily, usually in old age or illness.

samayika A desired state of equanimity; ritual practice of meditation.

samsara The endless cycle of rebirth from which Jainas seek release.

samyak darshan Right vision, faith, or intuition into the basic truth of the cosmos; spiritual growth depends on the attainment of *samyak darshan*.

shramana A renouncer; one who has given up worldly attachments to pursue spiritual release.

Svetambara One of the two early sectarian nodes within Jainism; mendicants wear simple white robes.

Tattvartha Sutra An important philosophical text accepted by all Jaina sects, composed by Umasvati in the second century CE.

Tirthankara Literally, "ford-maker"; epithet for the 24 Jinas who, through their teachings, created a ford across the ocean of *samsara*.

Suggested Readings

Babb, Lawrence A. 1996. *Absent Lord: Ascetics and Kings in a Jain Ritual Culture.* Berkeley: University of California Press. A wonderful exploration of the place of worship in Jaina ritual culture.

Banks, Marcus. 1992. *Organizing Jainism in India and England.* Oxford: Clarendon. An ethnographic study of the historical, sociological, and cultural ties between the Jaina communities of Leicester, England, and Saurashtra, India.

Carrithers, Michael, and Caroline Humphrey, eds. 1991. *The Assembly of Listeners: Jains in Society.* Cambridge: Cambridge University Press. An outstanding edited volume exploring the sociological dimensions of the Jaina community by leading scholars in the field.

Cort, John E. 2001. *Jains in the World: Religious Values and Ideology in India.* New York: Oxford University Press. A detailed and insightful ethnographic study of the religious lives of contemporary lay Jainas.

Dundas, Paul. 2002. *The Jains.* 2nd ed. London: Routledge. A comprehensive overview of Jainism and an excellent introduction to the subject.

Jaini, Padmanabh S. 1979. *The Jaina Path of Purification.* Berkeley: University of California Press. The standard general study of Jainism.

Laidlaw, James. 1995. *Riches and Renunciation: Religion, Economy, and Society among the Jains.* Oxford: Oxford University Press. An exploration of the place of renunciation in the life of North India's thriving Jaina business community.

Recommended Websites

http://www.jaindharmonline.com

A portal dedicated to Jainism and Jaina dharma containing information and links to news articles.

http://www.jainstudies.org

The website of the International Summer School for Jain Studies.

http://www.jainworld.com

The website of the Jainism Global Resource Center, based in the United States.

http://pluralism.org/wrgb/traditions/jainism

A site offering resources from Harvard University's Pluralism Project.

References

Cort, John E. 2001. *Jains in the World: Religious Values and Ideology in India*. New York: Oxford University Press.

Cort, John E. 2005. "Devotional Culture in Jainism: Manatunga and His *Bhaktamara Stotra*." In *Incompatible Visions: South Asian Religions in History and Culture*, ed. James Blumenthal. Madison: Center for South Asia, University of Wisconsin–Madison. 93–115.

Flügel, Peter. 2005. The invention of Jainism: A short history of Jaina Studies. *International Journal of Jain Studies* 1, no. 1: 1–14.

Jacobi, Hermann, trans. 1884. *Jaina Sutras*, Part I. In *Sacred Books of the East*, vol. 22, ed. F. Max Müller. Oxford: Clarendon Press.

Jacobi, Hermann, and Max Muller. 2001 [1895–1910]. *Jaina Sutras*. Richmond, UK: Curzon Press.

Jain, S. C. 2008. "Jain Festivals." Unpublished manuscript prepared for the International Summer School of Jain Studies.

Jaini, Padmanabh S. 1979. *The Jaina Path of Purification*. Berkeley: University of California Press.

Kundakunda. 1950. *Samayasara*. Ed. and trans. A. Chakravarti. Benaras: Bharatiya Jnanapitha, Kashi.

Note

1. This text was compiled by Jinendra Varni and published by Sarva Seva Sangh Prakashan, India. It was translated into English in 1993 by T. K. Tukol and K. K. Dixit.

10 Buddhist Traditions

Roy C. Amore

Traditions at a Glance

Numbers

Most estimates of the number of Buddhists today range between 200 and 300 million.

Distribution

Buddhists can be found in South, Southeast, and East Asia, and also comprise minorities on all continents.

Founder

Shakyamuni Buddha, who taught in northern India 2,500 years ago, is the founder of the tradition and is believed to be the most recent in a long line of major buddhas.

Principal Historical Periods

Early Indian Buddhism and the roots of the Theravada tradition, which eventually spread to Sri Lanka and Southeast Asia, emerged between the fifth and first centuries BCE. Mahayana emerged in the first century CE and later spread to Southeast, Central, and East Asia. Vajrayana emerged in the fifth century CE and then spread to the Himalayan region.

Deities

The Buddha is not worshiped as a god; he is venerated as a fully enlightened human being. Regional variants of Buddhism have often incorporated local gods and spirits. Mahayana developed a theory of three bodies of the Buddha, linking the historic buddhas to a cosmic force.

Authoritative Texts

Theravada has the *Tripitaka* ("Three Baskets"): *vinaya* (monastic rules), *sutras* (discourses), and *abhidharma* (systematic treatises). Mahayana has many texts in various languages, including Chinese, Japanese, and Tibetan. Vajrayana has the *Kanjur* (tantric texts) and *Tanjur* (commentaries).

Noteworthy Teachings

The Three Characteristics of Existence are suffering, impermanence, and no-self. The Four Noble Truths are suffering, origin of suffering, cessation of suffering, and the Eightfold Path. Other notable teachings include karma, rebirth, and nirvana. In addition, the Mahayana and Vajrayana schools stress the emptiness (nonabsoluteness) of all things. All schools emphasize nonviolence and compassion for all living beings.

In this chapter you will learn about:

- The origins of Buddhism in ancient India as part of an ascetic spirituality
- The life and teachings of Shakyamuni Buddha
- The spread of the conservative Theravada school of Buddhism into Southeast Asia and beyond
- The rise of the Mahayana school and its spread into East Asia and beyond
- The rise of the Vajrayana school and its current status in the Tibet Autonomous Region of China
- The nature and impact of Buddhism in the West
- Some of the issues facing Buddhism today

At the heart of Buddhism are the "Three Gems": the Buddha, the **dharma** (teachings), and the **sangha** (congregation). Buddhists express their faith in these elements by saying they "take refuge" in them. Many Buddhist ceremonies include a recitation of the "Triple Refuge" mantra.

 Novice monks at Bagan, Myanmar (Burma) (Martin Puddy/Getty Images).

⊕ Overview

With his last words to his disciples—"Everything that arises also passes away, so strive for what has not arisen"—the Buddha passed into **nirvana** some 2,500 years ago. After experiencing enlightenment at the age of 35, he had spent the rest of his life teaching that all worldly phenomena are transient. He set the wheel of dharma (teaching) in motion, established a community (sangha) of disciples, and charged his followers to carry the dharma to all regions of the world. Today there are Buddhists in nearly every country, and Buddhism is the dominant religion in many parts of East, South, and Southeast Asia.

Buddhism has three main traditions, or "vehicles," all of which originated in India. The earliest is **Theravada** (also known as **Hinayana**), which spread to Sri Lanka and Southeast Asia; the second is **Mahayana**, which became the principal school in East Asia; and the third is **Vajrayana**, which developed out of Mahayana and became closely associated with the Himalayan region. All three traditions also have followers in most parts of the world.

⊕ The First Gem: The Buddha

Religious Life in Ancient India

By 500 BCE, a "Ganges Spirituality" tradition was flourishing in northern India. Located halfway between the Bay of Bengal and the Arabian Sea, the region had easy access to a trading route that stretched across the subcontinent. Trade enriched the merchant (vaishya) class and gave rise to a new money-based economy, while agriculture flourished on large estates owned by the two highest classes (brahmins and kshatriyas) and worked by lower castes.

Beneath the prosperity, however, were both social and ideological tensions. The new money economy had created a large merchant class that had financial power but neither the land nor the social status of the traditional landowning classes, who looked down on the new urban rich. At the same time there was tension between the religion of the brahmins and the other religious traditions of the region. While the brahmins considered animal sacrifice essential, the ascetics—among them the Jaina master Mahavira—denounced it.

Another major difference between the brahmin and ascetic traditions had to do with the role of deities. It was believed that the deities of the brahmins would respond to devotees' requests for assistance in exchange for regular praise and ritual offerings. Some of the major deities were recognized by the ascetic traditions as well—especially the creator god Brahma and the storm god Indra. But they played quite a small role in the nonbrahminic traditions. Minor gods might provide practical help from time to time, but the liberation that the ascetics sought could be achieved only through their own efforts. It was in this environment that Buddhism originated. Some Buddhist concepts were major innovations: the impermanence of the human self or soul, for instance, and social egalitarianism. But others—including the notions of **karma** and successive reincarnations, the ideal of ascetic withdrawal from the world, and the belief that numerous gods, demons, and spirits play active roles in human life—were common to all the Ganges traditions.

The Bodhisattva Vow and Previous Lives

Buddhism, like Hinduism and Jainism, understands the cosmos in terms of an endless succession of universes arising and passing away. Our current universe was already in the declining phase of its life cycle when the buddha of the present age, Siddhartha Gautama—better known as **Shakyamuni**, the "sage of the Shakya clan"—was born. In every era, when dharma (morality and truth) has declined, a highly developed being is born to become the buddha for that era. Buddhists understand that there were buddhas in previous eras and will be buddhas in subsequent ones. In addition, in every age there are numerouss other beings who achieve some degree of enlightenment. Among them are **Arhats** ("worthy ones" or "saints") and **bodhisattvas** (those who have dedicated themselves to achieving buddhahood).

All Buddhist traditions agree that Shakyamuni lived to the age of 80, but no one is certain when he lived. Some believe he was born in 566 BCE; others argue for 563 BCE. In Sri Lanka and Southeast Asia, the standard birth date is 624 BCE, while Japanese scholars, relying on Chinese and Tibetan texts, have adopted a later date of 448 BCE.

Although Shakyamuni achieved enlightenment through his own efforts, he is understood to have nearly perfected his "mind of enlightenment" through hundreds of previous lives. Unlike the Hindu *avatara* or Jesus Christ, the Buddha is simply a human being who fulfilled the spiritual potential of all living creatures. What is special about him is the power of his insight to free people from suffering. This is what Buddhists have in mind when they say that they "take refuge" in the Buddha.

Siddhartha's Birth and Childhood

The story of the Buddha's birth and childhood varies somewhat among the Buddhist traditions. What follows is a very brief version, based on the early Pali-language account preserved in the Theravada tradition. According to this account, the queen of the Shakya people, Mahamaya, is keeping a vow of sexual abstinence in observance of a festival. One afternoon she takes a nap and dreams that four minor gods, the World Protectors, carry her to a pleasant grove of trees. There a spiritual being in the form of a sacred white elephant (an animal associated with good fortune) miraculously enters her body and becomes the embryo of the Buddha-to-be. After a pregnancy marked by supernatural signs, Mahamaya sets out for her home city, intending to give birth there. But along the way she stops to rest at a park known as Lumbini, and the baby is born through her side as she holds on to a tree branch for support. In the Theravada tradition, the birth takes place on the full-moon day of the month called **Vaishakha**, which usually falls in April or May of the Western calendar. (East Asian Buddhists follow a different tradition.) That night a bright light illuminates the world to mark the holy event.

The infant bodhisattva is named Siddhartha, "he who achieves success." But Buddhists rarely use that name, preferring titles related to his spiritual role, such as Shakyamuni or (Lord) Buddha. During the naming ceremony, brahmin sages offer predictions based on his physical features. His unusually long earlobes are seen as a sign of great spiritual wisdom, his golden complexion is said to show his inner tranquility, and the wheel patterns on the soles of his feet point to his role as "wheel-turner." On the basis of these signs, the brahmins predict the young prince will become either a great emperor or a fully enlightened buddha.

Timeline

c. 531 (or 589 or 413) BCE	Shakyamuni's enlightenment
c. 496 (or 544 or 368)	Shakyamuni's *parinirvana*, or passing
c. 395	First Buddhist council
c. 273	Accession of King Ashoka
c. 225	Mahendra takes Theravada Buddhism to Sri Lanka
c. 67 CE	Buddhism takes root in China
c. 100	Emergence of Indian Mahayana
c. 200	Life of Nagarjuna, Madhyamika philosopher
c. 350	Lives of Asanga and Vasubandhu, Yogacara philosophers
372	Buddhism introduced to Korea from China
c. 500	Emergence of tantra in India
604	"Prince" Shotoku, Japanese regent and patron of Buddhism, issues Seventeen-Article Constitution
c. 750	Padmasambhava takes Vajrayana Buddhism to Tibet
806	Shingon (tantric) Buddhism introduced to Japan
845	Persecution of Buddhism in China
1173	Birth of Shinran, Japanese Pure Land thinker (d. 1262)
1222	Birth of Nichiren, founder of the Japanese sect devoted to the *Lotus Sutra* (d. 1282)
1603	Tokugawa regime takes power in Japan; Buddhism put under strict state control
c. 1617	Dalai Lamas become rulers of Tibet
c. 1900	Beginnings of Buddhist missionary activity in the West
1956	B. R. Ambedkar (1891–1956) converts to Buddhism, leading to the conversion of 380,000 other Dalits and reestablishing Buddhism in India
1959	China takes over Tibet; the Dalai Lama and many other Tibetans flee to India
1963	Thich Quang Duc immolates himself in protest against the persecution of Buddhists in South Vietnam
2001	Taliban forces destroy colossal Buddhist statues along ancient trade route in Afghanistan
2008	Tibetan protests against Han Chinese domination erupt into violence in the lead-up to the Beijing Summer Olympics; Dalai Lama denounces the violence while sympathizing with Tibetans' concerns
2011	The Dalai Lama renounces his role as the temporal ruler of Tibet
2017	UN report criticizes the military in Buddhist-majority Myanmar for violence against the Islamic-minority Rohingya population

His father orders that no evidence of life's suffering be allowed near the boy, lest it lead him to renounce the world and become a monk. Evidently the early Buddhists who told this story shared the view of those modern scholars who suggest that in the absence of adversity, humans would have little reason to pursue the spiritual path.

There are only a few stories of the bodhisattva's childhood. In one of them his first teacher is amazed to find that he already knows the various alphabets. In another he wins a martial arts tournament even though he has shown little interest in war. In the most significant story, he is sitting in the shade of a rose-apple tree watching his father perform a spring ground-breaking ritual when he enters a meditational trance, during which the shadow of the tree miraculously stands still even though the sun moves. The memory of this wakeful meditation state will later play a role in Siddhartha's achievement of enlightenment.

The Four Sights and the Great Departure

Despite all the king's precautions, Siddhartha learns the bitter truth about life around the time of his thirtieth birthday. By then he is happily married and the father of a son. During a chariot ride through the royal park, the prince happens to see four sights that will alter the course of his life. The first three—a sick man, a suffering old man, and a dead man—awaken him to life's sorrows. When he asks what is wrong with these men, his chariot driver answers honestly, revealing to him for the first time the harsh realities of life.

The fourth and final sight is an ascetic whose aura of tranquil detachment from the world suggests that there is a way to overcome the suffering of life after all. To this day, Buddhist monks often say that what first attracted them to join the sangha was seeing, as children, the serenity of the older monks and nuns as they passed through the streets on their daily alms-seeking rounds.

On returning home, the bodhisattva ponders the four sights, and that night he flees the palace. He exchanges his princely clothes for those of a poor hunter, obtains an alms bowl, and begins a new life as one of the wandering students seeking spiritual truth along the banks of the Ganges. With five other students, he begins a program of rigorous ascetic discipline. After six years he is able to subsist on one palmful each of water and food per day.

Enlightenment

Now convinced that even the most extreme asceticism cannot produce the enlightenment he seeks, the bodhisattva goes to a town now called Bodh Gaya. There he resumes eating and drinking, but he still needs a method to achieve the state he desires. Then he remembers the wakeful meditational trance he experienced spontaneously as a child:

> I thought of a time when my Sakyan father was working and I was sitting in the cool shade of a rose-apple tree: quite secluded from sensual desires, secluded from unprofitable things I had entered upon and abided in the first meditation, which is accompanied by thinking and exploring with happiness and pleasure born of seclusion. I thought: Might that be the way to enlightenment? Then, following up that memory there came the recognition that this was the way to enlightenment. (*Majjhima Nikaya*; Nanamoli 1972: 21)

Choosing a pleasant spot beside a cool river, under a *pipal* tree (known thereafter to Buddhists as the Bodhi tree), he sits to meditate and vows that he will not get up until he has achieved nirvana.

Document

From the *Dhammapada*

Many sutras include one or more verses that sum up the teaching. These "memory verses" were eventually collected as a separate work called the Dhammapada, *"fundamentals of dhamma." Dhamma is the Pali spelling for dharma. The following verses from its first chapter concern the pure mind.*

1. The mind is the source of all mental actions [dharmas],
   mind is the chief of the mental actions, and they are made by the mind.
   If, by an impure mind, one speaks or acts, then suffering follows the mind as a cartwheel follows the footprint of the ox.

2. The mind is the source of all mental states, mind is their leader, and they are made by the mind.
   If, by a pure mind, one speaks or acts, then happiness follows the mind like a shadow.

3. "I was abused." "I was beaten." "I was hurt." "I was robbed."
   Those who dwell excessively on such thoughts never get out of their hating state of mind.

4. "I was abused." "I was beaten." "I was hurt." "I was robbed."
   Those who leave such thoughts behind get out of their hating state of mind.

5. In this world hatreds are never ended by more hating.
   Hatreds are only ended by loving kindness. This is an eternal truth [dharma].

6. Some people do not know that we must restrain ourselves.
   But others know this and settle their quarrels.

7. One who dwells on personal gratifications, overindulges the senses, overeats, is indolent and lazy, that person is overthrown by Mara [Death] like an old, weak tree in a windstorm.

8. One who dwells in meditation on the bodily impurities, keeps the senses under control, eats moderately, has faith and disciplined energy, that person stands against Mara like a rocky mountain.

9. Whoever puts on the ochre robe but lacks purity, self-control, and truthfulness, that person is not worthy of the robe.

10. Whoever puts on the ochre robe and is pure, self-controlled, and truthful, that person is truly worthy of the robe.

11. Mistaking the unessential for the important, and mistaking the essential for the unimportant,
    some persons, dwelling in wrong-mindedness, never realize that which is really essential.

12. Knowing the essential to be important, and knowing the unessential to be unimportant,
    other persons, dwelling in right-mindedness, reach that which is really essential. (1:1–12)

In some versions of the story, it is just before dusk on the full-moon day in the month of Vaishakha that Mara, the lord of death, arrives. Determined to thwart the bodhisattva's attempt to achieve enlightenment, Mara summons his daughters—whose names suggest greed, boredom, and desire—to tempt him. When that fails, Mara offers him any worldly wish, if only he will return home and live a life of good karma (merit) as a householder. The bodhisattva refuses.

Now Mara becomes violent. He sends in his sons—whose names suggest fear and anger—to assault the bodhisattva. But the bodhisattva's spiritual power surrounds and protects him like a force field.

Having failed in his efforts to tempt and threaten the bodhisattva, Mara challenges him to a debate. Mara himself claims to be the one worthy to sit on the Bodhi Seat—the place of enlightenment—on this auspicious night, and he accuses the bodhisattva of being unworthy. But the bodhisattva has the vast store of merit from the generosity, courage, and wisdom he has perfected through countless previous lives, and he calls on the earth goddess to stand witness on his behalf. The resulting earthquake drives Mara away. Buddhists today may understand this story as symbolic of the mind recognizing and overcoming its deepest impurities, which the bodhisattva must conquer before he can attain liberation.

Now the bodhisattva begins to meditate in his own way. First he remembers his own past lives. Then he acquires deeper insight into the working of karma, understanding how the past lives of various people have been reflected in later incarnations. Finally he contemplates how to put an end to suffering and arrives at what will come to be known as the Four Noble Truths.

Just before dawn, the bodhisattva enters the state of total insight into the nature of reality. After hundreds of lives, he has fulfilled his bodhisattva vow. He is no longer a being striving for enlightenment; now he is a buddha, a "fully enlightened one": "I had direct knowledge. Birth is exhausted, the Holy Life has been lived out, what was to be done is done, there is no more of this to come" (*Majjhima Nikaya*; Nanamoli 1972: 25).

Having completed his journey to enlightenment, he has earned the title Tathagata ("thus-gone one"), and it is by this title that he will most often refer to himself. Another term for the state he has reached is "nirvana" (*nibbana* in Pali). This state has two aspects, negative and positive. In its negative aspect nirvana has the sense of "putting out the fires" of greed, hatred, and delusion. In its positive aspect nirvana is the experience of transcendent happiness. Reflecting on his experience,

Young Tibetan monks pay their respects to the Buddha by circumambulating the Bodh Gaya Bodhi tree (© Gianni Muratore/Alamy).

the new Buddha concludes that the way to enlightenment can be taught, and so he begins a teaching career motivated by compassion for all living beings.

Setting the Wheel in Motion

Shakyamuni's first impulse is to seek out and teach his five former companions. Perceiving that they can be found at a deer park called Sarnath near Varanasi, he sets out and on the way encounters two merchants who show their respect by offering him food. In a sense, this act marks the beginning of institutional Buddhism, which depends on the material support (food, medicine, robes, financial donations) given by laypeople in return for the spiritual gifts offered by ordained Buddhists (dharma teaching, chanting, guidance). This pattern of reciprocal giving remains central to all forms of Buddhism.

On arriving at the deer park, the Buddha is at first shunned by his friends because he has abandoned their rigorous discipline, but when they see his aura they recognize that he has attained nirvana and ask to know how he did it. He responds with his first *sutra*, often referred to as the

Shakyamuni and his five fellow ascetics in the deer park at Sarnath, the site of his first sermon; from a series of illustrations of the life of Buddha on a temple wall (Roy C. Amore).

"Wheel Turning" discourse because it marks the moment when the wheel of true dharma is once again set in motion.

Another name for this teaching is the "Instruction on the Middle Path." As long as the Buddha lived the life of a pampered prince, he could not advance spiritually. Yet his years of ascetic discipline left him too weak to make any real progress. Only after he began to eat, drink, and sleep in moderation was he able to reach enlightenment. In time, this principle of moderation would be developed into a general ethic of the Middle Way.

Now the Buddha begins to explain the insight into suffering that he has gained. After a few days of instruction in the Four Noble Truths and the Eightfold Path for overcoming suffering, the Buddha ordains the five as his first disciples and sends them out to teach the dharma to others.

Entering *Parinirvana*

For the next 45 years the Buddha travels, ordaining disciples and teaching thousands of lay followers. He also ordains several members of his own family.

As he nears 80, his body weakens, but he continues to travel until one day, as he and his disciples are dining with the leader of a local tribal group, an odd-smelling dish is brought to the table. He asks his host to serve it only to him, not to his disciples, and on eating it he falls ill. The Compassionate One tells his disciples not to blame the host, who meant well. They ask whom they should follow if he dies, and he tells them to follow the dharma; thus, in Buddhism no individual has absolute authority. Finally, in a grove of trees at Kushinagar, at the moment of death, the Buddha experiences *parinirvana*: the final end of the cycle of rebirth, the total cessation of suffering, the perfection of happiness.

⊕ The Second Gem: The Dharma

> Avoid doing all evil deeds,
> cultivate doing good deeds,
> and purify the mind—
> this is the teaching of all buddhas.

(*Dhammapada* 183)

The crystallization of the Buddhist tradition began with the transformation of the Buddha's discourses into a set of doctrinal teachings—the dharma—and the movement toward an institutionalized monastic system. "Dharma" is a central concept in Buddhist thought, and the range of its meanings extends well beyond the meaning of "dharma" in the Hindu context.

In classical Indian culture generally, "dharma" carries the sense of social and moral obligation, but Buddhist usage reflects its root meaning: "that which holds." Thus in English we could understand "dharma" to mean eternal truth, which for Buddhists includes the laws of nature, the reality of spiritual forces such as karma, and the rules of moral duty. Believing the Buddha's understanding of those realities to be definitive, generations of thinkers studied and systematized his insights, creating a program of instruction that anyone seeking enlightenment could follow.

The Four Noble Truths and Eightfold Path

At the core of the Buddha's first sermon in the deer park are the Four Noble Truths about suffering and the Eightfold Path to overcoming it. The Truths are:

1. The Noble Truth of Suffering: No living being can escape suffering (*dukkha*). Birth, sickness, senility, and death are all occasions of suffering, whether physical or psychological.
2. The Noble Truth of Origin: Suffering arises from excessive desire.
3. The Noble Truth of Cessation: Suffering will cease when desire ceases.
4. The Noble Truth of the Eightfold Path: It is possible to put an end to desire, and hence to suffering, by following eight principles of self-improvement.

The eight principles that make up the Eightfold Path are not sequential, like the steps on a ladder. All are equally important, and each depends on all the rest. Thus none of them can be properly observed in isolation. They must work in concord, like the petals of a flower unfolding together. They are:

1. Right understanding (specifically of the Four Noble Truths)
2. Right thought (freedom from sensuous desire, ill will, and cruelty)
3. Right speech
4. Right conduct
5. Right livelihood
6. Right effort
7. Right mindfulness
8. Right meditation

Document

From the *Itivuttaka*

The Itivuttaka *("So I heard") is a collection of the Buddha's teachings said to have been made by Khujjuttara, a woman of the servant class who was held up by the Buddha himself as an exemplary lay disciple. She used the teachings she had heard to teach other women; hence the phrase "So I heard" ("Itivuttaka"), which begins each section of the collection and became its title.*

Even if one should seize the hem of my robe and walk step by step behind me, if he is covetous in his desires, fierce in his longings, malevolent of heart, with corrupt mind, careless and unrestrained, noisy and distracted and with sense uncontrolled, he is far from me. And why? He does not see the Dhamma, and not seeing the Dhamma, he does not see me. Even if one lives a hundred miles away, if he is not covetous in his desires, not fierce in his longings, with a kind heart and pure mind, mindful, composed, calmed, one-pointed and with senses restrained, then indeed, he is near to me and I am near to him. And why? He sees the Dhamma, and seeing the Dhamma, sees me. (Dhammika 1989: 49–50)

The Three Characteristics of Existence

Existence has three characteristics, according to the Buddhist dharma: suffering, impermanence, and no-self. "Suffering" refers to all the varieties of pain and deprivation, physical and psychological, that humans are subject to; "impermanence" is the passing nature of all things; and "no-self" (*anatman* in Sanskrit) refers to the psychological implications of that existential impermanence. Literally, **anatman** means "without Atman," but what is Atman? The Hindu understanding of this term is reflected in the *Upanishads*, in which Atman represents the eternal self or soul and is related to Brahman, the underlying energy of the universe. For many Hindus, the innermost self is the most stable and abidingly real feature of the individual, because it participates in the reality of the universe.

The Buddha proposed that no such eternal, unchanging self exists. And in denying the existence of a self, he made the concept of ownership radically unsustainable for his followers: if there is no "I," there can be no "mine." The *anatman* concept does not mean that there is "no person" or "no personality" in the ordinary English sense of those terms. In fact, Buddhist teachings address the components of personality, the *skandhas*, in some detail, suggesting that personality is the product of shifting, arbitrary circumstance. Buddhist personality theory implies that wise people, recognizing the impermanence of all things—including themselves—will not become emotionally attached to fixed images of themselves.

Dependent Origination

The principle of causality is a thread that runs throughout the Buddha's dharma. To appreciate its function, think of a pool table where the balls are colliding with one another and the cushions, repeatedly causing one another to change directions; each time you blink, you see a new configuration caused by the previous configuration.

The standard term for this understanding of causality—in which everything that arises does so in response to other factors and will in turn cause changes in other things—is "dependent origination." Buddhist dharma uses the image of a 12-spoked "wheel of becoming" (not to be confused with the eight-spoked Dharma Chakra, the wheel that symbolizes the Eightfold Path) to express the view of life as a cycle of interdependent stages or dimensions.

The 12 links of the chain may be further divided into three stages, reflecting the movement from a past life through the present one and on to the future:

Past
1. Ignorance, leading to
2. karma formations, leading to

Present
3. a new individual "consciousness," leading to
4. a new body-mind complex, leading to
5. the bases of sensing, leading to
6. sense impressions, leading to
7. conscious feelings, leading to
8. craving, leading to
9. clinging to (grasping for) things, leading to
10. "becoming" (the drive to be reborn), leading to

Future
11. rebirth, leading to
12. old age and death

The process does not stop with the twelfth link, of course, since old age and death lead to rebirth, and so the wheel of life turns on and on. All living beings are in this process and will be reborn over and over again until they realize nirvana.

The *Tripitaka*: Three Baskets of Sacred Texts

Shakyamuni did not write down his teachings, nor did anyone record them. For the first four centuries or so after his death, the Buddha's teachings were recited from memory. Different **bhikshus** (monks) memorized different portions, and at the early conferences of sangha members, one of the most important tasks was to recite the teachings in their entirety.

The Wheel of Becoming (Bhava-Chakra) represents the 12 stages of dependent origination. At the center are three animals representing the three evil root tendencies of human consciousness: greed, represented by a rooster with endless desire for more hens; hate, represented by a snake spitting venom; and delusion, represented by a boar (perhaps because boars were thought to have poor eyesight or bad judgment). The surrounding 12 pictures illustrate the spokes of the Wheel of Becoming (see text). The wheel is held in the teeth of the demon of death, whose head, hands, and feet are visible behind it. (The Buddhist Society)

At the first council, held not long after Shakyamuni's death, Bhikshu Ananda is said to have recited the discourses (*sutras*) on dharma ascribed to Shakyamuni. Bhikshu Upali is credited with reciting the section on monastic rules (**vinaya**). The systematic treatises (*abhidharma*) composed after Shakyamuni's *parinirvana* were recited at a later meeting. The oral teachings were finally put into writing by the Theravada monks of Sri Lanka in the first century CE, after a famine had so reduced the monks' numbers that the survival of the oral tradition was threatened. The fact that Theravada Buddhists refer to their scriptures as the **Tripitaka** ("Three Baskets") suggests that the manuscripts of the three types of texts—written on palm leaves strung together and bundled like Venetian blinds—may have been stored in three baskets. The collection survives in the Pali language and is therefore referred to as the Pali canon.

The *Sutra Pitaka*, or "discourse basket," contains the talks on dharma attributed to Shakyamuni or his early disciples. Many *sutras* are presented as responses to questions from disciples. The opening of the "Discourse on the Lesser Analysis of Deeds" is typical: "Thus have I heard: At one time . . . the brahmin youth Subha, Todeyya's son, spoke thus to the Lord: 'Now, good Gotama, what is the cause, what the reason that lowness and excellence are to be seen among human beings while they are in human form?'" (Horner 1967: 248–249). Subha has asked the timeless question of why bad things happen to apparently good people. Shakyamuni then explains to Subha how the karma accumulated through actions in past lives causes some people to suffer short, unhappy lives and others to enjoy long, blessed lives.

There are five sections (*nikayas*) of the *Sutra Pitaka*, the first "basket." The second basket, the *Vinaya* ("discipline") *Pitaka*, contains both the rules of monastic discipline and stories about how Shakyamuni came to institute each rule. Finally, the *Abhidharma* ("further discourses") *Pitaka* contains seven books by unnamed early Buddhists who systematically analyzed every conceivable aspect of reality in light of Buddhist principles. For example, the first book of *abhidharma* classifies all mental phenomena according to their karmic consequences—good, bad, or neutral. Other books deal with the various physical elements of nature.

⊕ The Third Gem: The Sangha

The third part of the Triple Gem has two components: the monastic community of ordained men (*bhikshus*) and women (*bhikshunis*), and the broader community, the universal sangha of all those who follow the Buddha's path.

Bhikshus and *Bhikshunis*

Shakyamuni began accepting disciples in the deer park at Varanasi. Soon an ordination ritual took shape in which the new disciples recited the Triple Refuge; took vows of chastity, poverty, and obedience; and put on the distinctive robes of a monk. Later, a more rigorous preliminary level of ordination was introducd during which novices were required to master the basics of dharma. Each novice was assigned both a demanding teacher and a supportive spiritual guide.

The full ordination ritual for *bhikshus* and *bhikshunis* (nuns) takes several hours. Friends and relatives pay their respects to the new sangha members, who give presents to their teachers and counselors in gratitude for their assistance. Because seniority plays a large role in monastic life, careful attention is paid to the exact time and date of every ordination.

Lay Buddhists are considered members of the sangha in its wider sense. The sangha of all disciples includes eight categories of "noble persons," into which people fall according to the progress they have made toward nirvana. There are four levels: "those who have entered the stream" to nirvana, those who have advanced enough to return (be reborn) just once more, those who are so advanced that they will never return, and those who have advanced to the state of realizing the Arhat (worthy) path. For each level, those who have just reached the new level are distinguished from those who have matured there, making a total of eight classifications.

Ordained and Lay Women

Unlike many other religious traditions, Buddhism never defined women as the "property" of men. Nevertheless, the early texts indicate a profound ambiguity about the status of women in Buddhism, and Shakyamuni is said to have resisted the formation of an order for women on the grounds that it would be detrimental to the survival of his teachings. On the other hand, he did permit it, and he encouraged close relatives to join it, maintaining that women were no less capable than men of becoming Arhats (saints), and that the way to nirvana was the same regardless of gender:

> And be it woman, be it man for whom
> Such chariot doth wait, by that same car
> Into Nirvana's presence shall they come. (Horner 1930: 104)

Other early Buddhist texts are similarly ambiguous about women. On the positive side, they describe approvingly the support provided to the early sangha by some wealthy women, and one book of the Pali canon, the *Therigatha*, contains poems by early *bhikshunis*. On the negative side, there was a distinct difference in status between *bhikshus* and *bhikshunis*, who were not allowed to teach their male counterparts.

Controversies, Councils, and Sects

Because there was no central authority in the tradition, the monks had to settle disputes collectively on the basis of their interpretations of the Buddha's discourses—a challenging task in the era before the scriptures were written down. In the fourth century BCE, for instance, a *bhikshu* visiting the city of Vaishali found that his colleagues there were accepting donations of gold and silver. He criticized them publicly, and they demanded that he apologize in front of their lay supporters. As a consequence, a meeting of all the *bhikshus* in the area had to be convened.

The meeting, called the Vaishali Council, decided that monastic discipline did indeed forbid the acceptance of gold and silver. Most of the Vaishali *bhikshus* agreed to abide by the ruling, but a schism developed later when one dissident monk raised several points of controversy concerning the status of Arhats. Was an Arhat subject to the same limitations as an ordinary *bhikshu*? Was an Arhat susceptible to sexual misconduct? Was it possible for an Arhat to have doubts about doctrine? Could one become an Arhat merely by instruction, without spiritual practice?

Behind those questions lay an issue that was to fuel serious divisions later on: the level of spiritual attainment possible for Buddhists in this life. Most of the monks held out the prospect of enlightenment for ordinary people, but some of the *sthavira* ("elders") argued that the Arhat level was beyond the reach of all but a few. In this way a division arose between the majority group, who formed the Mahasanghika or "Great Sangha" sect, and the Sthavira group, who formed the Sthaviravada or Theravada sect. This debate foreshadowed the split that would lead to the development of the Mahayana and Theravada schools as distinctly different "vehicles."

By the third century BCE there were 18 sects, each with its own oral version of the teachings, although all shared a similar ordination tradition and all followed more or less the same *vinaya* rules. Monks of different sects sometimes lived together in one monastery, especially at the major training centers, and the same was true of the *bhikshunis*, who always lived in their own monasteries, separate from the men.

A Theravada *bhikkhu* with a palm-leaf umbrella (Roy C. Amore).

King Ashoka's Conversion

The spread of Buddhism within India was remarkable. Unlike many reformers, Shakyamuni gained converts across the social spectrum, from the lowest laborers to powerful kings. Among the latter was Ashoka (r. c. 273–232 BCE), who had waged a series of wars to expand his territory and eventually came to rule an empire that included most of modern India. Buddhist accounts claim that it was the carnage of his war with the kingdom of Kalinga that led Ashoka to convert to Buddhism and begin promoting the ethic of nonviolence.

Under Ashoka's patronage Buddhism enjoyed its golden age in India. To spread the dharma of nonviolence, the king ordered that large stones or pillars be erected at the main crossroads throughout his empire, and that messages be carved on them for the moral instruction of his subjects. Some of these messages are still readable. One, a from a pillar in the Kalinga region, expresses Ashoka's remorse for the death and suffering he had caused to its people:

> When the king, Beloved of the Gods and of Gracious Mien, had been consecrated eight years Kalinga was conquered, 150,000 people were deported, 100,000 were killed, and many times that number died. But after the conquest of Kalinga, the Beloved of the Gods began to follow Righteousness (dharma), to love Righteousness, and to give instruction in Righteousness. Now the Beloved of the Gods regrets the conquest of Kalinga, for when an independent country is conquered people are killed, they die, or are deported, and that the Beloved of the Gods finds painful and grievous. . . . (*Thirteenth Rock Edict*; de Bary 1958: 146)

In the remainder of the message Ashoka lays out his ideals for governance, saying that he desires security, self-control, impartiality, and cheerfulness for all living creatures in his empire. He spells out his "conquest by dharma" and claims that it is spreading not only within the Indian continent but to the west, to lands whose kings he names.

Although he reminds his subjects that he will not hesitate to deal firmly with rebels and criminals, he promises that his punishments will be just and moderate. Ashoka's promotion of dharma became a model for later Buddhist rulers, who were willing to sentence criminals (and rebels) to punishment or even death, but remained committed to nonviolence in other matters.

Buddhism and the State

From the time of Shakyamuni, Buddhism expected rulers not only to provide for the physical welfare of their subjects (e.g., by distributing food in times of need) but to promote dharma by setting a good example and sponsoring lectures, translations, and the distribution of literature. The king who promoted dharma would be a true successor to the Buddha.

As Buddhism spread throughout Asia, so did its social and moral ideals regarding kingship. A Zen Buddhist story tells of a Chinese king named Wu who has dedicated himself to doing all the good works expected of a Buddhist king, probably with the goal of winning a long and pleasant rebirth in heaven. When Wu learns that a monk named Bodhidharma has arrived from India, he summons the monk to court and proudly shows him the rice kitchens he has established for feeding the poor, the new wing of the palace filled with scribes who are busy translating and copying the sacred texts, and the altar he has set up for daily worship.

Map 10.1 The Spread of Buddhism

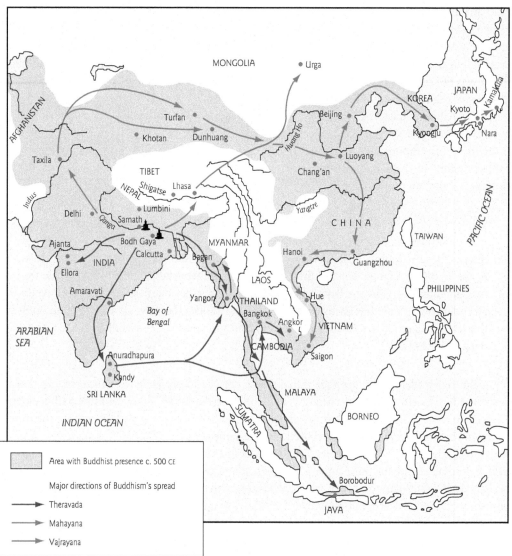

Source: Adapted from Nielsen et al. 1993: 196.

After the tour, the emperor asks Bodhidharma how much merit he has made. "None whatso-ever!" is the famous response. Bodhidharma explains that true merit comes only from activities that increase one's wisdom and purify one's mind. It seems that the emperor has been doing all the right things for the wrong reason. What this story tells us is that although rulers were encouraged to support the sangha and promote dharma in their realms, the ultimate goal of these activities was the ruler's own spiritual advancement. This helps to explain why Buddhist kings sometimes abdicated to undergo ordination as *bhikshus*.

Nonviolence as a Public Ethic

One characteristic of Buddhist political rule, at least ideally, was promotion of nonviolence. Unnecessarily harsh punishment was forbidden, and kings were expected to release prisoners during Buddhist festivals. Justice was to be administered fairly, regardless of the social status of the accused, and quickly.

At the same time, the Buddhist king was expected to maintain an army and a police force to defend the people. There is no such thing in Buddhist scripture as a "just war" of aggression, but many Buddhists have believed that a defensive war is not against dharma, and that the state may use force to maintain law and order.

With very few exceptions, Buddhism spread by missionary conversion rather than by force. The adoption of Buddhism in new regions was helped by the dedicated, spiritual lifestyle of the monks and nuns and the fact that Buddhist missionaries allowed new converts to continue venerating their traditional deities as well as the spirits of their ancestors. There were territorial wars between Buddhist kingdoms in Southeast Asia, however, and Sri Lanka has a long history of conflict between the Buddhist Sinhalese and the Hindu Tamils.

⊕ Early Buddhism: The First Vehicle ("Hinayana")

By Ashoka's time, Buddhism had split into 18 distinct sects. Over the following centuries most of these disappeared. The main survivor, Theravada, is one of the three major divisions of Buddhism that exist today. The second major school, which emerged around the first century CE, called itself Mahayana, "Great Vehicle," in contrast to what it considered the Hinayana, "Lesser Vehicle," of Theravada and its contemporaries. The third division, Vajrayana, emerged some 500 years later and considers itself the third vehicle.

Focus

Buddhist Vehicles and Schools

1. Theravada (sometimes called Hinayana, the "Little Vehicle"), now dominant in Sri Lanka and Southeast Asia: a survivor of the 18 sects that existed in the third century BCE
2. Mahayana (the "Great Vehicle"), now dominant in East Asia and Vietnam:
   • Madhyamika in India, Sanlun in China
   • Yogacara in India, Faxiang in China
   • Tiantai in China, Tendai in Japan
   • Huayan in China, Kegon in Japan
   • Zhenyan in China, Shingon in Japan
   • Pure Land, Jingtu in China, Jodo in Japan
   • Chan in China, Seon in Korea, Zen in Japan
   • Linji in China, Rinzai in Japan
   • Caodong in China, Soto in Japan
   • Nichiren in Japan
3. Vajrayana (the "Diamond Vehicle"), now dominant in Tibet and the Himalayas:
   • Gelugpa ("Yellow Hats")
   • Kargyu ("Red Hats")
   • Karma-pa ("Black Hats")
   • Nyingma ("Ancient" school)

⊕ Theravada Buddhism

We know very little about the early history of Theravada, although it appears to have been widespread in India by the time of Ashoka. We do know that the Theravada tradition was conservative. Rejecting all scriptures composed after the formation of the *Tripitaka*, it considers itself the preserver of Buddhism in its original form.

Theravada in Sri Lanka

A monk named Mahinda, who was Ashoka's son, is said to have taken Theravada Buddhism to Sri Lanka in the third century BCE. In this story Mahinda and his assistant monks use psychic powers to travel through the air and arrive on a large hill near the island's capital, Anuradhapura. There the king of Sri Lanka and his hunting party discover the monks and are soon converted to the Buddha's dharma. The next day, Mahinda enters the capital and teaches dharma to the members of the king's court, who are also converted. On the following day the largest space available—the royal elephant stable—is put into service as a hall of dharma instruction, whereupon everyone is converted.

These legends are presumably based on historical events, since one of Ashoka's inscriptions claims that he sent missionaries in groups of five to seek converts far and wide, even in the Hellenistic kingdoms to the west. The king of Sri Lanka could well have been receptive to the idea of an alliance with the great emperor on the mainland, in which case adopting the empire's religion and court rituals would have indicated willingness to comply with the greater power. The Sri Lankan king ordered the building of a proper temple, dharma hall, and **stupa**, and the temple grounds were made complete with the arrival of a Bodhi tree sapling brought from India by Mahinda's sister, herself a *bhikshuni*.

The king underwent a new enthronement ritual, carried out according to Ashoka's instructions, and in this way the island became a cultural extension of Ashoka's empire while maintaining its sovereignty. This uniting of Buddhist leadership and Indian forms of kingship set the pattern for subsequent Buddhist rulers across mainland Southeast Asia. Theravada Buddhism is still the main religion of Sri Lanka.

Theravada in Southeast Asia

The spread of Buddhism into Southeast Asia took place over many centuries. Today Buddhist culture remains dominant in much of the mainland, including Cambodia, Laos, Thailand, and Myanmar. It was also influential (as was Hinduism) in the Indonesian islands and the Malay peninsula, although Islamic religion and culture eventually became dominant there.

An account written by a Chinese Buddhist pilgrim in the seventh century suggests that several of the early Buddhist sects were already established in Southeast Asia by that time. Until about 1000, various early Buddhist sects as well as Mahayana and Vajrayana schools competed for support, but by the fifteenth century all the region's major rulers had embraced Theravada, perhaps because, in adopting it, they could bring their kingdoms into political alignment with other powerful kingdoms in Sri Lanka and mainland Southeast Asia. Other forms of Buddhism gradually died out, and Theravada training centers and temples of national importance flourished under royal patronage. Today Theravada remains the majority religion of the Thai, Khmer (Cambodian), Burmese, and Lao (Laotian) peoples.

Island Southeast Asia, by contrast, is now predominantly Muslim, but both Buddhist monuments and Buddhist minorities survive. In Indonesia, for example, tourists still flock to the ruins of the majestic temple of Borobudur, which covers a hilltop with a geometrical arrangement of stupas representing the mountains that, according to traditional Buddhist cosmology, anchor the world. Malaysia also has a sizable Buddhist minority, mainly among the Chinese population.

Theravada Practice: Rituals and Mindfulness

The most common Theravada ritual is the Buddha-puja, in which Buddhists chant praise to the Buddha and promise to observe the Five Precepts, vowing to refrain from:

- Taking life
- Taking that which is not given
- Sensual misconduct (sexual immorality)
- Wrong speech (lying, slander, and the like)
- Intoxicants leading to the loss of mindfulness

Merit-Making Rituals

Theravadins also perform a number of more elaborate "merit-making" rituals specifically designed to produce good karma. Of these, two of the most important are almsgiving and the *dana* ritual.

Lay Buddhists in Laos lower themselves in respect as they offer food to monks, who silently make their alms rounds early in the morning (© Robert Harding Picture Library Ltd/Alamy).

Traditionally, members of the sangha would leave the monastery early each morning carrying bowls to collect their daily food. As they moved silently through the streets, their eyes downcast to maintain a tranquil, composed state of mind, laypeople would come out of their houses, put cooked food into the alms bowls, and then bow low or prostrate themselves as a sign of respect. The practice of going out to collect alms is rare today, but it is still common in Thailand, and efforts have been made to revive it in Sri Lanka.

Life-Cycle and Death Rituals

Early Indian Buddhists continued to follow the life-cycle rituals of what we now call Hinduism, and as Buddhism spread, converts in other regions also retained their own traditions. Thus there are no specifically Buddhist wedding or childhood rituals. It is in part for this reason that Buddhism has been able to exist alongside different traditional belief systems: Sri Lankan Buddhists continue to observe Indian rituals, Thai Buddhists still worship their traditional spirits, and Japanese Buddhists still visit Shinto shrines.

There is a Theravada funeral ritual, however, based on the ancient Indian cremation ceremony. Although the pattern varies from country to country (and where the cost of wood is prohibitive, cremation is replaced by burial), the principal features of the ceremony are similar. The corpse is taken in a procession to the cemetery along a route prepared in advance by filling in potholes, cutting the grass and weeds beside the road, and placing flowers along the way.

At the cemetery the body is placed in a wooden structure above a funeral pyre. A brief service is then held that includes chants, prayers, and a ritual in which family members and friends take turns pouring holy water from one container into another while a long prayer is chanted. Then the

Practice

Dana-Giving

In time, the practice of giving alms to monks and nuns developed into a ritual called **dana**, from the Sanskrit word for "giving." A *dana* might be held at a temple or a pilgrimage site, but it is often held by a family in the home to celebrate some important occasion. The following description of a *dana* ceremony in a Sri Lankan home offers a glimpse of several other Buddhist rituals as well.

As the **bhikkhus** (the Pali term for *bhikshus*) arrive at the door, their feet are washed by the men of the family. (If the guests are **bhikkhunis**, the Pali term for *bhikshunis*, this hospitality ritual is performed by the women.) On entering, the monks first bow before the Buddha altar. A string is run from the Buddha image on the altar to a pot of water, then to the monks, and finally to the laypeople, so that all are holding the string in their right hand. The monks lead a Buddha-puja and then chant from a collection of scriptures called *paritta* before offering a dharma talk. The water and the string become sacred through the power of the chanting. Then a merit transfer ritual is performed in which the merit made by those present through their participation is transferred "to all living beings": "May the merit made by me now or at some other time be shared among all beings here infinite, immeasurable; those dear to me and virtuous as mothers or as fathers are, . . . to others neutral, hostile too. . . ."

Practice

Vipassana: Mindfulness Meditation

Theravada Buddhists practice a form of meditation called **vipassana** ("insight" or "mindfulness"). Practitioners concentrate on their breathing, focusing either on the sensation of air passing through the nostrils or on the rising and falling of the abdomen. Unlike some forms of yoga, the practitioner does not try to slow down the breaths or to regulate the length of the in-breaths in relation to the out-breaths. The meditator counts each breath from 1 to 10 and then starts counting again from 1. The point is not to keep count but to focus the mind. If one's mind is distracted by an outside noise such as an airplane or mosquito buzzing, a mental thought such as remembering something to do, or an itch or muscle pain, the meditator should not pretend the disturbance didn't happen. Rather, the meditation master will instruct the meditator to acknowledge the distraction three times and then refocus on breathing. For example, if the distraction happens to be the noise of an airplane, one should think "airplane, airplane, airplane," and then start counting the breaths again from "one."

Practitioners may also cultivate mindfulness of other parts of the body, personal emotions, or relationships with others. The goal is to live in a totally mindful way, being more calm and maintaining a heightened awareness of one's body, one's emotions, and the external world.

pyre is lit, ideally by the eldest son of the deceased. In the event that a crematorium is used instead of a funeral pyre, one or more monks will come to recite prayers over the body.

On the sixth night after the death, a dharma-preaching service is held at the home, followed by a *dana* on the morning of the seventh day. Other memorial *dana* rituals are held at the home of the deceased after three months and one year. Family members and friends who were unable to attend the funeral may participate in these memorials. After time has lessened the pain of the loss, the memorial services provide occasions to remember the deceased and enjoy a family reunion.

The Buddha Day Festival

Many Buddhist festivals developed out of earlier seasonal festivals, and there are regional variations of each. However, Buddhists in most places celebrate the day on which three major events in the life of Shakyamuni are said to have occurred: his birth, his enlightenment, and his *parinirvana*. Known in Theravada countries as Vesak or Wesak (and as Vaishakha in Sanskrit), this day is called "Buddha Day" in English.

⊕ Mahayana: The Second Vehicle

The Mahayana ("Greater Vehicle") movement appears to have emerged around the first century CE. We know that its members were dismissing older forms of Buddhism as Hinayana ("Lesser Vehicle") by the third or fourth century, and that around the same time it was becoming the dominant form of Buddhism across the region traversed by the Silk Road, stretching from Central Asia to northern China. It remains the main form of Buddhism in China, Korea, and Japan.

Mahayana differed from Theravada in everything from the doctrines and scriptures it emphasized to its rituals and meditation practices. Whereas Theravada saw the discipline of the *bhikshu* as a precondition for enlightenment and liberation, Mahayana offered laypeople the opportunity to strive for those goals as well. Whereas Theravada focused on the historical Shakyamuni, in Mahayana he represented only one manifestation of buddhahood. Furthermore, whereas Theravada insisted that there was no supernatural force on which human beings could call for assistance, Mahayana populated the heavens with bodhisattvas dedicated to helping all those who prayed to them.

How did these differences arise? A possible explanation is that Mahayana Buddhism developed from one or more of the 18 early Indian sects. There is some evidence for a close connection between early Mahayana and two or three of those sects, but it seems more likely that Mahayana emerged in southern India as part of a movement toward more liberal interpretation that spread across several of them.

Despite their differences, Mahayana and the earlier sects share a common core of values and moral teachings, practices (such as meditation, chanting, scripture study, and veneration of relics), and forms of monastic life. In short, Theravada and Mahayana are different vehicles for traveling the same path to enlightenment.

Mahayana Doctrine

Mahayana Buddhism begins with the same basic teachings as Theravada but gives more emphasis to some doctrines, such as emptiness (see the section on "Madhyamaka"); interprets others, such as the role of the lay sangha and the doctrine of the three Buddha bodies, in new ways; and includes additional elements, such as the bodhisattva vow.

The Lay Sangha

The practice of venerating Shakyamuni at the stupas enshrining his relics began soon after his death. In time, many laypeople began making pilgrimages to places with major relics, and new stupas were built in all Mahayana countries. Lay Buddhists came to believe that they could earn valuable karmic merit by making a pilgrimage to these sites.

This development marked a major shift away from early Buddhism, in which the religious role of laypeople had been restricted to providing material support for the sangha, and the prospects for lay progress along the spiritual path were limited. Anyone who wished to seek enlightenment more seriously was expected to "depart the world" for the monastic life. Mahayana, by contrast, offered laypeople the possibility of attaining enlightenment even while living in the world.

Doctrine of the Three Bodies (*Trikaya*)

To account for the various ways in which Buddha could be experienced, Mahayana developed a doctrine of "three bodies" (*trikaya*). The earthly manifestation of a buddha is called the Appearance or Transformation Body (*nirmanakaya*). The heavenly body that presides over a buddha-realm and is an object of devotion for Mahayana Buddhists is called the Body of Bliss (*sambhogakaya*). These are supported by the buddha as the absolute essence of the universe, called the Dharma Body (*dharmakaya*).

The three bodies doctrine calls attention not only to the oneness of all the buddhas that have appeared on earth, but also to the unity of the buddha-nature or potential in all its forms. That is, the *trikaya* doctrine envisions one cosmic reality (Dharma Body) that manifests itself in the form both of heavenly beings (Body of Bliss) and of humans such as Shakyamuni (Appearance Body). By connecting the earthly Buddha to the Dharma Body or Absolute, the doctrine of the three bodies also moved Mahayana Buddhism in the direction of theistic religion—in sharp contrast to the Theravada school, which continued to revere the Buddha not as a deity but as an exceptional human being.

Teaching by Expedient Means: The *Lotus Sutra*

The Sanskrit word *upaya* forms part of an expression frequently translated as "skill in means" or "skillful means." Shakyamuni's teachings were pragmatic, and he tailored his presentation of them to suit each audience's capacity. He urged his followers to use skill in guiding people to spiritual attainment, like the boatman who ferries people to the other side of the river. The analogy implies that once one has reached the other side, there is no further need of the boat for the onward journey.

A Mahayana text that emphasizes *upaya* is the *Lotus Sutra*. It treats many Buddhist teachings as steps toward a more complete understanding. As an illustration of this perspective, it tells of a father whose children are inside a burning house. He persuades them to come out by promising them chariots that he does not actually have; this false promise may be a lie, but it serves an important purpose. Similarly, those just starting on the path are taught not the ultimate truth, but temporary formulations that will allow them to advance to a point at which they will be able to see the purpose of the earlier stages. From this perspective, even Shakyamuni's teaching is provisional—simply an expedient means of persuading human beings to start along the path. By treating earlier teachings as expedient means, Mahayana thinkers were able to shift the emphasis from Shakyamuni to celestial buddha figures and a notion of cosmic wisdom.

Bodhisattvas and Merit Transfer

Early Buddhism taught that every individual makes his or her own karma, and that there is no supernatural source of grace. By contrast, the Mahayana school proposed that grace is available in the form of merit transferred to humans from bodhisattvas. Mahayana cosmology envisions a multitude of spiritually advanced beings, all of whom are prepared to share their great merit with anyone who prays for help.

Even though Shakyamuni himself had remained a bodhisattva until the night of his enlightenment, for most Theravadins the highest goal was to reach the status of an Arhat. The Mahayana school criticized this goal as self-centered because it was focused on personal liberation. Thus all Mahayana Buddhists are encouraged to take the bodhisattva vow, pledging not only to attain buddhahood themselves but also to work toward the liberation of all beings.

The corollary of this innovation in Buddhist thought was the Mahayana idea that humans can appeal to merit-filled beings in the heavens for assistance. Early Indian Buddhism had considered Shakyamuni after his *parinirvana* to be beyond the realm of direct involvement with human lives, and therefore it had no tradition of appealing to him for assistance. In some Mahayana schools, by contrast, worshipers not only venerate the bodhisattvas but petition them for blessings.

Another important characteristic of Mahayana Buddhism is its extension of the concept of merit transfer. As we have seen, early Buddhism taught that merit—that is, good karma—is made solely by the individual. The only exception involves the merit transfer ritual. In Mahayana, by contrast, the buddhas and the bodhisattvas are believed to be capable of transferring merit from themselves to human beings.

Some important bodhisattvas have special functions. For example, Bodhisattva Manjusri is the guardian of Buddhist wisdom, and novices entering Buddhist training often call on him to guide and inspire them. The bodhisattva of compassion, Avalokiteshvara ("the Lord who looks down"), is popular in all Mahayana countries. Originally Avalokiteshvara was masculine, but in China he came to be venerated in female form under the name Guanyin. This change of gender is an example of the bodhisattva's power to take any shape necessary to benefit believers.

Bodhisattva Maitreya ("the Friendly One") is expected to be the next buddha, the one who will turn the dharma wheel once again after the wheel set in motion by Shakyamuni has stopped turning. Some Mahayana Buddhists pray to Maitreya as the "future buddha," requesting that they be reborn when he comes because it will be easier to achieve enlightenment when there is a living buddha to follow.

The heavens in which the buddhas and bodhisattvas reside are known as "fields" or "realms." Those who venerate a certain buddha may be reborn into his heaven. As we shall see, this is a central belief of the **Pure Land** movement, which venerates a celestial buddha of "infinite life" and "infinite light" known in Sanskrit as Amitayus or Amitabha, in Chinese as Amituofo, and in Japanese as Amida (the Japanese spelling is the one most commonly used in English).

Bodhisattva Vows

The practice of taking bodhisattva vows reflects the Mahayana emphasis on giving oneself to help others. As we have seen, early Indian Buddhists rarely aspired to become buddhas themselves; they were content to hope that in some future life they could achieve the status of Arhat. It was the self-centered nature of this focus on personal liberation that Mahayana philosophers criticized. All Mahayana Buddhists—male or female, lay or monastic—were encouraged to declare their intention to become buddhas someday, but also to remain active in efforts to help liberate all beings.

In practical terms, taking the bodhisattva vow meant vowing to be reborn in a heaven from which one can transfer merit to others. Although the possibility of helping others by accepting rebirth as a human was not ruled out, the advanced bodhisattvas were thought to live in their own heavenly realms.

Mahayana Schools

The preceding overview of Mahayana doctrine suggests some substantial differences from Theravada Buddhism. But there are also pronounced differences among the various Mahayana ordination lineages or "schools" that developed first in India and later across East Asia. For example, the **Chan** (**Zen** in Japan) school downplays Buddha veneration and has much in common with Theravada, whereas the Pure Land school stresses the necessity of Amida Buddha's help. We will briefly discuss some of the more important schools of Mahayana thought, focusing on their beginnings (usually in India) and noting the names they assumed as they spread across East Asia.

Madhyamaka

Early Buddhism taught that there were six perfections, the last and most important of which was the perfection of a kind of wisdom known as **prajna**. This wisdom—not to be confused with worldly wisdom or scientific knowledge—is accessible only to those with a highly developed consciousness.

Mahayana thinkers wrote a number of texts on *prajna*, beginning as early as the first century BCE with the *Perfection of Wisdom in Eight Thousand Verses*. The two that were to become the most important were the *Heart* and *Diamond Cutter Sutras*. In all these texts, the key to the highest spiritual wisdom is awareness of the emptiness or nothingness (**shunyata**) of all things.

Sometime in the second century, a brahmin from southern India converted to Buddhism and took the ordination name Nagarjuna. He wrote Buddhist devotional hymns and ethical guides, but his fame is based on philosophical works such as the *Mulamadhyamaka-karika* ("Fundamentals of the Middle Way").

Nagarjuna's philosophical position is called the "Middle Way" (Madhyamaka) because it refuses either to affirm or to deny any statement about reality on the grounds that all such statements necessarily fall short of ultimate truth. All realities (dharmas) are equally "empty" of absolute truth or "self-essence." According to Nagarjuna's doctrine of emptiness, everything in the phenomenal world is ultimately unreal. By a process of paradoxical logic he claims that Emptiness as ultimate reality is itself unreal, although it may be experienced directly in meditation. Nagarjuna summed up this paradox in a famous eightfold negation:

> Nothing comes into being,
> Nor does anything disappear.
> Nothing is eternal,
> Nor has anything an end.
> Nothing is identical,
> Or differentiated,
> Nothing moves hither,
> Nor moves anything thither.
> (Chen 1964: 84)

For Madhyamaka and the later Mahayana schools that developed under its influence, including Zen, enlightenment demands recognition of the *shunyata* of all dharmas.

Of course Nagarjuna recognized that his own thinking was no less empty than any other. Thus he made it his philosophical "position" to refrain from taking any dogmatic position. According to his paradoxical logic, nirvana is dialectically identical to *samsara*, or the phenomenal world: each is present in the other. In China the Madhyamaka school was called Sanlun ("three treatises") after its main texts.

Yogacara, or "Consciousness Only"

In the late fourth century, three Indian *bhikshus* named Maitreyanatha, Asanga, and Vasubandhu founded a new Mahayana school. Though usually called Yogacara ("Practice of Yoga") because it stresses meditation and uses a text by that name, it is also known as "Consciousness Only" (Vijnanavada), because it argues that what most people assume to be realities are merely images taken from a "storehouse consciousness" shaped by past karmic actions and attachments. As a consequence, we can never know if external objects exist.

For Yogacara, both the universe and the perceiver exist only in the process of perceiving. Even our "selves" and our karma are merely reifications of momentary awareness. Sensory impressions are "seeds" that lead to acts or thoughts:

> A seed produces a manifestation,
> A manifestation perfumes a seed.
> The three elements (seed, manifestation, and
> perfume) turn on and on,
> The cause and effect occur at the same time.
> (Chen 1964: 323)

According to this theory, the only way to avoid false substantialization is to so exhaust the consciousness, through yoga and spiritual cultivation, that it becomes identical to the ultimate reality called "thusness," which corresponds to the "emptiness" of Madhyamaka. Critics from rival schools argued that the storehouse consciousness concept seemed to come close to affirming the Hindu notion of the Atman (eternal soul) that the Buddha had rejected. But the Yogacara writers argued that the storehouse consciousness has no eternal, unchanging substance. Buddhist ideas of the link between one birth and the next as a "karma complex" or "migrating consciousness" were developed by Yogacara into the notion of a storehouse consciousness.

Pure Land Buddhism

The school dedicated to Amitabha (Amida) most likely began to take shape around the first century. According to an account in the *Larger Sutra on the Pure Land*, attributed to Shakyamuni himself, Amitabha was a buddha of a previous age who in an earlier life, as a young prince named Dharmakara, took 48 bodhisattva vows detailing his intention to strive for enlightenment and help others in specific ways. In the eighteenth vow, Amitabha promised to establish a heavenly region—the "Pure Land" or "Western Paradise"—into which all beings who so desired could be reborn. No extraordinary effort would be required to earn rebirth in that land: admission would be free to all who had faith in Amitabha's compassionate power and made their desire for rebirth in his heaven known by thinking of him.

Followers of this school believe that suffering, old age, and death will be unknown in the Pure Land, as opposed to the land of suffering that is the world. There will be food, drink, and music for all, and the buddha's followers will be so uplifted by his merit that their progress toward nirvana will be easy. This notion of the "Pure Land" marked a transformation in the Buddhist idea of heaven. In early Buddhism, meritorious individuals could hope to be reborn in a paradise, but they would be unable to "make" new merit or develop their higher wisdom while there. In other words, there was no path leading from heaven to nirvana: once the inhabitants' store of merit was exhausted, they would have to be reborn in human form to make more. But for those in the Pure Land, rebirth on earth will no longer be necessary.

The *Smaller Sutra on the Pure Land* spells out what is required to benefit from Amitabha's store of merit. Those who have remembered and repeated his name before death will be reborn in his Pure Land. This rebirth cannot be earned by any meritorious works: it is a gift made available through the infinite merits of Amitabha.

A third early Pure Land text, the *Meditation on Amitayus Sutra*, offers detailed instruction in vision meditation. But for those unable to undertake the rigorous training required to achieve a vision, it also offers an easier path. Even the meritless or wicked could gain rebirth in the Pure Land through sincere repetition of the sacred formula "Homage to Amitabha Buddha."

The Pure Land school introduced a path to salvation based solely on faith. There is no equivalent in the Theravada tradition. The *Smaller Sutra on the Pure Land* teaches that the only condition for rebirth in the Pure Land is faith in Amitabha's infinite compassion, shown through prayerful repetition of his name. This reliance on an external or "other" power stands in sharp contrast to the self-reliance emphasized in early Buddhism. Over the centuries that followed, Pure Land spread from India to China, Korea, and Japan, becoming the most popular of all Buddhist schools in East Asia.

The monk Honin and his disciple Shinran (1173–1262) underlined the need for the "other power" of Amida's grace in a "degenerate" age when Buddhist dharma was thought to be in decline. Condemning the magical and syncretic tendencies that he saw in other schools, Shinran taught the *nembutsu*, a chant praising the name of Amida Buddha, as an act of faith and thanksgiving.

Both Honen and Shinran faced opposition from rival schools and were exiled by the authorities, but they found wide support among the people. Shinran founded a new sect called "True Pure Land" (Jodo Shinsu) or Shin Buddhism. He also did something revolutionary: he chose to marry, maintaining that husband and wife are to each other as the bodhisattva Kannon (Avalokiteshvara) is to the believer. In so doing he laicized Buddhism. Although this break with the tradition of monastic celibacy was widely opposed, today most Buddhist priests in Japan are married, and temples are usually passed down through their families; the oldest son is typically expected to train for the priesthood so that he can continue the family tradition.

Chan (Zen) Buddhism

The founder of Chan Buddhism (better known in the West by its Japanese name, Zen) was Bodhidharma—the same sixth-century Indian monk who told King Wu that all his good works had earned him no merit at all. In sharp contrast to the Pure Land sect's emphasis on "other

Document

Pure Land Buddhism: Honen's Testament

In this passage Honen explains that the faithful repetition of homage to Amida Buddha, rather than more complex Buddhist practices, is sufficient for birth in Amida's Pure Land.

The method of final salvation that I have propounded is neither a sort of meditation, such as has been practiced by many scholars in China or Japan, nor is it a repetition of the Buddha's name by those who have studied and understood the deep meaning of it. It is nothing but the mere repetition of the "Namu Amida Butsu," without a doubt of his mercy, whereby one may be born into the Land of Perfect Bliss. The mere repetition with firm faith includes all the practical details, such as the three-fold preparation of mind and the four primordial truths. If I as an individual had any doctrine more profound than this, I should . . . be left out of the Vow of the Amida Buddha. (Tsunoda 1958: 208)

power," Chan emphasized "self-power" and the attainment of personal enlightenment through rigorous practice of meditation. Although there is no surviving evidence that a similar school existed in India, Chan tradition traces Bodhidharma's lineage to the Buddha's disciple Kashyapa, whose intuitive insight is celebrated in the story of the "flower sermon" (see Focus box).

The Chinese pronunciation of the word *dhyana* was *chan*—hence the name of the school that Bodhidharma founded in China, centered in what he called a "mind to mind, direct transmission" of enlightenment, with "no dependence on words." Just as the Buddha relied on a single enigmatic gesture to deliver his "flower sermon," so Bodhidharma and later Chan masters used surprising, shocking, paradoxical, or even violent actions to bring about the state of mind best known in the West by the Japanese term *satori*. One master is said to have twisted a disciple's nose so hard that the pain and indignity led to a breakthrough. Another is said to have shoved his disciple into a thorn bush, with the same result. Another apparently simply held up a finger. Many made impossible demands on their students, including the master who held up one hand and demanded to be told what sound it made; this was the origin of the familiar Zen **koan** "What is the sound of one hand clapping?" One master would instruct his disciples to imagine hanging by their teeth from a branch suspended over some danger and then being asked a question that demands a response—for example, "Do all persons have Buddha-nature?" If the disciple correctly answers, "Yes," he will fall and die. But if he refuses to answer, he will seem to communicate an untruth. The master demands to know: "What would you do?" Since there is no logical way out of this dilemma, the correct answer must be found in some place other than the rational mind.

In the early sixth century, Bodhidharma took this school of thought to China and settled into a cave in the mountains above the village of Shaolin. His teaching is summed up in these four lines attributed to him: "A special transmission outside of doctrines. Not setting up the written word as an authority. Pointing directly at the human heart. Seeing one's nature and becoming a buddha" (Robinson 1959: 332). These lines put into words Kashyapa's "flower sermon" experience of the transmission of enlightened consciousness by direct contact between master and disciple, without textual or doctrinal study.

Because of its distaste for book learning, Chan became known for its transmission of enlightenment "outside the scriptures," independent of "words or letters." The special Chan state of consciousness is transmitted only "from mind to mind"—from master to disciple—without the

Focus

The Flower Sermon

This story begins with the disciples asking Shakyamuni for a dharma talk. He agrees, and as he takes his seat on the teaching throne, all grow silent, eagerly waiting to hear his words. Instead of speaking, however, Shakyamuni simply holds up a white lotus flower.

All are dumbfounded except for Kashyapa, who in that moment experiences an intuitive flash of enlightenment. The Buddha acknowledges his understanding with a smile, and Kashyapa becomes the first patriarch in a lineage that stresses the achievement of the state of mind called *dhyana* in Sanskrit: the state reached by the young Shakyamuni while meditating under the rose-apple tree.

Dozens of elementary and high schools in the town of Shaolin combine academic studies in the morning with martial arts training in the afternoon. Although most of the schools are Buddhist in orientation, two are Muslim; there are also some schools for girls, although the majority are male-only. The best students from each age group perform hourly for tourists, as in this photo (© VISUM Foto GmbH/Alamy).

intervention of rational argumentation. It advocates the "absence of thoughts" to free the mind from external influences.

In the late seventh century, a young boy from southern China named Huineng arrived at the Shaolin monastery seeking admission as a novice. He was not accepted, perhaps because he spoke a different dialect, but he stayed to work in the kitchen. Huineng had made the journey because he had learned that the monastery taught a radical new form of Buddhism that offered the possibility of a direct breakthrough to a higher level of consciousness, without undue dependence on knowledge of scriptures or the performance of rituals. He understood the essence of Buddhism to involve an intuitive, mystical experience, the "direct pointing of the mind" that Bodhidharma had taught.

It was Huineng who spread Chan into southern China, from which it was eventually taken to Korea, where it is known as Seon, and Japan, where it is called Zen.

Zen Sects: Linji (Rinzai) and Caodong (Soto)

There are two main Zen sects, Linji (Rinzai in Japan) and Caodong (Soto in Japan). The first is named after Linji, a ninth-century Chan monk who is said to have entered training as a shy young boy. After training diligently for more than a year, he was permitted to meet with the master,

Document

Chan Buddhism

The Platform Sutra *is attributed to Huineng and was compiled by one of his disciples in the early 700s.*

Meditation and Wisdom

Good friends, how then are meditation and wisdom alike? They are like the lamp and the light it gives forth. If there is a lamp there is light; if there is no lamp there is no light. The lamp is the substance of light; the light is the function of the lamp. Thus, although they have two names, in substance they are not two. Meditation and wisdom are like this. (*The Platform Sutra of the Sixth Patriarch*, sec. 15; Yampolsky 1976: 137)

On Saving Oneself

Good friends, when I say "I vow to save all sentient beings everywhere," it is not that I will save you, but that sentient beings, each with their own natures, must save themselves. What is meant by "saving yourselves with your own natures"? Despite heterodox views, passions, ignorance, and delusions, in your own physical bodies you have in yourselves the attributes of inherent enlightenment, so that with correct views you can be saved. (*The Platform Sutra of the Sixth Patriarch*, sec. 21; Yampolsky 1976: 143)

Huangbo. When the master asked why he had come, Linji humbly requested instruction in enlightenment, whereupon the master hit him hard with his stick.

When Linji told his teacher what had happened, he was advised to try again, which led to a second beating. After three such beatings Linji concluded that he was not worthy. The master granted his request to leave but asked that he first visit an old hermit monk who lived farther up the mountain. After hearing Linji describe what had happened, the hermit exclaimed, "Poor old Huangbo, he must have nearly exhausted himself hitting you!" This lack of sympathy so shocked and angered Linji that he experienced a breakthrough and burst out laughing. "Why the sudden change?" demanded the hermit. "There's not so much to old Huangbo's Zen after all" was the reply. On returning to Huangbo, Linji threatened to hit the master with his own stick. "Just get back to your training," said the master.

When Huangbo died, Linji succeeded him as master and gave his name to a new ordination lineage that emphasized exactly the kind of "sudden enlightenment," or *satori*, that he had experienced in response to Huangbo's apparently irrational behavior. Later Linji/Rinzai masters continued to find that they could stimulate a breakthrough to Chan (Zen) consciousness by delivering unexpected blows and shouts or otherwise confounding their pupils.

At the center of this approach is the koan: a paradoxical anecdote that is specifically designed to defy rational understanding and force the student out of the reason- or word-centered state of mind into a more intuitive, body-centered mode. The typical koan retells an incident in which, by doing something unexpected, a master sparked an enlightenment experience in his student. The point of the retelling is to evoke the same experience in successive generations of disciples (see Practice box).

Practice

Koan Training

The first koan presented to Zen disciples is known as "Joshu's *Mu*." In this story the ancient master Joshu and a disciple are walking through the monastery grounds and see one of the stray dogs that lives there. The disciple asks Joshu, "Does a dog have buddha-nature?" Joshu replies, "*Mu*" ("no"; *wu* in the Chinese original). There are many layers to this reply. We might think that the standard Buddhist answer to this question would be "yes," since all living beings have buddha-nature. Yet Joshu answers with a word that seems to deny that fundamental doctrine. The key to this paradox lies in the fact that *mu*, "no," is the very word used in

Buddhism to express emptiness, the "nothingness" state of mind that characterizes the buddha mind. Thus Joshu's negation is in reality an affirmation.

The correct response to the koan lies not in a rational answer to the master's question but in the experience of breaking through the confines of the rational mind to a new level of consciousness. It is the master's task to reject all false responses to the koan until the breakthrough is achieved. Disciples must report to the master regularly to respond to the assigned koan and may be hit or shouted at if their "answers" are inadequate. Mastering one's first koan can take years.

The second Zen sect, Caodong/Soto, seeks "gradual enlightenment" through long hours of *zazen* (sitting meditation). Both sects use koans and *zazen*, so the differences between them lie mainly in their emphasis, with Linji/Rinzai relying more on koans and Caodong/Soto on *zazen*.

The practice of meditation is particularly intense in the Soto Zen school. Typically, after half an hour of *zazen*, during which attention is focused on breathing, a bell is rung to signal that it is time to rise and practice walking meditation—focused on the slow lifting of the feet high off the ground—for a similar length of time. Then another bell signals a return to *zazen*.

Mahayana Holidays

In Mahayana countries, the Buddha's birth, enlightenment, and *parinirvana* are remembered on separate days, determined by the lunar calendar. Festivals honoring other buddhas and bodhisattvas are also observed, especially Guanyin's birthday. Different sects also celebrate the anniversaries of their patriarchs (e.g., Nichiren in Japan).

Under the influence of the ancestor cults of China and Japan, the dead are honored by an "all souls' day." In China this day is celebrated by burning paper boats to free "hungry ghosts" who have perished in violence. At the Japanese feast called Obon, two altars are built, one for offerings to the dead ancestors and the other for the "ghosts." Traditionally, Chinese Buddhists avoided nonessential outside activity during the "ghosts'" month, to lessen the risk of a ghostly encounter.

Buddhism has also adopted local customs surrounding occasions such as the beginning of the new year. In China pilgrimages are made to four sacred mountains, each dedicated to a different bodhisattva. In Japan the temple gong is struck 108 times on New Year's Eve, symbolizing forgiveness of the 108 kinds of bad deeds.

Mount Putuo, off the southern coast of China, is one of the four mountains that Chinese Buddhists hold most sacred, each of which is associated with a particular bodhisattva. Putuo is dedicated to Guanyin, and it includes a temple and a huge Guanyin statue (Sanguis1973/Dreamstime.com/GetStock).

⊕ Vajrayana: The Third Vehicle

"Vajrayana"—from *vajra*, meaning both "diamond" and "thunderbolt"—is just one of several names for the third vehicle of Buddhism. The diamond image suggests something so hard that it cannot be broken or split, while the thunderbolt suggests a very particular kind of power, although its symbolism is not physical or astronomical. The thunderbolt remains a central symbol in the principal Vajrayana school today, Tibetan Buddhism.

Followers of Vajrayana refer to it as the "third turning of the wheel of dharma," the culmination of the two earlier vehicles, Theravada and Mahayana. This is exemplified in a system of Vajrayana training that takes place in three stages named after the three vehicles. In the "Hinayana" phase (corresponding to Theravada), beginners concentrate on basic moral discipline. In the "Mahayana" stage, they receive instruction in basic Mahayana doctrines. And in the third and highest stage, the Vajrayana, they learn the doctrines and practices that Vajrayana itself considers the most advanced.

The view of Vajrayana as the third turning of the wheel also makes sense in historical terms, for it is the most recent vehicle. Emerging in India during or after the third century, it spread to

Practice

Mantras

Vajrayana incorporates numerous elements that originated in India, in both Hindu and Buddhist practice, but in many cases gives them its own emphasis. An example is its use of mantras, sacred syllables or phrases thought to evoke great spiritual blessings when properly spoken or chanted. Although mantras are also central to the Pure Land ("Homage to Amida Buddha") and Nichiren ("Homage to the *Lotus Sutra*") schools, the Vajrayana (also known as Mantrayana) tradition puts an emphasis on sound that recalls the ancient brahminic idea that the priests' chanting of the ritual formulas in itself has a particular acoustic efficacy.

The best-known Vajrayana mantra is the Sanskrit phrase *Om mani padme hum*. *Mani* means "jewel" and *padme* "lotus," while *om* and *hum* are not words but sacred syllables. In English we might say, "O the jewel in the lotus" or simply "Om jewel lotus hum." But the phrase can be interpreted in several ways. Some Vajrayana practitioners see the jewel and lotus as symbolic of the male and female principles, and understand their union to represent the harmony of the cosmic forces. Others believe that the phrase refers to the bodhisattva Avalokiteshvara in feminine form as the "jeweled-lotus lady." Some think that its six syllables refer to six realms of rebirth or six spiritual perfections. Whatever the interpretation, the mantra evokes a cosmic harmony.

Mantras need not be spoken to be effective; they can also be written on banners or slips of paper and hung on trees or lines, or rotated in cylindrical containers called prayer wheels. The repetition achieved through rotation is thought to provide additional benefit.

virtually all parts of the Buddhist world, although it disappeared from Southeast Asia centuries ago and in East Asia assumed a minor role in relation to the more popular Mahayana schools. Where Vajrayana became the majority religion was in the region of Nepal and Bhutan, and across the Himalayas in Tibet and Mongolia. Hence some refer to Vajrayana as "northern" Buddhism—northern from the point of view of the Ganges region where Buddhism first developed (from that perspective, Theravada is "southern" and Mahayana "eastern").

Vajrayana Practice

Tantras

Another Indian tradition that Vajrayana incorporated is tantrism. "Tantric" Buddhism, like Hindu tantrism, envisions cosmic reality as the interplay of male and female forces and teaches a set of practical techniques for tapping into the spiritual energy produced by that interplay. The image of a male figure in sexual embrace with his female consort is common in Vajrayana art. Known in Tibetan as the *yab–yum* (father–mother), this union of male and female symbolizes the coming together of the complementary elements essential to enlightenment, such as compassion and wisdom.

Given the centrality of sexual union to tantric Buddhism, some tantric texts suggest that since the world is bound by lust, it must be released by lust as well. While the "right-hand" school

The eyes of the Swayambhunath Buddha survey the Kathmandu Valley in all four directions. The Nepali script for the number one, symbolizing unity, forms the "nose" (© Tuul/Hemis/Corbis).

understood this principle symbolically, the "left-hand" school interpreted it more literally, practicing ritual unions in which the man and woman visualized themselves as divine beings. It was thought that such practices, properly undertaken according to tantra texts, would defeat lust and transcend it.

The Vajrayana tantras classify the many buddhas and bodhisattvas in various families, which are often depicted in a sacred geometric design called a **mandala**. The "head" of the family occupies the center of the design and is surrounded by the other members, each of whom occupies a specific position.

Practitioners meditate on their chosen buddhas or bodhisattvas in order to achieve visions that will help them along the path to enlightenment. The Vajrayana guru initiates the disciple into the symbolic meanings of the various members of the family and their relationships, as well as the rituals required to develop inner wisdom.

Having built up a visualization, practitioners begin to identify with their chosen figures and tap into their energies. Visualizing themselves as identical with them, practitioners become aware of the centers of power ("chakras") in their own bodies and may perceive themselves to be at the center of a sacred space defined by a mandala. At the culmination of this process of gradual enlightenment, initiates aspire to dissolve slowly into emptiness, liberated from ego attachment.

A classic mandala pattern reflects tantric Buddhism's emphasis on the *Mahavairocana* ("Great Sun") *Sutra*. In this pattern, the mandala centers on Mahavairocana, surrounded by the buddhas of the four directions: Aksobhya in the east, Amida in the west, Amoghasiddhi in the north, and Ratnasambhava in the south, all of whom together represent the various emanations of buddha-hood itself. It is also characteristic of tantric Buddhism to give female counterparts not only to the buddhas but to the bodhisattvas who accompany them; thus, mandalas often include numerous figures.

These deities have dual aspects, pacific and angry, depending on their functions (e.g., to assist in beneficial activities or to repel evil forces). The union of wisdom and compassion, considered the key to enlightenment, is represented by the father–mother image evoked by the embrace of deities and their consorts.

Vajrayana in East Asia

Introduced to China in the eighth century under the name Zhenyan ("true word" or "mantra"), tantric Buddhism enjoyed only a brief period of popularity there, but in 806, a Japanese monk who had been studying in China introduced it to his homeland, where it flourished under the name Shingon. Shingon Buddhists practice a "right-handed" tantrism and believe that enlightenment comes with the realization that one's own Buddha-nature is identical with the Great Sun Buddha, Mahavairocana, and can be achieved in this life.

Monks from Tibet paint a mandala in sand as part of a ritual performed while visiting Mexico in 2016. (AGCuesta/ Shutterstock)

Zhenyan was transmitted to Korea in the same period. Known there as Milgyo, it maintained a distinctive identity until the fourteenth century, when it was amalgamated with Mahayana schools.

Vajrayana in Tibet

Shakyamuni was born in the foothills of the Himalayas and converted his home region (now part of Nepal) a few years after his enlightenment. But the high Himalayan plateau was so difficult to reach that Buddhism made little headway there for the first 1,200 years of its history. It was not until the late eighth century that a few Buddhist missionaries found their way there at the invitation of Tibetan kings.

Vajrayana is said to have been established in Tibet by a *bhikshu* named Padmasambhava, who combined instruction in dharma with magic involving the world of the spirits. Revered as Guru Rinpoche ("precious teacher"), Padmasambhava is particularly identified with a school of Tibetan Buddhism known as the Nyingma ("ancient"), which traces its origins to his time.

Tibetan Buddhism is divided among three main ordination lineages or orders. The best known, the Gelugpa, was founded by the reformer Tsongkhapa (1357–1419). On ceremonial occasions, members of this order wear large yellow hats, whereas the Kargyu and Karma-pa orders wear red and black hats, respectively.

The Tibetan Book of the Dead

A unique feature of Tibetan Buddhism is the text called the *Bardo Thodol*, better known as *The Tibetan Book of the Dead*. A set of written instructions concerning the afterlife, the *Bardo Thodol* was to be read aloud to the dying in order to help them achieve liberation during the three stages of the *bardo* state between death and rebirth.

During the first stage the dying person loses consciousness, experiences a transitional time of darkness, and then emerges into a world filled with objects unknown on the earthly plane. A brilliant light then appears. If the person recognizes the light as the Dharma Body of Buddha, he or she will attain liberation and experience nirvana rather than rebirth. More often, however, bad karma prevents people from recognizing the true nature of the light, and instead they turn away in fear. Thus most people then pass on to a second *bardo* stage, in which some consciousness is regained. One may be aware of one's own funeral, for example. Peaceful deities appear for seven days, then wrathful deities appear for seven more days. These are all the Buddha in the Body of Bliss form, and those who meditate on them as such will experience liberation. Those who do not recognize them will gradually assume a new bodily form within a few weeks of death. Liberation is possible right up to the moment of rebirth, but karma keeps most people in the grip of *samsara*, the wheel of death and rebirth. In the third stage the individual's karma is judged and the appropriate rebirth is determined.

The Office of the Dalai Lama

To understand the office of the Dalai **Lama** and the controversial Chinese claim that Tibet is a part of China, we need to understand the historic relationship between Tibet and the Mongols. As the rulers of China from 1222 to 1368, the Mongols did not invade Tibet, but they appointed the head of the Shakya monastery there to serve as their viceroy for the region. Some two centuries later, a Gelugpa missionary named Sonam Gyatso (1543–1588) went to Mongolia and converted

Buddhist nuns during morning chanting service in Lhasa, Tibet (© Tom Salyer/Alamy).

its ruler, Altan Khan, who created the title Dalai Lama ("Ocean of Wisdom") and bestowed it posthumously on Gyatso's two predecessors, designating Gyatso the third in the succession. With the sponsorship of the Mongol princes, the Gelugpas soon became the dominant sect in both Mongolia and Tibet.

The first Dalai Lama to become the temporal as well as the spiritual leader of Tibet was the fifth, Ngawang Lobsang Gyatso (1617–1682). With Mongol aid he subdued the challenge of the rival Karma-pa lineage and constructed the famous Potala Palace in Lhasa. He recognized his teacher, Lobsang Chogye Gyaltsen (1569–1662), as an incarnation of Amida Buddha and gave him the title Panchen Lama. The position still exists but has become controversial because the Dalai Lama and the Chinese government disagree on the identity of the legitimate Panchen Lama.

The fifth Dalai Lama also established diplomatic relations with the Manchu (Qing) dynasty, which came to power in China in 1644. As a result, Tibet became embroiled in the eighteenth-century rivalry between the Manchus in Beijing and the Oirots of Mongolia, and it eventually was made a Manchu protectorate. Those old Tibetan ties with Mongolia and China are the basis of modern China's claim to Tibet. The former Tibet is now divided into three Chinese provinces known collectively as the Tibetan Autonomous Region, or TAR.

Considered to be a manifestation of the bodhisattva Avalokiteshvara, each Dalai Lama is said to be the reincarnation of the previous one. When a Dalai Lama dies, a search is undertaken to

Focus

The Fourteenth Dalai Lama

Born: July 6, 1935, in a peasant farming village northeast of Lhasa. His name was Lhamo Thondup.

Signs: After the death of the thirteenth Dalai Lama in 1933, the head of his corpse turned to the northeast, and a senior monk had a vision that included a monastery and a house with a distinctive guttering. When the search party found the house in 1938, the three-year-old boy who lived there called one member of the party by name and picked out toys and other objects that had been loved by the thirteenth Dalai Lama. He was then taken from his family to the monastery to begin training.

Instruction: After 18 months the boy was reunited with his family, who moved with him to Lhasa. In 1940 he was ordained as a novice and installed as the spiritual leader of Tibet. A long course of Buddhist studies followed.

High Office: An earthquake and threats of invasion from China prompted his installation as the political leader of Tibet in 1950, at age 15.

Exile: By 1959 the Chinese had taken over Tibet. To avoid arrest or worse, the Dalai Lama crossed the Himalayas to Dharamsala in northern India. From there he led the Tibetan government in exile until 2011, when he officially turned over the leadership to Lobsang Sangay, a Harvard-trained legal scholar. This brought to an end the tradition of joint religious and political leadership that had begun in the seventeenth century.

Writings: The Dalai Lama has written numerous books on Tibetan Buddhism, meditation, and philosophy, as well as an autobiography, *Freedom in Exile*.

Politics: The Dalai Lama continues to use nonviolent means to advocate for the well-being of the Tibetan people. Negotiations with the Chinese government have so far not been fruitful. It remains to be seen whether his formal renunciation of political power will ease the tensions with China.

find a boy who shows intellectual qualities and personality characteristics similar to those of the deceased; then various objects are presented to him to see if he chooses those that were the prior Lama's favorites. Finally, the state oracle enters a trance to contact the spirits who must confirm the selection. The fourteenth and current Dalai Lama, Tenzin Gyatso, was chosen in this way from a family of Tibetan descent living in China. A senior monk's vision played a key role in locating the boy.

⊕ Interaction and Adaptation in East Asia

China

Chinese converts interpreted a number of Buddhist ideas in ways that harmonized them with Indigenous teachings (see Chapter 11, "Chinese and Korean Traditions"). The Buddhist concept of rebirth on a higher or lower level of life was combined with the Chinese concepts of retribution for good and evil and the existence of a home after death with the ancestors to produce a system of many-layered heavens and hells, with a variety of savior figures, including Guanyin and the bodhisattva Dizang, who could relieve the suffering of those reborn in hell. The scripture *Yulanpenjing* tells of a monk named Mulian, who after his enlightenment sought to rescue his mother from hell. This Buddhist expression of filial piety was the basis for the "All Souls' Day" celebrated on the fifteenth day of the seventh month in China, Korea, and Japan, where it is known as Obon.

Nevertheless, Buddhist monasticism was deeply alien to a social system based on kinship and veneration of ancestors. The practice of celibacy put the family lineage in jeopardy, and Chinese society looked down on those who did not work to support themselves. Thus Chinese monks eventually started to grow their own food. As a Chinese Zen master proclaimed, "A day without work is a day without eating."

At the same time, imperial officials saw Buddhism as a direct threat to the state's authority. In 845, the Chinese state launched a campaign of persecution against Buddhism that, according to a report prepared for the emperor, led to the destruction of more than 40,000 temples and the laicization of 260,500 monks and nuns.

Folk Buddhism and the Milo Cult

The image of the "friendly" bodhisattva Maitreya underwent a transformation in China not unlike that of the Indian Avalokiteshvara into the Chinese Guanyin. Before the seventh century, Maitreya had been a heroic figure, and he has more than once been the focus of political rebellions in China, including the one that led to the founding of the Ming dynasty in 1368. In the fifteenth century, however, he began to appear as Milo, a laughing monk with a potbelly who would travel from village to village, putting interesting objects into his hemp bag and then giving them out to children, like Santa Claus. With his happy-go-lucky nature (*maitri* means "friendly" in Sanskrit), his large belly, and his affinity for children, the "Happy Buddha" reflects the importance that Chinese culture attached both to children and to worldly prosperity.

Korea

Physical proximity created close links between China and Korea. The Han dynasty conquered the northern part of the peninsula in the late second century BCE, and Buddhism was introduced roughly two centuries later, spreading from the northern kingdom of Goguryeo first to Baekche in the southwest and then to Silla in the southeast. It became most influential after Silla conquered the two other kingdoms and united the country in 668.

The new religion expanded on an unprecedented scale during the Silla period, which lasted until 935. Among the major schools of Buddhism introduced from China were the Theravada tradition of the *vinaya* (monastic discipline) and the Faxiang (Yogacara) school, which eventually developed into a syncretic tradition. The most influential school, however, was Chan ("Seon" in Korea), introduced in the early seventh century. Nine Seon monasteries, known as the Nine Mountains, were eventually established.

In the late twelfth century, a monk named Chinul united the various schools to create the Jogye sect, which became the orthodox form of Buddhism in Korea. Nevertheless, Buddhist influence withered for several centuries after Confucianism was adopted as Korea's state ideology in the 1400s. To facilitate state control, Confucian scholars petitioned the court to restrict the number of

Buddhist temples, supervise the selection of monks, and reorganize the ecclesiastical system while reducing the number of sects allowed to practice. Accordingly, temple properties were confiscated, the serfs attached to monasteries were drafted into the army, and Buddhist monks were banned from Seoul, the capital. Chapter 11 has more detail about Buddhism in China and Korea.

Japan

Buddhism reached Japan from Korea in the sixth century—almost 900 years after Shakyamuni's time. Along the way, it had been transformed. A turning point in its adoption was the warm reception it received from the regent, "Prince" Shotoku, who welcomed it (and Confucianism) for its civilizing effects and in 604 issued the "Seventeen-Article Constitution," a set of moral guidelines for the ruling class that urged reverence for the Three Gems. How Buddhism developed in Japan is explored in detail in Chapter 12.

⊕ Cultural Expressions

Stupas and Pagodas

After the Buddha's *parinirvana*, several kings requested the honor of enshrining his cremated remains in their kingdoms. Accordingly, the remains were divided into seven portions. The urn that had held them and the cloth that had covered it were also given the status of primary relics, and so nine memorials were built in total. Then, as Buddhism spread, additional memorials were built over other sacred objects, including the remains of major disciples and portions of scriptures.

When asked before his death how he ought to be buried, the Buddha had said that a Tathagata's remains should be enshrined in a memorial stupa like that of a great ruler. Thus each portion of his remains was placed in a small casket, richly decorated with jewels, and interred in an aboveground crypt, which was covered with a large earth mound, faced with bricks, and then plastered and whitewashed. Finally, a pole was erected over the mound to represent Mount Meru, a cosmic mountain that in Indian mythology reaches from earth toward the pole star, and around whose axis the world is thought to turn. There are several terms for these memorial mounds, including the Sanskrit *stupa* and its Pali equivalent, *thupa*. The term used throughout East Asia is **pagoda**, which derives from the Sanskrit *dagoba* and connotes "womb" in the sense that burial is the forerunner of a rebirth. Whatever the local term, there are stupas on the grounds of nearly every Buddhist temple in the world, and it is the custom for devotees to circumambulate them (always in a clockwise direction, with the right side of the body facing the holy structure).

The shape of the stupa or pagoda underwent changes through the centuries. In East Asia, the pagoda developed into an elegant stone or wooden tower with either five or seven stories representing the levels of the heavens symbolized by the wooden disks of the original Indian stupas; thus, pagoda architecture made the "heavenly section" of the original stupa the dominant part of the structure.

Temples

Buddhist monasteries grew out of the simple refuges—usually a collection of thatched huts—in which early monks lived during the rainy season, when they settled down for a period of intense study and meditation. Wealthy devotees could earn merit by paying for the construction of permanent buildings, and so over time a temple complex consisting of living quarters, a small shrine, and a meeting hall often took shape. Eventually, to accommodate lay worshipers, the shrine would develop into a large temple housing images of the Buddha. Today, besides the stupa and temple, the grounds of such sites usually contain a Bodhi tree, dharma hall, monastery, library, and refectory.

Early cave temples carved in stone were clearly modeled after the simple huts of the early sangha. By the Gupta period (c. 320–540), Buddhist temples had taken on the rectangular shape and other architectural features of Hindu temples of the time. In some regions cliffside cave complexes were developed that included all the essentials of a temple complex, including separate caves for shrines, living areas, and even large dharma halls. In China, the rectangular wooden buddha hall reflected the influence of the tile-roofed imperial hall of state, with the buddha statue enshrined in the posture of an emperor. This style was the one that made its way to Japan, where the best-known example, the Todaiji temple in Nara, houses a bronze image of the cosmic buddha Vairocana more than 52 feet high.

Images of the Buddha

The first images of the Buddha date from the first century CE, a time when the devotional aspects of Mahayana Buddhism were becoming increasingly popular. Until then, it was apparently assumed that no physical form could or should depict him. Instead, the Buddha and his teaching were symbolized by the stupa and symbols such as his footprint, the Wheel of the Law, the Bodhi tree, or an empty seat. Early statues and reliefs show the Buddha standing, seated either with dangling legs or in the lotus position of yogic meditation, or reclining at the moment of the *parinirvana*.

Hand gestures, or **mudras**, similar to those found in Hindu portrayals of deities, became an important feature of Buddhist art. Buddhist iconography also includes the 32 major signs of Shakyamuni's status, the most obvious of which are the *usnisa* (the protuberance on the top of his head that was supposed to be the locus of his supernatural wisdom) and elongated earlobes. Some art historians think that these features were associated with royalty (who were often depicted with elaborate hairstyles and earlobes stretched by heavy earrings), but Buddhists see them as signs of Shakyamuni's supernatural nature. Other signs include wheel images on the soles of his feet and fingers that are all the same length.

In China the Buddha is often depicted like an emperor surrounded by his court, seated in a serene posture and flanked by his disciples Kashyapa and Ananda. Often the bodhisattvas and stern-looking Arhats (*lohans* in Chinese) also appear nearby, while the four World Protectors stand guard.

Story Illustrations

Buddhist paintings and relief carvings often illustrate scenes from the life of the Buddha or the *Jataka* collections recounting Shakyamuni's previous lives. The walls of temples are often lined with such images, so that circumambulating visitors can see the story of the Buddha's life unfold.

As Buddhism spread, other cultures developed their own distinctive iconography. In China, images of Shakyamuni gradually took on a more Chinese appearance, and the figure of Guanyin developed into the graceful, standing feminine form now found throughout East Asia. There is a distinctive Korean representation of Maitreya as a pensive prince with one leg crossed over the other knee. This pose spread to Japan and can be seen in the famous wooden statue of Maitreya in Kyoto's Koryuji temple, which was founded in 622 for the repose of "Prince" Shotoku.

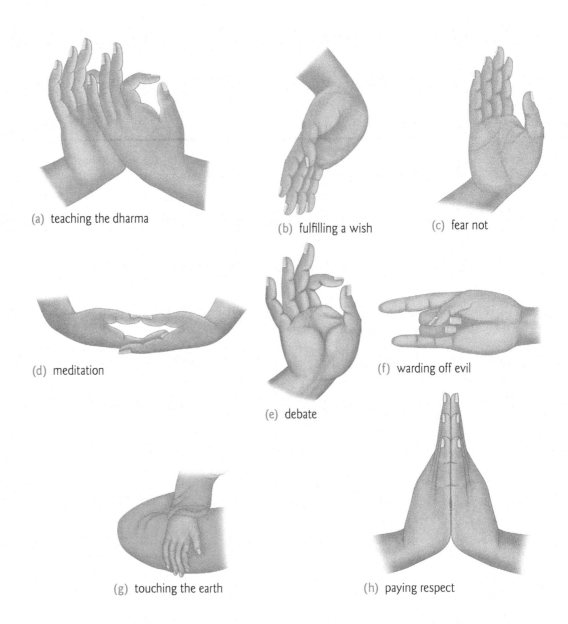

(a) teaching the dharma

(b) fulfilling a wish

(c) fear not

(d) meditation

(e) debate

(f) warding off evil

(g) touching the earth

(h) paying respect

Figure 10.1 Hand *Mudras*

Source: Adapted from www.buddhanet.net/mudras.htm

Zen Art and the Tea Ceremony

The highly ritualized tea ceremony was introduced by Zen monks and spread from monasteries to become one of the most familiar symbols of Japanese culture. The Zen influence is also reflected in the minimalism of Japanese painting, in which empty space plays a central role, and the raked-sand gardens (accented only by the occasional boulder) typically found in the courtyards of Zen temples. Another cultural expression of Zen values is the Japanese art of flower arranging, which originated in the practice of creating floral offerings for altars and special ceremonies.

⊕ Buddhism in the Modern World

India

Buddhism's intellectual and institutional influence within India lasted until the seventh century, but its royal support disappeared as Buddhist kings were replaced by Muslim rulers. A related factor may have been the loss of lay support as Hinduism absorbed a number of elements from Buddhism, including its ascetic dimension. Hindus understood the Buddha as an *avatara* of Vishnu: while some saw him in a positive light as a champion of nonviolence, others thought it was his role to attract insufficiently committed Hindus away from the "true" religion. Monasteries throughout India were abandoned or repurposed by other traditions, and some of the most famous Buddhist scholar-monks left for Tibet beginning in the eleventh century. As a result of this migration and the loss of lay adherents, Buddhism largely disappeared from India until the mid-twentieth century, although it did survive in a few eastern regions, as well as in Tibet, Nepal, Bhutan, Sikkim, and Assam.

B. R. Ambedkar and the Mass Conversion of Dalits

One catalyst for the revival of Buddhism in India was Dr. Bhimrao R. Ambedkar (1891–1956), the lead author of the Indian constitution. Although he was born into the **Dalit** (the "oppressed"

A mass conversion ceremony held in Mumbai in 2007 recalls the original mass conversion of Dalits to Buddhism under Ambedkar's leadership in 1956. The people in red robes are Tibetan monks and nuns, many of whom now reside in India (© AP Photo/Rajesh Nirgude, File).

class once known as "untouchables"), his intelligence led a brahmin teacher named Ambedkar to formally adopt him. With the help of that teacher and the local Muslim ruler, the young Ambedkar earned an undergraduate degree in India and eventually a doctorate from the London School of Economics. On his return to India he became an advocate for Dalit rights at a time when his older contemporary M. K. Gandhi was pursuing the same goal. The two disagreed, however, on the best way to achieve that goal.

Ambedkar blamed Hinduism for the discrimination that Dalits faced. Hindu leaders such as Gandhi hoped that Hinduism could be reformed to eliminate, or at least greatly reduce, that discrimination, but Ambedkar foresaw that entrenched social and economic interests would make substantial reform impossible. Setting out to find a religion that would not discriminate against his people, he recognized in Buddhism a form of spirituality that was compatible with Indian cultural values, but that from its origins had taught the equality of all humans, regardless of birth status.

The history of Buddhism supports Ambedkar's view. The Buddha accepted followers without any regard for their caste. Seniority in the sangha was based solely on date of ordination, and the names of early Buddhist leaders suggest that they came from all social classes.

In 1956, at a large rally in the city of Nagpur, in the heart of Hindu India, Ambedkar and his wife recited the Triple Refuge mantra and took the Five Precepts vow from a Buddhist monk, and thousands of Dalits followed their example. Since then, many more Dalits have converted to Buddhism.

Shakyamuni's critique of social inequity has also contributed to a growing appreciation of his place in Indian history. As noted previously, there was a time during the period of Buddhist–Hindu competition when Hindus thought of the Buddha as an *avatara* of Vishnu. That some modern Hindu scholars recognize the Buddha as an important and admirable figure in his own right marks a significant change.

Document

Ambedkar on Religion and Democracy

Here Dr. Ambedkar argues the necessity of fraternity for democracy.

What sustains equality and liberty is fellow-feeling. What the French Revolutionists called fraternity . . . [and] the Buddha called, Maitree [friendship or love]. Without Fraternity Liberty would destroy equality and equality would destroy liberty. If in Democracy liberty does not destroy equality and equality does not destroy liberty, it is because at the basis of both there is fraternity. . . .

In examining the possibilities of [democracy's] functioning successfully one must go to the Religion of the people and ask—does it teach fraternity or does it not? . . . If it does not, the chances are poor. . . . Why did Democracy not grow in India? . . . The answer is quite simple. The Hindu Religion does not teach fraternity. Instead it teaches division of society into classes or varnas and the maintenance of separate class consciousness. In such a system where is the room for democracy? (Ambedkar 2008: 270)

Theravada in Modern Sri Lanka

After the fifteenth century, Sri Lanka was colonized by the Portuguese, Dutch, and British in turn, all of whom promoted some form of Christianity. Buddhism declined in prestige but hung on, and in the late 1800s it received an important boost from the founders of the Theosophical Society, Helena P. Blavatsky and Henry S. Olcott. Sinhalese Buddhists have been active ever since in publishing English-language materials on Buddhism, and they remain loyal to the Theravada tradition despite the presence of largely Hindu India to the north and 500 years of Christian missionary efforts under colonial rulers.

Since independence in 1948, Buddhism has had considerable influence on the policies of Sri Lanka's ruling parties, which draw support from the Sinhalese majority. This has led to feelings of oppression among the Hindu minority, most of whom are descendants of South Indian Tamils who migrated to the island over the past two millennia. (The Sinhalese are thought to have come from North India.) Conflict between the government and Tamil separatists led to more than two decades of bloodshed, even though both Hinduism and Buddhism teach nonviolence. Although the civil war finally came to an end in 2009, relations between the two religious communities remain severely strained.

The Kandy Perahera features torchlit processions in which more than 100 elaborately costumed elephants are paraded through the streets. Musicians and dancers come from surrounding villages, each with its own distinctive attire and dance style (© M.A. PUSHPA KUMARA/epa/Corbis).

This conflict also sparked a resurgence of Buddhist fervor among the Sinhalese majority in reaction to perceived Muslim assertiveness, aggressive Christian missionary tactics, and a general erosion of traditional Buddhist values in the public sphere. Under the leadership of conservative monks and a supportive laity, a new political party known in English as the National Heritage Party, or JHU (Jathika Hela Urumaya), was founded in 2004. The founding monks broke with Buddhist tradition when they ran for public office without first disrobing and resuming lay status. Some other monks and Buddhist laity objected to this breach of traditional practice, but the JHU won enough support to gain nine seats in the 2004 parliamentary elections. The JHU advocates against "impious" practices such as alcohol consumption on Buddhist holidays and aggressive forms of Christian missionizing. It favors laws and practices protecting the environment and has been active in promoting forest protection, tree planting, and related measures.

Interview

Sulak Sivaraksa

Sulak Sivaraksa.

Sulak Sivaraksa is a Thai Buddhist activist known for his many efforts to bring Buddhist and spiritual solutions to modern problems. Known as Ajarn ("professor") Sulak, he is an influential social critic whose many recognitions include the Right Livelihood Award—sometimes referred to as the Nobel Prize equivalent for Buddhists.

Q: Ajarn Sulak, you are a leader in the activist movement called Engaged Buddhism. Tell us about that.

A: I started in my own country with Buddhists, then worked with Christians, Muslims, and agnostics. Later, I expanded to my neighboring countries. In making Buddhism more relevant for the contemporary world, it is important not to compromise on the essentials, such as the ethical precepts (*sila*). However, these ethical precepts need to be rethought in order to make sense of life in contemporary societies.

Q: What are some examples of Engaged Buddhist activities currently in Siam?

A: To follow the first Buddhist ethical precept, to refrain from killing living beings, is not so simple now. Do we allow our tax money to go for armaments? Do we keep ourselves separate from the political realm? Should we breed animals for consumption?

Our understanding of the second precept, to refrain from taking what is not ours, must also be extended. Do we allow the rich countries to exploit the poor countries through the workings of the international banking system and the international economic order? Do we allow industrial societies to exploit agrarian societies? The First World to exploit the Third World? The rich to exploit the poor generally?

Q: What Engaged Buddhist projects are ongoing in other countries?
A: A real highlight was to see and to build networks of friendships. Good friends are those who tell you what you don't want to hear. Some Buddhists, for example, the Japanese, are wonderful with funerals and with thinking of the next world, but they have no care for the present world. Now they care more for the present world, and I am happy for that. The Taiwanese Buddhists have begun to help the poor in Bangladesh and Cambodia. That's good, but not good enough. To help the poor is social welfare, but Buddhism demands social change. The First [Noble] Truth is the truth of suffering. You have to find out the course of suffering, and to overcome suffering nonviolently.

Also, in India, the Buddhists are the poorest of the poor. For 50 years, the Tibetan Buddhists have been in India, although they have never met those Indian Buddhists. I was the one to bring the Dalai Lama to meet the poor Buddhists. So he came four years ago to meet our Buddhist groups, and now the Buddhists in India are learning with the Tibetans, and are being helped.

Q: You have taken a strong stance against "consumerism." Why?
A: From the Buddhist point of view, the three root causes of suffering are greed, hatred, and delusion. Consumerism promotes greed. Greed now dominates global society, through advertising in the media and because transnational corporations are in control. It is linked with hatred and violence. Violence is on the whole controlled by politicians, [and

by] transnational corporations. Greed and hatred go together. People want more and more, and if they don't get it, violence takes place. But underneath everything is delusion.

We Buddhists should not simply preach. We should concretize it. That's why I keep saying consumerism is an expression of greed. Mainstream education never teaches people to know who they are. They don't teach how to breathe properly. If people are taught to breathe properly and mindfully, we can tackle greed, hatred, and delusion. That's why His Holiness the Dalai Lama is such an important example. He is a simple monk who gets up every morning, breathing properly. You can see his wisdom and compassion shining. We must learn from science too, and bring it together with wisdom and compassion. We must come together now to change ourselves and also change this world.

Q: Is there something within Theravada, or Buddhism as a whole, that you would like to see change?
A: Dr. Ambedkar (who led thousands of the Dalit "untouchable" people to Buddhism) was great because he emerged from beneath the four *varnas* [social classes]. Unless that system is tackled, India will remain un-liberated. [Over] 60 years after independence, the social structure is still awful. The suffering of India's poor carries on and on. This is why more and more so-called untouchable people become Buddhist. I say [to them], "You became Buddhists, that's great. But if you still hate the brahmins, that doesn't help. You must learn to cultivate compassion and wisdom, and how to change the social structure—rather than hating the Brahmin oppressor."

Q: Do you support the efforts made recently to restart the Theravada *bhikkhuni* sangha?
A: The absence of *bhikkhuni* [in Thailand] over the last century has led to the perception among many Thais that women are not meant to play a monastic role in life

Continued

other than being a lay follower, or becoming a Mae Ji or nun. Although a Mae Ji is higher than a layperson, their place within the monastic hierarchy tends to be seen as subservient to monks. Wat Songhammakalyan [a monastery] has differentiated itself from male-dominated monasteries in Thailand in that the *bhikkhuni* have developed a strong rapport with the communities around them, and an exemplary empathy and ability to address the needs of the local residents. The *bhikkhuni* directly engage the community, not just helping in their spiritual needs, but rendering assistance in many other ways, especially to the needy, sick, and infirmed. The *bhikkhuni* were there giving assistance when floods hit their community a couple of years ago.

This restricts women in the monastic hierarchy to only participating in activities of obtaining merit through collective rituals, and undertaking the housekeeping activities within a temple. Basically, they are there to serve the monks.

Q: What is the most important thing for non-Buddhists to know about or learn from Buddhist dharma?
A: The Ministry of Education unfortunately teaches people to climb up the social ladder—socially, economically, and politically. I think that for people to become clever without being good is very dangerous. The Ministry of Education cannot teach people to be good. Only spiritual, religious people can do this. Religious people can be too dogmatic and too churchy, and so you need the spiritual people to help. When I received the Right Livelihood Award in 1995, I used that money to start an education movement. It has done so much now for education. Education must linger in both the heart and the head. It must be meditative and include contemplation. You don't need to be Buddhist, or you don't need to be Christian. The idea is to be spiritual in the heart and the head. You have to expose yourself to suffering, and if you are middle class, you need to work with the poor.

The Buddha taught that men and women are equal, but we have oppressed women over the years. We now have women ordinations, but we are the only country to do so in mainland Southeast Asia. There are also women ordained by a man in Perth, Australia, but he was ostracized by his order. In Burma, they put the women in jail for being ordained. The monk who ordained the women was also shut out from his village and community. They are much more backwards than in my country. There are still very few women monks.

The most radical of the Sri Lankan Buddhist organizations is known as BBS, an acronym for the Bodu Bala Sena, which is usually translated as "Buddhist Power Force." The BBS was started by two Buddhist monks who broke away from the JHU in order to lead a more activist and militant protest against Islam and Christianity. The new movement held its organizational convention in 2012 and has since grown in influence and controversy.

Nevertheless, Sri Lankan Buddhism continues its rich intellectual and ritual life. The symbolic center of that life is the Temple of the Tooth in Kandy, where an eyetooth said to be a relic of Shakyamuni himself is enshrined. At the time of the Perahera festival, one of the miniature gold stupas that house the tooth is placed in a howdah on the back of an elephant and paraded through the streets of Kandy for several nights.

Theravada in Modern Southeast Asia

Theravada remains the most important vehicle across most of mainland Southeast Asia, though East Asian Mahayana traditions are dominant in Vietnam, Malaysia, and Singapore.

The end of Burmese kingship in the late nineteenth century, the years of British colonialism, and long periods of military rule since independence have severely weakened the Burmese sangha's traditional political influence. Its members have been cut off from significant contact with other Buddhist countries, and its temples have fallen into disrepair. Yet the *bhikshus* are still important in the traditional village-centered society, and the recent easing of military control offers some hope for renewal of Buddhist values.

One of the most well-known religious conflicts in recent years has occurred in Myanmar. The Rohingyas are an ethnic population who most likely migrated into Rakhine State in western Myanmar from the Bengal region now known as Bangladesh several generations ago. They share a religious culture with the Muslims of Bangladesh and speak a dialect related to Bengali. Even though their ancestors migrated to Myanmar long ago, the current government recognizes only those ethnic groups who were resident in Myanmar before it became a British colony. The ancestors of many of the current Rohingya residents were encouraged by the British to settle in Rakhine State during the period of British rule. Recently some Rohingya were issued white cards, rather than full citizenship papers, and in theory they were allowed to apply for full citizenship if they had documentation that their ancestors had immigrated before the British period. However, the Rohingyas are a poor, rural population, and many lacked the sufficient documentation papers even if they would have qualified. This left most in a stateless condition, being citizens of neither Myanmar nor modern Bangladesh. The Myanmar government calls them "Bengalis" rather than Rohingyas in an attempt to support its case that their true home is Bangladesh.

By 2016 the international media and human rights activists had become concerned that elements of the Myanmar military not only had been persecuting some Rohingyas for several years but may have begun a systematic plan to drive them from Myanmar. International attention to the group's plight increased when the prime minister of Bangladesh and several prominent international figures, including Nobel laureates, publicly lamented the miserable state of the Rohingya refugees. Media interviews with Rohingyas in Bangladeshi refugee camps revealed that elements of the Myanmar army were apparently behind the burning of Rohingya villages and the rape, torture, and murder of Rohingyas. The UN Human Rights Council subsequently established a commission of inquiry that denounced these actions as ethnic cleansing.

The flow of Rohingyas into Bangladesh's refugee camps increased in 2017. They brought with them stories of military helicopters hovering over their villages and shooting at them as they fled. The military or men from the local Buddhist population would then loot and set fire to the villages. Many refugees were children, and over 1,000 of them arrived without parents or relatives.

The majority of Myanmar's population is Theravada Buddhist, so the effort to drive out the Rohingyas was seen by some as a Buddhist attack on Islam. Ashin Wirathu, a Buddhist monk and leader of an organization of ultranationalist monks known as Ma Ba Tha, the Association for Race and Religion, emerged as the leader of the Buddhist movement to expel the Rohingyas. Ma Ba Tha has been active in providing various development and legal services to help the poor, so it has some support among moderate Buddhists despite its stance against Muslims in Myanmar. Wirathu was sentenced to a long prison term in 2003 for the crime of inciting hatred toward Muslims, but he was freed from prison in 2010 and resumed his verbal attacks. He claims to be against the Islamization of Myanmar rather than being against Islam itself. Wirathu also claims, contrary to many international news reports, that the Muslims started the conflict. His many followers, cultivated via public talks and social media, include hundreds of monks and even more lay Buddhists. Wirathu's talks are filled with claims of Muslim rape and mistreatment of Buddhists, which have incited some Buddhists to take revenge on Muslims.

Map 10.2 Rohingya Refugees

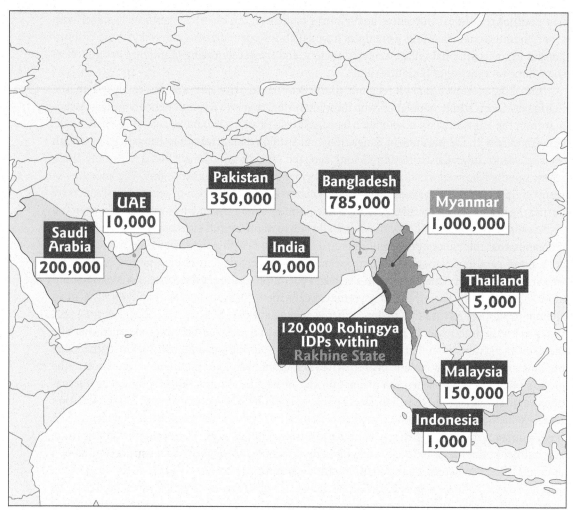

While the majority of the approximately 1 million Rohingya refugees from Myanmar have taken shelter in Bangladesh, at least seven other nations have accepted some Rohingya refugees. Numbers based on data from Al Jazeera and international agencies.

Source: Al Jazeera (http://sonna.so/en/?p=9943)

Some Rohingyas reacted to the persecution by organizing into militant resistance movements. Their defense efforts provided an excuse for Myanmar's military to burn more villages and drive out more Rohingyas. Several foreign Islamic organizations also called for a *jihad* against Myanmar.

The international community eventually accused Myanmar's government of the crime of ethnic cleansing, even as spokespersons for the government maintained that the military was only combating insurgencies. International attention came to focus on Aung San Suu Kyi, the de facto head of the government who holds the title of state counselor. Suu Kyi has been the leading figure of Myanmar's democracy movement since the student uprising known as 8888 because it began on August 8, 1988. Even though she led her National League for Democracy Party to a decisive electoral victory in 1990, she was kept under house arrest or severely restricted for decades until the recent "Road to Democracy," a plan to transition from military to more democratic rule, set the scene for new elections and brought her party into power in 2015.

For her peaceful defense of her people, Suu Kyi was awarded the Nobel Peace Prize in 1991. Muslims and the international community consequently expected her to denounce the actions of the military and Buddhist looters in regard to the Rohingyas, but she has not done so. Wirathu has bragged that Suu Kyi wants to end the expulsion of the Rohingyas, but that he has blocked such a move. Outsiders have expressed disappointment that she has not had the political strength to take a stand against the military, which holds the real power in the country. Some people have called upon the Nobel Committee to revoke her Nobel Peace Prize, and in 2018 the Canadian government revoked the honorary citizenship it previously bestowed on her.

In modern Cambodia, the overthrow of Prince Norodom Sihanouk (r. 1941–1955) meant the end of the Buddhist kingship ideal of a government that provides for the basic human needs of all citizens. Since then, the political influence of the Cambodian sangha has been limited. Under the communist regime of Pol Pot (r. 1975–1979) and the Khmer Rouge, many *bhikshus* were among the innocents slaughtered in the "killing fields." Yet by the late 1980s Khmer Rouge soldiers and *bhikshus* were working together on village projects. Today Buddhism continues to play its traditional role at the village level, most laypeople of all political stripes remain Buddhists, and all political factions appeal to Buddhist values to legitimate their claims to power.

In Thailand the tradition of monastic training for the king continues, and members of the royal family take part in rituals that symbolize the close ties between Buddhism and the monarchy. At the beginning of each season, the king changes the clothing on the Buddha image in the Temple of the Emerald Buddha and gives it a ceremonial bath.

In Laos—which has been under communist rule since the 1960s—Buddhism has lost the governmental support that it traditionally enjoyed. The traditional relationship of *bhikshus* and laity continues in the villages, however.

Finally, although Theravada has never gained a foothold in Vietnam, Theravada missionaries have recently had some success in Singapore and Malaysia, especially among English-speaking Chinese. Apparently some Mahayana Buddhists in Singapore have been attracted to Theravada as a purer form of the tradition than the Chinese schools that incorporated elements of Chinese folk religion. The Young Buddhist Association of Malaysia has been very active in encouraging dharma study.

Several reform movements are having an impact on Theravada Buddhism in the region today. Retreat centers have been established in Thailand in an effort to reintroduce the practice of meditation among laypeople, and the Thai intellectual Sulak Sivaraksa (see Interview box) has argued for a Buddhist vision of society in which the means of development are harnessed for the good of everyone rather than the profit of a few capitalists. He has founded several organizations dedicated to that goal, including the Asian Cultural Forum on Development and the International Network of Engaged Buddhists.

Mahayana in Vietnam

Theravada images and monastery foundations dating from before the ninth century have been found in Vietnam, but Chinese Mahayana traditions—notably Thien (from Chan) and Tinh-do (from Chinese Jingtu, "Pure Land")—have been dominant ever since then. Although Thien is largely a monastic tradition and Tinh-do mainly a lay movement, the two have influenced each other, and all Thien monasteries also teach Pure Land practices.

Twentieth-century efforts to reform Vietnamese Buddhism were interrupted by the Second World War. Then, in 1954, the country was divided into a communist North and an anticommunist South, with the Roman Catholic president of the latter, Ngo Dinh Diem (r. 1954–1963), imposing restrictions on Buddhists. It was in protest against these restrictions that, in May 1963, an elderly monk named Thich Quang Duc assumed the lotus position on a busy street in Saigon, had gasoline poured over him, and then calmly struck a match and became a human torch. A number of monks and nuns followed his example, attracting worldwide attention and contributing to the fall of the Diem government.

Self-sacrifice is an important theme in the thought of Thich Nhat Hanh (b. 1926), a Vietnamese monk who became not only a Thien (Chan–Zen) master but a poet and peace activist. In response to the atrocities of the Vietnam War, he developed what he called an "engaged Buddhism" to bring the resources of Buddhist wisdom to bear on contemporary conflicts. For him, the self-immolations of 1963 must be understood in the context of the Buddhist belief in the continuity of life beyond one human life span. He believes that changing the world requires that we first change our awareness, especially through meditation and the "art of mindful living." Commenting on the *Heart Sutra*, he says:

> If you are a poet, you will see clearly that there is a cloud floating in this sheet of paper. Without a cloud, there will be no rain; without rain, the trees cannot grow; and without trees, we cannot make paper. If we look even more deeply, we can see the sunshine, the logger who cut the tree, the wheat that became his bread, and the logger's father and mother. Without all of these things, this sheet of paper cannot exist. . . . Everything co-exists with this sheet of paper. So we can say that the cloud and the paper "inter-are." We cannot just be by ourselves alone; we have to inter-be with every other thing. (Nhat Hanh 1988: 3)

Buddhism in Modern China, Korea, and Japan

In the 1920s, while Chinese intellectuals were advocating greater openness to Western ideas, a Chan monk named Taixu ("Great Emptiness") called for both political and monastic reform, as well as a restatement of dharma in such a way as to speak to modern Chinese society. Like other Buddhist modernists, he believed that Buddhism should aspire to establish the heavenly Pure Land on earth.

Government policy regarding Buddhist communities varies with their ethnicity. Temples of the majority Han Chinese population are mostly self-governing, but minority Buddhist communities, especially Tibetans, are strictly regulated because they are perceived to constitute a potentially threatening separatist movement. For that reason, any display of support for the Dalai Lama is prohibited. Even so, many Tibetan Buddhists took part in antigovernment protests during the run-up to the Beijing Olympics in 2008, and in recent years dozens of people (most of them monks and nuns) have sacrificed themselves in what may be the ultimate form of nonviolent protest: self-immolation.

In Korea, the overthrow of the pro-Confucian Joseon dynasty by Japan in 1910 freed Buddhism from the restrictions that had been imposed on it for centuries. Throughout the occupation (1910–1945), however, religion was controlled and manipulated by the Japanese, and the influence of Japanese Buddhism led some Korean monks to abandon their vows of celibacy. The renewal of Korean Buddhism had to await the country's liberation from Japan, and the process was further delayed by the devastating civil war of 1950–1953. The more conservative Jogye struggled to restore the traditions of Korean Buddhism and in 1954 regained control of virtually all the major Korean monasteries.

Today in Japan Buddhism is often described as the religion of the dead, whereas Shinto is called the religion of the living because of its association with the joys of life. So closely is Buddhism associated with the memorialization of the dead that the family shrine dedicated to the ancestors is called the *butsudan*—literally, "the Buddhist altar." (For more on the complex interactions between Buddhism and other Japanese traditions, see Chapter 11.)

An interesting development in modern Japan has been the emergence of the Kyoto school of Buddhist philosophy. Its founder was Nishida Kitaro (1875–1945), who came of age in the period when Japan was looking to the West for ideas to help it modernize, and who sought to fuse Japanese Zen ideas with continental European philosophy. In keeping with Zen's emphasis on direct experience, he wrote of what he called "pure experience"—"experience just as it is without the addition of the slightest thought or reflection," such as "the moment of seeing a color or hearing a sound that takes place . . . before one has added the judgment that this seeing or hearing is related to something external. . . . When one has experienced one's conscious state directly, there is not as yet any subject or object; knowing and its object are completely at one. This is the purest form of experience" (*Zen no kenkyu*; Takeuchi 1987: 456). This approach is consistent with Zen founder Bodhidharma's call for a "direct pointing of the mind." Among Nishida's successors was Nishitani Keiji (1900–1990), who played a role in the emergence of an international Buddhist–Christian dialogue movement in the 1970s.

Buddhism in the West

Alfred North Whitehead (1861–1947), the Anglo-American philosopher, once said that Christianity was "a religion seeking a metaphysic," whereas Buddhism was "a metaphysic generating a religion." For a long time, Western scholars were not certain whether Buddhism fitted their definition of "religion" at all, since—despite its rituals, scriptures, and monastic traditions—it did not center on a personal deity.

Knowledge of Buddhism in the West was almost nonexistent before the mid-nineteenth century, but in 1879 a book entitled *The Light of Asia*—a moving poetic account of the Buddha's life by Edwin Arnold—attracted wide public attention. Even so, it was not until the beginning of the twentieth century that a few Western seekers began to publish firsthand accounts of Buddhist meditational practice. By the 1930s, Buddhist societies had been established in Great Britain, France, and Germany.

Buddhist influences in North America have tended to come more from the Mahayana and Vajrayana traditions than the Theravada. This has been the case ever since the World's Parliament of Religions Conference in Chicago in 1893. Among the delegates was a Zen monk named Shaku Soyen (1856–1919), who later returned to America to spread Buddhism there. His young translator, Daisetsu T. Suzuki (1870–1966), became the most influential Buddhist writer in North America. Suzuki made two extended visits to the United States and wrote many popular books sprinkled with stories of Zen masters and koans. Popularized by Alan Watts, these writings caught the attention of Westerners looking for alternatives to Christianity.

Some Westerners have considered Zen a form of mysticism. Though others have argued that there is no experience of union with a personal god in Zen, if "mysticism" is understood in the broader sense of spiritual experience as a transformation of human consciousness, then Zen practitioners may well share something in common with Christian mystics. Catholic missionaries and theologians, coming from a long contemplative tradition, have sought to learn from Zen insights and techniques. Zen meditation has also attracted the attention of experts in depth psychology.

Zen was the first form of Buddhism to make significant inroads in North America, but it was not the only one. Immigrants from Japan also brought with them Nichiren Shoshu and various Pure Land sects. In addition, two lineages of Vajrayana or Tibetan Buddhism have gained converts in North America since the 1960s. The Kargyu lineage is represented both by the Naropa Institute in Boulder, Colorado, and by a community of Tibetans and converts based in Halifax, Nova Scotia, while the Dalai Lama's Gelugpa lineage has centers in New York and elsewhere.

Ethnic Congregations

Existing alongside the Western converts are East Asian Buddhists who, beginning in the late 1880s, settled along the West Coast of North America, especially in California and British Columbia, and gradually obtained the financial resources to build their own temples. These ethnic congregations represented many branches of Buddhism, although the popularity of Pure Land in East Asia is reflected among ethnic Buddhists in North America.

There are also organizations such as the Buddhist Association of America and the Buddhist Association of Canada, which serve mainly immigrants of Chinese origin, and the Buddhist Churches of America (and of Canada), which serve True Pure Land followers, who are mainly ethnic Japanese. Similar groups with roots in Vietnam and Laos also have their own networks. Over time, some congregations have adopted Christian styles of worship, with pews, hymnals, and group leaders who take on all the responsibilities of North American clergy. There are now Buddhist Sunday schools, cemeteries, and wedding rituals conducted by *bhikshus* who are referred to as "priests."

In North America, ethnic Buddhist temples serve as community centers. Visitors are welcome, but the emphasis on community affairs tends to limit congregation membership to people from the same ethnic community. Buddhist meditation centers, on the other hand, have attracted many Western converts. Umbrella organizations are helping to bring Western "meditation Buddhists" into closer contact with ethnic congregations.

The influence of Buddhist thought in the West has been greater than the relatively small number of Western Buddhists might suggest. Without necessarily becoming Buddhists, many people in the West use modified versions of Buddhist meditational practices to calm their minds or improve their concentration before athletic or artistic performances. At the same time, Buddhist (and Hindu and Jaina) values such as nonviolence and concepts such as rebirth and karma have spread well beyond their traditional religious context.

⊕ Recent Developments

Buddhism continues to spread far beyond the land of its origin, but it has also faced setbacks in recent decades. In Sri Lanka and Southeast Asia it was weakened and challenged by the Christian missions and Western values introduced during the colonial era. Furthermore, the loss of kingship in most of the Buddhist countries of southern Asia has undermined the political support system underpinning the tradition that existed for many centuries. Like other religions, Buddhism has also been challenged by modern, secular ways of life. Buddhists generally do not see the scientific worldview as a serious challenge, since the Buddha himself emphasized rational thought. Still, the concepts of karma and rebirth do not fit comfortably into the standard scientific worldview.

It is also true that *bhikshus* are no longer the main educators, social workers, dispute settlers, and advisors in Buddhist countries, especially in the major cities; their roles are mainly limited to those of ritual leaders and directors of religious education. Yet Buddhists are not converting in any significant numbers to other religions, and most do make some effort to live according to Buddhist values.

The Female Sangha

Over time the *bhikshuni* sangha died out in many Buddhist countries. The specific reasons for its disappearance may have varied, but in general the female order was vulnerable simply because it was smaller and less well connected to political power than the male order. In Sri Lanka, for instance, when both sanghas were devastated by famine, the king imported monks from Siam to revive the male order, but there is no evidence of similar action that was taken on behalf of the female sangha.

Recently, though, some effort has been made to revive the practice of *bhikshuni* ordination in Theravada countries. Some Theravada women take the same 10 precept vows as male novices, consisting of the 5 precepts that laypersons take, plus 5 more. In Sri Lanka a female order observing 10 precepts was started in 1905 with the help of women from Myanmar, and a new order of *bhikshunis* adhering to all 235 precepts (the 227 that monks take plus 8 specific to women) was established in 1996 with the help of *bhikshus* from Sri Lanka and Korea.

Even without ordination, many Theravada women pursue a very active religious life both at home and in the temples. In Thailand, laywomen can take vows of poverty and service similar to those taken by Roman Catholic nuns. Some of these women say they would not seek ordination if it were available, because they would have less freedom to serve others if they were bound by the *vinaya* rules. In modern times, Theravada has also moved toward greater acceptance of women's capacity for high religious achievement. A Thai laywoman named Upasika Kee Nanayon (1901–1979), for instance, was revered by Buddhists of both sexes for her mastery of meditation and her instructional talks.

Even in the vehicle's early years the status of women in the Mahayana tradition tended to be higher than that of women in other traditions. Certainly Mahayana took a more sympathetic view of laypeople in general than earlier forms of Buddhism did. The fact that Mahayana encouraged women as well as men to take the bodhisattva vow indicates that it considered women capable of enlightenment in a way that Theravada did not.

An order of Mahayana nuns following a *vinaya* of the Dharmagupta sect has continued as an unbroken lineage in China and Taiwan, and some of its *bhikshunis* may now be found in many countries. The founder of the Soto Zen school, Dogen, taught females as well as males, and although the Soto convents died out, the Rinzai school today has both nuns and female masters. Outside Japan, Zen masters give equal status to practitioners of both sexes.

Tibetan Buddhism has a long tradition of ordained women, several of whom have been at the forefront of Tibet's struggle against Chinese domination. Ani Pachen ("Great Courage") was known as Tibet's Joan of Arc after she led her clan in rebellion against the Chinese takeover in 1949. She was imprisoned and tortured, but refused to renounce Buddhism or her loyalty to the Dalai Lama. On her release from prison in 1981, she again played a leading role in Tibetan demonstrations against Hanification before escaping to join the exile community in Dharamsala, India.

Women in the Traditions

The *Bhikshuni* Sangha Controversy

During his teaching years the Buddha instituted an order (sangha) of fully ordained females, or *bhikshuni* sangha, and the poems of several female elders (*theri*) are preserved in the Theravada canon. Over time the *bhikshuni* sangha died out or never was instituted in many Buddhist countries. The specific reasons for this varied, but in general the female order was vulnerable simply because it was relatively small and less well connected to political power than the male order. In Sri Lanka, for instance, after both sanghas were devastated by famine, the king imported the required elders from Siam to revive the male order, but there was no equivalent female sangha from which female elders could be brought to Sri Lanka.

Recently, an effort has been made to revive the practice of *bhikkhuni* ordination in Theravada countries such as Sri Lanka and Thailand. This has been controversial because according to Buddhist rules the ritual of higher ordination can only be properly conducted by a committee of *theras* (male elders, or senior monks) for male candidates or *theris* (female elders) for female candidates. So, strictly speaking, there is no way to restart the ordination lineage once it has ended. In this "catch-22" situation, conservative monks have insisted that the *bhikkhuni* sangha cannot be restarted. More liberal Buddhists who take the contrary position that the order for women should be reinstituted have organized ordination ceremonies for women. The controversy over whether the validity of these recently ordained Theravada *bhikkhuni* should be recognized continues today.

A Renewed Sense of Mission

According to the Buddhist understanding of long-term historical cycles, the dharma will continue to decline until the next buddha restarts the wheel. This somewhat pessimistic view of the future stands in sharp contrast to the views of many other religions. Yet it does not in any way diminish Buddhists' zeal or sense of mission.

In a sense, the many volunteer associations promoting Buddhist solutions to modern problems are performing the same functions as the Buddhist kings of the past who provided leadership in education, economic development, and social values. Meditation centers offer help with modern problems such as stress and overdependence on material possessions, and most of them emphasize the importance of breaking through the normal bonds of ego, self-centeredness, and the assumption of permanence. Bhikshu Buddhadasa (1906–1993), a Thai reformer, identified the fundamental problem with modern society as the attitude of "me and mine." This attitude may be part of the human condition, but Buddhists believe it is made worse by the materialistic and individualistic emphasis of contemporary values.

Buddhist Economics

Another problem that some Buddhists are addressing is the need for alternatives to modern patterns of economic development. The term "Buddhist economics" was first used by the economist E. F. Schumacher, who had exposure both to Gandhi's advocacy of small-scale, people-oriented development and to the efforts of U Nu to implement "Buddhist Socialism" in Burma as a middle path between communism and capitalism. (U Nu was a devout Buddhist who in 1947 became the country's first prime minister.) Not surprisingly, Buddhist economics proposes a middle path between the environmental and social disasters of over- and underdevelopment. It advocates local-level, low-tech, people-oriented projects that will help everyone and criticizes all projects that serve to make the rich richer and the poor poorer. Other advocates of Buddhist economics include the Thai monks Ven. Prayudh Payutto, who sees this middle path as the best form of sustainable development, and Ven. Prabhavanaviriyakhun, whose book *Buddhist Economics* argues that sustainable development will require (as he puts it in the title of another book) "reforming human nature." This theme is also central to the social critic Sivaraksa, who laments the spread of consumer greed throughout the world. In a variation on Descartes's "I think, therefore I am," Sivaraksa says that the slogan of consumerism is "I shop, therefore I am."

Cooperation among Buddhists

Buddhists in various countries are now forming networks across national borders, such as the International Network of Engaged Buddhists, based in Bangkok. Many Buddhists now identify themselves first as Buddhists and only secondarily as Zen or Theravada Buddhists. This trend is strengthened by the growing tendency of Buddhist periodicals and Internet sites to feature articles by writers from a variety of traditions.

This sense of common purpose has been strengthened by the international exposure of the Dalai Lama, who has traveled to most Buddhist countries and in every case has been very well received. Strictly speaking, he is the spiritual head of just one Tibetan order, but Buddhists everywhere recognize Tenzin Gyatso as their spokesperson in some sense. His forced exile is seen as a loss for Tibet, but in the long run it may provide the impetus that Buddhism needs to regain its traditional role as one of the world's most vigorous and successful religions.

⊕ Summary

Buddhists understand Shakyamuni, the sage of the Shakya clan, to be the latest in a long line of spiritual masters who have become fully enlightened, teaching buddhas. In the 2,500 years since his birth, his followers have preserved the teachings of the Buddha and others as sacred texts, selections from which are chanted to bring understanding and blessings to all. Buddhist thought makes no sharp distinction between animals and humans, and holds that all living beings are reborn according to their karma and progress along the path to enlightenment. Buddhism is organized by ordination lineages as subdivisions among three vehicles: Theravada, Mahayana, and Vajrayana. No one individual holds authority over all Buddhists, but the current Dalai Lama is renowned throughout the world as the face of Buddhism today. Although Buddhism is a missionary religion, its approach to non-Buddhists today is generally low-key, centered on activities such as meditation training and informal "dharma talks."

What gives Buddhism its energy? What has made it work for so many people in so many different times and cultures? The answer may lie in the continuing power of the Triple Gem to shape people's spiritual lives. Buddhists feel confident "taking refuge" in the Buddha, not as a god but as a great human being; in the dharma as a set of living teachings that go to the heart of reality; and in the sangha as a community of people committed to following the Buddha's path as closely as possible. They also feel confident that, in the distant future, when the wheel of dharma set in motion by Shakyamuni ceases to turn, the future buddha Maitreya will appear on earth and turn the wheel yet again for the benefit of all beings.

Sites

Lumbini Park, Nepal

Lumbini Park is the site of the Buddha's birth, with the pond where Mahamaya is said to have bathed, a Bodhi tree, and a park surrounded by monasteries for visiting monks.

Bodh Gaya, Bihar, India

Bodh Gaya is the site of the Buddha's enlightenment. In addition to a huge Bodhi tree (said to be descended from the one under which he sat), there is a temple, and the park is surrounded by temples and monasteries representing different schools of Buddhism.

Sarnath, Uttar Pradesh, India

The deer park near Varanasi where the newly enlightened Buddha preached his first sermon and ordained his former companions is called Sarnath.

Bangkok, Thailand

On the grounds of the Grand Palace in Bangkok is the temple housing a jade sculpture known as the Emerald Buddha. The nearby Wat Pho temple complex is filled with interesting temples, and across the river is the picturesque Wat Arun, "Temple of the Dawn," where a tall pagoda sparkles at dawn and sunset.

Angkor, Cambodia

Angkor (from a Sanskrit word meaning "city") was the heart of the Khmer Empire. Of the hundreds of religious temples and shrines it is home to, the most famous is the (originally Hindu) Angkor Wat.

Shaolin, China

The Shaolin monastery is the home of Chan (Zen) Buddhism, as well as many East Asian martial arts traditions. A two-hour hike up a mountain path leads to Bodhidharma's cave.

Kathmandu, Nepal

There are two great Buddhist temples in Kathmandu. Swayambhunath sits high on a hill, its Nepali-style "eyes" overlooking the countryside. The other, Bodhanath, is a Tibetan-style stupa surrounded by shops and cafés.

Lhasa, Tibet

Lhasa is the home of the Potala Palace (the home of the Dalai Lamas before the Chinese occupation) and the Jokhang temple.

Ajanta Caves, Maharashtra, India

The Ajanta Caves contain a complex of stone temples carved into a cliffside, filled with Buddhist sculptures and paintings.

Kandy, Sri Lanka

The Temple of the Tooth in Kandy, northeast of Colombo, is the most important Buddhist site in Sri Lanka. The Perahera festival is a spectacular 10-day event in which some Hindus also participate.

Sacred Texts

Religion	Texts	Composition/Compilation	Compilation/Revision	Use
Buddhism: Theravada	*Tripitaka: vinaya* (discipline), *sutras* (sermons), and *abhidharma* (further dharma)	Each of the various early sects had its own collection of texts, which were transmitted orally for several centuries before they were first written down in the 1st century BCE, in Sri Lanka.	Only the Theravada versions of the texts survive in full; commentaries include Buddhaghosa's *The Path of Purification* (5th century).	Study and discussion; selections called *parittas* chanted as blessings in various rituals; verses from the *Dhammapada* (part of the *Sutra* collection) often used for guidance in everyday life

Sacred Texts (Continued)

Religion	Texts	Composition/Compilation	Compilation/Revision	Use
Buddhism: Mahayana	*Lotus* and *Heart Sutras*, as well as hundreds of other *sutras* and commentaries	Some written in early 1st century CE; others said to have been recovered from hiding	Commentaries written on many major sutras	Chanted for study or blessing rituals; different Mahayana schools have their own favorite texts
Buddhism: Mahayana, Pure Land	*Sukhavati* (Pure Land) *Sutras*, of various lengths	Composed during early centuries of Common Era	Commentaries written by major thinkers	Studied and chanted; the source of the bodhisattva vows that Pure Land practitioners take
Buddhism: Mahayana, Chan	*Platform* and *Lankavatara Sutras*, among others; *Mumonkan* (koan collection)	Favorite Mahayana scriptures, plus stories of masters unique to Chan tradition	Numerous translations of teachings, updated frequently over time	Doctrinal, ritual, inspirational, educational; it can take years for students to work their way through the 48 koans of the *Mumonkan*.
Buddhism: Vajrayana	*Kanjur* (sutras and tantras)	Includes many Tibetan translations of Mahayana *sutras*	Commentaries called *Tanjur* expand on the *Kanjur* texts	Study, chanting, rituals

Discussion Questions

1. How does the life of the Buddha compare with that of Christ (or the leader of some other spiritual tradition)?

2. What were the main elements of the brahmin tradition that Buddhism rejected?

3. What role, if any, do deities play in Buddhism?

4. What does Buddhism mean by the goal of purifying the mind?

5. What is the status of Tibetan Buddhist culture in contemporary China?

6. Why does the Chinese government object when the leaders of other countries meet with the Dalai Lama?

7. Why has the *bhikshuni* sangha been lost in several Buddhist countries? What efforts are being made to restore it?

8. What is "Engaged Buddhism"?

9. Why did Ambedkar and many other Dalits past and present convert from Hinduism to Buddhism?

10. Is it fair to call Buddhism a system of self-development rather than a religion?

Glossary

anatman "No-soul"; the doctrine that the human person is impermanent, a changing combination of components.

Arhat/lohan A worthy one or saint; someone who has realized the ideal of spiritual perfection.

bhikkhu, bhikkhuni The Pali spellings for the Sanskrit *bhikshu* and *bhikshuni*.

bhikshu, bhikshuni An ordained Buddhist monk and nun, respectively.

bodhisattva In Theravada, a being who is on the way to enlightenment or buddhahood but has not yet achieved it; in Mahayana, a celestial being who forgoes nirvana in order to save others.

Chan/Zen A tradition centered on the practice of meditation and the teaching that ultimate reality is not expressible in words or logic, but must be grasped through direct intuition; see also **koan** and **zazen**.

Dalit "Oppressed person"; a member of any one of the lowest castes in the hierarchical Indian caste system.

dana A "giving" ritual in which Theravada families present gifts of food, at their homes or a temple, to *bhikshus* who conduct rituals including chanting and merit transfer.

dharma In Buddhist usage, teaching or truth concerning the ultimate nature of things.

dukkha The suffering, psychological as well as physical, that characterizes human life.

Hinayana "Lesser Vehicle"; the pejorative name given by the Mahayana ("Greater Vehicle") school to earlier Indian Buddhist sects, of which Theravada became the most important.

karma The energy of the individual's past thoughts and actions, good or bad; it determines rebirth within the "wheel" of *samsara*, the cycle of rebirth that ends only when *parinirvana* is achieved. Good karma is also called "merit."

koan A paradoxical thought exercise used in the Chan–Zen tradition to provoke a breakthrough in understanding by forcing students past the limitations of verbal formulations and logic.

lama "Wise teacher"; a title given to advanced teachers as well as the heads of various Tibetan ordination lineages.

Mahayana "Greater Vehicle"; the form of Buddhism that emerged around the first century in India and spread first to China and then to Korea and Japan.

mandala A chart-like representation of cosmic buddha figures that often serves as a focus of meditation and devotion in the Mahayana and Vajrayana traditions.

mudra A pose or gesture in artistic representations of Buddha figures; by convention, each *mudra* has a specific symbolic meaning.

nirvana The state of bliss associated with final enlightenment; nirvana "with remainder" is the highest level possible in this life, and nirvana "without remainder" is the ultimate state. See also *parinirvana*.

pagoda A multi-story tower, characteristic of Southeast and East Asian Buddhism, that developed out of the South Asian mound or stupa.

parinirvana The ultimate perfection of bliss, achievable only on departing this life, as distinct from the nirvana with the "remainder" achievable while one is still in the present existence.

prajna The spiritual wisdom or insight necessary for enlightenment.

Pure Land The comfortable realm in the western region of the heavens reserved for those who trust in the merit and grace of its lord, the celestial buddha Amitabha (Amida).

sangha The "congregation" or community of Buddhist monks and nuns. Some schools also refer to the congregation of laypersons as a sangha.

Shakyamuni "Sage of the Shakya clan"; a title used to refer to the historical Siddhartha Gautama, the Buddha.

shunyata The teaching that emptiness is held to be ultimately characteristic of all things, stressed especially by Madhyamaka doctrine.

stupa Originally a hemispherical mound built to contain cremation ashes or a sacred relic; in East Asia the stupa developed into the tower-like pagoda.

sutra A discourse attributed either to Shakyamuni himself or to an important disciple.

Theravada "Teaching of the Elders"; the dominant form of Buddhism in Sri Lanka and Southeast Asia.

Tripitaka "Three baskets"; the collection of early sacred writings whose three sections consist of discourses attributed to the Buddha, rules of monastic discipline, and treatises on doctrine.

Vaishakha/Vesak A Theravada festival held at the full moon around early May, marking Shakyamuni's birth, enlightenment, and *parinirvana*.

Vajrayana The tantric branch of Buddhism that became established in Tibet and the Himalayan region, and later spread to Mongolia and eventually India.

vinaya The rules of practice and conduct for monks; a section of the Pali canon.

vipassana "Insight" or "mindfulness" meditation practiced by Theravada Buddhists.

zazen Sitting meditation in the Chan–Zen tradition.

Zen See **Chan**.

Further Reading

Adiele, Faith. 2004. *Meeting Faith: The Forest Journals of a Black Buddhist Nun.* London: W. W. Norton and Company. The story of a Western woman's challenging and rewarding experiences as a nun in a remote retreat center in Thailand.

Amore, Roy C. 1978. *Two Masters, One Message.* Nashville, TN: Abingdon. A work that compares and contrasts the figures of Buddha and Jesus.

Batchelor, Martine. 2006. *Women in Korean Zen: Lives and Practices.* Syracuse, NY: Syracuse University Press. A good account based on 10 years of Zen practice in Korea.

Dalai Lama. 1990. *Freedom in Exile: The Autobiography of the Dalai Lama.* New York: HarperCollins. The Dalai Lama tells about his life's work and wisdom.

Dalai Lama. 2002. *How to Practice: The Way to a Meaningful Life.* Trans. and ed. Jeffrey Hopkins. New York: Pocket Books. The Dalai Lama writes about how to practice a spiritual path that leads to transformation.

Gross, Rita M. 1993. *Buddhism after Patriarchy: A Feminist History, Analysis, and Reconstruction of Buddhism.* Albany: State University of New York Press. Material for provocative debate.

Lopez, Donald S., Jr. 2002. *The Story of Buddhism: A Concise Guide to Its History and Teachings.* New York: HarperCollins. A good introduction to Buddhism.

Queen, Christopher S., and Sallie B. King, eds. 1996. *Engaged Buddhism: Liberation Movements in Asia.* Albany: State University of New York Press. A work charting twentieth-century activism from India and Thailand to Tibet and Japan.

Seager, Richard Hughes. 2000. *Buddhism in America.* New York: Columbia University Press. The story of Buddhists and Buddhist traditions in America.

Shaw, Ronald D. M., trans. 1961. *The Blue Cliff Records: The Hekigan Roku [Pi yen lu] Containing One Hundred Stories of Zen Masters of Ancient China.* London: M. Joseph. A collection of koans especially prized by the Japanese.

Sivaraksa, Sulak. 2005. *Conflict, Culture, Change: Engaged Buddhism in a Globalizing World.* Somerville, MA: Wisdom Publications. A book by an important Thai Buddhist social critic.

Toomey, Christine. 2017. *In Search of Buddha's Daughters: The Hidden Lives and Fearless Work of Buddhist Nuns.* New York: Experiment. A set of engaging biographies of nuns.

Recommended Websites

http://lhamo.tripod.com

A good but dated site focusing on women in Buddhism.

http://www.americanbuddhist.net

A site that offers a broad overview of Buddhism, including Buddhist activism.

http://www.buddhamind.info

A comprehensive site including an e-zine with cartoons, pictures, and much more.

http://www.dharmanet.org

A useful overview of the history and varieties of Buddhism in China that does not address current issues.

http://www.dhamma.org

A good source on Theravada-style *vipassana* meditation.

http://www.freetibet.org

The site of the Free Tibet Campaign, a movement started by Tibetans in exile and their supporters.

http://www.sakyadhita.org

The site of the International Association of Buddhist Women, with links to various country sites including those of the United States and Canada.

References

Ambedkar, Bhimrao Ramji. 2008. *Riddles in Hinduism.* Scotts Valley, CA: CreateSpace.

Chen, Kenneth. 1964. *Buddhism in China: A Historical Survey.* Princeton, NJ: Princeton University Press.

de Bary, William Theodore, ed. 1958. *Sources of Indian Tradition.* New York: Columbia University Press.

Dhammika, Sravasti, ed. 1989. *Buddha Vacana.* Singapore: Buddha Dhamma Mandala Society.

Horner, I. B. 1930. *Women under Primitive Buddhism: Laywomen and Almswomen.* New York: Dutton.

Horner, I. B., trans. 1967. *The Collection of the Middle Length Sayings (Majjhimanikaya).* Vol. 3. London: Luzac.

Nanamoli [formerly Osborne Moore], trans. 1972. *The Life of the Buddha as It Appears in the Pali Canon, the Oldest Authentic Record.* Kandy: Buddhist Publication Society.

Nhat Hanh, Thich. 1988. *The Heart of Understanding: Commentaries on the* Prajnaparamita Heart Sutra. Berkeley, CA: Parallax Press.

Robinson, Richard H. 1959. "Buddhism: In China and Japan." In *The Concise Encyclopedia of Living Faiths,* ed. R. C. Zaehner, 321–347. London: Joseph.

Takeuchi, Yoshinori. 1987. "Nishida Kitaro." In *The Encyclopedia of Religion,* ed. Mircea Eliade, 10:456–457. New York: Macmillan.

Tsunoda, Ryusaku. 1958. *Sources of Japanese Tradition.* New York: Columbia University Press.

Yampolsky, Philip, trans. 1976. *The* Platform Sutra *of the Sixth Patriarch.* New York: Columbia University Press.

11 Chinese and Korean Traditions

Terry Tak-ling Woo

Traditions at a Glance

Numbers

East Asian traditions such as shamanism, Confucianism, and Daoism do not require exclusive membership; they also tend to be less institutionalized than monotheistic religions. Their membership is therefore very difficult to count. For Confucianism, most estimates are in the range of 6 million, but because East Asians generally do not consider Confucianism to be a religion, the true number is impossible to gauge. For Daoism, as for Confucianism, exact numbers are impossible to determine because of issues around definition, but estimates range from 20 million to as many as 400 million. Daoism is sometimes counted as a folk or popular religion. This latter category also includes numerous new religious movements and traditional sects whose devotees may consider their practices and beliefs to be more cultural than religious. Estimates of adherents range from 225 to 445 million. Finally, for Korean shamanism and popular religion, estimates range from 1 to 7 million.

Distribution

Confucians and Daoists live mainly in East and Southeast Asia, Australia and New Zealand, western Europe, and North America. Adherents of popular religions remain primarily in East Asia, with small pockets in diasporic communities in Australia, New Zealand, North America, and Europe.

Founders and Teachers

Mythical founders and heroes include Yao, Shun, and Yu in China, and Dangun in Korea. Famous first teachers—some mythical, some historic—include the Yellow Emperor, Confucius, and Laozi in China, and Choe Chung in Korea.

Deities

For Confucians, the place of a deity is filled either by Heaven or by Heaven and Earth together. Some Daoists see the Dao, or Way, as a deity, while others look to a bureaucracy of deities. Popular religions, both Korean and Chinese, include hundreds if not thousands of deities.

Authoritative Texts

Popular and shamanistic religions are not textually oriented. For Confucians, the classics from the Zhou and Han dynasties are the foundational texts. For Daoists, Laozi and, to a lesser degree, Zhuangzi are fundamental, but otherwise different groups focus on different texts, including the *Unity of the Three* and the Classics of *Great Peace* and *Purity and Tranquility*. For Buddhists, Mahayana texts such as the *Lotus*, *Vimalakirti*, *Heart*, *Diamond*, *Pure Land*, and *Flower Garland Sutras* are central. The only Chinese text considered "canonical" in the monotheistic sense is the *Platform Sutra* of the Chan school.

Noteworthy Teachings

No East Asian tradition is exclusive; many believers attend temples and shrines of various kinds. The three elite or institutional traditions—Daoism, Confucianism, and Buddhism—differ fundamentally in doctrine and vary greatly in practice, but they share a utopian view of a peaceful and harmonious society whose members are devoted to self-cultivation and discipline. In addition, some schools of Buddhism look to an afterlife in the Pure Land of a celestial buddha such as Amituofo (Amitabha). Popular religions syncretize teachings from all three traditions, as well as from more recently introduced religions such as Christianity and Islam.

The Dragon and Tiger pagodas, Lotus Lake, Kaohsiung, Taiwan (© Pat Behnke/Alamy).

In this chapter you will learn about:

- Syncretism and the role it has played in the development of Chinese and Korean religiosity
- Popular religions and how they continue to thrive and express the syncretic spirit
- Confucianism, Daoism, and Buddhism and how they have argued against, influenced, and developed in relation to one another
- The development and acceptance of a wide range of texts for a variety of needs
- Brutal challenges that Chinese and Korean religions have faced in modern times and how they have responded
- Women and the importance of the feminine principle in Chinese and Korean religions

From the beginning, religion in East Asia has been inextricably linked to politics. Social harmony and stability in governance have always been central concerns, along with physical sustenance and security.

⊕ Overview

The foundational layers of animism and shamanism remain visible in East Asian religions today in traces of tribal practices focused on dealing with the insecurities of life. Philosophers, shamans, and "masters of the methods" such as prognosticians and geomancers all sought to bring people and societies peace. Early Confucian and Daoist writings thus included political teachings along with metaphysical ruminations, advice on cultivating good health and moral character, and instructions for achieving mystical union with the divine. It was into this religious landscape that Buddhism was later introduced from India and Central Asia. The central focus on peace and harmony of all the various religions in this region led them to embrace a generally tolerant, inclusive, and syncretic ethos.

When the Chinese speak of *sanjiao*, they are talking about the three (*san*) teachings, philosophies, or religions (*jiao*) of Confucianism, Daoism, and Buddhism. Collectively, these are sometimes described as the "elite tradition." A much more diffuse fourth tradition, often described as folk or popular religion, honors an assortment of spirits that varies from place to place. For the most part the four traditions have coexisted in peace, and many people consult specialists from across the spectrum—Confucian teachers, Daoist priests, Buddhist monks, spirit mediums, astrologers, and *feng-shui* practitioners. In general, Chinese religions agree on the importance of avoiding sociopolitical conflict and chaos and encourage actions that bring stability and security.

⊕ The Classical Period to the Qin (c. 2300 BCE–206 BCE)
Confucian Beginnings

Origins

Not all of the philosophy that the West calls Confucianism originated with Kongzi, or **Confucius** (c. 551–479 BCE).[1] Some of its seminal ideas can be found in the Five Classics: the *Classic* (or *Book*) *of Changes*, the *Classic of Documents* or *Book of History*, the *Classic of Odes* or *Book of Poetry*, the *Records* (or *Book*) *of Rites*, and the *Spring and Autumn Annals*. (A sixth work, the *Classic of Music*, is now lost.) Some parts of these works may predate Confucius himself, and others were likely written after his time. Nevertheless Confucius is revered as the first of three foremost classical

The three tiers of the Temple of Heaven (Tiantan) in Beijing symbolize the relationship between Heaven, Earth, and human beings; the circular shape reflects the belief that Heaven is round, whereas the Earth is square. It was here that the emperor made offerings to Heaven and prayed for bountiful harvests (© Imagemore Co., Ltd./Corbis).

philosophers in the Confucian tradition; the other two are Mengzi (**Mencius**; c. 343–289 BCE) and **Xunzi** (c. 310–219 BCE).

Originating during the Zhou dynasty (c. 1046–256 BCE), the Classics were first standardized during the Han period (202 BCE–220 CE), and they have been central to the state examination curriculum since the establishment of the first state-supported Confucian college in 124 BCE. Historically, they provided the ideology behind government policy for some 2,000 years in addition to serving as blueprints for family relations and guides to individual moral and spiritual transformation.

The Classics record a society in transition. During the Shang era (c. 1750–1040 BCE) the world was understood to be under the control of deities, ghosts, and spirits. In the Zhou era this "supernatural" worldview was gradually replaced by the understanding that the world operated according

Timeline

24th century BCE	Time of China's "sage kings" Yao, Shun, and Yu; some accounts place Dangun, the mythical founder of Old Joseon (Korea), in the same period
c. 2200–1750	Xia dynasty (China)
c. 1750–1046	Shang (Yin) dynasty (China)
c. 1046–256	Zhou dynasty (China)
722–479	Spring and Autumn period
551	Birth of Confucius (d. 479); some accounts place Laozi around the same time, some place him earlier, and others say that he never existed
479–221	Warring States period
c. 400–100	Active period of Huang–Lao school
c. 343	Birth of Mengzi (Mencius; d. 289); Zhuangzi (369?–286?) was a slightly older contemporary
c. 310	Birth of Xunzi (d. 219), who witnessed the carnage of the late Zhou period
c. 300	Old Joseon suffers major losses (Korea)
221–206	Qin dynasty (China); destruction of Confucian texts by the first Qin emperor
202 BCE–9 CE	Early (also Former or Western) Han dynasty; Confucian texts recovered and edited based on copies that had been preserved and the recitations of scholars who had memorized them
124 BCE	Emperor Wu establishes Confucian state college and state examination system
108 BCE	Old Joseon defeated by the Han
c. 50 BCE–668 CE	Three Kingdoms of Goguryeo, Baekje, and Silla (Korea)
25 BCE–220 CE	Latter or Eastern Han
c. 48 CE	Birth of Ban Zhao (d. 112), who advocated education for women
142	Zhang Daoling founds the Daoist Celestial Masters (later Orthodox Unity)
220–589	Period of North–South disunion or Six Dynasties (China)
317	Northern China falls to invaders from North and Central Asia
c. 370–380	Buddhism introduced to Goguryeo, Baekje, and (later) Silla (Korea)
527	Buddhism made state religion of Silla
c. 530	Baekje monks introduce Buddhism to Japan
618–907	Tang dynasty (China)
600s	Tang rulers send Daoist priests, texts, and images to Goguryeo
629–630	Chinese monk Xuanzang makes pilgrimage to India
647	Second Tang emperor orders construction of Confucian temples with tablets commemorating 22 orthodox Confucians
661	Korean monks Wonhyo and Uisang start out for China
668–936	Kingdom of United Silla (Korea)

682	United Silla establishes National Confucian College
824	Death of Han Yu, defender of Confucianism
890–936	Later Three Kingdoms (Korea)
918–1392	Goryeo period (Korea), with Buddhism as state religion
960–1279	Song dynasty (China)
1158–1250	Jinul synthesizes the practice-focused Seon (Chan) school and doctrinal schools like Hwaeom (Flower Garland)
1368–1644	Ming dynasty (China)
1392–1897	Joseon persecution of Buddhism (Korea)
1400s	Both China's Empress Xu and Joseon's Queen Sohye write texts entitled *Instructions for the Inner Quarters*
1500s	Emergence of Joseon neo-Confucianism
1529	Death of Confucian Wang Yangming
1644–1911	Qing (Manchu) dynasty (China)
1900s	East Asia reconfigured in response to Western challenges; new religions established and traditional ones renewed
1910–1945	Japanese occupation of Korea
1911	Qing dynasty falls and China becomes a republic
1945	Korea divided between Democratic People's Republic (North) and Republic (South)
1949	People's Republic of China (PRC) established
1950s	New Confucian movement finds a home in Hong Kong
1966–1976	Communist government promotes "Great Proletarian Cultural Revolution" in attempt to eradicate traditional Chinese values and practices
1980s	Revival of Daoism in PRC after more than a century of persecution
1989	Confucius's birthday officially celebrated in PRC for the first time since 1949
2004	First Confucius Institute opens in Seoul
2006	First World Buddhist Forum—the first government-sponsored religious conference held in China since 1949—opens in Hangzhou
2007	Privately funded international forum on the *Daodejing* approved by the PRC government
2011	First International Daoism Forum held at the foot of Hengshan, one of the five sacred Daoist mountains

to impersonal natural principles. The content of the Classics therefore ranges from descriptions of deities, ghosts, and spirits and the rites (**li**) performed for them to philosophical explanations of the natural principles underlying those rites. The ultimate goal was the creation of a harmonious society through careful self-cultivation. Over time, the Classics were reinterpreted with this goal in mind.

Confucian Concerns

The concerns addressed in the Five Classics can be categorized into four broad areas: individual, familial, political, and cosmic. The first duty of the exemplary Confucian (*junzi*) is to promote a peaceful, prosperous, and harmonious society. The Classics make it clear that such a society cannot be achieved by men alone, for there can be no harmony in the public world without harmony in the private world of the family—the domain of the Confucian woman. They also explain how sacrifices and rituals give symbolic expression to the relationship between the outer and inner worlds. The essential function of ancestor rituals in particular was to encourage right relationships, especially between men and women.

Confucians believe that correctness in human relationships is crucial to a stable society. There are five types of relationship—ruler and minister (state official), parent and child (traditionally, father and son), husband and wife, elder and younger siblings (often translated as "brothers"), and friends—all of which must be guided by *ren* (usually translated as "goodness," "humaneness," "benevolence," or "compassion"). Except in the case of the relationship between friends, the first member of each pair is deemed "senior" and is expected to take into account the effect of his or her actions on others in general; the second person is "junior" and is expected to be upright and loyal.

Confucian Exemplars and Sages

The prototypes of the Confucian sage are three mythical "sage kings" named Yao, Shun, and Yu, whose stories are told in the *Classic of Documents*. The virtues they embody are civil, familial, and filial rather than military, and their stories are understood as implicit critiques of rule by force.

Yao is admired for bringing harmony to his domain and making sure that the common people were well fed and prosperous. In the simple agrarian society of his day, Yao's virtue was said to have radiated throughout the land. The *Classic of Documents* recounts how Yao, when he recognized that his own son was not virtuous enough to be a good ruler, asked his ministers to find a more appropriate successor. They recommended a man of humble status named Shun because he had managed to live in harmony with his family and fulfill his filial duties even though his father was blind (literally and figuratively) and stupid, his stepmother deceitful, and his half-brother arrogant. In other words, Shun had triumphed over adversity. Accordingly, Yao married his two daughters to Shun, observed his conduct for three years, and then offered him the throne.

The last sage king, Yu, is associated with the largely legendary Xia dynasty—the predecessors of the Shang. Yu's father was said to have thrown the natural cycle into chaos by building dams to contain floodwaters, but Yu worked with nature by digging deep canals to channel the water away. According to the *Classic of Documents*, this story was told to Wu, the first king of Zhou, as a lesson in governance.

Divination and the Pantheon of Spirits

At least two related elements from the stories of the sage kings survived into the Shang dynasty: an intense interest in "right" governance and a belief in divine intervention through revelation to the king. The Shang kings served as shamans, practicing divination and communicating directly with the spirits that were believed to hold the real power over the empire. Religious ritual was thus an indispensable part of governance.

At the apex of the Shang pantheon of spirits sat the Lord-on-High, also known as Shangdi. Thought to be the ancestor of the Shang clan, he was the sky god who commanded rain, thunder,

Table 11.1 Major Chinese (C) and Korean (K) Historical Periods at a Glance

C		c. 2300 BCE–206 BCE: Classical period through Qin dynasty
K		?–108 BCE: Old Joseon
C		202 BCE–220 CE: Han dynasty
K		c. 50 BCE–668 CE: Three Kingdoms period
C		220 CE–589 CE: Six Dynasties period
C		589–907: Sui and Tang dynasties
K		668–1392: United Silla, Later Three Kingdoms, and Goryeo
C		960–1644: Song, Yuan, and Ming dynasties
K		1392–1910: Joseon and the Korean Empire
C		1644–present: Qing dynasty and republican period
K		1910–1945: Japanese occupation
K		1945–present: Korea partitioned between North and South

and wind. Below him were the nature spirits believed to animate natural phenomena, followed by celestial spirits such as the sun and moon; "Former Lords" who were associated with the Shang but were not royal clan members; and, finally, direct human ancestors, both male and female.

The Mandate of Heaven

After more than 700 years in power, the Shang dynasty fell to the Zhou in 1046 BCE. It was in the context of this power shift that the concept of the Mandate of Heaven was developed. When the first Zhou ruler, King Wu, died, leaving a young son, his brother the Duke of Zhou served as regent, but he returned the throne to the boy once he was old enough to rule. Such loyalty was revered by the early Confucians, and the duke's popularity rivaled that of Confucius himself. The personification of restraint, humility, and willingness to listen to advice, the duke declared that Heaven had withdrawn the Mandate of Heaven from the later Shang kings because they had failed to provide for the people.

In this way moral character became the primary determinant of the right to rule. The idea that good governance was a duty to Heaven reflected the Zhou belief in a moral force or supreme deity that took an interest in human affairs. How to encourage kings to rule ethically became a central concern for Confucians. In the *Classic of Odes*, King Wen (the father of Wu) is imagined addressing the last Shang king:

> King Wen said, Woe!
> Woe upon you, Yin and Shang!
> You have been the harsh oppressor,
> you have been grasping and crushing.
> You have been in the places of power,
> you have held the functions.
> Heaven sent recklessness down in you,
> and you rise by acts of force. (Owen 1996: 20)

Document
On the Mandate of Heaven

The Mandate of Heaven appears in the Classic of Documents *in the form of a public announcement legitimating the Zhou overthrow of the Yin (an alternative name for the Shang).*

Heaven has rejected and ended the Mandate of this great state of Yin. Thus, although Yin has many former wise kings in Heaven, when their successor kings and successor people undertook their Mandate, in the end wise and good men lived in misery. Knowing that they must care for and sustain their wives and children, they then called out in anguish to Heaven and fled to places where they could not be caught. Ah! Heaven too grieved for the people of all the lands, wanting, with affection, in giving its Mandate to employ those who are deeply committed. The king should have reverent care for his virtue. (D. Nivison, in de Bary and Bloom 1999: 36)

Thus the mandate to rule was taken away from the cruel Shang and passed to the virtuous Zhou. In this political transition, the term "god" became associated with the earthly political ruler, while Heaven came to be portrayed as an impartial universal power, a cosmic moral force that cares for human welfare and so gives the people a wise and good king.

Humanization: The Transition from Shang to Zhou

With the establishment of the Zhou dynasty, the concept of Heaven displaced the more personal Lord-on-High of the Shang. Although divination continued, the methods and materials used in the practice changed, reflecting a simultaneous change in the understanding of the universe.

This shift did not mean that ancient beliefs and practices disappeared. The understanding that the world is controlled by ghosts, nature spirits, and celestial beings remains an integral part of Chinese religion, especially in folk traditions. Nevertheless, new schools of thought developed. Legalists stressed the power of law in the advancement of human well-being, Naturalists concentrated on natural elements and processes (see Focus box on "The Yin–Yang School"), and Confucians focused on human relationships. Philosophers came to see the world as regulated by impersonal processes, which they sought to understand in order to use them as models for human society.

The quest to understand natural processes was driven in part by the desire to find a natural—hence "correct"—foundation on which to structure human society. The 64 hexagrams that are the basis of the *Classic of Changes* (also known as the *Yijing*), a divination text originating around 1000 BCE, were said to capture the metaphysical structure, transformations, and "Way" of the universe, providing both a general blueprint and a specific guide for humans facing a cosmos in continual flux.

Confucius

Confucius spoke of himself as a transmitter of tradition rather than an innovator. On the connection between goodness and ritual, he famously said: "Respect without ritual becomes tiresome, circumspection without ritual becomes timidity, bold fortitude without ritual becomes unruly, and directness without ritual becomes twisted" (Sommer 1995: 46).

Focus

The Yin–Yang School

The Naturalists, also known as the Yin–Yang school, believed that those who followed the laws of nature would thrive while those who did not would perish. Yin–yang theory was later combined with the theory of the five "agents," also called "elements" or "processes" (**wuxing**)—metal, wood, earth, water, and fire—to form a theory of cycles that are generated and overcome. Thus metal generates water, water generates wood, wood generates fire, fire generates earth, and earth generates metal; then the cycle begins again. This cosmology suggests there is nothing in the world that cannot be defeated, and, at the same time, that there is no destruction from which growth cannot come.

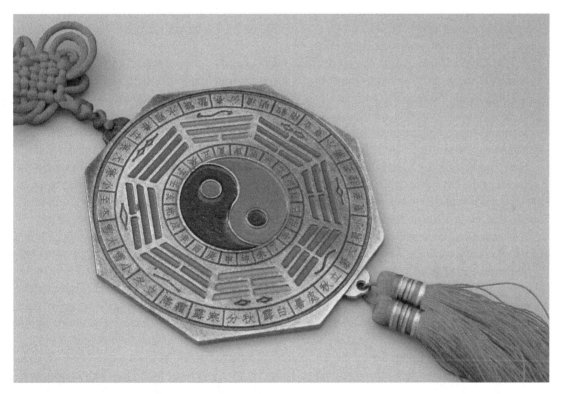

A *bagua* (eight trigrams) mirror is said to ward off evil spirits. This one contains the yin-yang symbol at its center, surrounded by the eight trigrams and two circles (iStockphoto/Thinkstock).

Confucius used the word *li* ("rites" or "ritual") to mean not only religious ritual but also the rules of social etiquette and everyday courtesy. He encouraged his students to practice *li* in all five fundamental relationships and urged them to seek the spirit and principles behind the rites. Central to the Confucian understanding of history was the perfection that the sage kings had achieved by governing in accordance with the Way. Confucius believed that the time of the sage kings had been preceded by a utopian age:

> When the Great Way was practiced, the world was shared by all alike. The worthy and the able were promoted to office and men practiced good faith and lived in affection. Therefore they did not regard as parents only their own parents, or as sons only their own sons. The aged found a fitting close to their lives, the robust their proper employment; the young were provided with an upbringing, and the widow and widower, the orphaned and the sick, with proper care. Men had their tasks and women their hearths. . . . [A]ll evil plotting was prevented and thieves and rebels did not arise, so that the people could leave their outer gates unbolted. This was the age of Grand Commonality [*Datong*]. ("Evolution of Rites," trans. B. Watson, in de Bary and Bloom 1999: 342–343)

In time, greed and selfishness ended the Grand Commonality and ushered in the "Period of Lesser Prosperity," during which the sage kings emerged as exemplars of correct, ethical governance. The primary source of Confucius's teachings on how to govern in such a potentially chaotic era is the collection known as the *Analects*.

The Confucian ideal was the *junzi* (translated variously as "gentleman," "noble," or "superior person"). Although the standard meaning of *junzi* was "son of a lord," indicating inherited social nobility, in the *Analects* the *junzi* is a person of noble character, committed to the development of **de**—another word that underwent a shift in meaning with Confucius. Originally referring to a kind of magical charismatic power, in the *Analects* it signifies a moral power rooted in ethical behavior. The fact that Confucius used these words in nontraditional ways did not mean that the meanings he gave them were new; the sociopolitical ideals he promoted were already present in the classic texts (*Odes*, *Documents*, *Spring and Autumn Annals*, and *Changes*). Confucius used the single word *ren* to capture virtues such as respect, liberality, trustworthiness, earnestness, and kindness. He believed that the most effective way to cultivate *ren* was through careful observance of *li*.

Above all, Confucius emphasized filial piety or devotion, explained in the *Rites* as "caring for" one's parents according to the Way—that is, to the greatest extent possible without neglecting one's responsibilities in other relationships (8.2.1). For Confucius, ritual observance was essential to the maintenance of harmony, for he believed that those who treat their parents with the proper respect will be equally loyal to a government ruling with the Mandate of Heaven. Above all, humaneness is reflected in loyalty and empathetic understanding or reciprocity (*Analects* 4:15). Confucius summed up his teachings in the "silver rule": "What you would not want for yourself, do not do to others" (15:23).

Since all human beings are by nature similar, all have the potential to be noble; however, individuals set themselves apart through their habits and actions (*Analects* 17:2). Thus even as he democratized the idea of nobility, Confucius created a hierarchy of character based on moral cultivation. This hierarchy was all about the mastery of the "heart-mind" (**xin**): "Through mastering oneself and returning to ritual one becomes humane. If for a single day one can master oneself and return to ritual, the whole world will return to humaneness. . . . Look at nothing contrary to ritual; listen to nothing contrary to ritual; say nothing contrary to ritual; do nothing contrary to ritual" (12:1).

Confucius believed that if the ruler wants goodness, the people will be good: "The virtue of the exemplary person is like the wind, and the virtue of small people is like grass: When the wind blows over the grass, the grass must bend" (*Analects* 12:19). To re-create the Grand Commonality, therefore, the good, wise, and humane must rule over the small-minded and morally inferior.

The Confucian mandate is to limit the negative consequences of ignoble behavior. In one story, when a recluse describes Confucius as "a scholar who withdraws from particular men" and suggests that instead he should withdraw from society, Confucius sighs and responds: "If the Way prevailed in the world, [I] would not be trying to change it" (*Analects* 18:6). Personal goodness is not enough: ethical nobility must be expressed through action in the public realm.

Mengzi

The second most prominent classical thinker after Confucius was Meng Ke, whose name was Latinized as Mencius. He lived more than a century after Confucius, by which time large armies of conscripts had been formed and the human costs of war had increased accordingly. Mengzi traveled from state to state, trying to persuade rulers to stop the carnage for the sake of the people. At the same time he emphasized the practical value of humaneness (*ren*) and the importance of the moral sense of what is right (**yi**).

The book *Mencius* is a collection of conversations between Mencius and his disciples, his opponents, and feudal rulers. Among the issues discussed are human nature and government. Mencius traced many of the problems of his day to the human heart-mind (*xin*), of which he identified four types. The heart-mind of compassion yields benevolence, that of shame leads to observance of rites, that of respect moves people to duty or right behavior, and that of right and wrong brings wisdom (Mencius, 6.A.6: 163).

Mencius taught that sensitivity to others' suffering is innate but must be consciously developed if a ruler is to govern as the sage kings did. In later times, a great man was needed to encourage the ruler to cultivate the heart-mind; then, once the prince had become benevolent and dutiful, everyone would emulate him. Mencius did not believe that the effect of the prince's character on the people was automatic or magical, however. Even though human nature was essentially good, the common people needed supervision; otherwise they would be driven only by material needs and desires, with no higher consciousness. The best way of nurturing the heart-mind of the people, Mencius taught, was to teach them to reduce their desires.

Mencius's belief in the potential of the mature heart-mind allowed him to take some unconventional positions. For example, he rejected the notion that filial piety demanded blind obedience. When someone suggested that Shun, the son-in-law of King Yao, had failed in filial piety because he had not informed his parents of his marriage to Yao's daughters, Mencius argued that the parents' heart-minds had not been sufficiently developed for them to consent to his marriage, while Shun's own heart-mind had been so well developed that he could act according to his own conscience.

Similarly, Mencius once remarked that it would be better if the *Documents* had never been written if its contents had to be accepted without critical thought. Most famously, he argued that rebellion by loyal subjects is justified when the ruler has lost the Mandate of Heaven. For Mencius it was not enough simply to follow the classical teachings; we must also use our heart-minds to determine the morally correct course of action.

Mencius was not only a political thinker. He has also been described as a mystic because of his emphasis on **qi** (or *ch'i*): the "flood-like vital force, energy or ether" that appears simultaneously to give substance to virtue and to be nourished by it: "This is a *ch'i* which is . . . vast and unyielding . . . which unites rightness and the Way. Deprive it of these and it will collapse. It is born of accumulated rightness and cannot be appropriated by anyone through a sporadic show of rightness. Whenever one acts in a way that falls below the standard set in one's heart, it will collapse" (Mencius, 2.A.2: 77–78).

Xunzi

Xun Kuang or Xun Qing (c. 310–219 BCE), better known as Master Xun or Xunzi, was a generation younger than Mencius. Living at the end of the Warring States period, he likely witnessed the bloody conflict that ended in the conquest of the last feudal states by the first Qin emperor, Qin Shi Huang. So perhaps it is not surprising that he did not agree with Mencius on the innate goodness of human beings; rather, he believed that human nature was evil, and goodness required conscious effort. Nevertheless, he did share the core Confucian beliefs in the possibility of sagehood and the value of culture and learning.

Xunzi believed that education and ritual were essential to the maintenance of the hierarchy required for an orderly society. But he was not blind to the misuse and corruption of Confucian values. Like Confucius, who says in the *Analects* that the "village paragon is the thief of virtue" (17:13), and Mencius, who describes such a paragon as an honest man who "might be confused with the virtuous" but in fact "cringingly (tries to please) the world" (Lau 1970: 203), Xunzi spoke out against contemporary officials and scholars who had "all become confused" (Watson 1963: 141).

The collection known as the *Xunzi* was compiled more than a century after Xunzi's time, during the Han dynasty. Its form marks a major departure from the recorded conversations of the *Analects* and *Mencius*: it consists mainly of essays on topics such as the original nature of human beings, learning, self-cultivation, government, and military affairs. The first chapter, "Encouraging Learning," underlines the necessity of effort to achieve moral progress: "Learning should never cease. . . . A piece of wood as straight as a plumb line may be bent into a circle as true as any drawn with a compass and, even after the wood has dried, it will not straighten out again" (Watson 1963: 15).

Why did Xunzi think that human beings need to be "straightened out"? Because they are "warped" with innate desires that must be curbed through education and ritual. In his chapter "A Discussion of Heaven," Xunzi continues Confucius's effort to humanize the Zhou tradition, rejecting the supernatural in favor of the rational and natural. He describes Heaven, Earth, and humanity as forming a trinity in which each component has its own function. As human beings, even sages do not seek to understand Heaven, let alone to take over its "godlike" role. Rather, humans should simply focus on living well.

Even though Xunzi believed the world to operate without supernatural intervention, he supported the performance of traditional rituals because he believed they had been perfected by the ancient kings. Only a sage can fully understand the rites, he said, but the noble person finds comfort in performing them, while the common person accepts them as a reflection of the reality of the spirit world. Xunzi took ritual and music out of the realm of magic, interpreting their functions in practical terms. Thus the purpose of teaching the rites is to cultivate the virtues that promote harmony, such as courtesy and humility.

Daoism

Origins

Not everyone believed in the Confucian way. Daoists developed a counterpoint to the Confucian focus on social hierarchy, political involvement, emotional and moral discipline, and ritual regimentation, a counterpoint based on the concept of the **Dao** ("Way"; also spelled **Tao**). Although they did not seek to overturn Confucianism, they pointed out its limitations.

Historically, Daoism was understood to have two branches, philosophical and religious. Daoist philosophy traced its origins to the third and fourth centuries BCE, but Daoist religion was thought to have emerged only in the second century CE, with the formation of two millenarian groups, the

Celestial Masters and Yellow Kerchiefs. Recent research, however, shows that philosophers in the northeastern state of Qi (present-day Shandong) were discussing ideas related to both philosophical and religious Daoism as early as the fourth century BCE.

Although the literature of that time does not use the term "Daoist," it does refer to a Huang–Lao school, named for the mythical "Yellow Emperor" (Huangdi), and the legendary philosopher **Laozi**. Huang–Lao teachings correspond roughly to what we now consider philosophical Daoism. They took shape around the early fourth century BCE, when King Xuan of Qi (r. 319–301 BCE) offered appointments at the Jixia Academy to scholars from various states, north and south, in the hope that they would find solutions to the problems of the day. Among those scholars were Mencius, Xunzi, the Naturalist Zou Yan of the Yin-yang Five Phases (*Wuxing*, or "Five Elements") school, and a student of the Huang–Lao teachings named Huan Yuan.

Daoist nuns from the Quanzhen (Complete Truth) sect perform daily rituals on Wudang Mountain. The three head officiates wear the lotus crown and robes embroidered with trigrams. The yellow banners in the background mark the space as sacred and contain writing that resembles Chinese characters but is "heavenly," not of the human realm (© Michael Saso).

Philosophical Daoism

The term "philosophical Daoism" refers to an early prototypical Daoism concerned with ideas such as the nature of virtue, cultivation of the heart-mind, and good governance. Its early history has conventionally been associated with two main sources: the **Daodejing** (*Classic of the Way and Power*), a multilayered, multi-authored verse text traditionally attributed to the "old master" Laozi, and the **Zhuangzi**, named for the thinker whose ideas it purports to represent (in fact, both works are collections of texts written at different times by different authors).

At least three other sources have proved helpful in reconstructing the early development of philosophical Daoism. Two of them are found in the *Guanzi*, a collection of writings traditionally attributed to a very early (seventh century BCE) figure named Guan Zhong. The third, the *Huang–Lao* manuscripts, is a recently discovered bundle of silk manuscripts, dating from the second century BCE, that include illustrations of "guiding and stretching" exercises similar to modern-day *taiji* (the sequence of slow-motion movements known in the West as Tai Chi).

Development Toward Religious Expression

Religious Daoism is widely associated with colorful rituals; belief in deities, ghosts, and spirits; meditation in search of union with the Dao; and the use of drugs in pursuit of immortality or transcendence. Thus it may appear to be diametrically opposed to philosophical Daoism. Yet the two streams do share several fundamental elements: self-discipline, the quest for transcendence of the ordinary self, the ideal of nonaction (**wuwei**), and the assumption that religion and politics are inseparable.

What makes it difficult to recognize these common elements is the fact that religious Daoism also incorporates two traditions that are clearly not philosophical: a southern Chinese tradition of shamanism and a northern Chinese tradition known as the "way of recipes, methods, and immortality." Unlike the (northern) divinatory shamanism of the Shang and Zhou eras, this southern shamanism was distinctly religious and nonphilosophical. Its character can be seen in a collection called *Songs of the South*, which features lavish descriptions of gods and goddesses, "soaring phoenixes," and fabulous unions between humans and gods. The northern "way of recipes, methods, and immortality," for its part, centered on a quest for an elixir of everlasting life conducted by "masters of technical methods" such as magicians, doctors, diviners, and astrologists. The integration of these very different traditions only adds to the difficulty of understanding the early history of "religious" Daoism.

Different Streams of Daoism

The conjunction of these diverse traditions produced several distinctive streams in early Daoism. Three elements recur in the classical texts: the concept of the Dao as "the One," the primary force in the universe; the need for inner discipline to reach the deep tranquility necessary to experience unity with that force; and, finally, the use of the first two elements to achieve benevolent government.

It has been suggested that the concerns of the classical texts can be classified in three streams: individualist, primitivist, and syncretist. The individualist stream is mystical; concerned mainly with inner cultivation and union with the cosmos, it is basic to all six of the classical texts. To this the primitivist stream, which can be seen in the *Laozi* as well as parts of the *Zhuangzi* (ch. 8–10 and the first part of 11), adds an appeal for a simple agrarian way of life. Finally, the syncretist stream, found in the later chapters of the *Zhuangzi*, *Techniques of the Mind I*, and the *Huang–Lao* manuscripts, combines teachings of Laozi and Zhuangzi with those of other schools. The exact chronology of the various writings is not known, but the *Daodejing* and *Inward Training* are generally considered to be the earliest. Anecdotes in the *Zhuangzi* that describe encounters between Confucius and Laozi would make the two men contemporaries, but their historical authenticity is questionable. The first seven chapters of the *Zhuangzi*, if they were in fact composed by Zhuang Zhou (Zhuangzi, 369?–286? BCE), are also of some antiquity. Finally, the *Songs of the South* are traditionally attributed in part to Qu Yuan, a famously righteous minister who is remembered in the Dragon Boat festival, though most of them were probably written about a century after his death in 278 BCE. Brief descriptions of the six sources follow.

Inward Training in Daoist and Confucian Contexts

Inward Training, a short text on cultivation of the heart-mind embedded in the *Guanzi*, serves as a bridge between philosophical and religious Daoism and provides examples of the cultural beliefs and practices from the Zhou era that Confucians and Daoists shared.

Like the *Daodejing*, *Zhuangzi*, *Techniques of the Mind I*, and *Huang–Lao* sources, *Inward Training* recommends a type of meditation known as "holding fast to the One." But it also refers to concepts uncommon in those philosophical texts—the vital essence (*jing*), vital energy or breath (*qi*), and the numinous or the spirit (*shen*)—that became core features of religious Daoism, in which the integration of these three elements (through meditation and dietary practices) was believed to confer longevity and even physical immortality or spiritual transcendence.

The Dragon Boat festival (*Duanwujie*), held on the fifth day of the fifth month of the lunar calendar, commemorates the loyal Chu minister Qu Yuan (c. 340–278 BCE), who drowned himself after he was unjustly banished. The boat races recall the efforts made to keep fish from eating Qu's body (© Imaginechina/Corbis).

Inward Training recalls early Confucianism when it suggests that the virtue of an exemplary person has a kind of mystical efficacy. The emperor in particular is believed to be capable of "righting" conditions in the empire by virtue of the harmony he embodies. Section 9 of this work uses the same terms that Confucians do to describe the exemplary person (*junzi*) who cultivates this power-virtue (*de*). Like the ideal Confucian ruler, his Daoist counterpart possesses a virtue-power that influences lesser persons.

Whereas *Laozi* and *Zhuangzi* suggest some antipathy toward Confucians, *Inward Training* hints at a shared desire for tranquility and recovery of our original or Heavenly nature. Later forms of Daoism, however, did include practices that some Confucians found abhorrent, including the use of esoteric sexual practices, the ingestion of poisonous cinnabar to attain immortality, and an emphasis on escaping or transcending the world rather than serving it.

Laozi and the Daodejing

If the apparent incongruity of such practices seems puzzling, it may be helpful to remember the famous first lines of the *Daodejing*: "The way that can be spoken of/Is not the constant way" (Lau 1963: 57). The fluidity implied by this holy ineffability is characteristic of Daoism.

Unlike the authors (or editors) of *Inward Training*, Laozi takes a dim view of Confucian rites: "The rites are the wearing thin of loyalty and good faith/And the beginning of disorder" (Lau 1963: 99). Yet, like the Confucians, he wants to ensure that "the offering of sacrifice by descendants will never come to an end" (115). The sage of the *Daodejing* shares with Confucius the ideal of discipline; the only difference is that he seeks to achieve it not through human-created rites but through the all-embracing cosmic Way.

The term *de* in the *Daodejing*, as in Confucianism, refers to the virtue-power that embodies the mystic inner power attained through alignment with the unseen world, the power that allows a sage ruler to infuse his realm with the harmony he has achieved by "doing nothing," *wuwei*. (It's important not to take this phrase literally: in this context, "doing nothing" refers to a state of mind or being in which one is so permeated by the Way that one acts in concert with it, free of self or intention.)

The Daoist sage invites the Dao to dwell in him by making himself as empty as the hollow of a cup or the space in a room. Soft as the water that flows over rocks yet in time wears them down, he is spare in his desires. Overturning convention, he knows the honored male but keeps to the traditionally subservient role of the humble female. He knows the symbolic goodness of white but keeps to the unenlightened black (Lau 1963: 127). He embraces the One and remains an uncarved block, transcending dichotomies. He refuses to be sculpted with conventional virtues—though Laozi makes it clear that he also teaches conventional values:

> What others teach I also teach.
> "The violent will not come to a natural end."
> I shall take this as my precept. (103)

Yet even as the *Daodejing* counsels against violence—just as the Confucian sages do—it criticizes as "false adornments" the Confucian concepts of the wise sage and righteous benevolence. It also finds fault with profit, ingenuity, and learning. Simplicity should replace false values: "Exhibit the unadorned and embrace the uncarved block,/Have little thought of self and as few desires as possible" (Lau 1963: 75).

Unlike the Confucian who concentrates on the virtuous, the Daoist sage "abandons no one" (Lau 1963: 84). "He is "drowsy," "muddled," and "foolish" (77), and does not claim to be right (79); he is self-effacing and "avoids . . . arrogance" (87). Such a sage is capable of surviving even the tumult of the Warring States.

Zhuangzi

Unlike the sage of the *Laozi*, the sage of the *Zhuangzi* shuns politics. Even more strikingly, in the *Zhuangzi* great sages are not the only ones with wisdom: a humble cook may also be wise. The fanciful and the historical exist side by side, like black and white, or female and male. The aspiration to transcend dichotomies is at the core of Zhuangzi's teachings: he "recognizes . . . a 'this' which is also 'that,' a 'that' which is also 'this'" (Watson 1968: 39).

This sage allows his mind to wander, blending with the vastness that is the Way. He follows things as they are. In contrast to Laozi's *wuwei*, or "nonaction," Zhuangzi describes a state of "self-so-ness," or spontaneity (**ziran**). Although the principle is not inconsistent with the Confucian ideal of following nature, it is expressed in remarkably different terms. The story of Cook Ding illustrates the Daoist position. When a prince asks the cook for advice, Ding counsels the same approach to governance that a cook would take to carving an ox: instead of hacking at the carcass, he would look for the hollows in the joints. In the same way, the ruler should not rely on preconceived rules and principles, but should examine the situation at hand to understand its natural structure. The condition in which it is possible to assess a situation clearly is that of Oneness through emptiness.

The Huang–Lao Silk Manuscripts, Techniques of the Mind I, and Songs of the South

The last three textual sources of early Daoism were likely compiled throughout the late Zhou, Qin, and early Han periods. The ideas recorded in the *Huang–Lao Silk Manuscripts* are drawn from a variety of schools, but their underlying theme is Laozi's ideal of the tranquil sage king who governs through nonaction. The prototypical Daoist Huang–Lao scholars were active at court during the early Han, although they disappeared after Emperor Wu (r. 140–87 BCE) made Confucianism the state religion. Sealed in a tomb in 168 BCE, the manuscripts were unknown until 1973.

Like the *Huang–Lao* teachings, *Techniques of the Mind I* reflects the Daoist concerns outlined in *Inward Training*, the *Daodejing*, and the *Zhuangzi*. It explains how self-cultivation—specifically, restraining desire and emptying the mind—can help a ruler attain the tranquility necessary to respond harmoniously to any situation in its "self-so-ness."

Women and the Feminine in the Classical Texts

Neither *Inward Training* nor the *Daodejing* discusses women. The latter talks abstractly about the "mother" and the "spirit of the valley," which is both the "root of heaven and earth" and the "mysterious female" that never dies (Lau 1963: 62). Nor is the *Zhuangzi* much concerned with women: wives are mentioned only as companions in life who are mourned in death, and conventional gender roles are accepted. The Daoist Liezi is described as taking over the domestic realm of the feminine after he has attained mature spiritual understanding:

> He went home and for three years did not go out. He replaced his wife at the stove, fed the pigs as though he were feeding people, and showed no preferences in the things he did. He got rid of the carving and polishing and returned to plainness, letting his body stand alone like a clod. In the midst of entanglement he remained sealed, and in this oneness he ended his life. (Watson 1968: 97)

This association of sacred oneness with animals and the feminine is not surprising. Nor is the *Zhuangzi*'s implied criticism of Confucian-style "carving and polishing," given the Daoist preference for nonaction and the natural. Images of female power and divinity in themselves—without reference to men—are limited to a teacher called the Woman Crookback and a Queen Mother of the West, who heads the pantheon of goddesses. These are mythical characters, however; unlike the Confucian classics, the *Zhuangzi* does not celebrate any historical women. In the *Songs of the South*, by contrast, the theme of mystical oneness with deities, of men seeking union with the feminine, and women with the masculine, becomes prominent.

⊕ The Han Dynasty (202 BCE–220 CE)
State Confucianism, Huang–Lao, and Religious Daoism

During the Han period, ancient shamanic traditions endured, and interest in divination using the *Yijing* persisted. Although eclipsed by Confucianism at court, Daoism reemerged in the form of religious anti-Han rebel groups like the Yellow Kerchiefs and Celestial Masters. It was into this varied religious landscape that Buddhism was introduced.

The Assimilation of Popular Beliefs and Practices

The worship of deities continued into the Han. During a drought, ordinary folk appealed to the Queen Mother of the West for help. By the Latter Han, she had become the head deity of a paradise in the far west that was believed to connect Heaven and Earth, as well as the goddess who bestowed immortality and a protector-deity who granted wealth and children—a precursor of the Buddhist **pusa** (bodhisattva, or enlightened being) Guanyin (Avalokiteshvara).

Political Daoism

The influence of the Huang–Lao thinkers during the early Han is seen in a collection of Huang–Lao writings called the *Masters of Huainan* (*Huainanzi*), a copy of which was presented to Emperor Wu in 139 BCE. A comprehensive guide to just governance, it emphasizes the ruler's need to still his passions and rid himself of prejudice so that he can respond appropriately to all situations.

The court historian Sima Tan (d. 110 BCE) was also a follower of the Huang–Lao school. In his discourse "On the Six Lineages of Thought" he describes the Daoists approvingly as "mov[ing] in unison with the Formless and provid[ing] adequately for all living things" (Roth 1999; S. Queen, in de Bary and Bloom 1999: 279). By contrast, he writes that the New Text Confucians, who favor strength especially in men and tend to focus on ritual performance in the social and political realms, "labor much yet achieve little." By distancing himself from purposeful "right" action, Sima Tan makes clear his preference for the Daoists.

Nevertheless, underlying both traditions is a fundamental renunciation of avarice and an emphasis on self-cultivation for the sake of harmony in the universe. Both Confucians and Daoists seek to control the heart-mind in order to attain the tranquility necessary to achieve union with the Way. Both believe that oneness with the Dao, and hence with Heaven and Earth, allows human beings to transcend their ordinary selves in order to serve others.

The Introduction of Buddhism

Buddhism, like Daoism, emphasizes meditation, breath control, and abstinence from certain foods. Like both Indigenous religions, it focuses on purity of the heart-mind and mastery of the passions. But its trajectory and methods tend to be more extreme. For example, the *Sutra in Forty-Two Sections* stresses the hindrance that lust poses for a man seeking enlightenment, and the Buddha instructs

This sixth-century mural from the Mogao Caves (or Grottoes) at Dunhuang, in western China, shows four divinities, including, at left, the Queen Mother of the West—the preeminent female immortal in Daoism. In spite of her presence, Mogao is renowned as a Buddhist site, one of three extraordinary Buddhist cave-temple systems in north-central and western China; the others are Yungang and Longmen. Beginning in 366 CE, more than 400 grottoes were carved out of the rock at Mogao alone and filled with Buddhist paintings, sculptures, and manuscripts. Among the subjects they depict are Amituofo in his western Pure Land, the bodhisattvas who help suffering, and celestial beings who fly through the air. (Pierre Colombel/CORBIS)

his monks not to look at women, let alone talk to them. During the Han dynasty, the features that Buddhism appeared to share with Confucianism and Daoism helped to mask its more fundamental differences. Sometimes Daoist terms and ideas were used to convey Buddhism to potential converts.

Confucianism

The Birth of Political State Confucianism

The victory of the Qin unified the Warring States. To minimize dissent, however, the first emperor ordered the destruction of almost all the scholarly books that might encourage deep reflection on social and political values, among them the Confucian Classics. Although one copy of each work was preserved in the imperial library, those copies were destroyed in a fire when the capital was sacked. Thus when the Han dynasty (202 BCE–220 CE) replaced the short-lived Qin, a great many works had to be reconstructed.

The political and intellectual changes that took place during the Han would continue to shape imperial ideology as well as religious beliefs and practices for the next 2,000 years. To the four virtues identified by Mencius—humaneness, right action, ritual appropriateness, and wisdom—was added a fifth: trustworthiness. Also central to Han ideology were the notions that Heaven, Earth, and humankind form a trinity, and that the celestial and terrestrial powers respond to human entreaty. Confucian thinkers reflected the influence both of Xunzi and of a chapter in the *Rites* called "Centrality and Equilibrium" in their belief that humans who are sincere in their efforts to bring about peace and harmony can share in the creative, transformative powers of Heaven and Earth.

Echoing Mencius and Xunzi, Han Confucians identified economic welfare as the basis of morality. The government, and in particular the emperor, was obliged to provide both the physical sustenance and the moral education necessary for people to lead secure and happy lives. Following Xunzi, Han Confucians also promoted moral education through ritual, music, and literature.

Both a Confucian canon (in the form of the Five Classics) and political or state Confucianism were established during the Han. Philosophers seeking a holistic account of the universe and humankind's place in it tried to syncretize the Confucian tradition with other philosophies. The result was a Confucianism that blended ideas from traditional texts with those of thinkers such as the masters of technical methods, who sought to manipulate the cosmos, and the Naturalists, who developed the notions of *qi* and **yin-yang–five phases**. It was also during the Han that a number of influential noncanonical texts were written or compiled and edited, among them the *Biographies of Exemplary* (or *Virtuous*) *Women, Admonitions* (or *Lessons*) *for Women*, and the *Classic of Filiality*. The first two in particular defined what was expected of women and formed the foundation of a specifically female Confucian tradition.

The Compilation of the Five Classics

Han Confucians believed that Confucius himself had transmitted the Zhou tradition through the canonical texts, and that he had had a hand in the selection, compilation, and editing of all five Classics. However, later scholars have shown that a good portion of their content originated after Confucius's time.

The first Classic, the *Changes*, assumed particular importance during the Han. It is divided into two parts: a series of short passages interpreting the 64 hexagrams and 10 appendices, or "wings" (traditionally attributed to Confucius), that elaborate on those interpretations. Confucius is also said to have edited or written a short introduction to each section of the second Classic, the *Documents*. Although some of the content is now thought to date from as late as the fourth century CE, this volume was historically considered an accurate account of China's ancient rulers, from the sage kings to the early Zhou.

The third Classic, the *Odes*, consists of roughly 300 poems, mostly from the early Zhou, that Confucius is believed to have chosen and edited. They include songs from both ordinary people and the aristocracy and were often interpreted politically as expressions of popular sentiment—praising virtuous rulers and criticizing bad ones.

The fourth Classic, the *Rites*, consists of three separate texts, some of which Confucius is credited with compiling and editing: *Rites of Etiquette and Ceremonials*, intended for minor officials; *Rites* (or *Institutions*) *of Zhou*; and the *Records* (or *Book*) *of Rites*, which explores the principles behind particular rites. The contents, which likely date from the mid- to late Zhou and the early Han and took their current form over time, range from minutely detailed advice on how to live daily life to broad philosophical discussions of the meaning of state rituals.

The fifth and last Classic, the *Spring and Autumn Annals*, is a terse chronicle of events in Confucius's native state of Lu from 722 to 481 BCE that Confucius is said to have compiled to express his judgment of them. It was therefore used as a guide to moral laws and principles.

Map 11.1 Indigenous Chinese Religions

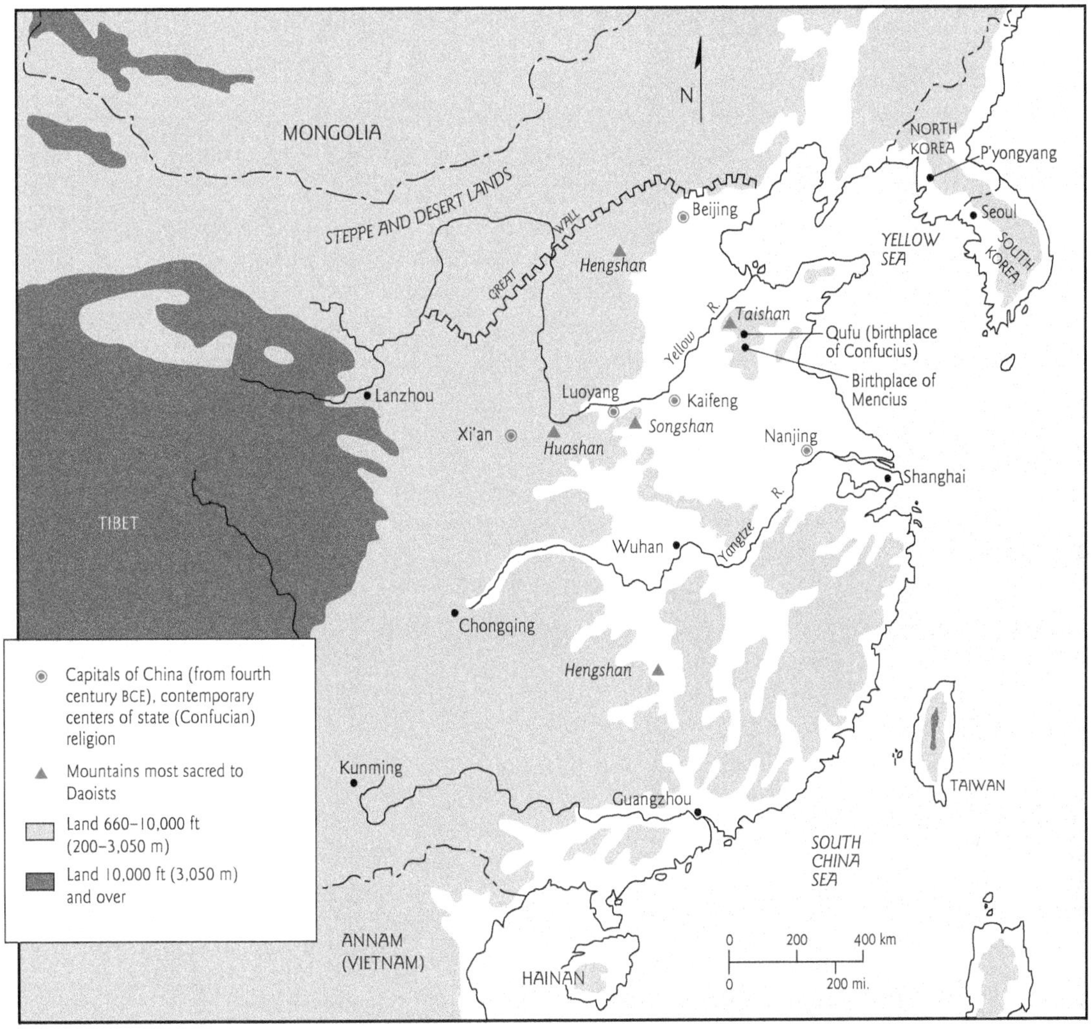

Source: Adapted from al-Faruqi and Sopher 1974: 111.

The text-focused Confucians were the hardest hit by the Qin emperor's book burning. And it was the Confucians of the third and second centuries BCE who took up the task of retrieving and reassembling the lost texts, including those of other schools.

Dong Zhongshu

The most influential Confucian at the court of Emperor Wu was **Dong Zhongshu** (195?–105? BCE). He promoted a "natural model" of the way the world works, based on the idea of correlation between the macrocosm of Heaven and Earth and the microcosm of the human body.

Dong set out to integrate Confucian thought with the supernatural thinking of court diviners, the correlative thinking of the Huang–Lao movement (see "Daoism" in the section on "The Classical Period to the Qin"), and the yin-yang thinking of the Naturalist school. Dong took ideas from

Mencius and Xunzi and combined them with the Naturalist concept of vital force (*qi*) operating through the dynamics of yin and yang.

The Classic of Filiality

A version of the five relationships known as the three bonds was central to Han Confucianism; they concentrated on the distinction between the senior and junior roles encapsulated in the emperor–minister, parent–child, and husband–wife relationships. The importance of the minister's role was especially clear in the *Classic of Filiality* (traditionally traced to Confucius's disciple Zengzi). Presented in the form of a conversation between Zengzi and Confucius, the *Classic of Filiality* extends the notion of continuity between the human and spirit worlds through the veneration of ancestors and connects filial piety to the idea of the triad formed by Heaven, Earth, and human beings. Following ideas laid out in the *Rites*, the work establishes filiality as the foundation of all virtues and the basis of public morality. By the Latter Han, *Filiality* and the *Analects* had been added to the list of Classics.

Women and Confucianism

Liu Xiang (79–8 BCE) is said to have written the *Biographies of Exemplary Women* because he believed that women (beginning with the empress) had a critical, albeit indirect, role to play in government through their influence on their husbands. Drawing on the *Odes* and *Documents*, he identified seven types of women, six of whom contributed to peace and prosperity, and one of whom destroyed dynasties (Raphals 1998: 19):

1. Women of maternal rectitude
2. Women of sage intelligence
3. Women of benevolent wisdom
4. Chaste and obedient women
5. Chaste and righteous women
6. Women with skill in argument
7. Vicious and depraved women

Under the section on "Maternal Rectitude" he tells the famous story of Mengmu, the widowed mother of Mencius. She is said to have moved three times to facilitate her son's education. On one occasion, when Mengmu asked how his day at school had gone and Mencius answered nonchalantly, "As usual," she took a knife and destroyed the cloth she had been weaving to teach him that a man who does not take learning seriously is like a woman who neglects her responsibility to her family.

Like a man's moral development, a woman's cultivation began at home, in the family. Self-cultivation was especially important for women because of the influence a mother was thought to have on her fetus. According to the *Rites*, boys and girls should be separated after the age of seven. At 10, boys were sent out to study the six arts (rites, music, archery, chariot racing, calligraphy, and mathematics), while girls were kept at home to learn domestic skills and develop the mental discipline they would need to care for their future families. In addition to learning how to weave, sew, and prepare food, girls were taught etiquette—the social conventions required for harmonious relations—and how to perform particular rituals, including the sacrifices required to keep peace with the ancestors.

Born into a family of scholars, **Ban Zhao** (c. 48–112 CE) said that she wrote *Admonitions for Women* for her daughters, who had not had the benefit of systematic training in their roles either as wives or as daughters- and sisters-in-law in their husbands' families. Well educated, socially prominent, and politically influential, Ban Zhao was typical of aristocratic women in Han society. According to one later history, she worked in the imperial libraries and supervised the writing of treatises on astronomy and the chronological tables of nobles. Recognizing Ban's erudition, the emperor appointed her as tutor to the women at court, and she later served as an advisor to Empress Deng. *Admonitions* is divided into seven chapters:

1. Humility
2. Husband and Wife
3. Respect and Caution
4. Womanly Qualifications
5. Whole-Hearted Devotion
6. Implicit Obedience
7. Harmony with Younger Brothers- and Sisters-in-Law

Ban describes three rituals performed at the birth of a girl and explains the principles behind them. First, whereas a baby boy was placed on the bed, a girl was placed below it, to signify her lowliness; second, she was given broken pieces of pottery to play with to signify that she must work hard; and third, her birth was announced to the ancestors to draw attention to her future role in their veneration.

Ban belongs firmly in the Confucian lineage. She believed that relationships are founded on the cosmic principles of yin and yang; because yang is rigid, a man is to be honored for his strength, and because yin is yielding, a woman is considered beautiful for her gentleness. Over time, the name Ban Zhao became synonymous with womanly erudition. Some 400 years after her death, she was included in a list of exemplary women venerated in state sacrifices.

Daoism

Although the Huang–Lao school disappeared from the Han court after Confucianism was made the state religion, Daoist practice continued to develop outside the palace, among the common people.

Inner and Outer Alchemy

The first text on inner alchemy was published in the mid-second century. Traditionally ascribed to Wei Boyang, an alchemist from the south, *The Seal of the Unity of the Three* took its name from its three main subjects: cosmology from the *Changes*, *wuwei* from Daoism, and alchemy. Wei fused the three elements into a single doctrine. Like Dong Zhongshu, Wei used correlative cosmology, drawing on the concepts of yin-yang and five phases to describe the cosmos in relation to the Dao, the relative to the absolute, multiplicity to oneness, and time to timelessness.

The classical Daoist texts taught that the three vital elements of essence, energy, and numinous spirit, which have been broken by worldly activity and the disruptive awareness of things as separate from one another, must be returned to their original wholeness by meditation: "holding fast to the One," "sitting and forgetting," visualizing the cosmos within one's body, and following the internal circulation of vital energy. According to Wei, practitioners of inner alchemy sought to return to the Dao by reversing the processes of disunion—as though they were sculptures "unsculpting" themselves to recover their original unity as uncarved blocks. In practice, through meditative visualization devotees sought to move from form to essence, from essence to vital energy, from vital energy to spirit, and from spirit to emptiness or the Void, which, though formless, can be visualized as the highest deity: the Great One, Supreme Unity, or Supreme Oneness.

Belief in physical immortality was strong during the Han period. It was thought that after a long period of inward concentration, when the spirit had been purified, a "spirit embryo" containing or representing the True Self would be born. There were also some who believed that immortality could be achieved through the ingestion of cinnabar.

The Celestial Masters and Yellow Kerchiefs

Over time, the Confucian underpinnings of the Han regime were challenged by political corruption, natural disasters, and military turbulence. The resulting economic and social turmoil provoked uprisings, some of which reflected Daoist influences. At the same time, the *Classic of the Great Peace* (*Taipingjing*) was circulating, prophesying the coming of a celestial master who would bring peace to a time of surging chaos.

The Great Peace likely influenced both the Celestial Masters and the Yellow Kerchiefs (*Taiping Dao*, or "Way of Taiping"). Founded in 142 CE, the Celestial Masters (*Tianshi*; later renamed Orthodox Unity) traced its origins to a deified Laozi, who was said to have revealed to **Zhang Daoling** the teachings of Orthodox Unity and to have given him a covenant establishing a new relationship between the gods and humans. A central feature of this covenant was the abolition of traditional blood sacrifices; no longer would the gods be influenced by animal offerings. Instead, they would operate as a kind of celestial bureaucracy, modeled after the governmental bureaucracy, to whom believers could present their appeals. The priests were expected to provide their services in return for an annual donation of five bushels of rice from devotees.

Initiates of the Celestial Masters gained access to esoteric sacred texts. The *Daodejing* was used in liturgy, practices included chanting and meditation, and purity chambers were provided for the cultivation of the spirit embryo. The sect established a theocracy in the state of Shu (Sichuan) and was the state religion of the Wei kingdom until it was dispersed across northern China, unintentionally aiding the spread of Daoism.

The Yellow Kerchiefs movement, based in Shandong, was established with the express purpose of challenging the Han regime in the name of the Yellow Emperor. Like the Celestial Masters, the Yellow Kerchiefs practiced confession, repentance of sins, meditation, and chanting; they also believed in inherited guilt, passed on from ancestors to descendants. They attracted a massive following, but when they rose in rebellion in the year 184 they were crushed, and the movement disappeared.

Buddhism

Buddhism was first introduced to China shortly before Confucianism became the official religion and the various prototypical Daoist elements were synthesized. At first the Chinese had difficulty understanding the relationship between rebirth and the idea of no-self (*wuwo*, or *anatman*; see Chapter 7 on Hinduism). If there was no enduring soul, what was reborn? Misunderstanding of this concept led Han Buddhists to erroneously teach the indestructibility of a soul that is bound to the cycle of rebirth through cause and effect (**yinguo**, or karma). The idea of an enduring soul was familiar to China, but the idea of karma was something new. Contrary to the Indigenous idea that descendants would inherit the sins of their ancestors, Buddhism suggested that reward and punishment would be bound to the individual alone.

Though Daoism and Buddhism were initially understood as belonging to one religious family, the *Taipingjing* attacked Buddhism on four counts that reflected core Chinese concerns: it encouraged the abandonment of parents, to become a monk it was necessary to abandon one's wife and children, the requirement of celibacy defied the duty to continue the family lineage, and the monks' dependence on alms promoted begging.

In time, Buddhism disentangled itself from Daoism, established its own communities, and became more popular than its Daoist counterpart. As native teachings influenced the evolution of Buddhism, the tradition in turn had a profound influence on the development of both Confucianism and Daoism.

⊕ The Six Dynasties Period (220–589)

The Six Dynasties period, covering the era of the Three Kingdoms (220–280), the Jin dynasty (265–420), and the Southern and Northern dynasties (420–589), was politically fractured, marked by struggle against both "barbarian" invaders from North and Central Asia and a foreign religion, Buddhism. Religious teachings in this period were shaped by the tension between China's desire to preserve its traditional values and political independence and its sometimes-grudging admiration and acceptance of an increasingly Sinicized Buddhism.

Tensions notwithstanding, Buddhist ideas were attractive, and as they began to permeate Chinese society, different spheres were allocated to each religion. Buddhism was seen as medicine for spiritual disorders, and Confucianism continued to play an important role in family life despite its loss of official status. It survived over the next 400 years not only through individual study of the classic texts, but also in handbooks offering practical advice on everyday matters.

The development of large-scale religious organizations like the Celestial Masters was greatly strengthened by the new model of Buddhist monastic discipline. The nascent Daoist and Buddhist movements went far beyond the traditional state- and family-centered cults such as those dedicated to Heaven, the ancestors, or the gods of soil and grain. Although they respected the foundational values of filial piety and sociopolitical harmony, they did not show the traditional respect for hierarchies; thus monks and nuns refused to bow before kings.

Confucianism

Interaction with Daoism and Buddhism

The fall of the Han dynasty in 220 marked the beginning of the Six Dynasties, a period of almost four centuries of instability. During this time, China experienced repeated invasions from North and Central Asia, Confucianism lost state support, and those seeking religious guidance increasingly looked to Daoism and Buddhism.

Wang Bi

Among the Confucian literati was a man who has also been described as a neo-Daoist. In his short life (226–249), Wang Bi wrote extensive commentaries not only on the *Analects* and *Changes* (a text revered by Daoists as well as Confucians), but also on the *Daodejing*. Like the Seven Sages of the Bamboo Grove—famous neo-Daoist eccentrics who were near contemporaries—Wang was interested in *xuanxue* (study of the "dark" or mysterious and profound). Above all, he emphasized the concept of principle (**li**, written differently in Chinese than the *li* meaning "rites"), which would become the linchpin for the neo-Confucians of the Song period (960–1279) nearly 1,000 years later.

Criticism of Buddhism

As Daoism and Confucianism drew closer together, both criticized Buddhism on the same grounds that the *Taipingjing* had. They also raised questions about Buddhist practices. To shave one's head, for instance, was construed as an act of gross disrespect, since it amounted to harming the body given by one's ancestors. Industrious Confucians interpreted Buddhist monks' ascetic withdrawal from productive work as a shirking of responsibility, and the monastic tradition of begging for food as parasitism. In addition, Confucians and Daoists argued that Buddhism lacked authority because it was not mentioned in the Five Classics. Furthermore, the Buddhist renunciation of worldly pleasures went far beyond the Confucian ideal of moderation, effectively denying the value that Confucianism attributed to life in the world (de Bary and Hurvitz, in de Bary 1972: 125–138). Finally, there was the seemingly irrational nature of some Buddhist teachings. According to Mouzi, Confucians were baffled by the Buddhist practice of reflecting on the impurities of the body:

> The ascetic engages in contemplation of himself and observes that all the noxious seepage of his internal body is impure. Hair, skin, skull and flesh; tears from the blinking of the eyes and spittle; veins, arteries, sinew and marrow; liver, lungs, intestines and stomach; feces, urine, mucus and blood: such a mass of filth when combined produces a man. . . . [A]wakened to the detestability of the body, concentrating his mind, he gains *dhyana*. (de Bary 1972: 129)

This emphasis on the impurity of the body was especially harsh for women, given the additional defilements of menstruation and childbirth. Although it contradicted the Indigenous Chinese idea that the body is a fundamentally good gift from the ancestors, the negativity of other Buddhist ideas about women was not inconsistent with Chinese ideas. The depictions of females in the section titled "Vicious and Depraved" in Liu Xiang's *Biographies of Exemplary Women*, for example, are quite in line with Buddhist notions of women's physical and spiritual impurity.

Buddhism

Amid the chaos of the Six Dynasties era, Chinese Buddhism developed in two distinctive streams. In the north, where many states were under non-Han rule, Buddhist political dissenters were attracted by monks' claims of mysterious powers such as clairvoyance and the ability to make themselves invisible. In the south, where many Han scholars and officials had taken refuge and society was steeped in an apolitical neo-Daoism, Buddhism was only occasionally drawn into politics.

Hinayana (*Xiaocheng*, or "Small Vehicle") as well as Mahayana (*Dacheng*, or "Great Vehicle") traditions were practiced in China. In this early period, meditation was more closely associated with the Hinayana school, while Mahayana Buddhists were more interested in exploring what constitutes wisdom. Several texts on the "Perfection of Transcendental Wisdom," such as the *Heart* and *Diamond Sutras*, were translated into Chinese by the end of the 300s, and many Mahayana texts, including the *Lotus* and *Vimalakirti Sutras*, were translated after the famous scholar-monk Kumarajiva arrived in 401.

Buddhism and Daoism

Nevertheless, the Chinese continued to think of Buddhism as a variant of Daoism. The "Perfection of Transcendental Wisdom" writings teach a notion of emptiness or "the void" that recalls the Daoist belief in nonbeing. The monk Zhi Dun's idea that there is a transcendental absolute (*li*), an essence and ultimate truth that is expressed in the relative mundane world, found echoes in Wang

Bi's *li*, or principle. Moreover, just as a buddha is free of all attachments, a sage is free from all desires; in both, all dualities and distinctions disappear.

In addition, Buddhism's dual focus on wisdom and compassion echoed the traditional Chinese concern with security, stability, and harmony, while the Buddhist notion of impermanence was in tune with the Chinese assumption of continual change. At the same time, Buddhist teachings on suffering and the path to liberation resonated with people in a time of instability.

Reasons for the Popularity of Buddhism

People were attracted to Buddhism for many reasons, including its art (paintings and sculptures) and architecture (pagodas modeled after stupas); the promise of enlightenment, or at least a better chance at contentment and equanimity in this life; a well-tested, progressive program of precept taking, chanting, meditation, and study to help the faithful achieve that goal; and the sophisticated philosophy, literature, and erudition of its proponents. Even though some found the monastic life unfilial, others were positively attracted to the idea of a religious community that was separate from the family and clan.

As Buddhism became more popular, it also offered new possibilities to women. Baochang's *Lives of Nuns* is a testament to the devotion and accomplishments of the first Chinese nuns, many of whom were ordained in the fifth century by a quorum of nuns from Sri Lanka. Of course, their male counterparts were remembered as well, in parallel biographies like the *Lives of Famous Monks*, also by Baochang, and Huijiao's *Lives of Eminent Monks*.

Power Struggle Between Buddhism and the State

It was not long before the Buddhist community attracted charges of extravagant spending on its monasteries and monks were accused of moral laxity, graft, and corruption. According to a memorial submitted to Emperor An of the Eastern Jin dynasty in 389, "Monks [and] nuns . . . are vying with each other to enter into cliques and parties. . . . I have heard that the Buddha is a spirit of purity, far-reaching intelligence, and mysterious emptiness. . . . But nowadays the devotees are vile, rude, servile, and addicted to wine and women" (quoted in Chen 1964: 74–75).

Where government had been entrusted to monks and nuns, as under the Eastern Jin (317–420), they were accused of meddling in politics. In 403 Huan Xuan, who usurped power from the Eastern Jin, demanded that monks and nuns bow to him, as laypeople were obliged to, but the famous monk Hui Yuan (344–416) successfully argued against this command. The leader of a well-organized and strictly disciplined community that worshiped the celestial Amituofo of the Pure Land, he contended that Buddhists can be divided into two groups: the laity, who, because they remain in the world, should obey all rules, and the monastics, who, having left home, have abandoned the secular realm and therefore should not be required to adhere to its rules.

The first five stories of the Big Wild Goose Pagoda in Xian were built in 652 as part of a temple complex designed to house Buddhist artifacts brought from India (© GRANT ROONEY PREMIUM/Alamy).

Document
From *Lives of the Nuns*

Lives of the Nuns, by a sixth-century monk named Baochang, tells the stories of 65 Buddhist nuns who lived between 316 and 516. Two earlier efforts to capture the religious lives of women were the anonymous Buddhist Song of the Sisters *and Liu Xiang's Confucian* Biographies of Exemplary Women. *The following excerpt tells of a young devotee who rejected a marriage arranged by her family.*

Sengduan had vowed that she would leave the household life rather than be married off. Nevertheless, her beauty of face and figure were well known in the region, and a wealthy family had already received her mother and elder brother's agreement to a betrothal.

Three days before the marriage ceremony Sengduan fled in the middle of the night to a Buddhist convent whose abbess hid her . . . and supplied her with everything she needed. Sengduan also had a copy of the Bodhisattva Guanshiyin [another name for Guanyin] Sutra that she was able to chant from memory after only two days of study. She rained tears and made prostrations day and night without ceasing. Three days later, during her worship, she saw an image of the Buddha, who announced to her, "Your bridegroom's lifespan is coming to an end. You need only continue your ardent practice without harboring sorrowful thoughts." The next day her bridegroom was gored to death by an ox. (Tsai, 1994: 49–50)

Success and Subsequent Interreligious Conflict

The popularity of Buddhism proved to be its undoing. While in the south hostility toward it was channeled into written form, in the north it resulted in full-blown campaigns of persecution, once under Emperor Taiwu of Northern Wei in 446, and twice under Emperor Wu of Northern Zhou, in 574 and then again in 577.

Scholars suggest that Taiwu, who was likely of Turkish background, was predisposed against Buddhism because he wanted to prove his acculturation to Chinese values. His antipathy was aggravated when he discovered that weapons had been hidden in a monastery; that men were becoming monks to avoid *corvée* labor and conscription; and, worse yet, that monks were secretly living with women in subterranean apartments. He was further outraged when he learned that some monks had sold off grain intended for the poor in times of famine.

To make things worse, the monastic system was a powerful organization operating alongside the state, and even its architecture rivaled that of the imperial buildings. Taiwu's Daoist–Confucian prime minister Cui Hao, whose brother and wife were both Buddhists, encouraged him to take such harsh measures against Buddhists, both monastics and laypeople, that even the Daoist Kou Qianzhi counseled against them. The other northern ruler to torment the Buddhists was Emperor Wu of the Northern Zhou. Unlike Taiwu, however, he included Daoists in his persecutions.

A different ruler also named Wu, this one in the south, was a devout Buddhist himself. Liang Wudi (King Wu of Liang) (502–549) ceded the responsibilities of governance to the monks and nuns, abolished all Daoist temples, and returned all Daoist priests, men and women, to lay life. Many Daoists fled north.

A Sinification of Buddhism: Ideas Consistent with and Adopted by the Chinese

As Buddhism developed, it became acculturated to Indigenous Chinese values and grew into a distinctive branch of the originally foreign South and Central Asian Buddhism, marked in part by the following elements.

Nonduality and Emptiness

As more Buddhist teachings made their way into China, it became clear that the Hinayana and Mahayana doctrines sometimes contradicted one another (see Chapter 7 on Hinduism). The *Heart Sutra*, for example, presents the Madhyamaka (*zhonglun* or *sanlun*) teaching of nonduality, which negates Hinayana teachings such as the five components of personality (*skandhas* or *yun*). The second stanza of this short but essential sutra, often chanted in liturgy, begins with the bodhisattva of compassion, Avalokiteshvara or Guanyin, in a deep trance, recognizing that the five components are "in their own-being . . . empty," and that the same is true of "feelings, perceptions, impulses, and consciousness."

Doctrinal Categorization and Skillful Means

The *Lotus Sutra* offered a way of understanding these divergent teachings. Two ideas developed to account for the theoretical differences: doctrinal categorization or classification and skillful means, or *upaya*. The first term refers to the notion that the Buddha's talks can be classified into varying doctrines based on different periods and audiences. The second idea explains why: the Buddha's lectures reflected both his own development and his skillful shaping of his ideas to suit the capacities of his audience. The famous story of the burning house (see Chapter 10) is reinforced by the following passage, also in the *Lotus Sutra*, according to which there is only one Buddha vehicle: "The Buddhas of the past used countless numbers of expedient means, various causes and conditions, and words of simile and parable in order to expound the doctrines for the sake of living beings. These doctrines are all for the sake of the one Buddha vehicle" (Watson 2001: 9).

Guanyin

Over time, the Chinese accepted the Three Baskets of the Hinayana but gave priority to Mahayana teachings. In the *Lotus Sutra*, the Buddha himself says nothing about the classic Hinayana themes, but he does advise the faithful to call on Guanyin (see Chapter 10):

> If a woman wishes to give birth to a male child, she should offer obeisance and alms to Bodhisattva Perceiver of the World's Sounds [Guanyin] and then she will bear a son blessed with merit, virtue, and wisdom. And if she wishes to bear a daughter, she will bear one with all the marks of comeliness, one who in the past planted the roots of virtue and is loved and respected by many persons. (Watson 2001: 121)

The idea of a selfless being who defers enlightenment, is capable of taking on an infinite number of forms, and disregards sociocultural and religious boundaries in order to aid the suffering expanded and deepened Chinese religiosity. The *Lotus Sutra* continues: "If they [the people] need a monk, a nun, a layman believer, or a laywoman believer to be saved, immediately [Guanyin] becomes a monk, a nun, a layman believer, or a laywoman believer and preaches the Law for them" (Watson 2001: 123).

> The innumerable guises of Guanyin recall the first four lines of the *Daodejing*:
>
> The way that can be spoken of
> Is not the constant way;
> The name that can be named
> Is not the constant name. (Lau 1963: 57)

And the *pusa*'s compassion resonates with the ideal of the sage, central to both Confucianism and Daoism. But the Buddhist Guanyin introduced a stronger version of the Indigenous ideas of transformation implicit in the *Changes*: he/she can take any form necessary to rescue those in need.

Lay Practice

As part of its accommodation of local ideals, Buddhism shifted its focus from monasticism to lay practice. One of the most popular sutras, the *Vimalakirti*, teaches that there is no need to abandon home and family in order to become enlightened. In it the Buddha's students tell him that Vimalakirti—a wise, pure, celibate layman—understands the teachings better than they do. This lay orientation no doubt helped push forward the sinification of Buddhism.

The Mind in Both Aspects: Pure and Impure

The mind that is "upright," "deeply searching," and "aspires to *bodhi*" illustrates two core Mahayana ideas: that Mind or Consciousness is crucial in the alleviation of suffering, and that it has two aspects—which means that those three positive characteristics can never be separated from their opposites: non-uprightness, not deeply searching, and not aspiring to *bodhi*. The first idea belongs to the Yogacara, or Consciousness Only, school (see Chapter 7), known as Faxiang in China. The second is an expression of the concept of the nondual One Mind found in the teachings on the Matrix of the Tathagata (*Tathagatagarbha*) and discussed at length in the *Lankavatara Sutra* and a treatise entitled *The Awakening of Faith* (*Dacheng qixin lun*), which has no Sanskrit original.

The two aspects of the One Mind may take several forms: the universal and the particular, the transcendental and the phenomenal, the pure and the impure. The Matrix (*garbha*) also has two aspects, symbolizing both the seed of the Tathagata (the Buddha) and the womb in which it may grow. It represents the Buddha-nature and capacity for enlightenment that are inherent in all human beings (a concept that parallels Confucian and Daoist ideas about sagehood). But it is important to understand that (in line with the concept of no-self) Buddha-nature has no substance: it is not a thing, even in the sense that a soul would be a thing. When the One Mind is unhindered by defilements, the luminosity of Buddha-nature will be clear. Thus Buddha-nature is not something we possess, but something we are. The key to uncovering or cultivating the One Mind is meditation.

Mofa, or End-Time

From the beginning, Buddhism taught that the universe was in a phase of decline when Shakyamuni was born to set the wheel of dharma in motion again. The Three Stages School (*Sanjiejiao*), founded in the late sixth century, developed that idea, teaching that time was divided into three periods—those of the Correct Law, the Counterfeit Law, and the Decadent or Final Law—and that the Chinese were living during the last of the three, the end-times (*mofa*). During the time of the Buddha, people were able to attain enlightenment through practice, but during the time of false teachings Buddhism becomes increasingly formalized, so that fewer and fewer people are able to benefit from it. During the end-times, humans lose their aspiration for enlightenment and Buddhism is incapable of leading them to buddhahood.

Help from the Celestial Buddhas

So what if one is a layperson living in the end-time and cannot reach enlightenment? One group of practitioners offered a solution: when you cannot do it on your own, ask to be reborn in the Pure Land of a celestial buddha such as Amituofo (see Chapter 10).

The *Larger Pure Land Sutra*, or *Sutra on the Buddha of Infinite Life*, is one of three Pure Land (**Jingtu**) sutras; the other two are the *Smaller Pure Land* or *Amitayus Sutra* and the *Contemplation* (*Amitayurdhyana*) *Sutra*. According to the *Larger Sutra*, Amituofo, in a previous incarnation, vowed to bring into his Western Paradise all who "sincerely and joyfully entrust themselves to me, and call my Name even ten times" (Inagaki 1994: 244–245). And according to the *Contemplation Sutra*, one may simply repeat the mantra for rebirth into the Pure Land—"Homage to Amitayus Buddha" (*Namo Amituofo*)—10 times. The mantra can be used as a focus in silent meditation or chanted aloud.

Flower Garland

Another important idea that shaped Chinese Buddhism is found in the *Flower Garland Sutra* (*Avatamsaka* or **Huayan**): the belief that all things are interconnected.

Some Chinese schools, such as Tiantai and Huayan, were organized around a particular teaching or doctrine (those of the *Lotus* and *Flower Garland Sutras*, respectively), while others, such as **Chan** and Pure Land, were centered on a core practice (meditation and chanting, respectively). We will look at the most influential schools in the next section. But first we will return to Daoism and see how it was faring during this period.

Daoism

Buddhist Influences

Daoism assimilated beliefs and practices from Buddhism, blending them into the various streams of Daoist thought and developing them while remaining faithful to its own beliefs and practices. Thus Daoist teachings were reinterpreted in terms of *yinguo* (karma) and **lunhui** (rebirth), and Daoist rituals were adapted to reflect the new ideas about death that Buddhism had introduced. Both monastic and lay institutions were established, culminating in the construction of the first Daoist temple in the fifth century. Some Daoist leaders stayed active politically, but others turned inward and focused on individual cultivation.

The quest for transcendence took two forms: the pursuit of spiritual transcendence through meditation and the pursuit of physical immortality through methods that included a sexual ritual known as the joining of energy or the union of breaths and the ingestion of poisonous substances such as cinnabar.

Mysterious Learning and Outer Alchemy

The Seven Sages of the Bamboo Grove concentrated on private individual cultivation, and (like the Confucian Wang Bi) they were interested in *xuanxue*. Discouraged from participating in public life after the fall of the Han, and inspired by Zhuangzi's notions of spontaneity and spiritual freedom, they gained a reputation for eccentric behavior (one of them was said to have roamed around naked in his hermitage). Having fled the turmoil of northern China for the south, the Seven Sages engaged in "pure conversation" on metaphysical rather than political topics, in which they reflected Confucian and Buddhist as well as Daoist influences.

It was likely sometime in the 300s that the *Liezi*—the third most important Daoist "philosophical" text, after the *Daodejing* and *Zhuangzi*—was compiled, bringing together stories about one of the Daoist thinkers mentioned in the *Zhuangzi*. A less important but still informative text, probably written in the 320s, was Ge Hong's *Baopuzi* ("The master who embraces spontaneous nature"), a collection of essays on classic Daoist themes, including methods of driving away harmful spirits, reaching the gods, and achieving longevity and immortality using alchemical recipes.

The Highest Clarity and Numinous Treasure Schools

Two new religious Daoist schools emerged in the latter part of the fourth century. Yang Xi, a medium and shaman, formed the Highest Clarity (*Shangqing*) school when he received scriptures from the immortal Lady Wei of the Heaven of Highest Clarity. Yang and his followers sought to become "true beings" or "perfected persons" (*zhenren*) through practices that included the use of outer alchemy to facilitate flights to the star deities who controlled human destiny. Devotees ate very little, believing that fasting would make their bodies light and radiant for their ascent to the heavens.

The second new school, Numinous Treasure (*Lingbao*), was founded a few decades later by Ge Chaofu, a grandnephew of Ge Hong who received from his clan ancestors a series of revelations involving the Buddhist concepts of karma, rebirth, and cycles of time. Whereas Highest Clarity focused on the individual, Numinous Treasure looked outward to the local community and beyond to all of humanity, suggesting a synthesis of Daoist and Buddhist ideas. The *Scripture for the Salvation of Humanity* (*Durenjing*) illustrates this synthesis, describing a cosmic deity who sends an emissary to earth to reveal the *Durenjing* and ferries suffering humans to liberation and peace—paralleling the services performed by Amituofo and the historical Buddha Gautama himself.

Numinous Treasure focused especially on purification and communal renewal rituals. The goals of the former were typical of the era: prevention of disease, the warding off of natural calamities, and the salvation of ancestors. Performed around a temporary altar, they began with cleansing of the body and purification of the heart-mind through confession of sins; a communal feast was then held to celebrate the reinstatement of harmony between the gods and human beings. In community renewal rituals (which are still practiced today), deities were invited down to the altar, incense was offered, and the sponsors of the rituals were granted audiences with the gods, during which they would request favors for their communities.

⊕ The Sui and Tang Dynasties (589–907)

China Reunited

In 589 China was reunited for the first time since the fall of the Han nearly 400 years earlier, and in 618 the Tang came to power. Daoism and Buddhism both reached new heights of popularity over the next three centuries of relative peace and prosperity, and Confucianism experienced a renewal.

Confucianism

The second Tang emperor, Taizhong, established an academy for scholar-officials in which the curriculum was based on the classical texts of Confucianism. For the first time in Chinese history it became possible for a commoner to work his way into officialdom. Taizhong also ordered all districts to build Confucian temples and in 647 installed in each temple 22 tablets commemorating orthodox Confucians of the Han era. A century later, the title "King of Manifest Culture" was bestowed on Confucius, who now displaced the Duke of Zhou as the "uncrowned king" of Chinese civilization.

In time, the Confucian curriculum was expanded to include 12 works, among which were the *Analects* and the *Classic of Filiality*. The revival of interest in Confucian thought was reflected in the popularity of three writers: Madame Zheng, author of the late-seventh-century *Classic of Filiality for Women*; **Han Yu** (768–824), a prominent scholar-official intent on reintroducing Confucianism to the people; and Han's contemporary Song Ruozhao, who wrote the *Analects for Women*.

Madame Zheng's Classic of Filiality for Women

The wife of a government official, Madame Zheng set out to create a female Confucian tradition starting from Ban Zhao. Her *Classic of Filiality for Women* emphasizes the importance of chastity, filial piety, intelligence, and wisdom. Zheng imagines Ban Zhao teaching a group of women that a wife should encourage her husband in good behavior and guide him with "modesty and deference" (T. Kelleher, in de Bary and Bloom 1999: 826). When the women ask if they must obey their husbands' every command, Ban cites numerous historical examples of wives who corrected or criticized their husbands and explains: "If a husband has a remonstrating wife, then he won't fall into evil ways. Therefore, if a husband transgresses against the Way, you must correct him. How could it be that to obey your husband in everything would make you a virtuous person?" (827).

Han Yu's Defense of Confucianism

Han Yu marks an important point in the Confucian renewal. Although Confucian principles had been reintroduced into government, they initially had little popular currency. In an effort to bring Confucian teaching back to the people, Han Yu wrote *Essentials of the Moral Way*. In it he answers the question "What is the teaching of the former kings?" as follows:

> To love largely is called a sense of humaneness; to act according to what should be done is called rightness. To proceed from these principles is called the moral Way; to be sufficient unto oneself without relying on externals is called inner power. . . . Its methods are the rites, music, chastisement, and government. Its classes of people are scholars, peasants, craftsmen, and merchants. (C. Hartman, in de Bary and Bloom 1999: 569)

Song Ruozhao's Analects for Women

The *Analects for Women* is usually attributed to Song Ruozhao, though some say that the actual author was her sister Ruohua. Born into a scholarly family, Song was appointed to the court as a scholar and taught the imperial princesses. Her *Analects* consists of eight sections: establishing oneself as a person, learning how to work, ritual decorum (learning proper etiquette), rising early to begin household work, serving one's parents-in-law, serving a husband, instructing sons and daughters, and managing the household.

Daoism

The founder of the Tang dynasty, Li Yuan, claimed descent from Laozi, and under his family's rule Daoism once again became the state religion. Some patriarchs from the Highest Clarity school held government posts. The "Brilliant Emperor" Xuanzhong wrote a commentary on the *Daodejing* and invited the Highest Clarity patriarch Sima Chengzen to court, princesses were ordained as Daoist priestesses and performed state rituals, colleges of Daoism were established, and the *Daodejing* was briefly included in state examinations. By 739 there were 1,137 abbeys for male Daoist priests and 550 for female Daoist priests. Classical Daoism reached the height of its power and popularity during the Tang.

Buddhism

The first two centuries of the Tang dynasty are often seen as the apex of Buddhism in China. Monks visited the imperial court often, and several Chinese Buddhist schools developed around individual sutras. In addition, one sutra was used to legitimate the rise to power of China's first and only female emperor. The *Great Cloud Sutra* prophesied the imminent arrival of a female Maitreya (Milo), a salvational figure who would bring peace and prosperity to the land. After the death of her husband, the emperor Gaozong, Wu Zetian claimed to be that figure and took the throne as Empress Wu of the Zhou dynasty.

The two types of Buddhist schools, doctrinal and practical, were often described as two wings of a single bird. Among the doctrinal schools that were influential during the Tang were Tiantai, based on the *Lotus Sutra*; Huayan, based on the *Flower Garland Sutra*; and Faxiang (Yogacara, or Consciousness Only). Vajrayana Buddhism, known in China as Zhenyan (True Word or Mantra), was introduced in the 700s but was soon absorbed into other schools.

Toward the end of the dynasty, the scholar-monk Zongmi (780–841) integrated Confucianism and Daoism into a Buddhist framework in his *Treatise on the Original Nature of Man*—a classic example of the Chinese tendency toward syncretism.

The only female emperor in Chinese history, Wu Zetian (625–705) flouted more than one Confucian norm. She committed culturally defined "incest" when she married her son-in-law Gaozong, and then she ruled for a time from behind the throne as the empress-dowager after her second husband's death. Finally, encouraged by Buddhist monks and prophecies, she declared her own dynasty and took the throne outright (The Art Archive/British Library).

Late Tang Persecution of Buddhism

Zongmi's efforts notwithstanding, Daoist priests eventually persuaded Emperor Wuzong to put an end to the spread of Buddhism in China. In 845 Wuzong issued an edict that summarized the charges against the foreign religion that had "poisoned the customs of our nation": "At present there are an inestimable number of monks and nuns in the empire, each of them waiting for the farmers to feed him and the silkworms to clothe him, while the public temples and private chapels have reached boundless number, all with soaring towers and elegant ornamentation sufficient to outshine the imperial palace itself" (B. Watson, in de Bary and Bloom 1999: 585–586).

⊕ The Song, Yuan, and Ming Dynasties (960–1644)

In the aftermath of the late Tang persecution, the monastic community was decimated, and the only schools that retained strong followings among ordinary people were the two that focused on practice rather than study: Chan (which was based on meditation) and Jingtu (Pure Land). After the fall of the Tang, however, Daoism itself was stripped of its status as the state religion. The Song (960–1279) would prove to be a period of renewal for Confucianism, which synthesized ideas from both Daoism and Buddhism and reasserted itself at the state level as neo-Confucianism.

Daoism

The Complete Truth School

The Daoist school of Complete Truth (*Quanzhen*; also translated as "Perfect Realization," "Perfect Truth," or "Complete Perfection") was founded in the twelfth century and is still active today. Associated with the White Cloud Abbey in Beijing, it is distinctive in its monasticism—a feature that its founder, Wang Chongyang, modeled on the Buddhist tradition. Wang also argued against the superstitions and supernatural elements that had accrued within Daoism over time and taught a more down-to-earth understanding of transcendence or immortality:

> Leaving the world does not mean that the body departs. . . . When you realize the Tao, your body will be in the sphere of the ordinary, but your mind will be in the realm of the sages. Nowadays, people want to avoid death forever and at the same time leave the ordinary world. They are very foolish, indeed, and have not even glimpsed the true principle of the Tao. (Kirkland 2004: 188)

Document

From the *Platform Sutra*

The Platform Sutra *is the only "canonical" non-Indian Buddhist text. It records the teachings of Huineng, the sixth patriarch of the Chan school. In the following passages, he explains that practicing meditation and non-attachment does not mean having no thoughts, and that there is no "right" way to become enlightened.*

Learned Audience, some teachers of meditation instruct their disciples to keep a watch on their mind for tranquility, so that it will cease from activity. Henceforth the disciples give up all exertion of mind. Ignorant persons become insane from having too much confidence in such instruction.

Such cases are not rare, and it is a great mistake to teach others to do this. . . .

In orthodox Buddhism the distinction between the Sudden school and the Gradual school does not really exist; the only difference is that by nature some men are quick-witted, while others are dull in understanding. Those who are enlightened realize the truth in a sudden, while those who are under delusion have to train themselves gradually. But such a difference will disappear when we know our own mind and realize our own nature. Therefore these terms *gradual* and *sudden* are more apparent than real. (Price and Wong 1990 [1969]: 95)

Wang urged his disciples to read works from across all three major traditions, especially the Confucian *Classic of Filiality*, the Buddhist *Heart Sutra*, and the *Daodejing*. His "Fifteen Precepts for Establishing the Teaching" includes practical recommendations alongside more elevated principles. For example, he advises that to achieve harmony in spirit and vital energy, the body must be well rested. He also recommends using herbs for healing, living a simple life, and maintaining good Daoist friends. The "basic motif of the art of self-cultivation," he wrote, is the "search for the hidden meaning of Nature and mind" (Sommer 1995: 202).

Sun Buer

Where Confucians have Ban Zhao, the Daoists have Sun Buer (1119–1183), the wife of Wang Chongyang's disciple Ma Danyang. The following story is likely apocryphal, but it highlights the difficulties that women of Sun's time faced in their search for enlightenment.

One day Sun heard Wang say that an immortal was expected to emerge in the city of Luoyang, far from her home in Shandong. She asked Wang for permission to go there, but he refused, predicting that she would be molested and the shame would kill her. Undeterred, Sun went to her kitchen, heated some oil in a wok, poured cold water into it, and stood over the boiling oil as it spattered her face. When Wang saw her scars, he recognized her sincerity and agreed to teach her the methods of inner alchemy, but he advised her to hide her knowledge even from her husband. To ensure that she would be left alone, Sun pretended to be insane. Eventually, she slipped out of the house and travelled to Luoyang. There—as Wang had anticipated—two men accosted her. When a rain of enormous hailstones helped her escape, the men recognized her special nature and spread the story. Left in peace for 12 years, Sun became the only female among the famed seven masters of the Complete Truth school.

Revival of Orthodox Unity

Daoism continued to thrive until the twelfth century, when the Mongolian Kublai Khan extended his rule to the south. There he gave exclusive authority to the Orthodox Unity sect, which had been renamed for the revelations given to the Celestial Masters. After the Mongols were overthrown, Orthodox Unity was entrusted with the compilation of the Daoist canon (*Daozang*), which was printed in 1445.

Confucianism

The Emergence of Neo-Confucianism

Meanwhile, neo-Confucianism continued to develop and reached its apex with **Zhu Xi** (1130–1200), who synthesized numerous works from thinkers of the preceding century, including Zhou Dunyi, Zhang Zai, and the brothers Cheng Yi and Hao. Although neo-Confucianism traced its roots to the ancient writings, much of its philosophy reflected Buddhist and Daoist influences. Thus Zhou Dunyi (1017–1073) advocated what he called "quiet sitting"—a practice clearly modeled on Daoist and Buddhist meditation—and his most important work, "An Explanation of the Diagram of the Great Ultimate," was based on a Daoist representation of the creation of the material world.

For Zhou, the Great Ultimate and the Ultimate Nonbeing are identical. Through movement, yang is generated from the Ultimate Nonbeing/Great Ultimate. When its limit is reached, it becomes quiet and yin is generated. When yin reaches its limit, then activity, or yang, begins again. Thus the alternation between stillness and movement produces yin and yang, which in turn give rise to the five vital elements: fire, water, earth, metal, and wood. When Ultimate Nonbeing interacts with the essences of yin-yang and the five elements, a mysterious union occurs, from which Heaven and Earth come into being.

Document

From Zhang Zai's *Western Inscription*

Zhang Zai (1020–1077) took Zhou Dunyi's universal cosmology and expressed it in terms of a human family. The following excerpt shows how he correlated the essential Confucian elements of self, family, humanity, and virtue to the broader elements of nature and the cosmos.

Heaven is my father and Earth is my mother, and even such a small creature as I finds an intimate place in their midst.

Therefore that which fills the universe I regard as my body and that which directs the universe I consider as my nature.

All people are my brothers and sisters, and all things are my companions. The great ruler (the emperor) is the eldest son of my parents (Heaven and Earth), and the great ministers are his stewards. . . .

He who disobeys [the Principle of Nature] violates virtue. He who destroys humanity is a robber. He who promotes evil lacks [moral] capacity. But he who puts his moral nature into practice and brings his physical existence into complete fulfillment can match [Heaven and Earth]. (W. T. Chan, in Sommer 1995: 188)

Zhu Xi and the School of Principle

Working from Zhou's cosmology, the School of Principle explicitly linked *li*, the principles or patterns of nature, to human relationships and theories about education and government. Zhu Xi, considered the founder of this new school, synthesized the ideas of the earlier Song thinkers and gave Confucianism a metaphysical bent.

Zhu focused on the nature, place, and function of the self in the Great Ultimate. Like most Chinese philosophers, he understood human beings to be part of the fabric of the universe. Although he was interested in Buddhist-style "quiet sitting," Zhu was quintessentially Confucian in his focus on self-cultivation.

Zhu produced commentaries on "Centrality and Equilibrium" and "The Great Learning" (*Daxue*), two chapters from the *Rites*, in which self-discipline or self-cultivation is the first link in a chain that extends from the individual through the family to the state and recalls the ideal of the Grand Commonality. A famous passage from "The Great Learning" argues that proper self-cultivation begins with the acquisition of knowledge:

> In antiquity, those who wanted to clarify their bright virtue throughout the entire realm first had to govern their states well. Those who wanted to govern their states well first had to manage their own families, and those who wanted to manage their families first had to develop their own selves. Those who wanted to develop themselves first rectified their own minds, and those who wanted to rectify their minds first made their thoughts sincere. Those who wanted to make their thoughts sincere first extended their knowledge. Those who wanted to extend their knowledge first had to investigate things. (Sommer 1995: 39)

Approximately three centuries after Zhu Xi's death, **Wang Yangming** (1472–1529) challenged his view that the process of self-cultivation must begin with studying the classics and learning about the outside world. He argued that our moral sense is innate in our heart-minds and takes precedence over any external learning; this teaching became known as *Xinxue*, the School of the Heart-Mind.

Women in Neo-Confucianism

Neo-Confucianism continued to thrive into the Ming dynasty (1368–1644). After the Ming regained control from the Mongols, the education of women—esteemed as the transmitters of culture to the young—received renewed attention. Empress Xu, the wife of the third Ming emperor, wrote *Instructions for the Inner Quarters* (*Neixun*) under the inspiration of her mother-in-law Empress Ma, who had believed it her duty, as mother of the people, to challenge her cruel, hot-tempered husband. Empress Xu's book reflects the same sense of a woman's broader responsibility. When a set of "Four Books for Women" was compiled during the Ming period, Empress Xu's *Instructions* was one of them, along with Ban Zhao's *Admonitions*, Song Ruozhao's *Analects*, and Madame Zheng's *Filiality*.

Buddhism

Developments in Chan

Critics of Wang Yangming charged that his focus on the heart-mind reflected the influence of Buddhism. It is true that his emphasis on intuitive, innate knowing resonated with both the Chan view of enlightenment and the general Mahayana belief in the universality of Buddha-nature. The Chan of the early Tang period had developed broadly into two schools with different notions of how to achieve enlightenment: a northern "gradual" school and a southern "sudden" school associated with the sixth patriarch, Huineng (see Chapter 10). By the end of the Tang, the two schools were represented by two distinct lineages—Linji and Caodong—both of which survive today.

New literary genres also developed: discourse records (*yulu*) of individual masters, as well as "lamp" or "flame" records of lineages, which were later edited into collections of *gongan* (public documents or case records). A record of a Chan master's exchange with a student became a *gongan* when a living master wrote a commentary on it that "proved" him to be a part of the lineage of enlightened masters. Eventually, the cases became pedagogical tools used to bypass the student's intellect and spark sudden enlightenment. Famous collections of these stories and their commentaries include the *Book of Serenity*, the *Blue Cliff Record*, and the *Gateless Gate*, all of which were collected and edited in the twelfth and thirteenth centuries. (See the Document box on "Excerpts from the *Gateless Gate* and *Zhuangzi*" for a comparison of Chan and Daoist dialogues on the Buddha and the Dao, respectively.)

Popular Buddhism

The second school of Buddhism to survive the Tang persecution was Jingtu, which offered followers comfort with its promise of an afterlife in the "Pure Land" of Amituofo. In time, other forms of popular Buddhism developed, but they tended to be more prosaic in their promises. The monk Zhuhong (1535–1615), for example, classified actions in terms of merit and demerit: to "help a person recover from a slight illness" was worth 5 points, while to "rescue one person from the death penalty" was worth 100. Conversely, failure to help a sick person meant 2 demerit points, and the penalty for murder was 100 points. According to this scheme, those who earned 10,000 points would see their wishes granted, but if one died with more demerit than merit points, one's descendants would suffer for it (Chen 1964: 437–438). This system was adapted from a monk who

Document

Excerpts from the *Gateless Gate* and *Zhuangzi*

Scholars have noted a general eccentricity in Chan dialogues that is shared by the Daoist Zhuangzi. *The two excerpts that follow, the first from the Chan* Gateless Gate *and the second from the* Zhuangzi, *point to an earthy irreverence in both traditions.*

A Chan *gongan*:

A monk asked [Yunmen Wenyan, c. 863–949]: "What is Buddha?" [Yunmen] answered him: "Dried dung."

[Wumen's] comment: It seems to me [Yunmen] is so poor he cannot distinguish the taste of one food from another, or else he is too busy to write readable letters. Well, he tried to hold his school with dried dung. And his teaching was just as useless.

    Lightning flashes,
    Sparks shower.
    In one blink of your eyes
    You have missed seeing. (Reps 1989 [1960]: 106–107)

A dialogue from *Zhuangzi*:

Master Tung-kuo asked Chuang Tzu, "This thing called the Way—where does it exist?"

    Chuang Tzu said, "There's no place it doesn't exist."

    "Come," said Master Tung-kuo, "you must be more specific."

    "It is in the ant."
    "As low a thing as that?"
    "It is in the panic grass."
    "But that's lower still!"
    "It is in the tiles and shards."
    "How can it be so low?"
    "It is in the piss and shit!"
    Master Tung-kuo made no reply. (Watson 1968: 240–241)

had learned it when he had previously been a Daoist, which may explain the non-Buddhist idea of transference of ancestral demerit points.

Popular Religion

Folk beliefs and practices continued after the fall of the Tang in the form of spirit possession (shamanism) and fortune-telling (divination). Popular religion, sometimes called sectarian religion, also continued to thrive. One example, the White Lotus Society, is thought to have originated in the eleventh century as a lay movement dedicated to Amituofo that over time incorporated other elements, including Daoist longevity practices and millenarian expectations surrounding a messianic Milo. White Lotus members played a substantial role in overthrowing the Mongols, who had established Tibetan Buddhism as the state religion, and establishing the native Ming. But the first Ming emperor feared the Society's power and sought to suppress it. In time, "White Lotus" became a pejorative term, used by officials to refer to any religious group they considered suspect.

⊕ The Qing Dynasty and Republican Period (1644–Present)

The Challenges of Modernity

The Qing Manchus retained Tibetan Buddhism as the state religion, but they continued to use Confucian principles for government until 1911, when dynastic rule was replaced by republicanism. The end of the Qing was marked by hostility toward traditional beliefs and practices. By mid-century "China" had splintered into the People's Republic of China (PRC) on the mainland, the Republic of China on the island of Taiwan, and the British Crown Colony of Hong Kong, with sizable Chinese communities in the city-state of Singapore and elsewhere in Southeast Asia, as well as a global diaspora.

Yet despite the persecution that traditional institutions and folk spiritualties have suffered over the last 120 years, popular annual celebrations, folk religious practices, Confucianism, Daoism, and Buddhism continue to thrive outside the mainland. Moreover, many religious beliefs and practices have experienced a renaissance in the PRC itself since the 1980s.

Confucianism

Encounter with the West and Modernization

In 1838 the Qing emperor appointed Lin Zexu to put an end to the opium trade initiated by the British in hopes of balancing their trade deficit with China. In addition to confiscating and destroying vast quantities of the drug, Lin composed an open letter of protest to Queen Victoria in which, as a Confucian, he framed his argument in moral terms:

> The wealth of China is used to profit the barbarians [the British]. . . . By what right do they then in return use the poisonous drug [opium] to injure the Chinese people? Let us ask, where is your conscience? I have heard that the smoking of opium is very strictly forbidden by your country; that is because the harm caused by opium is clearly understood. Since it is not permitted to do harm to your own country, then even less should you let it be passed on to the harm of other countries—how much less to China! (S. Y. Teng and J. Fairbank, in deBary and Lufrano 2000: 203)

The British responded to this high-minded appeal with the First Opium War (1839–1842); a second war would follow in 1856–1860. The defeat of the hopelessly outgunned Chinese was a watershed moment in East Asian history, presaging the end of the dynastic system and leading to a profound reassessment of the traditional ways of thinking. The final nail in the military coffin was Japan's victory in the Sino-Japanese War of 1894–1895. That Japan—a former vassal state—not only had succeeded in modernizing along Western lines but had defeated China meant that radical reform was necessary. Some reformers urged the abandonment of all traditions; others argued that certain aspects of China's cultural heritage should be preserved. Among the latter was Kang Youwei (1858–1927), who believed that the adoption of Shinto as the state religion had saved Japan from the stultifying influence of Buddhism, given it a strong national identity, and helped it to focus on modernization. Although he argued that Confucianism could play a similar role for China, the ancient teaching continued to lose ground.

Interview

The Adaptation of Ancestor Veneration in Diaspora: Kent and Philip Mark—A Study in Flexibility

The syncretic practice of Chinese religions in the diaspora illustrates well their distinctive irreligious quality, the different levels at which the various elements of their practice function, and the weak ties that they have to ethnic identity in contrast to monotheistic religions. Kent and Philip Mark in Saskatoon offer a good case study of the statistically nonreligiously affiliated Chinese.

I met and interviewed Kent and Philip in 2007 when the father and son duo, along with a busload of members from the Chinese community, visited Woodlawn Cemetery in Saskatoon for *Qingming* (the Clear and Bright ritual) on a warm July day—instead of the cold April one that tradition requires—to remember all the ancestors of the community, and especially the earliest Chinese Canadians, many of whom had been bachelors with no descendants. When I asked Kent about the ritual's date change, he noted that it is the practice of remembering the people who passed before us that is important, and not the set traditional schedule.

When all the participants had gathered around the site where many of the early Chinese immigrants are buried, incense was lit to notify the ancestors, and everyone bowed three times. The incense sticks and a red wax candle were planted into the ground along with a plate of barbecue pork, a whole duck and chicken, and some fresh fruit, and then everyone made three more bows. Teacups and chopsticks were the next items to be placed on the ground, and all attending bowed three times again. Liquor was then offered, and the congregation bowed three times once more.

The ritual then turned personal for the Mark family: Philip's eldest son, Kent's grandson, brought a cup of liquor for his great-grandparents to their graves and bowed three times. Philip then took the cup and drizzled the contents in front of the

Qingming is a time for families to visit gravesites and pay respect to their ancestors. (© Hupeng/Dreamstime.com)

headstone before the cup was refilled for the next family whose ancestor was also buried there. After this was done, "hell banknotes" were burnt for the ancestors to spend in the afterlife, and the ritually engaged families received the offerings of food.

After he had completed the ritual, Philip turned to me and reported that ancestor veneration had in recent years become more individualized, reflecting a more benign and liberal Canada. Personal visits to the cemetery, he said, now tend to be spread throughout the year. In the past, more congregants from Chinatown had traveled to the cemetery in two busloads, but as the older generations have passed on, the need for the rites of community remembrance of the bachelor ancestors, who experienced such heartbreaking discrimination in forging the way for later generations, has gradually become more remote.

While both men observed the traditional practice of veneration, Kent did not keep an ancestral shrine and did not insist on traditional beliefs and practices at home. Philip professed no religion but remembered going to Roman Catholic Sunday School; his wife was Euro-Canadian, and they had been married in a church. Kent did, however, believe in Daoism, particularly in its ability to heal and to bring longevity and good health. He had taught tai chi for over 30 years at his own studio, and his students had created and maintained a website for him. Many knew him as *Sifu*, or "Teacher." Kent died in 2013, at age 87.

"New Confucians" in Postdynastic China

Soon after Kang made his argument for Confucianism, Sun Yatsen, the father of modern republican China, found precedents for democracy in the Confucian Mencius and the neo-Confucian Cheng Yi. He identified three principles as fundamental to democracy—nationalism, citizen rights, and human welfare—and argued that they represented "a completion of the development of . . . three thousand years of Chinese ideas about how to govern and maintain a peaceful world" (Bell and Hahm 2003: 9).

Sun Yatsen's insights notwithstanding, state Confucianism was disestablished following the formation of the Chinese Republic in 1911. But scholars such as Fang Dongmei—who settled in Taiwan after the Communist takeover of the mainland—encouraged the ongoing development of Confucianism in the diaspora.

Diaspora Attempts to Reconstruct Chinese Culture

In 1958 a group of "New Confucians" based in Hong Kong responded to Western critics of China with an English-language "Manifesto for a Reappraisal of Sinology and the Reconstruction of Chinese Culture." Following a discussion of "what the West can learn from Eastern thought," the authors concluded with a few remarks on the future "intellectual development of China and of the world." Noting the friction caused by the expansion of Western civilization, they called for "respect and sympathy toward other cultures" and "genuine compassion and commiseration." Second, since "scientific learning is inadequate," they called for "a different kind of learning, one that treats [Man] as a conscious, existential being [and] applies understanding to conduct, by which one may transcend existence to attain spiritual enlightenment." Finally, they suggested that the end product of that new learning would be "a moral being that . . . can truly embrace God" (quoted by J. Berthrong, in de Bary and Lufrano 2000: 559).

Even though they clearly identified themselves with the Confucian tradition, the authors included Daoism and Buddhism in their discussion, and their use of the Christian term "God" shows their willingness to adopt foreign concepts. Their efforts are reflected in the work of scholars such as Du Weiming of Harvard; John Berthrong of Boston University; the controversial Daniel A. Bell, a Canadian who describes himself as a Confucian philosopher and scholar and who teaches at the Center for International and Comparative Political Philosophy in Beijing; and Lee Kuan Yew, the first president of Singapore, who tried (unsuccessfully) to introduce both Confucian and religious studies into the new republic's high schools.

Winds of Change in the People's Republic of China

Since the 1980s, the PRC has reintroduced state celebrations of Confucius's birthday (the Republic of China, Taiwan, has always celebrated this day). Some elementary schools have integrated classical literature into their curricula, along with a focus on rites and ethics, and introduced traditional garb such as the scholar's robe into their classrooms.

Scholars also note that the Chinese government's emphasis on a "harmonious society," non-interference in foreign policy, soft diplomacy, the establishment of Confucius Institutes outside China, and the development of online sites for Chinese language and culture all reflect the Confucian concern for promoting social security and stability through the disciplined self-cultivation of individual persons.

Daoism and Popular Religion

Even as neo-Confucianism became entrenched as state ideology during the Qing dynasty (1644–1911), Daoism continued to inspire popular morality books and a variety of practices from meditation to *taiji* and **qigong** (breath exercises that help the movement of vital energy through the body). However, it suffered enormous setbacks after the Opium Wars, when Western-inspired reformers began to attack traditional beliefs and practices.

Daoism, with its Eight Immortals (legendary figures who play a role not unlike that of human saints) and its elaborate liturgies inviting the deities into this realm, can be difficult to distinguish from folk religion. Modernizers perceived both Daoism and folk religion as superstitious and hostile to progress, especially after the failure of the anti-Western uprising (1899–1901) known in the West as the "Boxer Rebellion." The Boxers had believed they could drive out the foreigners on the strength of their martial arts skills alone, which they thought would make them impervious to Western guns and cannon.

This Ming dynasty bottle shows Zhongli Quan, one of the eight Daoist "Immortals" who serve as patrons of various groups and trades. Recognizable by his two topknots, exposed belly, and fan, Zhongli is believed to have been a successful Han general who discovered the Dao only after he had experienced defeat for the first time; he is also said to have had an impressive knowledge of alchemy (© The Metropolitan Museum of Art, Image source: Art Resource, NY).

Buddhism

Reform and Modernization

Of the three elite religions, Buddhism has been the most successful in modernizing itself. A leader in that effort was a layman named Yang Wenhui (1837–1911), who published Buddhist texts, started a school for monastics in Nanjing, and inspired Tan Sitong (1865–1898) to propose a process through which millennia-old institutional and cultural barriers in Chinese society might be cleared away. In his book *Renxue* ("On Benevolence") Tan argued that the Confucian notion of *ren* was the same as Buddhism's compassion and Christianity's love. Appealing to Huayan ideas of interconnectedness, he described a state of oneness or nondifferentiation in which communication between people is always possible. Tragically, he was beheaded for plotting against the Qing government, but his wife, Li Run, remained true to his ideal of nondifferentiation and established a school for girls in rural Hunan—a feat unheard of in the early twentieth century.

Elsewhere, several monks also worked to revive and reform Buddhism. Yinguang (1861–1940) was a conservative monk credited with reviving the Pure Land school, while Taixu (1890–1947) argued that of all religions, Buddhism was the one most compatible with modern science; he also advocated a modern education for monastics. He made his reputation as an activist in 1912 when he and another monk, Renshan, announced that they had petitioned the government for permission to open a new school for monastics and planned to use the monastery's resources to run it.

The monk-officers of the temple successfully prevented the construction of the school, but the seeds of Humanistic Buddhism had been sown. Instead of retreating into meditation or scriptural study, monastics and laypeople alike were encouraged to become "engaged" in the world—in education, social work, medicine, and politics. In 1929 the Chinese Buddhist Association was established in Shanghai and charged with reforming and reviving Buddhism in China.

Government Treatment of Religion

In 1949 the PRC guaranteed freedom of religion. The official policy, in line with Marxist theory, stated that to coerce religious people to give up their beliefs and practices without material improvement of society was "useless and positively harmful." Nevertheless, in 1950 the Chinese Buddhist Association decamped to Taiwan with the Nationalist government and was replaced by a state-administered Buddhist Association. And in 1966 the government launched the Cultural Revolution. Fueled by the Marxist notion of religion as an opiate that blunts the masses' instinct for justice and hinders advancement, the "revolutionaries" systematically targeted all religious traditions. By the mid-1970s the social and economic foundations of traditional Chinese society had been destroyed, and the government acknowledged that a new approach was necessary. Today the Chinese government recognizes five religions as "legitimate": Buddhism, Daoism, Roman Catholicism, Protestantism, and Islam (Confucianism is considered a philosophy rather than a religion). At the same time, although it is not officially recognized, popular religion is experiencing a revival in the PRC.

Popular Religion

A loose collection of beliefs and practices centered on the power of deities, ghosts, and spirits, popular religion may draw elements from any of the more established traditions, including Christianity and Islam. Spirits of all kinds are seen as compassionate helpers, regardless of tradition.

The goals of practitioners of popular religion have remained stable through the ages: children (especially sons), happiness, academic success, prosperity, safety at work (especially in potentially dangerous occupations such as fishing and policing), and even political change. These goals can be divided into two streams: personal religiosity and political activism.

One important element of personal religiosity is the belief that the spirits of the deceased continue to intervene in the world, and that their power can be harnessed for the benefit of the living. This belief finds expression not only in ancestral tablets in temples and family altars dedicated to ancestors, but also in shrines in commercial establishments. Local folk heroes and heroines, buddhas, bodhisattvas, Daoist perfected beings—all can be called on for help. But popular religion can also be externalized in a less individual, more dogmatic, and more partisan way. When an idea such as the Mandate of Heaven or a messianic figure such as Milo (Maitreya) is incorporated into popular religion, it can give rise to politically charged movements like the White Lotus Society, the Boxers, or the Heavenly Kingdom of Great Peace.

Daoism and folk religion are reestablishing themselves in the PRC, and Daoism is especially popular in Europe and the Americas, where its dual focus on living a simple, balanced life and promoting health, longevity, and transcendence are increasingly valued. The *Daodejing* ranks only second to the Bible as the most translated book in the world.

Recent Developments

Study after study tells us that the Chinese, Koreans, Japanese, and Vietnamese are the least religious of all ethnic groups. This calls into question the term "religion." Clearly, Chinese traditions fit badly into the monotheistic frame of reference.

Revival of Confucianism

The first two generations of the twentieth-century New Confucians wrote from the cultural margins—Hong Kong, Taiwan, Singapore, Boston—while China lagged far behind the West developmentally. Yet by the late 1970s it was clear that communism had failed to improve life for the Chinese people. Thus in 1978 a process of economic and political reform was begun. Rapid industrial and economic growth lifted half a billion people out of poverty by 2004, and by 2012 China had achieved exceptional economic stability, despite the global financial disaster of 2008. Despite (or because of) this remarkable material success, some long-standing problems remained and some new ones surfaced, including social alienation, radical individualism, ecological degradation, and infractions of human rights. As antidotes, both political and academic leaders recommended the revival and integration of traditional Confucian values such as integrity, loving respect, and belief in the unity of human beings with the cosmos.

The New Confucianism that had developed in the diaspora was harnessed to neutralize international fears that economic success would turn China into an imperialistic superpower. In 1984, just six years after the reform process began, the state-supported China Confucius Foundation was created with the explicit mandate of expanding the influence of Confucianism both internally and internationally. By 2007 there were close to 200 Confucius Institutes around the globe, all supported by the Chinese government. None of this activity is "religious" in the Western sense. Yet the Chinese government's strategy of persuasion through education, both in and outside China, clearly recalls the traditional Confucian belief that moral development is fundamental to a peaceful society.

Daoism under Reconstruction

Daoism has been more popular than Confucianism in the West: Daoist teachings were integral to the counterculture movement of the 1960s, and some Westerners continue to cherish the Daoist ideals of *wuwei* and *ziran*. Daoism has also been used to encourage "green" thinking in Taiwan, and as the PRC becomes prosperous enough to turn its attention to the natural environment, the value of the Daoist emphasis on achieving harmony with the cosmos is being recognized in this sphere as well.

Popular Religious Movements

One recent popular movement that originated in the northeast PRC during the 1990s is the Buddho-Daoist Energy of the Wheel of Law, better known as Falun Dafa or Falun Gong. Its founder, Li Hongzhi, teaches the virtues of truthfulness, compassion, and forbearance, along with a form of meditation that he claims minimizes the need for doctors. The PRC government objects to this claim because of its potentially detrimental effect on believers and has punished some members for the group's frequent antigovernment demonstrations both in the PRC and in the diaspora.

Another successful sectarian group has been the Taiwan-based Yiguandao (Unity, Pervasive Truth, or Consistent Way) movement, which has survived persecution not only by the Communist government in the PRC but also by the Nationalist government in Taiwan until 1987. This group teaches that during these end-times, people must repent their sins, take up vegetarianism, and reunite with the Eternal Mother, a well-established Daoist deity. Still other movements have been syncretic, combining elements from Confucianism, Daoism, Buddhism, Christianity, and Islam; one of these movements, Tien De or Tiande (Heavenly Virtue), professes to use cosmic energy and spiritual healing to cure disease.

Humanistic Buddhism: A Religion for This World

Buddhism is the most successful "Chinese" religion in the West. Three "Humanistic" groups influenced by the reformer Taixu have been particularly active in growing global Buddhism, and all three have attracted strong lay participation. Foguangshan (Buddha's Light Mountain), which accepts all the teachings of eight traditional schools (Tiantai, Huayan, Sanlun, Faxiang, Lu, Zhenyan, Chan, and Jingtu), focuses on education and has three universities, one of which is the University of the West in Rosemead, California. The founder of Fagushan (Dharma Drum Mountain), Sheng Yen (1930–2009), was a modern scholar-monk who instituted an ongoing campaign for "Six Ethics of the Mind": family ethics, living ethics, school ethics, environmental ethics, workplace ethics, and ethics between ethnic groups.

The third group, Cizi or Tzu Chi (Compassionate Relief), is a charitable foundation based in Taiwan that is active in disaster relief around the world. It was founded by a Buddhist nun named Cheng Yen (1937–) after three Catholic nuns observed to her that Buddhism was not well organized to help the sick and the poor in her town. With the help of housewife-disciples, Cheng established Cizi in 1966.

Women in the Traditions

Sea Change for Chinese and Korean Women

The ideals of the "virtuous wife and good mother" (xianqi liangmu) and of devotion to a spiritual life detached from the mundane belong to neo-Confucianism and Buddhism, respectively. Traditionally, both discouraged women from becoming involved in public life in China and Korea. Women were participants and specialists in shamanism and Daoism, but neither of these roles challenged the status quo. Under the influence of Western ideals drawn from Christianity, Marxism, and liberal democracy, Korea and Taiwan have both voted in their first never-married, single female presidents: Park Geun-hye (elected in 2013) and Tsai Ing-wen (elected in 2016). Both countries have also seen their fair share of female corporate executives as well as female spiritual leaders.

The story of Park Geun-hye demonstrates well the traditional flexibility of South Korea's blend of East and West, old and new, religious and political. Choi Tae-min, a family friend who became

Park's mentor after her parents' assassinations in 1974 and 1979, was a Buddhist monk who converted to Roman Catholicism, started the Church of Eternal Life (Yongsaenggyo), and professed to be Mireuk Bosal (a Maitreya bodhisattva). He taught that all people are originally God and should strive for salvation to become God again and live eternally.

We do not know if Park was a member of the Church of Eternal Life, but Choi did help her run a volunteer group, Movement for a New Mind, as a step toward political power. Unfortunately, Park's later relationship with Choi's daughter, Soon-sil, led to charges of corruption and her impeachment in 2017.

Tsai Ing-wen is of mixed Chinese (Hakka) and Indigenous heritage and belongs to the Democratic Progressive Party, which includes sovereignty for the island in its platform. At the urging of her father, she pursued legal education in both Taiwan and the West. She professes no religion, though her vice president was a devout Roman Catholic epidemiologist, also educated in the West. She was defeated in the November 2018 election and has retired as the chairperson of her party. Her future in politics remains unclear.

A contemporary *mudang* dressed in traditional costume performs a ritual. (Jon Lusk/Redferns)

⊕ Korean Religions

Theoretically, traditional Korean religiosity can be classified as nontheistic at the elite level and polytheistic at the popular level, but in practice (like its Chinese counterpart) it tends to be syncretic. Thus neither of these categories necessarily excludes the other. It is even possible to identify a quasi-monotheistic belief in a purposeful and creative Way (or Heaven, or Heaven-and-Earth) coexisting with both the polytheistic belief in ancestral spirits and nature deities and the nontheistic belief in an impersonal natural Way.

Korea and China: A Shared History

Ancient Korean culture shows traces of influences from both continental East Asia and Central Asia. Migration from China to the Korean peninsula was underway as early as the Zhou dynasty

(1046–256 BCE), and political relations between the two populations have always reflected a mixture of kinship and antipathy, relatedness and differentiation.

The earliest written records of Korea are Chinese. Sima Qian's *Records of the Grand Historian* describes Wiman, one of the later kings of the proto-state of Old Joseon, as a refugee from northern China who ruled over Chinese refugees and Indigenous inhabitants at Wanggeom (present-day Pyongyang) in the sixth and fifth centuries BCE. Another Chinese source, the sixth-century *History of the Wei Dynasty*, tells how the mythical king Dangun founded Old Joseon during the time of China's legendary sage king Yao.

This early-twentieth-century painting shows the Mountain God with three symbols of longevity: a crane (left), a deer (right), and pine trees (foreground). An example of Korean syncretism, the Mountain God is variously portrayed as the legendary founder Dangun, a Confucian sage, a Daoist immortal, and a Buddhist bodhisattva (© The Trustees of the British Museum).

Old Joseon

An early Korean source, now lost, told of Dangun's divine grandfather Hwanin and father Hwanung. Hwanin knew that his son wanted to descend from heaven and live in the world of human beings, so he settled Hwanung in a cave on Mount Taebaek.

But Hwanung was not alone in the cave: a bear and a tiger were also living there, and they asked him to transform them into human beings. So Hwanung gave them a bundle of sacred mugworts and 20 cloves of garlic, with instructions to eat these foods and avoid the sunlight. After 21 days the bear became a woman, but the tiger had failed to avoid the light and therefore was not transformed. The woman remained alone, unable to find a husband, so she prayed for a child. In response to her prayers, Hwanung transformed himself, lay with her, and gave her a son, Dangun Wanggeom.

This foundation myth became a marker of national identity when Korea faced a series of Mongol invasions between 1231 and 1270). According to the thirteenth-century *Memorabilia of the Three Kingdoms*, the god Hwanung descended into the human world and married a she-bear who gave birth to Dangun (a bear cult still exists among the Ainu people of Japan). Yi Suenghyu in his *Songs of Emperors and Kings* (1287) gives a variant account in which the great king Hwanung gave medicine to his granddaughter to change her into a human being; she then married a tree god and bore Dangun (a tree cult was once prevalent in the southern portion of the Korean peninsula). Interestingly, there is no reference to Dangun in the official *History of the Three Kingdoms*, compiled a century earlier, under Confucian inspiration, by Gim Busik.

The Three Kingdoms (c. 50 BCE–668 CE)

The proto-state of Old Joseon was followed by the Three Kingdoms of Goguryeo, Baekje, and Silla. Goguryeo's foundation myth (found in a collection from the thirteenth century) recalls the *Songs of the South* in both form and content, telling how the founder Jumong, who eventually took the title King Dongmyeong, was born from an egg after the sun—Haemosu, the Son of Heaven—shone on the breast of his mother, the eldest daughter of the River Earl. After ruling for 19 years, Dongmyeong forsook his throne and rose to heaven. Goguryeo was closely linked to Baekje, whose founder, King Onjo, is said to have been Dongmyeong's son.

Silla's foundation myth, like Old Joseon's, was recorded in Iryeon's *Memorabilia*. Like King Dongmyeong, King Hyeokgeose ("Bright") was born from an egg. His birth was announced by an eerie lightning-like emanation from a well. When the people cracked open the egg, they found a beautiful boy inside. When they bathed him he emitted light, and the "birds and beasts danced for joy, heaven and earth shook, and the sun and the moon became bright" (Lee et al. 1993: 33). Soon after, a dragon appeared and presented an infant girl from under her left rib. When the two reached the age of 13, they married and became king and queen.

Daoism

Korea's foundation myths contain several elements reminiscent of the shamanist stream in Daoism, including nature deities (the River Earl), marriage between gods and human beings (Hwanung and the bear-woman), and the possibility of ascent into heaven (King Dongmyeong). In Silla, the people believed in the Holy Mother of Mount Fairy Peach: a goddess, the guardian of the country, who was said to live on a mountain to the west of the capital, recalling the Queen Mother of the West in the *Zhuangzi*. These apparently Daoist elements have led some scholars to suggest that her cult was a composite of an Indigenous mountain deity cult and a Daoist immortality cult. Her tale (see

Document
The Lay of King Dongmyeong

The following passages are drawn from the Collected
Works of Minister I of Korea.

In early summer, when the Great Bear stood in the
    Snake,
Haemosu came to Korea,
A true Son of Heaven.
He came down through the air
In a five-dragon chariot,
With a retinue of hundreds,
Robes streaming, riding on swans,
The atmosphere echoed with chiming music.
Banners floated on the tinted clouds.

. . .

North of the capital was the Green River,
Where the River Earl's three beautiful daughters
Rose from the drake-neck's green waves
To play in the Bear's Heart Pool.
Their jade ornaments tinkled.
Their flowerlike beauty was modest—
They might have been fairies of the Han River banks,
Or goddesses of the Lo River islets.
The king, out hunting, espied them,
Was fascinated and lost his heart.
Not from lust for girls,
But from eager desire for an heir. (Lee et al. 1993: 24)

Document box) underlines the syncretic nature of Korean religion, linking the Holy Mother with a Buddhist nun as well as a Chinese emperor and King Hyeokgeose (Hyokkose) of Silla.

This mythological syncretism is reinforced in Silla's history. In the 700s Gim Jiseong, a vice minister of state, kept one image each of Amitabha, the buddha of the west, and Maitreya, the buddha of the future. He read Mahayana literature but also enjoyed Laozi and the *Zhuangzi*. Echoes of Daoist scripture in Korean philosophy, religion, and politics continued into the 1400s, during the staunchly neo-Confucian Joseon or I dynasty, when many of the literati (much like the Seven Sages of the Bamboo Grove) retired from official life to engage in metaphysical conversation.

Murals in Goguryeo tombs suggest that the Daoist cult of immortality merged with local beliefs in prognostication. The early Tang court sent a Daoist adept and a copy of the *Daodejing* to Korea. In the same period, a Buddhist monastery near the border with China was converted into a Daoist temple, and in 643, at the request of the Goguryeo king, eight Daoist priests were sent there from China. By 650, the Daoist influence at the Goguryeo court was so strong that a monk who opposed the state's adoption of Daoism fled and sought refuge in Baekje.

Shamanism

With its focus on deities, ghosts, and spirits, Daoism found deep resonance in Korean shamanism (*mugyo*). Each village had its own deity: a local mountain god or goddess in inland regions and a dragon king by the sea. Traditional household deities included the gods of the hearth, the roof beam, and the outhouse. Shamans (*mudang*) regularly performed rituals at community celebrations and ceremonies.

Document

The Holy Mother of Mount Fairy Peach

The phrases "art of the immortals" and "art of longevity" suggest that the Holy Mother embraced Daoism as well as Buddhism.

During the reign of King Chinpyong [579–632], a nun . . . wished to repair a hall for the Buddha . . . but could not carry out her desire. A beautiful immortal fairy, her hair adorned with ornaments, appeared in the nun's dreams and consoled her: "I'm the holy goddess mother of Mount Fairy Peach [Mount West], and I am pleased that you would repair the Buddha Hall. I offer you ten *kun* of gold. . . ." The holy mother, originally the daughter of a Chinese emperor, was named Saso. Early in her life she learned the art of the immortals. . . . When Saso first came to Chinhan, she gave birth to a holy man who became the first ruler of Silla—perhaps he was Hyokkose. . . . Saso donated gold to make a Buddha image, lighted incense for the living beings, and initiated a religion. How could she be merely one who learned the art of longevity and became a prisoner in the boundless mist? (Lee et al. 1993: 94)

Buddhism

A Buddhism that was focused on karma and the search for happiness was introduced to Goguryeo by a Chinese monk in 372 and to Baekje by an Indian monk in 384; both received imperial support. In Silla, King Pophung and his minister Yi Chadon made Buddhism the state religion in the sixth century. In 540, when King Chinhung established a youth group, he made the Buddhist Five Precepts (p. 400) part of its ethical foundation. And in 661 two monks named Wonhyo and Uisang set out for China in search of new teachers.

In the end they did not travel far. One night, while waiting out a rainstorm, they unknowingly slept in an ancient tomb and drank water that had collected in a human skull. The next morning Wonhyo was horrified to see what he had used as a drinking vessel; then he realized that his response had been determined solely by his mind. Having achieved enlightenment, Wonhyo returned home, left the monastery, and developed what came to be known as "interpenetrated Buddhism" (*tongbulgyo*), harmonizing the teachings of the Samron (Sanlun or Madhyamaka) and Yusik or Yugagyo (Weishi or Yogacara) schools. Wonhyo's *tongbulgyo* reflected the teachings of his friend Uisang, who completed the trip to China and returned to found the Hwaeom school—the Korean version of the Huayan (Flower Garland) tradition.

United Silla, Later Three Kingdoms, and Goryeo (668–1392)

Confucianism

Today Korea has the largest network of Confucian shrines in the world. The process of Confucianization started around 600, but it was not until the Goryeo period (918–1392), when Buddhism was at its height, that Confucianism became firmly rooted. King Taejo ("Ultimate Ancestor"), the ruler who united the Later Three Kingdoms that splintered from Silla and founded Goryeo in 918, was an ardent Buddhist, but he also encouraged Confucian learning.

Taejo replaced Silla's tradition of governance by a hereditary aristocracy with the examination-based bureaucratic system of Tang China. He is also said to have left for his successors a list of "10 Injunctions" that brought together Buddhist, Confucian, and Indigenous perspectives. The first injunction, for example, clearly honors the Buddhist tradition: "The success of the great enterprise of founding our dynasty is entirely owing to the protective powers of the many Buddhas. We therefore must build temples for both Son [Meditation] and Kyo (Textual) Schools and appoint abbots, that they may perform the proper ceremonies and themselves cultivate the way" (Lee 1985: 132). But the third injunction pays tribute to the Confucian tradition: "If the eldest son is not worthy of the crown, let the second eldest succeed to the throne. If the second eldest, too, is unworthy, choose the brother the people consider the best qualified for the throne." And the fourth injunction emphasizes the primacy of Indigenous traditions: "In the past we have always had a deep attachment for the ways of China and all of our institutions have been modelled upon those of Tang. But our country occupies a different geographical location and our people's character is different from that of the Chinese. Hence, there is no reason to strain ourselves unreasonably to copy the Chinese way" (H. Kang, in Lee et al. 1993: 263).

Soon after this, the influence of Confucianism was further reinforced when Choe Chung (948–1068) established a private Confucian academy.

Buddhism

A new era of Korean Buddhism began around 800 CE with the establishment of the Seon (Chan) school. Although the established Gyo (doctrinal) schools resisted its innovations, two monks, Uicheon (1055–1101) and Jinul (1158–1210), effectively synthesized the Seon and Gyo traditions.

Jinul brought together the two views on enlightenment, sudden and gradual, with the dictum "sudden enlightenment followed by gradual practice." He integrated *gwanhwa* (meditating on the word) or *gongan* practice into Seon, turned his back on the excesses of other Buddhist schools, and established the Jogye order as a new community of pure-minded and disciplined Seon practitioners on Mount Jogye.

Joseon (1392–1910)

Confucian Antipathy to Buddhism

In Korea as in China, Buddhism's success eventually led to corruption and backlash. The founder of the Joseon dynasty, another Taejo, banned the building of new Buddhist temples; his son Taejong disestablished temples and confiscated their estates and workers, including slaves. Buddhist activities were confined to specific areas, largely outside the cities and on the mountains.

Around the same time, families began installing shrines for ancestral tablets in their homes in accordance with Confucian custom. Eventually, the responsibility for performing the rites of ancestor veneration was entrusted to the first son, who became the only one with the right of inheritance. This system of primogeniture put an end to the Goryeo system, under which daughters were also entitled to inherit and couples could hold property jointly.

Neo-Confucianism

In the early 1500s, the philosopher Jo Gwangjo continued to root out superstitions deemed incompatible with Confucianism. He encouraged government by moral suasion and instituted a system

The *Tripitaka Koreana* is the most complete collection of Buddhist texts in the world. Engraved in Chinese characters on 80,000 woodblocks, it was completed between 1237 and 1248. This immense government-sponsored project was undertaken in an effort to win the Buddha's protection against invasion by the Mongols (© John Van Hasselt/Sygma/Corbis).

of local self-government based on the idea of a village code or "Family Compact," which had been outlined by the Chinese neo-Confucian Zhu Xi. At the heart of this system was a notion of reciprocity expressed in mutual encouragement of morality, supervision of conduct, decorum in social relations, and aid in times of hardship or disaster.

Zhu Xi's influence extended into the metaphysical realm. He believed that human beings have in them both a principle or pattern of nature that is wholly good and a vital or material force that can be good or bad. The latter is good when desires and emotions are expressed in appropriate balance and bad when a lack or excess is expressed. This idea inspired a famous exchange of letters between the Korean philosophers I Hwang (Toegye) and I I (or Yulgok) in the mid-1500s.

At the center of this exchange, known as the "Four–Seven Debate," was the relationship between the four heart-minds—which, according to Mencius, reflect the fundamental goodness of human nature—and the seven emotions (happiness, anger, sorrow, fear, love, hate, and desire)—which, according to "Centrality and Equilibrium," cause some human actions to be less than good when they are not expressed in correct proportion.

Both taking Zhu Xi as their starting-point, I Hwang and I I arrived at different conclusions. I Hwang argued that principle or pattern in nature (*i*) rises and material force (*ki*) follows, implying that human nature is mixed from the beginning. Il Huang, on the other hand, argued that if principle pervades everything and is thus uniform and undifferentiated, then it must be material force that initiates action, implying that human nature is originally wholly good. Behind the philosophers' quest for a deeper understanding of human nature was the commitment to psychological–moral transformation of the self—the neo-Confucian equivalent of classic Confucian self-cultivation.

The quest for self-improvement was not limited to men. Three prominent documents written by or for women were Queen Sohyc's *Instructions for the Inner Quarters* (1475); a letter written by the seventeenth-century Confucian Song Siyol on the occasion of his daughter's marriage, emphasizing a mother's influence on her children; and a letter from Lady Hyegyeong (1735–1815) to her brother's son in which she sought to impress on him the Confucian virtues of filiality and respect for elders, as well as compassion for paternal aunts.

As neo-Confucianism became increasingly entrenched at the state level and Daoism was gradually assimilated into Joseon culture, Buddhist monastics argued for reconciliation of the various religions—in effect, syncretism. As the sixteenth-century monk Hyujeong wrote in his *Mirror of Three Religions*: "An ancient man said: 'Confucianists plant the root, Taoists grow the root, and Buddhists harvest the root'" (Lee et al. 1993: 662). Nevertheless, Confucianism retained its dominant position.

Recent Developments: 1897 to the Present

From the late nineteenth to the mid-twentieth century, Korea was forced to contend with both Japanese imperialism and the increasing presence of the West. Korean responses to the West varied. One of the few English-speaking politicians of the time, Yun Chiho (1864–1945), favored wholesale Westernization and an end to the historic relationship with China, which was then known as the "sick man of East Asia." Like his contemporaries in China, Yun argued that if Koreans were poor and oppressed, Confucianism was to blame.

Yun's antipathy toward Confucianism was not unreasonable, for in addition to being seen as regressive, the tradition was associated with Japanese imperialism. During Japan's occupation of Korea (1910–1945), the old Royal Confucian Academy was renovated and institutions like the Society for the Promotion of the Confucian Way were established to aid the imposition of Japanese culture on the Koreans.

Contemporary Confucianism

Other Korean scholars agreed that Korea's adherence to the conservative teachings of Zhu Xi, which focused on maintaining the status quo through mastery of classical literature, had held it back. However, like the Chinese New Confucians, they also believed that a renewed transnational Confucianism based on traditional values could help to bring peace and stability to the whole world. Among those scholars was Bak Eunsik (1859–1925), who preferred the Confucianism of Wang Yangming even though Wang had been overshadowed by Zhu Xi in Korea. Bak saw hope in Wang's emphasis on the "manifesting" of the naturally "clear character" through cultivation of the heart-mind and uncovering of the innate goodness in human beings. He was not alone in his choice of Wang's Confucianism as a response to modernity.

Gim Chungnyol, who studied with the New Confucian Fang Dongmei in the 1950s and 1960s, was an activist in the Korean democracy movement in the 1970s and 1980s. He believed that Confucianism could serve as an antidote to the excesses of capitalist industrialization. But the movement for the revival of Confucianism in Korea has not been monolithic. So Chonggi, for one, was critical of authoritarian rule even if it was Confucian, but he believed that a Confucianism of the people could be good for Korea. The recent establishment of an Institute of Confucian Philosophy and Culture at Sungkyunkwan University suggests a revival of scholarly interest in the Confucian tradition. Even so, popular support for Confucianism as a religion is not strong.

Buddhism

The 35 years of Japanese occupation were particularly difficult for Korean Buddhists. During this time the traditional temple system was replaced with the Japanese system. Temple abbots were given the right to private ownership and inheritance, and some monks adopted the Japanese customs of marrying and having children. In 1920 the 31 main temples were put under the oversight of the Japanese government. After the defeat of Japan in 1945, deep rifts developed between the "Japanized" monks and those who had remained celibate. In time the Jogye order became the dominant school and took over the management of the temples from the married priests. Beginning in the 1960s, Korean Buddhism adopted a Protestant model of active missionizing, encouraging lay associations, and focusing on youth, and the South Korean government devoted many resources to restoring and reconstructing historic temples.

North Korea

In 1953 the Korean peninsula was divided into two parts. North Korea, like the PRC, is communist, and although its laws support religious freedom, in practice religion is barely tolerated. There are reports that Buddhism fares a little better than Christianity there, but it still has a very limited presence in the country. Some contend that "Kim Il-sung-ism," North Koreans' worship of their current political leader, like "Maoism" in the PRC, is the most prominent demonstration of religious zeal in the country.

South Korea

In the early 2000s nearly half of South Korea's population professed to have no religion—a similar pattern to that seen among the Chinese. Those who did claim an institutional affiliation were almost equally divided between Buddhism and Christianity (mainly of the Protestant, especially Pentecostal, variety). Confucianism claimed only 0.3 percent of the population, and the Indigenous shamanic tradition was statistically invisible, even though both traditions still seem pervasive in Korean life.

There are more than 200 new religions in South Korea. Because their beliefs and practices are syncretic and are often more "cultural" than "religious," they may not be captured in census statistics. But they demonstrate the pervasiveness of Korean religiosity and its multiple influences. Some modern progressives urge the revival of folk traditions as a way of reclaiming Korean culture; others call for shamanism to be rooted out as mere superstition. A sampling of new religious movements in the country shows that Korean religious responses to modernity are diverse.

The oldest of the new movements, the Religion of the Heavenly Way, or Cheondogyo, was founded in 1860 in response to Catholicism. It syncretizes Korean, Chinese, and Christian values, and combines monotheism and belief in the equality of all human beings with the broad East Asian vision of religious practice as enabling humans to live in harmony with the universe.

Students wearing traditional costumes perform during one of the regular celebrations of Confucius held at Sungkyunkwan University in Seoul (© Seoul Shinmun/epa/Corbis).

Another response to Western culture and globalization has been the Religion of the Great Ancestors (Daejonggyo), which sees itself as a revival of ancient Korean shamanism. Founded in 1910, it depicts God as Korean and presents the heavenly triad of Indigenous ancestors—Hwanin, Hwanung, and Dangun—as an alternative to the Christian Trinity. Other new religions, such as Dahn Yoga, have been influenced by the Daoist practice of internal alchemy aimed at both physical longevity and spiritual transcendence.

Summary

The ancient popular beliefs and practices at the root of the elite religions of China and Korea do not claim exclusive truth. They come from many different places and cultures. Yet most of them share a single aspiration to harmony—individual and communal, earthly and cosmic. Furthermore, many see the achievement of harmony as dependent on the disciplined transcendence of the self. Although individual groups vary in their specific goals and methods, they have all tended to believe that basic human desires—for material well-being, health, familial joy, personal security, social stability, spiritual maturity, and, ultimately, release from the cycle of rebirth—should be harnessed and directed toward the care of others: family and friends, the community, the state, and the natural world.

Like Korea's, China's religious culture has undergone significant transformations over the last 1,500 years, incorporating new influences—primarily from Confucianism, Daoism, Buddhism, and Christianity—without abandoning its Indigenous shamanistic traditions. Today both societies remain pluralistic and syncretic. None of the traditional religions have disappeared. Buddhism has thrived in Taiwan, while Christianity has flourished in Hong Kong and South Korea. New religious movements have developed in Taiwan and Hong Kong, and there are now more than 200 active new ones in South Korea. But religious freedom remains elusive in the People's Republic and North Korea. How the various religions will continue to develop and interact with one another remains to be seen.

Sites

Beijing, People's Republic of China

The Imperial Palace complex (the "Forbidden City") includes the Altar or Temple of Heaven, where the Ming and Qing emperors performed the grandest sacrifices. Beijing is also home to the ancestral temple of both dynasties (the Taimiao), a Confucian temple dedicated to scholar-officials, and the tombs of the later Ming emperors.

Qufu, Shandong Province, PRC

Among the monuments in the birthplace of Confucius in Qufu are a temple, a family mansion, and a cemetery containing Confucius's tomb and the remains of more than 100,000 of his descendants.

Xian, Shaanxi Province, PRC

Xian (formerly Chang'an) was China's capital through many dynasties. The famous terracotta warrior guardians were discovered nearby.

Wudangshan, Hubei Province, PRC

Mount Wudang is home to many Daoist monasteries, as well as a complex of palaces and temples that contain some of the finest examples of Chinese art and architecture; most were built during the Ming dynasty (1368–1644), but some Daoist buildings date from as early as the seventh century.

Guangzhou, Guangdong Province, PRC

It was in Guangzhou that Huineng (638–713), the sixth Chan patriarch, was enlightened. His remains are enshrined in the Nanhua Temple, north of Guangzhou.

Cheongju City, South Korea

The first book in the world to be produced using movable metal type was printed in 1377 at the Heungdeok Temple in Cheongju. Entitled *The Monk Baegun's Anthology of the Great Buddhist Patriarchs' Seon Teachings* but better known as *Jikji* (*Straight Pointing*), this work is now housed in the National Library of France.

Seoul, South Korea

The Changdeokgung (Palace of Prospering Virtue) complex in Seoul was established by Taejong, the third Joseon king. It includes Jongmyo, the oldest of the surviving Confucian shrines dedicated to the ancestors of Joseon.

Sacred Texts

Religion	Text	Composition/ Compilation	Compilation/Revision	Use
Confucianism (texts understood to come from sages and not considered "sacred")	*Books of Music, Poetry, History, Changes, Rites* and the *Spring and Autumn Annals*	5th–3rd centuries BCE	Stone engraving of the Classics made in 175 CE after the burning of the books in 213 BCE; *Book of Music* is lost	Home education; curriculum assigned for state examination and official learning
Confucianism	*Classic of Filial Piety, Analects, Er Ya* (earliest Chinese dictionary), three commentaries on the *Spring* and *Autumn Annals* and *Rites* in three sections (*Rites of Zhou, Book of Rites,* and *Ceremonial Rites*)	7th–10th centuries	Five Classics increased to Nine and then Twelve and inscribed on stone	Home education; curriculum assigned for state examination and official learning
Confucianism	Zhu Xi formulates standard texts into the Four Books (*Great Learning, Centrality and Equilibrium* [both from the *Book of Rites*], *Mencius, Analects*) and Five Classics from ancient times	10th–13th centuries	With *Mencius*, the Twelve Classics become Thirteen	Home education; curriculum assigned for state examination and official learning
Confucianism	Four Books for women include *Admonitions for Women, Filial Piety for Women, Analects for Women,* and *Instructions for the Inner Quarters*	1st–2nd centuries	Two new additions in 7th–9th centuries; *Instructions* added in 15th century; *Filial Piety* replaced by a *Handy Record of Rules for Women*	Education for women
Daoism (early texts seen primarily as words of wisdom from sages)	*Daodejing*	Contested but early 3rd century BCE generally accepted	3rd century CE Wang Bi commentary	Liturgical; basis for movements seeking legitimacy from Laozi
Daoism	*Zhuangzi*, known as the Classic of South China (*Nanhuajing*)	First seven chapters attributed to namesake; 4th to 3rd centuries BCE	Guo Xiang believed to be compiler of the current text	Education
Daoism	*Techniques of the Mind* and *Inward Training*	4th century BCE	Both lost to the main tradition and "found" recently in the legalist *Guanzi*	Likely used as meditation manual
Daoism	*Classic of the Great Peace*	1st century CE	Reassembled in 6th century after destruction in 3rd century	Ritual; instructional manual
Daoism	*Master Who Embraces Spontaneous Nature or Simplicity*	320s	"Inner" and "outer" sections of current text combined in 14th century	Manual for external alchemy
Daoism	High Clarity scriptures	Revealed 364 to 379	Edited into *Pronouncements of the Perfected* by Tao Hongjing	Doctrinal, ritual
Daoism	*Scripture for the Salvation of Humanity* of the Lingbao school	Revealed 4th century	12th century 61-chapter version presented to Song emperor	Recitation

Daoism	*Fifteen Precepts for the Establishing of the Teaching*	12th century	Collected as part of Wang Chongyang's writings	Doctrinal for Complete Truth school
Buddhism	Three Baskets of Theravada/Hinayana	Originals from India	Most translated during 3rd to 6th centuries	Study, reference for monastic law
Buddhism	Core to Chinese and Korean practice are treatises like *The Awakening of Faith*; sutras such as the *Pure Land* (in three volumes), *Lotus, Flower Garland, Platform of Hui-neng,* and *Vimalakirti*; and recorded sayings by Chan masters like Baegun's *Jikji*, Wumen's *Gateless Gate*, and the *Blue Cliff Records*	Most from South Asia except for the *Platform Sutra*, records of sayings from masters of the Chan school, and *The Awakening of Faith*, which has no Sanskrit original	Most translated during 4th to 6th centuries	Doctrinal, ritual, inspirational, educational
Popular tradition	Innumerable tracts of religious rituals and devotion	Throughout history	New writings appear based on new movements	Instructional, ritual

Discussion Questions

1. How do changes in the elite or institutional religions, and beliefs and practices in popular movements like the White Lotus Society illustrate the syncretic quality of Chinese religion?

2. What assumptions and values do Confucianism and Daoism share? What sets them apart from one another?

3. Would you consider Confucianism to be patriarchal, misogynist, and oppressive for women? Explain your position using evidence from China and Korea.

4. What are some of the core spiritual concerns in the early prototypical Daoist texts? How did they influence the goals, methods of cultivation, and institutional development of religious Daoism?

5. Compare and contrast classical and neo-Confucianism. What accounts for their differences?

6. What qualities would an ideal Buddhist woman have?

7. Explore points of tension and convergence between Confucianism, Daoism, and Buddhism.

8. What allows such disparate groups as the Seven Sages of the Bamboo Grove and Complete Truth to coexist under the umbrella of Daoism? What makes them both Daoist?

9. Who are the "New Confucians"? What issues are they tackling? What are their goals?

10. How does Engaged or Humanistic Buddhism differ from traditional Buddhism?

11. What do the Korean foundation myths suggest about the nature of Korean culture and religiosity?

12. What are some of the challenges facing modern Korean Buddhism?

13. In this work, the religious traditions of East Asia have been organized geographically in two groups: "China and Korea" and "Japan." Would a different organization, based on the traditions—Indigenous shamanism (as in Shinto and *mugyo*), Daoism, Confucianism, and East Asian Buddhism—be more or less appropriate? Why?

Glossary

Ban Zhao (c. 48–112 CE) The influential female Confucian scholar who wrote *Admonitions* (or *Lessons*) *for Women*.

Chan From Sanskrit *dhyana* (meditation); the Buddhist school known as Seon in Korea and Zen in Japan.

Confucius (551–479 BCE) The first teacher of Confucianism, known in Chinese as Kongzi or Kongfuzi.

Dao/dao (also **Tao/tao**) Either the "Way" in the sense of the Ultimate or the "way" in the sense of the path taken by followers of a particular tradition.

Daodejing The *Classic of the Way and Power or Virtue*; the multi-authored foundational Daoist text purportedly written by Laozi.

de Power or virtue.

Dong Zhongshu (195?–105? BCE) The most prominent Confucian of the New Text school, who helped establish Confucianism as the state religion.

five phases The generative and destructive cycles between metal, wood, water, fire, and earth, representing a dynamic view of the cosmos. The concept is also translated as "five agents" or "elements" depending on the meaning. See **wuxing**.

Han Yu (768–824) A pivotal figure in the revival of Confucianism in a period when it was overshadowed by Daoism and Buddhism.

Huayan Flower Garland Buddhism; Hwaeom in Korea.

Jingtu Pure Land Buddhism.

junzi A person of exemplary or authoritative behavior, especially in Confucianism; traditionally translated in English as "gentleman," implying the virtues of the upper class; a superior person, or one of virtue and exceptional character.

Laozi The "Old Master"; the putative patriarch of Daoism and author of the *Daodejing*, who may or may not have been an actual historical figure.

li The single English transliteration used for two different Chinese words. *Li* in the first sense refers to ritual practice and decorum and is usually translated as "rites." *Li* in the second sense refers to the pattern in a natural material such as wood or stone; it was used by the neo-Confucians to designate the force that pervades the cosmos and is translated as "principle."

lunhui Rebirth or *samsara*.

Mencius (c. 343–289 BCE) The second most prominent Confucian thinker, known in Chinese as Meng Ke, Master Meng, or Mengzi; he believed that human nature is inherently good.

pusa Bodhisattva; an enlightened being who foregoes release/liberation to stay in the world and help others.

qi Material force or vital energy

qigong A "breath" discipline or set of exercises used to enhance health and spiritual well-being; also the vital or material energy or force that animates everything in the universe.

ren The central Confucian virtue, usually translated as "humaneness," "benevolence," "goodness," or "compassion."

taiji The "Great Ultimate," understood to coexist with the Ultimate of Nonbeing; also the term for the slow-motion exercise sequence widely known in English as tai chi.

Wang Yangming (1472–1529) The Ming Confucian who challenged Zhu Xi's understanding of self-cultivation and established the neo-Confucian School of Mind.

wuwei "Not-doing" as a way of being in the world: a state not of "doing nothing" but of acting without intention or self-interest; an ideal for both Daoists and Confucians, though most prominently associated with the former.

wuxing Five agents, elements, or phases. See also **five phases** and **yin-yang**.

xin The single English transliteration used for two different Chinese characters. The first is translated throughout this chapter as "heart-mind" when discussing Daoism and Confucianism and is associated with both the thinking and the feeling capacities; the same character also refers to Mind or Consciousness in Buddhism. The second character means trustworthiness, a quality valued by Daoists and Confucians alike.

Xunzi (c. 310–219 BCE) The third most important classical Confucian thinker; he believed that human nature is evil and that conscious effort is required to develop goodness.

yi A moral sense of what is right, what is required and appropriate for a situation; most often used in conjunction with *ren*.

yinguo Cause and effect, or karma.

yin-yang "Yin" and "yang" originally referred to the shady and sunny sides of a mountain, but in time they came to be associated with female and male qualities and, more broadly, complementary forces in the universe. When combined with the word *wuxing*, these terms specify the dynamic nature of the universe—a concept integral to the Naturalist school of thought, which was popular during the Han dynasty.

Zhang Daoling According to tradition, the founder of the oldest surviving Daoist school, the Way of the Celestial Masters, which he established after Laozi appeared to him in a vision in 142 CE.

Zhuangzi (369?–286?) The second most important early Daoist thinker, after Laozi; also the title of the book attributed to him.

Zhu Xi (1130–1200) The most important member of the neo-Confucian School of Principle. He synthesized early Song Confucian writings, focused on book learning, and sought to find the principle/pattern common to Nature.

ziran Spontaneity or "self-so-ness."

Further Reading

Baker, Donald L. 2008. *Korean Spirituality*. Honolulu: Hawai'i University Press. An interpretation of the layered multiplicity of religious ideas and practices.

Buswell, Robert E., ed. 2007. *Religions of Korea in Practice*. Princeton, NJ: Princeton University Press. A work presenting primary source selections regarding ordinary devotional beliefs and practices as well as critical analysis and a helpful introductory essay by Don Baker.

Komjathy, Louis. 2013. *The Daoist Tradition: An Introduction*. London: Bloomsbury. A multidisciplinary work that includes historical, ethnographic, and textual sources.

Lagerwey, John, and Pierre Marsone, eds. 2016. *Modern Chinese Religion II: 1850–2015*. Leiden: Brill. A continuation of *Modern Chinese Religion I: Song-Liao-Jin-Yuan (960–1368 AD)*, published in 2015, including essays on Daoism, Confucianism, Buddhism, popular religious movements, and the presence of the West in China through science and Christianity.

Lopez, Donald S., ed. 1996. *Religions of China in Practice*. Princeton, NJ: Princeton University Press. A collection of essays on the religious practices of ethnic minorities such as the Manchus and Yi; Stephen Teiser's introductory essay provides a helpful overview.

Wang, Robin. 2003. *Images of Women in Chinese Thought and Culture: Writings from the Pre-Qin Period Through the Song Dynasty*. Indianapolis: Hackett. A collection of primary documents written by, for, and about women that also apply to the Korean experience.

Yu, Anthony. 2005. *State and Religion in China*. Chicago and La Salle, IL: Open Court. A persuasive argument that religions in China have always been closely involved with worldly politics.

Recommended Websites

http://www.clickkorea.org/

A general interest site sponsored by the Korea Foundation; to access essays on Korean religions, select the main category "Thought & Religion" and then choose from six subcategories.

http://folkency.nfm.go.kr/eng/introduction.jsp

The Encyclopedia of Korean Folk Culture, offering short notes, images, and videos. Current sections provide information on seasonal customs, folk beliefs, and folk literature, with sections planned on rites of passage; folk arts; food, clothing, and housing; livelihood skills; and folk society.

http://afe.easia.columbia.edu/cosmos/ort/confucianism.htm

Part of the Columbia University website, Asia for Educators, and an excellent source for basic information on Chinese religions.

http://www.stanford.edu/~pregadio/index.html

A concise introduction to Daoism that includes an impressive list of sources on alchemical beliefs and practices in the tradition.

http://eng.taoism.org.hk

The website of the Taoist Culture and Information Centre, which offers an insider's view of Daoism's history and place in the world today. The site is sponsored by a Daoist temple in Hong Kong and maintained with the help of scholars from North America, Europe, and China.

http://www.chinakongzi.org

The Chinese-language site of the China Confucius Foundation (CCF). Established in 1984, the CCF is dedicated to promoting the teachings of Confucius.

http://www.ica.org.cn

The website of the International Confucian Association, which aims to advance the study of Confucianism in order to promote peace and prosperity around the world. The site is also available in Chinese.

http://english.hanban.org/node_10971.htm

Hanban is the abbreviation for Guojia Hanyu guoji tuiguang lingdao xiaozu bangongshi or Office of Chinese Language Council International. It is affiliated to the Ministry of Education. This is the official site of the Confucius Institute/Classroom, offering information on teaching materials, tests, teachers, and scholarships. French and Spanish are also available.

http://www.chinesecio.com

The English website of the Confucius Institute Online with subject-dedicated MOOCs for Putonghua (Mandarin) and also information about scholarships.

http://www.fgs.org.tw/english/index.html

The website of Foguangshan (Buddha's Light Mountain), an ecumenical group based in Gaoxiong in southern Taiwan that favors Pure Land teachings.

http://www.dharmadrum.org/

The website of Fagushan (Dharma Drum Mountain), a Chan group headquartered in New Taipei City in Taiwan.

http://tw.tzuchi.org/en/

The website of Tzu Chi (Compassionate Relief), also transliterated as Cizi, a Taiwanese group, led by the nun Zhengyan, involved primarily in health care.

References

al-Faruqi, I., and D. E. Sopher, eds. 1974. *Historical Atlas of the Religions of the World*. New York: Macmillan.

Bell, Daniel A., and Chaibong Hahm, eds. 2003. *Confucianism for the Modern World*. Cambridge: Cambridge University Press.

Chen, Kenneth. 1964. *Buddhism in China. A Historical Survey*. Princeton, NJ: Princeton University Press.

de Bary, Theodore, ed. 1972. *The Buddhist Tradition in India, China and Japan*. New York: Vintage Books.

de Bary, Theodore, and Irene Bloom, comps. 1999. *Sources of Chinese Tradition*. Vol. 1. 2nd ed. New York: Columbia University Press.

de Bary, Theodore, and Richard Lufrano, comps. 2000. *Sources of Chinese Tradition*. Vol. 2. 2nd ed. New York: Columbia University Press.

Inagaki, Hisao, trans. 1994. *The Three Pure Land Sutras*. Kyoto: Nagata Bunshodo.

Kirkland, Russell. 2004. *Taoism: The Enduring Tradition*. New York and London: Routledge.

Lau, D. C., trans. 1963. *Lao Tzu: Tao Te Ching*. Middlesex, UK: Penguin.

Lau, D. C., trans. 1970. *Mencius*. Middlesex, UK: Penguin.

Lee, Ki-Baik. 1985. *A New History of Korea*. Trans. Edward Wagner. Cambridge, MA: Harvard University Press.

Lee, Peter H., ed. with Donald Baker, Han-Kyokim, Hugh H.W. Kang, Yongho Ch'oe. 1993. *Sourcebook of Korean Civilization*. Vol. 1. New York: Columbia University Press.

Owen, Stephen, ed. and trans. 1996. *An Anthology of Chinese Literature*. New York: W. W. Norton.

Price, A. F., and Wong Mou-lam. 1990 [1969]. *The Diamond Sutra and the Sutra of Hui-neng*. Boston: Shambhala.

Raphals, Lisa. 1998. *Sharing the Light: Representations of Women and Virtue in Early China*. Albany: SUNY Press.

Reps, Paul, comp. 1989 [1960]. *Zen Flesh, Zen Bones: A Collection of Zen and Pre-Zen Writings*. New York: Anchor Books, Doubleday.

Roth, Harold D. 1999. *Original Tao: Inward Training and the Foundations of Taoist Mysticism*. New York: Columbia University Press.

Sommer, Deborah, ed. 1995. *Chinese Religion: An Anthology of Sources*. New York: Oxford University Press.

Tsai, Kathryn Ann. 1994. *Lives of the Nuns: Biographies of Chinese Buddhist Nuns From the Fourth to Sixth Centuries: A Translation of the Pi-ch'iu-ni Chuan*. Honolulu: University of Hawaii Press.

Watson, Burton. 1963. *Xunzi: Basic Writings.* New York: Columbia University Press.

Watson, Burton. 1968. *The Complete Works of Chuang Tzu.* New York: Columbia University Press.

Watson, Burton, trans. 2001. *The Essential Lotus: Selections from the Lotus Sutra.* New York: Columbia University Press.

Note

1. Some scholars prefer a birth date of 552 BCE, based on scientific dating of an eclipse mentioned in the records of the time.

12 Japanese Traditions

John K. Nelson

Traditions at a Glance

Numbers

All numbers are based on self-assessment by the groups concerned. Because most Japanese religions are complementary rather than exclusive, the numbers reported by various sects may reflect occasional participation rather than membership. For Shinto, estimates range from 3.5 million to more than 100 million if New Year's visits to shrines are counted as indicating "Shinto" affiliation. For Buddhism, estimates range from 84.8 million, based on a 2009 government assessment of membership in the major denominations, to more than 100 million, while for Christianity, just under 1 million people nationwide are estimated to be adherents. Finally, 10 to 30 million people worldwide are estimated to participate in "new" religions emerging from Japan.

Distribution

Buddhism, Shinto, and "new" religions are practiced in every part of Japan, as well as in overseas communities. Japan itself counts approximately 75,000 Buddhist temples and more than 80,000 Shinto shrines, although many of the latter do not have resident priests.

Founders

Shinto is an ethnic religion with no founder. Important founders of new Buddhist schools include Saicho (Tendai), Kukai (Shingon), Eisai (Rinzai Zen), Dogen (Soto Zen), Honen (Pure Land), Shinran (True Pure Land), and Nichiren (Nichiren).

Deities

Shinto has a vast number of deities, many of which are specific to local communities. The sun goddess Amaterasu has been promoted as the supreme deity since the late 1800s because of her affiliation with the imperial household. However, one of the most widely distributed deities is Hachiman, who is associated with military valor.

The primary Buddhist deities include the medicine buddha, the cosmic buddha, and Amida, the buddha of the Pure Land, along with various **bodhisattvas** (or Buddhist "saints") associated with compassion, healing, and deliverance from hell.

Authoritative Texts

Since the nineteenth century, the primary texts for Shinto have been the *Kojiki: Record of Ancient Matters* and the *Nihon Shoki*. The various Buddhist denominations and "new" religions all have their own primary texts.

Noteworthy Teachings

Shinto emphasizes harmony with nature, sincerity, and ritual purity. Each Buddhist denomination and "new" religion (Tenrikyo, Rissho Koseikai, etc.) likewise emphasizes its own distinctive teachings: secrets about the nature of reality, how universal salvation can be achieved through the buddha of the Pure Land, the perfection of the *Lotus Sutra*, the necessity of performing memorial rites for ancestral spirits, and so on.

In this chapter you will learn about:

- The interactivity of diverse religious traditions and practices in Japan
- The features and interventions of spiritual and religious agents in Japanese traditions
- The myths, history, and development of Japan's major religious traditions
- The strong influence that politics has had on religion in Japan
- The transitions and transformations of religious practice in the modern and contemporary periods

The great "floating" *torii* gate at the Itsukushima Shinto shrine. Each of the main posts is a giant camphor tree, said to be some 500 years old (GARDEL Bertrand/hemis.fr/Getty Images).

⊕ Overview

Long before the establishment of shrines to local deities and Buddhist temples in the third and sixth centuries, respectively, local clans developed close relationships with both deities of the natural world and the spirits of their ancestors. Reciprocity was a key dynamic of these relationships, in which humans sent their petitions to the deities, accompanied by ritual offerings, and the deities were expected to respond by providing bountiful harvests, plentiful children, and stable political and social conditions. People expressed loyalty to the ancestral spirits of their own household and clan, yet there was also acknowledgment of the powers of the many other deities (**kami**) associated with natural phenomena such as fire, water, and mountains, as well as the spirits of animals and plants. When the harmonious balance of the relationship between humans and spirits was disturbed—by plague, famine, earthquake, typhoons, war, or death—efforts to restore it via ritual were renewed. This pattern is common to all Japanese religions.

A discussion of Japan's religious traditions requires the perspectives of cultural studies, history, politics, and anthropology, as well as religious studies. Even then, to encompass all the traditions that inform Japanese society today is a challenge. Shinto, the "way of the *kami*," is often said to be more than 2,000 years old. Yet it has gone through several transformations, some as recently as 150 years ago. Buddhism likewise defies easy assumptions; for example, only a few denominations have anything to do with meditation. Layered on an even older tradition of venerating ancestral spirits, the seven major Buddhist denominations today have their roots in the medieval period and yet must continually reinvent themselves to retain the financial support of the Japanese people. Although many monks use social media to stay in touch with their flocks, there is no guarantee that a younger generation that is highly skeptical of religion in general will develop affiliations with local temples. It is no exaggeration to say that Japanese religious traditions force us to rethink the social, cultural, and individual dimensions of religion in a rapidly changing world.

Timeline

c. 8000 BCE	Hunter-gatherers produce sophisticated cord-pattern pottery, arrowheads, and human figures with possible religious significance
c. 450 BCE–250 CE	Immigration from northern Asia introduces new technology, cultural forms, language, religious rituals, etc.
c. 250–600	Kofun period; rulers interred in massive burial mounds (*kofun*), with grave goods and clay models of attendants that indicate complex local hierarchies in this life and the next
538	Introduction of Buddhism; Yamato clan establishes dominance
594	"Prince" Shotoku (*Shotoku taishi*) promotes Confucian principles alongside Buddhism; later acknowledged as patron saint of Buddhism in Japan
600s	Early temple building; ruler referred to as "heavenly sovereign" (*tenno*)
710–794	Nara period; capital city, Heijokyo, located on site of present-day Nara

712, 720	Compilation of two key texts (*Kojiki, Nihon Shoki*) used to legitimate imperial rule and aristocratic privileges; more than 1,000 years later, these texts would be used in the campaign to revitalize "Shinto"
752	Dedication of Todaiji temple and completion of its Great Buddha image
785	Saicho, founder of Tendai sect, establishes a temple on Mount Hiei near Kyoto
794–1184	Heian period; capital city, Heiankyo, moved to what is now Kyoto
834	Kukai, founder of Shingon sect, establishes a monastery on Mount Koya
1039	Tendai monks attack monasteries of rival Buddhist sects
1052	Beginning of the "Final Decline of the Buddhist Dharma" (age of *mappo*), marked by fires, famines, earthquakes, wars, pestilence, etc.
1175	Honen begins propagating "Pure Land" Buddhism
1185–1333	Kamakura period, characterized by dominance of the samurai class; capital moved to Kamakura
1200	Eisai establishes Rinzai Zen school with support of the samurai
1233	Dogen establishes Soto Zen school
1253	Nichiren forms sect centered on recitation of the *Lotus Sutra*
1254	Honen's disciple Shinran introduces "True Pure Land" Buddhism
1274, 1281	Attempted invasions by Mongol armies are thwarted when violent storms, called "divine winds" (*kamikaze*), sink many of their ships
1430–1500	Major fires, famine, epidemics, social disorder; Onin War (1467) devastates Kyoto and marks start of regional power struggles
1474–1550	True Pure Land peasant protest movement spreads throughout the country
1542	Systematization of Shinto shrines, beginning of priestly certification via Yoshida clan
1549	Christianity enters Japan with the Jesuit Francis Xavier
1573–1602	Gradual centralization of political power; Oda Nobunaga, Toyotomi Hideyoshi, and Tokugawa Ieyasu establish military regimes that subdue regional lords
1603–1867	Edo period; Tokugawa clan dominates all political, military, and bureaucratic activity; country closed to outside trade in 1633
1638	Shimabara rebellion; Christianity banned
1644–1860	Rise of neo-Confucian teachings as challenge to Buddhist dominance
1705	First major pilgrimage of commoners to Ise Grand Shrines
1812	Beginning of movement to revitalize Shinto
1853–1867	Commodore Matthew Perry arrives in Japan and demands open ports; Christian missionaries return; regional wars between feudal and imperial forces end with defeat of Tokugawa shogunate
1868	New Meiji government orders separation of *kami* and buddhas, resulting in destruction of temples and religious art throughout the country

1879	Establishment of Yasukuni Shrine, where the spirits of military dead are venerated
1890–1944	State launches campaign to establish ideology centered on notions of imperial divinity, the sacred nature of Japan, and military conquest
1936–1945	War in the Pacific, ending in the systematic destruction of most major and many minor Japanese cities
1945–1953	Allies occupy Japan; emperor renounces divinity; Shinto's status as state religion revoked
1995	Aum Shinrikyo attack on Tokyo subway; government passes new laws regulating religion organizations and activity
2011	Great Eastern Japan Earthquake of March 11 kills about 16,000 people and causes a meltdown of three nuclear reactors, as well as tremendous property damage; Japan's religious organizations provide substantial material and spiritual relief

⊕ Foundations

Japanese history has no written records from the first four centuries of the Common Era. However, Chinese accounts from the fourth century describe "the land of Wa" (Japan) as ruled by a female queen who used "black magic and witchcraft" to control the *kami* and maintain power. The early belief (second to fifth century CE) that rulers embodied the *kami* legitimized their rule as a function of divine will.

When these rulers died, earthen mounds were built to house their tombs, in which were placed items that they would need in the netherworld. The Miyazaki region of southeast Kyushu is particularly rich in earthen burial mounds. Unlike their counterparts in Egypt and China, however, the Japanese did not sacrifice human beings to accompany their masters into the afterlife. Instead, they relied on clay models to serve as the servants, musicians, shamans, and soldiers that the ruler would need in the next world. These early rulers became guardian spirits of the clans, communities, and regions they once ruled.

These traditions changed dramatically after 538 CE, when the ruler of what is today western Korea wrote to the Japanese king praising Buddhism as a religion "superior to all others" (see Document box). Buddhism offered a whole new set of deities that could be petitioned to protect the ruler and maintain the status quo.

For its first 150 years in Japan, Buddhism was sustained mainly by clans with ties to Korea. But in time its promises of "salvation" attracted state patronage. Meanwhile, a steady stream of immigrants fleeing wars in southern China and the Korean peninsula were arriving with cultural knowledge—in astrology, philosophy, divination, architecture, and courtly protocol—that contributed significantly to the development of the fledgling state. Among the concepts and practices brought from the mainland were several that we now associate with religious Daoism. Attention was paid to the movement of the stars, for example: the constellations painted on the ceilings of imperial tombs link the Japanese court to its counterparts in Korea and China, where the same constellations can be found portrayed. Stories about magical peaches ("Momotaro") and time travel ("Urashima Taro") also recall Daoist ideas about immortality and alchemy. Even elements of the material culture associated with the imperial household—the mirror, sword, and jewel, as well as the color purple—have roots in continental Daoism, which itself was influenced by the older traditions of shamanism (Senda 1988: 133–138).

Document

From the *Nihon Shoki* ("Chronicles of Japan")

Japan's second-oldest book after the Kojiki *(712), the* Nihon Shoki *(720) combines origin myths with more factual accounts. The following extract purports to be from a Korean document recommending Buddhism to the Japanese king.*

This Dharma is superior to all others. It is difficult to grasp and difficult to attain. Neither the Duke of Zhou nor Confucius was able to comprehend it. It can give rise to immeasurable, limitless merit and fruits of action, leading to the attainment of supreme enlightenment. The treasure of this marvelous Dharma is such that it is as if one owned a wish-fulfilling gem that granted every desire. Every prayer is granted and nothing is wanting. Moreover, from distant India to the three kingdoms of Korea, all receive these teachings and there is none who does not revere and honour them. (*Nihon Shoki*, in Bowring 2006: 15)

Japan's first Buddhist temple was constructed in 596 CE, with the assistance of Korean builders, and the first Buddhist rituals were conducted there by specialists (women as well as men) from the Korean kingdom of Baekje. Incredibly, temples established in those early years can still be seen in places like Osaka (Shitennoji) and Nara (Horyuji and Todaiji).

Persistent Themes

In Japan, religious belief generally takes a back seat to religious activity. Taking action—if only to purchase an amulet—may significantly reduce anxiety about an upcoming examination, a relationship problem, or a health condition. Which particular shrine or temple one visits depends on the situation that one wants a blessing for.

A conventional survey of Japanese religions would emphasize the doctrines, institutions, and leaders associated with the three major traditions: Buddhism, Confucianism, and Shinto. Although this chapter will certainly touch on these, many scholars now question the validity of this approach. Lack of specific "religion" does not mean that religious belief, feeling, or orientation is lacking (Pye 2004), and Japan has no fewer than 7 major and 16 minor schools of Buddhism, countless "new" religions, and more than 80,000 different *kami*. So it's not surprising that Japanese people might feel confused when asked which particular sect they belong to. Most have no trouble tolerating doctrinal diversity at the popular level. Nor do most of their religious traditions require adherence to one set of beliefs. In fact, those traditions have been subordinate to the themes outlined in the following sections for more than 1,000 years.

Seeking Benefits

Central to most Japanese religious traditions is the pragmatic desire to secure benefits, either in this world or in the next. It matters little whether a given place of worship is devoted to the Buddha or to a particular local *kami*; the important thing is that the prayers offered there help the individual resolve a conflict, start a new business, find a marriage partner, or conceive a child. A person may visit both temples and shrines, engage priests to perform rituals, and make regular offerings until the desired outcome is obtained—or until it seems clear that all those efforts have failed. Then he or she may have little to do with any organized religion until the next problem arises. "Turning to the gods in a time of trouble" is a well-known expression that summarizes Japan's pragmatic attitude toward religion.

One way to understand the diversity of religion in Japan is to imagine religious life as a marketplace in which consumers decide which shops to patronize on the basis of cost and product availability. Variables of time, place, and occasion also enter into consumers' calculations: thus a religious "product" appropriate for the end of summer—for example, the ritual prescribed to protect the ripening rice crop from insects, typhoons, or fire—is not the same ritual required to protect one's business from financial trouble or one's soul from the flames of hell. Just as consumers go to different stores depending on the kinds of goods they need to buy, so Japan's religious consumers know which traditions offer the appropriate assistance for the situation at hand.

Once the right religious "product" or service has been determined, a reciprocal relationship is initiated that entails certain obligations and expectations. In exchange for tangible assistance from a *kami*, *bodhisattva*, or buddha, one must show one's gratitude, not only by performing formal rituals but by treating that spiritual agent with special respect. Japanese literature is full of stories in which an ungrateful or arrogant person who has offended a deity ends up chastened and contrite.

Religious and Spiritual Agents

One of the most fundamental themes of Japanese culture and civilization is that there is a life-energy that circulates throughout the physical world, and that humans can align themselves with this energy through worship of the *kami*. Capable of entering any object to exercise their power, *kami* can be found in flowing water, rain, mountains, clouds, fire, earth, and wind, as well as in certain animals that serve as their agents, messengers, and avatars. Their peaceful side helps humans prosper, while their destructive side can only be endured and appeased through rituals.

Practice

The *Gomadaki* Ritual

The gomadaki *ritual (see photo) combines external, physical action and internal meditation. As participants place their offerings in the fire, they are instructed to perform a series of visualizations.*

First, visualize one's own body: form Amitabha's meditation hand gesture (*mudra*), and visualize the syllable KIRIKU . . . above the heart-moon energy centre (*chakra*). It becomes a fully open red lotus blossom . . . that emits a great clear light in the midst of which is the "form body" . . . of Amitabha. Next, form Amitabha's meditation *mudra* and imagine these ritual offerings entering the mouth of the chief deity, going to the lotus blossom of his heart, becoming vast numbers of brightly shining *chakras*; then from each and every one of his pores these brightly shining *chakras* flow out through the entirety of empty space. Next, the various buddhas and bodhisattvas of the world, having received the offerings, cause these brightly shining *chakras* to enter one's own and the donor's heads. As a result, the evil consequences of greed, hatred and ignorance are completely erased from our bodies, the calamities and unhappiness caused by evil people and evil destinies are destroyed, vitality and lifespan increase, and peace and tranquility are attained. (Payne 2006: 213–219)

Tendai and Shingon Buddhists perform a purification and blessing ritual that has its roots in ancient India. Participants in the "consecrated fire" ritual (*homa* in Sanskrit, *gomadaki* in Japanese) inscribe wooden slats with their names and a prayer or petition; their requests are then transported into the spirit realm via the fire and the chanting of the priests (John K. Nelson).

Mythology

We can see examples of these dynamics in the myths explaining the origins of Japan. The basic contours of the Japanese creation myth first took shape in the **Kojiki**, a collection of regional stories compiled in 712 CE to legitimate the dominance of the Yamato clan by associating it with the divine origins of the land. Yet these stories were not widely known until the late nineteenth century, when they were circulated as part of a state campaign to create a cultural heritage for the new nation.

In these tales, the positive and peaceful side of the primordial *kami* couple, Izanagi and his "wife" Izanami, can be seen in their creation of the islands that make up Japan and the primary elements of the natural world: seas, straits, winds, trees, mountains, plains. After a false start produces a "leech baby" that must be cast aside, Izanami dies giving birth to the deity of fire. As her grieving partner consigns her to the land of the dead, he laments: "Alas, I have given my beloved spouse in exchange for a mere child!" (Philipi 1985: 57).

The destructive side of the *kami* is then revealed. First, the enraged Izanagi kills the fire deity and journeys to the netherworld to beseech his wife to return. She agrees to negotiate with the gods of the underworld on the condition that Izanagi not look at her. But he cannot resist and is horrified to see her corpse full of "squirming and roaring maggots" (Philipi 1985: 62). As he flees, she cries out, "He has shamed me!" and sends her "hags" to stop him. After several narrow escapes, Izanagi reaches the land of the living and uses a huge boulder to block the opening to the netherworld, but not before Izanami vows that she will cause 1,000 of his subjects to die each day; he counters that he will cause 1,500 to be born.

To purify himself after this ghastly encounter with death, Izanagi bathes in a river. As he does so, the female *kami* of the sun, **Amaterasu**, is born from his left eye; she will become the primary deity associated with the imperial family. Then the male moon *kami* springs from his right eye, and the last imperial *kami*, associated with the land, issues from his nose.

What this myth tells us is that the *kami* are responsible for both the world's blessings and its destructive powers. Whenever human well-being is threatened, the *kami* can be petitioned for help.

Map 12.1 Japan: Major Cities and Religious Sites

Source: Adapted from Young 1995: 211.

The founding of the Todaiji temple brings together many of the themes we've been discussing. Designed to house a monumental bronze statue of the cosmic buddha (Vairocana), the temple was planned by the emperor Shomu in the early 740s in response to a series of earthquakes and poor harvests. Before starting construction, however, he sent a high-ranking monk to the distant island of Kyushu to ask a powerful *kami* there for his approval. Not only did the *kami* approve, but he demanded to be transported to the site so that he could keep the local deities from interfering with the project. His shrine still stands on a hillside overlooking the temple.

Aspects of this story remain relevant today. Temples and shrines still conduct rituals for the health of the emperor and the stability of the nation. And though Westerners tend to see Japan's two dominant religious traditions, Buddhism and Shinto, as discrete entities, most Japanese do not distinguish between them.

Other Spiritual Agents

The concept of the bodhisattva was discussed in Chapter 10. In Mahayana Buddhist thought, a bodhisattva is an enlightened being who delays entry into nirvana in order to help all living beings who have not yet been released from worldly suffering.

As part of an annual ritual, priests brush dust from the 50-foot-tall statue of the Buddha in Japan's Todaiji Temple. (Kimio Ida/EPA/Shutterstock)

The bodhisattva with the greatest reputation among the Japanese for intervening in human affairs is undoubtedly Kannon, who arrived in Japan from China under the name Guanyin. Countless "miracle" tales testify to Kannon's commitment to alleviating the suffering she perceives (*kan*) and hears (*on*). The economic golden years of the 1980s saw a revival of interest in Kannon: her cult was promoted at pilgrimage sites and in temples, and giant statues of her were erected in various places (Reader 1991: 191, 157, 36).[1] While all the traditional attributes of Kannon are still present in interpretations of her today, her all-embracing motherly qualities in particular have attracted a new generation of devotees.

Another bodhisattva who has provided comfort to millions of Japanese is Jizo (Ksitigarbha in Sanskrit) or (more respectfully and affectionately) Ojizo-sama. Known for his ability to free tormented souls from hell, he also protects children and travelers, and since the 1970s he has taken on the job of conducting the souls of deceased children and aborted fetuses to salvation. Anyone visiting a temple in Japan today is likely to see rows of Jizo statues, many with little berets on their shaved heads (he is a monk, after all) and offerings of coins or pebbles at their feet. A woman who has aborted a pregnancy or suffered a miscarriage may pay a monthly fee for a temple to care for the fetus's soul by performing periodic rituals and offerings to appease its unhappy and potentially dangerous spirit.

This somewhat unusual motif for a Jizo representation is at Mount Koya in southern Wakayama Prefecture. It shows two children together in death; they may be twins or siblings, but they are carved from one block. One interesting dimension of Jizo statues is that they are reclothed regularly over the course of hundreds of years. In an indication of the normal Japanese mixture of Shinto and Buddhism, sacred tree sprigs have been left as an offering at the base, and Sanskrit text in Siddham script can be seen on the column to the left. (Richard Mammana)

Unsettled Spirits

How can the spirit of an unborn child be dangerous? The roots of this tradition lie in a combination of native Japanese, Korean, and Chinese folk beliefs, Daoist dynamics, and Buddhist-inspired demonology. In ancient times, the spirits of people who had lost their lives to powers beyond their control were expected to become angry and vengeful, and rituals of pacification were believed to be required to calm them. One of Japan's most respected scholars of death and dying, Gorai Shigeru, believes that all Japanese funeral and memorial rites are rooted in the idea that the spirits of the dead must be placated before they can become benevolent ancestral influences (Gorai 1994: 105).

At the level of the state, to neglect or ignore the vengeance-seeking spirits of assassinated rivals or powerful enemies killed in battle was to invite retribution in the form of earthquakes, droughts, storms, sickness, or infertility. Thus spirit appeasement was high on the list of state-sponsored ritual activities. When Buddhism arrived in the early sixth century, it took up its share of that responsibility, which until then had been the exclusive domain of shamans.

⊕ Pivotal Developments in Japanese Religious History

During the formative Nara period (710–794), the government set up a ministry to manage the shrines of the *kami*. At the same time, a council of senior Buddhist monks formed the Sangha Office to oversee monastic conduct and training. The same basic administrative structure would remain in place for nearly 350 years, reasserting itself whenever a strong centralized government took charge. Knowing all too well from Chinese history how religious organizations and ideas could undermine the state, the early Japanese rulers carefully monitored all religious appointments and construction projects.

Tendai and Shingon

For three centuries Buddhism remained the preserve of the Nara elite, who commissioned temples dedicated to their ancestors, consigned their second or third sons to Buddhist monasteries, and sponsored Buddhist art as a way to earn merit. In 804, however, two monks named Saicho and Kukai traveled to China for further study in the tradition, and there they encountered some important new perspectives, one of which emphasized the written word. The *Lotus Sutra*, which

had originated in northern India and been translated into Chinese, taught that there is only one
vehicle to salvation—the body we live in, here and
now—and that we all have the potential to become
buddhas ourselves. The monks who had mastered
the teachings of the *Lotus Sutra* saw themselves as
instrumental to the welfare of the state.

When Saicho and Kukai returned to Japan, they
took with them volumes of teachings and commentaries, paintings, mandalas, and ritual implements.
The traditions they founded helped to domesticate
Buddhist teachings and rituals in very pragmatic
ways. For example, both Saicho's Tendai and Kukai's Shingon taught a kind of short-cut approach
that put the possibility of enlightenment and salvation within the reach of common people (not just
monks and nuns) in their own lifetime. Through
incantation, ritual gestures, meditation, visualization, and austerities, individuals could connect with
and obtain benefits from deities in other spheres of
existence. Whereas earlier Buddhist schools had
considered the human body problematic because
of its fragility, desires, and impermanence, the new
doctrines, which we now identify as "tantric" or
"esoteric," attributed a spiritual value to it: much
as geothermal steam and seismic activity can be
transformed into electricity, bodily desires could
be harnessed through ritual and directed toward
the quest for salvation and enlightenment.

The fact that both sects established their headquarters on sacred mountains near Kyoto—Tendai
on Mount Hiei and Shingon on Mount Koya—
suggests that they continued to respect the local
kami. The Japanese phrase **honji suijaku** (which
comes from the *Lotus Sutra* and means "manifestation from the original state") helps to explain the

A young *bugaku* dancer performs on the grounds of Osaka's
Shitennoji temple. Established in 593 CE, the temple has been in
continuous operation ever since (John K. Nelson).

implications of the relationship between the two traditions. *Honji*, meaning "original ground," refers
to the fundamental reality and power of a particular buddha or bodhisattva, while *suijaku* refers to
the "trace" or particular form in which that entity chooses to manifest him- or herself in Japan. Thus
the *kami* of a particular mountain or powerful clan came to be seen as the "provisional manifestation" of a particular buddha or bodhisattva. For many centuries, the *honji suijaku* principle made
Buddhist and Shinto deities interdependent, although the Buddhist deities were usually superior.

From the ninth century onward, Buddhism increasingly overshadowed the traditional ritual
practices centered on *kami*. The *honji suijaku* principle was applied to local shrines as a way both
to incorporate their deities and to allow worshipers to achieve salvation along more obviously

Practice

Taboo Terms at Shinto Shrines

In an effort to resist total assimilation into the new tradition, the priests and priestesses of major shrines developed a kind of code for referring to Buddhism without adopting its vocabulary. Thus Shakyamuni Buddha became the "Central One," a temple a "tiled roof," and sutras "dyed paper." Buddhist monks, with their shaved heads, were called "long hairs," death became "getting well," and illness was "slumber" (Felicia Bock, cited in Bowring 2006: 191).[2] Using these terms, the participants in a *kami* ritual could acknowledge the importance of Buddhist concepts while keeping a certain distance from them.

Buddhist lines. A number of rituals could be performed by officiants of either tradition. For example, the early-eleventh-century noblewoman who served for nearly four decades as the chief spiritual medium at the Kamo Shrine in Kyoto was a devout Pure Land Buddhist.

⊕ New Emphases in Japanese Religious Practice

New Sects in the Kamakura and Muromachi Periods

Around the world, people deeply affected by changing political, economic, and cultural conditions have often been open to innovations in religious belief or practice that promise to help them cope with challenging new circumstances. In Japan, three new types of Buddhist practice emerged during the Kamakura period (1185–1333): Pure Land, Nichiren, and Zen (the three principal forms of Buddhism still practiced in Japan today). At the same time, innovations in *kami* worship laid the foundations for what would eventually be known as Shinto.

The relative stability of the Heian period ended in 1185, when the courtly families in power since the early days of Japanese civilization were overthrown. Once the imperial capital of Kyoto was under the control of the new regime, which drew its power from the warrior elite, or **samurai**, the center of political power shifted north to Kamakura, near what is today Tokyo.

For the elites of the Kyoto region, the move was a disaster. Yet they were predisposed to expect conflict, corruption, and vice because a popular Buddhist teaching had predicted that the year 1052 would mark the beginning of the degenerate age known as **mappo**, during which the Buddhist dharma would decline. The social chaos and bloody political disorder that attended the transition to the Kamakura period were accompanied by earthquakes, typhoons, pestilence, and famine. Living at a time before the science behind such disasters was understood, people believed they were trapped in a kind of hell on earth.

Pure Land Salvation

It is no wonder, then, that a new interpretation of Buddhism promising salvation gained wide acceptance. For centuries, Buddhism had been almost exclusively the faith of the elite, but it began to attract the common people after Genshin (942–1017) organized Pure Land beliefs into a coherent

Document

From Genshin's "Essentials of Salvation" (985 CE)

The first division, the corrupt land that one must shun [in order to reach the Pure Land] comprises the three realms in which there is no peace. . . . The first of these, hell, is . . . divided into eight parts: the hell of repeated misery, the hell of black chains, the hell of mass suffering, the hell of wailing, the hell of great wailing, the hell of searing heat, the hell of great searing heat, the hell of incessant suffering.

The rewards of the Pure Land are of endless merit. . . . First is the pleasure of being welcomed by many saints. Second is the pleasure of the first opening of the lotus. Third is the pleasure of obtaining in one's own body the ubiquitous supernatural powers of a Buddha. Fourth is the pleasure of the realm of the five wonders. Fifth is the pleasure of everlasting enjoyment. Sixth is the pleasure of influencing others and introducing them to Buddhism. Seventh is the pleasure of assembling with the holy family. Eighth is the pleasure of beholding the Buddha and hearing the Law. Ninth is the pleasure of serving the Buddha according to the dictates of one's own heart. Tenth is the pleasure of progressing in the way of Buddhahood. (Yampolsky 2008: 726)

system. His *Essentials of Salvation* (completed in 985) describes in graphic detail the six realms of existence (hell, hungry ghosts, demonic beings, animals, human beings, and heavenly beings) through which all must pass, in multiple incarnations, before reaching the perfection of the Pure Land.

For the first time in Japan, Buddhist monks began to concern themselves with the salvation of ordinary people, although it would take another two centuries for a new institutional form to give practical expression to that concern. It was a Tendai monk, frustrated by his sect's preoccupation with politics, who developed Pure Land Buddhism as we know it today. Honen (1133–1212) believed that in an age of *mappo*, it was impossible to attain salvation by the traditional means (following the precepts, chanting, meditating). The only hope lay in the saving grace of Amida, who did not discriminate according to social rank, past karma, or present activity; for this buddha, sincere faith and repeated recitation of the **nembutsu**, "*Namu Amida Butsu*," alone were enough. In this way Honen opened the door to the notion of universal salvation.

At the time, this concept was seen as radical because it meant there was no fundamental difference between a layperson and a learned monk. Honen was banished from the Kyoto region in 1207, along with his disciple Shinran (1173–1262), who had just caused a scandal by marrying—a "degenerate" practice that was fairly common among monks (as was keeping a concubine) but had never been made public. Shinran reasoned that if the power of Amida Buddha was great enough to save even those of the lowest social status, then marriage would not be an obstacle to salvation.

Honen's exile lasted only four years, but Shinran was banished for seven, during which he is said to have preached among farmers and fishermen, refining his "True Pure Land" doctrine to the point of maintaining that a *single* sincere repetition of the *nembutsu* would secure salvation. Shinran believed humans were incapable of exercising the disciplined "self-power" (*jiriki*) necessary for attaining salvation and therefore must rely on "other-power" (**tariki**) for deliverance from suffering.

In the tumult of the Kamakura period (and subsequent years), Pure Land spread via small groups that emphasized *nembutsu* practice. Around 1450, the sect's eighth hereditary leader, Rennyo, began to systematize its teachings and organize the scattered Pure Land communities to create a kind of militant security force dedicated to protecting the Honganji temple in what is today Osaka.

Interview

Miura Akari

Reverend Miura Akari assumed control of her family's True Pure Land temple when she was 23 years old and still a university student. Located in a small city south of Nara, this temple is one of several in the area and thus competes for parishioners at a time of nationwide population decline. However, Reverend Miura's unique background as a singer/songwriter in several bands while at university, as well as an online video she made on "Connections/*En*" that has been used by the national True Pure Land Higashi Honganji denomination, has made her something of an up-and-coming "star" in the tradition.

Miura Akari. (Courtesy of Miura Akari)

How has your background as a musician and performer helped prepare you to lead a temple in ways that supplement traditional training?

When I was on stage during my university days, I sang to the audience in only one direction. I emphasized my personal experience about love and peace, topics I thought my generation could relate to. During that time, I developed confidence in front of a group of people that has carried over to speaking or lecturing, singing in a variety of musical styles, or chanting sutras. I now appreciate the Japanese saying about *ichigo-ichie*, or "one time, one meeting," which highlights both the uniqueness and impermanence of the moment when people meet.

What themes do you promote in your choice of songs when you perform solo, or when leading the temple chorus?

It's important to create a body of work that communicates ideas and experiences all people share. Making connections between people, understanding differences, appreciating our precious human lives and relationships—these are all important.

Has it been challenging to be accepted as a woman Buddhist priest in a profession that is largely dominated by men?

At first it was. But the warm relations I have with the parishioners (*danka*), the temple's board of directors, and of course my mother made the transition less bumpy than it might have been. When I visit the homes of temple members to perform a memorial or some other ritual, I see it as a kind of "stepping out on the town" that is rich with personal contacts, and so I enjoy it very much. I hear about all kinds of problems and difficulties in peoples' lives, and want to serve and collaborate with them to find solutions. I want Buddhist temples to be a place where people can meet and create new communities of shared interests, and where they can go to enjoy themselves.

They were not the first Buddhists to take aggressive action: as early as 1039, Tendai "monk warriors" had attacked rival sects and temples, and even challenged the legitimacy of the imperial court. Four centuries later, however, the True Pure Land insurrection was led not by monks, but by common people and leaderless samurai. With nothing to lose and salvation guaranteed through their faith, they held their own against experienced armies. By 1500 they controlled several provinces, although they were finally defeated and brought partially under control by the warlord Oda Nobunaga (1534–1582).

Rinzai Zen and Kamakura Culture

The word "Zen" is the Japanese version of the Chinese *chan*, which in turn is a translation of the Sanskrit term for meditation, *dhyana*. Whereas the Pure Land traditions prescribed recitation of the name of Amida Buddha, the Chan/Zen tradition emphasized seated meditation (**zazen**) as the path to enlightenment and, eventually, salvation.

Zen became established in much the same way as Pure Land, but with an important difference: it was imported directly from China, and its development was led by Chinese masters who settled in Japan in the thirteenth century. Although the seeds of Zen meditation can be found in Tendai as early as the ninth century (when the practice of "constantly sitting" was introduced), it was not until the later twelfth century that the tradition took root in Japan.

In 1168 a Tendai monk named Eisai (1141–1215) traveled to China expecting to find the traditions in which Tendai and Shingon had originated, only to discover that they had been superseded by Chan Buddhism. Chan had survived a nationwide campaign of persecution, launched in 845, that had targeted other Buddhist traditions because of their lavish wealth, landholdings, political meddling, and "parasitic" monks and nuns who did nothing for society. By contrast, Chan monks worked with their hands and displayed none of the elaborate trappings that characterized other traditions.

Eisai studied Chan for the next 20 years while continuing to serve as a Tendai monk. Then he made a second trip to China (1187–1191), during which he studied with a Linji (Rinzai in Japanese) Chan master who certified his enlightenment. In addition to Chan, Eisai imported other Buddhist and Confucian teachings to Japan—as well as a hot drink that helped to keep sleepy monks awake during meditation. His work "Drink Tea and Prolong Life" is credited with promoting tea in Japan, and the tea ceremony (developed a century later) was deeply influenced by Zen aesthetics and symbolism.

In an effort to attract the patronage of the military rulers in Kamakura, Eisai wrote a treatise, "The Propagation of Zen for the Protection of the Country," that led to his temporary exile from all Tendai temples in the Kyoto region. After a short time in Kamakura, where he secured patrons and established a small temple, he returned to Kyoto and in 1202 built Japan's first Zen temple, Kenninji. Its many reconstructions have preserved a number of cultural treasures as well as beautiful examples of classic Zen landscape gardens and architecture.

Why would samurai warriors have been attracted to an austere Chinese tradition focused on the achievement of "sudden enlightenment" through the practice of *zazen* and the mental exercise of the koan? One reason was that those practices were conducive to a particularly rich and refined type of artistic expression. Zen-inspired poetry, stories, paintings, and sculpture were valued for their subtle and elegant evocations of concepts such as emptiness, the cycle of rebirth (*samsara*), impermanence, and enlightenment (*satori* in Japanese). At the same time, in a society that accorded the highest status to the warrior, Zen-style discipline was valued as a way of training oneself to endure hardship, pain, and even the finality of death.

The Rinzai tradition was assisted in its institutional development by its ongoing relationship with the ruling samurai, but another factor in its success was the "Five Mountain" monastery system, which made leading Rinzai temples into administrative outposts that helped to monitor local conditions and implement new laws on behalf of the military rulers. Although the temples managed their own affairs without interference, they were expected to further the state's agenda in return for its patronage.

Soto Zen: The Gradual Path

The other major Zen school, Soto, promotes "gradual enlightenment" through the practice of "just sitting," without the mental stimulation of the koan. According to the standard accounts of its origins (which may or may not be true), the Tendai monk Dogen (1200–1253) was troubled by a persistent question: If humans are born with an innate buddha-nature, as Tendai taught, why should they need to make any effort to achieve enlightenment? After studying at Kenninji with Eisai's successor, in 1223 Dogen traveled with an official mission to China, where encounters with the Caodong tradition and a monastery cook led to his own spiritual awakening.

On his return to Japan in 1227, Dogen recognized that his Soto Zen could not compete with either Tendai or the increasingly influential Rinzai Zen school. Leaving Kyoto for the countryside, he found rural elites to be more receptive than urban samurai to his new way to liberation. The Eiheiji monastery, which he founded in 1244 near the present-day city of Fukui, is still the headquarters of the Soto school, and it continues to train young monks in *zazen* coupled with rigorous study and physical labor.

The popularity of Soto Zen grew rapidly after the early fifteenth century, when its monks began performing funerals for laypeople. At a time when only members of the clergy were entitled to funeral services, Soto monks would posthumously ordain deceased laypeople as monks or nuns and thereby assist them along the way to salvation (Bodiford 1992). This brilliant innovation helped to gain Soto a wide following.

The Kenninji temple in Kyoto marked its eight hundredth anniversary by commissioning this powerful painting by Koizumi Junkasu for its ceiling (John K. Nelson).

Nichiren

The last new Buddhist sect of the Kamakura period was founded by a charismatic monk who drew on the Tendai practice of reciting mantras but embraced the teachings of the *Lotus Sutra* as the path to salvation for both the nation and the individual. Believing that this sutra provided an all-encompassing guide to both secular and spiritual affairs, Nichiren (1222–1282) instructed his followers to study its teachings and chant the mantra "*Namu myoho renge kyo*" ("Hail the marvelous teaching of the *Lotus Sutra!*"). To Nichiren, all other Buddhist teachings were merely provisional, no longer relevant in the age of *mappo*.

Expelled from his monastery in Kyoto, he traveled to Kamakura, where he preached on street corners the radical message that "the *nembutsu* is hell, Zen is a devil, and Shingon is the nation's ruin." He was exiled twice for subversive teaching and claimed to have avoided execution only because of a divine intervention that shattered the executioner's sword as it was about to fall on his neck. His 1260 work "On Establishing the True Dharma to Bring Peace to the Nation" established him as a pioneer in the politicization of religion. If the nation suffered invasions, plagues, and social disorder, he argued, it was because the ruler had not adopted the *Lotus Sutra* as his guide to sound governance.

When the Mongol dynasty actually invaded Japan in 1274, Nichiren's warnings were seen as a kind of prophecy, and he was pardoned. Retiring to Mount Minobu (not far from Mount Fuji), he established a temple there that became a training facility for the next generation of clergy. In time, disciples such as Niko, Nissho, and Nichiko established their own sects, and centuries of factionalism followed. Several of Japan's most prominent "new" religions—Soka Gakkai, Rissho Koseikai, and Nichiren Shoshu—trace their roots to one or another of these denominations.

Confucianism and the Beginnings of Shinto

Another development that influenced the modern Japanese state was the introduction of Confucianism. Although Confucian ideas (dating from the fifth century BCE) had been present at the very beginning of Japanese civilization in the sixth century CE, they had not developed into a distinct body of knowledge or ritual practices. During the political and social disruptions of the Kamakura and Muromachi periods, however, Japan's ruling classes took a new interest in ideas that promoted order in society.

Confucianism laid out the "Way" that every member of society should follow, as determined by his or her position in that society. Awareness of the responsibilities in each relationship would promote reciprocity between superiors and subordinates, which in turn would foster a stable and harmonious society. Zen monks found that these teachings resonated with their own traditions, and so recommended them to rulers for nearly four centuries.

The Emergence of "Shinto"

And what of the older religion based on the ritual veneration of *kami*? Recent scholarship has demonstrated that it was only in the medieval period that Shinto began to take form as a distinct and self-conscious entity. Since the seventh century, the Grand Shrines at Ise (pronounced *ee-say*), dedicated to the sun goddess Amaterasu, had been the preserve of the imperial family. With the triumph of the samurai, however, the shrines lost their main source of financial support, and by the early 1400s they were in obvious decline. Therefore the priests opened up Ise to visits from samurai and lower-ranking officials and developed new rituals for them. Purification was of primary importance, but in the fifteenth century, in recognition of the institutional power of Tendai and Shingon and the *honji suijaku* doctrine, Ise ritual practices were coupled with Buddhist notions of enlightenment so that, instead of competing, the two traditions complemented one another. At one time there were more than 300 Buddhist temples on the Ise grounds.

The Itsukushima shrine complex on the island of Miyajima is about 90 minutes by train and ferry from Hiroshima (John K. Nelson).

With its emphasis on rituals rather than texts, the "way of the *kami*" lacked the kind of conceptual structure that was so central to Buddhism. Still, the Ise priests rejected the *honji suijaku* principle, arguing that although the indigenous *kami* could have Buddhist counterparts, they were not subordinate to them. With new doctrines in place, pilgrimage at an all-time high, and increasing interest in the power of Ise's deities to provide benefits even for common people, the *kami* tradition assumed a new importance in the life of the nation. An organized system began to emerge in 1542, when the central government granted the powerful Yoshida clan the authority to appoint and demote shrine priests outside Ise.

⊕ Continuities of Japanese Religious Practice

The variety of benefits that worshipers in Japan may seek is almost endless: from health and prosperity to fertility and good weather to enlightened governance and salvation in the afterlife. Equally diverse are the religious practices believed to produce these benefits. Here are just a few examples:

- Individuals, families, businesses, or entire communities can contract religious specialists to conduct rituals at a temple or shrine. Petitioners typically address their requests to a particular spiritual agent (buddha, bodhisattva, or *kami*) believed capable of exerting a beneficial influence on the situation in question. However, rituals may also be conducted at home, and until very recently, many families had both a Buddhist altar (where ancestral spirits were venerated alongside Buddhist deities) and a Shinto altar (honoring the local and regional *kami* thought to protect the family). The religious observances conducted at such altars have usually been the responsibility of the family's female members.

- By purchasing amulets or talismans, individuals can establish an informal relationship with the deity of a particular temple or shrine. Since the spiritual energy invested in these objects is believed to fade over time, purchasers must return regularly for replacements.
- Undertaking a pilgrimage is another way of accessing benefits in this world and beyond. Even today, the 88 sacred temples on the island of Shikoku are visited by more than 100,000 pilgrims a year. Some walk the entire 870-mile route at once, but most take buses or private transportation and complete the route in segments, as time permits. Smaller, less demanding pilgrimage routes exist all over Japan.
- Monetary donations and the performance of good deeds for a temple/shrine or its priests are thought to generate merit beneficial to one's spiritual condition.
- Grand festivals (*matsuri*) involving the entire community are believed to benefit even those who do not take part in them. Although many Buddhist temples have also adopted this practice, Shinto shrines in particular regularly parade their central object of worship through the community in a portable shrine. In large communities, the annual *matsuri* commands a staggering degree of financial, personal, and administrative commitment. Furukawa's "rousing drum" festival involves an entire city of 74,000, while Osaka's Tenjin Matsuri attracts crowds of nearly 2 million.

Another important practice is the veneration of spirits. East Asian religious traditions maintain that the spirits of the dead continue to play an active part in the world. Whoever a deceased person might have been in life—a religious leader, a soldier killed in war, a sweet-tempered grandmother—his or her spirit may become angry or vengeful in death; to prevent this, additional rituals must be performed long after the funeral. Only if the spirits are satisfied with the respect they receive will they become beneficial allies.

One of Japan's great holidays is the Obon festival, held in mid-August in most places, when the spirits of the dead are said to return to this world to receive ritual offerings of food and drink made by their loved ones. In addition, individuals and families regularly memorialize departed family members at household altars.

The household altar is just one example of the material impact that religious traditions have had on Japanese culture. From paintings and sculpture to architecture, landscape design, ritual attire, and habits of personal hygiene derived from purification rituals, the list of cultural influences that these traditions have exerted is almost endless. Let us consider just a few examples one might encounter in daily life in Japan.

The Japanese art of flower arranging, *ikebana*, was developed in Buddhist temples, where the deceptively simple arrangements were used in memorial services. Today there are many different styles of *ikebana*, but most still share a few basic features, including the use of organic materials (stems and leaves are at least as important as flowers), sensitivity to the season, balanced composition, and poetic or religious symbolism (a classic three-part arrangement, for instance, is likely to symbolize heaven, earth, and humanity).

A similar combination of natural materials, restrained composition, and religious symbolism is found in the Japanese garden. The art of garden design also originated at temples, where a few artfully placed rocks in a bed of gravel might symbolize islands in the sea of eternity. Gardens

Participants carry a portable Shinto shrine at the Kanda Matsuri Festival in Tokyo, Japan. (Picture Partners/Alamy Stock Photo)

were later constructed at imperial palaces and on the estates of the wealthy, and today even the most humble residence will often have a garden that evokes ancient cultural values. The temple, with its sweeping rooflines, overhanging eaves, and verandas, has also been a major influence on architecture. Historically, inside the house, one room would typically be modeled on the abbot's quarters in a temple, with a hanging scroll painting in an alcove, an *ikebana* arrangement, and open space conveying a sense of space in harmony with form. Even ultramodern condominiums today often include alcoves.

The influence of religious traditions can also be seen in literature and popular culture. The minimalism of the haiku, for example, is said to derive from Zen's emphasis on penetrating to the essence of reality. In its 17 syllables, the haiku typically offers both sharply defined detail and a connection to a wider universe, as in this example by Matsuo Basho (1644–1694):

The sea darkens;
the plaintive calls of the wild ducks
are faintly white.

Another art form that uses minimalism to evoke reflection on the nature of reality is Noh theater. The slow, mesmerizing cadences—reminiscent of Buddhist chanting—of the masked actors usually convey a lesson of some kind, whether about karma, the consequences of desire, or the spiritual power of monks. Even anime and manga stories refer to religious practices, spiritual powers gained through ascetic training (*shugyo*), and divinities who use their powers for both good and evil ends. The early comics of Osamu Tezuka (1928–1989) and the feature films of the animator Miyazaki Hayao (b. 1941; *Totoro, Princess Mononoke, Spirited Away*) are full of allusions to Japan's spiritual history.

⊕ Global and Domestic Trends

We often talk about "globalization" as a recent phenomenon, but the worldwide exchange of people, ideas, and goods actually began in the fifteenth century, when European powers began navigating the globe in search of new territory for their kings and the Christian church. The first Europeans to reach Japan were some shipwrecked Portuguese sailors who arrived there in 1543, but in 1549 they were followed by Jesuit missionaries, led by Francis Xavier.

Christianity's Rise and Fall

In the fifteenth century Japan was embroiled in ongoing internal conflict; had this not been the case, it is doubtful that the Jesuits would have been permitted to enter at all. Yet a unique convergence of social and political factors enabled them to broker agreements with a number of local warlords. It was also a stroke of luck that they arrived during the rise to power of Japan's first military unifier, Oda Nobunaga, who hoped that Christianity would weaken Buddhism in Japan.

In 1571 Nobunaga attacked Mount Hiei, killing more than 3,000 Tendai monks and attendants. The lesson was not lost on the True Pure Land militants: only one more major battle was required to bring them under control. Although Nobunaga died in 1582, his chief aide quickly established himself as a visionary leader and patron of religion. Toyotomi Hideyoshi (1537–1598) continued the unification effort that Nobunaga had begun and financed the construction of many temples and shrines. For a time, he even tolerated Christianity, which by 1590 may have acquired as many as 100,000 converts, though some conversions were forced by local warlords seeking to facilitate trade with Europeans. However, the situation changed dramatically in 1596, when the cargo of a Spanish ship was seized and its captain threatened military reprisals via an armada stationed in the Philippines. The Japanese authorities responded by expelling a number of European missionaries and putting some Japanese converts to death.

The third of Japan's unifiers, Tokugawa Ieyasu (1548–1616), at first tolerated the Catholic presence, largely because it facilitated trade, but in time he came to see the priests as disruptive of the social order he was trying to build. His successors cracked down hard in the 1620s, requiring all adults to register at the local Buddhist temple; those who resisted or refused to step on an image of Jesus or Mary were threatened with torture if they did not recant their Christian faith.

In 1637 an estimated 25,000 oppressed peasants and rogue samurai mounted an armed insurrection from Shimabara on the island of Kyushu. Using Christian symbols on their flags, these ragtag rebels held off the government's forces for nearly seven months until they ran out of food and gunpowder. With the defeat of the Shimabara rebels, the Tokugawa regime closed the door on both Christianity and Europe. From 1641 to 1853, the only port open to the outside world was Dejima, a small artificial island near Nagasaki, and it was rigidly controlled. Christianity went into hiding in remote valleys and on far-flung islands. Believers adopted Buddhist practices but continued reciting mass and worshiping images of the Virgin Mary disguised as Kannon.

Document

"Tidings from the West"

In 1709, a scholar named Arai Hakuseki interviewed Giovanni Battista Sidotti (1668–1714), a Jesuit missionary who had entered Japan illegally and been imprisoned to await execution. Respecting Sidotti's learning, Arai recorded the interviews, with his comments, in Seiyo kibun ("Tidings from the West"), and sought to persuade the authorities that such foreigners should be deported rather than put to death.

Sidotti: As a rule, in each section of the world, there is a doctrine that is held with esteem. There are only three different types of this doctrine. One of these is called Christian. The second type is called heathen or gentile. The third type is called Mohammedan.

Hakuseki: This is probably what is referred to in China as Huihuijia [Islam].

Sidotti: In the region known as Europe everyone is a Christian. However, each region has a different sect of Christianity. I belong to the Catholic sect. When that Christianity first came about, it was the original law and from it came various heresies.

Hakuseki: This is probably a reference to that teaching's various heterodoxies [*itan*].

Sidotti: Luther, Arius, Calvin, and Manichaeus, these are all heresies. In Holland they are followers of the heresy of Luther.

Hakuseki: Luther is a person's name. In Portuguese he is called Lutero. Originally, he was a Christian, but he established his own lineage. From what I understand . . . it is like how from the founder of the Zen School sprung up various esoteric lineages. . . . (adapted from Josephson 2012: 263–264)

Unification and Stability

As part of its effort to impose stability, the Tokugawa regime introduced laws designed to create four distinct classes: samurai, farmers, artisans, and merchants. This structure (like the temple registration law) was inspired by the Confucian doctrines introduced to Japan by Chinese Zen monks some four centuries earlier. In addition, a number of newer Confucian texts were reinterpreted to promote the stratification and regulation of society. Each social class was given specific guidelines regarding occupation, travel, and civic duties, and both Buddhist and Shinto institutions were required to adopt a hierarchical organizational model. The Tokugawa **shoguns** took Zen monks as some of their closest advisors in the early years of their rule, but as the regime tightened its control over the nation, it also sought advice from scholars influenced by Confucian texts.

The overall mood of society began to change under the shoguns as well. During the medieval period, Buddhism had flourished because its doctrines of salvation in the next life offered hope to people whose prospects in this life were bleak. Now, with growing economic prosperity in the cities and order imposed by a police state, neo-Confucian scholars began to criticize Buddhism.

We have already seen how Buddhism benefited from state patronage but also suffered because of its involvement in political affairs. Temple building increased dramatically with the imposition of the temple registration requirement; Soto Zen temples alone multiplied from several thousand to 17,500 in the early Tokugawa period. But the growing emphasis on political rather than spiritual matters was reflected in a breakdown of morality among many monks (Williams 2005). One seventeenth-century Confucian scholar commented that "the freedom with which they [Buddhist monks] eat meat and engage in romantic affairs surpasses that of even secular men" (Jansen 2000: 217). Although Buddhism remained central to ritual life, it increasingly lost its vitality as a force in society. It is not surprising, therefore, that alternative perspectives began to emerge.

Religion Meets Modernity

Scholars in particular were eager for new philosophies that would explain the meaning of life and the individual's purpose in society. Some embraced Confucian principles; among them was Yamaga Soko (1622–1685), who codified samurai ethics and combined them with Confucian values to create the "way of the warrior" known as **bushido**.

In the next century, however, the **Kokugaku** ("Native Learning") movement rejected Confucianism as well as Buddhism in favor of "true" Japanese spiritual traditions. Scholars like Motoori Norinaga (1730–1801) tried to use ancient texts such as the *Kojiki* (the source of the foundation myth of Izanagi and Izanami) to discover the will of the *kami* regarding the roles of a ruler and his subjects. The logical implication was that the solution to Japan's political problems and the threats it faced from abroad lay in direct imperial rule—although to voice this opinion publicly would surely have been considered treason.

Meanwhile, at the popular level, "new" religions began to appear. In 1838, for example, Nakayama Miki, the wife of a wealthy farmer, said that "God the Parent" had chosen her to transmit divine truths about how to live happily and honorably. She was imprisoned more than once, but as the Tokugawa regime was ending she succeeded in establishing the new religion known as Tenrikyo. Another new religion, Kurozumikyo, traced its origins to a revelation received by a Shinto priest who claimed to have experienced "divine union" with Amaterasu. And Konko-kyo, which emerged in 1859, was based on a privileged communication between a farmer and a *kami* he had discovered to be the savior of mankind.

In 1825, the scholar and samurai Aizawa Seishisai (1781–1863) advocated unification of religion and the state under one system, as could be seen in the European colonial powers that were encroaching on Japan's sovereignty. He urged the adoption of Shinto as the national faith and the sun deity Amaterasu as the primary *kami*. Although these ideas were controversial at the time, they would become central to the leaders of samurai clans in the far west and south.

In 1868, following a brief civil war, those clans overthrew the Tokugawa regime. Well aware of how far behind Japan had fallen during its period of isolation, and fearing colonization by the West, the new government embarked on an unprecedented program of industrialization, militarization, and nation building. This agenda, legitimized by a new emphasis on the emperor's status as a direct descendant of the *kami* (exactly as Aizawa had recommended four decades earlier), would dramatically alter Japan and the Asian region in both positive and negative ways.

⊕ Recent Developments

Nationalism and Shinto

How does a government create a nation of citizens where only feudal loyalties have previously existed? This was the challenge that faced the Meiji government (1868–1911). The term *meiji* means "enlightened rule," and its adoption signified a shift away from clan rule to a parliamentary system.

Document

The Great Way

The "father" of modern Shinto studies was Tanaka Yoshito (1872–1946). This excerpt comes from his 1936 book Shinto Gairon.

The Japanese people, being endowed with a true Japanese spirit, sincerely hold an absolute faith in shrines. . . . Buddhism and Christianity are merely religions and nothing more; but Shinto and shrines are politics, as well as morality, as well as a great religion. A combination of these three aspects, that is the Way of the Gods. It is the Great Way of the subjects of Japan. (Breen and Teeuwen 2000: 328)

In its effort to emulate those Western nations where religion served to legitimate policy, the Meiji government promoted a kind of national cult based on the emperor and his associations with various *kami*.

The Meiji state subjected Buddhism to a brief but dramatic period of persecution, in part because it had served the Tokugawa feudal regime so well. Institutions that had been fully syncretic, combining worship of buddhas and *kami*, were now divided. Their ritual specialists were either forced into lay life or reeducated as government-certified Shinto priests. Even more extreme was the brief period from 1868 to 1872 when many Buddhist temples, icons, and artifacts were destroyed by overzealous officials. The remains of Buddhist statues decapitated during this period can still be seen at temples all over Japan.

Shinto was designated the official state religion, although adherence to it was described as a matter of "civic duty" rather than religious conviction. Not everyone supported these policies, of course, but it became increasingly difficult to resist the state's agenda. A series of wars with China (1894–1895), Russia (1904–1905), and Korea (1910)—which cost some 80,000 lives while gaining Japan overseas resources that it would use to expand its manufacturing and military base—inspired a general patriotic fervor that drowned out all but the most courageous voices of opposition.

It was during this period that the government sponsored the establishment of a shrine to the soldiers who had died for the nation. Although Shinto shrines had traditionally avoided association with the impurity of death, the Yasukuni Shrine in Tokyo combined Shinto-style rituals with Buddhist ancestor worship and shamanic traditions of spirit appeasement and control. The imperial household, high-ranking government officials, and leading businessmen, intellectuals, and even Buddhist monks all visited the shrine regularly to pay their respects. According to the government, there was no greater glory than to die for the nation and be enshrined at Yasukuni. An imperial edict on education informed the youth of Japan that "should emergency arise," they were expected to "offer [themselves] courageously to the State; and thus guard and maintain the prosperity of Our Imperial Throne coeval with heaven and earth" (Hardacre 1989: 122). The "divine wind" (*kamikaze*) attacks on American naval vessels in the Pacific, undertaken in desperation at the end of the Second World War, were extreme expressions of this ideology.

Several of Japan's postwar prime ministers have visited Yasukuni Shrine despite constitutional guidelines that prohibit the state from favoring a particular religion. Each visit has set off anti-Japanese demonstrations in China and Korea, both of which were occupied by Japan during the war and whose leaders object to the honoring of 14 officers identified as "class-A" war criminals.[3] Debates over how to honor Japan's war dead continue.

Postwar Restructuring and Religious Adaptation

After Japan's defeat in 1945, eight years of occupation by Allied forces laid the groundwork for its transformation into a stable democracy. The emperor was obliged to renounce his claim to divinity, and Shinto was stripped of its status as the de facto state religion. In the spiritual void that followed the war, constitutional guarantees of religious freedom encouraged a proliferation of new religious movements. Among them were Soka Gakkai and Rissho Koseikai (both based on the *Lotus Sutra*), Shinnyo-en (derived from Shingon), Mahikari (True Light), and Perfect Liberty Kyodan (Obaku Zen), each of which claims to have more than a million followers today.

Much of the success of these movements can be attributed to their focus on dealing with life's problems, but they also offered a sense of community to people uprooted by postwar urbanization

A Japanese Buddhist temple can be compared to a franchise business in that it is affiliated with a particular brand yet operates independently. Each temple is required by law to have a board of trustees who work with the resident priest to ensure stability and continuity. Here, temple trustees relax after a ritual commemorating ancestral spirits (John K. Nelson).

and industrialization. Some smaller groups have seen it as their role to serve as agents of radical personal and social transformation. The most extreme example of this tendency has been the Aum Shinrikyo ("Supreme Truth of Aum") cult, which was established in 1987. Aum was responsible for a number of crimes and murders, including a sarin gas attack on the Tokyo subway system in 1995 that killed 12 people and injured 5,000. According to the group's leader, Asahara Shoko, Japanese society was so thoroughly corrupt that it needed to be "cleansed" by an apocalypse. As a result of these attacks, the Japanese government passed more rigorous laws to monitor all religious organizations.

Japan's 74,000 Buddhist temples benefited greatly from the rising tide of the Japanese economy. A number of Zen temples began offering retreats designed to foster a spiritual discipline that could help those competing for success in their careers or higher education. A growing desire to venerate the ancestors in style created a market for services ranging from elaborate funerals to rituals memorializing aborted fetuses or deceased household pets.

"Funeral Buddhism" has become a common derogatory term, applied to temples that have benefited from the income generated by funerals, memorials, and the sale of grave plots on their property. Many people have been turned off by this trend, seeing it as hypocritical for Buddhism—a tradition dedicated to the alleviation of suffering—to profit from people's grief and loss. Younger people in particular object to paying membership fees to local temples just so that they will be in good standing when they have to arrange a funeral. In urban areas especially, increasing numbers of people are holding nonreligious memorial services.

⊕ Summary

Today Japan's religious traditions appear to be entering an experimental phase. Ancient shrines and temples still attract many people, but most visitors are more interested in history and sacred art than in "religious experience." In response to negative perceptions of Buddhism, a number of progressive temples have been engaging more directly with social problems, offering community services, providing sanctuary for victims of domestic violence, and working for environmental causes. Following the earthquake and tsunami of March 11, 2011 (in which more than 16,000 people died), and the subsequent nuclear meltdown at Fukushima, clergy of all faiths provided both material and spiritual care for survivors. Many temples became shelters, and monks helped survivors cope with the emotional and psychological aftereffects of the trauma. The nuclear disaster led to much soul searching among Japan's religious leaders, and many have urged their denominations and parishioners to address the dangers of nuclear power.

The current period is one of great challenges for the Shinto tradition as well. In urban areas, Shinto festivals continue to attract broad-based participation, especially among women, who for generations were barred from joining in rituals because of their gender. In rural areas, however, it can be difficult to find enough people to carry a village's portable shrine in a procession.

Although new religions continue to develop, there is an increasing tendency among many to reject traditional religious affiliations, especially when they impose financial demands. It is predicted that as Japan's baby boom generation passes away, funeral rituals will become less identifiably Buddhist and more like the eclectic services typical of North America and Europe. Although young people appear to distrust organized religion in general, partly because of financial scandals and partly because of the Aum terror attack, many still seem interested in more individualistic expressions of spirituality. Books related to the occult, fortune-telling, and the spirit world always seem to sell well. This suggests that the ancient tradition of "turning to the gods in times of trouble" will likely remain a guiding paradigm.

Buddhist clergy provided material, psychological, and spiritual relief after the earthquake and tsunami of 2011. "Café de Monk" volunteers traveled between temporary housing settlements to offer victims a chance to speak with a monk (photo courtesy of the Rev. Kaneta Taiō).

Document

The Japan Buddhist Federation's Appeal for a Lifestyle Without Dependence on Nuclear Power

Issued in 2011, the declaration from which the following statement is taken represented a rare moment of cooperation between the various schools of Japanese Buddhism.

We, the Japan Buddhist Federation, will strive to reduce our dependence on such nuclear power that threatens life, and to realize a society based on sustainable energy. We must choose a path in which personal happiness is harmonized with human welfare, instead of wishing for prosperity at the expense of others. We would like to make an appeal for building societies that protect each and every life, [and for] letting go of excessive materialistic greed, finding contentment in the feeling of moderation, and living in humility with nature. (Sakai and Watts 2012)

Sites

Izumo Shrine, Shimane Prefecture

Mentioned in several ancient accounts of the nation's founding, Izumo is a registered "National Treasure." A visit is recommended to those seeking marriage partners.

Nara

Nara was Japan's capital from 710 to 784. Its Todaiji and Horyuji temples are said to be the world's largest and oldest wooden buildings, respectively.

Kamakura

This former fishing village near Tokyo was the capital of the samurai from 1185 to 1333 and has one of the world's most famous large Buddha statues.

Kyoto

Japan's capital for more than 1,000 years (794–1869), Kyoto is home to Japan's first Zen temple (Kenninji) and its second most important Shinto shrine (Kamigamo), as well as the picturesque Golden Pavilion, which was built as a shogun's palace and is now part of a Zen temple.

Ise Shrines

The Ise Shrines are the most important of all Shinto sites. The main sanctuaries are rebuilt every 20 years; in this way, ancient wood-joinery techniques are passed on to the next generation of builders.

Nikko

The same eighth-century Buddhist monk who founded the Rinnoji Temple in Nikko also established the nearby Futarasan Shrine, dedicated to the *kami* of the surrounding mountains.

Sacred Texts

Religion	Text	Composition/Compilation	Compilation/Revision	Use
Shinto	*Kojiki*	8th century; compiled by O no Yasumaro at emperor's request	13th-, 15th-, 19th-, and 20th-century versions	Legitimates imperial rule; provides myth for founding of Japan; select parts used in ritual purification and ideology
Shinto	*Nihon Shoki*	8th century; patronized by Prince Toneri and Ono Yasumaro	13th-, 15th-, 19th-, and 20th-century versions	Historical
Tendai Buddhism	*Lotus Sutra*; writings of founder, Saicho; other esoteric Buddhist texts	3rd-century China, brought to Japan in early 9th century	Translations are updated and commentaries added periodically	Ritual, doctrinal, ideological
Shingon Buddhism	*Mahavairocana* and *Vajrasekhara* sutras	7th century (India)	Periodic updates, translations, and commentaries	Doctrinal, ritual, inspirational, educational
Rinzai Zen Buddhism	Various sutras, including the *Lankavatara*; apocryphal stories of enlightened masters; koans	12th century (and earlier)	Numerous translations of teachings, updated frequently over time	Doctrinal, ritual, inspirational, educational

Sacred Texts (Continued)

Religion	Text	Composition/Compilation	Compilation/Revision	Use
Soto Zen Buddhism	*Heart*, *Diamond*, and *Lankavatara* sutras; writings of Dogen	13th-, 16th-, and 18th-century texts and commentaries	Periodic updates, translations, and commentaries	Doctrinal, ritual, inspirational, educational
Pure Land Buddhism	*"Infinite Life" Sutra*	3rd century (China)	Periodic updates, translations, and commentaries	Doctrinal, ritual, inspirational, educational
True Pure Land Buddhism	*Tannisho*, sayings of founder, Shinran	13th-century version	Periodic updates and commentaries	Doctrinal, ritual, inspirational, educational
Nichiren Buddhism	*Lotus Sutra*; writings of founder, Nichiren	13th-century version	Translations are updated and commentaries added periodically	Doctrinal, ritual, inspirational, educational

Discussion Questions

1. Why is it common among contemporary Japanese to visit a Buddhist temple and on the same trip stop at a Shinto shrine to purchase an amulet yet say that one is "not religious"?

2. What are several of the principal spiritual agents in Japan that interact with human beings and the natural world?

3. Identify two of Japan's most popular bodhisattvas and how they are said to help humans in moments of crisis.

4. How did the monks Saicho and Kukai help to establish what can be called "Japanese Buddhism" in the eighth century?

5. Identify and differentiate the three types of Buddhism that emerged in the medieval period.

6. What are some of the contributions of Zen Buddhism to Japanese culture? Be sure to reference both aesthetic and political contributions.

7. Explain why accessing spiritual benefits has more meaning for Japanese people than the teachings of particular religious denominations.

8. What role did religion play in the creation of a "modern Japan" between the late nineteenth century and the Second World War?

Glossary

Amaterasu Female deity of the sun, born from the eye of the primordial deity Izanagi following his purification; enshrined at Ise as the patron deity of the imperial family.

bodhisattva A Buddhist "saint" who has achieved spiritual liberation but chooses to remain in this world to help alleviate the suffering of individuals.

bushido Literally, the "way of the warrior"; an ethical code that combined a Confucian-style emphasis on loyalty with the discipline of Zen.

honji suijaku Literally, "manifestation from the original state"; the concept that *kami* are manifestations of buddhas or bodhisattvas.

jiriki Literally, "self-power"; the principle that individuals can attain liberation through their own abilities and devotional activities.

kami The spirits that animate all living things, natural phenomena, and natural forces. Shrines are built to accommodate their presence during rituals.

Kojiki A collection of stories commissioned to legitimate the imperial regime by linking it with Japan's mythical origins. It was published in 712 CE but was soon replaced by the *Nihongi* and remained largely forgotten until the nineteenth century.

Kokugaku Literally, "learning about one's country"; the intellectual movement of the eighteenth and nineteenth centuries that privileged Japanese culture and ideas over those from abroad.

mappo The period of "decline of the (Buddhist) dharma," thought to have begun in 1052; a time of social disorder, during which individuals could not achieve liberation without the aid of buddhas and bodhisattvas.

nembutsu The key prayer of the Pure Land traditions: *Namu Amida Butsu* ("Praise to the Amida Buddha").

samurai A popular term for the *bushi* ("warrior"), who served regional warlords in various capacities; samurai made up the top 5 percent of society during the Edo period (1603–1867).

shogun The supreme military commander of Japan, who was appointed by the emperor and effectively ruled in his name.

tariki The "outside power," offered by buddhas and bodhisattvas, without which individuals living in the age of the Buddhist dharma's decline (*mappo*) would be unable to achieve liberation.

zazen Seated meditation.

Further Reading

Ambros, Barbara. 2012. *Bones of Contention: Animals and Religion in Contemporary Japan*. Honolulu: University of Hawaii Press. A thorough exploration of the newly popular practice of memorializing pets and what it implies for both Japanese society and its Buddhist traditions.

Bowring, Richard. 2006. *The Religious Traditions of Japan, 500–1600*. Cambridge: Cambridge University Press. A comprehensive and highly readable account of Japanese religious history covering more than 1,000 years.

Covell, Stephen. 2005. *Japanese Temple Buddhism: Worldliness in a Religion of Renunciation*. Honolulu: University of Hawaii Press. A pioneering examination of contemporary temple Buddhism, with an emphasis on the Tendai denomination.

Jaffe, Richard. 2002. *Neither Monk nor Layman: Clerical Marriage in Modern Japanese Buddhism*. Princeton, NJ: Princeton University Press. An engaging analysis of the tension between the historical image of Buddhist clergy as celibate and the modern expectations that they will have families and run their temples like businesses.

Nelson, John. 1996. *A Year in the Life of a Shinto Shrine*. Honolulu: University of Hawaii Press. A study of what goes on behind the scenes at a major Shinto shrine in the city of Nagasaki.

Nelson, John. 2005. *Spirits of the State: Japan's Yasukuni Shrine*. Films for the Humanities, 28:00. A documentary, made for university audiences, about the controversy surrounding Yasukuni Shrine, where the spirits of the military dead are enshrined and venerated by the state.

Nelson, John. 2013. *Experimental Buddhism: Innovation and Activism in Contemporary Japan*. Honolulu: University of Hawaii Press. A study of priests from all of Japan's Buddhist denominations evaluating the crisis facing temples in Japan today and documenting some of their creative responses to their loss of patronage and declining social significance.

Prohl, Inken, and John Nelson, eds. 2012. *Handbook of Contemporary Japanese Religions*. Leiden: Brill. A volume containing chapters by more than 20 scholars surveying postwar and contemporary developments in Japanese religions and religious practices.

Reader, Ian. 2005. *Making Pilgrimages: Meaning and Practice in Shikoku*. Honolulu: University of Hawaii Press. A detailed study of the Shikoku pilgrimage, including the religious significance of the 88 sacred temples that make up the route.

Rowe, Mark. 2011. *Bonds of the Dead: Temples, Burial, and the Transformation of Contemporary Japanese Buddhism*. Chicago: University of Chicago Press. A groundbreaking book that explores Japanese Buddhism's reliance on mortuary rituals in the postwar period.

Schnell, Scott. 1999. *The Rousing Drum: Ritual Practice in a Japanese Community*. Honolulu: University of Hawaii Press. An ethnographic look at a major festival in a small mountain city and what it means to the cultural identity of the local people.

Swanson, Paul, and Clark Chilson, eds. 2006. *The Nanzan Guide to Japanese Religions*. Honolulu: University of Hawaii Press. A very useful compilation of scholarly articles on many topics related to Japanese religions.

Thal, Sarah. 2006. *Rearranging the Landscape of the Gods: The Politics of a Pilgrimage Site in Japan, 1573–1912*. Chicago: University of Chicago Press. A comprehensive history of the wrenching changes forced on a former Buddhist temple, now converted to a major Shinto shrine.

Watsky, Andrew. 2004. *Chikubushima: Deploying the Sacred Arts in Momoyama Japan*. Honolulu: University of Hawaii Press. One of the best studies of the artistic, architectural, and aesthetic contributions of the sixteenth-century Toyotomi regime to the religious landscape of Japan.

Williams, Duncan. 2005. *The Other Side of Zen: A Social History of Soto Zen in Tokugawa Japan*. Princeton, NJ: Princeton University Press. Surprising and often shocking in its account of corruption and exploitation among monks from the sixteenth to the nineteenth centuries, this study reveals the "dark" side of institutional Zen, which dominated Japanese society for more than 250 years.

Recommended Websites

http://nirc.nanzan-u.ac.jp/en/publications/jjrs/

The online edition of a semi-annual journal dedicated to the academic study of Japanese religions.

http://www2.kokugakuin.ac.jp/ijcc

The English-language website for the Institute of Japanese Culture and Classics at Kokugakuin University, specializing in Shinto studies and containing many online publications.

http://global.sotozen-net.or.jp/eng/index.html

The English-language website of the Soto Zen school, introducing key teachings and practices (each Buddhist denomination has a similar site, as do many temples).

http://www.jodo.org

An English-language website offering a variety of resources on Pure Land Buddhism.

http://www.onmarkproductions.com/html/buddhism.shtml

A photo library devoted to artwork, especially sculpture, depicting Buddhist and Shinto deities in Japan.

http://zen.rinnou.net

A brief overview of history, temples, and teachings from the Joint Council of Rinzai-Obaku Zen.

References

Bodiford, William M. 1992. "Zen in the Art of Funerals: Ritual Salvation in Japanese Buddhism." *History of Religions* 32: 146–164.

Bowring, Richard. 2006. *The Religious Traditions of Japan: 500–1600*. Cambridge: Cambridge University Press.

Breen, John, and Mark Teeuwen. 2000. *Shinto in History: Ways of the Kami*. Honolulu: University of Hawaii.

Gorai, Shigeru. 1994. *Nihonjin no shiseikan* ("Japanese views of death"). Tokyo: Kadokawa Shoten.

Hardacre, Helen. 1989. *Shinto and the State: 1868–1945*. Princeton, NJ: Princeton University Press.

Jansen, Marius. 2000. *The Making of Modern Japan*. Boston: Harvard University Press.

Josephson, Jason. 2012. *The Invention of Religion in Japan*. Chicago: University of Chicago Press.

Kamens, Edward. 1990. *The Buddhist Poetry of the Great Kamo Priestess: Daisaiin Senshi and Hosshin wakash*. Michigan Monograph Series in Japanese Studies no. 5. Ann Arbor: University of Michigan Press. .

Payne, Richard K. 2006. "The Shingon Subordinating Fire Offering for Amitabha, 'Amida Kei Ai Goma.'" *Pacific World: Journal of the Institute of Buddhist Studies* 8: 191–236.

Philipi, Donald L. 1985. *The Kojiki*. Tokyo: Tokyo University Press.

Pye, Michael. 2004. "The Structure of Religious Systems in Contemporary Japan: Shinto Variations on Buddhist Pilgrimage." Occasional Paper No. 30, University of Marburg, Centre for Japanese Studies.

Reader, Ian. 1991. *Religion in Contemporary Japan*. Honolulu: University of Hawaii Press.

Sakai, Jin, and Jonathan Watts. 2012. *This Precious Life: Buddhist Tsunami Relief and Anti-Nuclear Activism in Post 3/11 Japan*. Yokohama: International Buddhist Exchange Center.

Senda, Minoru. 1988. "Taoist Roots in Japanese Culture." *Japan Quarterly* 35, no. 2: 133–138.

Williams, Duncan. 2005. *The Other Side of Zen: A Social History of Soto Zen in Tokugawa Japan*. Princeton, NJ: Princeton University Press.

Yampolsky, Philip, trans. 2008. "The Essentials of Salvation." In *Sources of East Asian Traditions*, ed. Wm. Theodore De Bary. New York: Columbia University Press, 725–726.

Young, W. A. 1995. *The World's Religions*. Englewood Cliffs, NJ: Prentice-Hall.

Notes

1. One of these colossal statues of Kannon appears at the end of the 2006 film *Kamikaze Girls* as the backdrop for a battle between an all-girl motorcycle gang and one of the protagonists.

2. For more on the *saiin* tradition, see Kamens 1990.

3. For a treatment of this topic suitable for classroom use, see my documentary film *Spirits of the State: Japan's Yasukuni Shrine* (2005).

13 New Religions and Movements

Roy C. Amore

Timeline

1830 CE	Church of Jesus Christ of Latter-day Saints founded (United States)
1844	Baha'i Faith emerges (Iran)
1929	Nation of Islam founded (United States)
1930	Soka Gakkai founded (Japan)
1940s	Wicca appears (England)
1954	Church of Scientology founded (United States)
1965	International Society for Krishna Consciousness (ISKCON) founded (United States)
1965	Kabbalah Centre established (United States)
1974	Raëlian Movement emerges (France)
1991	Church of Almighty God (Eastern Lightning) founded (China)
1992	Falun Dafa founded (China)

In this chapter you will learn about:

- The differences between a religion, a sect, and a cult
- The origins, beliefs, and practices of Eastern movements that are now established in the West, such as Soka Gakkai, Falun Dafa, and the International Society for Krishna Consciousness
- The origins, beliefs, and practices of Western movements such as the Church of Jesus Christ of Latter-day Saints, the Baha'i Faith, the Nation of Islam, the Kabbalah Centre, and the Church of Almighty God.
- The origins, beliefs, and practices of new Western movements such as Wicca (modern witchcraft), Scientology, the Aetherius Society, the Raëlian Movement, and New Age traditions

The youngest of the Abrahamic religions covered in this volume is almost 1,500 years old, but innovations in religion did not end with Islam. The early nineteenth century saw the emergence of many new faiths, and more have developed since then. This chapter explores a selection of religions either newly coming to or arising in the West. First, though, we need to consider what distinguishes a "religion" from a "sect" or a "cult."

⊕ Defining New Religions, Sects, and Cults

What is a "new religion"? This question might be easier to answer if scholars could agree on what constitutes a religion. But there are countless ideas on that subject. Even a definition as seemingly basic as "belief in a god or goddess" would not take into account nontheistic traditions such as Buddhism and Jainism. As we learned in Chapter 1, while there has been no universal definition of religion, it is generally understood to imply a sense of obligation within a relationship, whether a communal bond among humans or one between humans and divinities. In this chapter, our task is not to define religion, but to understand what is meant by the terms "sect" and "cult," and how those terms are applied to new religious movements.

 Baha'i "Lotus" temple, New Delhi (Prisma by Dukas Presseagentur GmbH/Alamy Stock Photo).

Sociologists of religion such as Max Weber, writing in the early 1900s, used the word "**sect**" to refer to Christian splinter groups, new institutionalized movements that had broken away from mainstream denominations, usually to practice what they considered to be a purer form of the faith. Often the breakaway group would denounce its origins and set itself apart by adopting stricter rules, new modes of worship, or distinctive clothing. With the passage of time, however, most sectarian movements either faded away or moved back toward the mainstream. In other words, new movements would begin as sects (or sectarian movements) and evolve into churches (new denominations). A similar process can be seen in the histories of many other religions.

As for "**cult**," it was originally a neutral term, used as a synonym for "worship" or even "religion." Today, though, its connotations—at least in the popular media—are almost always negative: a cult is generally assumed to be a small group under the control of a charismatic leader who is suspected of brainwashing followers (especially the young) and promoting self-destructive, illegal, or immoral behavior.

A movement that is accepted by outsiders as a "new religion" will enjoy all the constitutional protections and tax exemptions afforded to established religions. But a movement that is labeled a "cult" is likely to attract scrutiny, if not harassment, from legal authorities and taxation officials. In 2017, for example, when Amy Coney Barrett became one of President Donald Trump's potential nominees to the Supreme Court, concern was aired about her membership in People of Praise, a small conservative Christian movement. And in the 2018 midterm elections, Democratic candidate Lissa Lucas was targeted by opponents for her membership in a Wiccan community and ultimately lost her race in West Virginia.

Yet the definitional lines between a cult and a sect (or new religion) are quite vague. By the usual definitions, for example, the **Hare Krishna** movement would be considered a sect of Hinduism in India, but in the West its members' unusual practices and dress soon led to its branding as a cult. This suggests that the "cult" label has less to do with the nature of the movement itself than with how sharply it differs from the mainstream religious culture—in other words, that one person's religion is another person's cult.

Yet there are several traits that many cults seem to share. Cults typically claim to have some special knowledge or insight, perhaps based on a new interpretation of an old scripture or revealed through contact with spirits (or even aliens). Their practice often includes rituals that promote ecstatic experiences, and they tend to emphasize individual spiritual experience more than institutional organization (Dawson 2006: 28–29).

Perhaps the most widely shared characteristic of cults, however, is a charismatic leader who demands extreme loyalty. Adherents may be required to work long hours for little or no pay, cut ties with family and friends from the past, denounce former religious beliefs, or even submit sexually to the leader. In extreme cases, leaders may go so far as to demand that followers be willing to die for the cause. The mass suicide (forced or voluntary) of more than 900 members of the Peoples Temple at Jonestown, Guyana, in 1978 is one infamous example. In most mass suicides, whether coerced or voluntary, the underlying belief has been that the current world order is about to be replaced by a new order in which the cult's members will be rewarded for their loyalty. That is, such movements have a **millenarian** belief in an imminent "end of time" or "apocalypse" leading to the dawning of a "new age."

Hundreds of new religious movements have established themselves over the past two centuries. This chapter focuses on a small selection of those that have been most successful or have attracted the most attention. We will discuss them in three groups, organized according to their spiritual roots: traditional Asian religions, Abrahamic traditions, and other forms of spirituality.

⊕ New Religions from the East

Soka Gakkai

Soka Gakkai was founded in Japan before the Second World War and emerged as an important force only after 1945—a period that saw a flowering of new Japanese religions. But its roots lie deep in Buddhist history, in the tradition of the controversial thirteenth-century monk Nichiren.

The dominant tradition of Nichiren's day was the Pure Land school of Mahayana Buddhism, which taught the saving power of Amida Buddha. Nichiren, however, believed that a Mahayana scripture called the *Lotus Sutra* represented the culmination of all Buddhist truths, and he warned that Japan would be doomed if the people ignored its teachings. At the same time he became so critical of the Pure Land sects that their leaders persuaded the emperor to exile him to a remote island, where he continued to write tracts criticizing other Buddhist sects and promoting his own.

Nichiren's prophecies of impending doom seemed to come true when the Mongols attempted to invade Japan in 1274. Thus he was allowed to return from exile and, with his followers, establish a sect based on his teachings, together with the *Lotus Sutra*. It is to this sect, eventually known as Nichiren Shoshu ("True Nichiren"), that Soka Gakkai traces its roots.

Soka Gakkai ("Association for Creating Values") was established in 1930 as a lay organization within Nichiren Shoshu. Its founder was a reform-minded schoolteacher named Makiguchi Tsunesaburo, who wanted to promote moral values among young people. Many of its leading figures were imprisoned during the Second World War because they refused to recognize the divinity of the emperor as required by the officially Shinto Japanese state, and Makiguchi himself died in prison before the war ended.

After the war, the organization's new leader, Josei Toda, adopted an aggressive recruitment strategy based on an ancient Buddhist missionary principle. To break down resistance to their message, Soka Gakkai members might gather outside the home of a potential convert and chant all day and all

Practice

Nichiren, "On Attaining Buddhahood in This Lifetime"

Soka Gakkai follows the Nichiren practice of chanting the mantra "Myoho-renge-kyo," "Homage to the Lotus Sutra." Here Nichiren explains the thinking behind that practice.

If you wish to free yourself from the sufferings of birth and death you have endured since time without beginning and to attain without fail unsurpassed enlightenment in this lifetime, you must perceive the mystic truth that is originally inherent in all living beings. This truth is *Myoho-renge-kyo*.

Chanting *Myoho-renge-kyo* will therefore enable you to grasp the mystic truth innate in all life.

The Lotus Sutra is the king of sutras, true and correct in both word and principle. Its words are the ultimate reality, and this reality is the Mystic Law (*myoho*). It is called the Mystic Law because it reveals the principle of the mutually inclusive relationship of a single moment of life and all phenomena. That is why this sutra is the wisdom of all Buddhas. (Nichiren 1999: 3)

night or point out to shop owners that Soka Gakkai members would shop at their stores if they converted. Although critics complained that this approach amounted to harassment and coercion, it was effective, and Soka Gakkai grew exponentially under Toda's leadership. Meanwhile, small groups of practitioners began to establish themselves throughout much of Asia, Europe, and the Americas. Often the leaders of these local groups were ethnic Japanese, but the majority of the members were not. As usual with new religious movements, young people made up the majority of the converts.

Today, Soka Gakkai International—founded in 1975 as a worldwide organization under the umbrella of Soka Gakkai in Japan—claims 12 million members. Most "new religions" in Japan promise this-worldly happiness, and Soka Gakkai is no exception. In particular, it stresses the here-and-now benefits of chanting the sacred mantra "*Namu myoho renge kyo*" (translated on the Sokka Gakkai website as "I devote myself to the Lotus Sutra of the Wonderful Law"), such as passing a test, getting a promotion, or improving one's outlook on life. Soka Gakkai is also active in youth activities. At the core of Soka Gakkai is the belief that the practice of Nichiren Buddhism can bring about a personal transformation that will empower the individual to take effective action toward achieving the goals of peace, justice, social harmony, and economic prosperity.

The profile of Soka Gakkai in Japan has been somewhat diminished since 1991, when Nichiren Shoshu officially severed its links with the group. This division was the climax of a long dispute between the conservative clergy and the reform-minded lay organization. But the international organization has continued to grow. Members continue to follow the religious teachings of Nichiren Shoshu, studying the *Lotus Sutra* and chanting the sacred mantra.

Falun Dafa (Falun Gong)

Falun Dafa ("Energy of the Wheel of Law"), popularly known as Falun Gong, developed out of a Chinese Buddhist *qigong* tradition. The term *qi* refers to unseen energy flowing through the body, while *qigong* refers to techniques of breathing and movement that are said to permit energy to flow properly through the body, promoting health and long life. Although Western science has been reluctant to incorporate the flow of energy into its worldview, the belief in *qi* has been part of East Asian cultures for centuries.

Li Hongzhi, the man who brought Falun Dafa to prominence in China in 1992, explains it as a system of Buddhist cultivation passed down through the centuries and considers himself only the most recent in a long line of teachers. The system's Buddhist roots are reflected in its name: the *falun*, or dharma wheel, is an auspicious symbol in Buddhism. Li's teachings of compassion and self-development are based on Buddhist principles, and he uses Buddhist symbols and terms, but Falun Dafa is not officially recognized as a traditional school of Chinese Buddhism. Thus the Chinese government has been able to outlaw Falun Dafa without contravening its policy on the five religions it does recognize.

Although Falun Dafa has traditional roots, Li Hongzhi adapted the practice to everyday life. It spread quickly in China and was openly accepted by the government as one of many recognized *qigong* practices. But Li's refusal to accept governmental control and the organization's rapid growth began to attract attention within the Communist Party, which was particularly concerned by Falun Dafa's popularity among younger party members and their children. When some senior party officials began expressing alarm in early 1999, the leaders of Falun Dafa organized a demonstration in Beijing. They intended only to call attention to their right to practice and to show that Falun Dafa was not a political threat, but the government was disturbed by the sudden presence of so large a gathering in the heart of Beijing.

Government officials persuaded the Falun Dafa leadership to send the demonstrators home. Then, three months later, the organization was banned on the grounds that it was an unregistered religion and discouraged people from seeking proper medical attention. Falun Dafa members throughout China were arrested, fired, imprisoned, sent to prison camps, tortured, or killed.

Li Hongzhi had left China two years before the ban was imposed. He now lives in New York City, which has become the base of a worldwide organization claiming more than 100 million followers in over 100 countries.

Although Falun Dafa teaches and practices nonviolence along Buddhist lines, practitioners have faced serious persecution in China, and therefore it remains an underground movement, regularly denounced as an evil cult working against the good of the people. Curiously, it has not been banned in Hong Kong, which has been a part of China since 1997. However, when the organization wanted to hold a major international rally there in 2007, Beijing blocked the event by refusing to grant visas to Falun Dafa members from abroad.

Outside China, Falun Dafa is openly practiced and has mounted a campaign of severe criticism of the Chinese government. According to Falun Dafa, many practitioners are imprisoned in long-term work camps, where they are used as what amounts to slave labor to produce various goods that are sold in the West. The organization also claims that organs are involuntarily removed from prisoners to be used for transplants. Groups such as Amnesty International have lent some credence to these accusations (Amnesty International n.d.).

Practice

Whereas some people practice *qigong* purely for its physiological benefits, Falun Dafa practitioners see it as a way to seek both physical and spiritual purification. The organization describes Falun Dafa as "a high-level cultivation practice guided by the characteristics of the universe—Truthfulness, Benevolence, and Forbearance" (Li 2000: "Introduction").

Practitioners are said to develop a *falun*, or "law wheel," in the abdomen. This is not the same as the *qi*, which is naturally present in everyone. Once acquired, the *falun* spins in synchrony with the universe. When rotating clockwise, the *falun* absorbs and transforms energy from the universe, and when rotating counterclockwise, it dispenses salvation to oneself, to others, and to the universe. The energy cluster emitted by the *falun* is called *gong*—hence the alternative name for the religion, Falun Gong.

Falun Dafa practices are divided into five sets, with names such as "Buddha showing a thousand hands," the foundational set of exercises intended to open the body's energy channels. When the exercises are done properly, it is said that the body will feel warm, indicating that the energies have been unblocked and energy is being absorbed from the universe.

The Falun Dafa symbol. Note the Daoist yin–yang (*taiji*) symbols and Buddhist rotating swastikas. The outer symbols rotate individually, and together they rotate around the central swastika, first in one direction and then in the other. The colors are said to vary depending on the level of visions experienced by the practitioner (courtesy of Falun Dafa Association, http://en.falundafa.org/introduction.html).

International Society for Krishna Consciousness (ISKCON)

In September 1965, a 70-year-old Hindu holy man from India named A. C. Bhaktivedanta Swami Prabhupada arrived in New York City. A few weeks later, he sat under a tree in a city park and began to chant:

> Hare Krishna Hare Krishna,
> Krishna Krishna Hare Hare,
> Hare Rama Hare Rama,
> Rama Rama Hare Hare.

This mantra, which he had learned from his guru, was said to have originated with a sixteenth-century Hindu mystic named Chaitanya, who was reputed to have entered a state of mystical ecstasy while chanting the three names of his god: Krishna, Hare, and Rama. Within a year of his arrival, Prabhupada had established the International Society for Krishna Consciousness (**ISKCON**) and the "Hare Krishna" movement had begun to take root in America.

The Hare Krishna movement was new to the West, but it was not a new religion. Rather, it was a Western mission of Vaishnava Hinduism, the school devoted to Vishnu. Traditional Vaishnavas worship Vishnu both as the Supreme Godhead and in the forms of his 10 major avatars. In this system, Krishna is the eighth avatar. However, Prabhupada belonged to a variant tradition in which Krishna himself is the Supreme Godhead—the source of everything, including other divine forces. As such, Krishna is understood to encourage a personal relationship between the devotee and himself. Like other forms of Hinduism, ISKCON teaches that the soul is eternal and subject to reincarnation according to the individual's karma; however, those who practice loving devotion to Krishna will go to his heaven when they die and thus escape the cycle of rebirth. The foundational texts for ISKCON are the *Bhagavad Gita* and a collection of stories about Krishna's life called the *Srimad Bhagavatam*.

Between the founding of ISKCON in 1966 and his death 11 years later, Prabhupada traveled around the world spreading his version of Hinduism. Soon the Hare Krishna movement was establishing centers across North America and abroad. Each center included a temple with an altar area featuring images of Krishna and his consort Radha, as the male and female aspects of the divine, as well as pictures of the guru, Prabhupada. In addition, schools were founded to educate the children of devotees in Vedic (ancient Hindu) culture, and farms were established that sought to work the land in traditional ways consistent with Vedic norms.

It is not uncommon for new religions to undergo a difficult period of adjustment after the death of the charismatic founder/leader. Following Prabhupada's death, ISKCON vested authority not in a single guru, but in the Governing Body Commission (GBC), which recognized 11 devotees who had risen to high positions under Prabhupada's leadership as gurus and authorized them to ordain recruits and oversee operations in 11 regional zones. Some of the gurus subsequently got into trouble with the law over matters including illegal guns, drugs, child abuse, and murder, and by the 1980s six of the original group had quit or been removed from office by the GBC.

Practice

As we saw in Chapter 7, the *Bhagavad Gita* depicts Krishna telling Arjuna that he, Krishna, is the highest of all gods, and that although the yoga (spiritual practice) of good karma actions and the yoga of spiritual wisdom are both valid paths, the best path is **bhakti** yoga: loving devotion to Krishna.

Document

From Swami Prabhupada

The following passage outlines the ethical ideals of Krishna consciousness.

A person in Krishna Consciousness, fully devoted in the transcendental loving service of the Lord, develops many good qualities. . . . Lord Chaitanya described only some of them to Sanatan Goswami: A devotee of the Lord is always kind to everyone. He does not pick a quarrel with anyone. He takes the essence of life, spiritual life. He is equal to everyone. Nobody can find fault in a devotee. His magnanimous mind is always fresh and clean and without any material obsessions. He is a benefactor to all living entities. He is peaceful and always surrendered to Krishna. He has no material desire. He is very humble and is fixed in his directions. He is victorious over the six material qualities such as lust and anger. He does not eat more than what he needs. He is always sane. He is respectful to others; but for himself he does not require any respect. He is grave. He is merciful. He is friendly. He is a poet. He is an expert. And he is silent. (Prabhupada 1968: 104)

These ideas, combined with Chaitanya's mystical practice of chanting the praises of Krishna while dancing in ecstasy, are at the heart of the tradition that Prabhupada introduced to the West. Devotional services (pujas) to Krishna are held several times a day. During them, one male or female devotee, acting as the puja leader, stands near the altar and makes offerings of fire and vegetarian food to the images on the altar, which include, in addition to Krishna himself, his consort Radha and his brother Balarama. While the puja leader performs these rituals, the other devotees chant and dance to the accompaniment of handheld cymbals and drums and a small organ called a harmonium. As the pace builds, the chanting becomes louder and the dancing more feverish, and when it reaches a climax, many devotees jump high into the air.

Devotees are given a Sanskrit name, wear saffron-colored robes, and show their devotion to Krishna by adorning their bodies with painted marks called *tilaka*, made of cream-colored clay from the banks of a holy lake in India. Two vertical marks represent Krishna's feet, or the walls of a temple, and below them is a leaf representing the sacred *tulasi* (basil) plant. Adherents' diet is strictly vegetarian, and recreational drugs of all kinds, including alcohol and caffeine, are avoided.

Great effort is put into keeping the temple clean, and every activity is to be done "for Krishna" as an act of devotional service. In this way the mental state known as Krishna consciousness is developed. Some devotees attend the temple only for major activities, but others live in or near it. Single male and female devotees have separate living quarters, while married couples and families often live in nearby houses or apartments. Sexual activity is allowed only within marriage and only for the purpose of procreation. Some devotees have outside employment and turn their wages over to the temple. Others work full-time for the movement.

Most temple-based male devotees shave their heads except for a pigtail at the back of the head. Women are required to dress very modestly. Devotees carry a small bag containing a string of 108 chanting beads (the number 108 is sacred in India partly because it represents the multiple of the 12 zodiac houses and 9 planetary bodies recognized in Indian astrology). Using the beads if their

Hare Krishna devotees try to recruit new members by chanting their mantra in public places; here, they are in front of a mural by R. Cronk at Southern California's popular Venice Beach (© LHB Photo/Alamy).

hands are free, devotees chant the Hare Krishna mantra hundreds of times each day as they go about their duties at the temple.

The Hare Krishnas provoked strong reactions. Some were in response to the movement's efforts to raise money by chanting in public places. Others centered on the fact that in the early years ISKCON discouraged contact between devotees and their former friends and family. As a consequence, the media quickly branded the movement a "cult," and a new profession known as "deprogrammer" came into existence. Hired by concerned parents, deprogrammers would kidnap young devotees in an effort to break the "cult program" that had been "brainwashed" into them. Sometimes these efforts succeeded, but many young people returned to the Hare Krishnas as soon as they were free to do so.

The schools operated by ISKCON for children of devotees also became controversial. In 2000 a class-action suit was filed in Dallas by 44 former students who claimed to have been victims of physical, emotional, and sexual abuse in ISKCON-operated schools in the United States and India. By the time the final settlement was reached, hundreds of others had joined the list of plaintiffs and ISKCON had been forced to seek bankruptcy protection. The claims, totaling $20 million, were settled by 2008.

ISKCON now runs approximately 350 temples and centers worldwide. It has been especially successful in the former states of the Soviet Union, including Russia, and in South America. The spread of ISKCON back to India has been a remarkable development. After starting his mission in America, Prabhupada established a number of temples in India, where ISKCON has been welcomed as a movement reviving Gaudiya Vaishnava devotion. Today Indian devotees may outnumber Western ones.

⊕ Religions Arising from the Abrahamic Lineage

We now turn our attention to some new religions arising from the three Abrahamic religions. The Church of Latter-day Saints can be classed either as a branch of Protestant Christianity or as a new religion developing out of Christianity. The Baha'i Faith originated in Iran in the context of Shi'i Islam. The Kabbalah Centre draws on a Jewish mystical tradition that is centuries old, while the Nation of Islam was established in the United States by leaders raised in the Christian tradition. Finally, the Church of Almighty God arose in China in the context of Protestant Christianity.

Church of Jesus Christ of Latter-day Saints (Mormons)

The founder of the **Church of Jesus Christ of Latter-day Saints**, Joseph Smith, Jr. (1805–1844), claimed that in 1820, as a boy in upstate New York, he had experienced a vision of God and Jesus in which he was told not to join any of the existing denominations. In subsequent visions, he said, an angel named Moroni had persuaded him that he had been divinely chosen to restore the true church of Christ. He founded his new church in 1830.

As a textual basis for his enterprise, Smith published the *Book of Mormon*, which he said he had translated from gold plates inscribed in "reformed Egyptian" that had been entrusted to him by Moroni during a hilltop meeting near Palmyra, New York. The *Book of Mormon* uses the language of the 1611 King James Bible to tell the otherwise undocumented story of two groups, both descended from one of the lost tribes of Israel that supposedly migrated from the Near East to the New World around 600 BCE and became the ancestors of the Indigenous peoples of the Americas. Including accounts of visitations by Christ sometime after his crucifixion, the book is understood by **Mormons** to be a scriptural account of God's activity in the Western Hemisphere, parallel with the Bible and its account of divine events in the Eastern Hemisphere.

Facing ridicule and persecution in New York, Smith led his followers westward. They established settlements in Ohio and Missouri, and, when driven out of the latter in 1839, moved on to Nauvoo, Illinois. By now they were calling themselves the Church of Jesus Christ of Latter-day Saints. It was in Nauvoo that Smith secretly introduced "plural marriage" (polygamy), rumors of which added to the suspicions of outsiders. He also declared himself a candidate for the US presidency in the 1844 elections, advocating a blend of democracy and religious authority that he called "theodemocracy." Some of these innovations caused strife between factions of the Latter-day Saints, and in 1844 Smith and his brother were killed by an anti-Mormon mob.

In 1847 many followers moved to Utah under the leadership of Brigham Young, who had been president of an inner council of 12 that Smith had organized on the pattern of the apostolic church. Although they were unsuccessful in their bid to make Utah a Mormon state, they dominated the Utah Territory, and the US government chose Young to serve as its governor.

A number of the antipolygamy members of the group stayed in the Midwest as the Reorganized Church of Latter-day Saints, with headquarters in Independence, Missouri. In 2001 they renamed themselves the Community of Christ.

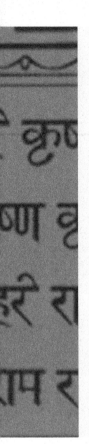

Document

From *The Book of Mormon*, Chapter 1

Here the prophet-historian named Mormon explains how he was instructed to recover the texts hidden by Ammaron, a recordkeeper among the Nephites—one of four groups said to have migrated from Jerusalem to the Western Hemisphere more than five centuries before the time of Jesus.

And now I, Mormon, make a record of the things which I have both seen and heard, and call it the Book of Mormon.

And about the time that Ammaron hid up the records unto the Lord, he came unto me, (I being about ten years of age, and I began to be learned somewhat after the manner of the learning of my people) and Ammaron said unto me: I perceive that thou art a sober child, and art quick to observe;

Therefore, when ye are about twenty and four years old I would that ye should remember the things that ye have observed concerning this people; and when ye are of that age go to the land Antum, unto a hill which shall be called Shim; and there have I deposited unto the Lord all the sacred engravings concerning this people.

And behold, ye shall take the plates of Nephi unto yourself, and the remainder shall ye leave in the place where they are; and ye shall engrave on the plates of Nephi all the things that ye have observed concerning this people.

And I, Mormon, being a descendent of Nephi, (and my father's name was Mormon) I remembered the things which Ammaron commanded me.

And I, being fifteen years of age and being somewhat of a sober mind, therefore I was visited of the Lord, and tasted and knew of the goodness of Jesus. (*Book of Mormon* 1961: 460–467)

Practice

The church's code of behavior includes not only a rigid sexual morality but strict abstinence from tea and coffee as well as alcohol and tobacco. Young adults are expected to serve as volunteer missionaries for two years—a practice that has helped spread awareness of the faith and attract new members around the world. Distinctive practices include the baptism (by proxy) of the deceased; because of this practice, Utah has become a world center for genealogical research. Members have also taken a keen interest in Western Hemisphere archaeology, in the hope that physical evidence of the events described by the *Book of Mormon* will be found.

The controversial practice of plural marriage was officially dropped in 1890, after the federal government threatened to abolish it, and soon faded among mainstream members. But a few congregations broke away to form independent sects known collectively as "Fundamentalist Mormons." The largest of these sects, the Fundamentalist Church of Jesus Christ of Latter-day Saints (FLDS), in particular is known for allowing its male leaders to have multiple wives. Because the women involved are often quite young, FLDS congregations have come under intense scrutiny. In 2011, FLDS leader Warren Jeffs was convicted of two felony counts of child sexual assault and sentenced to life plus 20 years in prison.

Whether the Mormons constitute a new religion or merely a new Christian denomination is open to question. Joseph Smith saw himself as reforming the Christian church, and the fact that

Mormons keep the Bible as scripture argues for their inclusion under the umbrella of Christianity. On the other hand, the Mormons' new postscriptural revelations, new scriptures, and new modes of worship (e.g., using water rather than wine for the Eucharist) suggest that they constitute a new religion. The issue came into focus during the lead-up to the 2000 federal election, when Massachusetts governor Mitt Romney sought nomination as the Republican candidate for president. Some conservative Christians who admired his strong family values were reluctant to support his candidacy because of his Mormon faith. However, in the 2012 presidential campaign, the Billy Graham Evangelistic Association removed Mormonism from its list of cults following a visit between Romney and Graham.

The Baha'i Faith

Baha'i developed out of Islam in the mid-nineteenth century, when Islam was already more than 1,200 years old. Although it has many elements in common with Islam, it gives those elements a new and more nearly universal configuration. The main point of divergence is that Baha'is believe that their leader, Baha'u'llah, was a new prophet, whereas Muslims believe that there can never be another prophet after Muhammad.

The roots of Baha'i lie in the eschatology of Iranian Shi'ism. Ever since the last imam disappeared in 874, Twelver Shi'a had been waiting for a figure known as the **Bab** ("Gateway") to appear and reopen communication with the hidden imam. After 10 centuries, most people no longer expected this to happen anytime soon. But seeds of messianic expectation germinated in the soil of political unrest.

Thus in 1844 Sayyid 'Ali Muhammad declared himself to be the Bab, the gateway to a new prophetic revelation. Although he was imprisoned in 1845, his followers, the Babis, repudiated the Islamic *shari'ah* law that was being practiced in the Persian Empire, and in 1848 the Bab proclaimed himself the hidden imam. He was executed by a firing squad in 1850 on orders from the prime minister of the empire, but he left behind a number of writings that Baha'is consider scriptural.

After the Bab's death, leadership passed to Mirza Husayn 'Ali Nuri (1817–1892), whose religious name was Baha'u'llah, "Glory of God." Although he had not met the Bab, he had experienced a profound feeling of divine support while imprisoned in Tehran in 1852. On his release the following year, he was banished, first to Baghdad, and then, in 1863, to Istanbul. Before departing for the latter, he declared himself to be "the one whom God shall manifest" as foretold by the Bab.

The transfer to the Mediterranean world expanded the sphere of Baha'u'llah's spiritual activity well beyond the horizons of Iranian Shi'ism. Now he was in a position to address the entire Ottoman Empire. Although he was banished to Acre in Palestine a few years later, his following continued to grow. Nearby Haifa (today in Israel) remains the world headquarters of the Baha'i Faith today, and since 1963 leadership has been vested in an elected body of representatives called the Universal House of Justice.

Baha'u'llah produced more than 100 texts that Baha'is believe to be God's revelation for this age. Among the most important are *Kitab-i Aqdas* ("The Most Holy Book," 1873), containing Baha'i laws; *Kitab-i Iqan* ("The Book of Certitude," 1861), the principal doctrinal work; and *Hidden Words* (1858), a discourse on ethics. *The Seven Valleys* (1856), a mystical treatise, enumerates seven spiritual stages: search, love, knowledge, unity, contentment, wonderment, and true poverty and absolute nothingness.

Baha'is have a major temple in every major region of the world. Architects are instructed to take their inspiration from the traditional culture and building styles of the region while incorporating the number nine (sacred to Baha'is) and formal gardens in the Iranian style. The temple above, in Haifa, Israel, is Middle Eastern in design. By contrast, the "Lotus Temple" in New Delhi evokes the sacred flower that is a symbol of Indian culture (© E Simanor/ Robert Harding World Imagery/Corbis).

The Baha'i notion of prophethood is in line with the Abrahamic religions. Prophets are sent by God to diagnose spiritual and moral disorder and to prescribe the appropriate remedy. Baha'is, like Muslims, believe that the world has known a sequence of prophets. However, they do not believe the prophets' messages to have been community-specific; instead, they understand the prophets to speak to the entire world. They also believe that, in accordance with their doctrine of "progressive revelation," more prophets will come in future ages.

It may well be their ideal of world community that has done the most to make the Baha'i tradition attractive to serious searchers. Baha'u'llah himself wrote that he came to "unify the world," and Baha'is have asserted the unity of religions. Baha'is actively advocate economic, sexual, and racial equality; proclaim unity of the races; and welcome interracial marriage. In recent decades these emphases have been a major factor of the appeal of the Baha'i Faith to African Americans. Extremes of poverty and wealth are to be eliminated, and slavery rooted out—along with priesthood and monasticism. Women are to enjoy rights and opportunities equal to those of men, marriage is to be strictly monogamous, and divorce is frowned on. World peace is to be achieved through disarmament, democracy, and the rule of law, along with the promotion of international education and human rights, and Baha'is have consultative status with the United Nations as an official nongovernmental organization. Although these goals are clearly compatible with modern secular values, they have a spiritual quality for Baha'is, who cite Baha'u'llah as saying that human well-being is unattainable until unity is firmly established.

Practice

Baha'is strive to live a peaceful and ethical life. Personal spiritual cultivation is encouraged, and recreational drugs and alcohol are forbidden. Since the Baha'i Faith sees itself as the fulfillment of other religions, Baha'is are unusually open to dialogue with other faiths.

Baha'is follow a distinctive calendar, in which the number 19 (which figured in the tradition's early mystical thinking) plays an important role. Beginning with the spring equinox (the time of the Iranian new year), there are 19 months of 19 days each, with 4 additional days (5 in leap years) to keep up with the solar year. Local Baha'is gather for a community feast on the first day of each month, and the final month, in early March, is devoted to dawn-to-dusk fasting, as in the Muslim observance of Ramadan.

Although the 19-day calendar does not recognize the 7-day week, many Baha'is in the West meet on Sundays for study and reflection. Important days in the annual cycle are essentially historical: several days in April and May are associated with Baha'u'llah's mission, for instance. In addition, the Bab's birth, mission, and martyrdom are commemorated, as are the birth and passing (or ascension) of Baha'u'llah.

Baha'i devotions at the monthly feasts feature singing but no instrumental music. Readings are mainly from Baha'i scriptural writings by Baha'u'llah or the Bab, but they may be supplemented with devotional readings from other traditions. Those who grow up as Baha'is may make a personal profession of faith at the age of 15. Converts simply sign a declaration card. Baha'i weddings vary depending on the tastes of the couple but always include the declaration "We will all, truly, abide by the will of God." At funerals there is a standard prayer for the departed, which is virtually the only prayer said in unison by Baha'is.

Personal devotions are similar to Islamic practice: the faithful wash their hands and face before praying, and set prayers are said at five times of the day. Also reminiscent of Islam is the practice of repeating the phrase "*Allahu-'l Abha*" ("God is the most glorious"). These similarities notwithstanding, the Baha'i Faith has gone its own way. Its revelation does not conclude with the Qur'an, and its ideals for society depart from those reflected in the *shari'ah*. There have also been political tensions between the two traditions. Muslims have tended to see the Baha'is as sympathetic to Israel, and in Iran the Baha'i community suffered serious losses in lives and property after the Islamic Revolution of 1979.

Since the end of the nineteenth century, the Baha'i Faith has spread around the world. It now claims some 7 million adherents in 235 countries. These include 750,000 in North America and several times that number in India. More than one-quarter of local councils are in Africa and a similar number in Asia. There are nearly as many councils in the southwestern Pacific as in Europe.

Document

Baha'i Prayer

The following prayer by 'Abdu'l-Bahá reflects the Baha'i belief that the oneness of humankind overrides any religious, racial, or national divisions.

Oh kind Lord! Thou Who art generous and merciful! We are the servants of Thy threshold and we are under the protection of Thy mercy. The Sun of Thy providence is shining upon all and the clouds of Thy mercy shower upon all. Thy gifts encompass all, Thy providence sustains all, Thy protection overshadows all and the glances of Thy favour illumine all. O Lord! Grant unto us Thine infinite bestowals and let Thy light of guidance shine. Illumine the eyes, make joyous the souls and confer a new spirit upon the hearts. Give them eternal life. Open the doors of Thy knowledge; let the light of faith shine. Unite and bring mankind into one shelter beneath the banner of Thy protection, so that they may become as waves of one sea, as leaves and branches of one tree, and may assemble beneath the shadow of the same tent. May they drink from the same fountain. May they be refreshed by the same breezes. May they obtain illumination from the same source of light and life. Thou art the Giver, the Merciful! (*Baha'i Prayers* 2002: 43–44)

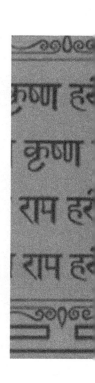

The Nation of Islam

It is estimated that at least 20 percent of the West Africans taken as slaves to the Americas were Muslims. One early promoter of Islam (or a version of it) among African Americans was Noble Drew Ali, who in 1913 founded the Moorish Science Temple of America in Newark, New Jersey. By the time of his death in 1929, major congregations had been established in cities including Chicago, Detroit, and Philadelphia.

Whether Wallace D. Fard (1893–1934?) was ever associated with this temple is unclear; his followers say he wasn't. But the idea that Islam was the appropriate religion for African Americans was in the air when he established the **Nation of Islam (NOI)** in Detroit in 1930. Fard's version of Islam bore little resemblance to either the Sunni or the Shi'i traditions. For Muslims, who understand Allah to be a purely spiritual entity, the most fundamental difference lay in the NOI's claim that Allah took human form in the person of Fard himself. These claims may have originated in Fard's first encounter with Elijah Poole (1897–1975), a young man who had felt called to a religious mission of some kind but had stopped attending church before his fateful 1923 meeting with Fard. Fard was so impressed with the young man—who later changed his name to Elijah Muhammad—that he authorized him to teach Islam with his blessing. Elijah quickly became Fard's favorite disciple.

The men who developed the theology of the Nation of Islam maintained that all humans were originally black and lived in harmony as one tribe called Shabazz for millions of years, until an evil man named Yakub rebelled and left Mecca for an island where he created the white race by killing all dark-skinned babies and selectively breeding light-skinned ones. Eventually, the evil white race returned to Arabia and subjugated the blacks, bringing oppression and disunity to humankind. God sent Moses to try to redeem them, but that effort failed. Now the blacks needed to undergo a "resurrection" and recognize themselves as proud members of the great and peaceful Shabazz people.

The Nation of Islam came to the attention of the authorities in Detroit when it was rumored that Fard had promised life in heaven for anyone who killed four whites. This was probably not true,

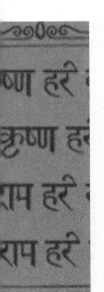

Document

Elijah Muhammad on the True God and the Tribe of Shabazz

After criticizing the Christian concept of God as a "mystery," Elijah Muhammad writes that the true God is now "making Himself manifest."

He is not anymore a mystery . . . but is known and can be seen and heard the earth over. This teaching of a mystery God enslaves the minds of the ignorant. My poor people are victims of every robbery. They are so pitifully blind, deaf and dumb that it hurts, but I am going to prove to them that Allah is with me. . . .

Allah (God) loves us, the so-called Negroes (Tribe of Shabazz), so that He will give lives for our sake today. Fear not, you are no more forsaken. God is in person, and stop looking for a dead Jesus for help, but pray to Him who Jesus prophesied would come after Him. He who is alive and not a spook. (Muhammad 1997 [1965]: 3) although he was known to have preached that anyone who killed four devils would go to heaven. In any event, Fard disappeared after he was expelled from Detroit in 1933. Elijah Muhammad took over the movement's leadership, but some factions were quite hostile to him, and it soon fragmented. In 1935, he moved to Washington, DC, where he preached under the name Elijah Rasool (Lee 1996: 26).

In 1942, however, he was convicted of sedition for counseling his followers not to register for the draft. His wife, Clara, directed the organization during the four years he spent in prison, and after his release in 1946 the NOI's numbers soon began to grow. Much of the credit for the movement's expansion in the 1950s has been given to a convert named Malcolm X.

Malcolm X

Malcolm Little (1925–1965) spent much of his childhood in Lansing, Michigan. When he was six, his father was run over by a streetcar; the coroner ruled it a suicide, but the Little family believed he had been killed by a white supremacist group. After his father's death, the family was impoverished and his mother suffered a nervous breakdown, so the children were put in foster care. Later, Malcolm moved to Boston and became involved with criminals. It was while he was serving time for theft that he was encouraged by his brother to join the NOI. He read widely while incarcerated, and after his release in 1952 he became a key disciple of Elijah Muhammad. Like other converts at that time, he took the surname X to protest the absence of an African name and to recall the X branded on some slaves. Before long he had become the leader of the Harlem NOI temple. His eloquence brought him national attention as an advocate for Black Power, and he came to symbolize black defiance of white racism in America.

Despite his success, however, Malcolm X became alienated from the movement. In 1964 he broke away from the NOI and founded Muslim Mosque, Inc. Increasingly aware of the differences between NOI theology and that of traditional Islam, he converted to Sunni Islam and made the pilgrimage to Mecca, where he learned that the tradition was not an exclusively black religion, as the NOI had taught. It was a life-changing experience. Renaming himself El Hajj Malik El-Shabazz, he began to teach an understanding of Islam as a religion for all races. Less than a year later, in February 1965, he was assassinated while giving a speech in New York. Three members of the NOI were convicted of the murder, although some people suspected that the Federal Bureau of Investigation had instigated it (Lee 1996: 44).

Warith Deen Muhammad

The early 1970s also saw a moderating of the NOI's attitude toward whites and an increasing willingness to work with other black organizations. When Elijah Muhammad died in 1975, the leadership passed to his son Wallace, who moved the NOI closer to the mainstream and helped put it on a more solid financial basis. Wallace also renamed the temples, adopting the Arabic word for mosque, *masjid*. This, together with a new emphasis on studying the Qur'an, brought the NOI into Sunni Islam. In 1975 Wallace renamed the organization the World Community of al-Islam in the West (WCIW), and in 1981 it became the American Muslim Mission. In 1985 the name was changed again to the American Society of Muslims. Wallace also renamed himself, and as Warith Deen Muhammad ("the inheritor of the religion of Muhammad") he became a mainstream American Sunni leader until his death in 2008.

Louis Farrakhan

Not all members of the former NOI agreed with these reforms, however. Among the dissenters was Louis Farrakhan, who in 1978 broke with WCIW and formed a new organization modeled on the NOI. He restored the original name, reinstituted earlier practices, and attracted many members.

In 2001 a former member of the revived NOI published an account of his experience that was particularly critical of Farrakhan's financial dealings. Members were pressured to donate large sums, and many struggling black-owned businesses were left with unpaid bills for their services to the organization, even as substantial amounts of money were finding their way to various members of the Farrakhan family (White 2001).

Farrakhan also appears to have courted African Muslim leaders, including Libya's Muammar Gaddafi, for support. Perhaps this helps to explain why he has moved the NOI toward the Islamic mainstream by encouraging Islamic-style daily prayers and study of the Qur'an. The most difficult change he made was to drop the doctrine that identified Fard as Allah and Elijah Muhammad as his Messenger. In a 1997 conference, Farrakhan publicly affirmed that Muhammad was the last and greatest prophet of Allah (Walker 2005: 495).

In 1995 Farrakhan organized a "Million Man March" on Washington, DC, to draw attention to the role of the black male in American society and to the need to unite for social and economic improvement. The march was a joint effort sponsored by many black organizations, and most of the participants had a Christian background. As the main organizer, however, Farrakhan set the agenda. Although the march was criticized for excluding black women and promoting a Muslim agenda, as well as for its lack of transparency in accounting, it did bring several African American organizations into fuller cooperation and helped draw public attention to the challenges faced by black people in the United States.

The Kabbalah Centre

The Kabbalah Centre in Los Angeles teaches a new form of spirituality based on traditional Jewish mysticism. As an organization, it traces its roots to a center for **Kabbalah** studies founded in Jerusalem in 1922 by Rabbi (or Rav) Yehuda Ashlag. But the tradition stretches back through the sixteenth-century master Isaac Luria to the (probably) thirteenth-century text called the Zohar and beyond. The Centre itself claims that its teachings go back some 4,000 years. However, in its current form, the National Institute for the Research of Kabbalah (later renamed the Kabbalah Centre) was founded in 1965 by Rabbi Philip S. Berg.

In itself, Berg's Kabbalah was not new, but his approach to it was radically different from what had come before. Traditionally, the study of Kabbalah had been restricted to mature male Jews, aged 40 or older, who had already completed years of Talmudic studies. Yet Berg taught Kabbalah to his secretary, who would later become his wife and a leading figure in the movement herself. Within a few years, the Bergs had set out to make Kabbalah available to the world at large: young and old, male and female, Jews and non-Jews alike. This was the new dimension of Berg's Kabbalah, and it sparked a great deal of controversy in traditional Jewish circles.

On its website the Centre defines Kabbalah as "ancient wisdom and practical tools for creating joy and lasting fulfillment now." The emphasis on "practical tools" is significant, for the purpose of Kabbalah study, as the Centre presents it, is to unlock the human potential for greatness. It is a fundamental tenet of Kabbalah (as it is of Eastern traditions such as Hinduism and Buddhism) that humans will be reincarnated over and over again, returning to this world as many times as necessary "until the task of transformation is done" (Kabbalah Centre n.d.).

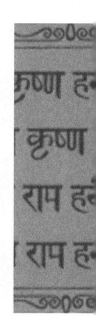

Document

Kabbalah: Thoughts on God

God's only desire is to reveal unity through diversity. That is, to reveal that all reality is unique in all its levels and all its details, and nevertheless united in a fundamental oneness. (Kabbalist Aharon Ha-Levi Horowitz [1766–1828], in Levi 2009: 929)

The essence of divinity is found in every single thing—nothing but It exists. Since It causes everything to be, no thing can live by anything else. It enlivens them. *Ein Sof* exists in each existent. Do not say, "This is a stone and not God." God forbid! Rather all existence is God, and the stone is a thing pervaded by divinity. (Moses Cordovero [1522–1570], in Levi 2009: 937)

Shards of Light are drawn out of the destructive entities that reside within my being. Their life force is cut off and I am then replenished with Divine energy. Life grows brighter each and every day as billions of sacred sparks return to my soul! ("Focus in Front")

Another fundamental principle is that the reality perceived by our five senses is only a tiny portion of the totality, and that events occurring in the knowable 1 percent of reality are the product of events in the unknown 99 percent. Berg's followers maintain that Kabbalah teachings give access to the larger reality that normally remains unknown.

Practice

Kabbalists experience God as the energy that underlies and permeates all things. To illustrate how God and the material world interrelate, Kabbalah uses a diagram usually referred to as the

Practice

Meditation

One of the practices of Kabbalah involves meditating on the 72 names for God, based on combinations of Hebrew letters that Kabbalah finds hidden in Exodus 14:19–21, the biblical account in which Moses calls on God for help before leading the Hebrews into the sea as the Egyptian army pursues them. Kabbalists took these three verses, each of which has 72 letters in Hebrew, and developed 72 names of God by combining these letters into triads of three letters each. To get the first name, they took the first letter of verse 19, the last of verse 20, and the first of verse 21. The next name was composed by taking the second letter of verse 19, the second from last letter of verse 20, and the second letter of verse 21, and so on for a total of 72. These 72 names were then arranged in a grid with eight columns and nine rows. According to the Kabbalah Centre, the 72 names of God "work as tuning forks to repair you on the soul level"; each three-letter sequence "act[s] like an index to specific, spiritual frequencies. By simply looking at the letters, as well as closing your eyes and visualizing them, you can connect with these frequencies" ("72 Names of God").

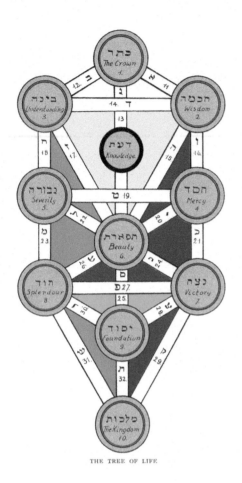

THE TREE OF LIFE

The Kabbalist Tree of Life (Mary Evans Picture Library/Alamy).

Tree of Life. The space above the tree represents God as *Ein Sof*, "The Endless." The tree itself pictures the 10 **spherot**, shining circles of fire, representing the 10 attributes of God in the world. The topmost circle represents the Crown (*Keter* or *Kether*). Below it the other nine circles are arranged in three sets, each with a circle in the left, center, and right columns. Read from the top down, these three sets represent the spiritual, intellectual, and material (earth-level) qualities of creation. The *spherot* in the right-hand column represent the masculine attributes of God, and those on the left feminine attributes. The *spherah* (singular) in the center of the nine *spherot* is "Glory," which brings harmony and interconnectedness among the lower nine *spherot*. The 10 *spherot* are numbered from top to bottom and are connected by 22 lines (corresponding to the 22 letters of the Hebrew alphabet) that show how they interact. Kabbalists believe that their practice facilitates the flow of divine energy into the world, and that God needs human effort to work in the world.

Kabbalists do not attempt to interpret the Bible literally; instead, they use a complex kind of numerology. The ancient Hebrews used letters as numbers, assigning them numerical values according to their position in the 22-letter Hebrew alphabet. Totaling the numbers in certain words could reveal hidden connections between them and lead to new interpretations. For example, the numerical values of YHWH, the name for God revealed to Moses, and *aleph*, the first letter of the alphabet, are both 26. For Kabbalists, this is significant because one of the words for "Lord" or "Master" in Hebrew, *aluph*, is based on the word *aleph*. Inspired by the numerological practices of ancient Kabbalah, modern Kabbalists maintain that determining the numerical value of one's name can lead to new insights.

Traditional Kabbalah employs a dualistic symbolism of light and darkness, and many of the Centre's teachings focus on moving from darkness to light. For example, the tradition stresses that instead of running away from adversaries, one should confront and learn from them, just as the biblical Jacob wrestled with the angel and gained light from the experience. Kabbalists see Jacob's angel as a personification of the personal darkness with which every individual must struggle in order to reach the light. Kabbalah practice is thought to help remove the darkness that covers the ego to reveal that light.

Like Scientology, the Kabbalah Centre has benefited from the media attention attracted by celebrity adherents. At the same time, the large sums of money donated by celebrities have raised questions about the Centre's finances and accounting. Some Jews have accused the Centre of exploiting Kabbalah for worldly gain, which the Kabbalist tradition explicitly forbids. Other criticisms have focused on the Centre's claims linking worldly happiness with Kabbalah practice. One Kabbalah leader in London, England, was heavily criticized for seeming to suggest that the 6 million Jews killed in the Holocaust died because they did not follow Kabbalah practices to unblock the light.

The Church of Almighty God (Eastern Lightning)

The Church of Almighty God is one of the newest movements to grow out of Christianity. Its roots go back to 1990 in China, when a man named Zhao Weishan led followers away from the House Church movement to form a revised version of Christianity so divergent from mainstream Christianity that it has been soundly rejected by other Christians. In China the term "house church" refers to Protestant churches that are not registered with the government and therefore usually hold services and Bible study sessions in private homes. House Church congregations are evangelical in nature and stress the coming of Judgment Day and the end-times.

The movement founded by Zhao has undergone several name changes. Since 1993 it has been formally known as the Church of Almighty God. In Chinese, it is known as Zhen Shen Church, which may be translated "Real God Church." However, the church is more popularly referred to as Eastern Lightning, a phrase derived from the movement's vision of itself as the lightning from the east mentioned in Matthew 24:23–27. In that text Jesus warns against false prophets and false Christs who will arise and lead people astray. Jesus then says that just as lightning comes from the east and goes to the west, so also will it be with the Son of Man. The usual understanding of this passage is that the coming of the Son of Man, taken to mean the return of Christ, will happen suddenly, like a flash of lightning. The Church of Almighty God, however, interprets the passage quite differently. It takes the reference to the lightning coming from the east to refer to China, and the reference to the return of Christ to refer to a Chinese woman revered by the group as the new Christ. From a traditional Christian point of view, it is ironic that a New Testament passage warning against following false Christs has become the favorite text of a new movement formed around a belief in a new incarnation of Christ.

The new Christ adored by Eastern Lightning is a woman named Yang Xiangbin, the wife of Zhao. Followers of Eastern Lightning refer to her as Almighty God, which is the origin of the group's name, the Church of Almighty God. They talk of her as the returned Christ or as the second of the "two incarnations." Mainstream Christians reject both the idea that there can be a new Christ and the idea that the returning Christ might be a woman.

Besides its belief in the return of Christ in China, other beliefs of Eastern Lightning deviate from those of traditional Christianity. Eastern Lightning considers the book authored by Yang Xiangbin, known in English as *The Word Appears in the Flesh*, to be a new scripture for this new age. The group divides human history into three periods: the time before Jesus, when the world was under the guidance of God (Yahweh); the period when the world was under the guidance of Jesus; and the current period, when the world is under the authority and guidance of the second Christ, Yang Xiangbin. Her role as Christ in the end-time is to judge and purify humans and to defeat Satan. According to Eastern Lightning, those who reject her and her book will suffer during the end-time judgment.

The church believes that this end-time is approaching. Followers of Eastern Lightning initially looked to a date in May 2012 as the beginning of the end-time, but when nothing of consequence occurred around that date, they were not discouraged in their belief that the end-time is imminent. They continue to use the phrase "Christ of the End-Times."

The actions of Eastern Lightning have been quite controversial in China. Members of the House Church congregations, as well as other citizens, have complained that Eastern Lightning followers use overly aggressive or even violent tactics in their efforts to recruit new members. In his book *Kidnapped by a Cult*, the Christian pastor Shen Xiaoming claims to have been kidnapped by Eastern

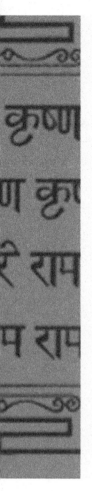

Document

From the Forty-Sixth Utterance

In this passage, drawn from Yang Xiangbin's Forty-Sixth Utterance, in The Word Appears in the Flesh, *the end-time Christ speaks for God, expressing God's dismay over human nature in the past and cautioning that things will not go well for those who do not heed the book's warnings. God seems to be comparing his disappointment with humans to a parent's worries about a child who doesn't show ambition in life.*

I tell people to hurry up and leave, to not stick to living in "poverty"; in the future it will be too late for regrets. Don't be too hard on yourself; why bother? Yet I also tell people that when they fail to gain blessings, no one may complain about Me. I have no time to waste My words on man. I hope that this sticks in people's minds, that they don't forget it—these words are the uncomfortable truth from Me. I have long since lost faith in man, I have long since lost hope in people, for they lack ambition, they have never been able to give Me a heart that loves God, and always give Me their motivations instead. I have said much to man, and since people still ignore My advice today, I tell them of My view to prevent them misunderstanding My heart in the future; whether they live or die in the times to come is their business, I have no control over this. I hope they find their own path to survival, and I am powerless in this. Since man does not truly love Me, we simply part ways; in future, no longer will there be any words between us, no longer will we have anything to talk about, we will not interfere with each other, we will each go our own way, people must not come looking for Me, never again will I ask for man's help. This is something that's between us, and we've spoken without equivocation to prevent there being any issues in the future. Doesn't this make things easier? We each go our own way and have nothing to do with each other—what's wrong with that? I hope people give this some consideration. (Xiangbin n.d.)

Lightning in 2002 as part of its practice of abducting Christian pastors to try to get them, and subsequently their congregations, to convert. And in 2014, when a woman refused to give a group of five Eastern Lightning recruiters her cell phone number while in a McDonald's restaurant, they beat her with a mop handle so violently that she died. The five were convicted of and two executed for murder. This incident caught international attention when it was featured on a BBC show about Eastern Lightning's extreme practices.

One typical characteristic of cults is that they use extreme measures to discourage adherents from leaving the organization. Such allegations have been made about Eastern Lightning. Besides allegedly harassing followers seeking to leave, Eastern Lightning has been accused of committing violence against such followers' family members.

Since 1995 Eastern Lightning has been officially banned in China by the Chinese government, which holds it responsible for various cases of murder, extortion, kidnapping, and harassment. In response, Eastern Lighting adherents claim that the accusations made against them are false and are simply being used by the government as an excuse to ban the group. The church refers to the Chinese Communist Party as the Great Red Dragon. That term is taken from Revelation 12, in which the Great Dragon is an evil monster that swats stars out of the sky with its tail while it waits to devour the baby Jesus.

Zhao Weishan left China before 1995 and, having been granted asylum in the United States, now lives in and runs the organization from New York State. Chinese sources claim that his wife immigrated with him, with both using false passports.

Missionaries have had some success in spreading Eastern Lightning beyond mainland China. The movement has adherents in Hong Kong and Taiwan and has made converts in some other Asian cities and, to a lesser extent, the West.

⊕ Religions Inspired by Other Forms of Spirituality

Not all new religions are offshoots of established mainstream religious traditions. We turn now to a selection of new religions deriving from unconventional sources. **Wicca** is a modern phenomenon inspired by pre-Christian European traditions, with a significant feminist component. Scientology and the **Raëlian Movement** draw on more secular sources, including science fiction and new forms of depth psychology. Finally, the **New Age** movement encompasses a variety of spiritualities.

Wicca: The Witchcraft Revival

In the late Middle Ages, after centuries of condemning the remnants of "pagan" tradition in northern Europe as "witchcraft," the Roman Catholic Church mounted a systematic campaign to eradicate those remnants once and for all. Although accusations of witchcraft were frequent well into the 1700s, by the early twentieth century witchcraft was widely considered a thing of the past in industrialized societies.

Around the time of the Second World War, however, a movement emerged in England that claimed that witchcraft was the original religion of Britain and sought to revive it. The leading figures in this movement were two men, Gerald B. Gardner and Aleister Crowley, but women's interest increased after 1948, when Robert Graves published *The White Goddess*, a work on myth that posited the existence of a mother goddess in European prehistory. In 1953 Doreen Valiente helped Gardner rewrite *The Book of Shadows*, a liturgical handbook for witchcraft.

The first modern use of the Old English word "Wicca" is attributed to Gardner in 1959, but it is a Gardner initiate named Ray Buckland who is credited with introducing Wicca to the United States. Soon people with no connection to the Gardner lineage were establishing covens, and the name Wicca was becoming known outside the "Craft" itself. It is difficult to estimate the current size of the Wicca movement, but sales of publications and various claims regarding coven attendance suggest that there are at least 85,000 adherents in North America and perhaps four times as many around the world.

The Covenant of the Goddess, which was organized in California in 1975, is an umbrella organization representing many but not all covens. It is open to any Wicca coven that worships the Goddess or ancient gods. It recognizes two levels of leadership (priestesses/priests and high priestesses/priests) and reports that approximately two-thirds of coven leaders are women.

The feminist movement had a major impact on Wicca in North America. After journalist Margot Adler listened to a tape sent by a witchcraft circle in Wales, she became interested in the movement and found that its visionary and aesthetic elements played an important role in women's involvement in the Craft, along with the mysteries of birth and growth, a concern for the natural environment, and particularly a sense of feminist empowerment. Feminism is also central to Starhawk (Miriam Simos), for whom the religion of the Goddess is the pulsating rhythm of life and human sexuality a reflection of the fundamentally sexual nature of the earth itself.

In general, the kind of neopagan witchcraft represented by Wicca seeks a return to primal nature and repudiates the classical Western religions that it holds responsible for repressing human sexuality. At the same time, its feminist emphasis challenges the patriarchal traditions of Judaism and Christianity. Although men can take an active part in it, Wicca is particularly empowering for women, and this has surely been part of its appeal.

Practice

Wiccans celebrate as many as eight *sabbats* (festivals) during the annual cycle or "wheel of the year." Four have fixed dates: Candlemas (February 1), May Day (May 1), Lammas (August 1), and Halloween (October 31). The other four mark important days of the solar cycle: the spring and autumn equinoxes and the fall and winter solstices.

Although the practices of different covens vary in their details, standard activities include healing rituals and the celebration of important life-cycle events, such as birth, coming of age, marriage, and death. Among the most important symbols are the circle, the four directions, and the four elements (earth, water, fire, and air). Some of the rituals are symbolically sacrificial, paralleling (or parodying) the Christian Eucharist. Some covens announce upcoming services only by word of mouth and require that strangers be introduced by a trusted friend.

Wiccans celebrate the winter solstice at Stonehenge (AP Photo/Matt Dunham/CP).

In 1993 members of the Covenant of the Goddess took part in the centennial World's Parliament of Religions in Chicago. In an age of interfaith acceptance, Wiccan priestesses and priests sought public and governmental recognition of their work as chaplains in hospitals, prisons, universities, and military units, but they could not provide any formal documentation of clerical training. To obtain the necessary credentials, some Wiccan leaders enrolled in Unitarian theological seminaries. Since then, the term "witch" has begun to be used to distinguish credentialed clergy (group leaders) from lay adherents.

Scientology

The Church of **Scientology** was founded in 1954 by L. Ron Hubbard (1911–1986). Official biographies emphasize the breadth of his experience and learning. As a boy in Montana, for instance, he was exposed to the traditional teachings of the Blackfoot nation. In his youth he was introduced to Freudian psychology by a mentor who had trained with Freud and, while traveling through Asia with his family, learned about a variety of ancient spiritual traditions. As an adult, he not only became a prolific author in various genres, including science fiction, but served as a naval officer in the Second World War and, after being severely wounded, assisted his return to health by discovering how to remove deep-seated blocks in his mind. Following his recovery he began to advocate a new theory of what the soul does to the body. He called this theory **dianetics**, from the Greek *dia* (through) and *nous* (mind or soul).

Hubbard's 1950 book *Dianetics: The Modern Science of Mental Health* sold millions of copies. Soon followers were forming groups across the United States, and in 1954 they became the first members of the Church of Scientology. The church's official website defines Scientology—a word derived from the Latin *scio* (knowing) and the Greek *logos* (study)—as "knowing about knowing" and describes it as an "applied religious philosophy."

The official creed of Scientology, reflecting Hubbard's belief that the underlying principle of all life forms is the drive to survive, asserts that all humans have the right to defend themselves and the duty to protect others. It also affirms that "the laws of God forbid" humans to destroy or enslave the souls of others, that the spirit alone can heal the body, and that the spirit can be saved.

Scientologists understand the universe to consist of eight intersecting planes, or "dynamics," beginning with the self and the family at the bottom and moving up to the spiritual universe (the seventh dynamic) and the Supreme Being or Infinity (the eighth). The nature of the Infinity or God dynamic is not clearly defined, but it seems to have less in common with the "personal God" of Christianity, who knows, wills, and acts like a (super)human person, than with "impersonal" principles or divinities such as the Dao of Daoism, the Brahman of the Hindu *Upanishads*, and the transcendent cosmic buddha of some forms of Mahayana Buddhism.

Scientology uses the term "**thetan**" (pronounced "thay-tan") for the soul. Each thetan is thought to be billions of years old. Like the Atman of Hindu belief, the thetan is reincarnated, passing from one body to another at death.

Scientologists prefer to think of the movement as originating with its practitioners rather than with Hubbard himself. But he was its inspiration, he gave it direction from the first, and his writings and lectures constitute its religious literature. In a sense, the spread of Scientology began with the publication of *Dianetics* and its translation into numerous languages, even before the official founding of the church in 1954. Various publications helped to spread Scientology to Britain and Europe. Today Scientologists have an organized presence in most countries.

As a strategy for spreading Scientology's influence, Hubbard decided to focus on high-profile celebrities. "Celebrity Centers" offering posh facilities for practice and training have attracted several celebrities, whose names have given the organization credibility.

Credibility has been important for Scientologists, because the movement has long been haunted by controversy. Several Scientologists, including Hubbard's wife, Mary Sue, were convicted of criminal activity involving the infiltration of various government agencies and the theft of documents thought to reflect badly on the operation. L. Ron Hubbard was named as a co-conspirator in this case (*United States vs. Mary Sue Hubbard et al.*, 1979) but was never indicted.

As early as 1982, some dissenting followers of Hubbard were beginning to form alternative organizations outside the Church of Scientology. These "heretical" organizations are known collectively as the "Free Zone." The name comes from Hubbard himself, who claimed that planet earth, under the galactic name Teegeeack, had been declared a "free zone" millions of years ago. In that context, "free" meant free of political or economic interference from other planets in the galaxy, but in the organizational context the term was meant to indicate that individuals were free to follow the teachings of Hubbard without either payment to or interference from the Church of Scientology. The Church of Scientology tries to maintain exclusive rights to Hubbard's practices and refers to **Free Zoners** as "squirrels"—the equivalent of heretics. But the International Free Zone Association claims that it is the Free Zoners who are faithful to Hubbard's original teachings and practices.

Practice

In the 1960s Hubbard developed a step-by-step method for clearing the mind, or thetan, of mental blocks (called **engrams**) and restoring it to a state referred to as "clear." Engrams are the result of traumatic experiences, and they remain with the thetan until they are cleared, even carrying over from one life to the next. Hubbard's process for clearing engrams, called "auditing," involves the use of a device called an "**E-meter**," which is supposed to indicate when an engram blockage has been discovered in the mind.

Another important Scientologist practice is the study of Hubbard's thought and writings. Students are encouraged to continue this "training," striving to reach ever-higher levels. Progress can take years of expensive auditing. After sufficient progress has been made to "go Clear," advanced training begins. This phase introduces some of Hubbard's imaginative science fiction concepts, among them the idea that an extraterrestrial named Xenu, the ruler of a galactic confederation, came to Teegeeack (earth) 75 million years ago, bringing with him thousands of aliens who had tried to revolt against his leadership. He put these political prisoners around volcanoes in which he detonated H-bombs. Then he captured the souls of the dead, now known as thetans, and implanted in them various ideas that we now associate with other religions. However, traces of their essences remain to this day, and some of their souls accumulated on the few bodies that were left. They are known as "body thetans." Those who complete all seven levels of training are known as "operating thetans" (OTs).

Scientology has come under intense public scrutiny and criticism. Psychologists and other scientists are not sympathetic to the underlying claims of dianetics, and the fact that each level of training costs additional money has given rise to accusations that it is just a pyramid scheme designed to bilk money from gullible people. Some observers have claimed that Hubbard once suggested to a meeting of science fiction writers that, instead of writing for a penny a word, they could make millions by starting a new religion.

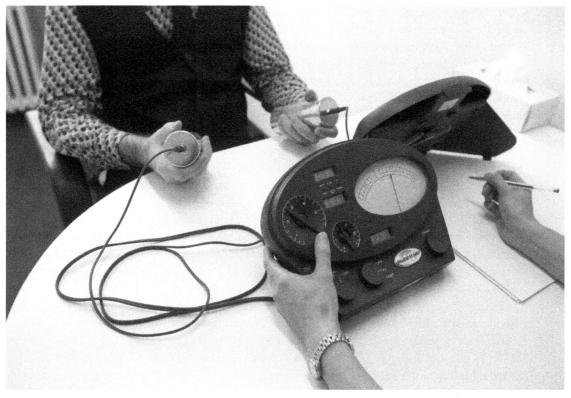

An E-meter auditing session at the Scientology church in Zurich (© ALESSANDRO DELLA BELLA/Keystone/Corbis).

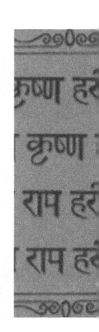

Document

L. Ron Hubbard on the Benefits of "Clearing"

A Clear can be tested for any and all psychoses, neuroses, compulsions and repressions (all aberrations) and can be examined for any autogenic (self-generated) diseases referred to as psychosomatic ills. These tests confirm the Clear to be entirely without such ills or aberrations. (Hubbard 1968: 13)

One of the incidental things which happen to a Clear is that his eyesight, if it had been bad . . ., generally improves markedly. (16)

Migraine headaches are psychosomatic and, with the others [arthritis, dermatitis, allergies, asthma, some coronary difficulties, eye trouble, bursitis, ulcers, sinusitis, etc.] are uniformly cured by Dianetic therapy. . . . Clears do not get colds. (113)

A Clear . . . has complete recall of everything which has ever happened to him or anything he has ever studied. (208)

In *Blown for Good: Behind the Iron Curtain of Scientology*, former Church of Scientology employee Marc Headley describes his early years as a child of Scientologists who sent him to Scientology schools whenever they could afford it. Eventually he took a job with the organization. Promoted to work at the headquarters where the tapes, E-meters, and other equipment were manufactured, he happened to be chosen as the subject on whom Tom Cruise would practice auditing. In an interview with the *Village Voice*, Headley explained that, as Cruise's trainee, he was instructed to tell inanimate objects such as bottles or ashtrays to move in a certain way; when they did not move, Headley was instructed to move the objects himself and then thank them for moving. The purpose of this exercise, according to Headley, was to rehabilitate the mind's ability to control things and be controlled (Ortega 2009). He also claimed that employees lived and worked in substandard conditions for little or no pay, and were not allowed to leave the premises. In Scientology circles, critics such as Headley are known as Suppressive Persons, or SPs.

In 2016, the American actor Leah Remini created a television show entitled *Scientology and the Aftermath*. Remini had been a Scientologist but had left the movement and written a book that was critical of it, called *Troublemaker: Surviving Hollywood and Scientology*. Scientology has been critical of the television series, which won an Emmy award in 2017 for an outstanding informational series or special.

Despite the controversies that surround it, Scientology has been recognized as a valid new religion in several countries, including South Africa, Spain, Portugal, and Sweden, and in the United States it was granted tax-free status as a religious organization in 1993. The movement has had problems elsewhere, however, especially in France, where a number of Scientology leaders, including Hubbard himself in 1978, have been convicted of fraud; a 2009 fraud conviction of the organization as a whole was upheld in 2013. Scientology now claims more than 12 million followers in over 100 countries. Critics who believe that number to be grossly exaggerated suggest that it is based on the number of people who have ever bought a Scientology book or taken a Scientology course since the movement's inception. Based on the quantities of E-meters and other supplies shipped during his time with the organization, Headley estimates that there were roughly 10,000 to 15,000 active Scientologists in the 1990s.

The Raëlian Movement

The Raëlian Movement traces its origins to a winter day in 1973 when a French journalist and racing enthusiast named Claude Vorilhon impulsively decided to drive to the site of an old volcano where he had enjoyed family picnics in the past. There he saw a small flying saucer hovering near the ground. An extraterrestrial creature—approximately four feet tall and resembling a bearded human with a greenish skin tone—walked over and spoke to Vorilhon in French. In the course of this and subsequent encounters, the alien, whom Vorilhon came to know as Yahweh, recounted details of Vorilhon's own life and explained that he had used telepathy to draw the Frenchman to this spot. Yahweh invited him inside the spaceship and told him that all life on earth had originally been created in a laboratory by aliens called Elohim—the plural form of the word for a god in biblical Hebrew (*eloh*), frequently used in the Torah to refer to the one God. The International Raëlian Movement translates "Elohim" as "those who came from the sky," replacing the traditional idea of creation by a deity with creation by sky people.

Yahweh explained that a few weeks earlier he had used telepathy to urge Vorilhon to refresh his memory of the book of Genesis because he wanted to talk to him about it; now Vorilhon understood why he had recently, for no apparent reason, purchased a Bible and started to read it. The alien interpreted the reference to God's creation of heaven and earth (in Genesis 1:1) as a reference to the aliens "from the sky," and the verse saying that the spirit of God moved over the face of the earth (Genesis 1:2) as a reference to the alien spacecraft. Yahweh said that a "day" in the context of the six days of creation was equal to 2,000 earth years, and that the aliens had used advanced scientific techniques to create the first plants and animals in such a way that they would be able to reproduce themselves thereafter.

Yahweh told Vorilhon that he had been chosen to receive the truth because he had a Jewish father and a Catholic mother, and was a free-thinking opponent of traditional religion. As a result of his UFO encounter, Vorilhon was told to change his name to Raël, "messenger of the Elohim." Feeling called to prophecy, he was told to write down the message in book form and to spread the word in anticipation of the Elohim's return.

Two years after his initial encounter, Raël says, he was transported to the planet of the Elohim, where he received further instruction and met with past religious leaders. He wrote an account of the visit in his book *They Took Me to Their Planet*.

In 1974 Raël called a press conference in Paris, at which he introduced his movement to the media. By 1980 the International Raëlian Movement had taken on most of the features of an organized religion: scripture, rituals, festival days, and a communal building. It is organized hierarchically on the model of the Roman Catholic Church, with Raël himself at the pinnacle of the group, like a pope, and lesser officials with titles such as bishop guide and priest guide beneath. Susan Jean Palmer (1995) notes that although the movement advocates gender equality and is libertarian on sexuality and gender roles, women are not well represented in the leadership hierarchy, especially at the upper levels.

The leadership hierarchy may reflect Roman Catholicism, but the Raëlian cosmology is nothing like that of traditional Christianity. Not only does it reject belief in gods of any kind, but it teaches that the whole of the observable universe is just a small atom of a larger structure, which is itself part of a larger one, and so on infinitely. At the same time every atom is itself a universe on the next smaller scale, with structures descending in size infinitely. Time and space are infinite in this cosmos, which runs on scientific principles without any need for divine command or intervention.

The Elohim are expected to return by 2035, but only on condition that humans are ready to welcome them, have tolerance for one another, and respect the environment. The movement hopes one day to create an "embassy" (ideally in Israel) where the Elohim can interact with humans.

The Raëlian symbol is a swastika inside a six-pointed star that is said to be based on a design of interlocking triangles that Raël saw on the UFO. In fact, though, it seems identical to the Jewish Star of David. Raëlians claim that their swastika has nothing to do with Nazism and point out that for thousands of years it was a symbol of good luck and prosperity used in religious traditions such as Buddhism and Jainism. They say that the symbol as a whole reflects the Raëlian belief that the universe is cyclical, without beginning or end.

Practice

Becoming a Raëlian involves two ceremonies. First, initiates must renounce all ties to theistic religions. This "Act of Apostasy" is followed by a baptismal ceremony in which information about the initiate's DNA is supposedly transmitted to the Elohim.

Raëlians practice a spiritual technique that Raël learned from the Elohim. "Sensual meditation" or "meditation of all senses" involves turning inward to experience the lesser universes within the atoms of one's own body and then turning outward to experience the greater universes beyond our own; eventually, the most adept will be able to visualize the planet of the Elohim. The goal is to awaken spiritual potential by first awakening the physical sensibilities.

There are four Raëlian holidays: the first Sunday in April, celebrated as the day the Elohim created Adam and Eve; August 6, the day of the Hiroshima bombing, which for Raëlians is the beginning of the apocalypse; October 7, the date that Raël is said to have met with Jesus, Buddha, and other past prophets aboard a spaceship during the second encounter; and December 13, the day when Raël first encountered the Elohim.

Raëlians are expected to avoid mind-altering drugs, coffee, and tobacco, and to use alcohol either in moderation or not at all. They celebrate sensuality, advocate free love, and discourage traditional marriage contracts. The movement's liberal policy regarding marriage and sexual partners has made it an attractive religious home for gays and lesbians.

As part of his effort to free humans from traditional religions, Raël has called for a massive "de-baptism" campaign across Africa or (as he calls it) the United Kingdom of Kama. He argues that "spiritual decolonization" is a prerequisite for future development. Raëlians also denounce the practice of clitorectomy, which is common in some parts of Africa, and have raised funds to pay for restorative surgery for those who have undergone this procedure.

Raël with a full-scale model of the spaceship he encountered in 1973 (© Clonaid/epa/Corbis).

Although Raëlians reject the concept of the soul, they believe that a kind of everlasting life can be attained through cloning. Clonaid, a Raëlian cloning enterprise founded in France in 1997, has announced the births of several cloned babies; however, none of these claims have been substantiated.

Because Raëlians do not believe in gods, their movement is not classified as a religion, but it does recognize religious leaders such as Jesus and Buddha as prophets inspired by the Elohim to communicate as much of the truth as humans were able to absorb in their time. Raël himself is identified with Maitreya, the future buddha, although Buddhists themselves reject this idea.

Just as Christianity sees itself as completing Judaism and Islam sees Muhammad as the "seal of the prophets," Raëlians see their movement as the culmination of earlier religions, which incorrectly understood the role of the Elohim. According to Raël, the Elohim say that only 4 percent of humans are advanced enough to understand the truth about them, so it is not surprising that his movement has not made converts by the millions. Nevertheless, it claims more than 65,000 members in 84 countries.

⊕ The New Age Movement

The expression "New Age" has had many connotations. For nineteenth-century millenarian Christian movements (among them the Jehovah's Witnesses), which looked forward to the literal fulfillment of the apocalyptic prophecies in the biblical books of Daniel and Revelation, the term referred to the end-time when the Kingdom of God would be established on earth. For the Nation of Islam, by contrast, the "new age" was the time when African Americans would emerge triumphant.

The term "New Age" was in use as early as 1907, when it appeared as the title of a progressive British political and literary journal that introduced its readers to topics such as Freudian psychoanalysis. But the "consciousness revolution" of the 1960s brought expectations of a different sort of "New Age." The transpersonal psychology movement, for instance, emphasized spiritual insights and therapeutic techniques that were diametrically opposed to the mechanistic approach of orthodox Freudianism. One center of transpersonal psychology was the Esalen Institute in Big Sur, California, founded in 1962, which offered seminars, workshops, and encounter groups.

To some, the idea of the Age of Aquarius, popularized in the 1967 musical *Hair!*, meant the advent of a universal religion that would replace the Christianity of the Piscean Age. To others, it meant little more than freely available music or drugs. Those varied expectations came together in 1969, when as many as half a million young people congregated in a farmer's field near Woodstock, New York. By the late 1980s, "New Age" had become a kind of shorthand for a variety of self-help practices promising spiritual insight, worldly success, physical healing, and psychological peace.

Scholars looking for the historical roots of New Age spirituality often point to Emanuel Swedenborg, an eighteenth-century Swedish mystic who wrote about the evolution of the human soul; the nineteenth-century American Transcendentalist Ralph Waldo Emerson; or the Russian founder of the Theosophical movement, Helena P. Blavatsky, who claimed to have discovered the wisdom of the ages in Asian teachings such as Hindu Vedanta. Those looking for antecedents of New Age therapeutic techniques often point to the Swiss physician Paracelsus (1493–1541), who claimed that humans were subject to the magnetism of the universe. Two centuries later, the German physician Franz Anton Mesmer postulated that healing takes place through a kind of magnetism in bodily fluids, analogous to ocean tides, which he sought to manipulate with magnets or the wave of a wand or a finger. The effort to direct their flow, called mesmerism, was reflected in the development of hypnosis. As for what New Agers call "channeling," it can be traced back at least as far as the nineteenth-century séance, in which the bereaved sought to make contact with their deceased loved ones through a "spirit medium." Together these practices opened the way for subjects that had been left on the sidelines of a scientific and technological age—such as astrology, hypnosis, and alternative healing—to enter the mainstream. All these could be seen as alternatives to orthodox religion, medicine, and society generally, and perhaps also to the exclusivist claims made by mainstream orthodoxies.

If any of the metaphysical and therapeutic resources sketched so far have connections with the major Western religious traditions, they are marginal at best. So how did the New Age movement come to be so closely associated with religion? At least part of the answer can be found in its connections with Eastern religious traditions.

A prominent feature of the 1960s was a fascination with the depths of awareness that Hindu yoga and Japanese Zen Buddhism in particular were believed to offer. The *Yijing* (or *I Ching*), an ancient Chinese divination manual, became a bestseller during this decade, and many people were introduced to Eastern religious symbolism through the writings of the Swiss psychologist Carl G. Jung and the Jungian comparative religion scholar Joseph Campbell. "Exotic" religions seemed to offer something that the familiar Western traditions did not. Across North America and Europe, people explored Chinese *qigong* and acupuncture, Indian yoga and ayurvedic medicine, and Buddhist meditation techniques. In India, Maharishi Mahesh Yogi's Transcendental Meditation movement attracted high-profile devotees, including the Beatles, Mia Farrow, and Clint Eastwood. Deepak Chopra, an endocrinologist practicing in the West, returned to his native India to explore traditional ayurvedic medicine and found it compatible with modern Western medicine.

The New Age movement is open to many possibilities, including female leadership. In this respect it stands in sharp contrast to the male-dominated structures of the established religions and professions. This may constitute one of its lasting contributions.

Is there any single word that sums up the spirit of the New Age? One candidate would be "holistic." Implying a quest for wholeness, sometimes with an overtone of holiness, this term was coined in the context of evolutionary biology to refer to the whole as something more than the sum of its parts. Thus holistic diets and therapies seek to treat the whole person, body and mind, and holistic principles are fundamental to the ecological movement; the Gaia hypothesis, for instance, sees the earth as a single organism whose survival depends on the interaction of all its components (a perspective central to James Cameron's film *Avatar*). New ages yet to come are bound to view ecological holism as an increasingly urgent goal.

⊕ Summary

None of the new religions we have discussed is seriously challenging the traditional religions for influence. Some seem to have already peaked in numbers, at least in North America. Since new religious movements typically need strong, charismatic leaders, most have trouble sustaining themselves after their founders have left the original organization or died. But others are still making significant gains in numbers, wealth, and influence.

The few new religions that survive and prosper will eventually become established as normal parts of the religious landscape, as "religions" without the "new." Judaism, Christianity, and Islam made this transition long ago. The Baha'i Faith and the Church of Jesus Christ of Latter-day Saints have made it more recently. Which, if any, of the new religions that emerged in the late twentieth century will survive into the twenty-second is impossible to tell from this vantage point, but it is surely an interesting topic for debate.

Sites

Baha'i Temple, Wilmette, Illinois

The Baha'i Temple for North America, located just north of Chicago, is a nine-sided building—nine being a sacred number to Baha'is—set in a beautiful park. It is open to the public.

Kabbalah Centre, Los Angeles

The Kabbalah Centre of Los Angeles offers classes, a bookstore, and related activities, as well as an online university. There are affiliated centers in many other large US cities, as well as Toronto and worldwide.

New Vrindaban, West Virginia

Located in a rural area near Moundsville, New Vrindaban is an ISKCON community named after Vrindaban, India—a place associated with Krishna. Its temple was constructed using traditional Indian tools and techniques and (like most Hare Krishna temples)

includes a vegetarian restaurant that is open to the public. The community grows its own organic food.

Soka University of America, Orange County, California

Founded by Soka Gakkai International, Soka University of America is located atop a hill with a beautiful view overlooking mountains and the Pacific Ocean in Orange County, California. Although affiliated with Soka Gakkai, the university welcomes students from all backgrounds.

Temple Square, Salt Lake City, Utah

The Tabernacle, Family History Library, Salt Lake Temple, and other Mormon-related museums in Temple Square are open to the public. The Tabernacle, renowned for its acoustics and architecture, is home to the famous Mormon Tabernacle Choir.

Sacred Texts

Religion	Texts	Composition/ Compilation	Compilation/ Revision	Use
Soka Gakkai	*Lotus Sutra*	Probably composed in the early 1st century CE; considered the highest expression of Mahayana thought	Supplemented by writings of Nichiren and modern leaders	Read and chanted; the phrase "Homage to the *Lotus Sutra*" is chanted as a mantra
Falun Dafa (Falun Gong)	*Falun Gong* by Li Hongzhi	First published in 1993 and translated into most major languages	The English translation has been revised several times	Guide to practice
ISKCON ("Hare Krishnas")	*Srimad Bhagavatam, Bhagavad Gita,* and other Krishna-centered devotional texts	Ancient Hindu texts of debatable date, now available in English and other major languages	Commentaries by Swami Prabhupada	Studied and chanted during puja

Continued

Sacred Texts (Continued)

Religion	Texts	Composition/ Compilation	Compilation/ Revision	Use
Church of Jesus Christ of Latter-day Saints (Mormons)	The Bible, plus Smith's *Book of Mormon, Doctrine and Covenants,* and *The Pearl of Great Price*	*Book of Mormon* published 1830; *Doctrine and Covenants* (selected writings) published 1835; *Pearl of Great Price* compiled by F. D. Richards and published in England in 1851	All three texts revised at various times	Worship; life guidance
Baha'i	The *Most Holy Book, The Book of Certitude, Hidden Words,* and *The Seven Valleys*	Written by Baha'u'llah between 1856 and 1873	Edited by 20th-century Baha'i leaders	Legal guidance (*Most Holy Book*); doctrine (*Book of Certitude*); ethical guidance (*Hidden Words*); mystical guidance (*Seven Valleys*)
Nation of Islam	The Qur'an, plus Elijah Muhammad's *Fall of America* and *Message to the Blackman*	Elijah Muhammad's works date from the 1950s and 60s	Louis Farrakhan's *A Torchlight for America* (1993)	The Qur'an is studied, recited, and used in Sunni services, along with Muslim daily prayers
Kabbalah Centre	Hebrew Bible, the Zohar	The Kabbalah Centre attributes the Zohar to Rav Shimon Bar Yochai rather than Moses de Léon	Bible is interpreted through numerology and the 72 names of God	Guidance in daily life
Wicca	Important early works include Graves's *The White Goddess* (1948) and *The Book of Shadows* (c. 1950)	Other publications added a feminist emphasis, such as *The Holy Book of Women's Mysteries*	Popularization by newer writers such as Starhawk	Rituals and *sabbats*
Scientology	Hubbard's *Dianetics: The Modern Science of Mental Health* and *Scientology: The Fundamentals of Thought*	1950s		"Auditing"
Raëlian Movement	*Intelligent Design: Message from the Designers*	Compilation of Raël's publications from the 1970s and 1980s published in 2005	Other texts include *The Maitreyya* and *Sensual Meditation*	Guidance for sensual meditation practice
Church of Almighty God	*The Word Appears in the Flesh*	1991–2014 yearly revisions		Used as new scripture

Discussion Questions

1. What kinds of social and economic factors may contribute to the rise of new religious movements?

2. Why is the line between a "cult" and a "religion" so difficult to define?

3. Why do Eastern religions appeal so strongly to many people in the West?

4. Do all "religions" have to involve belief in deities?

5. Can a set of beliefs and practices centered on extraterrestrial aliens be considered a "religion"?

6. What factors might attract people to new religious movements?

7. How do new religious movements gain acceptance?

8. How do new religious movements tend to change over time?

Glossary

Bab The individual expected to appear as the "Gateway" to the new prophet in the Baha'i Faith.

Baha'i Faith The religious tradition of those who call themselves Baha'i, meaning "adherents of Baha('u'llah)."

bhakti Devotional faith; the favored spiritual path in ISKCON.

Church of Jesus Christ of Latter-day Saints The formal name of the largest Mormon organization, abbreviated as "LDS."

cult Term for a new religion, typically demanding loyalty to a charismatic leader.

dianetics L. Ron Hubbard's term for the system he developed to clear mental blocks.

E-meter A device used in Scientology to detect mental blocks.

engrams The term for mental blocks in Scientology.

Falun Dafa The "law wheel" said to be acquired through Dafa practice.

Free Zoners Individuals or groups teaching Hubbard's thought independently of Scientology International.

Hare Krishnas Informal name for the members of ISKCON, based on their chant.

ISKCON International Society for Krishna Consciousness.

Kabbalah Traditional Jewish mysticism.

millenarian Term used to refer to the belief that the current social order will soon come to an end.

Mormons Another name for members of the Church of Jesus Christ of Latter-day Saints. In 2018 members were advised by President Russell Nelson to stop using the term "Mormon" when referring to the church, and instead to use its full name.

Nation of Islam (NOI) An African American movement that originated in Detroit in 1930. Its practice of Islam has become more aligned with the Sunni tradition in recent years.

New Age A vague term embracing a diversity of religious or spiritual movements providing alternatives to mainstream Western religions.

qi **(or chi)** Spiritual energy.

qigong Exercises to cultivate *qi*.

Raëlian Movement A new religion originating in France in the 1970s, based on the belief that an alien revealed previously unknown information about the creation of life on earth to a man named Raël.

Scientology A new religion devoted to clearing mental blockages founded by L. Ron Hubbard.

sect A sociological term for a group that breaks away from the main religion.

Soka Gakkai A lay movement that originated in the 1930s among Japanese adherents of Pure Land Buddhism; now an independent new religion teaching the power of chanting homage to the *Lotus Sutra*.

spherot The 10 attributes of God in Kabbalah.

thetan Term for the soul or mind in Scientology.

Wicca A name for witchcraft, or the Craft.

Further Reading

Baha'u'llah. 1952. *Gleanings from the Writings of Baha'u'llah*, rev. ed. Wilmette, IL: Baha'i Publishing Trust. A good selection of Baha'i writings.

Barrett, David V. 2003. *The New Believers: A Survey of Sects, Cults and Alternative Religions*. London: Octopus Publishing Group. A good place to start on the topic of cults versus new religions.

Dan, Joseph. 2005. *Kabbalah: A Very Short Introduction*. Oxford: Oxford University Press. A useful introduction to the subject.

Drew, A. J. 2003. *The Wiccan Bible: Exploring the Mysteries of the Craft from Birth to Summerland*. Franklin, NJ: Career Press. An overview of Wicca.

Dunn, Emily. 2015. *Lightning from the East: Heterodoxy and Christianity in Contemporary China*. Leiden: Brill. A work that explains Eastern Lightning in China.

Esslemont, John E. 1979. *Bahá'u'lláh and the New Era: An Introduction to the Bahá'í Faith*. 4th ed. Wilmette, IL: Baha'i Publishing Trust. The standard survey recommended by Baha'is.

Gallagher, Eugene V., William M. Ashcraft, and W. Michael Ashcraft, eds. 2006. *An Introduction to New and Alternative Religions in America*. 5 vols. Westport, CT: Greenwood Press. A work offering scholarly introductions to religious movements from the colonial era to the present.

Headley, Marc. 2009. *Blown for Good: Behind the Iron Curtain of Scientology*. Burbank, CA: BFG Books. The autobiography of a former Scientologist turned critic.

Hubbard, L. Ron. 2007 [1956]. *Scientology: The Fundamentals of Thought*. Los Angeles: Bridge Publications. The basic introduction to Scientology, by its founder.

Lewis, James R., and J. Gordon Melton, eds. 1992. *Perspectives on the New Age*. Albany: State University of New York Press. One of the best assessments of the New Age phenomenon.

Li Hongzhi. 2000. *Falun Gong*. 3rd ed. New York: University Publishing. Master Li's introduction to Falun Dafa.

Miller, William McElwee. 1974. *The Baha'i Faith: Its History and Teachings*. Pasadena, CA: William Carey Library. An outsider's view of Baha'i.

Muster, Nori J. 2001. *Betrayal of the Spirit: My Life Behind the Headlines of the Hare Krishna Movement*. Champaign: University of Illinois Press. A former member's critical view of ISKCON.

Ostling, Richard, and Joan K. Ostling. 2007. *Mormon America—Revised and Updated Edition: The Power and the Promise*. New York: HarperOne. An overview of the issues facing the Church of Jesus Christ of Latter-day Saints today.

Porter, Noah. 2003. *Falun Gong in the United States: An Ethnographic Study*. Ph.D. diss. An argument against the "cult" label given to Falun Gong based on interviews and publications.

Seager, Richard H. 2006. *Encountering the Dharma: Daisaku Ikeda, Soka Gakkai, and the Globalization of Buddhist Humanism*. Berkeley: University of California Press. A scholarly overview of Soka Gakkai and other new Buddhist sects.

Shinn, Larry D. 1987. *The Dark Lord: Cult Images and the Hare Krishnas in America*. Philadelphia: Westminster Press. An objective account of the Hare Krishna movement, based on extensive interviews.

Starhawk. 1982. *Dreaming the Dark*. Boston: Beacon Press. One of many works by an important Wicca leader.

White, Vibert L., Jr. 2001. *Inside the Nation of Islam: A Historical and Personal Testimony by a Black Muslim*. Gainesville: University Press of Florida. A particularly interesting work on the Nation of Islam whose author was involved in both the NOI and the organization of the 1995 march.

Wright, Lawrence. 2013. *Going Clear: Scientology, Hollywood, and the Prison of Belief*. New York: Alfred A. Knopf. A balanced but critical overview of Scientology, its leaders, and its celebrity followers.

Recommended Websites

http://www.bahai.org
The official website of the Baha'i religion.

http://www.falundafa.org
The official site of Falun Dafa.

http://www.finalcall.com
The news site of the Nation of Islam.

http://www.holyspiritspeaks.org
The official site of the Church of Almighty God.

http://www.internationfreezone.net
The portal for the Free Zoner alternative to Scientology.

http://www.iskcon.org
The site of the International Society for Krishna Consciousness.

http://www.kabbalah.com
The official site of the Kabbalah Centre International.

http://www.lds.org
The official site of the Church of Jesus Christ of Latter-day Saints, the Mormons.

http://www.rael.org

The official site of the International Raëlian Movement.

http://www.scientology.org

The official site of the international Scientology organization.

http://www.sgi.org

The official site of Soka Gakkai International.

http://www.wicca.org

The official site of the Church and School of Wicca.

References

"The 72 Names of God." n.d. http://www.kabbalah.com/node/432.

Amnesty International. n.d. "Human Rights in China." http://www.amnesty.ca/blog2.php?blog=keep_the_promise_2&page=7.

Baha'u'llah and The Bab. 2002. *Baha'i Prayers: A Selection of Prayers*. Bel Air, CA: Bahai Pub Trust.

The Book of Mormon. 1961. Salt Lake City: Church of Jesus Christ of Latter-day Saints.

Dawson, Lorne L. 2006. *Comprehending Cults: The Sociology of New Religious Movements*. Toronto: Oxford University Press.

"Focus in Front." n.d. http://www.kabbalah.com/newsletters/weekly-consciousness-tune-ups/focus-front.

Hubbard, L. Ron. 1968. *Dianetics: The Modern Science of Mental Health*. Los Angeles: Bridge Publications.

Kabbalah Centre. n.d. "Reincarnation." http://www.kabbalah.com/node/434.

Lee, Martha F. 1996. *The Nation of Islam: An American Millenarian Movement*. Syracuse, NY: Syracuse University Press.

Levi, Jerome M. 2009. "Structuralism and Kabbalah: Sciences of Mysticism or Mystifications of Science?" *Anthropological Quarterly* 82, no. 4: 929–984.

Li Hongzhi. 2000. *Falun Gong*. 3rd ed. New York: University Publishing. Kindle.

Muhammad, Elijah. 1997. *Message to the Blackman in America*. Phoenix, AZ: Secretarius Memps Publications.

Nichiren. 1999. *The Writings of Nichiren Daishonin*. Vol. 1. Trans. Gosho Translation Committee. Santa Monica, CA: Soka Gakkai.

Ortega, Tony. 2009. "Tom Cruise Told Me to Talk to a Bottle: Life at Scientology's Secret Headquarters." *Village Voice*. http://blogs.villagevoice.com/runninscared/archives/2009/11/tom_cruise_was.php.

Palmer, Susan Jean. 1995. "Women in the Raelian Movement: New Religious Experiments in Gender and Authority." In *The Gods Have Landed: New Religions from Other Worlds*, ed. James R. Lewis. Albany: State University of New York Press, 105–136.

Prabhupada, A. C. Bhaktivedanta. 1968. *Teachings of Lord Chaitanya: The Golden Avatar*. New York: Bhaktivedanta Book Trust.

Walker, Dennis. 2005. *Islam and the Search for African-American Nationhood: Elijah Muhammad, Louis Farrakhan and the Nation of Islam*. Atlanta: Clarity Press.

White, Vibert L., Jr. 2001. *Inside the Nation of Islam: A Historical and Personal Testimony by a Black Muslim*. Gainesville: University Press of Florida.

Yang, Xiangbin. (nd). *The Word Appears in the Flesh*. https://www.holyspiritspeaks.org/books/the-word-appears-in-the-flesh/.

Note

Parts of this chapter, especially the sections on the Mormons, the Baha'i Faith, Wicca, and New Age movements, incorporate material written by the late Will Oxtoby for earlier editions of the work.

Credits

The authors gratefully acknowledge the use of the following material:

Text Credits

Pages 168–69, Excerpt, Shlomo Pines (tr). *Guide of the Perplexed*. University of Chicago Press, 1963; Page 202, Excerpt, Copyright 1975, Sister Benedicta Ward, tr. A Cistercian Studies publication. Published by Liturgical Press, Collegeville MN; Page 316, The Second Teaching (Philosophy and Spiritual Discipline) from THE BHAGAVAD-GITA: KRISHNA'S COUNSEL IN TIME OF WAR by Barbara Miller, translation copyright © 1986 by Barbara Stoler Miller. Used by permission of Bantam Books, an imprint of Random House, a division of Penguin Random House LLC. All rights reserved; Pages 546 and 547, Excerpts, as cited in Lee, Peter H., et al., eds. 1993. *Sourcebook of Korean Civilization*. Vol. I. New York: Columbia University Press. Original source: "The Lay of King Tongmyong," from *The Korea Journal*, Vol. 13.7;

Design Photo Credits

Chapter opener backgrounds, timelines, and running heads: Chapter 2: Cenk Unver/Thinkstock.com; Chapter 3: Kirill Zdorov/Thinkstock.com; Chapter 4: Comstock/Thinkstock.com; Chapter 5: Michael Luhrenberg/Thinkstock.com; Chapter 6: Ingram Publishing/Thinkstock.com; Chapter 7: Hemera Technologies/AbleStock.com/Thinkstock; Chapter 8: Alan Lagadu/Thinkstock; Chapter 9: hanoded/iStockphoto.com; Chapter 10: Borirak/Thinkstock; Chapter 11: Sebastiaan de Steigter/Thinkstock; Chapter 12: Photos.com/Thinkstock; Chapter 13: tnotn/iStockPhoto.com

Focus and Practice boxes: moggara12/Thinkstock

Sites boxes; Chapter 1: Margaret and Alan Smeaton/Thinkstock.com; Chapter 2: Bernardo69/Dreamstime.com/ GetStock; Chapter 3: Nickolay Vinokurov/Thinkstock.com; Chapter 4: Paul Prescott/Thinkstock.com; Chapter 5: Olegusk/Dreamstime.com/GetStock; Chapter 6: José Antonio Sánchez Poy/Thinkstock .com; Chapter 7: javarman2/Thinkstock; Chapter 8: Nilesh Bhange/Thinkstock; Chapter 9: Caroline Vancoillie/Thinkstock; Chapter 10: eAlisa/Thinkstock; Chapter 11: javarman2/Thinkstock; Chapter 12: Urban angel/Dreamstime.com/GetStock.com; Chapter 13: Fabrizio Troiani/Thinkstock.com

Document boxes: Chapter 1: David Crowther/Thinkstock.com; Chapter 3: Yalçin Yener/Thinkstock.com; Chapter 4: Arkadiusz Komski/Thinkstock.com; Chapter 5: Spaceheater/Dreamstime.com/GetStock;Chapter6:Bbbar/Dreamstime.com/GetStock Chapter 7: Amanda Lewis/Thinkstock; Chapter 9: The Schøyen Collection, MS 4464, http://www.schoyencollection.com/religions_les/ms4464.jpg; Chapter 10: Alexander Studentschnig/Thinkstock; Chapter 11: emily2k/Thinkstock; Chapter 12: Ciprian Catusanu/ Thinkstock

Women in the Traditions boxes: Chapters 2–6: LeoPatrizi/iStockphoto; Chapters 7–12: Mlenny/iStockphoto

Index